Leading Schools With Social, Emotional, and Academic Development (SEAD)

Tara Madden-Dent
Sierra Nevada University, USA

Deborah Oliver
National University, USA & Mindful SEAD, USA

IGI Global
PUBLISHER of TIMELY KNOWLEDGE

A volume in the Advances in Educational Technologies and Instructional Design (AETID) Book Series

Published in the United States of America by
IGI Global
Information Science Reference (an imprint of IGI Global)
701 E. Chocolate Avenue
Hershey PA, USA 17033
Tel: 717-533-8845
Fax: 717-533-8661
E-mail: cust@igi-global.com
Web site: http://www.igi-global.com

Library of Congress Cataloging-in-Publication Data

Names: Madden-Dent, Tara, 1983- editor. | Oliver, Deborah, editor.
Title: Leading schools with social, emotional, and academic development (SEAD) / Tara Madden-Dent and Deborah Oliver, Editors.
Description: Hershey, Pennsylvania : Information Science Reference, [2021] | Includes bibliographical references and index. | Summary: "This book provides theoretical and applied frameworks for educators who seek to improve their understanding of evidence-based strategies to embed social, emotional, and academic development (SEAD) practices into sustainable and measurable high impact systems"-- Provided by publisher.

Identifiers: LCCN 2020046731 (print) | LCCN 2020046732 (ebook) | ISBN 9781799867289 (Hardcover) | ISBN 9781799867296 (Paperback) | ISBN 9781799867302 (eBook)
Subjects: LCSH: Affective education. | Social learning. | Emotional intelligence. | Academic achievement.
Classification: LCC LB1072 .L42 2021 (print) | LCC LB1072 (ebook) | DDC 370.15/34--dc23
LC record available at https://lccn.loc.gov/2020046731
LC ebook record available at https://lccn.loc.gov/2020046732

This book is published in the IGI Global book series Advances in Educational Technologies and Instructional Design (AETID) (ISSN: 2326-8905; eISSN: 2326-8913)

British Cataloguing in Publication Data
A Cataloguing in Publication record for this book is available from the British Library.

For electronic access to this publication, please contact: eresources@igi-global.com.

Advances in Educational Technologies and Instructional Design (AETID) Book Series

Lawrence A. Tomei
Robert Morris University, USA

ISSN:2326-8905
EISSN:2326-8913

Mission

Education has undergone, and continues to undergo, immense changes in the way it is enacted and distributed to both child and adult learners. In modern education, the traditional classroom learning experience has evolved to include technological resources and to provide online classroom opportunities to students of all ages regardless of their geographical locations. From distance education, Massive-Open-Online-Courses (MOOCs), and electronic tablets in the classroom, technology is now an integral part of learning and is also affecting the way educators communicate information to students.

The **Advances in Educational Technologies & Instructional Design (AETID) Book Series** explores new research and theories for facilitating learning and improving educational performance utilizing technological processes and resources. The series examines technologies that can be integrated into K-12 classrooms to improve skills and learning abilities in all subjects including STEM education and language learning. Additionally, it studies the emergence of fully online classrooms for young and adult learners alike, and the communication and accountability challenges that can arise. Trending topics that are covered include adaptive learning, game-based learning, virtual school environments, and social media effects. School administrators, educators, academicians, researchers, and students will find this series to be an excellent resource for the effective design and implementation of learning technologies in their classes.

Coverage

- Classroom Response Systems
- K-12 Educational Technologies
- Social Media Effects on Education
- Virtual School Environments
- Web 2.0 and Education
- Collaboration Tools
- Hybrid Learning
- Bring-Your-Own-Device
- Curriculum Development
- Instructional Design Models

The Advances in Educational Technologies and Instructional Design (AETID) Book Series (ISSN 2326-8905) is published by IGI Global, 701 E. Chocolate Avenue, Hershey, PA 17033-1240, USA, www.igi-global.com. This series is composed of titles available for purchase individually; each title is edited to be contextually exclusive from any other title within the series. For pricing and ordering information please visit http://www.igi-global.com/book-series/advances-educational-technologies-instructional-design/73678. Postmaster: Send all address changes to above address.

Titles in this Series

For a list of additional titles in this series, please visit: http://www.igi-global.com/book-series/advances-educational-technologies-instructional-design/73678

CALL Theory Applications for Online TESOL Education
Kenneth B. Kelch (Alliant International University, USA) Peter Byun (Alliant International University, USA) Setareh Safavi (Alliant International University, USA) and Seth Cervantes (Alliant International University, USA)
Information Science Reference • © 2021 • 440pp • H/C (ISBN: 9781799866091) • US $195.00

Handbook of Research on Environmental Education Strategies for Addressing Climate Change and Sustainability
Ahmed Karmaoui (Southern Center for Culture and Sciences, Morocco) Abdelkrim Ben Salem (Mohammed V University, Morocco) and Mohd Talha Anees (University of Malaya, Malaysia)
Engineering Science Reference • © 2021 • 416pp • H/C (ISBN: 9781799875123) • US $295.00

Challenges and Opportunities for the Global Implementation of E-Learning Frameworks
Badrul H. Khan (McWeadon Education, USA) Saida Affouneh (An-Najah National University, Palestine) Soheil Hussein Salha (An-Najah National University, Palestine) and Zuheir Najee Khlaif (An-Najah National University, Palestine)
Information Science Reference • © 2021 • 345pp • H/C (ISBN: 9781799876076) • US $195.00

Handbook of Research on Teaching With Virtual Environments and AI
Gianni Panconesi (Esplica, Italy) and Maria Guida (National Institute for Documentation, Innovation, and Educational Research, Italy)
Information Science Reference • © 2021 • 811pp • H/C (ISBN: 9781799876380) • US $265.00

Cases on Active Blended Learning in Higher Education
Brenda Cecilia Padilla Rodríguez (Universidad Autonoma de Nuevo Leon, Mexico) and Alejandro Armellini (University of Northampton, UK)
Information Science Reference • © 2021 • 375pp • H/C (ISBN: 9781799878568) • US $195.00

Applying Universal Design for Learning Across Disciplines Case Studies on Implementation
Frederic Fovet (Royal Roads University, Canada)
Information Science Reference • © 2021 • 335pp • H/C (ISBN: 9781799871064) • US $195.00

Advancing Online Course Design and Pedagogy for the 21st Century Learning Environment
Daniel Chatham (Middlebury Institute of International Studies at Monterey, USA)
Information Science Reference • © 2021 • 382pp • H/C (ISBN: 9781799855989) • US $195.00

IGI Global
PUBLISHER of TIMELY KNOWLEDGE

701 East Chocolate Avenue, Hershey, PA 17033, USA
Tel: 717-533-8845 x100 • Fax: 717-533-8661
E-Mail: cust@igi-global.com • www.igi-global.com

Table of Contents

Preface xiv

Acknowledgment xxiii

Chapter 1
Mindful Social Emotional Academic Development and Emotional Resilience 1
Deborah Oliver, National University & Mindful SEAD, USA
Molly Dahl, Mindful SEAD, USA

Chapter 2
Culturally Responsive Social, Emotional, and Academic Development (SEAD): Three Case Studies Implementing SEAD 20
Tara Madden-Dent, Sierra Nevada University, USA
Iesha Jackson, University of Nevada, Las Vegas, USA
Jo Ann L. Cason, Do More Living Now, LLC, USA

Chapter 3
Effective Social Emotional Learning Implementation: SEAD Starts With You 42
Ashley Wolfe Reilly, Independent Researcher, USA

Chapter 4
Higher Education Leading With Social, Emotional, and Academic Development: University Case Study on Explicit SEAD Coursework 56
Tara Madden-Dent, Sierra Nevada University, USA
Deborah Oliver, National University & Mindful SEAD, USA
Brooke Stratton, Sierra Nevada University, USA
Eleanor A. Strand, Sierra Nevada University, USA
Kimberly Reed, Sierra Nevada University, USA

Chapter 5
Implementing SEAD Statewide: A Three-Year Case Study of SEAD Support for Educators 78
Silvana Carolina (Diaz) Gorton, Nevada Department of Education, USA
Marie J. DuFresne, Nevada Department of Education, USA

Chapter 6
The Social and Emotional Issues of Teacher's Professional Identity Development 101
Michelle A. Arroyo, University of Nevada, Las Vegas, USA

Chapter 7
Elevating Social and Emotional Learning Throughout the Day: Ten Teaching Practices That Promote SEAD in Culturally Responsive Ways 119
Nick Yoder, National University, USA
Pat Conner, Collaborative for Academic, Social, and Emotional Learning, USA
Tyrone Martinez-Black, CASEL, USA
Richie Ressel, Inspire Teaching and Learning, USA

Chapter 8
Social Emotional Learning as a Lever for High School Student Mental Health and Academic Success: A Reflective Analysis 148
Kimberly Reed, Sierra Nevada University, USA
Tara Madden-Dent, Sierra Nevada University, USA

Chapter 9
Understanding the Why of Behavior Through Regulation 166
Kristin Martinsen Robison, Independent Researcher, USA

Chapter 10
Nurturing Spiritual Intelligence in the Classroom 187
V. Vineeth Kumar, Manipal University Jaipur, India
Geetika Tankha, Manipal University Jaipur, India

Chapter 11
Social and Emotional Learning (SEL) Assessment in After-School Care: How Accessible Evaluation Can Lead to Widespread Quality Implementation 202
Dana Minney, Texas State University, USA & St. Edward's University, USA

Chapter 12
A More Mindful Approach to College and Career Counseling 231
Alexandra Ellison, Davidson Academy of Nevada, USA

Chapter 13
Strengthening College and Career Readiness With Social and Emotional Learning: Integrating Explicit SEL in CTE 247
Kara Sidorowicz, IMAGO, USA
Anthony Yang, IMAGO, USA

Chapter 14
Developing Social Emotional Learning Competencies Through Virtual Internships 273
Daniel Basil Kerr, St. Joseph's College, USA
Tom Gore, Kaya Responsible Travel, UK

Compilation of References 297

About the Contributors 327

Index 333

Detailed Table of Contents

Preface xiv

Acknowledgment xxiii

Chapter 1
Mindful Social Emotional Academic Development and Emotional Resilience 1
Deborah Oliver, National University & Mindful SEAD, USA
Molly Dahl, Mindful SEAD, USA

This chapter will provide an overview of the history and the basics of SEL/SEAD, SEAD in current time, mindfulness as the foundation of SEL and SEAD, and emotional resilience as the key to successful SEAD implementation and application in all areas of education, from the legislative offices to the PK learning space. The hope is to increase the understanding that SEAD is not a passing fad, not a trend, not "one more thing" that teachers will feel overwhelmed by, and not something to be feared or dreaded.

Chapter 2
Culturally Responsive Social, Emotional, and Academic Development (SEAD): Three Case Studies Implementing SEAD 20
Tara Madden-Dent, Sierra Nevada University, USA
Iesha Jackson, University of Nevada, Las Vegas, USA
Jo Ann L. Cason, Do More Living Now, LLC, USA

Culturally responsive social-emotional competencies continue being essential skills for college, career, and life success, especially today, as the world seeks global citizens prepared to respectfully navigate relationships and interactions between people from different nations and ethnicities. These skills are more than valuable assets that a modern economy is dependent on, but skills that students, educators, employees, and society need in order for healthy and sustainable co-existence. In academia, educators are increasingly expected to bridge diverse cultural gaps and foster more equitable, respectful, and safe learning environments, but evidence-based implementation methods are limited. To contribute to the body of literature, this chapter presents three case studies and how each of their approaches can increase essential SEL skills at the high school, undergraduate, and graduate levels in addition to the in-service educator level. The chapter concludes with a discussion around themes that emerged from the three case studies, implications for practice, and recommendations.

Chapter 3
Effective Social Emotional Learning Implementation: SEAD Starts With You 42
Ashley Wolfe Reilly, Independent Researcher, USA

A growing interest and body of research in education in the United States has centered around the idea that students learn best when they have foundational social emotional learning skills. These skills, ranging from interpersonal skills to self-reflection and awareness skills to self-management skills, allow students and adults to engage with one another in productive, pro-social ways that can positively impact a classroom community and a school's culture at large. This chapter seeks to consider the ways that adult social emotional learning impacts the success of greater, school-wide implementation. Specifically, the chapter explores the impact that a purposeful, measured (six months to year-long) adult social emotional learning rollout has in successful school-wide adoption of a comprehensive social emotional learning program.

Chapter 4
Higher Education Leading With Social, Emotional, and Academic Development: University Case Study on Explicit SEAD Coursework 56
Tara Madden-Dent, Sierra Nevada University, USA
Deborah Oliver, National University & Mindful SEAD, USA
Brooke Stratton, Sierra Nevada University, USA
Eleanor A. Strand, Sierra Nevada University, USA
Kimberly Reed, Sierra Nevada University, USA

Institutions of higher learning serve as global catalysts for equitable educational systems as drivers of educator workforce that lead with social, emotional, and academic development (SEAD) practices. Colleges and universities are well-positioned to instruct on explicit social emotional learning (SEL) not only within pre-service programs of study, but have the unique opportunity to provide continuous education for in-service educators. This large-scale capacity to influence those who shape student experiences is more important today than ever before as schools seek safer, more inclusive campuses and digital learning environments with culturally responsive and respectful communication and interactions. The need for SEL skills across workforce sectors conflicts with the lack of SEL education in higher educational programs. To contribute to the body of literature around post-secondary SEL education, this chapter introduces new graduate-level SEAD courses and how they influenced pre-service and in-service teacher candidates.

Chapter 5
Implementing SEAD Statewide: A Three-Year Case Study of SEAD Support for Educators 78
Silvana Carolina (Diaz) Gorton, Nevada Department of Education, USA
Marie J. DuFresne, Nevada Department of Education, USA

School leaders play a significant role in shaping education, and their leadership practices are key in conveying professional learning priorities for districts and schools. Concurrently, the benefits of adult social emotional learning (SEL) on creating conditions for educator effectiveness, wellbeing, and success have been demonstrated in the literature. This chapter chronicles initiatives undertaken by the Nevada Department of Education (NDE) to establish a systemic, sustainable, multi-tiered professional development structure and infrastructure aimed to foster adult SEL across the teaching and learning continuum, and ultimately to positively change student outcomes. Four initiatives are described, including the innovative approach of bringing together multiple projects to provide a virtual comprehensive support system in response to increased educator need.

Chapter 6
The Social and Emotional Issues of Teacher's Professional Identity Development 101
Michelle A. Arroyo, University of Nevada, Las Vegas, USA

Teacher professional identity is an important factor in understanding professional lives and career decision making. Teacher professional identity may affect motivation, effectiveness, and most importantly, social and emotional well-being. Teacher identity lacks clarity with regards to a definition. This could contribute to the reason that it has not been studied as a key element for teacher social and emotional wellness during professional identity development. The process of how teachers view themselves as teachers and how their developing professional identity is shaped by their personal identity development and social identity connections has implications on their careers.

Chapter 7
Elevating Social and Emotional Learning Throughout the Day: Ten Teaching Practices That Promote SEAD in Culturally Responsive Ways 119
Nick Yoder, National University, USA
Pat Conner, Collaborative for Academic, Social, and Emotional Learning, USA
Tyrone Martinez-Black, CASEL, USA
Richie Ressel, Inspire Teaching and Learning, USA

The important role of social and emotional learning (SEL) to promote the holistic development of students, improve academic instruction, and prepare students for the world of work and civic life has been well-established. Although wide consensus has emerged about the importance of SEL, understanding the primary role SEL plays within academic learning and how to more fully embed SEL throughout the school day still appears to be elusive. Compounded by efforts to use SEL as a lever for equity and excellence, educators need practical tools and guidance about approaches that help them attune to the social, emotional, and academic needs of their students. In this chapter, the authors review 10 teaching practices that promote social, emotional, and academic development and ways in which each of these practices can be implemented in classrooms in a culturally responsive way.

Chapter 8
Social Emotional Learning as a Lever for High School Student Mental Health and Academic Success: A Reflective Analysis 148
Kimberly Reed, Sierra Nevada University, USA
Tara Madden-Dent, Sierra Nevada University, USA

The following case study demonstrates how one high school Social Studies teacher embedded social emotional learning (SEL) into content and classroom management practices for eight years at a large urban school in the American Southwest. The collected data (e.g., teacher reflections, student reflections) provide a variety of viewpoints around how SEL influenced the teacher and student experience. Through collective analysis, this study's qualitative data contributes to new understanding of the importance of social, emotional, and academic development practices in high schools for students and teachers, especially around supporting classroom safety, mental health, and wellness.

Chapter 9
Understanding the Why of Behavior Through Regulation 166
Kristin Martinsen Robison, Independent Researcher, USA

This chapter will review the many foundational theories that outline an historical understanding of behavior. Occupational therapy (OT) and psychology have provided a consistent framework for addressing and defining behavior. Behavior communicates self-awareness and self-management which are key competencies upon which social and emotional learning occur. Perception affects the definition and assumption of behavior, and this is affected by knowledge. Various considerations such as sensory processing, executive functioning, nervous system functions, and environmental factors affect the feedback loop that governs a child's ability to regulate. How we assess this process will determine our expectations and responses. When disciplinary programs do not address the whole child, behavior seldom improves. Embracing the big picture of behavior allows it to be viewed through a different lens to establish a supportive relationship with a student and empower them to achieve self-actualization and skills they will use for a lifetime.

Chapter 10
Nurturing Spiritual Intelligence in the Classroom 187
V. Vineeth Kumar, Manipal University Jaipur, India
Geetika Tankha, Manipal University Jaipur, India

Humans have a unique intelligence known as spiritual intelligence that tends to seek meaning and purpose in their lives, ask questions about one's existence, and render resolute conclusions to one's actions. Today, school teachings align with the industry's demands and are nurturing students' cognitive attributes. As the demand for technological innovations increases, the demand for focusing on vocational skill-focused education is also increasing. However, in the era of rapid technological innovations, nurturing the men's psyche behind the technology-driven progress is equally important. The chapter discusses the relevance of spiritual intelligence in schools. Further, the chapter explores spiritual intelligence's relationship with psychological wellbeing, mental health, quality of life (QOL), happiness, and academic performance. The way forward measures to enhance students' spiritual intelligence are also discussed for achieving students' holistic development.

Chapter 11
Social and Emotional Learning (SEL) Assessment in After-School Care: How Accessible Evaluation Can Lead to Widespread Quality Implementation 202
Dana Minney, Texas State University, USA & St. Edward's University, USA

An abundance of research links children's social-emotional competence with positive school and life outcomes, but many barriers to widespread, high quality social-emotional learning (SEL) exist. Studies also found SEL delivered consistently and in coordination with other programs, both in and out of school, is more effective, but lack of unified standards, a supportive framework, and systematic approach prevent consistency and coordination of delivery. Process monitoring and impact evaluation help overcome barriers and improve implementation. After-school programs provide opportunities for quality SEL delivery and evaluation. This chapter reports results of an evaluation comparing pre- and post-program survey data from elementary school children (n = 98) in an after-school program that has incorporated an SEL curriculum. Results showed significant increases in the SEL competencies of self-management, social awareness, and social skills. The author also explored advantages of providing both SEL instruction and low-cost evaluation in after-school care settings in addition to schools.

Chapter 12
A More Mindful Approach to College and Career Counseling 231
Alexandra Ellison, Davidson Academy of Nevada, USA

While social and emotional learning practices are now more common in American classrooms, counselors often have limited time and resources to devote to college counseling at all, let alone a type of counseling grounded in social and emotional awareness. The American School Counselor Association recommends a student-to-counselor ratio of 250 to 1, but the current ratio is 430 to 1. Few high school counselors have the rare luxury of only needing to focus on college and career readiness. They are up against pressures from parents, and sometimes administrators, who want to see more AP courses, higher GPAs, higher ACT and SAT scores, and more elite college acceptances. These pressures can blur a counselor's view of what is actually suitable for each individual student; this means the counselor needs to understand financial fit, social and emotional fit, and academic match for each college-bound student. This kind of holistic understanding of a student is the only way to restore a focus on student wellbeing to the college and career planning process.

Chapter 13
Strengthening College and Career Readiness With Social and Emotional Learning: Integrating Explicit SEL in CTE 247
Kara Sidorowicz, IMAGO, USA
Anthony Yang, IMAGO, USA

Social-emotional skills are essential for navigating the rapidly evolving world, especially for students who will become the makers and doers of tomorrow. The literature suggests that a technology-driven shift in needs is fueling a skills gap within a workforce needing social-emotional competencies. These shifts have grown the need for students to develop their social-emotional skills for professional and personal success. Experts suggest infusing social and emotional learning (SEL) in career and technical education (CTE) to address this. This study documents and explores a strategy for explicit SEL in CTE at Clark County School District in Nevada, USA during the 2019-2020 school year. Usage and student answers suggest promising value of SEL in CTE for student learning, but a need to better support teacher adoption. Findings from this study contribute preliminary guidance on program development and implementation upon which future educators and researchers can build.

Chapter 14
Developing Social Emotional Learning Competencies Through Virtual Internships 273
Daniel Basil Kerr, St. Joseph's College, USA
Tom Gore, Kaya Responsible Travel, UK

This chapter explores the experiences of four virtual interns working with organizations tackling social issues in Ecuador, Morocco, South Africa, and Vietnam. These internships provided a unique opportunity to develop and apply the social, emotional, and academic development (SEAD) competencies of self-awareness, self-management, social awareness, relationship skills, and responsible decision-making. Schlossberg's transition theory provides a framework for transitioning to another culture and cultural mapping is used as a tool to identify, plan, and mitigate differences in cultural orientations between interns and colleagues in their host countries. The chapter draws upon student narratives and reflections, and supervisor feedback to capture what they learned and the challenges they faced as they completed their virtual internships. The results contribute to the literature related to the development of SEAD competencies through virtual internships for high school and college students.

Compilation of References 297

About the Contributors 327

Index 333

Preface

AN OVERVIEW OF THE BOOK

Leading Schools With Social, Emotional, and Academic Development provides resource material to benefit educators, policymakers, and staff who work to create more equitable, culturally responsive learning environments within in-person and virtual settings. This book offers research-based findings and perspectives into how Social Emotional Learning (SEL) can improve youth and adult success through integrating SEL and academics that reinforce equitable and human-centered educational environments. As a data-driven research resource, this text contributes to current literature on culturally responsive SEL instruction, classroom management, college and career development, policy and funding considerations, and educator preparation and on-going professional learning strategies. A wide array of topics is included such as positive psychology and resiliency, explicit SEL instruction and after school time exemplars, sustainable systems at the higher education and state levels, culturally responsive SEL in virtual internships, and SEL impacts for educator effectiveness and retention. Creating an understanding of these issues through research-based inquiry is critical to effective SEL implementation through a multi-tiered system of supports framework where all educational stakeholders, (e.g., educators; students; families/caregivers; communities), gain the translatable skills that contribute to healthier, safer, and more equitable environments for all.

TARGET AUDIENCE

There is a growing need for social, emotional, and academic development (SEAD) in classrooms, schools, districts, and state offices of public education, but there has been an absence of resources that provide valid methods to better equip educators with evidence-based SEL applications for their respective roles to support student success in tangible ways. *Leading Schools With Social, Emotional, and Academic Development* is ideal for all educators including, but not limited to, pre-service and in-service teachers, school social workers, counselors, and psychologists, administrators and staff, educational practitioners, researchers, university faculty, and non-profit community organizations interested in implementing SEAD practices for youth and adult success.

DEFINING SOCIAL, EMOTIONAL, AND ACADEMIC DEVELOPMENT (SEAD)

Social, Emotional, and Academic Development (SEAD) is the systemic practice of integrating social emotional learning into academics that reinforce equitable, human-centered, and culturally responsive educational environments for youth and adults. The implementation of SEAD practices aims to increase Social Emotional Learning (SEL), the lifelong process of learning and applying the, "knowledge, skills, and attitudes to develop healthy identities, manage emotions and achieve personal and collective goals, feel and show empathy for others, establish and maintain supportive relationships, and make responsible and caring decisions" (CASEL, 2020). According to the Collaborative for Academic, Social, and Emotional Learning (CASEL), SEL encompasses five competencies: Self-Awareness, Self-Management, Social Awareness, Relationship Skills, and Responsible Decision-Making skills. These competencies have been found to be as predictive of academic and career achievement as is IQ (Almlund, Duckworth, Heckman, & Kautz, 2011).

Figure 1.

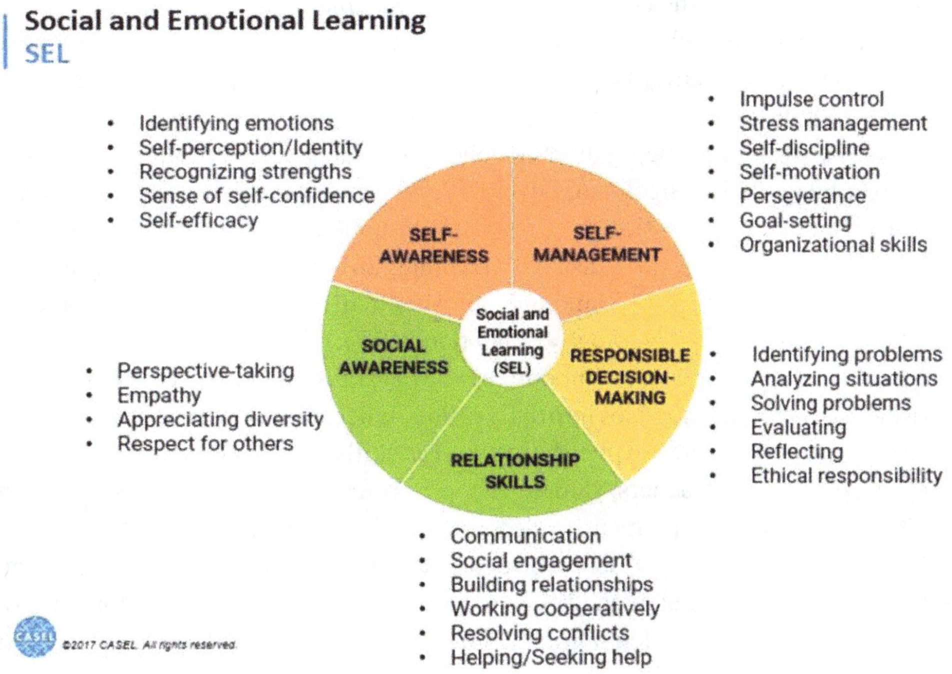

The field of social emotional learning emerged more than twenty-five years ago and through basic and applied research, has demonstrated that SEL contributes to safer and more equitable learning environments for youth and adults (Cantor et al., 2018; Durlak et al., 2011; Jones & Kahn, 2017; Madden-Dent, 2021b; Osher et al., 2018; Taylor et al., 2017), increases in cultural competence, linguistic skills, and academic success (Kerr, Madden-Dent, & Shalabi, 2020; Madden-Dent, 2021a), decreases in unhealthy behaviors, mental health issues, and drop-out rates (Kautz, Heckman, Diris, Bas ter Weel, & Borghans, 2014; Reed & Madden-Dent, 2021), increases of 11-14% point gains in grades and test scores (Durlak et al., 2011), and improved attitudes, emotional intelligence, and academic engagement (Li & Xu, 2019). The application of SEAD practices within educational systems improves school climate and culture through more culturally responsive environments that reinforce high school graduation rates and post-secondary enrollment and completion rates (Kautz, Heckman, Diris, Bas ter Weel, & Borghans, 2014), as well as increases in educator persistence and retention rates (Arroyo, 2020; Madden-Dent, Jackson, & Cason, 2021). Furthermore, both preventive and responsive SEL applications using a multi-tiered system of supports framework have been found to generate a financial return on educational investments that range from $11 to $104.90 for every dollar invested (Belfield, Bowden, Klapp, Levin, Shand, & Zander, 2015; Swain-Bradway, Lindstrom Johnson, Bradshaw, & McIntosh, 2017).

Of critical note, instead of SEAD practices and SEL competencies being exclusive to the values and preferences of a dominant culture, it is important that they are inclusive of diverse individual and community cultural orientations as means to create equitable educational environments, inclusive of home and community stakeholders. This is essential when school and government leaders develop social-emotional policies and practices (e.g., Restorative practices), so that they have a critical consciousness to how culture influences academic systems and incorporates stakeholder voice during early stages of policy development.

As students advance through the educational system, the graduates enter highly competitive and diverse, globalized environments, where universities and employers seek culturally intelligent applicants with SEL skills to respectfully navigate relationships and interactions between people from different backgrounds. These skills are far more than optional assets; they are requirements in today's modern academic systems and workforce sought after by school admissions and employers alike (Cunningham & Villasenor, 2016; Fitzgerald & Sigelman, 2018; Hart Research Associates, 2015; Job Outlook, 2016; Maldonado, 2019; National Association of Colleges & Employers, 2019). As SEL skills have been in increasing demand over the last several decades (Deming, 2017), research also suggests that business leaders will continue needing SEL skills among employees in the future (Yoder, Atwell, Godek, Dusenbury, Bridgeland, & Weissberg; 2020; Zogby Analytics, 2017).

But before we can expect students to embody these SEL skills, they must first engage within educational systems that infuse SEAD practices into daily norms, where they observe educators modeling these abilities, and have teachers/coaches explicitly teach SEL skills across all content subjects. This order of operations presupposes that teachers, student support professionals, staff, and school administrators learn what SEL is and how to implement evidence-based SEAD practices into their respective roles. This textbook, helps to address the absence of explicit SEL education within Colleges of Education (Schonert-Reichl, Kitil, Hanson-Peterson, 2017), to meet the increasing demand for educators to know and apply SEL, earn SEL micro-credentialing, and licensure endorsements (CASEL, 2021).

Chapter Organization

Leading Schools With Social, Emotional, and Academic Development consists of 14 chapters. Authors bring many years of experience teaching, researching, and implementing social-emotional applications within education for youth and adult success. A brief description of each of the chapters follows:

In Chapter 1, "Mindful Social Emotional Academic Development and Emotional Resilience," Debb Oliver and Molly Dahl provide an overview of the history of SEL and SEAD, mindfulness as the foundation of SEL and SEAD, and emotional resilience as the key to successful SEAD implementation and application in all areas of education.

In Chapter 2, "Culturally Responsive Social, Emotional, and Academic Development (SEAD): Three Case Studies Implementing SEAD," Tara Madden-Dent, Iesha Jackson, and Jo Ann Cason introduce culturally responsive social-emotional learning and how those skills continue being essential for college, career, and life success, as the world seeks global citizens prepared to respectfully navigate relationships and interactions between people from different nations and ethnicities. The chapter provides three case studies describing specific at the high school, undergraduate, graduate, and in-service educator levels.

In Chapter 3, "Effective Social Emotional Learning Implementation: SEAD Starts With You," Ashley Wolfe showcases an example of how adult social emotional learning impacts the success of school-wide SEL implementation. The chapter considers the educator elements during the adoption of a purposeful and comprehensive school-wide social emotional learning program.

In Chapter 4, "Higher Education Leading With Social, Emotional, and Academic Development: University Case Study on Explicit SEAD Coursework," Tara Madden-Dent, Debb Oliver, Brooke Stratton, Eleanor Strand, and Kimberly Reed, remind readers of how higher education institutions serve as drivers of educator workforce, those who shape the student experience, campus safety, and more inclusive, equitable learning environments. This chapter introduces four new graduate-level SEAD courses and how they influenced pre-service and in-service teacher candidates.

In Chapter 5, "Implementing SEAD Statewide: A Three-Year Case Study of SEAD Support for Educators," Silvana (Diaz) Gorton and Marie DuFresne provide initiatives undertaken by the Nevada Department of Education (NDE) to establish a systemic, sustainable, multi-tiered professional development structure and infrastructure aimed to foster adult SEL across the teaching and learning continuum, and ultimately to positively change student outcomes. Four initiatives are described, including the innovative approach of bringing together multiple projects to provide a virtual comprehensive support system in response to increased educator need.

In Chapter 6, "The Social and Emotional Issues of Teacher's Professional Identity Development," Michelle Arroyo examines teachers' professional identity and the importance of it in understanding their professional lives and career decision-making. The chapter's study demonstrates how teachers' professional identity may affect motivation, effectiveness, and most importantly, their social and emotional well-being.

In Chapter 7, "Elevating Social and Emotional Learning Throughout the Day: 10 Teaching Practices That Promote SEAD in Culturally Responsive Ways," Nick Yoder, Pat Conner, Tyrone Martinez-Black, and Richie Ressel, review 10 teaching practices that promote social, emotional, and academic development and ways in which each of these practices can be implemented in classrooms in a culturally responsive way.

In Chapter 8, "Social Emotional Learning as A Lever for High School Student Mental Health and Academic Success," Kimberly Reed and Tara Madden-Dent share a case study that demonstrates how one high school Social Studies teacher embedded social emotional learning (SEL) into content and classroom management practices for eight years at a large urban school in the American Southwest. The collected data (e.g., Teacher reflections; Student reflections), provide a variety of viewpoints around how SEL influenced the teacher and student experience. Through collective analysis, this study's qualitative data contributes to new understanding of the importance of Social, Emotional, and Academic Development practices in high schools for students and teachers, especially around supporting classroom safety, mental health, and wellness.

In Chapter 9, "Understanding the Why of Behavior Through Regulation," Kristin Robison reviews the many foundational theories that outline an historical understanding of behavior. Occupational therapy

(OT) and psychology have provided a consistent framework for addressing and defining behavior. Behavior communicates self-awareness and self-management which are key competencies upon which social and emotional learning occur. Perception affects the definition and assumption of behavior, and this is affected by knowledge. Various considerations such as sensory processing, executive functioning, nervous system functions, and environmental factors affect the feedback loop that governs a child's ability to regulate. How we assess this process will determine our expectations and responses. When disciplinary programs do not address the whole child, behavior seldom improves. Embracing the big picture of behavior allows it to be viewed through a different lens to establish a supportive relationship with a student and empower them to achieve self-actualization and skills they will use for a lifetime.

In Chapter 10, "Nurturing Spiritual Intelligence in the Classroom," V. Vineeth Kumar and Geetika Tankha, introduce spiritual intelligence and its importance in education. The chapter discusses the relevance of spiritual intelligence in schools and explores its relationship with psychological wellbeing, mental health, quality of life (QOL), happiness, and academic performance.

In Chapter 11, "Social and Emotional Learning (SEL) Assessment in After-School Care: How Accessible Evaluation Can Lead to Widespread Quality Implementation," Dana Minney introduces how after-school programs provide opportunities for quality SEL delivery and evaluation. This chapter reports results of an evaluation comparing pre- and post-program survey data from elementary school children (n = 98) in an after-school program that has incorporated an SEL curriculum. Results show significant increases in the SEL competencies of self-management, social awareness, and social skills.

In Chapter 12, "A More Mindful Approach to College and Career Counseling," Alexandra Ellison, identifies the intense role school counselors play in students' college & career planning and the critical approach to ensure a goodness-of-fit between the student and their post-graduation goals (e.g., College and career choice). The chapter describes the need for a holistic understanding of each student to support student wellbeing in the college and career planning process.

In Chapter 13, "Strengthening College and Career Readiness With Social and Emotional Learning: Integrating Explicit SEL in CTE," Kara Sidorowicz and Anthony Yang, document a strategy for explicit SEL in CTE. Findings from this study contribute preliminary guidance on program development and implementation upon which future educators and researchers can build.

In Chapter 14, "Developing Social Emotional Learning Competencies Through Virtual Internships," Daniel Kerr and Tom Gore explore the experiences of four virtual interns working with organizations tackling social issues in Ecuador, Morocco, South Africa and Vietnam. These internships provided a unique opportunity to develop and apply the Social, Emotional, and Academic Development (SEAD) competencies of self-awareness; self-management; social awareness; relationship skills; and responsible decision-making. Schlossberg's Transition Theory provides a framework for transitioning to another culture and Cultural Mapping is used as a tool to identify, plan, and mitigate differences in cultural orientations between interns and colleagues in their host countries. The chapter draws upon student narratives and reflections, and supervisor feedback to capture what they learned and the challenges they faced as they completed their virtual internships. The results contribute to the literature related to the development of SEAD competencies through virtual internships for high school and college students.

Tara Madden-Dent
Sierra Nevada University, USA

Deborah Oliver

National University, USA & Mindful SEAD, USA

REFERENCES

Arroyo, M. (2020). *The relationship between teacher identity and teacher retention in Title I schools: A multiple case study*. Dissertation from the University of Nevada, Las Vegas. ProQuest Number: 27999584.

Aspen Institute. (2018). *Pursuing Social and Emotional Development Through a Racial Equity Lens: A Call to Action*. Retrieved at https://www.aspeninstitute.org/publications/pursuing-social-and-emotional-development-through-a-racial-equity-lens-a-call-to-action/

Bailey. (2015). *Persistence and fadeout in the impacts of child and adolescent interventions*. Working paper in the ARC Center of Excellence for Children and Families over the Life Course, University of Queensland, Australia.

Busteed, B. (2019). *Why aren't graduates ready for work? They're the least working generation in U.S. history*. Retrieved at https://www.forbes.com/sites/brandonbusteed/2019/03/29/why-arent-graduates-ready-for-work-theyre-the-least-working-generation-in-us-history/#7cd974ae5e58

Cantor, P., Osher, D., Berg, J., Steyer, L., & Rose, T. (2018). Malleability, plasticity, and individuality: How children learn and develop in context. *Applied Developmental Science*. Advance online publication. doi:10.1080/10888691.2017.1398649

Cipriano, C., & Brackett, M. (2020). *How to support teachers' emotional needs right now. Schools can develop a plan to help teachers who are feeling anxious and overwhelmed*. Retrieved at https://greater-good.berkeley.edu/article/item/how_to_support_teachers_emotional_needs_right_now

Collaborative for Academic, Social, and Emotional Learning (CASEL). (2020). *CASEL's SEL framework: What are the core competence areas and where are they promoted?* Retrieved at https://casel.org/what-is-sel/

Collaborative for Academic, Social, and Emotional Learning (CASEL). (2021). *Collaborating States Initiative*. Retrieved at https://casel.org/collaborative-state-initiative/

Committee for Children Second Step. (2014). *Safe, Supported, and Ready to Learn*. Retrieved at https://www.cfchildren.org/wp-content/uploads/programs/docs/Second-Step_White-Paper_Safe-Supported-Ready-to-Learn_FA18.pdf

Cunningham, W., & Villasenor, P. (2016). Employer voices, employer demands, and implications for public skills development policy. Washington, DC: World Bank. doi:10.1596/1813-9450-7582

Deming, D. J. (2017). *The growing importance of social skills in the labor market* (NBER Working Paper No. 21473). Cambridge, MA: National Bureau of Economic Research.

Domitrovich, C. E., Syvertsen, A. K., & Calin, S. S. (2017). *Promoting social and emotional learning in the middle and high school years*. Edna Bennett Pierce Prevention Research Center, Pennsylvania State University.

Durlak, J. A., Weissberg, R. P., Dymnicki, A. B., Taylor, R. D., & Schellinger, K. (2011). The impact of enhancing students' social and emotional learning: A meta-analysis of school-based universal interventions. *Child Development, 82*(1), 405–432. doi:10.1111/j.1467-8624.2010.01564.x PMID:21291449

Educationlinks, U. S. A. I. D. (2018). *Education in crisis and conflict. Social and emotional learning in crisis and conflict settings*. Retrieved at https://www.edu-links.org/learning/social-and-emotional-learning-crisis-and-conflict-settings

Elias, M. J., Leverett, L., Duffell, J., Humphrey, N., Stepney, C. T., & Ferrito, J. J. (in press). Integrating social-emotional learning with related prevention and youth-development approaches. In J. A. Durlak, C. Domitrovich, R. P. Weissberg, & T. P. Gullotta (Eds.), Handbook of social and emotional learning (SEL): Research and practice. Academic Press.

Fitzgerald, B. K., & Sigelman, M. (2018). *The new foundational skills of the digital economy: Developing the professionals of the future*. Burning Glass Technologies. Retrieved from www.burning-glass.com

Fulbright Scholar Program. (2018). *About Fulbright*. Retrieved from https://www.cies.org/about-us/about-senator-j-william-fulbright

Grant, S., Hamilton, L. S., Wrabel, S. L., Gomez, C. J., Whitaker, A., Leschitz, J. T., Unlu, F., Chavez-Herrerias, E. R., & Baker, G. (2017). *Social and emotional learning interventions under Every Student Succeeds Act: Evidence Review*. Rand Education Commissioned by The Wallace Foundation. Retrieved at www.rand.org/t/RR2133

Gulbrandson, K. (2019). *Committee for children, high schoolers voice the value of social-emotional learning: Middle school SEL matters*. Retrieved at https://www.cfchildren.org/blog/2019/04/high-schoolers-voice-the-value-of-social-emotional-learning-middle-school-sel-matters/

Hart Research Associates. (2015). *Falling Short? College learning and career success*. Research conducted on behalf of the Association of American Colleges & Universities. Retrieved at https://www.aacu.org/leap/public-opinion-research/2015-survey-results

Hurley, K. (2020). *Social media and depression: New research links the problems, especially in teens*. Retrieved at https://www.psycom.net/social-media-depression-teens

Jones, D., Crowley, D. M., & Greenberg, M. T. (2017). *Improving social emotional skills in childhood enhances long-term well-being and economic outcomes*. Edna Bennet Pierce Prevention Research Center, Pennsylvania State University.

Jones, S., & Khan, J. (2017). *The evidence base for how we learn: Supporting students' social, emotional, and academic development*. Aspen Institute. Retrieved at http://nationathope.org/wp-content/uploads/final_cds-evidence-base.pdf

Kautz, Diris, & Borghans. (2014). Fostering and measuring skills: Improving cognitive and non-cognitive skills to promote lifetime success. Paris, France: Organization for Economic Cooperation and Development.

Kerr, D. B., Madden-Dent, T., & Shalabi, N. (2020). Cultural competency interventions: Three case studies with guiding theoretical frameworks. In *Cultural Competencies for Continuous Learning* (2nd ed.). Oxford University Press. Retrieved at https://www.oxfordhandbooks.com/view/10.1093/oxfordhb/9780197506707.001.0001/oxfordhb-9780197506707-e-6?utm_content=148183851&utm_medium=social&utm_source=linkedin&hss_channel=lcp-19900 doi:10.1093/oxfordhb/9780197506707.013.26

Madden-Dent, T. (2014). *A phenomenological study of cultural transition and adjustment of Asian undergraduate international students using different cross-cultural treatments. ProQuest*. UMI Dissertations Publishing.

Madden-Dent, T. (2021a). Advancing equity through culturally responsive social-emotional education: Addressing international student integration. In Advances in Motivation and Achievement. Motivating the SEL Field Forward Through Equity (Vol. 21). Emerald Publishing Limited. doi:10.1108/S0749-7423201719

Madden-Dent, T. (2021b). Bridging academic and industry skills gap via digital collaboration: Preparing scholars for international assignment. In *University-Industry Collaboration Strategies in the Digital Era*. Retrieved at https://www.igi-global.com/book/university-industry-collaboration-strategies-digital/244278 doi:10.4018/978-1-7998-3901-9

Madden-Dent, T., Jackson, I., & Cason, J. (2021). Culturally-responsive social emotional academic development. In *Leading Schools with Social Emotional Academic Development (SEAD)*. IGI Global Publication. Retrieved at https://www.igi-global.com/book/leading-schools-social-emotional-academic/256645

Maker, A. (2018). Screen time: The impact on kids and parenting. *Psychology Today*. Retrieved from https://www.psychologytoday.com/us/blog/helping-kids-cope/201808/screen-time-the-impact-kids-and-parenting

Maldonado, C. (2019). *Integrating workforce development practices in higher education*. Workforce Development Center, University of Nevada.

Mayo Foundation for Medical Education and Research (MFMER). (2017). *Mayo Clinic*. Retrieved from https://www.mayoclinic.org/diseases-conditions/depression/in-depth/depression-and-exercise/art-20046495

Miller, J. S. (2020). *Confident parents, confident kids: Raising emotional intelligence in ourselves and our kids from toddlers to teenagers*. Fair Winds Press. Retrieved at https://confidentparentsconfidentkids.org/the-book/

National Alliance on Mental Illness (NAMI). (2020). *Mental health by the numbers*. Retrieved at https://nami.org/mhstats

National Association of Colleges and Employers. (2019). *Career readiness for the new college graduate: A definition of competencies (revised)*. Retrieved from, https://www.naceweb.org/career-readiness/competencies/career-readiness-defined/

National Center on Safe Supportive Learning Environments. (2020). *Emotional Safety. American Institutes for Research*. Retrieved at https://safesupportivelearning.ed.gov/topic-research/safety/emotional-safety

National Coalition Against Domestic Violence (NCADV). (2020). *Domestic violence statistics*. Retrieved at https://ncadv.org/statistics

National Institutes of Health (NIH). (2020). *National Institute on Drug Abuse*. Retrieved at https://www.drugabuse.gov/drug-topics/opioids/opioid-overdose-crisis

Osgood, D. W., Feinberg, M. E., Gest, S. D., Moody, J., Ragan, D. T., Spoth, R., Greenberg, M., & Redmond, C. (2013). Effects of PROSPER on the influence potential of prosocial versus antisocial youth in adolescent friendship networks. *The Journal of Adolescent Health*, *53*(2), 174–179. doi:10.1016/j.jadohealth.2013.02.013 PMID:23885960

Outlook, J. (2016). *The attributes employers want to see on new college graduates' resumes*. National Association of Colleges and Employers. Retrieved from https://www.naceweb.org/career-development/trends-and-predictions/job-outlook-2016-attributes-employers-want-to-see-on-new-college-graduates-resumes/

Reed, K., & Madden-Dent, T. (2021). Social emotional learning as a lever for high school student mental health and academic success: A reflective analysis. In *Leading Schools with Social Emotional Academic Development (SEAD)*. IGI Global Publication. Retrieved at https://www.igi-global.com/book/leading-schools-social-emotional-academic/256645

Schonert-Reichi, K. A., Kitil, J., & Hanson-Peterson, J. (2017). To reach the students, teach the teachers: A national scan of teacher preparation and social & emotional learning. Report prepared for the Collaborative for Academic, Social, and Emotional Learning. University of British Columbia.

Spoth, R., Guyll, M., & Shin, C. (2009). Universal intervention as a protective shield against exposure to substance use: Long-term outcomes and public health significance. *American Journal of Public Health*, *99*(11), 2026–2033. doi:10.2105/AJPH.2007.133298 PMID:19762678

Swain-Bradway, J., Lindstrom Johnson, S., Bradshaw, C., & McIntosh, K. (2017). *What are the economic costs of implementing SWPBIS in comparison to the benefits from reducing suspensions?* Technical Brief from Center for Positive Behavioral Interventions and Supports. https://assets-global.website-files.com/5d3725188825e071f1670246/5d76c00cb9339d5f3f267ee7_economiccostsswpbis.pdf

Taylor, R. D., Oberle, E., Durlak, J. A., & Weissberg, R. P. (2017). Promoting positive youth development through school-based social and emotional learning interventions: A meta-analysis of follow-up effects. *Child Development*, *88*(4), 1156–1171. doi:10.1111/cdev.12864 PMID:28685826

Yoder, N., Atwell, M. N., Godek, D., Dusenbury, L., Bridgeland, J. M., & Weissberg, R. (2020). *Preparing youth for the workforce of tomorrow: Culturivating the social and emotional skills employers demand*. CASEL publication. Retrieved at https://casel.org/collaborative-state-initiative/

Yoder, N., Dusenbury, L., Martinez-Black, T., & Weissberg, R. P. (2020). *Emerging insights: From insights to action, redefining state efforts to support social and emotional learning*. Collaborative for Academic, Social, and Emotional Learning. Retrieved from www.casel.org

Zogby, J., Bohnert, C., Penz, M., & Buturovic, Z. (2017). *Business decision-makers view of the importance of early childhood in promoting social-emotional skills in the adult workforce*. Zogby Analytics. Retrieved at https://zogbyanalytics.com/case-studies-2

Acknowledgment

The editors would like to acknowledge the help of all the people involved in this project. First, the editors would like to thank each one of the authors for their chapter contributions. We sincerely appreciate the authors' time and expertise which is shared with the world through this book. Second, the editors wish to acknowledge the valuable contributions of the external reviewers who elevated the quality, coherence, and content presentation of each chapter. Most of the authors also served as referees; we highly appreciate their double contribution. Without the authors and reviewers' support, this book would not have become a reality.

The editors would also like to acknowledge the help of the Collaborative for Academic, Social, and Emotional Learning (CASEL), which helps identify the need for SEAD in education through rigorous research, open and on-going communication between U.S. states and school districts, and connecting education with policy and business stakeholders. This textbook was inspired by its advocacy for more explicit social-emotional instruction in higher education. Our hope is that this research-based resource will bridge higher education with educational workforce development, school policies, instruction and classroom management practices around the world by helping infuse SEL into educator preparation programs.

Lastly, but with the upmost importance, the editors would like to thank our families and friends for their encouragement and support during our endeavor to produce an academic textbook. A project of this magnitude requires significant time and energy. We are grateful for your support, encouragement, and your love.

Tara Madden-Dent
Sierra Nevada University, USA

Deborah Oliver
National University, USA & Mindful SEAD, USA

Chapter 1
Mindful Social Emotional Academic Development and Emotional Resilience

Deborah Oliver
National University & Mindful SEAD, USA

Molly Dahl
Mindful SEAD, USA

ABSTRACT

This chapter will provide an overview of the history and the basics of SEL/SEAD, SEAD in current time, mindfulness as the foundation of SEL and SEAD, and emotional resilience as the key to successful SEAD implementation and application in all areas of education, from the legislative offices to the PK learning space. The hope is to increase the understanding that SEAD is not a passing fad, not a trend, not "one more thing" that teachers will feel overwhelmed by, and not something to be feared or dreaded.

INTRODUCTION

By 2015, Mindfulness-Based Stress Reduction (MBSR) had gained a foot hold and was being taught in clinics, hospitals, and schools around the world. In the 1970s, Jon Kabat-Zinn, Ph.D., spent years at the University of Massachusetts Medical Center creating a mindfulness meditation program, MBSR, (what was then called Stress Reduction and Relaxation Program) to support those who suffered health problems. The results of his MBSR program are far-reaching and profound. Adults, teens, and children have experienced improvements in the cultivation of attention skills and emotional regulation as well as reductions in stress, anxiety, and worry. (Kabat-Zinn, 2013).

Herein, we borrow Kabat-Zinn's concept of Mindfulness-Based and apply that to social, emotional learning (SEL), and to social, emotional, and academic development (SEAD) to focus our approach through a different, more personalized lens. Each educator, administrator, and school counselor must stand on an unshakeable foundation of mindfulness; only by and through the focused application of at-

DOI: 10.4018/978-1-7998-6728-9.ch001

tentional awareness can one know their emotional state and inner landscape, and then make responsible decisions of how to best manage the self and interact with others. As the adults in education reinforce their foundation with Mindfulness-Based SEAD, used in conjunction with Mindful Social, Emotional Learning (M-SEL), their influence on their students, as well as their colleagues, will increase in its positive effect.

According to Dr. Mary Helen Immordino-Yang, "all learning in emotional." (Immordino-Yang, 2016). If the emotional component of learning, and teaching, is neglected, the educational process and the outcomes will not be as positively powerful as the potential they hold—that potential being the observable thriving, flourishing, and holistic well-being of each individual in the education system.

This chapter will provide an overview of the history and the basics of SEL/SEAD, SEAD in current time, mindfulness as the foundation of SEL and SEAD, and emotional resilience as the key to successful SEAD implementation and application in all areas of education, from the offices to the PK learning space. In The Aspen Institutes *The Evidence Base of How We Learn* report, "social, emotional, and academic development is an essential part of pre-K-12 education that can transform schools into places that foster academic excellence, collaboration and communication, creativity and innovation, empathy and respect, civic engagement, and other skills and dispositions needed for success in the 21st Century." (Jones & Kahn, 2017).

As education embraces SEAD and cultivates a dynamic relationship with it, we will enjoy the reality of Dr. Martin Seligman's perspective:

The time has come for a new prosperity, on that takes flourishing seriously as the goal of education and of parenting. Learning to value and to attain flourishing must start early—in the formative years of schooling—and it is this new prosperity, kindled by positive education, that the world can now choose. (Seligman, 2011).

BASICS OF SEL

Education is a changing phenomenon, based on the changing dynamic of human progress and growth. When a society is mainly agrarian and performing work and labor with the physical body, classroom education might be of little importance. Yet as societies have progressed beyond a focus on agriculture, and through the industrial age into the technological age and beyond, education has both shaped that progress and become a product of it.

At this current point in the history of educating societies, by educating their children, we have moved into the realm of the inner world. Advancements in technology, science, and human potential have necessitated a shift in the way we educate our children in the 21st Century. Whereas once the focus was on mastering outer, hard skills with myriad tools, the shift has moved us inward to the essential skills of human potential, the amazing plasticity of the brain, and the infinite realm of the mind. The tools now most needed by our young are those that will enable them to "contribute to and thrive in this new environment." (Goleman & Senge, 2014).

Social Emotional Learning entered the education scene in the late 1980s in New Haven, Connecticut with the Social Development curriculum created by Yale psychologist, Roger Weissberg. Dr. Daniel Goleman, psychologist, best-selling author, and presenter, along with Dr. Mark Greenberg, professor, developmental psychologist, and author, are among the original founders of the SEL, Social Emotional

Learning, movement. These three psychologists and professors, along with many others, were able to use their depth of knowledge of the human psyche and what leads a person to thriving and flourishing to influence the current educational landscape.

According to the Collaborative for Academic, Social, and Emotional Learning (CASEL), the organization co-founded by Goleman, Greenberg, and others, one of the most well-known resources for social and emotional learning, "Social and emotional learning (SEL) is an integral part of education and human development. SEL is the process through which all young people and adults acquire and apply the knowledge, skills, and attitudes to develop healthy identities, manage emotions and achieve personal and collective goals, feel and show empathy for others, establish and maintain supportive relationships, and make responsible and caring decisions." (CASEL).

Several additional prominent psychologists, psychiatrists, researchers, and professors have all contributed greatly to the body of research and effective practices of Social Emotional Academic Development. Dr. Richard Davidson at the University of Wisconsin-Madison, Dr. Daniel Siegel at UCLA, and Dr. Mary Helen Immordino-Yang at the University of Southern California have made profound contributions to how we understand not only the emotional nature of learning, but the neuroscience and neuropsychology of it as well. Much additional research around the globe is solidifying that mindfulness is indeed a key component of increasing learning outcomes. An Australian study highlights the importance of teaching to the affective domain; "what we know will influence what we feel, and affective teaching can therefore be used to optimize the cognitive domain and improve learning outcomes." (Zianian, Sawyer, Evans, & Gillham, 2015).

These thought leaders, with their years of research and application of tools, practices, and protocols, along with legions of classroom educators who are joining the ranks, are the supporting pillars of SEL/SEAD, which is fast establishing itself as the foundation of 21st Century Learning.

IS THERE A DIFFERENCE BETWEEN SEL AND SEAD?

Looking at the elements of SEAD we see that they are not so different from SEL (as outlined above), yet SEAD expands to include how the social and emotional factors of learning directly influence and impact the academic nature of what education is and can be. The importance of social awareness as well as emotional intelligence are underscored as vital to academic achievement. It is through a solid understanding and regular application of SEL strategies and practices that students can move beyond mere achievement into academic success and then on to academic thriving.

According to the Aspen Institute, the process of learning must include all components of the hierarchy of needs as laid out by Maslow in his Theory of Human Motivation first published in 1943. (Maslow, 1943). Now, in the current climate of education, the direct, explicit instruction of SEL is a valid and indispensable undertaking. From the Aspen Institute's report, A Nation at Hope, we read that *"Children learn best when we treat them as human beings, with social and emotional as well as academic needs." "Children require a broad array of skills, attitudes, and values to succeed in school, careers, and in life. They require skills such as paying attention, setting goals, collaboration, and planning for the future. They require attitudes such as internal motivation, perseverance, and a sense of purpose. They require values such as responsibility, honesty, and integrity. They require the abilities to think critically, consider different views, and problem solve. And these social, emotional, and academic capacities are increasingly demanded in the American workplace, which puts a premium on the ability to work in diverse teams, to grapple with difficult problems, and to adjust to rapid change.*" (Nation at Hope).

Again, the necessity of addressing the emotional well-being of the learner is of predominant importance. *"The promotion of social, emotional, and academic learning is not a shifting educational fad; it is the substance of education itself. It is not a distraction from the "real work" of math and English instruction; it is how instruction can succeed.... a mindset that should inform the entire educational enterprise"*. (IBID).

FROM ANCIENT TO CURRENT TIME IN SEAD

The Greek philosopher Aristotle's understanding of education almost 2,500 years ago revolved around a central question, "What makes for human flourishing?"

Roughly eighty years ago, Abraham Maslow was also on to something in terms of SEL and SEAD. In his 1943 paper, *A Theory of Human Motivation,* he may have been among the first of the current SEL proponents to emphasize the possibility of self-actualization. *"A musician must make music, an artist must paint, a poet must write, if he is to be ultimately happy. What a man can be, he must be. This need we may call self-actualization. It refers to the desire for self-fulfillment, namely, to the tendency for him to become actualized in what he is potentially. This tendency might be phrased as the desire to become more and more what one is, to become everything that one is capable of becoming."*

The more recent study of Positive Psychology, a field established and led by Dr. Martin Seligman, also has well-being as its primary focus: not only of each individual, but societies and all humankind as well. Dr. Seligman's interest in what makes life worth living has become a world-wide movement—initiating and growing a sea-change in the way we do education. Now, the goal of education is being re-written. Those with interest in and understanding of the cardinal importance of inner skills and the actualization of human potential are crafting that new definition.

Two primary organizations, CASEL and The Aspen Institute, exist as "clearing houses" for all things SEAD, providing ample resources, research, and support for educators to reconnect with some of the most critical and long-established goal of education.

CASEL was founded in "1994 with the goal of establishing high-quality, evidence-based social and emotional learning (SEL) as an essential part of preschool through high school education." (CASEL). Three years later, in 1997, the CASEL organization published *Promoting Social and Emotional Learning' Guidelines for Educators,* a book providing practical strategies for teachers to "create comprehensive and coordinated SEL programming." (CASEL). In 2015, they released *the Handbook of Social and Emotional Learning: Research and Practice.*

CASEL has been working since those early years to support the education community with evidence-based programs for all levels of students pre-K through year 12. They have established a set of competencies, a framework, that identifies five core areas of social and emotional learning.

- Self-awareness
- Self-management
- Social awareness
- Relationship Skills
- Responsible Decision-Making

Based on these, and the ever-changing dynamic in education, CASEL's definition (see Glossary) of SEL provides a solid framework for educators to guide the cultivation of emotional intelligence, responsibility, and self-regulation in each student. As we move steadily and incrementally away from standards-based education, which we now know does not serve the growth and highest potential of the individual, toward a competency-based model, we better understand the value and importance of competencies, and degrees of mastery within each competency, and the ability of each individual to thrive and flourish.

The Aspen Institute is an organization with many branches and a comprehensive, international outreach. Founded in 1949 by Chicago Industrialist, Walter Paepcke as The Aspen Institute for Humanistic Studies, it now includes not only a focus on education and intellectual understandings, but development in areas such as communications and culture, and philanthropy and social enterprise (to name a few) as well. As founder Paepcke said at the Executive Seminary in the year of its founding, the seminar is intended "to help a leader gain access to his or her own humanity by becoming more self-aware, more self-correcting, and more self-fulfilling." (The Aspen Institute, 2020).

We no longer see education as a way to turn out factory-ready workers, less inclined to think and make decision on their own accord. As Aristotle believed that "all human action was to achieve happiness" (Seligman, 2011) we now appreciate that the human being is a richly nuanced creation, capable of both extreme evil and supreme good. We now know that it behooves us to educate toward the inner resources of each child we teach. We no longer simply focus on facts and figures but include instruction and guided practice on the "five elements of well-being: positive emotion, engagement, meaning, positive relationships, and accomplishment." (Seligman, 2011). We delve deep into what it means to thrive, to flourish, and how to accomplish a life worth living. We are free, and even encouraged, to explore just such questions: "How do successful individuals and organizations become successful?" "What is success?" "What encourages students to seek success?" "How can we teach inner motivation?" "What does well-being look like on an individual level? On a societal level?" "How can education positively influence the well-being of both students and teachers?"

Through the inquiry into deep questions such as these, we come to see that SEAD practices can help educators shape their students into individuals who are autonomous, self-motivated, self-evaluative, self-responsible, and eventually, self-actualized, guided by a sense of meaning and purpose established on the cultivation of personal values, strengths, and talents. We also learn to appreciate that the thriving of any society is based on the number of individuals within that society who flourish. And none of this can happen without mindfulness.

MINDFULNESS AS THE FOUNDATION

No single, common, agreed upon definition of mindful is to be found in the research literature. Yet many definitions exist. For our purposes here, we will base our common understanding on the definitions of two mindfulness experts: Jon Kabat-Zinn's explanations: "moment-to-moment, non-judgmental awareness" and "being in the present on purpose," (Kabat-Zinn, 2013) and Daniel Goleman's: "paying attention to what [they] think and feel without being carried away by those inner stirrings." (Goleman & Senge, 2014). *Mindfulness is choosing to paying attention in current time.* As the attentional awareness is focused on the present, and we let go of judgement (this is good, or this is bad), we come into an open space of mind, neither consumed by the past, nor anxious about the future, but calm and focused on the here and now. And in the world of teaching and learning, this mindful awareness is of paramount importance. We know that "the brain's centers for learning operate at their peak when we are focused and calm." (Goleman & Senge, 2014).

This long-established foundation of a mindfulness-based approach is built on solid ground, not on sand but on years of careful, reliable research, with proven results. Richard Davidson and Daniel Goleman, in their recent work together, *Altered Traits,* explain that "every aspect of attention involves the prefrontal cortex in some way." (Goleman & Davidson, 2017). The prefrontal cortex is a primary brain region associated with learning: what the education system has been addressing since day one. As educators, we know—even if we have never really stopped to think about it—that if our students are not paying attention, they will not, they cannot learn.

Being mindful can help both the brain and the mind slow down. It is by going slowly, mindfully, that the executive function centers of the brain, the pre-frontal cortex, can assume control. Executive functioning comprises a number of responsibilities including "focusing and ignoring distractions, remembering and using new information, planning action and revising the plan, and inhibiting fast, impulsive thoughts and actions" (Seligman, 2011) as well as emotional impulses. This slower, more focused awareness can help learners sustain their attention for longer periods of time.

Learning takes time and patience. When students, and teachers, become frustrated if the learning task is too difficult or bored if the task is too easy, mindful self-awareness can facilitate the shift in attentional focus back to an engaged state. Self-awareness can help student internalize the teachings of any subject area and understand on a personal level why they matter and how they affect each individual. Self-awareness can be the well-spring of personal responsibility and motivation that we, as the educators, hope each student will come to possess and develop to full capacity.

Just as all academic learning occurs, so too the practices of mindfulness and the five SEL CASEL competencies—training the mind also need repetition, guided instruction with gentle correction, and finally, multiple opportunities for independent practice in the area of self: awareness, management/regulation, motivation, responsibility, and discipline. In such a way, over time, the student attains mastery of these "self" skills. Diligently cultivated, that attentional shift away from frustration, boredom, or any emotional extreme, becomes an exemplary display of self-regulation. That self-regulation has as its source a mindfulness-based practice that reflects self-understanding, positive decision-making skills, and social awareness.

EMOTIONS AND ATTENTIONAL AWARENESS

We learn best when we are calm and focused. Emotional upsets throw a wrench into the learning process. If we are, or become, emotionally triggered by something—a past event, getting the answer wrong, making a mistake in front of others, being distressed by events at home or outside the classroom—the cognitive centers of the brain, the prefrontal cortex, are not available. We are overwhelmed by the chemical cascade of the powerful emotion, most often fear or anger, (in any degree from mild frustration to full-blown rage). In such situations, the prefrontal cortex goes offline and the amygdala and hippocampus work in tandem to send an "all functions go" message to the brain to keep us alive. Our survival mechanisms kick in and quickly co-opt the functions of the rational, thinking brain. Several current research studies (Immordio-Lang & Damasio, 207; Li, Gow & Zou, 2020) suggest that the brain under stress or threat, real or perceived, cannot learn. It is engaged in keeping the human organism alive, which does not leave room for cognitive tasks.

For this reason, education professionals must help learners of all ages to emotionally self-regulate. The progression of developing self-regulations skills works much the same as learning to recall information, then integrate and apply that information to synthesize self-generated responses and solutions. The establishment of dependent, or supported, self-regulation is the first achievement benchmark. And the establishment and sustained application of independent self-regulation is the second benchmark, allowing learners to demonstrate their emotional regulation skills.

Educators must begin with direct instruction, explicitly teaching learners the vocabulary, "formula", and application of emotional self-regulation strategies and methods. This is best accomplished in a safe and engaging environment with sufficient opportunities for guided practice. As foundational levels of competency are achieved, students will be prepared for further advancements into independent practice, reinforced through accountability and self-evaluation check ins, to ownership of emotional regulation and management. Working continuously with students over time, during the entire course of the academic "career", they will develop and demonstrate their own emotional self-management and self-regulation skills.

By learning to quiet the storms of emotional distress, students can re-focus their attentional awareness to the learning task at hand. Again, the stages of the development of emotional maturity and self-management are based on age and developmental progress. Adults would certainly not expect a kindergartener to expound upon the trigger that set off a tantrum with tears and shouting. Adults can facilitate the self-regulation of that child with compassionate understanding and guiding the child through the process of coming into current time, settling the breath, and calming the mind.

Adults can help the child identify strong feelings with images or icons of facial expressions that align with child's felt emotions, as well as locating physical sensations of the emotion in the body (i.e.: rapid breathing, tight fists, or heat in the cheeks are all physical experiences of strong emotions). Learning to name the emotion, feel it in the physical body, and talk the self through releasing that emotion are all steps on the path of emotional resilience. Overcoming the meltdown, getting a hold of oneself, and being able to refocus on the (learning) task at hand are the components of emotional resilience. As the child brings mindful awareness to the experience of the current moment, and with help from the teacher, can settle the strong emotions, he or she is laying down a neural pathway of emotional self-regulation and resilience.

Like academic learning, emotional self-regulation and resilience can be learned and cultivated.

EMOTIONAL RESILIENCE – WHAT IT IS AND WHY IT IS NECESSARY

All learning involves making mistakes. All learning necessarily involves failure. But what we have failed to recognize is that by not teaching our students how to fail, they then fail to learn. Dr. Tal Ben-Shahar concisely sums up this concept with his phrase, "Learn to fail or fail to learn."

Students, and their teachers, must know that it is OK to need help. They must know that it is accepted not to know and to be wrong. By coddling our children and teens and not teaching them how to fail, they are set up for a difficult life, one that is not reflective of the reality they will face post-classroom. Resilience is a learned skill. Some individuals come with a bit more natural propensity toward it, but it can be learned by all. Resilience is a vital component of any SEL or SEAD program or instruction. It starts with self-awareness.

Most children want things to go their way. Most adults do too. As individuals incorporate more and more SEAD strategies, practices, and protocols, there is an increased understanding that things will not always "go your way". When things do not go your way, it does not mean that you are bad, or there is something wrong with you. Our children must have this understanding woven into their hearts, and into their self-concept.

Learning to fail involves understanding that sometimes a wrong answer is derived, sometimes the individual just does not know, and sometimes the individual will lose. When children are taught that there is a "second winner" or that everyone wins, the children are being taught lies. They are not learning the realities of life. They are ultimately set up for failure, without a single tool to manage that failure.

They must be taught truth. They must be provided with the tools and strategies for self-management, for demonstrated resilience. It is important to guide them through the development of these tools until they achieve a level mastery in their demonstrated behaviors. This is how education professionals should teach students and guide them toward a life of thriving and flourishing and self-actualization.

Begin by teaching that failure is a wonderful opportunity for learning and for growth. Teach that there is nothing wrong with getting the wrong answer, or not knowing an answer. Provide direct instruction on the fact that when a student is "wrong" it does not mean that the student is bad, or that there is anything wrong with that student. These are the seeds of emotional resilience—knowing what one is worth, understanding that self-concept and self-perception are characteristics that can be cultivated, can be shaped by experience, by self-talk, and by perspective taking.

These characteristics are also the seeds of a growth mindset, for a growth mindset is necessarily resilient. It contains within its definition the idea that abilities and skills are changeable, can be influenced by both inside and outside factors, and that effort and hard work matter. Resilience is the capacity to bounce back after a struggle, challenge, or defeat. Is the ability to take perspective and to understand that things will change, and that personal effort can affect that change. Resilience is being nimble in the ever-change events that happen in the ever-present moment of now. Resilience is a learned skill. Every individual has the ability to cultivate it, no matter how much or how little of it is naturally possessed to being with.

RESILIENCE AS THE PROCESS AND THE PRODUCT

How is resilience cultivated? Let us explore a phenomenon that at first glance, is rather simple. But as it is unpacked, the depth will be revealed as will be the profound effects as it is put into practice.

If there is a quality or characteristic or disposition that we would like to develop, the only way to develop it is to "be" it. For example, we become kind by *being* kind. We become patient by *being* patient. And on the flip side of that coin, we become angry by being angry. That same principle applies here—we become resilient by *being* resilient. We become that quality by demonstrating the same quality in our behavior.

We would not expect an apple tree to bear oranges. Just so, we cannot expect ourselves to *be* patient if we have a noticeably short fuse and our demonstrated behavior is often anger. Many times, becoming angry is the result of a lack of patience. If we can take a deep breath, slow down, and come into current time, we allow the prefrontal cortex to come back to focus, and we then see that choices are available to us. We can choose to be patient. Or resilient. Or kind. When we are run over by strong feeling a lack of time, or a lack of resources, or a lack of energy, the first thing to go is our patience. And when patience is gone, a wide variety of strong negative emotions rise to the surface, eager to display their power.

And how do we simply *be* resilient?

There might not be anything simple about it. Yet, with even a small degree of mindful self-awareness, we can corral our strong emotions and display a measure of self-management. As Seligman stated, slowing our emotional impulses, and going slow in general, "allows our executive function to take over" (Seligman, 2011). Our executive function is made visible, demonstrated, in the calling forth of our patience by settling down with a couple of slow, deep breaths. Because our decision-making ability is an executive function, not an emotional one, we see that demonstrated patience reflects active executive functioning.

And how do we get to the point where we can choose to "turn off" the survival mechanisms of the fight or flight reactions of the brain and "turn on" our executive functioning region instead?

First, we need to have a clear picture of what resilience looks like as opposed to unrestrained emotional displays. Students need to see, to observe and witness, demonstrated resilience to grasp that picture, which can then become a personal understanding. Here we lean heavily on the old teaching adage "what you model is what you get." Teachers, counselors, administrators, and office personnel all need to model resilient behaviors for students to know what it looks like, and thus what it means to be resilient.

An example might help us get a clearer idea.

Suzie is a first-year teacher with a handful of rambunctious, precocious children in her 5th grade classroom. Having little experience with classroom management, she often loses her patience and yells at this small group of rowdy students. Unaware yet that the rowdiness is probably caused by boredom, she sends these students to a timeout where they continue to display behaviors that are a distraction to the learning environment. Suzie frets that the "good kids" in her class are being affected by the disorder and are not learning all that they are capable of learning.

Suzie has not demonstrated emotionally resilient behavior, but has let her strong emotions dictate her automatic, negative reactions. She has not been able to provide a positive model for her students.

And the "troublemakers"? Suzie's demonstrated impatience and frustration, her yelling and belittling, simply provides an example of how those students can "get their way".

Flipping the situation, if Suzie were to demonstrate patience, talking her students through her own experience, she could provide a model to her students of what effective self-management and resilience could look like. She might stop the academic instruction, ask for the attention of all students, and explain her emotional as well as her thinking processes to them.

It might look like this: "Young ladies and gentlemen. May I please have your attention?"

Suzie waits for the children to settle down and to have all eyes on her eyes.

"Thank you. I appreciate your attention. Our classroom is a little loud and disruptive today. That makes it hard for me to keep my thoughts in order. Have you ever experienced a time when your thoughts were a jumble, and it was hard for you to learn?"

Suzie opens a classroom discussion, inviting the comments of only one or two students who raise their hands to share. She carefully monitors the attention of the rest of the students and keeps the sharing short. Then she continues with her explanation:

"Thank you for sharing. Yes, it can be hard to pay attention when it is so loud. When it is so loud that I cannot hear what Karen is saying, then it is too loud. I being to lose my patience. When I lose my patience, I raise my voice. That does not feel good to me. It hurts my throat! And I get more frustrated. Can anyone tell me what often happens when someone gets frustrated?"

Again, she asks for volunteers to share their understanding of what frustrated behavior looks like. Then, she can own her behavior, modeling maturity and social intelligence, by sharing: "Yes, people often yell when they are frustrated. That is what happens for me. I yell. Can you help me think of some other options that might be better next time I feel frustrated?"

Continuing with the class discussion where all are invited to participate and share their ideas demonstrates that Suzie trusts her students to help her find a more effective solution. This entire discussion is a positive model of how we both learn and demonstrate resilience.

Suzie then wraps up the short discussion on classroom behavior, patience, and resilience by explicitly instructing students on the vocabulary of these qualities and characteristics.

"Young ladies and gentlemen, thank you for your quiet attention during this impromptu discussion. Having your help to process my impatience and my strong emotion toward anger is important to me. When we are facing a challenge or a struggle and we do not know what to do next, asking for help from trusted friends can be especially useful. Instead of losing my patience and yelling at you, I was able to calm myself and use my words to explain what was happening for me. By not losing my patience, I demonstrated resilience. Can anyone explain what *resilience* is?"

Allowing a final opportunity for students to share can help solidify their understanding of the value of working together to find solutions to challenges and problems.

Suzie can either affirm the students' responses, add important points that were not stated by the students, or clarify any misunderstandings. She can conclude the discussion with a stated definition or positively challenge her students to work together for the rest of the day, or the week, to help each other demonstrate resilience.

The first option might sound like, "Resilience is the ability to bounce back after a big struggle or after you get something wrong or make a mistake. It takes some effort and a big belief in yourself that you can work hard enough to overcome your challenges. It also includes knowing when to ask for help."

The second option might sound like, "It looks like most of us have a better understanding now of what resilience is and what it looks like when someone is being resilient. So that we can all be resilient together, and each one of us be resilient by ourselves, let us work together the rest of this week to support each other in demonstrating resilient behavior. We can support others by listening, by being patient, and by keeping a calm and settled mind."

As students have a concrete example of and direct instruction on the process of learning and then demonstrating resilience, they are learning to self-manage the emotional reactions that stem from an activated amygdala. As they can progressively improve their self-management skills by controlling their strong emotions, the prefrontal cortex develops a powerful pathway of self-regulation and positive decision-making skills.

Decision-making skills is one of the five CASEL competencies. When the prefrontal cortex, our executive function region, is offline, hijacked by potent emotional reactions...we are not making decisions. In our brain, flooded by the neurochemistry of runaway emotions, the amygdala is calling the shots. Overwhelmed by the flood, the chemical cascade of fear or anger, the demonstrated behaviors are emotional reactions, not considered and chosen responses. Learning to be aware of and then self-manage these reactions by slowing down in current time and choosing a constructive response is emotional resilience.

STRATEGIES FOR CULTIVATING SELF-AWARENESS

Below are three strategies for developing mindful self-awareness, the first of the competencies needs as the cornerstone to support the others. The first of these strategies, a basic breathing practice—Diaphragmatic Breathing—lays the foundation upon which the other two are scaffolded. These can be used as a script, read directly from the page to the students. As the teacher becomes comfortable with the strategy, having practiced it to a personal level of competency, he or she will be more fluid and natural as they guide their own students.

1. Diaphragmatic Breathing:

   a. Sit up tall, lengthening the spine. Relax the face, the mouth, and the shoulders.
   b. Look down at the front edge of your desk or your lap. Keep your eyes soft.
   c. Feel your seat in the chair and your feet on the floor.
   d. Come into current time with yourself—notice how you feel physically, mentally, and emotionally.
   e. Slowly release your breath in a long, slow exhale. Pull the belly in slightly toward the spine as push out all the air.
   f. Soften the belly and let it expand wide in front of you as you take in a slow deep inhale.
   g. Keep the face and shoulders relaxed.
   h. Exhale long and slowly, squeezing the belly in.
   i. Inhale, with a big round belly.
   j. And one more time…Exhale.
   k. And inhale.
   l. Exhale, letting breath come its own natural rhythm.
   m. Check in with how you feel now. Are you ready to proceed with your task? Or do you need a few more deep breaths?

The following strategies are self-evaluation that deepen the awareness of the self in the current moment. These will need to be explicitly taught to students and practiced often together as students become more and more familiar are enabled to practice on their own to self-manage strong emotions, whether anxiety, fear, frustration, anger, or sadness, before they come inappropriate or destructive displays of behavior.

As you get your students settled, remind them that you are all practicing together the new skill of mindful awareness which is a powerful tool for helping them with their academic learning and goals.

2. 5+1=Right Now Awareness (Dahl, 2018) Adapted with permission from the author.

   a. Sit up tall, lengthening the spine. Relax the face, the mouth, and the shoulders.
   b. Look down at the front edge of your desk or your lap. Keep your eyes soft.
   c. Feel the seat in the chair and the feet on the floor.
   d. Come into current time with yourself—notice how you feel physically, mentally, and emotionally. Become aware of your close environment.
   e. Find the breath—notice where the breath moves the body.
   f. Soften the belly and let the breath sink from the chest and shoulders to the belly. This helps your mind let go of stress and anxiety and to relax.
   g. Take a slow, deep breath in.
   h. And out, slowly, slowly.
   i. Take a deep breath in.
   j. And out.

k. In.
l. And out.
m. Now, look around you. What do you see? Look at just one object. See its shape and color and texture. (Give 5-8 seconds of silence.)
n. What is one thing you can hear? Focus on this sound. Can you identify its source? (Give 5-8 seconds of silence.)
o. What is one thing you can feel or touch? Is the texture rough or smooth? Maybe you can feel the air on your skin. Is it warm or cool? (Give 5-8 seconds of silence.)
p. What is one thing you can smell? Does that smell remind you of anything? (Give 5-8 seconds of silence.)
q. What do you taste if anything? (Give 5-8 seconds of silence.)
r. And finally, how do you feel? Are you settled? Calm? (Give 5-8- seconds of silence.)
s. Please bring your attention back to your breath. Take a deep breath, image that it moves all the way to the outside edge of your skin.
t. Feel your seat on the chair and your feet on the floor.
u. Mentally become aware of the space around you.
v. Quietly open your eyes and get ready for our next learning task.
w. Thank you for your respectful participation. I feel settled, calm, and ready to learn more exciting information.

This check-in helps bring the awareness into the immediate surroundings in the present moment. The mind can let go of emotional upset or distress more easily when it can focus on the objects of the five senses. By the time the individual has progressed through checking in with all the senses and has come to the inner state of being, indicated by the question, "How do you feel?", it is common that the emotional state is mostly settled and calmed.

3. inSPIRE Check-in (Dahl, 2019)

inSPIRE is an advantageous way to settle into current time and assess the well-being of each of the "layers" of the self. Being by looking *in*—inward with a sharply focused lens of self-awareness. S signifies social well-being, P denotes physical well-being, I stands for intellectual or mental well-being, R for relationship well-being (which can be either relationship with the self or close, familial relationships. Note that relationships with friends, peers, teachers, and other school personnel is under Social), and finally E is emotional well-being.

The check-in entails going mentally through each letter, which represents the parts that make up the whole of each individual, and rating the self, using a 1-5 sliding scale. One is low and five is high. For example, when checking in with P, the physical self, the participant might notice that he or she is hungry and remember that it has been several hours since eating. The self-rating might be a 2. And so forth through each letter.

(Note before starting…students will need a piece of scratch paper or the inSPIRE Check-in worksheet to track their level of well-being for each of the 5 categories.

a. Begin with breathing as mentioned above.

b. We will use a rating system for this check-in, from 1-5. One is low and 5 is high. Please write down the number as you check in with each area of yourself.
c. Being with S, your social well-being. How are you at school, with your friends, and/or with your teachers? Note the number that best corresponds with how you are doing socially. (Give about 5 seconds of quiet think time.)
d. Next, please check in with your physical well-being, the letter P. Are you hungry? Did you get enough sleep last night? How are doing physically? (Think time.)
e. And now, the I, the intellectual or mental part of yourself. How is your intellectual processing, your thinking? Do you understand the academic instruction in your class(es)? Is it too hard and you might be confused? Or too easy and you might be bored? Or is it just right? Again, rate yourself from 1 to 5. (Think time.)
f. Moving to R, your relationships. How are you doing with your close people? Do you feel supported? Loved? Do you need support? Rate yourself here, in relationships, from 1 to 5. (Think time.)
g. And finally, the E, your emotional well-being. How are you doing? How are you feeling? Rate yourself 1 to 5. (Think time.)
h. Now look at your overall ratings. What is your highest? Take a little moment to celebrate what is going well for you. Maybe you had a great conversation with your dad on the way to school today and you have a 5 for R. Give yourself a high-five. (Pay close attention as you walk around to those students who might not have remarkably high numbers in any of the areas. They may need extra support from you today, or you might consider pairing them with another student for additional support during certain learning tasks.
i. And now, let us look at the low number. It is OK to have low numbers! Not everything is going to go smoothly for everyone, every day. When you have identified the area where you need a little support, write down one, just one thing that would help you get a higher number here. You might need to go to be early tonight if your P, physical was low. Maybe you need to ask a teacher for extra help with something you are struggling with. (Think time.) Whatever that one thing is that would help, can you make a goal for yourself to do that? (As students are finishing up, do a check for understanding, or if any of the students need clarification or help. Walk around and let students know that you see where they are and provide appropriate or necessary feedback on their ideas to improve their low number. When you are satisfied that students are comfortable with their self-assessment and have a plan for improving the low area, finish up with any of your own thoughts or ideas.
j. Thank you, class for being attentive and focused on this task. It is useful for each of us to know how we are doing on the inside so we can know how to best manage ourselves. Are we ready to move on to our next learning task?

Using the inSPIRE Check-in can be a useful tool at the beginning of each day, if a child is sent to the discipline center as a way for that child to settle into current time and "blow off steam" before speaking with the counselor, or as a quick check-in at the end of the day. The SPIRE can even be broken apart, a single letter used to do a quick check-in, using "fist-to-five" in front of the heart to indicate how each student is in the chosen area. For example, when instructing a new concept, as a check for preliminary understanding, the teacher could ask students to do a fist-to-five check in at the intellectual level, indicating the level of early comprehension of the material.

These three strategies allow students to move into a place of calm and focused awareness which then allows them to make beneficial or advantageous choices. Mindful behaviors do not happen without mindful inner awareness. Being mindful of ourselves and who we are is the foundation for the SEL and SEAD. Without knowing about mindful practices, being mindful, and paying attention, students are missing the foundation to practice solid social and emotional awareness and intelligence.

Teaching children and teens to be mindful is a necessary, yet often excluded, ingredient of SEAD. It is a necessary element of becoming self-aware in current time. Self-awareness requires mindfulness—that each individual pay attention to him or herself in the current moment, sensing the emotions being experienced, how he or she thinks about those emotions, as well as the breathing rate.

Using the breath to settle an emotional tempest is a secularized approach to an ancient tradition that has been validated through scientific research and study. (Kabat-Zinn, 2013*)*. The breath is a powerful tool to facilitate slowing down, to regain composure, and to become available to the possibility of the choice offered in the moment.

In the ancient world of Tibetan Yoga, students were taught to use the breath to calm and steady the mind. The Tibetan phrase, lung sem jukpa chikpa, (Yoga Studies Institute). "The mind rides the breath like a rider on a horse", creates a vivid image which those of us in modern times, with busy and harried minds, can appreciate. The thoughts are the rider. The breath is the horse. If the thoughts are chaotic, scattered hither and yon, or a jumbled mess, and metaphorically pulling on the reins or the horse (the breath), the breath will be fast and somewhat ragged, slightly jerky, and high in the chest, all of which create a more anxious state of mind.

When we can calm the breath by exhaling long and slowly, we naturally calm the mind. If we can use the analogy of a rider on a horse, we can see that the rider is the mind riding the currents of the breath. We can use the breath to slow the racing mind, to settle the frantic, scattered mind and to waken the dull and lethargic mind. The breath is a powerful tool, so easily at our disposal. Everyone can learn to regulate the breath and bring the mind into a calm and settled place.

This breath regulation, based on mindful self-awareness of your current inner state, is a preliminary step to demonstrating emotional resilience. The chain of events looks like this:

1. Emotional upset which can lead to a regrettable emotional episode (Goleman, 2003).
2. Become aware through mindful attention – notice the physical sensations and feelings, tight fists, fast heartbeat, heat in the cheeks or face, etc.
3. Intentionally pause
4. Exhale, then slow the breath through diaphragmatic breathing (explained above)
5. As the breath slows, come into current time
6. Self-evaluate with a personal "status update"
7. inSPIRE Check-in (Dahl, 2019) (explained above)
8. Allow the 90 second for the chemical cascade to dissipate
9. Consider how you are working on your emotional self-regulation and resilience
10. Consider your options and choices
11. Make the best choice available in the moment (which might be to excuse yourself and resume the conversation later when cooler heads prevail)

Building resilience, on a stable foundation of self-awareness and self-regulation through regulation of the breath and then through positive decision-making, places one squarely on the path of emotional and social intelligence. Development of these skills must also include a self-evaluative component. One cannot spend his or her entire life waiting for reinforcement or correction from outside sources. It is highly beneficial for everyone, students, and adults alike, to be able to self-assess, to self-evaluate, in order to adjust behaviors and attitudes.

The Self-Perception Theory, coined by Dr. Daryl Bem in (1972) helps us lay down a foundation of the self, built on the reality of self-evaluation and the creation of self-concept. Dr. Bem's theory explains that we place labels on and identify the self in the same way that we do with others—based on observable behaviors. We watch others and based on the behaviors they exhibit, we infer attitudes, character traits, and dispositions about that person.

And so, with the self. When we become self-aware and can self-evaluate our behavior, we can knowingly cultivate our own positive self-perception. If I observe myself holding open a door for someone with both hands full, I will label myself as helpful or kind. If I observe my demonstration of kindness on a regular basis, I begin to see myself with the character trait of kindness.

If I continually observe things about myself that I do not like, for example I see myself disrupting the learning environment and learn to see myself as disruptive, I end up with a self-perception that I do not like. I do not like myself. The encouraging part of this theory is that if I end up not liking myself, based on the behavior that I observe, I can change my behavior to something that I do find likeable or pleasing. As I self-evaluate my own social interactions, I can see how I either contribute to the well-being of the group or not. And based on how I feel about my contributions, either good or not, I can decide whether to change my outward behaviors. As I chose to change these behaviors to something more positive and likeable, I change the perception I have about myself, and thus my self-concept.

In the academic realm, we can cultivate within our students the practice of self-evaluation to help them understand how their efforts impact their learning. If a student is not attentive during the learning time and does not focus awareness during the practice-the-new-skill time, that student will see him or herself as not engaged or off-task. We know that students do not learn if they are not attentive to the instruction and the practice. What a student will come to learn is that his or her efforts during the learning process directly affect how much he or she takes in, assimilates, and can recall and apply—which of course his or her academic success.

In such a manner, we can support our students in what we traditionally think of as academic success, but we are providing them with so much more than just intellect and "smarts".

This process of self-evaluation can foster within each student a sense of personal responsibility, and a sense of academic ownership. As we support students in the cultivation of academic responsibility and ownership, we are providing them a skillset that is a necessary component of 21st Century learning and workplace success.

How can educators best teach, monitor, and assess the growth and progress of emotional skills and intelligence? Many will find it useful to first start with a rubric of what demonstrated SEL skills look like and then work backward. The authors of this chapter have created a Competency Benchmark rubric with performance indicators upon which to reference student behaviors, based on the identified areas of the five CASEL competencies, with one critical addition—Mindfulness. The M-SEL (Mindful Social Emotional Learning) Competency Benchmarks rubric is below.

SELF-EVALUATION RUBRIC

The M-SEL (Mindful SEL) Competency Benchmarks shown below takes the CASEL competencies and defines the categories with observable behaviors as self-evaluated by the student. Based on age and developmental stage, the authors have determined how much and how often an individual will demonstrate the benchmark behaviors. A younger learner will not demonstrate a high level of awareness, but as that individual matures through their academic years, they will end up with a full complement of SEL competencies and will demonstrate those up to 100% of the time.

M-SEL COMPETENCY BENCHMARKS

Student Self-Reflection

Competency progression is based on student self-reflection of observable behavior and awareness of inner states of being and mental/cognitive processes. Students will use their mindfulness as the foundation for the other five competencies, demonstrated beneficial or useful actions that proceed from that base-level of self-awareness. All performance levels are based on age and developmentally appropriate behaviors and cognitive processes. Those included here are for upper-high school students and adults.

Figure 1.

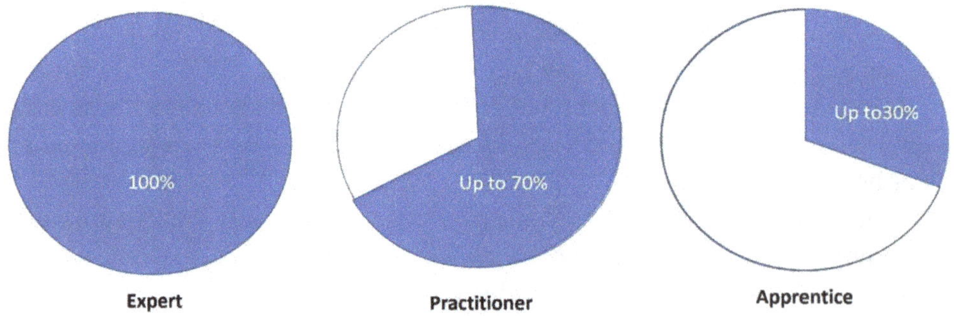

Competency **Mindfulness** – is choosing to pay attention to current time with focused awareness.	• I can bring my awareness into the current moment and let go of worrying about the past and being anxious about the future. • I can use my breath to settle a busy, troubled, or upset mind. • I am able to check in Socially, Spiritually, Physically, Emotionally, about Relationships, and Mentally/Intellectually. • I have and can utilize strategies to shut out distractions and stay engaged and focused on the task at hand.
Competency **Self-Awareness** – is an ability to clearly and accurate see, label, and identify the self, based on observable behaviors, including spoken words and recognition of cognitive processes	• I know my strengths, motives, and desires. I am conscious of my inner and outer states of being based on the inSPIRE check-in. • I am aware of my emotional state and can identify physical signals as manifestations of emotional occurrences. • I can see myself clearly and objectively based on observation of my demonstrated behaviors and can successfully navigate a full range of thoughts about myself including cognitive awareness and control, beliefs and belief structure, and interactive social and relationship awareness.
Competency **Self-Management** – is an ability to consciously manage behavior and words, (with an awareness on how these words and behaviors influence and impact others) and take responsibility for thoughts, actions, and attitudes	• I am conscious of my thoughts and feelings and respond with appropriate actions. • I take responsibility for my own choices, which I careful consider before reacting. • I can manage and discipline myself in situations that are potentially frustrating or difficult. • I can consciously change patterned reactions and respond in constructive and considerate ways.
Competency **Decision-Making Skills** – is a cognitive process of sorting information (facts, figures, and opinions) and then choosing from available options. Decisions can be based on reasoned process or intuition or a combination of the two.	• I make decisions based on relevant data including facts, primary sources of research and information, and my own intuition. • I consider the effects of my decisions on my own life and the long-term impact they potentially have. • I weigh the impact of social pressures on my decisions. • I carefully consider the potential consequences, including unintended consequences, of my choices on myself and others.
Competency **Relationship Skills** – involve the consideration of the feelings, values, and interests of others when relating on a social or familial level. Relationships of trust are built on several key components: communication, listening, cooperation, and mutual understanding.	• I can skillfully negotiate complex dynamics with others and/ or groups of people. • I can offer help or support when needed. • My awareness of the needs, values, and contributions of others support me in cultivating relationships of trust and shared humanity.
Competency **Social Awareness** – includes an awareness and comprehension of the different perspectives, beliefs, attitudes, and social norms of others. It is being aware of and understanding the emotional signals of others and accurately interpreting these signals and responding in self- and other-aware ways based on the locus of control.	• I can be in a social situation and understand the influence it has on my behavior and self-perception. • I can self-manage my emotions and understand that others' actions do not need to influence my feelings toward self. • I own my emotions, feelings, beliefs, values, and attitudes and understand how these influence my behaviors.

We can have the SEL competencies, but without mindful strategies, without being mindful about self-talk, self-concept, and demonstrated behaviors, students will make little progress toward academic success and a life of thriving and flourishing.

CONCLUSION

Emotional resilience allows learners to successfully navigate the challenging times, both in school and away from school. An element of 21st Century education is to instill within our students a solid sense of positive self-regard in order to face the struggles of life and to overcome them with any degree of success.

Positive self-regard is established on observable behaviors that are useful, beneficial, or advantageous to self and others.

The ability to bounce back after a struggle is how *resilience* is typically explained. A more well-rounded perspective includes being nimble in the ever-changing experiences that happen in the constantly-present moment of now. Today, it is necessary to pay close attention to the inner states of being to be emotionally and socially resilient, in myriad situations and circumstance both inside and out of the classroom. Knowing what emotions are felt, what message they offer, and being aware of the breath and how it can either exacerbate the strong emotion or soothe it, are skills that can be taught and learned, and cultivated to high levels of competency.

Teacher SEL and SEAD is just as important, if not more so than for the students. In the classroom it is critical to remember that what we model is what we get. If we, as the adults in the room, cannot model emotional resilience, we have little chance of our students being able to demonstrate their own emotional resilience. We also know that we teach who we are. We each have our own unique personality and mannerisms, attitudes, and worldviews that we bring into the classroom with us. As we can learn and then cultivate our emotional resilience skills, we are altering our character traits and dispositions to lean a little more to the positive.

We are capable of creating inner changes that bolster our determination and commitment to educational excellence. Our inner resources of taking perspective, emotional resilience, and hope are what we need now more than ever in the classroom. Our students need it. And they need to see it modeled, in action, from a caring and compassionate adult whom they trust. We learn from people we trust. We, and young children especially, mimic the behavior that they see modeled for them. And those behaviors that are modeled more frequently, which are seen more often, are the behaviors that most students will likewise demonstrate.

REFERENCES

Bem, D. J. (1972). Self-Perception Theory. In L. Berkowitz (Ed.), (pp. 1–63). Advances in Experimental Social Psychology. Academic Press.

Dahl, M. (2018). *YOUTH positive middle school workbook.* YOUTH Positive Publishing.

Dahl, M. (2019). *YOUTH positive teacher's guide: A deep dive into mindfulness, positive education, and SEL.* YOUTH Positive Publishing.

Dunning, D. L., Griffiths, K., Kuyken, W., Crane, C., Foulkes, L., Parker, J., & Dalgleish, T. (2019). Research Review: The effects of mindfulness-based interventions on cognition and mental health in children and adolescents - a meta-analysis of randomized controlled trials. *Journal of Child Psychology and Psychiatry, and Allied Disciplines*, *60*(3), 244–258. doi:10.1111/jcpp.12980 PMID:30345511

Goleman, D. (2003). *Destructive emotions: A scientific dialogue with the Dalai Lama.* Bantam Dell.

Goleman, D., & Davidson, R. J. (2017). *Altered traits, Science reveals how meditation changes your mind, brain, and body.* Avery.

Goleman, D., & Senge, P. (2014). *The triple focus; A new approach to education.* More Than Sound.

Immordino-Yang, M. H. (2016). *Emotions, learning, and the brain: exploring the educational implications of affective neuroscience.* W. W. Norton & Company, Inc.

Immordino-Yang, M. H., & Damasio, A. (2007). We feel, therefore we learn: The relevance of affective and social neuroscience to education. *Mind, Brain and Education: the Official Journal of the International Mind, Brain, and Education Society*, *1*(1), 3–10. doi:10.1111/j.1751-228X.2007.00004.x

Jones, S. M. & Kahn, J. (2017, September 13.) *The evidence base for how we learn: Supporting students' social, emotional, and academic development.* Academic Press.

Kabat-Zinn, J. (2013). *Full catastrophe living: Using the wisdom of your body and mind to face stress, pain, and illness.* Bantam Dell.

Li, L., Gow, A. D. I., & Zhou, J. (2020). The role of positive emotions in education: A neuroscience perspective. *Mind, Brain and Education: the Official Journal of the International Mind, Brain, and Education Society*, *14*(3), 220–234. doi:10.1111/mbe.12244

Seligman, M. E. P. (2011). *Flourish, A visionary new understanding of happiness and well-being*. Atria Paperback.

Smith, M. K. (2020, January 24). *Aristotle and education*. Retrieved from https://infed.org/mobi/aristotle-and-education/

Weissberg, R. P., Shriver, T. P., Sharmistha, B., & DeFalco, K. (1997). Creating a districtwide social development project. *Educational Leadership*, *54*, 37–39.

Zianian, T., Sawyer, J., Evans, N., & Gillham, D. (2015, November 25). The Impact of mindfulness meditation on academic well-being and affective teaching practice. *Creative Education*, *6*(20), 2174–2185. doi:10.4236/ce.2015.620222

KEY TERMS AND DEFINITIONS

Inspire Check-In: A reflective self-check-in designed to assess the current state of well-being in all the layers of an individual. Each participant will look *in*side and rate the self from 1-5, 5 being high, in the areas of spiritual or social, physical, intellectual, relational, and emotional.

M-SEL: Mindfulness-based social, emotional learning.

Mindfulness-Based SEAD: Social, emotional, academic development based on a foundation of mindfulness.

Mindfulness-Based Stress Reduction (MBSR): A stress reduction program based on mindfulness created by Jon Kabat-Zinn at the University of Massachusetts Medical Center in 1979.

SEAD: Social emotional academic development

Chapter 2
Culturally Responsive Social, Emotional, and Academic Development (SEAD):
Three Case Studies Implementing SEAD

Tara Madden-Dent
Sierra Nevada University, USA

Iesha Jackson
University of Nevada, Las Vegas, USA

Jo Ann L. Cason
Do More Living Now, LLC, USA

ABSTRACT

Culturally responsive social-emotional competencies continue being essential skills for college, career, and life success, especially today, as the world seeks global citizens prepared to respectfully navigate relationships and interactions between people from different nations and ethnicities. These skills are more than valuable assets that a modern economy is dependent on, but skills that students, educators, employees, and society need in order for healthy and sustainable co-existence. In academia, educators are increasingly expected to bridge diverse cultural gaps and foster more equitable, respectful, and safe learning environments, but evidence-based implementation methods are limited. To contribute to the body of literature, this chapter presents three case studies and how each of their approaches can increase essential SEL skills at the high school, undergraduate, and graduate levels in addition to the in-service educator level. The chapter concludes with a discussion around themes that emerged from the three case studies, implications for practice, and recommendations.

DOI: 10.4018/978-1-7998-6728-9.ch002

INTRODUCTION

In today's globalized and interconnected world, culturally responsive social and emotional competencies are increasingly recognized as core essential skills that help prepare global citizens for equitable twenty-first century education, workforce, civic health, and holistic wellbeing (Cunningham & Villasenor, 2016; Jagers, Rivas-Drake, & Williams, 2019; Jones, Crowley, & Greenberg, 2017; Mahoney, Weissberg, Greenberg, Dusenbury, Jagers, Niemi, Schlinger, et al., 2020). Employers and universities are seeking these skillsets (Fitzgerald & Sigelman, 2018; Maldonado, 2019), that youth and adults can learn to increase college and career readiness through cultural competence and social-emotional learning (Kerr & Gore, 2021; Kerr & Madden-Dent, 2019; Kerr, Madden-Dent, & Shalabi, 2020; Madden-Dent, 2021b).

According to Rose, Leverson, and Smith, (2020), cultural responsiveness from an educators' lens, is a "process of developing awareness of the significance of our students' backgrounds (including historical context), then intentionally integrating their customs and values into our curriculum, instruction, and school environment" (p. 1). Once established, this awareness becomes more of a mindset, an approach that respects students' cultural and linguistic backgrounds while holding them to high expectations for academic success, than a set of best practices (Banks, 1991; Gay, 2018; Hammond, 2015). According to Gay (2018), culturally responsive praxis is validating, multidimensional, empowering, transformative and emancipatory. By centering on the strengths and assets of students, considering the complex dynamics of teaching and learning, and positioning students as co-constructors of knowledge, culturally responsive practitioners create environments where success is accessible to all and learning is liberatory.

At the core of being culturally responsive is a willingness and ability to develop meaningful relationships across cultural difference. Such relationships consider individuals' holistic well-being as well as cultural norms in mutually defining and enacting care (Jackson, Sealey-Ruiz, & Watson, 2014). These caring relationships require an investment in students that results in knowledge of their families, communities, and heritages and how those influence students' ecological realities. In other words, culturally responsive practices are the lens through which self-awareness, self-management, social awareness, relationship skills, and responsible decision-making skills are fostered within equitable education systems.

Social, Emotional, and Academic Development (SEAD) is the integration of social-emotional learning (SEL) and academics that reinforces equitable and human-centered educational environments (Aspen Institute, 2018). The implementation of SEAD practices is aimed to increase SEL, a lifelong process through which all people learn and apply culturally responsive, "knowledge, skills, and attitudes to develop healthy identities, manage emotions and achieve personal and collective goals, feel and show empathy for others, establish and maintain supportive relationships, and make responsible and caring decisions" (CASEL, 2020). According to the Collaborative for Academic, Social, and Emotional Learning (CASEL), the five SEL competencies include Self-Awareness, Self-Management, Social Awareness, Relationship Skills, and Responsible Decision-Making skills; all of which are as predictive of academic and career achievement as is IQ (Almlund, Duckworth, Heckman, & Kautz, 2011). The competencies are illustrated and described below.

Figure 1.

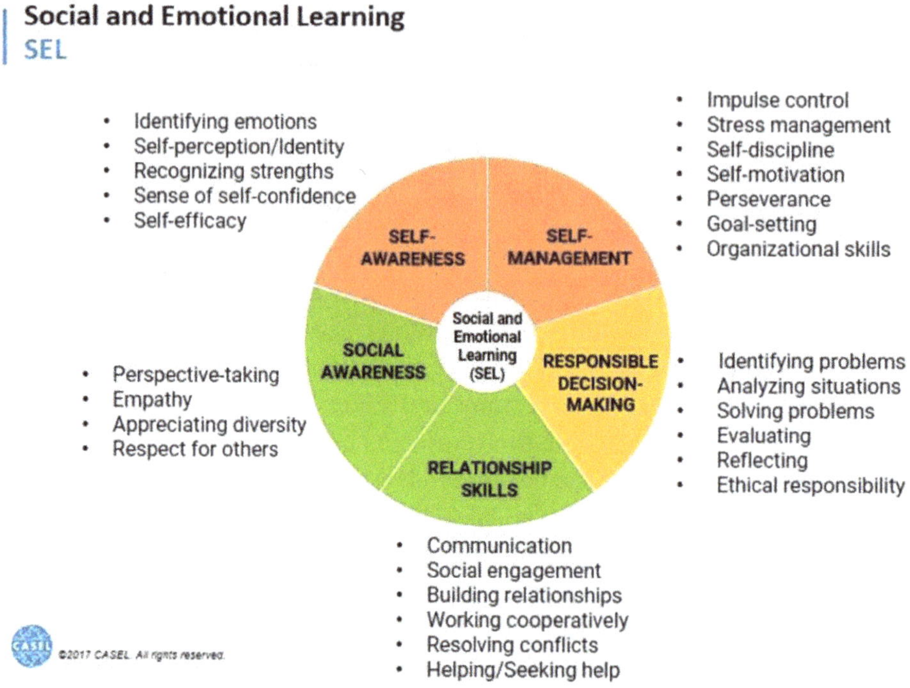

IMPORTANCE OF CULTURALLY RESPONSIVE SEL

Twenty-five years of basic and applied research has demonstrated that SEL contributes to more equitable and safe educational environments for youth and adults (Cantor et al., 2018; Durlak et al., 2011; Jones & Kahn, 2017; Madden-Dent, 2021a; Osher et al., 2018; Taylor et al., 2017). More specifically, SEAD practices are linked with increased cultural competencies, linguistic skills, and academic success (Madden-Dent, 2014; Madden-Dent & Donaburska, 2019), decreases in unhealthy behaviors, mental health issues, and drop-out rates (Kautz, Heckman, Diris, Bas ter Weel, & Borghans, 2014; Reed & Madden-Dent, 2021), increases of 11-14% point gains in grades and test scores (Durlak et al., 2011), increases in high school graduation rates and post-secondary enrollment and completion rates (Kautz, Heckman, Diris, Bas ter Weel, & Borghans, 2014), and improved attitudes, emotional intelligence, and academic engagement (Li & Xu, 2019). Furthermore, in educational environments where resources are often limited, preventive and responsive SEAD applications used with a multi-tiered system of supports framework have been found to generate a financial return on educational investment ranging from $11 to $104.90 for each dollar invested (Belfield, Bowden, Klapp, Levin, Shand, & Zander, 2015; Swain-Bradway, Lindstrom Johnson, Bradshaw, & McIntosh, 2017).

Although research findings point to SEAD practices producing significant benefits, SEL competencies are not fixed to any one cultural value-set and educators are advised to embed inclusive, multicultural values into their SEL instruction and policy work as to avoid teaching and/or assessing SEL with only the dominant culture's values. The absence of cultural responsiveness when modeling, teaching, or grading SEL concepts can inflict harm to others from different cultural backgrounds and an absence of critical consciousness, the complex intellectual capacity to think holistically, reflect on, and identify institutionalized constructs for effectiveness, inequalities, and social and political contradictions (Pollard, 2020; Rossatto, 2020), may perpetuate institutionalized inequities and oppressive educational systems. Instead, lessons or activities inclusive of diverse individual and community cultural orientations can foster greater cultural awareness, critical consciousness, cultural intelligence, and guide culturally responsive dialog between stakeholders (e.g., students; families/parents/caregivers; educators; community members). The importance of establishing a culturally responsive approach to SEL is summarized by Howard (2019), in the following statement:

Culture is an undeniable part of everything we do as humans, and SEL is a major platform for how we knowingly, and unknowingly, share values and norms with students. The work inside of schools has to become a fusion of both. Every day, students enter our space with values and beliefs that may cause them to see the world uniquely… It's tough to do this work if one hasn't explored their own cultural identity and biases. As educators, we have to predetermine that we will not allow cultural differences to be perceived as human deficits. An educator's SEL programming will be completely ineffective unless it starts with the cultural uniqueness that makes us different, yet in the pursuit of a full humanity, makes us equally the same (p. 2).

Having culturally responsive SEL embedded throughout classrooms and campuses requires intentional and conscious effort by educators who both understand the significance of SEL skills for academic, personal, societal, and professional success, and also who can model and explicitly teach those skills. This is reflected by Leverson et al. (2019), in the following statement:

Establishing a positive school culture includes setting up the school's social environment (either intentionally or unintentionally) to reflect a shared vision of common values, beliefs, and behavior expectations. However, for students who are not from the dominant culture, the school environment can expose them to unintentional slights, which devalue their backgrounds and diminish school connectedness (p. 2).

Research is still needed to better understand the impacts of explicit culturally responsive SEL education and professional development that incorporates individual cultural values, recognizes cultural assets, and abilities to bridge cultural gaps for academic and professional success. A goal of this chapter is to introduce research-based methods to assist students (e.g., high school, undergraduate, graduate) and active educators in gaining culturally responsive SEL skills and how that process influenced them personally, academically, and professionally. What follows are three case studies, chosen for the unique ways each one demonstrates the need for culturally responsive SEL with adult learners in a specific context (international college students in a cultural studies course; graduate students from various backgrounds in a teacher leadership SEL course; and experienced educators in a professional development setting). We highlight the need for SEAD as an integral aspect of a life-long learning process. This chapter concludes with recommendations for school leaders based on the insights from our case studies.

CASE STUDIES

First Case Study: Secondary and Post-Secondary Culturally Responsive SEAD Education

In an effort to demonstrate the influences of culturally responsive SEL education, this case study design identifies themes from descriptive data and a narrative research inquiry, that illustrate increases in students' cultural awareness, sensitivities, and competencies, their critical consciousness to systemic processes, and social-emotional skills. The following case study describes a method used by one mid-western university to support incoming international students, though a three-credit, online cultural studies and college readiness course entitled, "U.S. Academics and Culture". Through twenty lessons, quizzes, assignments, and one paper (*My Action Plan*), students examined their own cultural orientations and values (SEL Skill: Self-Awareness), explored how their cultural preferences differed to other cultural norms (SEL Skill: Social-Awareness), strategies to respectfully and effectively bridge cultural and linguistic differences (SEL Skill: Relationship), methods to manage feelings and behaviors at school, online, at work, and with peers (SEL Skill: Self-Management), and how to set and achieve goals for college and career success (SEL Skill: Responsible Decision-Making).

Purposive sampling was used to select twenty-five participants, (incoming international high school and undergraduate students preparing to study in the U.S. for four years), who had completed the online course between 2017 and 2019, and who had self-identified as an English Language Learner. Of the twenty-five participants, ages ranged from 17 to 23, twelve self-identified as male, and thirteen as female. Participants' home countries or Special Regions included Brazil, China, Hong Kong, India, Kazakhstan, Japan, Singapore, South Korea, Taiwan, Thailand, and Vietnam. All participants received instruction from the same university professor, guided by a regionally accredited course syllabi that included the same data sources.

The four sources of data used in this case study design included descriptive data and a narrative research inquiry to identify themes related to student experiences and outcomes from the online university course. Descriptive data was collected from a short quantifiable survey and a cultural self-assessment report, and used in partnership with qualitative narratives (students' written reflections and a paper entitled, *My Action Plan*), to create a triangulated body of data for collective analysis. The first data source was the *Cultural Orientations Indicator®* (COI), a web-based psychometrically validated and reliable self-reporting instrument used to identify and analyze cultural preferences (Interaction Style; Thinking Style; Sense of Self). The COI was developed by the *Training Management Corporation©* (TMC), for the purpose of training employees for international work assignments by increasing cultural awareness and improving communication and collaboration skills. The COI is hosted by a software program called the Cultural Navigator™, designed by the Berlitz Corporation, a global leadership training and language education company.

The COI's psychometric assessment uses a six-point Likert scale from low to high that identifies and analyzes cultural orientations from 83 items (questions) that were designed to measure an individual's preference for the given cultural orientation that defines each scale. Immediately after completing the COI assessment, in English or the participants' native language, synthesized results were organized into a personalized COI cultural preference report which demonstrated how participants are likely to communicate and engage with others (Interaction Style), how they tend to process information (Thinking Style), and how they tend to view identity and motivation (Sense of Self) (TMC, 2020).

All participants used their personalized COI report in conjunction with course homework assignments (e.g., written reflections; paper: *My Action Plan*). The report was used to guide student reflection about their own cultural styles (SEL Skill: Self-Awareness), and stimulate thought and awareness about institutionalized system differences and cultural norm differences between their home country and the U.S. (SEL Skill: Social Awareness), before developing personalized strategies to overcome likely cultural and linguistic barriers during students' first semester in the U.S. (SEL Skills: Relationship Skills & Responsible Decision-Making). Moreover, the COI was used in partnership with the Cultural Navigator's Country Comparison Report, which helped international students gain strategies to effectively bridge cultural gaps in Interaction Styles (SEL Skills: Social Awareness; Self-Management; Responsive Decision-Making). This report included recommendations of relevant resources for students to further study and prepare for shifting into socially diverse and unfamiliar environments.

The second and third data sources were artifacts that collected students' reflections through writing assignments. One data source included the twenty written homework reflections that responded to culturally responsive SEL prompts relating to students' individual cultural orientations and personal goals. These prompts allowed students to make meaning of their online academic and cultural studies to best prepare for integration and first semester success in ways that met their individualized needs. Through these prompts, students explored their own culture and social-emotional skills (SEL Skills: Self-Awareness), studied other cultural values, orientations, and preferences (SEL Skill: Social Awareness), collected and articulated culturally responsive methods to communicate and collaborate with others with different cultural and linguistic backgrounds (SEL Skills: Social Awareness; Self-Management; Relationship Skills), and their intentional action steps to investigate, plan for, and execute academic and professional goals (SEL Skill: Responsible Decision-Making).

The other artifact was this study's third data source, the capstone paper entitled, *My Action Plan*. This final project activity was designed to allow participants the space to articulate what they had learned in class and how they were using the information, or were strategically planning to apply the gained information during their first semester in the U.S. In this final paper, participants described specific academic, social, and professional goals before identifying research-based methods to achieve each goal using culturally responsive SEL skills. This rigorous college-level writing assignment was written in English, formatted in the American Psychological Association (APA), and graded for grammar, formatting, and content.

The fourth data source was a voluntary, online course evaluation survey completed during the last two weeks of the course. The survey used a five-point Likert scale to measure participants' perceptions of how much they agreed or disagreed with fifteen items. Items included statements on course topic, the distance education class delivery structure, student learning objectives, course instruments (e.g., COI), faculty knowledge and customer service skills, and student outcomes. The survey was completed through the University's online learning management platform and an administrative office manager transferred anonymous open-ended responses into a course evaluation summary report. Data was then used in partnership with the other three data sources for collective analysis.

There were two major themes that emerged from the data: *Gains in Cultural Intelligence* and *Gains in Critical Consciousness*. The first theme, *Gains in Cultural Intelligence* describes consistencies found within the data sources pertaining to increased awareness and understanding of culture and culturally responsive social-emotional skills. Through students' written reflections, the capstone paper (*My Action Plan*), and the course evaluation survey, participants demonstrated a gained awareness and sensitivity to their own culture, other cultures, culture's impacts on relationships, academic achievement, and professional success, and strategies to navigate diverse groups of people through the biomechanics of culturally responsive code shifting. This theme is summarized in the following series of student written expressions.

In India time has a Fluid orientation, whereas in the US, time is often Fixed. Communication is more formal and traditional in India whereas in the US the communication is much more informal, casual and laid back. Being born and have lived in India for 19 years of my life, it is going to be extremely difficult for me to get used to the Fixed time expectations and interaction styles in the US. The informal and laid-back communication styles in the US comes across as a contributor to culture shock for me.

Another student demonstrated gains in cultural intelligence within his reflection on Thinking Styles. The South Korean student wrote, "I'm a Being style and US often is generally more of a Doing style. I should try more "doing" not just "being" or "thinking" to get out of my comfort zone. I think it relates with participating and talking in class. I need to talk and ask questions more in class (Doing style), not just think quietly by myself (Being style)." Another eastern Asian student demonstrated her new understanding of communication style differences in her following statement,

Differences in high context and low context thinking styles when communicating with colleagues will make me think about the words of others more carefully to seek the true meaning of them. However, low context preferences may not have my kind of thinking style, they may just speak things directly. In this case, sometimes I will be confused or upset by the words of others when they don't have the intention to offend me.

It is important to note that students often expressed relationships between culturally responsive SEL education, culturally intelligence, and self-efficacy. One graduating high school student, while still in Japan had written about his online class preparation experience.

I am really lucky to have this class before I go to my U.S.A. university. I am concerned about academic performances the most, but this class taught me ways to attend class and participate, do my assignments, and prepare for exams... I thank you a lot for letting me have this amazing class and giving me opportunities to think about how to prepare before studying and living in the U.S. I will try to do my best in academics and social activities. Thank you so much.

Many students echoed similar experiences of increased confidence or self-assurance with the new cultural and academic knowledge from the course. One student wrote, "Although studying in a country which I'm not familiar with has a lot of challenges, by applying the information from class and my three action plans in my final paper, I feel more confident for facing the academic and culture challenges." A student from South Korea shared, "Since I've learned these things through U.S. Academics and Culture class, I know myself better and understand their [U.S.] culture and styles better. I have confidence that this will make my study easier and happier." Within an open-ended course evaluation survey, one student reflected on her perception of her online class experience. She wrote, "I found it very helpful taking this class, it helped me a lot to understand the culture differences better and gave me more ideas of how to get along with people from the U.S. better, and how to participate in school better."

The second theme, *Gains in Critical Consciousness* describes consistencies found within the research findings pertaining to international students' self-described gains in an awareness to how culture plays foundational roles in societal and academic constructs shaping their educational experience as international students. Students' intellectual capacity to think holistically, reflect on and recognize culturally-relevant institutionalized constructs, and engage in dialogs around equity and wellness for social transformation were articulated through written reflections, the capstone paper, and a course evaluation survey. Furthermore, students expressed new perspectives and awareness to educational equity issues (e.g., academic access; health and safety; international student barriers in the U.S.), and how being an international student often felt isolating and marginalized compared to domestic peers. Participants new in the U.S., were able to express their own hardship experiences during integration (e.g., discrimination), while participants preparing to arrive in the U.S. for their first semester, were able to express their anticipated challenges related to institutionalized system differences. This theme is summarized in the following series of students' written expressions.

Many participants expressed their new understanding of U.S. systems and institutionalized norms, and how they differed from their home country. After reflecting about how educational systems and student expectations are influenced by cultural values and norms, one student from northern China wrote about his plan to prepare for academic achievement in the U.S.; a much more independent system compared to his home country's collectivistic system.

Because of the cultural differences between China and the United States, there are many places where I need to learn how to live in the United States. For example, the Chinese and American learning methods. In China we will have many teachers to supervise and check our study. But in the United States, they prefer to study independently. You need to finish the tasks by yourself. In China, there will be teachers to urge you to finish it. So I have to learn how to finish my study more autonomously.

The following Japanese high school student demonstrates his gained awareness to how common systems of U.S. communication differ from his own and how the differences could affect him in the U.S.

Also I like to observe specific rules of etiquette and protocol. Since people in the U.S. tend to use informal communications and dispense formal etiquette, I might have difficulties not following the exact rule and opening my field of view when it comes to business situations.

Within one capstone paper (*My Action Plan*), a participant from Vietnam describes a common struggle for international students and his plan to address it during international relocation and academic integration.

When one moves and settles into a new region, culture shock is often inevitable. It can be caused by changing schools or towns. However, what is more challenging is moving into a different country with an entirely different culture in the pursuit of education. I am well aware of the challenges involved, so I have determined to first learn about the dynamics of integrating in the Western culture and about the American lifestyle.

Another student wrote about what she anticipated as cultural barriers and challenges within a U.S. academic environment since school settings and student expectations were different than in her home country. She summarizes this in her following statement.

As an international student from China, asking questions in front of the class will be hard for me. Also, questioning others in a group project will give me a hard time. I think speaking in front of the class and interacting with teacher will be my biggest problem because I'm so used to just sitting at the back of the classroom in China and listening.

A Brazilian student expressed a need for earlier support, unique for international students' needs to avoid the hardships she experienced as a new international student in the U.S. She wrote,

I started to learn everything (like literary everything!) here in the States. I had no idea how to pay rent/gas/phone/water/electricity, use transportation (buses and metro), 'what's insurance?', etc. because I didn't know I needed to know that. I just thought I could ask my parents later or my eldest sister would be the one who would take control of this anyway. By assuming this, I started learning everything from the basics. I was embarrassed and ashamed as to why I didn't know this before, but now feel proud that I know what to do and what I should do from now on.

Similarly, a student from South Korea shared how an absence of having accurate expectations about life in the U.S. and integration support services had influenced his isolation away from English speakers and kept only among home country peers. He wrote,

I had a year to get prepared to study abroad and I mostly focused on learning the English language. I had no idea about culture shock. When I first came to U.S., I felt like a traveler, which means, I wasn't quite involved or invested in the U.S. society. I looked for many Korean friends from my home country, and made Korean friends ONLY. However, since I always hung out with Korean friends, I had no chance to speak English except in class. When I tried to make local friends, the cultural wall felt so high that I couldn't jump it. I felt lonely, depressed, and unstable.

Another student echoed this theme in his statement,

As an international student who was born and raised in an Asian country, I experience the difference in culture, academic system and social interaction. Everything seems new and unfamiliar to me, so it's quite a struggle in how to deal with these when I first come to the United States. However, with the knowledge and action plan strategies that I mention in this paper, I believe that they can help me conquer challenges and gain a more success and social life in the U.S.

Emerging from the data, the two themes described above, reinforce current research that SEL education can support students' academic and professional readiness (Kerr, Madden-Dent, & Shalabi, 2020), while influencing safer and more equitable educational conditions (see, Cantor et al., 2018; Durlak et al., Jones & Kahn, 2017; Madden-Dent, 2021a; Osher et al., 2018; 2011; Taylor et al., 2017). The two themes illustrate how explicit culturally responsive SEL education can also influence cultural intelligence and a critical consciousness to culture's roles in institutionalized educational systems for international students' preparing for, or new in the U.S. during their first-semester.

This study's findings reaffirm a need for U.S. academic systems to offer more accessible support options for international students; a current systemic shortfall across the U.S. (Madden-Dent, Wood, & Roskina, 2019). As demonstrated in this study, participants who completed the class while in the U.S. during their first semester, often expressed having the academic and cultural studies information too late and wished to have completed the online course before arriving in the U.S. According to participants who completed the online class before arriving to the U.S., the culturally responsive social-emotional information had better prepared them for study, work, and life in the U.S. by developing culturally relevant skills to intentionally apply it in meaningful ways during their first semester. Participants were acutely aware of the differences between their home county culture styles and U.S. cultural styles (SEL Skills: Self-Awareness; Social Awareness), and discussed how cultural styles impacted their study skills, classroom engagement, communication skills, health and safety (SEL Skill: Self-Management). Participants often described intentionally alternating between their home cultural styles and U.S. cultural styles (SEL Skill: Relationship Skills) to more strategically interact and communicate with U.S students, teachers, and peers (SEL Skills: Relationship Skills; Responsible Decision-Making). Future research and educational applications may consider incorporating explicit culturally responsive SEL education into high school and higher education classes as one way to strengthen cultural intelligence and critical consciousness.

Second Case Study: Planning for Culturally Responsive SEAD at the Graduate Level

At the graduate level, it is easy to forget how important it is for learners to engage in SEAD for themselves in addition to them learning how to apply it to their professional lives. This case study describes the process of providing space for M.Ed. students to simultaneously learn and practice SEL competencies in a course titled *Social Emotional Competence for Teachers and Professional Leaders*. This course was offered to graduate students across majors at a research intensive institution in the western United States. While 11 out of 14 students were current, aspiring, and former classroom teachers, other program areas included social work and interaction and media sciences. The course, a three-credit seminar offered asynchronously online, was designed for students to understand basic tenets of social and emotional learning, connect those tenets to academic achievement, and develop skills to lead SEL development with children and adult learners.

For this student population, an important and often ignored aspect of culture is age; many of the graduate students in this course were coming back to the classroom as learners after an extended absence. This experience created a level of anxiety that had to be acknowledged and addressed early in the semester to establish meaningful relationships. Another important characteristic of students in this learning environment is that all but one was employed full-time while taking the course. Because culturally responsive SEAD is concerned with the various contexts in which learning takes place, including individual circumstances and barriers to success that students may need to overcome, planning and implementing a culturally responsive SEAD course for graduate students is a complex process. One approach to this work is described below.

Culturally Responsive Mindset

The professor of the course began with an outline of learning outcomes aligned with the university program's goal to develop teacher leaders. The overarching objective was to support students in developing skills to lead SEL development with children and adults. In understanding that the graduate students in the course would enter with varying degrees of knowledge of and experience with SEL, the professor first considered how to plan asynchronous online instruction in a manner that would increase learning for all students and encourage application of SEL competencies in different work environments. Foundational to this process was self-reflection regarding the professor's SEL practices in both teaching courses and working with colleagues. The professor had to hone her own competencies and apply them to planning for this course in order to anticipate learning hurdles that graduate students might face. This required collaborating with colleagues, identifying personal strengths, planning to build empathetic and supportive relationships with and among students, and constructing the syllabus in a manner that encouraged student reflection and feedback.

Equally important was embedding multiple opportunities for the students to self reflect, build community as a class, and practice then evaluate SEL strategies. This approach reflects a culturally responsive mindset in that it can lead to personal transformation of philosophies, beliefs, and values that impact one's relationships with others (see Fullam, 2017). The syllabus and learning opportunities required students to examine themselves, reflect on how their backgrounds and beliefs show up in their engagements with others. Students shared most of their assignments with the entire class and were required to read and respond to their peers. The process of self-disclosing and learning together help to establish an affirming, supportive learning environment.

The Syllabus

Because the course was being taught for the first time, the syllabus was built from scratch. To achieve the overarching goal of using the same culturally responsive SEAD principals that students were expected to learn and apply, the assignments centered around self-perception, reflection, respect for others, and social engagement in a virtual setting. There were seven assignments: a personal introduction, weekly SEL activities and reflections, a written response to a documentary, a mid-semester reflection, a Social and Emotional Learning literature review, a final project, and a final reflection.

The personal introduction allowed for self-expression by inviting students to upload a video, PowerPoint slide, poem, paragraph, or other form of story-telling that explained their background information such as where students were from, where and what they were teaching (if applicable), primary interests/hobbies, and what they hoped to learn in the course. This was followed by weekly SEL activities each designed to highlight a different aspect of CASEL's SEL competencies. Examples include "Discover Your Rules for Life" (Analyzing situations), "Gratitude Journal" (Identifying emotions), and "Virtual High Fives" (Building relationships). Following the completion of an activity, students responded to the following guiding questions: What is your personal take away from this activity? What did you learn from your peers' responses that you might not have considered before? Is this an activity you can imagine using at your job (with adults and/or children)? Guiding questions were also used to structure the reflection of video response assignments. For the final project, students were given a menu of options that included the opportunity to design their own final.

The Semester

As an asynchronous online course, students had the option of working through 13 modules at their own pace with the exception of needing to reflect on their peer's weekly SEL activities. Supplementary resources including videos, links to websites, and readings provided scaffolding for students who were new to SEL concepts while allowing those more familiar to further explore required readings. In addition, the literature review assignment was designed to support the development and implementation of students' chosen final project.

Within the first three weeks of the course, student assignments, communication with the professor, and engagement in online discussions demonstrated a developing sense of trust, respect, and understanding of one another. Students shared personal experiences of failure, regret, fear, and fatigue and empathetically responded to each other, offering solutions to personal challenges or commiserating as relevant. By the end of the first month of class, all fourteen students had stated that they felt comfortable sharing in this course things that they had never shared in other courses. They said they were surprised at how close they felt to people they had never met in person.

Using SEL competencies to structure learning opportunities created an environment in which students not only self-reflected but also developed collaborative relationships that enhanced their learning. Because Covid-19 closed schools in the middle of the spring semester, the last months of class were filled with responses of how the learning community was helping students cope with change and how important they felt the SEL activities were for their personal well-being in the midst of a global pandemic. All students performed exceptionally well; more importantly, they all commented on how much they benefited from the weekly SEL activities and looked forward to completing course assignments that they could use in their personal and professional lives.

Outcomes: Insights from a SEAD Instructor

When students' individual needs, strengths, and backgrounds are at the center of the learning environment (from course planning to the implementation of instruction), it is possible to establish a classroom culture that humanizes the individual and bolsters a collective good. In such an environment, connectedness is a hallmark of teaching and learning, and SEL competencies are more than theoretical ideas; they become concrete ways of engaging oneself and others in the classroom. The professor of this course began with the intention to help graduate students understand SEL as more than a set of strategies to use with children and more of an approach to a healthy lifestyle that can positively impact one's relationships inside and outside of the workplace. An unanticipated insight from teaching this course was that culturally responsive SEAD has ripple effects; when a person regularly practices SEL competencies, they are better able to identify their needs, communicate and work with others, and lead those around them to do the same. The potential positive impact is immeasurable. From one semester teaching 14 adult learners who designed projects to teach and lead others in socially and emotionally healthy manners, the course in this case study may reach much further than one professor could alone.

One of the challenges of designing and implementing a culturally responsive approach to an SEL course is planning to meet the learning needs of students you have not met, particularly in a graduate course that is open to all students regardless of academic major. Cultural considerations extend beyond race/ethnicity, gender, language, and socioeconomic status to include age and, in an online setting, technological socialization. This challenge was mediated by an emphasis on self-awareness, social awareness, and relationships skills as foundational to the course structure.

Third Case Study: Culturally Responsive SEAD at the In-Service Educator Level

In 2020, the global pandemic known as COVID-19, caused significant trauma to families around the world ranging from the loss of loved ones, financial hardships, and the severed physical and emotional connection to others during quarantine. In response to COVID-19, schools across the United States closed in March, 2020 and long-term quarantine practices kept educators, students and their families distanced from normal human contact. According to Holt-Lunstad (2020), "The pandemic has shown the world how fundamental social contact is in our lives, and how every aspect of life has changed to create social distance" (p. 1). In this uncertain era, the Pandemic created widespread fear causing people to think: "Who will be the next victim? Will it be me? Will it be my loved ones?"

The practice of social distancing in response to the Pandemic, caused a shift in how people interacted within their local communities, schools, and districts. Educators began changing how instruction was delivered to incorporate distance teaching and learning and established these practices as the "new norm." The use of technologies within distance education has made it possible for remote learning to take place in safe environments and allows for flexibility of instruction (Terzi & Celik, 2005). Although this shift to virtual learning spaces met the immediate need to deliver academic curriculum and programs, unintended outcomes have since illuminated human-centered need which in-person schooling had provided. While social distancing and distance learning have become the new norm for most schools, it has caused educators to look closer at their own social and emotional learning (SEL), how SEL is implemented in their work for both youth and adults, and how virtual spaces could focus on developing authentic relationships and support resources. This closer look placed a greater focus on ensuring that educators and support staff acquired and implemented SEL competencies.

As part of SEL implementation, educators have also begun to look at mindfulness as a useful tool that can be readily implemented by teachers and students. Research suggests that mindfulness lessons can help increase concentration time, reduce stress, and lengthen attention spans (Taters, 2019). Mindfulness, is a state of active, open attention to the present, can be taught in a variety of approaches including in-person or asynchronous self-paced virtual environments. The combination of intentional SEL support for educators and school staff with additional applications of mindfulness techniques were the foundational framework for the following case study.

SEAD Support for Educators: The HeartBeat Teams

In an effort to strengthen virtual interaction and decrease negative impacts of social isolation within one midwestern elementary school community, this case study provided a method to implement social-emotional support to the school's adult educators and staff. The method was an online SEL group activity called, The HeartBeat Team; a name recognizing that educators are the heartbeat of a school. The activity's purpose was to create new capacity for ongoing SEL supports that would increase positive social interaction among and between school teachers and staff and that could be easily embedded into the school's practices and reinforce an inclusive culture for all.

The HeartBeat Team activity allowed one large elementary school to offer culturally responsive SEL support to seventy teachers and staff who were seeking to build relationships and engage in supportive virtual cultures within their school community during the fall semester's distance education requirements. In the beginning of the fall semester, the school's administration and the lead school counselor began the activity by randomly assigning 6 - 7 school adults to each HeartBeat Team as a way to encourage new interactions with school members and develop relationships across the campus. Once the teams were formed, a group leader was selected randomly from each group. In these groups, educators had the opportunity to share values and beliefs within the structure of the team (Draeger, 2017), to develop positive workplace relationships and increase feelings of respect and collaboration that benefit everyone (Donahue, 2020). The participants met in weekly virtual small groups to discuss themed topics, exchanged resources, and provide support to each team member. Conversations and activities were supported by intentional strategies grounded on mindful SEL strategies to strengthen self-awareness, self-management, social awareness, relationship skills, and responsible decision-making skills.

During the first week of school in August, 2020 the HeartBeat Team Facilitator provided an orientation to the fall semester's virtual activity that included the purpose, process, and expectations. The Facilitator presented on topics, Why have a HeartBeat Team?; What is a HeartBeat Team?; Who is a member of the HeartBeat Team?; When do the HeartBeat Teams meet?; Where do they meet? The HeartBeat Norm, or salute of respect, was also introduced as the "HeartBeat Affirmation Tap". This tap was a symbolic gesture for team members to practice after participants shared in group discussions as a way to honor contributions. It was also used as a kinesthetic movement, to check-in with the participant's present state of mind and being (Self Awareness). The HeartBeat Team Facilitator modeled the tap by forming the shape of a heart with fingers from both hands and then concluding with two fingers from one hand, providing a double-tap on the shoulder: "Tap - Tap." The faculty responded by performing the HeartBeat Affirmation Tap together.

It was the understanding of the Facilitator that because of the composition of teams was made up of people from different SEL and mindfulness knowledge and experience, homework was assigned at the end of the orientation that included an introduction to the SEL competencies, Self-Awareness and Self-Management through a series of reflective prompts and small activity. The homework assignment was titled, the "HeartBeat Show & Tell". Participants were to prepare for the first HeartBeat Team meeting by bringing an object or symbol that helped them feel calm, relaxed, or helped them feel happiness, peace, or confidence. At the first HeartBeat Team meeting, the Team Leader gave each member one minute to share their object and why it was important to them. This activity helped establish an understanding of these SEL competencies, helped the adults make personalized meaning of one SEL activity, and contributed to SEL competencies of Social Awareness and Relationship Skills during the team meeting while learning about and honoring peer backgrounds, cultures, and stories.

The HeartBeat Team was well-received by school administrators, teachers, and staff. The project Facilitator observed and noted participants' smiling faces, positive body language, and staff independently practicing the Heartbeat Affirmation Tap. Participants shared positive comments reaffirming the an excitement and appreciation for culturally responsive SEL support for the school educators. This is reflected in a few statements such as, "This is much needed!", "This is going to be fun!", and "I can't wait to meet with my group!". Of note, the HeartBeat Team activity officially launched on the school-wide day dedicated to SEL.

Implementation

This was the first time a HeartBeat Team had ever operated in a school before. The project's Facilitator applied mindful and culturally responsive SEL competencies development strategies into a HeartBeat Team template for each Team Lead to use and help increase positive social interaction and relationships among diverse groups of educators within virtual environments. The Heartbeat Team Facilitator contacted with each of the Team Leaders and went over the basic Template guidance for their semester meetings. The Template included:

- Deep-Breath activities. Participants work for one minute - concentrating on Inhale, 1-2-3 and Exhale, 3-2-1, encouraging everyone to focus on the Breath… then what they can hear around them… what they can see…. And smell.
- Mindfulness activities that opened and/or concluded with the Heartbeat Affirmation Tap.
- Culturally responsive SEL resources. This included shared resources from all members.
- Reading and committing to the Heartbeat Team's Social-Emotional Contract; a verbal commitment to help build community, recognize commitment to each other, strengthen relationships, and build trust (Jkorderm, 2017).
- Check-in activities that focused on self-awareness and relationship skill building to connect with other team members.
- Exit Ticket activity with intention setting questions such as, "What day will you be connecting with your Teammates?" or reflective questions, such as "Today, I am feeling really ….".
- Ongoing support where participants could indicate if they wanted someone to follow-up with them after the meeting.

All participants in each of the 10 teams participated in the weekly HeartBeat Team meetings. Team Leaders and the Heartbeat Team Facilitator used participant feedback to continually improve the virtual HeartBeat Team experience and guide future Heartbeat Team meetings.

Outcomes: Insights from the HeartBeat Team Facilitator

Due to the social distancing caused by the COVID-19 pandemic, educators had truly missed interacting with each other and the connections made in the school's campus-based Professional Learning Communities. When given an opportunity to work in small, diverse groups intentionally focused on the human connection through culturally responsive SEL and mindfulness strategies, the school's educators experienced positive social interactions, felt valued and care for. Participants shared that it was uplifting to know that others were thinking about their wellness. Additionally, participants shared that they gained awareness of new social-emotional and mindfulness strategies to help support them in all areas of their lives, but especially to support them with teaching via distance learning. Feedback shared with the Heartbeat Team Leaders, which then was given to the project Facilitator, revealed a great appreciation of the Heartbeat Team system as a multi-tiered system of support to meet their needs, when they needed it during all of the changes that Distance Learning and Teaching had brought during school re-entry. Moreover, the staff expressed an overwhelming positive response to the implementation of the Heartbeat Team and a greater appreciation of schoolwide implementation of SEL. One staff member said, "SEL is not an add on, it is essential to everyone's success in life!"

When Heartbeat Team Facilitators collected ongoing participant feedback such as, "How did the meeting go? What is a need for increasing social interaction within your team? How did team members express any self-awareness needs?", Team Leaders reported positive experiences from their team members and identified a common theme in participant feedback described as, "We really need this!". Of the ten teams, one Team Leader reported that although most participants were consistently engaged, there were cases in which participant engagement levels fluctuated. This particular Team Leader shared, "My team felt good about meeting and seemed to really enjoy this, but a couple of people didn't contribute a lot. We might need some ideas to help them get started sharing." The administrative team would reinforce the activity by showing their support and encouraging open-communication with them about the project. Additionally, support materials were provided to all team members.

At the conclusion of the fall semester, participant's feedback and overall positive adoption of the Heartbeat Team activity inspired the school's leadership to incorporate the Heartbeat Team activity into regular faculty meetings hosted online, once a month. These faculty meetings would extend its agenda so that faculty could have intentional time to engage in, culturally responsive SEL activities, titled, "Celebrations & Conversations", the "Heartbeat- Hang Out", and the "Virtual Host Seat". Each activity would practice and develop SEL skills using a culturally responsive lens. The activities would focus on engaging deeper level conversations among team members through open-ended questions, celebrating SEL and mindfulness successes, and circulating positive feedback and support resources.

This case study's Heartbeat Team activity helped to increase social interaction midst a highly socially distant environment, provided culturally responsive SEL activities to support distance teaching, provided an emotionally safe virtual space for educators of all backgrounds to gain a new sense of community, and practice SEL and mindfulness strategies. Outcomes of this case study illuminates the need to address virtual social interaction for students in a distance learning. The Heartbeat Team *for students* is a future next step.

DISCUSSION

Supported by literature, the case studies presented in this chapter further illuminate how intentional culturally responsive SEAD practices can help create opportunities for students and adults to safely and respectfully explore their values and identities, discover socio-cultural variances and develop skills to bridge cultural gaps, build relationships and school climate, and constructively question systemic inequities while sharpening critical consciousness (NC-SEAD, 2019; Jagers, Rivas-Drake, and Borowski, 2018; Schlund, Jagers & Schlinger, 2020; Madden-Dent, 2021a). Across all three case study groups, their contributions lend to how different SEAD practices and SEL implementation methods strengthen youth and adult cultural awareness, SEL skills, self-efficacy and collective-efficacy, and student safety. Whether it be that culturally responsive SEL adds to distance education's ability to foster college readiness skills, cultural competence, and SEL skills (Case Study #1), contributes to safe and trusting classroom climates and co-creator relationships between students and professors (Case Study #2), or provide meaningful and satisfying ongoing professional development and support for in-service educators (Case Study #3), the need for SEAD in education is undeniable.

This study's findings advance current research demonstrating that cultural training and study increases self-awareness and management skills, cultural knowledge and social awareness, cross-cultural sensitivity and relationship skills, and responsible decision making (Altshuler, Sussman, & Kachur, 2003; Madden-Dent, 2021b; Pitts, 2009; Zhu, 2008). Based on this study, recommendations for practice encourage schools and school districts to consider increasing intentional and explicit culturally responsive social-emotional learning and professional development practices within in-person and virtual environments. The outcomes of the three case studies described in this chapter suggest that institutions of higher education may also consider supporting culturally responsive SEAD training in pre-service programs of study and ongoing faculty development to embed SEL competencies into instruction using a culturally responsive lens. Future research may consider examining each of the above case studies on a larger scale through a mixed-methods design to collect longitudinal data on the influence of culturally responsive SEL interventions.

CONCLUSION

This chapter provided an introduction to culturally responsive social, emotional, and academic development. It additionally provided three case studies demonstrating how culturally responsive SEAD can be implemented into high school, undergraduate, graduate, and in-service educator applications. The research findings shared in this chapter contribute to the understanding of how intentional practice and development of social-emotional competencies, framed within an inclusive cultural lens, can allow safe spaces to explore oneself and means to practice self-development (SEL Skills: Self-Awareness; Self-Management), discover other cultures and value diversity while better navigating relationships with people from different backgrounds (SEL Skills: Social Awareness; Relationship Skills), how to plan for and achieve goals that improve the quality of life for the individual and society at large (SEL Skills: Responsible Decision-Making).

As our world seeks global citizens who embody knowledge and skills to co-exist in a safe, respectful, and efficient society, our need to foster culturally responsive SEL skills in students, educators, and global economy will continue to increase. One consideration is to incorporate explicit culturally responsive SEL education into PreK – Grade 12 school curriculum, colleges of education for all programs of studies that influence educational systems, and within continual professional development as the foundation for the building essential skills for twenty-first century success.

REFERENCES

Almlund, M., Duckworth, A. L., Heckman, J. J., & Kautz, T. (2011). Personality psychology and economics. In E. A. Hanushek, S. Machin, & L. Wößmann (Eds.), *Handbook of the economics of education*. Elsevier. doi:10.1016/B978-0-444-53444-6.00001-8

Altay, I. F. (2005). Developing cultural awareness. *Journal of Language and Linguistic Studies*, *1*(2), 171–182.

Aspen Institute. (2018). *Pursuing Social and Emotional Development Through a Racial Equity Lens: A Call to Action.* Retrieved at https://www.aspeninstitute.org/publications/pursuing-social-and-emotional-development-through-a-racial-equity-lens-a-call-to-action/

Balcazar, F. E., Suarez-Balcazar, Y., & Taylor-Ritzler, T. (2009). Cultural competence: Development of a conceptual framework. *Disability and Rehabilitation*, *31*(14), 1153–1160. doi:10.1080/09638280902773752 PMID:19802931

Banks, J. A. (1991). A curriculum for empowerment, action, and change. In C. E. Sleeter (Ed.), *Empowerment through multicultural education* (pp. 76–88). Southern Illinois University Press.

Belfield, B., & Klapp, L. (2015). The economic value of social and emotional learning. New York, NY: Center for Benefit-Cost Studies in Education: Teachers College, Columbia University.

Cantor, P., Osher, D., Berg, J., Steyer, L., & Rose, T. (2018). Malleability, plasticity, and individuality: How children learn and develop in context. *Applied Developmental Science*. Advance online publication. doi:10.1080/10888691.2017.1398649

Collaborative for Academic, Social, and Emotional Learning (CASEL). (2017). *Making the case for SEL* [PowerPoint slides]. CASEL. https://docs.google.com/presentation/d/1Tb9WundNcsURexo2RTvVGVIVlzD_q9i6Vv4jcNtqZjI/edit#slide=id.p4

Collaborative for Academic, Social, and Emotional Learning (CASEL). (2020). *What is SEL?* Retrieved at https://casel.org/what-is-sel/

Cunningham, W. V., & Villasenor, P. (2016). Employer voices, employer demands, and implications for public skills development policy connecting the labor and education sectors. *The World Bank Research Observer*, *31*(1), 102–134. doi:10.1093/wbro/lkv019

Donahue, C. (2020). *Advice: Building positive relationships with fellow educators*. Retrieved at www.nea.org

Draeger, C. (2017). Developing professional relationships that work. *Education Week*. Retrieved at https://www.edweek.org/education/opinion-developing-professional-relationships-that-work/2017/09

Durlak, J. A., Weissberg, R. P., Dymnicki, A. B., Taylor, R. D., & Schellinger, K. (2011). The impact of enhancing students' social and emotional learning: A meta-analysis of school-based universal interventions. *Child Development*, *82*(1), 405–432. doi:10.1111/j.1467-8624.2010.01564.x PMID:21291449

Fitzgerald, B. K., & Sigelman, M. (2018). *The new foundational skills of the digital economy: Developing the professionals of the future*. Burning Glass Technologies. Retrieved from www.burning-glass.com

Fullam, J. P. (2017). From seeing to believing: Using instructional video to develop culturally responsive teaching. *Journal for Multicultural Education*, *11*(2), 131–148. doi:10.1108/JME-09-2016-0053

Gay, G. (2018). *Culturally responsive teaching: Theory, research, and practice* (3rd ed.). Teachers College Press.

Hall, E. T. (1976). *Beyond culture*. Doubleday.

Hammond, Z. (2015). *Culturally responsive teaching and the brain: Promoting authentic engagement and rigor among culturally and linguistically diverse students*. Corwin Press.

Hofstede, G. (2001). *Cultural consequences. Comparing values, behaviors, institutions, and organizations across nations* (2nd ed.). Sage.

Holt-Lunstad, J. (2020). *The double pandemic of social isolation and COVID: Cross-sector policy must address both*. Health Affairs Blog., doi:10.1377//hblog2020609.53823

Howard, D. C. (2019). Social-emotional learning won't happen without a culturally relevant start. *Education Week*. Retrieved from https://blogs.edweek.org/teachers/intersection-culture-and-race-ineducation/2019/02/social_emotional_learning_wont_happen_without_culturally_relevant_pedagogy.html

Jackson, I., Sealey-Ruiz, Y., & Watson, W. (2014). Reciprocal love: Mentoring Black and Latino males through an ethos of care. *Urban Education*, *49*(4), 394–417. doi:10.1177/0042085913519336

Jagers, R.-D., Rivas-Drake, D., & Williams, B. (2019). Transformative Social and Emotional Learning (SEL): Toward SEL in Service of Educational Equity and Excellence. *Educational Psychologist, 54*(3), 162–184. doi:10.1080/00461520.2019.1623032

Jkorderm, C. (2017). *Social contract: Capturing kids hearts.* Casey Jkorderm. Retrieved at https://rumblepups.wordpress.com/

Jones, D., Crowley, D. M., & Greenberg, M. T. (2017). *Improving social emotional skills in childhood enhances long-term well-being and economic outcomes.* Edna Bennet Pierce Prevention Research Center, Pennsylvania State University.

Jones, S., & Khan, J. (2017). *The evidence base for how we learn: Supporting students' social, emotional, and academic development.* Aspen Institute. Retrieved from http://nationathope.org/wp-content/uploads/final_cds-evidence-base.pdf

Kautz, Diris, & Borghans. (2014). Fostering and measuring skills: Improving cognitive and non-cognitive skills to promote lifetime success. Paris, France: Organization for Economic Cooperation and Development.

Kerr, D. B., & Gore, T. (2021). Developing Social Emotional Learning Competencies Through Virtual Internships. In *Leading Schools with Social, Emotional, and Academic Development (SEAD).* IGI Global Publication. Retrieved at https://www.igi-global.com/book/leading-schools-social-emotional-academic/256645

Kerr, D. B., & Madden-Dent, T. (2019). Cultural Transition and Adjustment of International East Asian Undergraduate Students. In S. E. Brock & P. J. McAliney (Eds.), *Discourses on Business Education at the College Level: On the Boundaries of Content and Praxis.* Touro University Press Books.

Kerr, D. B., Madden-Dent, T., & Shalabi, N. (2020). Cultural Competency Interventions: Three Case Studies with Guiding Theoretical Frameworks. In *Cultural intelligence and social-emotional competencies across the lifespan: Cultural Competencies for Continuous Learning* (2nd ed.). Oxford University Press. Retrieved at https://www.oxfordhandbooks.com/view/10.1093/oxfordhb/9780197506707.001.0001/oxfordhb-9780197506707-e-6?utm_content=148183851&utm_medium=social&utm_source=linkedin&hss_channel=lcp-19900 doi:10.1093/oxfordhb/9780197506707.013.26

Kim, Y. Y. (2001). Becoming intercultural: An integrative theory of communication and cross-cultural adaptation. *Sage (Atlanta, Ga.).*

Kluckhohn, C. (1951). *The study of culture: The policy sciences.* Stanford University Press.

Leverson, M., Smith, K., McIntosh, K., Rose, J., & Pinkelman, S. (2019). *PBIS cultural responsiveness field guide: Resources for trainers and coaches.* OSEP Technical Assistance Center. https://www.pbis.org/school/equity-pbis

Li, C., & Xu, J. (2019). Trait emotional intelligence and classroom emotions: A positive psychology investigation and intervention among Chinese EFL learners. *Frontiers in Psychology, 10*, 1–17. doi:10.3389/fpsyg.2019.02453 PMID:31736840

Lustig, M. W., & Koester, J. (2003). *Intercultural competence: Interpersonal communication across cultures* (4th ed.). Pearson Education, Inc.

Madden-Dent, T. (2014). *A phenomenological study of cultural transition and adjustment of Asian undergraduate international students using different cross-cultural treatments. ProQuest.* UMI Dissertations Publishing.

Madden-Dent, T. (2021a). Advancing equity through culturally responsive social-emotional education: Addressing international student integration. In Advances in Motivation and Achievement. Motivating the SEL Field Forward Through Equity (Vol. 21). Emerald Publishing Limited. doi:10.1108/S0749-7423201719

Madden-Dent, T. (2021b). Bridging academic and industry skills gap via digital collaboration: Preparing scholars for international assignment. In *University-Industry Collaboration Strategies in the Digital Era*. Retrieved at https://www.igi-global.com/book/university-industry-collaboration-strategies-digital/244278 doi:10.4018/978-1-7998-3901-9

Madden-Dent, T., & Donaburska, P. (2019). *Beyond Orientation: International Student Integration.* NAFSA: Association of International Educators National Conference.

Madden-Dent, T., Wood, D., & Roskina, K. (2019). A survey of international student services at 200 U.S. universities and colleges. *Journal of International Students*, *9*(4), 346–362. doi:10.32674/jis.v9i4.346

Maldonado, C. (2019). *Integrating workforce development practices in higher education.* Workforce Development Center, University of Nevada.

Medina-López-Portillo, A. (2004). Intercultural learning assessment: The link between program duration and the development of intercultural sensitivity. *Frontiers: The Interdisciplinary Journal of Study Abroad*, *10*(1), 179–200. doi:10.36366/frontiers.v10i1.141

National Commission on Social, Emotional, and Academic Development (NC-SEAD). (2019). *Nation at hope*. Aspen, CO: Aspen Institute. Retrieved from http://nationathope.org/

Osher, D., Cantor, P., Berg, J., Steyer, L., & Rose, T. (2018). Drivers of human development: How relationships and context shape learning and development. *Applied Developmental Science*, *1*. Advance online publication. doi:10.1080/10888691.2017.1398650

Osher, D., Moroney, D., & Williamson, S. (2018). *Creating safe, equitable, engaging schools: A comprehensive, evidence-based approach to supporting students.* Harvard Education Press.

Pilhofer, K. (2010). *Cultural knowledge: An ethical deconstruction of the concept as a foundation for respect for cultural differences from a post-colonial and Levinasian perspective.* Copenhagen Business School. Retrieved at http://studenttheses.cbs.dk/bitstream/handle/10417/1677/katharina_pilhofer.pdf?sequence=1

Pitts, M. J. (2009). Identity and the role of expectations, stress, and talk in short-term student sojourner adjustment: An application of the integrative theory of communication and cross-cultural adaptation. *International Journal of Intercultural Relations*, *33*(6), 450–462. doi:10.1016/j.ijintrel.2009.07.002

Pollard, B. A. (2020). What Sparks Critical Learning?: Exploring the Dialogical Teaching Context Facilitated in the LEAD Course. In G. Salinitri (Ed.), *Handbook of Research on Leadership Experience for Academic Direction (LEAD) Programs for Student Success* (pp. 297–322). IGI Global. doi:10.4018/978-1-7998-2430-5.ch016

Reed, K., & Madden-Dent, T. (2021). Social emotional learning as a lever for high school student mental health and academic success: A reflective analysis. In *Leading Schools with Social Emotional Academic Development (SEAD)*. IGI Global Publication. Retrieved at https://www.igi-global.com/book/leading-schools-social-emotional-academic/256645

Rew, L., Becker, H., Cookston, J., Khosropour, S., & Martinez, S. (2003). Measuring cultural awareness in nursing students. *The Journal of Nursing Education*, *42*(6), 249–257. doi:10.3928/0148-4834-20030601-07 PMID:12814215

Rose, J., Leverson, M., & Smith, K. (2020). *Embedding culturally responsive practices in Tier I.* Center on Positive Behavioral Interventions & Supports. Retrieved at www.pbis.org

Rossatto, C. A. (2020). Challenging fear and hate: Caring and compassion as essential components of a critical pedagogy school curriculum. In J. Keengwe (Ed.), *Handbook of Research on Diversity and Social Justice in Higher Education* (pp. 149–159). IGI Global. doi:10.4018/978-1-7998-5268-1.ch009

Spradley, J. P. (1980). *Participant observation*. Harcourt Brace Jovanovich College Publishers.

Swain-Bradway, J., Lindstrom Johnson, S., Bradshaw, C., & McIntosh, K. (2017). *What are the economic costs of implementing SWPBIS in comparison to the benefits from reducing suspensions?* Technical Brief from Center for Positive Behavioral Interventions and Supports. https://assets-global.website-files.com/5d3725188825e071f1670246/5d76c00cb9339d5f3f267ee7_economiccostsswpbis.pdf

Taters, G. (2019). *Making time for mindfulness*. Harvard Graduate School of Education. Retrieved at https://www.gse.harvard.edu/news/uk/19/01/making-time-mindfulness

Taylor, R. D., Oberle, E., Durlak, J. A., & Weissberg, R. P. (2017). Promoting positive youth development through school-based social and emotional learning interventions: A meta-analysis of follow-up effects. *Child Development*, *88*(4), 1156–1171. doi:10.1111/cdev.12864 PMID:28685826

Terzi, S., & Celik, A. (2005). Teacher-student interactions in distance learning. *The Turkish Online Journal of Educational Technology*, *4*(1), 54–56.

Training Management Corporation©. (2013). *Cultural Orientations Indicator® technical manual summary*. Retrieved by request from http://www.tmcorp.com/

Training Management Corporation©. (2020). *Cultural Orientations Indicator®*. Retrieved from http://www.tmcorp.com/Online-Learning/Assessments/Cultural-Orientations-Indicator-COI/76/

Trompenaars, F. (1993). Riding the waves of culture: Understanding cultural diversity in business. *Economica Books*.

Wehling, S. (2008). Cross-cultural competency through service-learning. *Journal of Community Practice*, *16*(3), 293–315. doi:10.1080/10705420802255080

Wohl, A. F. (2012). *Citizenship and social activism: A mixed method case study to understand cultural competence in students of a service-learning based course* (Thesis). North Dakota State University.

Zhu, Y. (2008). From cultural adaptation to cross-cultural discursive competence. *Discourse & Communication*, *2*(2), 185–204. doi:10.1177/1750481307088483

KEY TERMS AND DEFINITIONS

Critical Consciousness: The intellectual capacity to think holistically, recognize, and analyze institutionalized constructs for effectiveness and inequalities, and the commitment to take action to improve the system through critical reflection and dialog that promotes social transformation. This complex educational process of learning focuses on achieving an in-depth understanding of the world that in turn allows for the exposure of social and political contradictions. (Modified from Pollard, 2020; Rossatto, 2020).

Cultural Awareness: A means toward gradually increasing a person's power, energy and freedom of choice in a multicultural world (Pederson, 1998) by developing inner senses of the equality of cultures, increasing an understanding of the individual's orientations, other people's orientations, and a positive interest in how cultures are similar, interconnected, and differ (Tomlinson, 2001) through "increasing a person's intentional and purposive decision-making ability by accounting for the many ways that culture influences different perceptions of the same situation" (Altay 2005, p. 171).

Cultural Competence: The multifaceted, evolving capacity to interact and communicate with others having different cultural backgrounds (Balcazar, Suarex-Balcazar, & Taylor-Ritzler, 2009; IHEAC, 2008; Wehling, 2008).

Cultural Knowledge: The awareness and sensitivity to existing cultural preferences, values, and behaviors interpreted by an individual that generates cross-cultural competencies aiming to decrease emotional discomfort while increasing respect for other cultures (Hall, 1976; Hofstede, 2001; Pilhofer, 2010; Spradley, 1980; Trompenaars, 1993).

Cultural Responsiveness: Refers to the process of developing awareness of the significance of our students' backgrounds (including historical context), then intentionally integrating their customs and values into our curriculum, instruction, and school environment (Rose, Leverson, & Smith, 2020).

Cultural Sensitivity: The degree of an individual's psychological ability to deal with cultural differences (Medina-López-Portillo, 2004); and to value and respect these cultural differences (Rew, Becker, Cookston, Khosropour, & Martinez, 2003).

Culture: Sets of socially transmitted ways of thinking, feeling, interacting, and communicating through shared value in traditions and customs distinguishing members of one organization from another (Hofstede, 2001, Kluckhohn, 1951; Lustig & Koester, 2003; Wohl, 2012).

Social, Emotional, and Academic Development (SEAD): The integration of social-emotional learning (SEL) and academics that reinforces equitable and human-centered educational environments (Aspen Institute, 2019).

Social-Emotional Learning (SEL): A lifelong process through which all people learn and apply culturally responsive, "knowledge, skills, and attitudes to develop healthy identities, manage emotions and achieve personal and collective goals, feel and show empathy for others, establish and maintain supportive relationships, make responsible and caring decisions" (CASEL, 2020).

Chapter 3
Effective Social Emotional Learning Implementation:
SEAD Starts With You

Ashley Wolfe Reilly
Independent Researcher, USA

ABSTRACT

A growing interest and body of research in education in the United States has centered around the idea that students learn best when they have foundational social emotional learning skills. These skills, ranging from interpersonal skills to self-reflection and awareness skills to self-management skills, allow students and adults to engage with one another in productive, pro-social ways that can positively impact a classroom community and a school's culture at large. This chapter seeks to consider the ways that adult social emotional learning impacts the success of greater, school-wide implementation. Specifically, the chapter explores the impact that a purposeful, measured (six months to year-long) adult social emotional learning rollout has in successful school-wide adoption of a comprehensive social emotional learning program.

INTRODUCTION

To implement a Social, Emotional, and Academic Development (SEAD) program, also known widely as Social Emotional Learning (SEL), effectively and with fidelity, a school, district, charter management organization, or other educational institution must examine what it means for their organization to live and breathe the skills highlighted in social emotional learning frameworks. According to the Collaborative for Academic, Social, and Emotional Learning (CASEL), social emotional competencies include self-awareness, self-management, social awareness, relationship skills, and responsible decision-making (CASEL, 2021). It is essential that adults on school campuses embody these skills in order to appropriately model them for children. In the most successful SEL programs, implementation starts with adults long before administrators, teachers, and support staff are expected to engage students in social emotional learning. According to the Aspen Institute, the success of a social, emotional, and academic program

DOI: 10.4018/978-1-7998-6728-9.ch003

"depends upon consistent implementation, modeling by adults and peers, and professional development that deepens school staff's social and emotional skills" (Berman, Chaffee, & Sarmiento, 2018).

In a 2008 exploration of implementation barriers and facilitators, researchers identified several key factors that influence the success of these programs. The majority of these factors involve the adults on school campuses. First and foremost, the availability and training of leaders and administrators is identified as a critical need in the implementation process. Once that foundation has been established, the support and buy-in of school staff, particularly the educators responsible for the student-facing phase of implementation is emphasized. Other important adult-centered factors include ongoing, consistent training and coaching, collaboration with teammates to align on goals related to the implementation, and communication with stakeholders including school teammates (Forman, Olin, Hoagwood, Crowe, & Saka, 2008).

In a report entitled, "To Reach the Students, Teach the Teachers, prepared for CASEL in 2017, the authors observe that while graduate level and credentialing programs in education consistently incorporate social emotional learning into their curriculum, educators continually struggle to apply these principles to their classrooms. Teachers do not feel appropriately prepared to engage students in social emotional learning and consistently advocate for additional professional development and coaching (Schonert-Reichl, K.A., Kitil, M.J., Hanson-Peterson, J., 2017). By dedicating six months to a year to purposeful practice with adults, educators have an opportunity to experience this training and coaching. Collaboration facilitates buy-in and support for implementing SEL programs with fidelity. Staff on campuses are better equipped to understand how to integrate SEL tools into their daily lessons and how to lead SEL lessons in their classrooms. After all, a school leader should not and would not expect an English teacher to walk in and successfully lead an Algebra II course with no exposure to the material or preparation. In the same way, teachers and support staff should not be expected to teach students social emotional skills without appropriate preparation and support to do so.

Year after year educational institutions introduce new initiatives to integrate the newest research and adapt to best support students. With ongoing updates to curriculum, the push to meet state and national standards, and continuous additions of new strategies and models, schools and staff regularly report feeling overwhelmed. In fact, according to Gallup's report on American schools (2014), "Nearly half of K-12 teachers (46%) report high daily stress during the school year. That figure matches those from other highly demanding professions, such as nurses (46%) and physicians (45%), for the highest stress levels among all occupational groups surveyed" (p. 24). For these reasons, SEAD may seem like "just another thing on my plate" for staff and schools.

This chapter presents strategies to support all staff in creating a shared vision for SEAD on your campus, reflecting on their own social and emotional competencies, learning to model social and emotional skills as leaders, and supporting the emotional and mental wellness needs of adults. By practicing these strategies before implementing SEAD with students, SEAD will become a naturally integrated part staffs' practice, rather than an addition to it. Further, there are many positive implications for adult and school culture at large that result from the adoption of a comprehensive adult SEAD implementation. This chapter will explore five areas to support adult social and emotional development before beginning to implement SEAD with students, as well as several case examples under each section to support integration. First, the topic of engagement is explored, with particular emphasis on consistent barriers to engagement experienced by adults on school campuses. The chapter then transitions to focusing on how to establish a baseline and measure progress in adult social emotional learning. Developing buy-in through collaborative processes is then explored as a means of continuing to develop your social emotional program with the adults on campus. Then, a discussion around integrating SEAD into adult practices is had. Finally, the chapter explores how to address the wellness needs of staff in a wholistic and support manner as you implement a social emotional learning program on your campus.

Engaging Adults in Social Emotional Learning

The notion of engagement is not new to educators. Within the field, engagement is measured by looking at a student's attention, interest, and passion when presented with subject matter (Education Reform, 2016). Engagement is directly correlated with the amount of motivation a student has to learn and progress in a particular subject. As with students, engagement and motivation are key elements of the learning process for adult learners. Connection is a tremendous driver of both engagement and motivation. It is well known that adults who are uninterested will simply "tune out" what is being presented or de-prioritize it among the growing lists of tasks they must accomplish. Understanding some of the reasons why adults may struggle to engage in social emotional learning will help individuals responsible for implementing these programs in working through these challenges.

New Initiative Fatigue

The first and most frequently encountered barrier to implementing SEL with adults on a campus is simple: schools and districts have a long history of over-committing to new initiatives. In just a few short years, educators in many California schools were introduced to SEL, PBIS, MTSS, RtI, Restorative Practices, just to name a few. And those were only the student services focused initiatives. Educators and school leaders are simultaneously adapting to seemingly annual demands to shift curriculum, adapt to new standards, and integrate new rubrics and frameworks into their lesson planning and curriculum evaluation. This creates a "this too shall pass" attitude among educators, resulting in a lack of commitment to SEL programming.

There are many ways to combat new initiative fatigue in teammates. The most effective of these is to remind teammates that SEL is far from new. Educators and school staff have been shaping students' emotional intelligence, relationship skills, and values for as long as schools have existed. This process is no exception. Rather, it is a purposeful, dedicated time to focus on the skills that teachers have already been instilling in students. In many ways, this can serve as a relief. Finally, as educators, there is a time and place to have character-developing conversations. There is a time and a place to focus on wellness and "soft-skills" that will support students in becoming successful adults with healthy values, relationships, and coping skills.

For leaders reading this, listen well. This also means that designated social emotional learning time must exist. Teachers cannot be asked to add "one more thing" to their growing list of demands during each class period, as this almost certainly contributes to the feeling of initiative fatigue. "Although 87 percent of educators are aware of the importance of SEL, less than half of practicing teachers report being provided with resources, training, or professional development in SEL" (Woolf, 2020). As school leaders, time for SEL must be designated and purposeful. This begins by designating time to practice social emotional learning skills consistently in staff gatherings and meetings. Slowly, this becomes integrated into coaching sessions and educator development. Eventually, this evolves into school-wide times that are carved out and held for social emotional learning, all supported by ongoing professional development and coaching. After several years of implementation, these become norms and routines on campuses, even sacred time, for students and staff alike.

It can also be valuable to remind staff that SEL can be integrated into everything else they do and can be used to supplement other content areas. For example, when evaluating students' experiences of a particular assessment, SEL tools can guide that process. Yale's Center for Emotional Intelligence's SEL Curriculum, RULER, uses a tool called the "Mood Meter" to help students evaluate their current mood on 2 axises: energy and pleasantness (RULER, 2021). Teachers using this tool might ask students in their math class, "Where were you on the mood meter while taking this exam?" to evaluate students' mindset while completing the exam. Educators can also use these tools while diving into content directly. Using the same tool, a high school English teacher might ask, "Where on the mood meter might Scout have been when the mob arrived at Tom Robinson's jail cell?" Recognizing how social emotional learning tools can complement other content instruction (rather than live alone in a dedicated series of lessons) can help build buy-in and interest.

Finally, it is important to highlight why social emotional learning can be impactful for a teacher of any grade level and content area. In a 2009 Gallup study looking at almost 80,000 scholars across the country, it was found that "a one percentage-point increase in student engagement score was associated with a six-point increase in reading achievement and an eight-point increase in math achievement' (Gallup, 2014, p. 7). Educators who may be focused on student performance and who may consider SEL to be a distraction from their subject area might be more interested once they understand the impact engagement and connection can have on student achievement. Practically as school leaders, this phenomenon is easy to see. When students feel connected and engaged with their teacher, peers, and community, educators see an increase in belonging and motivation.

Case Example 1

Mr. Jones was a high school humanities teacher focused on teaching U.S. and World History. He would be the first to tell you that he was "over" all of the new initiatives on campus and usually ignored them until the initiatives inevitably fizzled out. Social emotional learning was presented on his campus the year after multi-tiered systems of support (MTSS) and restorative practices had been prioritized by his school district and site. Mr. Jones shared his skepticism and frustration with the site counselor who was on the implementation team. This counselor, using much of the above-mentioned data, helped this educator develop an understanding of the reasons behind SEL implementation, how social emotional skills can be easily integrated into existing curriculum, and the structure of the long-term roll out and plans.

In talking more with Mr. Jones, the counselor learned that by far, the most important part of implementation for him was consistency and support. It became clear that in past initiatives, he felt pressured to implement strategies or frameworks he was not confident in using. Then, by the time he developed some of this confidence by researching and practicing the strategies on his own, the initiatives shifted on campus. This was incredibly useful information for the SEL implementation team on this campus. It helped guide the team in their decision to present the long-term plans for rolling out this curriculum in a transparent way that helped increase engagement and adult buy-in. It also helped the leadership team understand the need for consistency in professional development and coaching around implementation. Leaders on campus committed to staff that when professional development needs around SEL were identified, there would be a corresponding training conducted. The outcome on campus after a year was clear: educators were prepared and had practiced with the SEL materials and tools before ever bringing them into their classrooms. Mr. Jones even ended up being one of the greatest proponents of social emotional learning on campus, coaching other teachers in how to use SEL tools in their classrooms to build stronger connections with students.

"I'm not an SEL Person"

How many times have educational leaders heard (or said) comments like, "SEL just isn't my thing" or "I'm not an emotional person, so SEL isn't for me." Trust that all administrators have likely heard it, and frequently, it comes from individuals who live and breathe social emotional skills without even knowing it.

It is essential that everyone on campus, from facilities staff to principals, view themselves as SEL people and understand the responsibility they hold in implementing social emotional learning on your campus. That ownership leads to fidelity and commitment to implementation. Yet it is equally important that educators feel empowered to implement SEL in a way that reflects and respects who they are. This respect for each of your teammates is reflective of the social emotional learning process itself. As your staff builds self-awareness about their own strengths and relationship-building style, they will also build capacity for building the skills of their students.

Although most school leaders would agree that a healthy respect for individual styles and differences is essential, when implementing a program with fidelity, sometimes leaders can develop a certain focus or even rigidity. This deserves mention here because many social emotional programs are already fairly prescriptive and emphasize consistency and adherence to the curriculum. After all, in a data-driven world searching for evidence of efficacy, program evaluators are interested in understanding if their programs are effective. However, when combined with a very focused leader, this rigidity can sometimes make individuals on campus feel as though there is little or no room to infuse their own personalities into the SEL process. To support buy-in and excitement, leaders must be creative and find ways to emphasize places in the curriculum where personalities can shine. A great way to model this is by presenting parts of lessons in staff meetings during your adult phase of implementation.

Case Example 2

Mrs. Allison was a Calculus teacher who prided herself on having open, honest conversations with students and being a teacher they could count on. When her school started to roll out social emotional learning for adults on campus, she was clear. "I'm never going to sit in a circle and do some touchy-feely stuff to get kids to open up." My response, "Okay. You don't have to, but let me ask you this - do you care about your students?" Her face was confused initially, but her answer was obvious. "Of course." I responded, "And how do you show them?" She described her honesty, the respect she holds for each student, and how she communicates with them as young adults and individuals. She also communicated around the boundaries and consistency she holds for students and her high expectations for them. I quickly retorted, "So you do SEL everyday. You're teaching self-awareness, social awareness, relationship skills, etc. all the time. You're helping students learn how to advocate for themselves and communicate in healthy ways. You are holding them accountable and helping them work through disappointment, fear, overwhelm, etc. This is all SEL, and all you had to do was show up and be who you are." As our conversation continued, Mrs. Allison looked more and more surprised, yet relieved to hear that SEL often looks like natural, positive relationship-building. All we were doing was putting a name to the teacher moves Allison was already making and helping her build her own awareness and competency to be able to use SEL interventions purposefully and intentionally. As Mrs. Allison's exposure to the SEL material grew throughout our year-long adult implementation, she began to be more vocal about alternative strategies and ways to use the tools in a math setting. By the time we began our student-facing implementation, Mrs. Allison was considered a resource for ways to integrate SEL into a math classroom and for general relationship-building strategies. The hidden beauty of this experience was also that Mrs. Allison had developed her own social emotional and communication skills through this process, skills that ultimately helped her in being more successful as a leader and eventual head of the math department at another school.

The Danger of the "SEL Point Person"

Before upsetting the SEL point people or leaders of the world, let us be the first to say that every SEL program needs strong leadership and backing from administrators. Sometimes the designated SEL leaders are not the administrative team, and this can be a great thing. There is a danger, however, in specifying a single point person for a school or district without explicitly stating and confirming understanding that social emotional learning is a school-wide initiative. Then, say this again. And again. And again. Social emotional learning is a school-wide initiative. It does not live in any department, classroom, or office. When an individual leader or driver is identified, it can come with a sense of ownership that should actually be shared with the greater community.

In order to create broader ownership among school teammates, it can be helpful to advocate for a school-wide roll out with SEAD/SEL champions and coaches banding together to form a task force of sorts. These individuals can be the cheerleaders, the supports, and the problem-solvers as the program implementation occurs. Ideally, this group will range in school role, grade levels, and interests in order to create stronger buy-in and representation. In the initial years of school-wide implementation, these coaches can hold bi-weekly or monthly SEL check ins with their multi-disciplinary teams. These coaches can regularly present in staff meetings to maintain adult engagement and to model upcoming lessons. Finally, the coaches can be responsible for finding ways to measure progress in the SEL implementation and report out to school staff.

Case Example 3

Not all case examples in this chapter have a fairytale ending with a newly developed SEL champion. In this case, we instead explore the potential downfalls of having a single SEL leader or point person on a campus or in a district. Ms. Stuart is a mental health counselor on a school campus. As with many counselors, she finds herself a "Jill of all trades." She is involved in the school's MTSS process, student government, restorative practices, teacher consultation and support, parent support and outreach, and crisis intervention, in addition to her main role as the preventative and responsive mental health provider on campus. When social emotional learning was planned in her district, site leaders were charged with identifying a responsible individual who would lead the implementation process for each school. Because of her natural strengths in social emotional skill building, Ms. Stuart was considered a perfect fit for the role. When her principal suggested it, her internal process involved 1) considering her current obligations and time constraints, 2) thinking about who else could or would hold that role on campus, 3) evaluating the scope of her role and accepting this fit into it, and 4) feeling a sense of guilt about potentially saying no mixed with a strong sense of obligation given her expertise in the subject area. Ultimately, Ms. Stuart agreed.

There were several problems that arose through the implementation process that deserve exploration here. First and foremost, the person selected to lead the implementation efforts simply did not have the time to do so. While Ms. Stuart was the natural choice and school leaders knew she would accept the role, her commitment to many other time-consuming tasks on campus gave her little time to commit to a thoughtful, school-wide roll out. Beyond attending district planning meetings and making occasional staff meeting announcements, Ms. Stuart was unable to dedicate time to school-based collaboration efforts or significant professional development for herself or her staff.

Outside of the selected individual's lack of time to dedicate, one of the largest concerns with implementation from Ms. Stuart's perspective was the lack of leadership and support for the initiative on the part of her administrators. Ms. Stuart believed that in order to effectively generate buy-in from stakeholders on campus, she would need leadership support in facilitating professional development, allocating adequate time in staff meetings, and reinforcing the use of social emotional learning skills. Unfortunately, she did not experience any of these forms of support. In case example after case example, this is an ongoing concern when a non-administrator/school leader is responsible for implementation of a program. While on one hand, Ms. Stuart could leverage her close relationships with teachers, students, and families to help her in her implementation efforts, she needed the support and shared credibility of the school leaders to help inspire and hold the team accountable. As a result, on Ms. Stuart's campus, SEL had the reputation of being a "counselor thing" that lived in counselor-generated curriculum within a year of beginning the implementation process.

What is particularly interesting for school leaders to consider about this scenario is the aftermath and associated consequences, the most important of which was the challenge of resurrecting this program once that label took hold. From Ms. Stuart's perspective, because professional development time and administrator energy did not accompany the initiative from infancy, the message that the program was not exceptionally important was received by staff. When mentions of social emotional learning happened monthly at best in all-staff meetings, and typically in mere ten to fifteen-minute PSAs, the message felt more like a preview and less like preparation for a comprehensive program roll out. When staff were then presented with the plan for student-facing curriculum implementation for the following year, they expressed overwhelm and a lack of preparedness. This became a new hurdle to overcome in the process of beginning this SEL program. This example is shared as a cautionary tale and a reminder that a team approach that fosters strong leadership, collaboration, and shared ownership from the beginning is bound to create a more successful experience for your teams.

Establishing a Baseline

As with any program implementation, establishing a baseline is a critical step in being able to accurately measure progress. Because social emotional learning is so vast and encompasses traditionally challenging areas to measure (like self-awareness and relationship skills), truly understanding how to establish a baseline is essential. This process will also support leaders in being able to understand what their school staff need in order to effectively launch an SEL program. While understanding the baseline and subsequent progress of students on campus is the ultimate goal of a social emotional learning program, it is recommended to establish school staff baselines in the year prior to your student-facing implementation.

The first step is to support staff in beginning to consider their own readiness for teaching SEL. Tools such as CASEL's "Personal Assessment and Reflection - SEL Competencies for School Leaders, Staff, and Adults" (CASEL Assessment, 2021), part of their Guide to School-Wide SEL, help adults reflect on their own strengths and needs in the various social emotional competencies. As CASEL notes, it is imperative that these reflective exercises be conducted in a supportive environment and never incorporated into any formal employee review processes. Rather, tools like this one can be a springboard for discussions about SEL competencies that adults on campus may be more or less comfortable with. This data can give school leaders essential information about areas of need and focus for future professional development.

Anytime leaders are asking staff to explore strengths and vulnerabilities, there is an opportunity to have conversations about self-care and building our own resiliency as adults. The Center on Great Teachers & Leaders published "Educator Resilience and Trauma-Informed Self-Care Self-Assessment and Planning Tool" (2020). This is another example of a baseline that can be established and regularly revisited to explore how educational teams are managing their own emotional histories and needs. Having a strong understanding of this is advantageous because it allows school leaders to identify individuals who may struggle with presenting emotionally-oriented content due to their own needs. This is not to say these individuals cannot or should not present SEL material. Quite the opposite is true, in fact. People with lived experiences who have overcome struggle often present SEL material in the most authentic ways. However, sometimes SEL materials and lessons will bring up thoughts, memories, and emotions for the adults presenting the material. An individual does not want this to happen for the first time when they are student-facing.

As school leaders and coaches, it is incredibly important to identify staff with vulnerabilities, as it allows us to structure support collaboratively with each individual. Notice this sentence deliberately does not say that leaders or coaches structure support for an individual. Adults on campuses deserve support, but they also deserve unwavering respect. That means that each individual is able to set their own boundaries and pacing for how to practice this material in a way that feels attainable and healthy for them. Leaders want to promote growth in their staff as school leaders, and sometimes that requires discomfort. Acknowledge this discomfort while providing leadership, and look for signs that it either is or is not being well tolerated by your teammates. It is possible to gently guide teams toward growth while maintaining respect for their boundaries and openness to change. This requires leaders to also develop skills in emotional attunement, relational awareness, and empathy. You can see how this process truly facilitates social emotional growth on all levels.

Another benefit to having staff engage in self-assessments like those named above is that these processes create natural insight for staff to better see how they already use social emotional competencies in their life. There are other ways to support teammates in building this insight and confidence. For example, many schools have incorporated "educational rounds" of some kind, where leaders and peers use targeted observations to look for and highlight specific practices. Conducting these classroom walks with an SEL focus during this "adult SEL" phase can really help to emphasize and share successful practices that staff are already using in their day-to-day work with students. It also helps leaders further establish (both qualitatively and potentially quantitatively if a rubric is used) a baseline around pre/early SEL implementation practices. This information can be used to help leaders determine what professional development needs exist and identify both strengths and gaps in existing knowledge or understanding around SEL.

Finally, never underestimate the simple power of asking questions in establishing a baseline among school teams. Whether using formal instruments like surveys to collect data or informal conversations about comfort with SEL implementation, teammates should feel heard. This creates a sense of ownership over the implementation process. When staff become invested in identifying gaps in knowledge and helping to bridge them, they automatically become part of the SEL team. Everyone needs to be on this team. Leaders can create this environment purposefully by strategically asking for feedback and input from those who might struggle most with the implementation.

Because of the growing popularity of social emotional learning across disciplines, but especially in education, significant research on how to maximize implementation and evaluate the process has been occurring for over a decade. This includes how to measure the baseline and the various phases of implementation itself. According to Domitrovich et. al. (2008), "Despite the existing research linking quality of program implementation with student outcomes, the process of monitoring the quality of implementation is often overlooked, or given lower priority than measuring outcomes." He and his colleagues went on to suggest that in the process of implementation, schools and districts should consider a multi-level framework in their progress monitoring processes. The first evaluates the impact of macro-level factors that can impact implementation. These would include things like educational and district policies, district leadership, and human capital. He then encourages consideration of school-level factors, including important elements such as decision structure, experience of staff, leadership among administrators, and the school and community culture. This particular level of the framework is where many of the strategies listed in this chapter reside. Finally, the individual-level factors like attitudes toward the program and professional values and strengths should be monitored (Domitrovich et al., 2008). Establishing a baseline is a critical step in the process of understanding the success of your implementation process, and continued mechanisms to measure the elements of the various levels of this framework will support successful adoption of a comprehensive SEL program.

Developing Buy-In Collaboratively

Education is full of new initiatives which can create resistance to implementing new SEAD programs. It is important to create a shared understanding and path for the school community and to do so in a collaborative manner that creates ownership from the beginning. You can facilitate a process of future school student SEAD success by first creating a shared vision with staff, developing a collaborative plan for implementation, and supporting staff to create SMART goals to work towards.

There are many practical resources available for school leaders looking for guidance in implementing a comprehensive social emotional learning program. Nearly all of them begin with a focus on building buy-in and enthusiasm among staff. The Collaborative for Academic, Social, and Emotional Learning (CASEL) is responsible for publishing many resources to help educators. A great starting point is "CASEL Schoolwide SEL Essentials: A printable compilation of key activities and tools for school teams." In the essentials resource, CASEL encourages school leaders to initially focus on "building foundational knowledge among staff, developing a shared vision, and engaging in collaborative planning" (CASEL Essentials, 2020). Many specific tools are offered for creating this shared idea of what SEL implementation looks like, feels like, sounds like, etc. on a school campus. Also, many specific social emotional learning programs have implementation guides and activities as part of their training phase. These can be particularly useful as they often mirror activities that educators will be doing in classrooms with students in the coming year.

Once your team has created a shared vision for how to move forward, setting specific, measurable, attainable, relevant, and time-based (SMART) goals for implementation of your SEAD program is a critical next step as a school leader. Several timelines and rubrics exist to guide schools and districts in this work. It is important to customize the goals to the needs identified in your school community. This can include a timeline for implementation, details around who holds what responsibilities, plans for strengthening the adult capacity for rolling out the program on campus, and goals for integrating feedback from your students, families, and community around the program. Though often the overarching plans around implementation are held by school leaders or designated social emotional learning leads, the goals and timelines should be regularly communicated with the entire school team. By doing so, school leaders further emphasize the shared ownership of the program.

A final important component of developing the support and buy-in of a school team is regularly, consistently modeling and integrating SEAD tools in collaborative meeting spaces. As competing priorities and needs arise through the school year, this is one of the easiest components to slowly neglect. Avoid falling into that pattern. If school leaders dedicate this time and energy into modeling these tools into meeting spaces, staff will begin to recognize the importance and value being put into these practices. By creating intentional space in all-staff meeting agendas throughout the school year, adults will be exposed to social emotional learning content with enough regularity to build comfort and eventually confidence in the material. Research demonstrates that consistent opportunities for professional development facilitates improved fidelity in implementation, while a lack of training becomes a barrier to successful implementation (Forman, Olin, Hoagwood, Crowe, & Saka, 2008).

SEAD Integration with Adults - Live, Breath, Train, and Teach SEAD

Integrating social and emotional development into already existing systems should not be a burden or cumbersome. Schools will find that as they find small opportunities to integrate elements of social and emotional development for adults, they will also see a reduction in stress, burnout, and 'new-initiative fatigue,' as well as an increase in comradery and positive staff culture. Simply put, practicing social emotional learning skills is just as beneficial to adults as it is to the children they serve. Research has demonstrated that SEL training for educators helps strengthens culturally responsive skills, collective teacher efficacy, and staff relationships (Kerr, Madden-Dent, & Shalabi, 2020; Madden-Dent, Jackson, & Cason, 2021). This section of the chapter will give practical, easy to use, and natural ideas of ways in which to incorporate SE development into already existing infrastructures.

The simplest way to naturally integrate social emotional learning is by incorporating language, site/district SEAD goals for staff, and activities into every meeting. As mentioned in the previous section, this consistent process helps staff feel prepared for the student-facing elements of SEL and facilitates productive implementation with high fidelity (Forman, Olin, Hoagwood, Crowe, & Saka, 2008). Whether using strategies like a welcoming activity, optimistic closure, or specific modeling of future student-facing lessons, these moments can support staff's involvement and learning (CASEL Essentials, 2020). Some schools even assign rotating staff members to facilitate these meeting practices in order to support them in developing facilitation skills. It is important to note that staff's reactions to these requests for their participation will correlate with their level of collaboration in the planning process. For example, a school where it was the staff's idea to facilitate or co-facilitate these new meeting activities may have more buy-in and enthusiastic participation than a school that mandates and assigns these new roles. By being collaborative from the beginning rather than forcing staff into roles they may not feel prepared for or comfortable in, administrators and leaders can avoid having to "right the ship."

Another important element of supporting adult learning that teachers and staff ask for time and time again is modeling. Show us what this looks like, sounds like, feels like in classrooms. The best social emotional learning coaches do this naturally through their everyday interactions. However, it is the naming and demonstration of the specific moves that staff frequently point to as most helpful. This can happen in staff meetings, classrooms, hallways, and cafeterias. The most important thing about modeling is that staff see it consistently from school leaders and have time to process what they saw and how they might integrate it into their practices. This may mean leaders need additional training as well. Not every administrator is well versed in strategies for modeling social emotional learning, and that is okay. Both CASEL and most evidence-based SEL programs provide offerings to support administrator development.

As a follow up to intentional modeling of SEAD practices, a step in the adult learning and integration process is providing regular coaching sessions for all staff with the SEL coaches/champions on campus. These coaching sessions can be individual or in small groups (or a targeted combination for staff who need more support and/or benefit from both learning modalities). Sessions should be focused on developing specific skills, as articulated in the goals and timelines developed by the SEL team on campus. It is important that staff have time and space to work through challenges associated with delivering new material and to ask questions. School leaders should meet at least monthly with their SEL coaches in order to evaluate the progress of the staff's integration and consider needs for professional development and training.

Finally, the importance of ongoing, varied professional development and training that meets the specific areas of need identified by your staff cannot be emphasized enough. It is a critical step in reaching true integration among staff. How often do school administrators hear, "Well, we have been asking for PD about this," from staff? Too often. This means school leaders must find mechanisms to gather this information, whether formally or informally, from school staff. As the individuals charged with delivering the information to students, school staff are uniquely positioned to articulate what training needs they have. Your job is to listen to and meet their needs (Forman, Olin, Hoagwood, Crowe, & Saka, 2008).

Supporting Staff's Wellness Needs

Naturally, as leaders are exploring and reflecting on staffs' social and emotional strengths and challenges, they will certainly begin hearing from staff that are struggling socially, emotionally, or mentally. This is to be expected, and leaders should be prepared to remind their teams that struggle is an essential element of growth. There are parallel processes that take place when supporting teacher and staff social and emotional needs. When adults feel better and know how to identify and navigate their social and emotional needs, these adults will be better equipped to support SEAD on a school campus (Woolf, 2020).

Schools must support staff burnout, address their high stress, and teach them how to navigate their own Social and Emotional needs. Over 40% of teachers report feeling high stress every day during the school year, which ties teaching with nursing as having the highest stress rate of any career (Yang, Ge, Hu, Chi, & Wang, 2009). Recent studies have found that teacher stress levels are at an all-time high (Gallup, 2014). Leaders cannot expect the adults to teach SEL without practicing it for themselves. Schools ask more and more from teachers and stretch their capacities as professionals, and this is one positive skill that can be taught to educators to support their wellness.

An additional way that school leaders can promote wellness among their educators is by creating opportunities to allow staff to connect. Through integrating SEL skills that incorporate talking with one another, small groups, opening activities, gratitude, and optimistic closure, leaders are building in moments for connection and comradery. Activities that explore personality types, strengths, and communication or learning styles can build empathy and foster positive connections. These moments can even support staff in developing a stronger understanding of teammates that can influence positive school culture (CASEL Essentials, 2020).

School leaders must also find ways to promote and integrate school-wide self-care practices for their educators and staff. This goes beyond the traditional annual mention of self-care and discussion of self-care activities. It goes beyond the round-robin share out of your favorite self-care activity in a staff meeting. Interesting ways schools have incorporated self-care include assigning self-care partners that regularly check in on one another throughout a designated time period, integrating mindfulness practices into staff meetings, and shortening all-staff meeting times to respect the need for educators to plan and grade. Self-care is extremely individual, and leaders should consider their staff as they determine what strategies might be most effective in promoting this wellness on their campus.

Finally, there are some staff wellness needs that exceed the support available from SEL coaches or school leaders. In these instances, it is important for school leaders to be aware of the mental health resources available to their staff, such as Employee Assistance Programs (EAP) and local mental health clinics. Understanding the different healthcare insurance options available to staff and the associated mental health providers who accept that coverage can also be beneficial. It can be difficult to encourage staff to pursue this type of support, however oftentimes staff will come to their leaders to ask for advice or options. These moments can present opportunities to have conversations about the various types of services available. It is also important to consider the relationship between you and the individual in need when making decisions about the best ways to support and suggestions to make. Ultimately, helping each individual connect with the right level of support is a critical step in maintaining staff wellness.

CONCLUSION

The process of preparing a school staff to implement a Social Emotional Learning program is complex and has many considerations for educators and leaders that are highlighted in this chapter. At the very least, readers should leave with considerations and questions to guide their social emotional learning planning and implementation. Because SEL material can feel new, emotionally driven, and extremely different than an educator's typical content area, it is essential to invest time and energy into your staff's learning and preparation. Each and every adult is a key participant and stakeholder in successful social, emotional, and academic development on your campus. Programs that appropriately prepare and collaborate with their full staff reflect more fidelity to the model. Their implementation also has a longevity unseen in programs where educators report feeling less equipped and less included in the process. Most importantly, the skills learned in social emotional programs benefit everyone on a school campus, including staff and educators.

REFERENCES

Berman, S., Chaffee, S., & Sarmiento, J. (2018). *The Practice Base for How we Lear: Supporting Students' Social, Emotional, and Academic Development.* https://www.aspeninstitute.org/wp-content/uploads/2018/03/CDE-Practice-Base_FINAL.pdf

CASEL. (2021). *Adult SEL Self-Assessment.* Retrieved January 8, 2021, from https://schoolguide.casel.org/resource/adult-sel-self-assessment/

CASEL. (2020, March). *The CASEL Guide to Schoolwide SEL Essentials.* Retrieved January 8, 2021, from https://schoolguide.casel.org/uploads/sites/2/2019/09/School-Guide-Essentials-5.2020.pdf

Center on Great Teachers & Leaders. (2020, April). *Educator Resilience and Trauma-Informed Self-Care Self-Assessment and Planning Tool.* Retrieved from https://gtlcenter.org/sites/default/files/Educator-Resilience-Trauma-Informed-Self-Care-Self-Assessment.pdf

Domitrovich, C., Bradshaw, C., Poduska, J., Hoagwood, K., Buckley, J., Olin, S., Romanelli, L. H., Leaf, P. J., Greenberg, M. T., & Ialongo, N. (2008). Maximizing the Implementation Quality of Evidence-Based Preventive Interventions in Schools: A Conceptual Framework. *Advances in School Mental Health Promotion, 1*(3), 6–28. doi:10.1080/1754730X.2008.9715730 PMID:27182282

Forman, S. G., Olin, S. S., Hoagwood, K. E., Crowe, M., & Saka, N. (2008). Evidence-Based Interventions in Schools: Developers' Views of Implementation Barriers and Facilitators. *School Mental Health, 1*(1), 26–36. doi:10.100712310-008-9002-5

Gallup. (2014). *State of American Schools.* Retrieved from https://www.gallup.com/education/269648/state-america-schools-report.aspx

Kerr, D. B., Madden-Dent, T., & Shalabi, N. (2020). Cultural Competency Interventions: Three Case Studies with Guiding Theoretical Frameworks. In Cultural Competencies for Continuous Learning (2nd ed.). Oxford University Press. doi:10.1093/oxfordhb/9780197506707.013.26

Madden-Dent, T., Jackson, I., & Cason, J. (2021). Culturally-responsive social emotional academic development. In *Leading Schools with Social Emotional Academic Development (SEAD).* IGI Global Publication. Retrieved at https://www.igi-global.com/book/leading-schools-social-emotional-academic/256645

RULER. (n.d.). Retrieved January 4, 2021, from https://www.rulerapproach.org/about/what-is-ruler/

Schonert-Reichl, K., Kitil, M. J., & Hanson-Peterson, J. (2017). To reach the students, teach the teachers: A national scan of teacher preparation and social and emotional learning. A report prepared for the Collaborative for Academic, Social, and Emotional Learning (CASEL). University of British Columbia.

SEL. What Are the Core Competence Areas and Where are they Promoted? (n.d.). Retrieved January 11, 2021, from https://casel.org/sel-framework/

The Glossary of Education Reform. (2016, February 18). Retrieved from https://www.edglossary.org/student-engagement/

Woolf, N. (2020). *A Comprehensive Guide to Adult SEL.* Panorama Education. Retrieved from https://www.panoramaed.com/blog/comprehensive-guide-adult-sel

Yang, X., Ge, C., Hu, B., Chi, T., & Wang, L. (2009). Relationship between quality of life and occupational stress among teachers. *Public Health*, *123*(11), 750–755. doi:10.1016/j.puhe.2009.09.018 PMID:19883926

KEY TERMS AND DEFINITIONS

Engagement: It refers to either a student or adult's attention, interest, and passion when presented with subject matter. In this particular case, engagement relates to how educators on a school campus dedicate attention, interest, and passion to social emotional learning and key strategies to build that engagement for school leaders.

Fidelity: The degree of faithfulness and consistency with which a social emotional curriculum is followed is known as fidelity. Each model has its own standards, rubrics, and curriculum that support educators in implementing the curriculum with enough consistency to reliably measure whether or not the program is meeting its goals for outcomes.

Implementation: The process of executing a specific program or plan is known as implementation.

Social, Emotional, and Academic Development: This specifically refers to the integration of social development, emotional development, and academic development. Proponents of SEAD tend to focus on integration of these elements of development into core classes on a school campus, rather than isolating "Social Emotional Learning" as a separate entity.

Social Emotional Learning: The process through which individuals at all phases of development learn skills in healthy relationships, awareness of self, emotional regulation, care for others, and responsibility.

Chapter 4
Higher Education Leading With Social, Emotional, and Academic Development:
University Case Study on Explicit SEAD Coursework

Tara Madden-Dent
Sierra Nevada University, USA

Deborah Oliver
National University & Mindful SEAD, USA

Brooke Stratton
Sierra Nevada University, USA

Eleanor A. Strand
Sierra Nevada University, USA

Kimberly Reed
Sierra Nevada University, USA

ABSTRACT

Institutions of higher learning serve as global catalysts for equitable educational systems as drivers of educator workforce that lead with social, emotional, and academic development (SEAD) practices. Colleges and universities are well-positioned to instruct on explicit social emotional learning (SEL) not only within pre-service programs of study, but have the unique opportunity to provide continuous education for in-service educators. This large-scale capacity to influence those who shape student experiences is more important today than ever before as schools seek safer, more inclusive campuses and digital learning environments with culturally responsive and respectful communication and interactions. The need for SEL skills across workforce sectors conflicts with the lack of SEL education in higher educational programs. To contribute to the body of literature around post-secondary SEL education, this chapter introduces new graduate-level SEAD courses and how they influenced pre-service and in-service teacher candidates.

DOI: 10.4018/978-1-7998-6728-9.ch004

BACKGROUND

Social, Emotional, and Academic Development (SEAD) is the integration of social-emotional learning (SEL) and academics that reinforces equitable and human-centered educational environments (Aspen Institute, 2018). The positive contributions of social-emotional interventions and practices has been well established through decades of basic and applied research demonstrating that SEAD contributes to more equitable and safe educational environments (Cantor et al., 2018; Jones & Kahn, 2017; Osher et al., 2018; Durlak et al., 2011; Madden-Dent, 2014; Madden-Dent, 2021a; Taylor et al., 2017), and reinforces cultural competence and college/workforce readiness (Kerr, Madden-Dent, & Shalabi, 2020; Madden-Dent, 2021b). Social-emotional education is linked with decreases in unhealthy behaviors, mental health issues, and drop-out rates (Kautz, Heckman, Diris, Bas ter Weel, & Borghans, 2014), increases of up to 14%-point gains in grades and test scores (Durlak, Weissberg, Dymnicki, Taylor, & Schellinger, 2011), improved attitudes, emotional intelligence, and academic engagement (Li & Xu, 2019), and can save educational institutions a range of $11 - $104.90 for each dollar invested when applied within a multi-tiered system of supports framework (Belfield, Bowden, Klapp, Levin, Shand, & Zander, 2015; Swain-Bradway, Lindstrom Johnson, Bradshaw, & McIntosh, 2017).

The implementation of SEAD practices aims to increase social-emotional learning (SEL), a lifelong process through which all people learn and apply culturally responsive, "knowledge, skills, and attitudes to develop healthy identities, manage emotions and achieve personal and collective goals, feel and show empathy for others, establish and maintain supportive relationships, and make responsible and caring decisions" (CASEL, 2020). According to the Collaborative for Academic, Social, and Emotional Learning (CASEL), SEL includes five competencies (SEC) which are as predictive of academic and career achievement as is IQ (Almlund, Duckworth, Heckman., & Kautz. 2011; Duckworth & Seligman, 2005). The SECs described below, include Self-Awareness, Self-Management, Social Awareness, Relationship Skills, and Responsible Decision-Making skills.

According to CASEL (2020), the competencies are implemented within a framework that takes, "a systemic approach that emphasizes the importance of establishing equitable learning environments and coordinating practices across key settings to enhance all students' social, emotional, and academic learning. We believe it is most beneficial to integrate SEL throughout the school's academic curricula and culture, across the broader contexts of schoolwide practices and policies, and through ongoing collaboration with families and community organizations. These coordinated efforts should foster youth voice, agency, and engagement; establish supportive classroom and school climates and approaches to discipline; enhance adult SEL competence; and establish authentic family and community partnerships" (p.3). It goes on to state, "To integrate SEL efforts across the school day and out-of-school time, school staff and community partners should align on common language and coordinate strategies and communication around SEL-related efforts and initiatives." (p.4).

One contributing out-of-school time sector that drives the need for SEAD in education is our global economy. The CASEL Five SECs have been of increasing need from employers for from across industry spectrums over the past decades and will continue to be in-demand skills (Cunningham & Villasenor, 2016; Deming, 2015; Fitzgerald & Sigelman, 2018; Hart Research Associates, 2015; HR Vision, 2019; Job Outlook, 2016; Maldonado, 2019; National Association of Colleges & Employers, 2019; Yoder, Atwell, Godek, Dusenbury, Bridgeland, & Weissberg, 2020).

Figure 1.

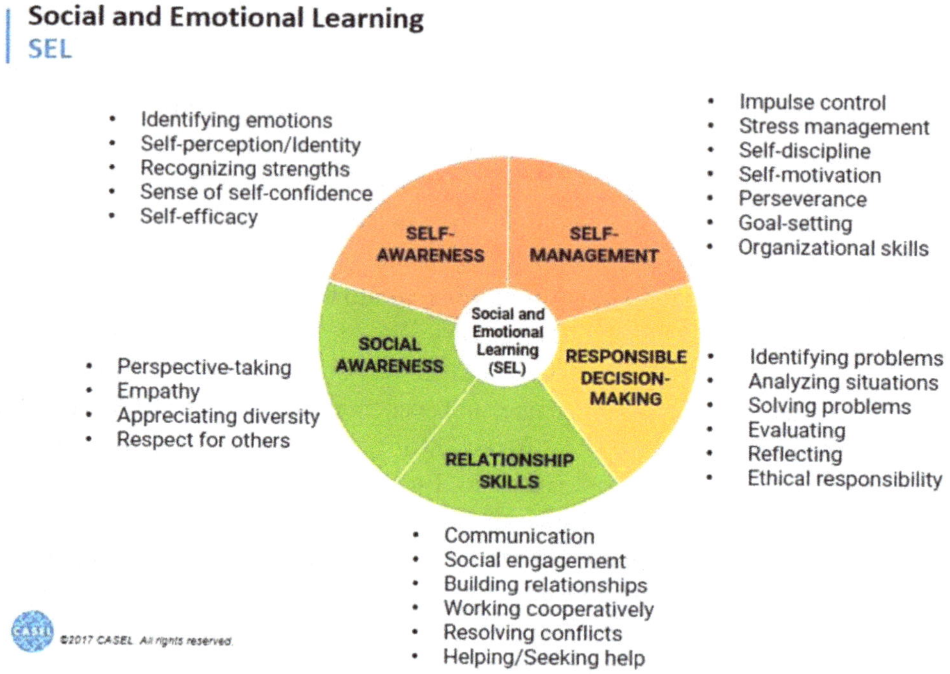

According to the National Association of Colleges and Employers (2019), there are eight competencies associated with career readiness which all require SECs: Critical Thinking/Problem Solving; Oral/Written Communication; Teamwork/Collaboration; Digital Technology; Leadership; Professionalism/Work Ethic; Career Management; and Global/Intercultural Fluency. In addition to those workforce readiness skills, HR Vision (2020) added that employees must be able to manage oneself and demonstrate psychological flexibility; again, behaviors made possible through social-emotional skills. In alignment, Cunningham & Villasenor (2016) reported,

While employers value all skill sets, there is a greater demand for socio-emotional skills and higher-order cognitive skills than for basic cognitive or technical skills. These results are robust across region, industry, occupation, and education level. Employers perceive that the greatest skills gaps are in socio-emotional and higher-order cognitive skills (p. 1).

To help meet the global workforce development need, schools can serve as workforce pipelines, fostering essential SECs in students and active professionals (Madden-Dent, Jackson, Cason, 2021). According to a national scan of teacher preparation and social and emotional Learning by CASEL (2017), one challenge is that limited SEL coursework in higher education is not reflective of what educators need to know, model, and instruct in the academic workforce. After a statewide and campus-wide scan for SEL courses, Sierra Nevada University recognized the need for more explicit SEL instruction to prepare Nevada's educators for workplace expectations and to establish the first higher education option for teachers to complete SEL classes and satisfy a State SEAD endorsement for licensure.

Figure 2.

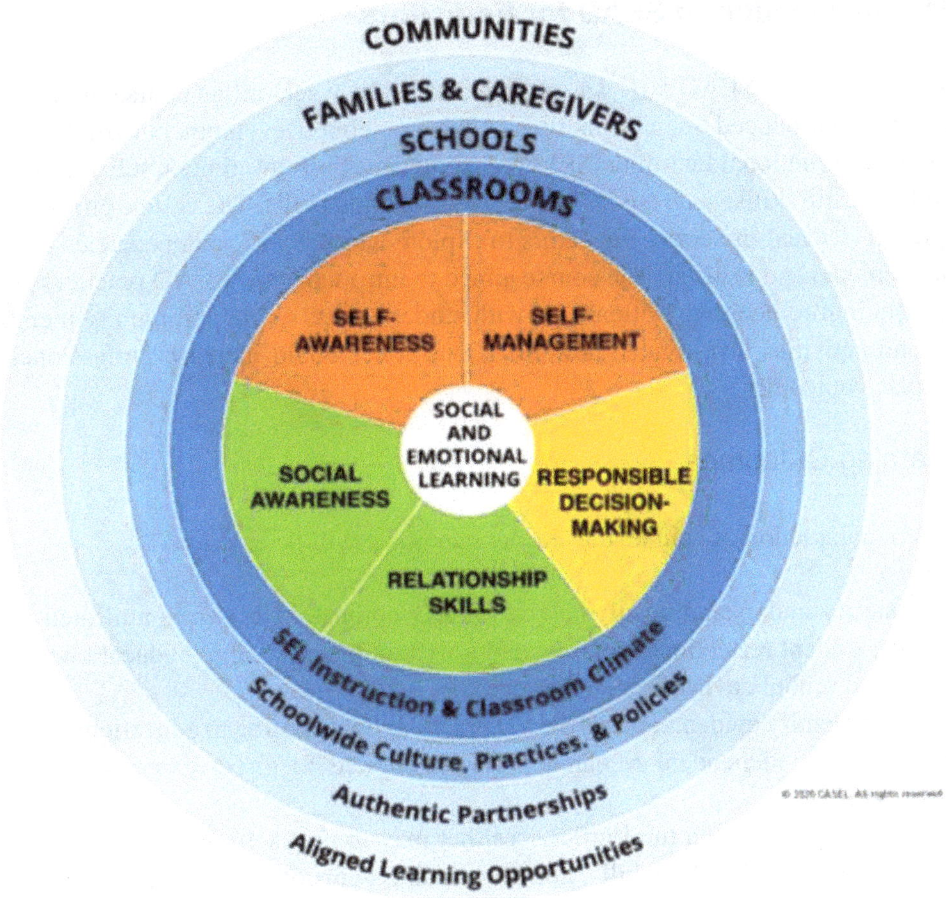

The purpose of this chapter is to introduce a case study demonstrating one university's approach to design and offer a series of explicit SEAD graduate classes to support pre-service and in-service educators. This chapter describes four new online graduate-level courses offered during the 2019/2020 academic year offered at Sierra Nevada University (SNU), a private, accredited, undergraduate and graduate level liberal arts institution located in Incline Village, Nevada. Educators who complete all four courses become eligible for State SEAD Endorsement on their licensure from the Nevada Department of Education. The four courses include, SEAD 501: Intro to SEAD for Educators; SEAD 502: Practices that Support Nevada Policies, Equity, and Critical Issues; SEAD 503: Methods & Curriculum for Modeling, Teaching, & Implementing SEAD; SEAD 504: Assessment, Evaluation, Monitoring, & Improvement Planning. Course professors collected data sources (e.g., written reflections, student assignments, course evaluation surveys) from each class, to collectively analyze common themes that emerged from the data.

CASE STUDIES

SEAD 501: Introduction to SEAD for Educators

The graduate-level course, SEAD 501, was offered as a seven-week online course in the summer, 2020 semester. The class introduced Social, Emotional, and Academic Development (SEAD) and its accompanying five Social Emotional Learning (SEL) competencies: Self- awareness, self-management, social awareness, relationship skills, and responsible decision-making skills. The course provided a safe space for twenty pre-service and in-service educators to explore why the SEL competencies were significant for educators to model and instruct. The course aimed to introduce how SEAD practices could contribute towards meaningful, healthy relationships with students, peers, and community members. Course assignments and activities investigated how SEAD practices could increase professional impact and desired workplace outcomes.

Course Learning Outcomes

Upon successful completion of course, the teacher candidate will be able to:

1. Demonstrate an understanding of the five SEAD competencies, communicated through class discussions, student reflections, quizzes, and a written paper, to apply educational content in the context of real school environment experiences.
2. Examine and identify evidence-based SEAD practices contributing to educational success through case studies and independent research projects, applied to direct experiences in educational environments.
3. Assess and interpret intracultural influences that may impact self-awareness, self- management, social awareness, relationship skills, and responsible decision-making skills, by exploring self-identity, values, beliefs, and behaviors demonstrated through written reflection assignments and class discussions.
4. Demonstrate, by means of class discussions and written assignments, a knowledge of how to intentionally implement evidence-based SEAD practices throughout educational work settings.
5. Gain a strategic and practical action plan to embed SEAD competencies throughout professional practices that achieve teacher candidates' unique goals (academic, personal, and professional), while using most current SEAD resources for supporting their goals and the strategies to sustain newly imbedded SEAD activities into daily work.

Course Assignments

Ten assignments were completed during this course and covered the following topics: The history of SEAD and its significance in Nevada, SEAD Research and its Impacts in Education, Field Experience journals, and the five SEL competencies. Students committed to completing an array of interactive and independent activities including, written research reflections, group discussions, quizzes, journal entries, and a final paper "My Action Plan".

An example of one interactive activity were group discussions. The group discussion activities reinforced personal reflection and professional application of SEAD competencies. The discussions allowed for student feedback, engagement, and collaborative learning through rich dialogue that recognized and valued each other's different perspectives in a confidential, human-centered, and respectful learning environment.

An example of an independent activity included the capstone paper. This final paper, *My Action Plan*, specifically described how course content had been interpreted and applied in their personal and professional environments. Each student set SMART goals that were measurable and achievable, that addressed specific challenges in their workplace, and reinforced their professional impact. The *My Action Plan* paper was designed to reinforce clear, consistent action steps to implement SEAD practices as a method of fostering healthy relationships and more effective communication skills at the school or district setting. Students in this course were asked to describe specific resources or practices that supported each of their action plan steps.

Student Artifacts

The majority of students found the work in this course very valuable. They saw an immediate improvement in their personal lives and knew it would translate to increased positive outcomes in their classrooms. The following student excerpts were retrieved from capstone papers, *My Action Plan*, to exemplify personal applications of explicit SEL instruction from SEAD 501.

Self-care is an area of my life that I have felt the great need to improve to better my health and wellness, both mentally and physically. In taking this course, I had to intentionally practice different competencies, which helped me understand the great need I have for these competencies in my life. Moving forward, I have decided I need to reinforce the competencies of self-awareness, self-management, and relationship skills. These competencies are areas that I feel would be most beneficial in improving my personal life and, in turn, improve my professional life.- L.

During the course of a six-week time frame I have learned exactly what SEAD stands for, along with its principles and application skills. I have tested myself and challenged myself to be as honest as I can be and to really dive deep for a clear understanding of the entire SEAD framework. Research has been conducted to illustrate best practices and skills that will prove valuable during an implementation of SEAD competencies. SEAD allows for mutual respect to all parties involved, which is something that classrooms will always need. I have opened my mind and body to the intentional practice of SEAD and all of its competencies. - J.

I have thoroughly enjoyed this class and have learned an enormous amount of information and strategies that I plan to put to work in my classroom. Research shows that taking the time from teaching academics and focusing on social and emotional learning has a direct, positive, impact on student attendance and achievement. If our goal as educators is to help students succeed, then it seems fairly obvious that we must take the time to incorporate SEL into our classrooms on a daily basis. In fact, it seems like the easiest way to increase student attendance and achievement, so why are so few schools and teachers willing to trade in some academic learning time for SEL? The time is now! I must make the choice to do what is best for my students and that means making SEL a priority in my classroom every day! – J.G.

SEAD competencies are crucial to control emotions and behaviors. Teachers and school authorities should emphasize the importance of these competencies. Students should be taught to develop SEAD competencies. Thus, they will grow socially and academically. It will reduce the rate of dropout from school. In our global society, it is important to honor diversity. For this reason, all individuals should learn the importance to apply SEAD competencies in their daily life. - V.

Professor Reflections

Overall, SEAD 501, Introduction to SEAD, was very effective to introduce and explore SEAD in education and the role educators play in modeling and instructing SEL competencies. The majority of the feedback was positive and students expressed their excitement about practicing SEL skills in their personal lives and in their classrooms. Ideally, we want students to take their learning from theory to application and this course design encouraged that process. Through each online module lesson, students had the opportunity to reflect and apply the learning objective to their personal and professional lives as demonstrated by one student who stated,

Professionally, I know my impact will be enhanced when I achieve success with all of the goals I have outlined. Improvement in Self-Awareness, Self-Management, Relationship and Social Skills will better all aspects of my life. I am excited to begin this journey more consciously with goals in writing. I am literally going to begin my meditative practice right now! I am happy to have had a chance to think about these things and reflect more fully upon each one. – T.

The series of the University's four new online SEAD courses were created to facilitate students' (pre-service and in-service educators) growth around SEL skills. First, with my course, SEAD 501, they learn what SEL is and then evidence-based SEL strategies to transfer within their professional practice; hence, supporting greater student success. Each of the University's courses build upon the previous course to facilitate a pathway of deeper learning and more intentional practice of embedding SEL skills into academic work behaviors.

SEAD 502: SEAD Practices Supporting Nevada Policies, Equity, and Critical Issues

This course was first offered as an eight-week spring, 2020 semester course via an online asynchronous format. This course introduced educators to current state policies and future state needs related to Social, Emotional, Academic Development (SEAD) and it's five Social-Emotional Learning (SEL) competencies (self- awareness, self-management, social awareness, relationship skills, and responsible decision-making skills). Class participants examined the relationship between Nevada-centered hot topics (e.g., Chronic Absenteeism; Restorative Practices; Equity) and SEAD practices to support youth, adults, educators, and community members. Course assignments investigated how SEAD programming positively supports school, district, and state priorities (e.g., Graduation rates; School safety; Campus climate).

Course Learning Outcomes

Upon successful completion of course, the teacher candidate will be able to:

1. Demonstrate an understanding of the five SEAD competencies and their meaningful impact within educator candidates' work in real school environments.
2. Examine and identify evidence-based SEAD practices contributing to educational success that meet identified local and state needs, policies, equity, and critical issues, through case studies and independent research projects, applied to direct experiences in educational environments.
3. Assess and interpret how intracultural influences may impact work experiences with various student, colleague, and community groups by exploring SEAD applications that address identity, values, beliefs, communication, and behaviors.
4. Demonstrate, by means of class discussions and written assignments, a knowledge of how to intentionally implement meaningful evidence-based SEAD practices throughout educational work settings to foster collaboration, supportive interaction, and positive social engagement that reinforce state policies, equity, and critical issues.
5. Gain a strategic and practical action plan to embed SEAD competencies and practices throughout educational system and workplace norms that achieve educator candidates' unique goals (academic, personal, and professional), while using most current SEAD resources for supporting their goals and the strategies to sustain newly imbedded SEAD activities into daily work.

This SEAD 502 course enrolled twenty graduate who began their studies during the time when the COVID-19 pandemic had forced school closures in Nevada and California (states that this course's students were living/working). The course's students (pre-service and in-service educators) were experiencing several simultaneous stressors due to the changing environments and associated stressors (e.g., managing distance teaching/learning; new family dynamics; job loss/lay off; etc.). The students shared that their situations presented a greater need/appreciation for meaningful social emotional learning. Specifically, the in-service teachers enrolled in this course were practice to manage their own stress while trying to support students during a world crisis.

Student Assignments

Course assignments were completed as independent and collaborative activities through the University's online management platform and ZOOM. As an online course, the learning activities included, virtual Socratic collaborative dialogues, case studies, independent study, small group work, reflective work, reading and writing assignments, video conferencing, and ongoing constructive feedback from peers and instructors.

An example of one independent assignment activity is the Field Experience. This weekly assignment was to implement an action step or activity at their school which focused on a topic discussed in class. Some students conducted interviews/discussions with a colleague (e.g., School Principal) to discuss adding new SEAD assessments at their school or educational setting. The students took note of the barriers, benefits, and needs around implementing SEAD assessment and then reflect on root causes of the school/district limits and barriers. Afterwards, students shared their notes in small group discussions in class and the professor provided feedback. According to students' group discussions, these field experiences and reflections were moments of critical student growth. They shared that when they were challenged every week to implement what they were learning about SEAD into their work and personal life, they were shared meaningful reflections and practical realizations.

Another example of an independent assignment activity is the capstone paper, *My Action Plan*. The final paper required each student to create a personalized action plan which defined intentional progress towards specific SEAD goals framed around the course topic. The personalized action plan was a culmination of field experiences and lessons learned from the field experiences. They were assigned to create intentional and mindful action steps to ensure sustainability of incorporating SEAD into their personal and professional life.

Specifically, students were asked to address three purposeful writing categories: how they would reinforce SEAD practices that improve quality of life (health/safety/wellness); Strengthen communication and interaction skills (e.g., relationships); and increase professional impact. The paper had students set a minimum of three achievable goals for each of the three purpose categories (nine goals total). The paper was to describe specific strategies that students would carry-out and the evidence-based resources that would support goal achievement.

Examples of guiding questions for paper development included, "Out of the class lesson topics, which ones do I want to practice or incorporate more on a regular basis and why?", "What are some ways that I can support SEAD development in my colleagues or students?", "In what ways can I more consistently model SEAD skills that both benefit me, while creating learning opportunities for students and/or peers to observe SEAD practices?". This assignment connected course content with actional steps for direct SEAD application in the workforce.

Student Artifacts

Insights and ideas emerged on a weekly basis with students implementing their field experiences and sharing reflections in group discussions. The timing of the Spring, 2020 course brought incredible perspective for teachers reflecting on the topics of chronic absenteeism, restorative practices, and school climate. Due to COVID-19, as schools closed and teachers' interactions with students and families were forced to be virtual, the concern for social-emotional wellbeing was apparent. One teacher was able to summarize this within a field experience post,

I thought it was useful to analyze my school, district, and personal use of SEL during this crisis. There have been so many demands on teachers now that we've moved to distance learning, it was good to step back for a moment and see how different efforts might be working/not-working in this moment. The second take-away I had was, I was exhausted just analyzing all the efforts we've made to engage students. I don't know how sustainable this is over the long-term.

The course topics and assignments had resonated with many students who were active teachers especially during field experiences with their school leaders and colleagues. The action of talking with work peers and then bringing the information back to class for discussion generated a lot of positive and constructive SEAD application ideas. For example, one teacher was moved to discuss chronic absenteeism at his school and used the field experience task and constructive ideas and suggestions from classmates to further conversations with his administration. His post was insightful and a good example of the type of application seen throughout the course,

I see this issue affecting my classroom and students everyday which is why I deeply connected with this topic. Even before I knew that we had a field experience coming up, I had already started talking to one of my school administrators about the absenteeism issue. I set up a video conference with an assistant principal...to discuss chronic absenteeism and how we are addressing it.

Professor Reflections

Teaching the SEAD course was a great opportunity to learn from educator about their deep real-time concerns, motivations, and future SEL plans. Course evaluation responses aligned with the amount of work, enthusiasm, and level of participation observed from students throughout the course which reflected student discussion topics in online discussions. Based on survey responses, 100% of the students agreed that the course helped them fulfill their purpose at the college, 90% of the respondents found that the course was exciting and were interested in the subject, and 90% either strongly agreed or agreed that the course had helped them think independently about SEAD in their roles as educators.

Open-ended comments shared statements including, "The curriculum was great and I enjoyed this course.". Another student wrote, "Really enjoyed the content and course. Not just busy work either, felt meaningful to me." There were several comments related COVID-19s impact on the course experience. One participant shared, "I did enjoy talking to my peers, but it would have been much more difficult to do this if we were not teaching from home. The field experiences were also difficult to do remotely."

SEAD 503: Methods & Curriculum for Modeling, Teaching, and Implementing SEAD

Over seven weeks in the 2020 semester, thirteen students from school districts across Nevada, participated and successfully completed this online graduate level course. The purpose of SEAD 503 was to introduce pre-service and in-service educators to practical, evidence-based SEAD strategies to teach and continuously improve instruction that embedded Social Emotional Learning (SEL) competencies (self- awareness, self-management, social awareness, relationship skills, and responsible decision- making skills). The students investigated various SEL curriculum and programs and then considered the application of those within a multi-tiered system of support framework to reinforce Pre-K - grade 12 instruction and support services, campus safety, and school-community relationships. Course assignments, including a personalized action plan paper, were designed to translate course content into daily activities leveraging SEAD practices to increase professional impact and achieve more positive workplace outcomes (e.g., modeling, teaching, and instructing SEL skills).

Course Learning Outcomes

Upon successful completion of course, the teacher candidate will be able to:

1. Demonstrate an understanding of SEAD, the associated five SEL competencies, and their meaningful impact within educator candidates' work in real school environments, communicated through class discussions, student reflections, quizzes, and a written paper.

2. Examine and identify evidence-based SEAD practices contributing to educational success that meet identified local and state needs, through case studies and independent research projects, applied to direct experiences in educational environments.
3. Assess and interpret how intracultural influences may impact work experiences with various student, colleague, and community groups by exploring SEAD applications that address identity, values, beliefs, communication, and behaviors demonstrated through written reflection assignments and class discussions.
4. Demonstrate, by means of class discussions and written assignments, a knowledge of how to intentionally implement meaningful evidence-based SEAD practices throughout educational work settings to foster collaboration, supportive interaction, and positive social engagement.
5. Gain a strategic and practical action plan to embed SEAD competencies throughout professional practices that achieve educator candidates' unique goals (academic, personal, and professional), while using most current SEAD resources for supporting their goals and the strategies to sustain newly imbedded SEAD activities into daily work.

Student Assignments

Students were asked to complete ten homework assignments that investigated research-based SEL monitoring instruments and practices. Each homework assignment had a corresponding quiz and was supported by collaborative group discussions guided by reflective prompts. After studying a particular assessment or evaluation and its applicability within their educational context, students were asked to further explore the possibility of embedding it into their classroom or school-site. To assist with this process, students were asked to interview local and state SEL leaders on the instrument of interest, test the assess if possible on themselves or pilot it through an online demo, and meet with school-site colleagues to discuss the logistics, benefits, and potential barriers of implementing SEAD assessment at their school site.

Another course activity which built upon the ten assignments was a capstone paper titled, *My Action Plan*. In this APA formatted paper, students deconstructed class content and discussions with a design-thinking approach for individualize measurable steps for embedding SEAD practices into daily work roles. These plans addressed their strengths and opportunities for growth to leverage SEAD practices that support students, their families, the campus and external community stakeholders. Each paper was relevant to the unique educational role and school site of the student in the course.

Student Artifacts

When observing difference between students' earlier homework assignment submissions and their reflective capstone papers, there was increases in awareness and ability to articulate SEAD and SEL, as well as the understanding of various applications to utilize for SEL instruction and support. This was demonstrated in the following students' written submissions.

Homework Assignment #2: What are three main take-aways that you gained from the article, *The Future of Children*? Student's Response: "…My third take-away came from the section that discussed strategies that impact the success of SEL interventions. The strategies were professional development for teachers (including support for teacher SEL development), embedded practice in the classroom, and family engagement."

In this assignment, the student was new to how SEAD could be intentionally incorporated into classroom and school-site practices. The student was beginning to realize both the importance of SEAD as well understand how SEAD could holistically address the whole child. Professional and personal growth can be seen in SEAD awareness when the homework except above is compared to the student's final paper, *My Action Plan*. In the following student submission, detailed and intentional steps are outlined for incorporating new SEAD practices.

I would also like to learn more about the Choose Love Enrichment Program (2020) and the Good Behavior Game (2018). Choose Love is a free program that is strictly online resources (2020), which will be perfect to try out in the fall. I am guessing that we will use Google Classroom for our virtual learning, and I liked that this program works with that platform. I was just introduced to the Good Behavior Game in a behavior training at the end of the school year and had never heard of it before. I had tried something similar in my classroom using our PBIS (2019) expectations this year, so I was excited to come across the curriculum again. I spoke with my school counselor and she has the program, so I am going to ask her if I can look it over now that my curiosity is piqued. I would like to incorporate some fun ways for students to practice the [SEL] skills we are learning.

Not only does this student demonstrate a greater awareness to specific SEL instruments, but demonstrates an ability to connect them with Positive Behavioral Interventions & Systems (PBIS) and her school counselor. This student can articulate what programs are considered most relevant to specific goals and school-site needs.

Professor Reflections

Students expressed having meaningful learning experiences in SEAD 503 and noted that it took a commitment to be vulnerable, sensitive, and honest during personal SEL exploration. Students and professor must remember to exchange in respectful and considerate dialog that recognizes and values each person's lived experiences and SEL journey. Course topics such as chronic absenteeism, ineffective teaching methods, trauma-informed classrooms, and reflective teaching processes were particular class discussions that students acknowledged stronger emotional connection with. Students acknowledged that the personal discomfort discussing sensitive topics was well worth it since by strengthening their SEL skills, they would become more effective educators to support student success.

SEAD 504: Assessment, Evaluation, Monitor, and Improvement Planning

Over seven weeks, twelve students completed the fully online course SEAD 504: Assessments, Evaluation, Monitoring, & Improvement Planning. Students from all over Nevada school districts set out to formally study practical SEAD assessments that measured self-awareness, self-management, social awareness, relationship skills, and responsible decision-making skills in youth and adults. This course identified methods to monitor SEAD competency development and help improve future SEAD programming across educational levels. Course participants gained practical skills to evaluate SEAD growth and its relationship to whole-student success. Finally, assessment-focused action planning helped ensure that class participants were making intentional progress towards achieving their professional goals and SEAD related outcomes.

Course Learning Outcomes

Upon successful completion of course, the teacher candidate will be able to:

1. Demonstrate an understanding of the five SEL competencies and their meaningful impact within educator candidates' work in real school environments, communicated through class discussions, student reflections, quizzes, and a written paper.
2. Examine and identify evidence-based SEAD assessment, evaluation, and monitoring practices contributing to educational success that meet identified local and state needs, through case studies and independent research projects, applied to direct experiences in educational environments.
3. Assess and interpret how intracultural influences may impact work experiences with various student, colleague, and community groups by exploring SEAD applications that address identity, values, beliefs, communication, and behaviors demonstrated through written reflection assignments and class discussions.
4. Demonstrate, by means of class discussions and written assignments, a knowledge of how to intentionally implement meaningful evidence-based SEAD assessment and monitoring practices throughout educational work settings to foster collaboration, supportive interaction, and positive social engagement.
5. Gain a strategic and practical action plan to embed SEAD competencies and evaluation methods throughout professional practices that achieve educator candidates' unique goals (academic, personal, and professional), while using most current SEAD resources for supporting their goals and the strategies to sustain newly imbedded SEAD activities into daily work.

Student Assignments

Students were asked to complete ten collaborative and independent homework assignments, five quizzes, five group discussions, and one capstone project. Students had an option for the capstone project. The first was an APA formatted paper on their own journey with SEL assessment, monitoring, evaluation, and improvement practices and the importance of culturally responsiveness when developing SEAD assessment rubrics. The second option was a research activity that developed a culturally responsive SEAD rubric for youth and adults to share with their respective schools.

Throughout the ten homework assignments, students researched and reflected on current SEAD assessments, monitoring strategies, and discussed the political, cultural, and environmental aspects of existing assessments. Students were asked to reflect on systemic inequalities and practice a critical consciousness during their studies and group discussions. Assignments asked students to explore the current SEAD assessments at their own school sites and how they served all student populations. Short competency quizzes were paired with homework assignments as quick checks for understanding, and reflective discussions with small groups helped students reflect, grasp, and consider the SEAD assessment process in the classroom and professional environments. Some assignments asked students to apply class content within their professional roles via field experiences.

Student Artifacts

When observing differences in students' earlier homework assignment submissions and their reflective capstone papers, there was increases in awareness to SEAD assessments and the ability to articulate evidence-based interventions. This was demonstrated in the following students' two submissions. The first submission was a written reflection responding to a prompted question within an early homework assignment. The homework prompt asked, "What are three main take-aways that you gained from the article: *Social and Emotional Learning Assessment Guidance/Washoe County School District?"* The student responded,

I noticed for the first time that the graphic CASEL uses to define SEL or SEAD has the three outer rings surrounding the five categories. These three rings represent classrooms where SEL is taught, schools that are unified in their "school wide practices and policies" that are SEL centered, and homes and communities because "these competencies are not learned through a single program or teaching approach. Rather SEL involves coordinating strategies across the entire educational environment… [which includes] the playground, school bus, at home and in the community" (p. 1-2). As was mentioned in Group 1's online Discussion, SEL is still in its infancy and common language is needed so that everyone understands the vocabulary in the same way. Washoe is attempting to do that when they adopted CASEL's SEL framework. I like that Washoe County has not only listed characteristics that fall within each competency, but they have also identified indicators of those characteristics. Thus, we have a goal and we have a way of monitoring the achievement of those goals.

As outlined above, the student was beginning to gain an understanding of how SEAD assessment and SEL competencies are discussed currently in local and state education. This student was observed connecting their homework assignments to their reflective group discussion, as well as connecting SEAD assessment application to regional school districts. The goals of the first homework assignments are always to lay a knowledge foundation down with which students are then asked to apply to their professional and personal SEAD journeys. In comparison to the students' early reflective submission, growth was identified in this student's capstone paper, *My Action Plan*. The student submitted the following reflective analysis on three sub-categories (Educators, Students, & Survey Analysis),

Educators. *There are many purposes for [SEAD] assessment. Surveys open the conversation between administration the teachers/staff, create opportunities for self-reflection, begin to educate the person taking the survey as they read the questions and begin to understand the scope of how SEAD can be incorporated throughout the school, and identify areas where training needs to be done. As demonstrated above in my personal reflection, my colleagues will gain a better understanding of how to embed SEL in the classroom by taking surveys. Those surveys will not only create opportunities for self-reflection but will start the conversation in the school about why SEL is important and how we can address the social and emotional needs of our students. To start the teachers and staff on this SEAD journey, I would use the set of surveys in the Self-Assessing Social and Emotional Instruction and Competencies (Yoder, 2014) as well as the SEL Site Visit Walk-Through (Metropolitan Nashville Public Schools). I believe that these two sets of surveys will have much of the same impact on teachers and staff as they had on me as discussed above.*

Students. *One of my biggest frustrations as a teacher is the perceived lack of intrinsic motivation to do well in a class. It makes me wonder why my students come to school. Is it because they want to learn, because they want to see their friends, because of the safe environment and free food, or because they are forced to attend school? For this reason, I want to use the Academic Motivation Scale (AMS-HS 28) (Vallerand, et al.) assessment not only for my class, but school-wide.*

I think there are two ways you can use the data from this survey. First, you can use the students' primary motivations to encourage them to do their best, i.e. address what motivates them. Second, you could try to move them to a high level of motivation which would be intrinsic motivation. How that is accomplished, is another conversation. If we had an answer for how to move motivation from extrinsic to intrinsic our students would all be excelling in school.

Survey Analysis. *For the teachers and staff surveys, I would not analyze this data. Instead, I would use it as a jumping off point for self-reflection and to start conversations. I would ask the teachers for input into which areas they felt they needed more training and I would set up professional developments for these areas of interest. These surveys could be re-administered at the end of the year or in subsequent years to gauge improvement.*

The AMS-HS 28 survey uses a Likert Scale of 7 starting with "Does not correspond at all" to "Corresponds exactly." I would change this to a Likert Scale of 5 and I would add a question at the end for the students to tell me in their own words why they come to school because I thought this would give insight into their inner motivations. To analyze the data from this survey, one needs to recognize that the questions target different forms of motivation: Intrinsic motivation - to know, intrinsic motivation - toward accomplishment, intrinsic motivation - to experience stimulation, extrinsic motivation – identified, extrinsic motivation – introjected, external motivation – external regulation, amotivation. There are four questions for each of these 7 categories, therefore, one analyzing the data needs to look at the students' responses to the four questions in each category.

Like the student exemplified in the above submission comparison, all students in SEAD 504 demonstrated gains in complex and nuanced understanding of SEAD assessment, evaluation, monitoring and improvement. From there, synthesis of their own professional and personal lives in relation to SEAD occurred.

While teaching SEAD 504, the option of another final project was brought up by students via classroom discussion. As a result of this discussion, SEAD 504 also offered the following final option with the same rubric expectations:

Final Project Option: SEAD Assessment Reflection, Application, and Rubric Building

The purpose of SEAD Assessment Reflection, Application, and Rubric Building Project is to specifically and intentionally apply *what and how you will incorporate* more SEAD assessment practices in your personal and/or professional life to 1) Reinforce SEAD practices that improve personal and student quality of life (health/safety/wellness); 2) Strengthen communication and interaction skills (e.g. relationships); and 3) Increase professional impact (what you consider to be professional "successes"). In a Word Document or other Format of your choice (PowerPoint, Prezi, or other approved presentation format) please attend to the following three parts of the SEAD Assessment Application, Reflection, and Rubric Building. The three parts of this final project are as follows:

1. Reflect back on your work throughout this class while using the following SEC assessment rubric: WCSD Social and Emotional Competency Short Form 2018.pdf

While reflecting on your work for SEAD 503 and personal Social Emotional Competency development, please provide evidence of growth in each of the areas outlined on the WCSD Social and Emotional Competency Short-Form Assessment through personal reflection and evidence of your work in this class.

How have you grown to understand what your strengths and areas of growth are in relation to Social Emotional Competency and SEAD assessment? Think back to the countless SEAD self-assessments you have taken. How have you grown with them? How have you responded to the results?

Some questions to ask yourself are: "What were my steps of getting through something difficult" compared to: "what is my plan to get through something when it is difficult?" Please attend to all areas of the WCSD Social and Emotional Competency Short-Form Assessment, with specific attention to at least three of the numbered areas.

2. Apply your growth to your professional learning community: While sifting through the resources provided to you throughout this course, please choose a particular SEAD assessment for your school site students and staff that you believe to be an effective and authentic assessment choice. Please defend your choice with college level thinking and reasoning. Although we may not have total access to assessment materials, choose as assessment you believe fits the needs of your students and staff.
3. Build a culturally responsive SEAD rubric for your student assessment: Using this article as the framework of your assessment rubric building: Frameworks-Equity.pdf please build a student-focused rubric that provides success criteria of Social Emotional Competency reflective of your classes. Your success criteria columns should be based off of CASEL's Social Emotional Competency Wheel. Please reference the following link if you have questions: https://casel.org/core-competencies/

Your rubric should be designed so that students can understand how to exemplify social emotional competency within the classroom by providing concrete relevant behavioral examples. Happy learning!

One exemplar student artifact which demonstrated an acute understanding of SEL assessment included one student's capstone project. The student cross-walked a rubric with the Washoe County School District's SEL Competency Short-form Assessment.

Exemplar Capstone Project: SEL Competencies Rubric. Each rating area of this rubric is intended to align with the WCSD SEL competency short-form assessment.

CASEL Social and Emotional Competencies				
	4	**3**	**2**	**1**
Self-Awareness	Student can identify many personal strengths, identify how emotions affect their actions, can self-regulate, and can understand their cultural identity	Student can identify some strengths, make some connections between emotions and actions, sometimes self-regulate, and is beginning to recognize cultural identity	Student can identify one strength, struggles to make connections between emotions and actions, struggles to self-regulate and cannot recognize cultural identity	Student is unaware of strengths, cannot connect emotions and actions, cannot self-regulate, and is unaware of cultural identity
Social Awareness	Student can learn from others with differing opinions, understand what others are feeling and communicating, offer help when needed, and can identify cultural supports	Student sometimes learns from others with differing opinions, has some understanding of what others are feeling and communicating, is willing to offer help, and is aware of some cultural supports	Student is attempting to learn from others with differing opinions, is beginning to understand what others are feeling and communicating, sometimes offers help, and knows cultural supports exist	Student cannot learn from others with differing options, does not understand what others are feeling or communicating, does not offer help when needed, and does not know about cultural supports
Self-Management	Student can set goals and stay focused to achieve them, work through difficulties and challenges, and has the skills to manage stress	Student can set some goals and sometimes stay focused, can sometimes work through difficulties and challenges, and has some stress-management skills	Student struggles to set goals or stay focused, struggles to work through difficulties and challenges, and has only a few skills to manage stress	Student cannot set goals or focus on achieving them, cannot work through difficulties and challenges, and lacks stress-management skills
Relationship Skills	Student respects classmates' opinions in a disagreement, gets along well with staff and peers, can navigate differing social norms, and is a team player	Student respects some classmates' opinions, gets along with some staff and peers, attempts to navigate social norms, and is a selective team player	Student struggles to respect classmates' opinions, struggles to get along with others, doesn't understand social norms, and struggles to be a team player	Student does not respect classmates' opinions, cannot get along with staff and peers, can't navigate social norms, and is not a team player
Responsible Decision-Making	Student is able to consider the consequences before making a decision, is aware of how decisions will affect others, and can judge between right and wrong	Student sometimes considers the consequences of a decision, is somewhat aware of how decisions affect others, and is aware of what is right and wrong	Student struggles to consider consequences of decisions, is vaguely aware of how decisions affect others, and struggles to know right from wrong	Student does not consider consequences of decisions, is unaware of how decisions affect others, and cannot judge between right and wrong

Another student artifact with an elementary level focus includes the following student's rubric which broke down SEL competencies and provided student-focused language so students could engage in the self-assessment process.

Self -Awareness	**When I think about myself…**	I am not sure what the name of my emotion is.	I can name the emotions I am feeling.	I can name the emotions I am feeling. I can identify the cause of my emotions.	I can name the emotions I am feeling. I can identify the cause of my emotions. I understand the importance of me being me.
Self-Management	**When I feel big emotions I…**	I don't know what to do.	I use several different strategies to manage my emotions.	I use several different strategies to manage my emotions. I stop and think before I act.	I use several different strategies to manage my emotions. I stop and think before I act. I try to understand why I feel this way and I know what to do about it.
Social Awareness	**When I am with other people…**	I do not know how other people are feeling.	I can identify how others are feeling based on facial expressions and body language.	I can identify how others are feeling based on facial expressions and body language. I think about how other people may feel in a situation.	I can identify how others are feeling based on facial expressions and body language. I think about how other people may feel in a situation. I understand that other people are different than me and have different feelings that I do.
Relationship Skills	**When I am working in a group…**	I can never get along with the other group members.	I can get along with others by respectfully work out disagreement.	I can get along with others by respectfully work out disagreement. I can clearly communicate my ideas and I listen respectfully to other's ideas.	I can get along with others by respectfully work out disagreement. I can clearly communicate my ideas and I listen respectfully to other's ideas. I identify if another member is feeling left out and I respectfully include that person in the group.
Responsible Decision-Making	**When I am faced with a decision…**	I just do the first thing that pops in my head.	I think through all parts of the problem before I act.	I think through all parts of the problem before I act. I consider all consequences of the decisions I make.	I think through all parts of the problem before I act. I consider all consequences of the decisions I make. I think about how my decision might make others feel and I work toward a solution that is best for everyone.

Professor Reflections

Through group discussions, students shared that they thoroughly enjoyed the "face-to-face" online discussions rather than written discussions. Student discussions were often embedded in personal classroom practices and field experiences. Oftentimes, class discussions would run over the required time with students connecting and building professional relationships would continue to meet during their personal time. Successful SEAD-focused assessment research and studies were exchanged during group discussions to which students later shared their gained knowledge with colleague at their school. Finally, students kept in touch after the course ended with both the instructor and with each other as the course experience had developed trusting relationships.

Discussion

This study's findings advance available literature demonstrating examples of explicit SEAD coursework for educators at the higher education level. Student artifacts from the four graduate level online SEAD classes reinforce current research demonstrating that adult SEL skills support effective instructional workforce (Arroyo, 2020), and thus, student success. This case study aligns with current literature demonstrating that explicit SEL education at the post-secondary level contributes to increases in SEL skills, cultural competency, and professional development (Madden-Dent, 2021a; Madden-Dent, 2021b; Madden-Dent, Jackson, & Cason, 2021).

Based on this case study, implications for practice encourage colleges and universities to offer more explicit SEAD and SEL coursework within pre-service and in-service programs of study within Colleges of Education which will address the limited SEL coursework in higher education (Schonert-Reichi, Kitil, & Hanson-Peterson, 2017). It is further encouraged from this case study, that institutions of higher learning establish common social emotional language with its State Office of Public Instruction to align statewide expectations, norms, and credentialing options across PreK – grade 12 (Gorton & DuFresne, 2021). Furthermore, in light of this study's student artifacts, State Offices of Public Instruction are encouraged to offer its educators virtual SEL supports including, but not limited to, free SEL resources, professional development, and professional learning communities to support them personally and professionally.

Building on this case study's discussion of the four graduate level courses, there is a need for continued investigation of how online SEAD courses influence educators' professional development and advancement, employment and persistence rates, and professional effectiveness. Current literature would appreciate the addition of longitudinal data identifying how educators' professional abilities and experiences were influenced over time after completing one, multiple, or all of the presented SEAD classes in this case study. Another direction of future research includes how online SEAD classes serve as a support resource for educators during state emergencies such as the COVID-19 pandemic.

CONCLUSION

This chapter provided an introduction to four new explicit Social, Emotional, and Academic Development courses at the higher educational level. Both pre-service and in-service educators engaged in independent and collaborate formal SEL studies aimed to increase knowledge of social-emotional concepts and how to implement them into daily work practices. The chapter provided examples of how colleges and universities can replicate similar online classes and some of the intended outcomes (e.g., increased SEL skills) and unintended outcomes (e.g., Virtual support for educators during COVID-19 pandemic). This chapter contributes to the current literature by adding a new understanding of how educators experienced online SEAD classwork and their perceptions of its importance for them becoming stronger and more effective educators.

As our institutions of higher learning continue shaping equitable educational systems as drivers of educator workforce development, it is imperative that they lead with SEAD practices within their educational programs of study and continuing education extension programs. Their role in encouraging SEL within our educational workforce is more important today than ever before, as schools seek safer, more inclusive campuses and digital learning environments with culturally responsive and respectful communication and interactions.

REFERENCES

Almlund, M., Duckworth, A. L., Heckman, J. J., & Kautz, T. (2011). Personality psychology and economics. In E. A. Hanushek, S. Machin, & L. Wößmann (Eds.), *Handbook of the economics of SEADation*. Elsevier. doi:10.3386/w16822

Arroyo, M. (2020). *The relationship between teacher identity and teacher retention in Title I schools: A multiple case study.* Dissertation from the University of Nevada, Las Vegas. ProQuest Number: 27999584.

Aspen Institute. (2018). *Pursuing Social and Emotional Development Through a Racial Equity Lens: A Call to Action.* Retrieved at https://www.aspeninstitute.org/publications/pursuing-social-and-emotional-development-through-a-racial-equity-lens-a-call-to-action/

Belfield, B., & Klapp, L. (2015). The economic value of social and emotional learning. New York, NY: Center for Benefit-Cost Studies in SEADation: Teachers College, Columbia University.

Cantor, P., Osher, D., Berg, J., Steyer, L., & Rose, T. (2018). Malleability, plasticity, and individuality: How children learn and develop in context. *Applied Developmental Science*. Advance online publication. doi:10.1080/10888691.2017.1398649

Collaborative for Academic, Social, and Emotional Learning (CASEL). (2020). *What is SEL?* Retrieved at https://casel.org/what-is-sel/

Cunningham, W. V., & Villasenor, P. (2016). Employer voices, employer demands, and implications for public skills development policy connecting the labor and education sectors. The World Bank Research Observer. (2016). *The World Bank Research Observer*, *31*(1), 102–134. doi:10.1093/wbro/lkv019

Deming, D. J. (2015). *The growing importance of social skills in the labor market* (NBER Working Paper No. 21473). Cambridge, MA: National Bureau of Economic Research.

Duckworth, A. L., & Seligman, M. E. P. (2005). Self-discipline outdoes IQ in predicting academic performance of adolescents. *Psychological Science*, *16*(12), 939–944. doi:10.1111/j.1467-9280.2005.01641.x PMID:16313657

Durlak, J. A., Weissberg, R. P., Dymnicki, A. B., Taylor, R. D., & Schellinger, K. (2011). The impact of enhancing students' social and emotional learning: A meta-analysis of school-based universal interventions. *Child Development, 82*(1), 405–432. doi:10.1111/j.1467-8624.2010.01564.x PMID:21291449

Fitzgerald, B. K., & Sigelman, M. (2018). *The new foundational skills of the digital economy: Developing the professionals of the future.* Burning Glass Technologies. Retrieved from www.burning-glass.com

Gorton, S. D., & DuFresne, M. (2021). Implementing SEAD statewide: A three-year case study of SEAD support for educators. In *Leading Schools with Social Emotional Academic Development (SEAD).* IGI Global Publication. Retrieved at https://www.igi-global.com/book/leading-schools-social-emotional-academic/256645

Jones, D., Crowley, D. M., & Greenberg, M. T. (2017). *Improving social emotional skills in childhood enhances long-term well-being and economic outcomes.* Edna Bennet Pierce Prevention Research Center, Pennsylvania State University.

Kautz, Diris, & Borghans. (2014). Fostering and measuring skills: Improving cognitive and non-cognitive skills to promote lifetime success. Paris, France: Organization for Economic Cooperation and Development.

Kerr, D. B., Madden-Dent, T., & Shalabi, N. (2020). Cultural Competency Interventions: Three Case Studies with Guiding Theoretical Frameworks. In *Cultural intelligence and social-emotional competencies across the lifespan: Cultural Competencies for Continuous Learning* (2nd ed.). Oxford University Press. Retrieved at https://www.oxfordhandbooks.com/view/10.1093/oxfordhb/9780197506707.001.0001/oxfordhb-9780197506707-e-6?utm_content=148183851&utm_medium=social&utm_source=linkedin&hss_channel=lcp-19900 doi:10.1093/oxfordhb/9780197506707.013.26

Leverson, M., Smith, K., McIntosh, K., Rose, J., & Pinkelman, S. (2019). *PBIS Cultural Responsiveness Field Guide: Resources for Trainers and Coaches.* OSEP Technical Assistance Center. Retrieved at: https://www.pbis.org/school/equity-pbis

Li, C., & Xu, J. (2019). Trait emotional intelligence and classroom emotions: A positive psychology investigation and intervention among Chinese EFL learners. *Frontiers in Psychology, 10*, 1–17. doi:10.3389/fpsyg.2019.02453 PMID:31736840

Madden-Dent, T. (2014). *A phenomenological study of cultural transition and adjustment of Asian undergraduate international students using different cross-cultural treatments. ProQuest.* UMI Dissertations Publishing.

Madden-Dent, T. (2020). Bridging academic and industry skills gap via digital collaboration: Preparing scholars for international assignment. In *University-Industry Collaboration Strategies in the Digital Era.* Retrieved at https://www.igi-global.com/book/university-industry-collaboration-strategies-digital/244278 doi:10.4018/978-1-7998-3901-9

Madden-Dent, T. (2021). Advancing equity through culturally responsive social-emotional education: Addressing international student integration. In *Advances in Motivation and Achievement. Motivating the SEL Field Forward Through Equity* (Vol. 21). Emerald Publishing Limited. Retrieved at https://www.emerald.com/insight/publication/issn/0749-7423 doi:10.1108/S0749-7423201719

Madden-Dent, T., Jackson, I., & Cason, J. (2021). Culturally-responsive social emotional academic development. In *Leading Schools with Social Emotional Academic Development (SEAD)*. IGI Global Publication. Retrieved at https://www.igi-global.com/book/leading-schools-social-emotional-academic/256645

Maldonado, C. (2019). *Integrating workforce development practices in higher education*. Workforce Development Center, University of Nevada.

National Association of Colleges and Employers. (2019). *Career readiness for the new college graduate: A definition of competencies (revised)*. Retrieved from https://www.naceweb.org/career-readiness/competencies/career-readiness-defined/

Neill, J. (2008). *The expatriate venture: What role does cross-cultural training play and what theories guide research in the field?* Schmidt Labor Research Center Seminar Research Series. University of Rhode Island.

Pieter Van Oudenhoven, J., & Van der Zee, K. I. (2002). Predicting multicultural effectiveness of international students: The Multicultural Personality Questionnaire. *International Journal of Intercultural Relations*, *26*(6), 679–694. doi:10.1016/S0147-1767(02)00041-X

Rose, J., Leverson, M., & Smith, K. (2020). *Embedding culturally responsive practices in Tier I*. Center on Positive Behavioral Interventions & Supports. Retrieved at www.pbis.org

Schonert-Reichi, K. A., Kitil, J., & Hanson-Peterson, J. (2017). To reach the students, teach the teachers: A national scan of teacher preparation and social & emotional learning. Report prepared for the Collaborative for Academic, Social, and Emotional Learning (CASEL). University of British Columbia.

Swain-Bradway, J., Lindstrom Johnson, S., Bradshaw, C., & McIntosh, K. (2017). *What are the economic costs of implementing SWPBIS in comparison to the benefits from reducing suspensions?* Technical Brief from Center for Positive Behavioral Interventions and Supports. https://assets-global.website-files.com/5d3725188825e071f1670246/5d76c00cb9339d5f3f267ee7_economiccostsswpbis.pdf

Yoder, N., Atwell, M. N., Godek, D., Dusenbury, L., Bridgeland, J. M., & Weissberg, R. (2020). *Preparing youth for the workforce of tomorrow: Culturivating the social and emotional skills employers demand*. CASEL publication. Retrieved at https://casel.org/collaborative-state-initiative/

Chapter 5
Implementing SEAD Statewide:
A Three-Year Case Study of SEAD Support for Educators

Silvana Carolina (Diaz) Gorton
Nevada Department of Education, USA

Marie J. DuFresne
Nevada Department of Education, USA

ABSTRACT

School leaders play a significant role in shaping education, and their leadership practices are key in conveying professional learning priorities for districts and schools. Concurrently, the benefits of adult social emotional learning (SEL) on creating conditions for educator effectiveness, wellbeing, and success have been demonstrated in the literature. This chapter chronicles initiatives undertaken by the Nevada Department of Education (NDE) to establish a systemic, sustainable, multi-tiered professional development structure and infrastructure aimed to foster adult SEL across the teaching and learning continuum, and ultimately to positively change student outcomes. Four initiatives are described, including the innovative approach of bringing together multiple projects to provide a virtual comprehensive support system in response to increased educator need.

INTRODUCTION

In the fall of 2018, the Nevada Department of Education (NDE) seized the opportunity to conceive, develop, and implement a statewide systemic structure intended to bolster the professional learning and development of school leaders and educators in the area of adult social emotional learning (SEL) and social, emotional, and academic development (SEAD) Adult SEL is the process by which one gains the knowledge, skills, and abilities to successfully navigate society and the world (Collaborative for Academic, Social, and Emotional Learning [CASEL], 2005). Similarly, SEAD is the connection between academics and social emotional skills that emphasize whole-child development in support of positive outcomes for students (Aspen Institute, 2019).

DOI: 10.4018/978-1-7998-6728-9.ch005

The objective of this chapter is to chronicle the development and eventual implementation of four adult SEAD initiatives: the SEAD Leadership Summit, SEAD for Educators Professional Learning, the SEAD Champions Cadre, and the SEAD Center. These SEAD initiatives represent the joining of two areas of work, SEAD education and educator development. A shared vision guided the development and implementation of the SEAD initiatives that would shape school leadership practices to create the conditions for increased success of teachers, other educators, and ultimately students, supported by a SEAD embedded, sustainable, and high-impact systemic structure. The background section explains common goals central to the collaborative work of the SEAD initiatives, which emerged from the momentum sparked by two projects which are described in the following section.

BACKGROUND

The NDE Office for a Safe and Respectful Learning Environment (OSRLE) has spearheaded the development of SEAD in Nevada. In cooperation and collaboration with partners, such as the Office of Educator Development, Licensure, and Family Engagement (EDLiFE), SEAD has become an important priority. The mission of OSRLE is: We collaborate to ensure that all work and learn in a safe and respectful environment. OSRLE's teams include: Health and Wellness, SEAD/SEL, School Climate and Safety, and Multi-Tiered System of Supports (MTSS).

The NDE Office of Educator Development, Licensure, and Family Engagement (EDLiFE) leverages and strengthens human resources to improve student outcomes. The mission of EDLiFE is aligned with that of the Department: To improve student achievement and educator effectiveness by ensuring opportunities, facilitating learning, and promoting excellence. Developing adult SEL and SEAD for school leaders and educators was prioritized as a high-impact approach for increased effective instructional practices.

Therefore, Adult SEL and SEAD emerged as a common interest for the OSRLE and EDLiFE offices, establishing a cross-office collaboration. Researchers were illuminating the systemic approach for coordinating strategies, resources, and supports as critical in efforts aimed to highlight SEL practices for the benefit of school leaders, educators, and ultimately student outcomes (Meyers et al., 2019; Allensworth et al., 2018; Aspen Institute, 2019; Jones et al., 2017; Shriver & Weissberg, 2020).

The opportunities identified at the intersecting priorities of the two offices were almost directly aligned to recommendations emerging from research focused on the effects of SEL on educators (Hamilton & Doss, 2020). Examples of findings from the research of Hamilton and Doss (2020) and Thessin and Louis (2020) strongly related to the eventual goals of the SEAD initiatives and include:

- Teacher burnout as impacted by the degree of job satisfaction and happiness, and work-related social and emotional wellbeing;
- Teacher sentiment regarding the importance of SEL-focused school leadership related to the impact that principals have on school climate; and
- Building instructional leadership capacity to address the expanding role of school leaders beyond the focus on academic development to include social and emotional development.

Of particular importance was the finding that teachers ultimately depend on principals for access to training, instructional resources, support for their own wellbeing, and professional encouragement and guidance for providing high-quality SEL for children (Hamilton & Doss, 2020; Allensworth & Hart,

2018). The three original initiatives aimed to establish a state-level multi-tiered professional development structure focused on adult SEL and SEAD instructional practices for school leaders and educators. In the early stages of development, the intention was for school leaders and educators with access to resources to gain increased understanding of adult SEL and SEAD, and then lead the implementation of systemic supports to increase effective SEAD instructional practices. The four SEAD initiatives developed to this end and discussed here are:

SEAD Initiative One: The SEAD Leadership Summit
SEAD Initiative Two: SEAD for Educators Professional Learning
SEAD Initiative Three: The Cadre of SEAD Champions
SEAD Initiative Four: The SEAD Center

In the face of the COVID-19 pandemic, the three original SEAD initiatives were synergistically reimagined into the fourth initiative, accessed exclusively online: the SEAD Center. The four SEAD initiatives aspire to foster adult SEL competencies in school leaders that are then demonstrated through effective SEAD instructional practices across all educators. The next section describes two foundational NDE projects instrumental in establishing the foundation for the structure of the four SEAD initiatives.

Building Adult SEL and SEAD Momentum

While ramping up adult SEL and SEAD momentum, it was clear that educators with a passion for SEAD were clamoring for a place to meet collaboratively, to share ideas, and to support one another. The SEAD Community of Practice project was formed. Ferguson (2012) describes Community of Practice as:

Groups of people who join together to work on a common project [with] [t]he purpose and nature of the common project to share concerns about an issue, to deepen their knowledge and expertise about the issue by interacting or cooperating with others, in an ongoing way. (p. 138)

The SEAD Community of Practice weekly meetings focused on how educators and educator leaders from across the state could become SEAD Champions to better improve the lives of students, families, communities, colleagues, and themselves in a safe and supportive environment. Using robust discussion prompts, self and system examinations, and action planning, participants worked together toward a common goal: student, family, staff, and self wellness. Tackling today's most challenging issues, such as racial injustice, equity, and the COVID-19 pandemic, the SEAD community of practice members continue to advocate and lead the way for systems change.

The second foundational project was the SEAD endorsement pathway. To elevate the importance of the SEL competencies (see *SEAD Initiatives Areas of Focus*) in the preparation and professional development of educators, it was recognized that SEAD knowledge and expertise merited formal recognition. Therefore, an endorsement as a specialist in social, emotional, and academic development was established in 2019 (NDE, 2019b) as a specialty subject area to the professional teacher license. Receiving this endorsement required the completion of at least three semester-hours of credit in each of the following areas of study: (1) Introduction to SEAD; (2) Curriculum and methods for modeling, teaching, and implementing SEAD; (3) Assessment, evaluation, monitoring, and plan improvement of SEAD; and (4) Best practices that support policies, equity, and critical issues for SEAD. This pathway was developed in cooperation with a local university to provide the endorsement program recognized by the state. The momentum resulting from these key projects led to the four SEAD initiatives, subsequently described.

NEW SEAD INITIATIVES PROJECT DESIGN: BUILDING THE STRUCTURE

This section describes three structural elements which encompassed the four SEAD initiatives. The first, which served as the overarching scope across projects, was based on the purpose of Title II, Part A (Every Student Succeeds Act of 2015) and set the vision: to improve educator effectiveness and increase the number of educators through quality professional learning and support. The second element consisted of the five core SEL competencies identified at the time, by CASEL (2005). The SEL competencies gave the SEAD initiatives intentional focus. The third element was the state-adopted, equitably integrated MTSS framework (NDE, 2018), an instrumental part of the structure in the implementation of the SEAD initiatives.

SEAD Initiatives' Overarching Scope

The guiding vision for the SEAD initiatives was strongly informed by the purpose of the Every Student Succeeds Act (ESSA) of 2015, Title II, Part A, commonly referred to as Title IIA (2015). The purpose of Title IIA includes four points:

- To increase student achievement consistent with state academic standards.
- To improve the quality and effectiveness of teachers, principals, and other school leaders.
- To increase the number of teachers, principals, and other school leaders who are effective in improving student academic achievement in schools.
- To provide low-income and minority students greater access to effective teachers, principals, and other school leaders (ESSA Title IIA, 2015, 20 U.S.C. 6601).

School leaders were identified as the primary participants in the SEAD initiatives, as they play a significant role in shaping education at the macro level. The Title IIA definition of school leader is:

a principal, assistant principal, or other individual who is, (1) an employee or officer of an elementary school or secondary school, local educational agency, or other entity operating an elementary school or secondary school; and (2) responsible for the daily instructional leadership and managerial operations in the elementary school or secondary school building. (ESSA section 8101(44))

Each SEAD initiative was designed as an ongoing series of related activities aligned with Title IIA requirements "that professional development be sustained, intensive, collaborative, job-embedded, data-driven, and classroom-focused" (ESSA section 8101(42)). The Title IIA definition of professional development offered leverage for ensuring that adequate time was reserved to realize the complex and high-level learning objectives and outcomes. During the process of project design, consideration was given to the distinct professional development needs of school leaders, as highlighted by Mizell (2010):

Principals who are instructional leaders often choose to participate in professional development designed primarily for teachers so that they can support its outcomes. In addition, principals need professional development to address their specific roles and responsibilities. . . . Many experts believe principals do not have adequate access to professional development related to their roles as school leaders. (p. 10)

Supporting school leaders relative to the improvement and ongoing success of educators was commonly identified as a need by teachers, and experts pointed to the positive benefits of leadership addressing the needs of educators and students (Yoder et al., 2020; New Leaders, 2017; Civic Enterprises et al., 2013).

The SEAD initiatives adopted the school-leader perspective, and the learning objectives of each SEAD initiative aimed to establish shared macro-level common understandings about adult SEL and SEAD-embedded leadership and instructional practices. These common understandings supported school leaders in the complex learning and action-planning process of developing a sustainable, multi-tiered, professional development structure to prioritize the learning, modeling, and teaching of SEL competencies.

SEAD Initiatives' Areas of Focus

The favorable implications of using SEL competencies for creating conditions for educator success are well established in the literature (Carver-Thomas et al., 2017; Durlak et al., 2011; Podolsky et al., 2016; Yoder et al., 2020). The SEL competencies were the focus of learning across the SEAD initiatives, each of which underscored the potential efficacy of leadership and instructional practices when related to the five SEL competencies identified by CASEL (2005) and adopted by Nevada in 2017:

- **Self-Awareness:** The capability to notice and observe one's feelings, values, and actions.
- **Social Awareness:** The ability to understand another's perspective and respect different cultures, backgrounds, and social norms.
- **Relationship Skills:** The ability to connect and sustain healthy and strong relationships with others.
- **Self-Management:** The capacity to regulate one's emotions, thinking, and behavior in regard to impulse control, managing stress, goal setting, and self-discipline.
- **Responsible Decision-Making:** The ability to make positive choices in consideration of oneself and others.

Each SEAD initiative highlighted the research-based academic, social, and individual benefits of prioritizing the SEL competencies in leadership practices. School leaders learned about improved teacher retention and increased teacher attendance and instructional excellence, increased student attendance and engagement in learning and decreased discipline issues, and ultimately increased quality of opportunities for learning and academic achievement (Carver-Thomas & Darling-Hammond, 2017, p. 29; Podolsky et al., 2016, p. 39; Yoder et al., 2020, p. 26).

The SEL competencies were the central focus of two overarching learning objectives across the SEAD initiatives. The first established that SEL competencies are based in rigorous research and supported by the hard sciences, as in the focus on the power of SEL on brain function (Immordino-Yang et al., 2018). The second established the powerful congruence of SEL competencies to ideal leading and learning conditions based on the positive effect of SEL competencies across academic, social, and individual professional and personal dimensions. As a result, an underlying tenet to the SEAD initiatives was that school leaders knowledgeable about the positive impact of SEL competencies would be more likely to create conditions to empower teachers, counselors, and school social workers with the tools, strategies, and skills to facilitate change in a positive, healthful, and sustainable way (Podolsky et al., 2016; Carver-Thomas & Darling-Hammond, 2017; Civic Enterprises et al., 2013).

MTSS Framework: SEAD In Action

The third essential element applied across the SEAD initiatives was the state-adopted equitable integrated MTSS framework (NDE, 2018). Similar to the SEL competencies, the benefits of practical application through a multi-tiered approach is strongly rooted in research (Aspen Institute, 2017, 2018; see also Allensworth et al., 2018; Center on Positive Behavioral Interventions and Supports, 2017; Freeman et al., 2017; McIntosh & Goodman, 2016). Each SEAD initiative used the MTSS framework to contextualize the action-planning process for the development and implementation of a structure to establish and sustain effective instructional practices. In each SEAD initiative, activities were explicitly correlated to the tiers of the MTSS framework presented in Figure 1.

Tier 1 supports for statewide SEAD implementation included: the online SEAD module series, weekly SEL/SEAD live office hours, bi-monthly lunchbox learning sessions, monthly guest speakers, SEAD training as requested, and a state website that provided SEAD resources and links. The weekly SEL/SEAD office hours provided an open forum for any educator or pilot-study participant to speak with a supportive SEL/SEAD professional for advising and support (see *The SEAD Center: SEAD Hope in the Midst of Crisis*). The lunchbox learning sessions provided an array of expert presenters on topics, such as SEL competencies, equity, restorative practices, implementation through integration, trauma, virtual and distance learning, cultural competency, and workforce development. The monthly guest speaker series included experts in early childhood education, family engagement, trauma-informed distance learning, and grief and loss. All presentations were recorded and added to the resource library, where articles, webinar links, exemplars, and tips could also be found.

Tier 2 targeted supports for statewide SEAD implementation, including the SEAD Leadership Summit, statewide Community of Practice, the SEAD ongoing professional development pilot study, and the SEAD Center pilot study. The SEAD Center pilot study included discussion and reflection threads directly related to the online SEAD module series, access to daily wellness sessions emphasizing yoga, guided imagery, positive self-talk, and intention-setting to assist in self-care strategies, and were provided the book *All Learning is Social and Emotional: Helping Students Develop Essential Skills for the Classroom and Beyond* by Frey, Fisher, and Smith (2019) to increase knowledge and provide an additional foundation in SEAD. Using the online platform, pilot-study participants responded to weekly prompts designed to engage them in thought-provoking, rich discussions.

Individualized support for Tier 3 statewide implementation provided pilot study participants with one-to-one personal coaching and advising, prompts for positive self-talk through hand-written notes of encouragement or inspirational quotes, and support throughout the pilot study. At Tier 3, participants received more intensive, individualized support, such as assistance for SEAD action planning. Monitoring the fidelity of implementation was prioritized to increase confidence in attributing positive outcomes to interventions (Center on Positive Behavioral Interventions and Supports, 2019). The MTSS framework (NDE, 2018), along with the other two structural elements described in this section, were central in the SEAD initiatives, each of which is described in the next section.

Figure 1. A triangle divided into three tiers: the bottom is a universal tier, the middle is a targeted tier, and the top is an individualized support tier

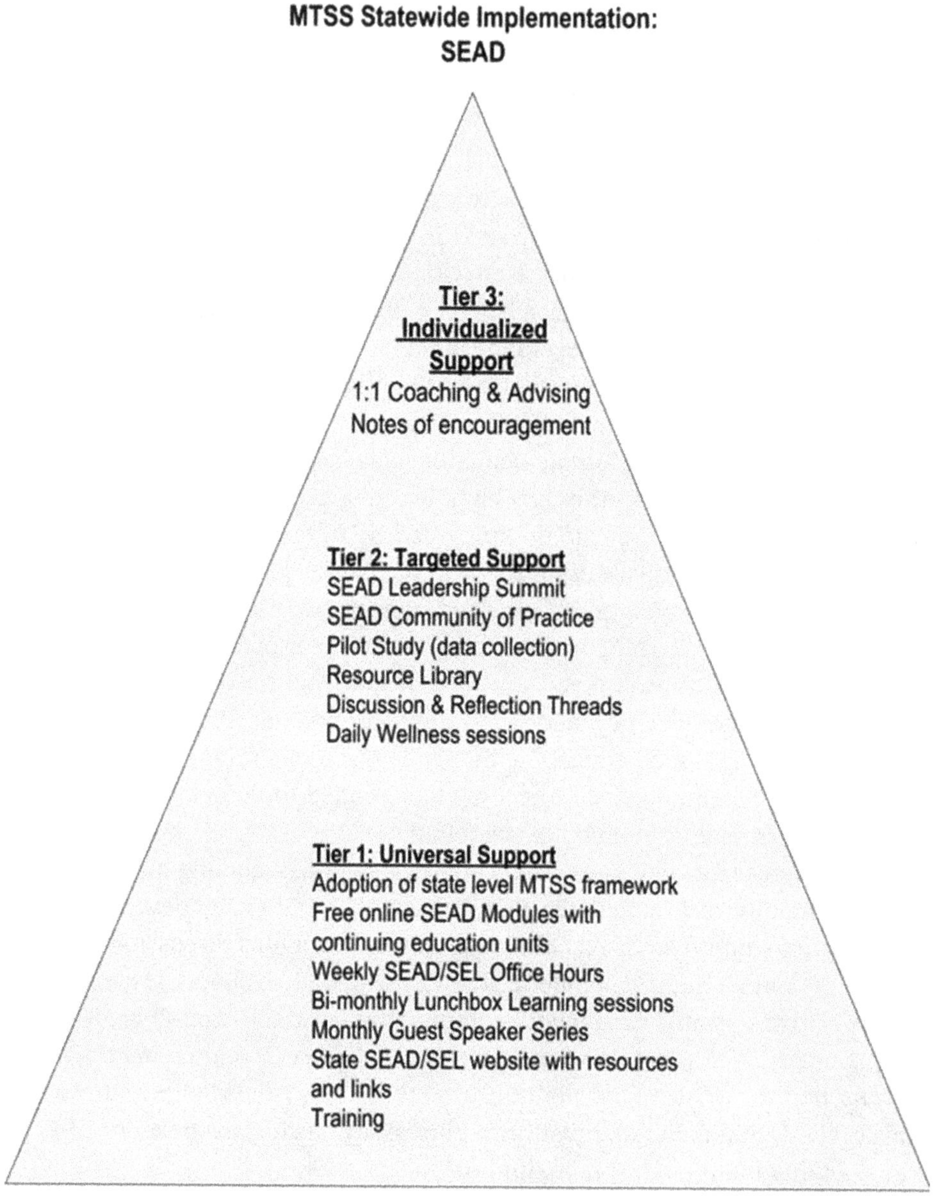

THE FOUR STATE SEAD INITIATIVES

The SEAD Leadership Summit

The first initiative, the SEAD Leadership Summit, assembled adult SEL and SEAD experts with a statewide cohort of school leaders interested in learning about the potential for the positive impact of SEAD in the school context, and inclined to support the development of a cadre of SEAD Champions. In the summer of 2019, 49 educational leaders representing 60% of the state's school districts, as well as NDE and at least two institutions of higher education, attended the three-day SEAD Leadership Summit. Participants included sitting and aspiring school leaders, professional learning specialists, teacher leaders, and other educators with direct influence on school climate and culture.

The content was designed with broad appeal to educators, and aligned to Title IIA, correlated to one or more of the CASEL five SEL competencies, and to one or more tiers of the MTSS framework. The primary objective was to empower teachers, counselors, and social workers with the tools, strategies, and skills to facilitate change in a positive, healthful, and sustainable way. Three learner outcomes were articulated: (1) to engage in reflective thought to better understand feelings and perspectives prompted by the learning experience, and to apply the principles and practices of SEAD, both personally and with departmental leadership; (2) to feel supported and prepared with easy-to-implement strategies to turn leadership ideas into action; and (3) to create a culture empowering leaders to improve educator effectiveness through positive long-term development, success, and wellbeing of educational support teams and, ultimately, students (Sierra Nevada University, 2019). The SEAD Leadership Summit was an experience described by many participants as unlike any other.

The SEAD Leadership Summit: Modeling The Action Plan

Throughout the Summit, school leaders were provided time and support for action planning. With the support of subject-matter experts, school leaders developed ideas for actionable application of the learned skills and practices across the tiers of the MTSS framework. Each session provided participants with perspectives that underscored the positive force of SEL competencies across a broad spectrum of personal and professional aspects. Dr. Carole Griggs was the first keynote speaker of the Summit, and she intentionally embedded multi-tiered strategies throughout the session. Dr. Griggs drew from a wealth of experiences as an executive coach, leadership development consultant, university professor, and developer of transformative technology tools "focused on human potential and consciousness evolution" (Sierra Nevada University, 2019a, p. 18). Summit participants explored the individual, collective, internal, and external perspectives through the use of a four-quadrant framework, with self-awareness as the central SEL competency. Educators learned about the roles of the conscious and unconscious, analyzed and reflected on their own thought filters, and were provided a safe space to discover a deeper level of self-awareness where negative aspects could be challenged with strategies to "deepen the positive and collaborative nature of your influence" in the ongoing process of personal transformation (Sierra Nevada University, 2019a, p. 24). A fascinating perspective shared by Dr. Griggs was the direct involvement in and contribution to the field of artificial intelligence (AI), particularly the scholar's commitment to ensure SEL competencies are prioritized as AI continues to develop (see Griggs & Strauss, 2018).

Another keynote speaker, Milton Chen, Ph.D., shared professional experiences to inspire in participants an emotional connection to the whole-child perspective. Dr. Chen described several projects that have profoundly impacted the development of children, including the George Lucas Educational Foundation, Edutopia, Sesame Street, and more recent initiatives supporting youth and science, technology, engineering, and math (STEM) learning with the Panasonic Foundation and the National Park System (Sierra Nevada University, 2019a, p. 18). Participants delved into a deeper understanding of whole-child instruction from the perspective of their own leadership capacity and through developing a systemic learning action plan integrated with exemplar social emotional and academic learning practices and resources.

A few SEL implementation examples mentioned by Dr. Chen included the Find My Role Model tool (Academy of Achievement, 1961), where the sentence structure, "Show me the achievers like me that wanted to _____, had a personality that was____ and have faced challenges like____," with the instructions, "Fill in the blanks and discover which of the world's greatest achievers match aspects of your own life." The resulting menu of "extraordinary achievers" provided a personalized roadmap toward a personal quest for excellence. Another example highlighted by Dr. Chen was Edutopia (2010), where entering the keywords "social and emotional learning" generated 1,548 results, including stories and videos that describe and model transformational strategies and best practices (for an example strategy, see Korbey, 2017). Dr. Chen's use of many web-based resources to illustrate the limitless possibilities of integrating SEL with academic content was well highlighted in his statement, "educating the heart is as important as educating the mind" (personal communication, June 26, 2019). Dr. Chen effectively addressed the learner outcome, as follows: "understand and build foundational capacity in the integration strategies available to support high-quality SEAD implementation across all academic subjects and instructional methods" (Sierra Nevada University, 2019a, p. 29). The thoughtful selection of speakers and presenters was strongly supported with attention to detail in other aspects of the SEAD Leadership Summit. The following section describes the importance of the program and journal, the enrichment activities, and the conditions set for the three-day Summit.

The SEAD Leadership Summit: Program and Journal

The 44-page Summit Program and Journal included multi-sensory artistic details to draw the participant into a mindset open to the experience from the outset. The Program included quotations to spark inspiration and positivity, images to conjure feelings of happiness and possibility, and embedded areas encouraging scribbles and doodles to support the process of deep thinking and reflection. The Program also included foundational SEAD and adult SEL information components, such as the CASEL competencies, the components of the MTSS framework, and useful summaries of key models applied throughout the Summit. For example, a half-page description of the experiential learning model was provided to lend context to the planned outdoor learning experiences: "Learning research shows us that deep, personalized, and lasting learning occurs through direct experience and reflection on those experiences and later, application of that learning to future experiences" (Sierra Nevada University, 2019a, p. 32). Throughout the Program, participants found areas for reflective journaling, intentional spaces created for participants to capture their personalized notes about experiences, feelings, ideas, intentions, and action-plan steps emanating from the process of deep learning throughout the Summit. Participants also found many prompts and sentence stems, places to ground them in the essence of the experience. For example, one prompt asked participants to indicate, "This afternoon I hope to be: an active listener, constructive, motivated, introspective, collaborative, challenged, other______."

The SEAD Leadership Summit: Enrichment Activities

The Summit provided lodging and meals, which allowed participants to experience a SEAD-embedded routine from morning to night. Each morning, participants could join yoga, walking, or meditation groups. A facilitator led participants through each step of the session and explicitly narrated the benefits of the practice relative to the stated Summit purposes. In other words, facilitators guided participants to experience the connection from a mind–body practice to the process of deepened learning, and the potential application through instructional practice in a school/learner context. These activities demonstrated the efficacy of activity-based SEL competency development. Likewise, breakfast was used to create conditions for networking. Participants were encouraged to meet new colleagues, and table-top tents provided discussion-starter topics. Facilitators modeled an immediately actionable strategy for creating conditions supportive of positive peer communication and relationship building, whether it be colleague-with-colleague or student-with-student. Throughout the Summit, integration or brain breaks were scheduled to provide participants with the opportunity to process and integrate new learning, and to teach and model what an integration break is and how it can be effective during instruction, transition, and at other key points in the school context. Consistent with other design elements, the integration breaks were facilitated by an expert, and participants learned about specific benefits for including cross-body movements, kinesthetic awareness movements, mindful breathing, and other techniques in instructional practice. Summit participants experienced several immediately actionable tools and techniques with the potential for applications across the school day, both in direct instruction to students, as well as through educator-to-educator peer modeling, mentoring, and coaching.

The SEAD Leadership Summit: Conditions for Success

The effort to create conditions for successful SEL competency development and actionable practice was a priority in every aspect of the Summit. One participant commented, "Not only did I learn the importance of SEAD practices, I also learned it through everyone's actions'" (personal communication, June 27, 2019). This captured the intended outcome of the many facilitated experiences meant to provide participants with the space, information, modeling, support, and structures for practicing SEL competencies. For example, Sierra Nevada University (SNU) was intentionally selected as the ideal climate for the Summit due to the health, wellness, and nurturing surroundings of the location, in close proximity to Lake Tahoe, Nevada. The climate also included positive words and phrases seen on t-shirts, on sidewalks, within discussion and reflection prompts, and during social conventions at mealtimes, transition times, beginning and ending of activities, and for group and paired interactions. The fireside chat was an opportunity for participants to talk with an expert at a time and place unlike a typical formal setting. The environment included a fireplace, comfortable seating, and with the general topic established, minimal expectations about interaction. While the informality might suggest that learning was not taking place, the opportunity to practice SEL competencies was effective. Participants witnessed and practiced respectful expressions of opinion, authentic listening, thoughtful participation, an effort to ensure that everyone had the opportunity to participate, and the practice of empathy. This description is key when considering the significant positive benefit to adults and students who are supported to learn, practice, and model effective communication skills across formal and informal settings.

The SEAD Leadership Summit: Participant Impact

Participants were continuously engaged in describing what they learned, how they might apply this knowledge, what additional supports might be needed, and offering additional comments. They were given two evaluations, one as part of the concluding session of the Summit, and a final evaluation sent to participants ten days after the close of the Summit. Evaluation data suggest that, overall, participants found the content to be engaging and useful, affirmed that knowledge and tools were gained, and agreed that SEAD helps improve school safety, student success, and school climate; reduce teacher stress; and reinforce complementary practices to reduce discipline issues.

The reflections included here demonstrate a theme around the interest in SEL skills as essential for creating equitable, respectful learning environments. One example of feedback shared a few weeks after the Summit read:

Over the past several weeks my thoughts keep returning to the incredible SEAD Summit. Truthfully, I didn't even know what SEAD stood for prior to our Summit. I hope to learn more and to positively influence SEAD awareness and practice within my organization. (personal communication, July 15, 2019)

Other participant descriptions of their biggest take-away included, "SEAD should be implemented with staff too! It is important for building a happy staff culture"; "Self awareness affects the understanding of others"; "Cultural inclusiveness is an integral part of SEAD"; "The importance of family engagement and understanding students' culture"; "Understanding culture (identifying bias) is essential to creating psychological safety—which lays a foundation for learning"; "Students can connect to teaching and learning if they are respected, can drop their guard and participate in a relationship"; and last, "Building mindful leadership is not by chance" (Sierra Nevada University, 2019a). The positive response to the first initiative signaled statewide interest for the next impending SEAD initiative, described next.

SEAD for Educators' Professional Learning

The second initiative was to develop an online SEAD module series, released in December 2019. This module series aimed to elevate the degree of interest across educators, school leaders, and any interested individual across the state by providing a no-cost, open-access, asynchronous, and facilitated learning option. The participants could determine for themselves the degree to which they would use the modules, as they could review the content at a cursory level to increase awareness, or to a deeper level to establish foundational knowledge. The SEAD module series represented a synthesis of major SEL research personalized to include the local perspective by addressing the following topics (NDE, 2019a):

- **Introduction to SEAD/SEAD and SEL: What Are They and Why Are They Important?:** Defined terms and provided a selection of articles; provided prompts for posting responses in the Discussion Community.
- **SEAD and the Brain: How We Learn:** Provided the science on how the brain develops and helped explain how social, emotional, and academic development are connected. For example, a growing brain needs social connections, emotional experiences, and intellectual capital. Supporting the whole child is an idea that educators need to embrace for students to learn and develop their brains (Immordino-Yang et al., 2018).

- **SEAD and Equity:** Provided information on how SEAD is directly related to equity. For example, by placing attention on equity, educators can use SEL to help students utilize their unique experiences, culture, and backgrounds to build strengths and achieve goals (Regional Educational Laboratory (REL) Midwest, 2018).
- **SEAD, Cultural Intelligence, and Cultural Responsiveness**: Defined terms and discussed the importance of educators having an understanding and awareness of culture and implicit (unconscious) bias, which is necessary when teaching and modeling SEL and creating welcoming, safe, inclusive, and culturally responsive classrooms (CASEL, n.d.a).
- **SEAD Starts With the Adult:** Provided information about the importance of building SEL competencies in adults and educators.
- **Evidence-Based SEAD Interventions:** Introduced evidence-based practices to guide the selection and implementation of SEAD interventions for various education levels and provided examples of SEAD interventions and supports.
- **Measuring and Assessing SEAD:** Introduced these important components to incorporate into SEAD practices and provided supportive resources to facilitate assessment, including students' social emotional competence, student progress on social and emotional development in the classroom, and implementation fidelity of SEL programs and practices.
- **Implementing SEAD Using an MTSS Framework:** Defined MTSS and the use of core elements to build a system for strong, effective, and sustainable implementation of evidence-based practices to ensure the most impactful services, practices, and resources based upon responsiveness to effective instruction and intervention (NDE, 2018).
- **SEAD and Hot Topics:** Provided information and resources on current topics, including attendance, the COVID-19 pandemic, restorative practices, family/parent engagement, and workforce readiness skills.
- **Optimistic Closures and Next Steps:** Offered closure to participants and opportunities to continue professional growth. CASEL (2019) states that optimistic closure "highlights an individual and shared understanding of the importance of the work, and can provide a sense of accomplishment and support forward-thinking" (p. 3).

Each series module was enriched with content-specific articles, videos, engagement activities, and an extensive resource list for each section. The knowledge conveyed by the modules was designed to establish a foundational understanding of SEL competencies and SEAD. The initial module series offered educators the benefit of earning continuing education hours to support licensure renewal requirements.

SEAD Initiative Collaborations

Efforts to elevate interest in adult SEL and SEAD across school leaders and educators expanded with opportunities to collaborate with already established professional organizations within the state. The rich content of the SEAD modules provided a foundation on which to customize content for professional learning events intended for sitting and aspiring school and district leaders, teacher leaders, school leadership teams, and state education leaders. Two examples of these collaborations are described below.

Teacher Leaders

First, the NDE and the Nevada Teach to Lead Network brought education leaders with diverse perspectives to the Powered By Teach to Lead: Nevada Summit. Teams represented teachers at all levels of pre-K–12 education, educator preparation programs from at least four institutions of higher education, non-profit teacher network organizations, educator professional development specialists, the state Teacher of the Year chapter, non-profit community organizations, and a team of developing student leaders. Each team was tasked with creating an action plan to implement MTSS and SEAD practices to "create and sustain a positive school climate and positively impact the retention of high-quality educators" (NDE & The Nevada Teach to Lead Team (NTTL), personal communication, October 12, 2019).

Each team was assigned a Critical Friend—that is, a subject-matter expert to facilitate engagement throughout the day-long process and to encourage critical thinking and innovative problem solving. The strong alignment between the Powered By Summit event and the SEAD for Educators Professional Learning initiative created a natural opportunity to collaborate. To that end, SEAD initiative leaders served as Critical Friends. During the event, the opportunity to underscore the importance of integrating and implementing adult SEL and SEAD competencies in the learning context was added as a valuable perspective.

School Leaders

A collaborative partnership was cemented with the self-described "only statewide administrative association" (Nevada Association of School Administrators [NASA], 2020). Over a 12-month span, SEAD initiative content was customized for three activities hosted by NASA for sitting and aspiring administrators statewide. The first activity was a one-day proceeding geared toward aspiring administrators (NDE, personal communication, September 20, 2019). The second was a one-and-one-half-day part of the opening session in a four-part leadership institute (NDE & The Nevada PBIS Technical Assistance Center, personal communication, January 16–17, 2020). The third activity was a two-hour session during the annual three-day spring conference (NDE & The Nevada PBIS Technical Assistance Center, personal communication, June 16, 2020).

The SEAD initiative learning objectives were applied across the NASA activities, and more than 200 school leaders and educators learned at a deeper level that, "when integrated fully into a school culture and taught explicitly and with fidelity, SEAD competencies have shown to improve academic achievement, student behavior, attendance, and overall student and staff morale" (NDE & The Nevada PBIS Technical Assistance Center, 2020). Further, the NASA Leadership Institute session incorporated a noteworthy structure to foster peer consultation and collaboration opportunities for participants, as school leaders, to work together and to learn with and from each other. The World Café conversation method (The World Café Community Foundation, 2015) provided school leaders the opportunity to practice strategies and to dialogue about circumstances ripe for immediate actionable application of the learned SEAD embedded practices.

The SEAD Champions Cadre

The third SEAD initiative, the SEAD Champions Cadre, began by identifying education leaders with a passion for SEAD who were interested in becoming SEAD subject-matter experts. The SEAD Champions initiative aimed to increase the number of SEAD subject-matter experts who could serve as resources statewide. As with the Summit, the SEAD Champions Cadre initiative was aligned to Title IIA (ESSA, 2015) and explicitly correlated to the five SEL competencies (CASEL, 2005) and to the MTSS framework (NDE, 2018). It was made accessible to educators in rural areas of the state, as the disparity in access to professional learning opportunities for educators in these regions was identified as a need by educators.

The results of a pre-workshop survey helped to tailor the learning objectives of the SEAD Champions coaching and advising workshops to address the needs identified as most important by the 72 pre-registered participants. Central to the professional learning, educational resources, supports, and ongoing coaching and advising offered to the SEAD Champions was the tenet that student outcomes are more likely to change if and when adult behaviors change. The primary objective of the initiative was to empower teachers, counselors, and school social workers with the tools, strategies, and skills to facilitate change in a positive, healthful, and sustainable way. The three articulated learner outcomes were focused on the understanding and implementation of the explicit integration of adult SEL and SEAD, applying the principles and practices of SEAD both personally and with students, feeling supported and prepared with easy-to-implement strategies for the classroom or office to promote an environment where all students thrive and flourish, and to create a culture empowering teachers, counselors, and school social workers to improve effectiveness through positive long-term development, success, and the wellbeing of educational support teams and ultimately students (Mindful SEAD, 2020a).

SEAD Champions Cadre: Journal and Reference Tool

Similar to the SEAD Leadership Summit, each participant received a 31-page journal and reference tool to deepen their professional learning and to support the ongoing application of learned strategies and skills (Mindful SEAD, 2020b). The implementation of explicitly integrated SEL competencies in leadership and teaching practices was emphasized throughout the learning experience. The workshop consisted of modeling effective teaching strategies for use in the classroom, followed by group reflection of the new strategy, and action planning with time for group brainstorming about the potential impact of the strategy on students. According to CASEL (n.d.b.),

As part of high-quality SEL continuous improvement, districts use what was learned throughout the year and during data reflection to determine next steps and engage stakeholders. This may mean building on or expanding strategies that worked, making changes to a strategy to address implementation challenges, or attempting new strategies when previous efforts were unsuccessful. (para. 2)

The multi-sensory artistic detail of the booklet provided was designed to create conditions for participants to adopt intentionality, positivity, and innovation as the frame for learning. Several techniques were presented to initiate the growth of the educator, and ultimately for use with students. A sampling of the techniques learned included mindfulness, intentional breathing, and maximizing the use of existing opportunities in a daily routine. One technique learned was the "InSPIRE Check-In'" (Dahl, 2019), which supports self-reflection and increases self-awareness (Mindful SEAD, 2020b, pp. 3–5). The InSPIRE acronym starts with "in," for inside evaluation of each of five areas of ourselves that make up the whole; "S," for social, or a sense of meaning and enjoying a sense of belonging and connection; "P," for physical, or listening to, honoring, and caring for the body; "I," for intellectual, or cultivating a positive attitude toward learning and balancing work and life; "R," for relational, or contributing to and benefitting from community, friends, and family; and "E," for emotional, or developing emotional intelligence, balance, and resilience, and enjoying positive emotions on a regular basis. Participants learned about each area and selected a self-rating along a Likert-type scale, where 5 was "excellent" and 1 was "not so much." The self-reflection was completed by "celebrating the area that's going well" as indicated by a high rating, and for areas with low ratings, considering "What is one thing you could do to boost yourself in this area?" (Mindful SEAD, 2020b, p. 4).

The participants learned to use the techniques with flexibility, by practicing the check-in verbally or with annotation, as part of an established routine or used spontaneously. Participants also learned how to use the tool at all three tiers of the MTSS framework. For example, in Tier 1, verbal application of the inSPIRE tool can be used as a formative assessment by having a teacher ask students to "hold up 'fist to five' in front of their heart" for one or more of the letters representing the areas (Mindful SEAD, 2020b, p. 3). A teacher could use the tool at Tier 2 with students who appear disengaged from a lesson by prompting them to do an inSPIRE check-in, and then follow up as necessary with a brief conference to connect directly and to "guide them toward making a 3% change that will get them back on track scholastically" (Mindful SEAD, 2020b, p. 3). In a Tier 3 application, as part of a discipline procedure, a teacher or administrator could use the inSPIRE tool as an "intake strategy" and use the ratings to inform about issues that need further attention and "talking points, to help recalibrate the student to their 'Why' of being in school" (Mindful SEAD, 2020b, p. 3).

SEAD Champions Cadre: Prioritizing Educators in Rural Sites

The SEAD Champions ongoing coaching and advising workshops were successfully implemented in three rural sites, impacting six rural districts, one additional district, and the NDE. Forty-two educational leaders, counselors, and teachers from school districts and charter schools statewide attended one of three one-day professional development workshops. Each participant who completed the six-hour workshop was given a Certification of Completion, and continuing education units were an option for participants. Educators who participated expressed great enthusiasm about the learning experience. Participant feedback suggested that not only were the learning objectives met, but the participants also were affected in a deep, authentic manner, as described by one comment:

Coming into the training, I was in need of practices to incorporate into my own personal and professional life. After completing the training, the instructors made me feel confident in leaving with multiple techniques to utilize both on a daily basis as well as for ongoing permanent growth. (Mindful SEAD, 2020a, Appendix B)

Another commented:

This workshop gave practical and useful tools that I am confident to use as soon as I walk into my classroom on Monday morning and as soon as I walk out to my car. (Mindful SEAD, 2020a, Appendix B)

Participant responses prominently highlighted the continued need for SEAD professional learning, and described participant requests for ongoing coaching and advising. Initially, embedded classroom coaching sessions were scheduled. The pandemic forced the transition from in-person sessions to virtual sessions in March 2020, and through quickly adapting to meet participant needs, the circumstances gave rise to video chatting and email support (Mindful SEAD, 2020a). The initiative was further modified for greater benefit to participants, and coaching and advising sessions occurred weekly or as requested by participants. The outcome proved significantly positive.

Mindful SEAD provided weekly group coaching and advising sessions via Facebook Live. During these sessions participants could watch a coaching/training session in the live feed, and participate in the comment area. This strategy proved to be very beneficial as the reach of these live sessions spanned much greater than the 42 participants as evidenced in the reach of the 190 to 560 individuals. (Mindful SEAD, 2020a, p. 5)

The positive response and request for more professional learning was considered with the commitment to increase access to educators in rural areas, and a fourth session was scheduled. Unfortunately, this fourth session was also impacted by the pandemic and was subsequently canceled. Highlighting this fourth session was an important exemplar of modeling the SEL competencies. While this session was beyond the scope of the project parameters, the project manager and workshop facilitators were compelled by the need for SEAD and adult SEL professional learning opportunities in rural communities, and intended to offer this valuable training to educators in an additional rural area.

The SEAD Center: SEAD Hope in the Midst of Crisis

The fourth initiative, the SEAD Center, was developed in direct response to the COVID-19 pandemic. The brunt of the crisis devastated communities in unimaginable ways. The debilitating impact quickly became apparent through daily anecdotal reports about physical and mental health, economic wellbeing, and overwhelming stressors due to the disruption of the most basic of societal structures and conventions, as Schlund and Weissberg describe (2020):

The pandemic has further illuminated the need for SEL to care for ourselves, our students, and their families. COVID-19 has also exposed existing inequities in education and may fundamentally change how we conceive of school. Now more than ever, we must call upon our empathy, resilience, relationship building, and collective resolve as we innovate and rebuild our education systems. (para. 2)

The progress of the three original SEAD initiatives was directly impacted by official directives at local, state, and federal levels, especially for planned in-person professional development. Faced with challenges that few anticipated, March 2020 brought a sudden and overwhelming need to quickly improve and innovate the existing initiatives. From June 2019 to March 2020, the progress of the three original SEAD initiatives helped create the conditions for the NDE's systemic response to COVID-19. The emerging needs were largely relevant to the adult SEL and SEAD work already undertaken by the initiatives. Through novel thinking, existing supports and resources were quickly repurposed and adapted to better meet the needs of educators statewide. The guiding questions were many: How can we use already existing structures and activities to provide guidance and support? What can be leveraged strategically for the greatest impact now, in the fall, and for the long-term?

SEAD: Rooting Optimism

The immediate response to the pandemic included the creation of the SEAD Center at the intersection of three significant conditions: the rich and versatile content of the online modules, the commitment from NDE leadership to repurpose the existing initiatives for a digital platform, and access to a team of experts with the capacity to quickly pivot the work of the SEAD Champions cadre to an online platform. Additionally, established and new positive working relationships were instrumental in ensuring that the quality of the SEAD Center resources was data-based and meaningful.

The SEAD Center pilot study was implemented from June to December 2020. An initial cohort of 100 educators participated in a safe virtual space and statewide community, with access to SEAD information, resources, and guidance. By the end of the pilot, the SEAD Center had added 50 additional participants; thus, more than 150 educators, representing at least 11 school districts, had continuous opportunities for personal growth and depth of professional knowledge rooted in the most current and practical social emotional evidence-based resources. Preliminary feedback suggests that the SEAD Center made a difference, as illustrated by the following participant comment (Mindful SEAD, 2021):

The SEAD Center came into my life at a time when I needed social emotional support the most. This has been a transformative experience for me as well as others who have become connected to me through my journey on self-care. Thank you is not enough.

Additional feedback noted: "I began to see how I could create lessons in the beginning of the year to build relationships with my students to decrease their stress," and, "With so many kids having anxiety especially during this pandemic, SEAD practices are super important to incorporate into the class lessons!" (Mindful SEAD, 2021).

The SEAD Center served to improve educator leadership and effectiveness through quality professional learning and support. Educators described growth facilitated by virtual wellness sessions, training and workshops, state and national guest speakers, expert implementation coaches, a resource library, advising, and access to the SEAD module series. Educators expressed more confidence in creating conditions for adult and youth success. The SEAD initiatives expended the foundation to support more SEAD initiatives to meet Nevada's diverse and growing needs.

NURTURING INSPIRATION YET TO BLOOM: FUTURE DIRECTIONS

A comprehensive evaluation of the SEAD initiatives is underway, with preliminary outcomes informing the strengthening of the SEAD Center. The SEAD Center is becoming an integral part of the Nevada Digital Learning Collaborative, the digital learning platform that can be widely accessed. This transition will facilitate the expansion content for the module series and for professional learning opportunities and resources.

Ongoing collaborations, outreach efforts, and newly established new partnerships will expand the reach of the SEAD Center to school leaders and educators across every role. Preliminary outcomes point to the need for SEAD initiatives to include early learning and development, secondary education, and education preparation programs. Broadened efforts of future initiatives will advocate and educate adults and students in SEAD, and continue to advance MTSS.

A more intentional training-of-trainer model will bolster the expertise of the SEAD Champions Cadre. SEAD Champions will be coached and mentored to facilitate learning activities, such as book studies and wellness sessions. SEAD Champions will increase access to expertise around current topics, and will develop new content on topics such as safe, respectful, and equitable digital learning environments, and the importance of adult SEL on educator recruitment and retention.

Similarly, the scope of the EDLiFE and OSRLE collaboration is expanding beyond the four SEAD initiatives toward more strategic alignment with the NDE Statewide Plan for the Improvement of Pupils (STIP). SEAD work in Nevada will focus on developing and implementing transformative SEL (coined by CASEL in 2019). According to Jagers et al. (2018):

Consistent with the pursuit of educational equity, we recently offered the concept of transformative SEL to reflect our interest in making explicit issues such as power, privilege, prejudice, discrimination, social justice, empowerment, and self-determination in the field of SEL. Transformative SEL connotes a process whereby students and teachers build strong, respectful relationships founded on an appreciation of similarities and differences, learn to critically examine root causes of inequity, and develop collaborative solutions to community and societal problems. (p. 3)

Additionally, an NDE and CASEL partnership has established the Nevada SEL Workforce Development Coalition to increase equity-focused, evidence-based, systemic SEL within college and career readiness initiatives that reinforce Nevada's economic health. This two-year grant (2020 and 2021) has built an alliance including the governor's office, business and industry, school districts, higher education, and the State Department of Education, to explore innovative SEL and workforce readiness practices and policies that meet the growing need for culturally responsive SEL across Nevada's workforce.

The OSRLE has assembled a network of educators and professionals throughout the state to begin considering the adoption of pre-K–12 SEL Standards for the state of Nevada. This work will link the importance of high-quality adult SEL and SEAD, such as that provided by the SEAD Center, with the critical need to ensure that all students receive the knowledge, skills, and abilities to be successful in today's world. Just as a seed takes tending to grow, so does statewide SEAD. What will you plant today?

ACKNOWLEDGMENT

The authors extend our gratitude and appreciation to the Nevada Department of Education and, in particular, to the OSRLE and EDLiFE staff, especially Director Jason Dietrich. In addition, we recognize and thank the Collaborative for Academic, Social, and Emotional Learning (CASEL), Panorama Education, the Nevada Association of School Administrators, and Public Consulting Group, Inc.: Pepper PD for their support. A hearty thank-you to Dr. Tara Madden-Dent and Dr. Deborah Oliver for this opportunity to contribute to work we care deeply about, and to our respective families for their unconditional love and encouragement.

Initiatives reported in this chapter were partially supported by the Nevada Department of Education, Title II, Part A State Activities funds under award 84.367A.

REFERENCES

Academy of Achievement. (1961). *Find my role model*. https://achievement.org/find-my-role-model/

Allensworth, E. M., Farrington, C. A., Gordon, M. F., Johnson, D. W., Klein, K., McDaniel, B., & Nagaoka, J. (2018). *Supporting social, emotional, & academic development: Research implications for educators*. University of Chicago Consortium on School Research.

Allensworth, E. M., & Hart, H. (2018). *How do principals influence student achievement?* University of Chicago Consortium on School Research.

Anti-Defamation League. (n.d.). *What do safe, respectful and inclusive virtual classrooms look like?* https://www.adl.org/education/resources/tools-and-strategies/what-do-safe-respectful-and-inclusive-virtual-classrooms

Aspen Institute. (2017). *Leading for equity: Opportunities for state education chiefs*. https://www.aspeninstitute.org/publications/leading-equity-opportunities-state-education-chiefs/

Aspen Institute. (2018). *Equity statement*. https://assets.aspeninstitute.org/content/uploads/2018/06/Aspen-Education-equity-statement_6.27.2018_Final.pdf

Aspen Institute. (2019). *Integrating social, emotional and academic development: An action guide for school leadership teams*. Education and Society Program. https://www.aspeninstitute.org/publications/integrating-social-emotional-and-academic-development-sead-an-action-guide-for-school-leadership-teams/

Bridgeland, J., Bruce, M., & Hariharan, A. (2013). *The missing piece: A national teacher survey on how social and emotional learning can empower children and transform schools*. Collaborative for Academic, Social, and Emotional Learning. https://www.casel.org/wp-content/uploads/2016/01/the-missing-piece.pdf

Carver-Thomas, D., & Darling-Hammond, L. (2017). *Teacher turnover: Why it matters and what we can do about it*. Learning Policy Institute. https://learningpolicyinstitute.org/sites/default/files/product-files/Teacher_Turnover_REPORT.pdf

Center on Positive Behavioral Interventions and Supports. (2019). *Tier 3*. https://www.pbis.org/pbis/tier-3

Collaborative for Academic, Social, and Emotional Learning. (2005). *Safe and sound: An educational leader's guide to evidence-based social and emotional learning (SEL) programs*. https://casel.org/wp-content/uploads/2016/06/safe-and-sound.pdf

Collaborative for Academic, Social, and Emotional Learning. (2019). *SEL 3 signature practices playbook: A tool that supports systemic SEL*. https://schoolguide.casel.org/resource/three-signature-sel-practices-for-adult-learning/

Collaborative for Academic, Social, and Emotional Learning. (n.d.a). *Examining biases for cultural competence*. https://schoolguide.casel.org/focus-area-2/learn/examining-biases-for-cultural-competence/

Collaborative for Academic, Social, and Emotional Learning. (n.d.b). *Focus area 4 – practice data for continuous improvement*. https://drc.casel.org/practice-continuous-improvement/share-with-stakeholders-and-take-action/

Dahl, M. (2019). *InSPIRE check-in*. Mindful SEAD. https://www.mindfulsead.org/uploads/1/7/1/7/17176054/inspire_check-in_for_srs_copy.pdf

Durlak, J. A., Weissberg, R. P., Dymnicki, A. B., Taylor, R. D., & Schellinger, K. (2011). The impact of enhancing students' social and emotional learning: A meta-analysis of school-based universal interventions. *Child Development, 82*(1), 405–432. doi:10.1111/j.1467-8624.2010.01564.x PMID:21291449

Edutopia. (2010). *Social emotional learning*. https://www.edutopia.org/social-emotional-learning

Every Student Succeeds Act of 2015, Title II Part A, 20 U.S.C. §6601 *et seq*. https://www2.ed.gov/policy/elsec/leg/essa/legislation/title-ii.pdf

Every Student Succeeds Act of 2015, 20 U.S.C. § 8101(42). https://www2.ed.gov/policy/elsec/leg/essa/legislation/title-ii.pdf

Every Student Succeeds Act of 2015, 20 U.S.C. § 8101(44). https://www2.ed.gov/policy/elsec/leg/essa/legislation/title-ii.pdf

Ferguson, R. (2012). Let's find a way to learn about our rights: Communities of practice as "spaces" for women and girls to learn about their human rights. In C. R. Roux (Ed.), *Safe spaces: Human rights education in diverse contexts* (pp. 131–150). Sense. doi:10.1007/978-94-6091-936-7_9

Freeman, J., Sugai, G., Simonsen, B., & Everett, S. (2017). MTSS coaching: Bridging knowing to doing. *Theory into Practice, 56*(1), 29–37. doi:10.1080/00405841.2016.1241946

Frey, N., Fisher, D., & Smith, D. (2019). *All learning is social and emotional: Helping students develop essential skills for the classroom and beyond*. ASCD.

Griggs, C., & Strauss, T. (2018). *iConscious*. https://drcarolegriggs.com/about-iconscious

Hamilton, L. S., & Doss, C. J. (2020). *Supports for social and emotional learning in American schools and classrooms: Findings from the American teacher panel*. RAND Corporation. https://www.rand.org/pubs/research_reports/RRA397-1.html

Immordino-Yang, M. H., Darling-Hammond, L., & Krone, C. (2018). *The brain basis for integrated social, emotional, and academic development: How emotions and social relationships drive learning*. The Aspen Institute National Commission on Social, Emotional, and Academic Development. https://www.aspeninstitute.org/publications/the-brain-basis-for-integrated-social-emotional-and-academic-development/

Jagers, J. J., Rivas-Drake, D., & Borowski, T. (2018). *Equity & social and emotional learning: A cultural analysis*. Collaborative for Academic, Social, and Emotional Learning (CASEL) Frameworks Briefs. https://measuringsel.casel.org/wp-content/uploads/2018/11/Frameworks-Equity.pdf

Jones, S., Bailey, R., Brush, K., & Kahn, J. (2017). Kernels of practice for SEL: Low-cost, low-burden strategies. EASEL Lab, Harvard Graduate School of Education.

Korbey, H. (2017). *The power of being seen: How well do you know your students?* Edutopia. https://www.edutopia.org/article/power-being-seen

Lucas Education Research. (2017). *Home page*. https://www.lucasedresearch.org/

McIntosh, K., & Goodman, S. (2016). *Integrated multi-tiered systems of supports: Blending RTI and PBIS*. Guilford Press. https://www.guilford.com/books/Integrated-Multi-Tiered-Systems-of-Support/McIntosh-Goodman/9781462524747/reviews

Meyers, D. C., Domitrovich, C. E., Dissi, R., Trejo, J., & Greenberg, M. T. (2019). Supporting systemic social and emotional learning with a schoolwide implementation model. *Evaluation and Program Planning*, *73*, 53–61. doi:10.1016/j.evalprogplan.2018.11.005 PMID:30513463

Mindful SEAD. (2020a). *Comprehensive report: Ongoing SEAD professional development*. Author.

Mindful SEAD. (2020b). *Journal and reference tool: Ongoing SEAD professional development*. Author.

Mindful SEAD. (2021). *Comprehensive report: The Nevada Department of Education SEAD Center*. Manuscript in preparation.

Mizell, H. (2010). *Why professional development matters*. Learning Forward. https://learningforward.org/wp-content/uploads/2017/08/professional-development-matters.pdf

National School Reform Faculty. (2020). *Critical friend*. https://nsrfharmony.org/faq-items/critical-friend/

Nevada Association of School Administrators. (2020). *Home page*. https://nvadministrator.org/

Nevada Department of Education. (2018). *Nevada's framework for equitable integrated system of student supports*. http://www.doe.nv.gov/uploadedFiles/ndedoenvgov/content/SafeRespectfulLearning/MTSSGuidanceDoc508.pdf

Nevada Department of Education. (2019a). *SEAD 101 SEAD center* [MOOC]. Pepper PD. https://www.pepperpd.com/courses/NDE/SEAD101/SU2020/cabout

Nevada Department of Education. (2019b, June 26). *Social Emotional, and Academic Development (SEAD)*. http://www.doe.nv.gov/Educator_Licensure/Special_Licenses-Endorsements-Various_Grade_Levels/

Nevada Digital Learning. (2020). *Home page*. https://nvdigitallearning.org/

New Leaders. (2017). *Prioritizing leadership: Opportunities in ESSA for chief state school officers*. https://newleaders.org/wp-content/uploads/2016/10/PrioritizingLeadership_OpportunitiesESSAChief-StateSchoolOfficers.pdf

Podolsky, A., Kini, T., Bishop, J., & Darling-Hammond, L. (2016). *Solving the teacher shortage: How to attract and retain excellent educators*. Learning Policy Institute. https://learningpolicyinstitute.org/sites/default/files/product-files/Solving_Teacher_Shortage_Attract_Retain_Educators_REPORT.pdf

Regional Educational Laboratory (REL) Midwest. (2018). *Integrating a focus on equity into social and emotional learning*. https://ies.ed.gov/ncee/edlabs/infographics/pdf/REL_MW_Integrating_a_Focus_on_Equity_into_Social_and_Emotional_Learning.pdf

Schlund, J., & Weissberg, R. P. (2020). *Leveraging social and emotional learning to support students and families in the time of COVID-19*. Learning Policy Institute. https://learningpolicyinstitute.org/blog/leveraging-social-emotional-learning-support-students-families-covid-19

Shriver, T. P., & Weissberg, R. P. (2020). A response to constructive criticism of social and emotional learning. *Phi Delta Kappan, 101*(7), 52–57. doi:10.1177/0031721720917543

Sierra Nevada University. (2019a). *Comprehensive report: Sierra Nevada College pilot 2019 SEAD leadership summit*. Author.

Sierra Nevada University. (2019b). *SEAD educational leadership summit program and journal*. Author.

Social, Emotional and Academic Development Endorsements. (2019). *NRS 391.019*. https://www.leg.state.nv.us/Register/2018Register/R154-18AP.pdf

Thessin, R. A., & Louis, K. S. (2020, April). The principal's role has changed: Is professional learning keeping up? *The Learning Professional, 41*(2). https://learningforward.org/journal/beyond-the-basics/the-principals-role-has-changed/

World Café Community Foundation. (2015). *Café to go! A quick reference guide for hosting world café*. http://www.theworldcafe.com/wp-content/uploads/2015/07/Cafe-To-Go-Revised.pdf

Yoder, N., Martinez-Black, T., Dusenbury, L., & Weissberg, R. P. (2020). *Systemic social and emotional learning for states: CASEL state theory of action*. Collaborative for Academic, Social, and Emotional Learning. https://casel.org/wp-content/uploads/2020/03/State-Theory-of-Action-Mar.pdf

Yoder, N., Posamentier, J., Godek, D., Seibel, K., & Dusenbury, L. (2020). *From response to reopening: State efforts to elevate social and emotional learning during the pandemic*. CASEL Committee for Children. https://www.cfchildren.org/wp-content/uploads/policy-advocacy/casel-cfc-covid19-response-plan-brief.pdf

KEY TERMS AND DEFINITIONS

Community of Practice: A group of like-minded individuals coming together for a common purpose or goal in support of one another.

COVID-19 Pandemic: The global outbreak of the SARS-CoV-2 virus that caused major disruptions in everyday life where society came to a standstill for several months.

Critical Friend: The role of facilitating reflection and growth by creating opportunities for deep and honest examination aimed to improve outcomes, and encouraging actionable steps to realize change.

Equity: The ability to recognize that each person is an individual who may have different needs, values, or beliefs that should be respected, understood, and accommodated.

Multi-Tiered System of Supports (MTSS): A structure that provides and defines three levels of supports. The first level is global supports, the next level is targeted supports, and the final level is personalized supports.

Social Emotional Academic Development (SEAD): The connection between academics and social emotional skills that emphasize whole-child development in support of positive outcomes for students.

Social Emotional Learning (SEL): The process by which one gains the knowledge, skills, and abilities to successfully navigate society and the world.

Social Emotional Learning (SEL) Competencies: A set of five qualities developed by the Collaborative for Academic, Social and Emotional Learning (CASEL) that seek to develop one's capacity to understand, relate, and regulate oneself and one's interactions with others.

Systemic: Considering the effect on the whole, such as state-level decisions that affect all districts, and district-level decisions that affect all schools.

Transformative SEL: Focuses on being more reflective and increasing understanding of the history of the dominant culture and society, and how it impacts and affects equity and racial justice today in order to be more responsive in advocating for change.

Chapter 6
The Social and Emotional Issues of Teacher's Professional Identity Development

Michelle A. Arroyo
University of Nevada, Las Vegas, USA

ABSTRACT

Teacher professional identity is an important factor in understanding professional lives and career decision making. Teacher professional identity may affect motivation, effectiveness, and most importantly, social and emotional well-being. Teacher identity lacks clarity with regards to a definition. This could contribute to the reason that it has not been studied as a key element for teacher social and emotional wellness during professional identity development. The process of how teachers view themselves as teachers and how their developing professional identity is shaped by their personal identity development and social identity connections has implications on their careers.

INTRODUCTION

Identity is approached from a socio-cultural point of view, which holds that teachers do not develop their identity alone and in a 'vacuum,' but rather in a context that brings social and cultural forces to allow that development (Holland & Lachicotte, 2007). Teachers develop and dynamically maintain their identity in relation to the 'collective regard' that others have for their role (Holland & Lachicotte, 2007). Teacher identity development is a process that may involve periods of exploration, uncertainty, and conflict, eventuating in some incorporation of personal identity with professional identity (Meijer, 2011).

Teachers' professional identity is an important factor in understanding their professional lives and career decision making. Teachers' professional identity may affect their motivation, effectiveness and most importantly, their social and emotional well-being. Teacher identity lacks clarity with regards to a definition. This could contribute to the reason that it has not been studied as a key element for teacher social and emotional wellness during professional identity development. The process of how teachers

DOI: 10.4018/978-1-7998-6728-9.ch006

view themselves as teachers and how their developing professional identity is shaped by their personal identity development and social identity connections has implications on their careers.

Social and emotional learning (SEL) commonly refers to a process through which people acquire and effectively apply knowledge, attitudes, and skills necessary to understand and manage emotions, set and achieve positive goals, feel and show empathy for others, establish and maintain positive relationships, and make responsible decisions (Weissberg, Durlak, Domitrovich, & Gullotta, 2015). SEL has been studied to understand the impact and influences the SEL efforts have on academic, social, and emotional competence development of adults.

School climate plays a critical role in teacher social and emotional development. Being a part of a culture shapes how the teachers fit in and what their roles may be. Working with other educators and building positive working relationships empowers teachers. Having mentors, strong student relationships, and a supportive administration has proven to be key components to teacher well-being. Administrators that include teachers in decision making and foster a positive school culture are more likely to retain teachers at their schools because the teachers feel appreciated and included.

SEC is the capacity to coordinate cognition, affect, and behavior that allows individuals to thrive in diverse cultures and contexts and achieve specific tasks and positive developmental outcomes. CASEL identified five core SEC clusters: self-awareness, self-management, social awareness, relationship skills, and responsible decision making (CASEL, 2013, 2015; Weissberg et al., 2015). The CASEL 5 emphasize intrapersonal skills and attitudes (i.e., self-awareness and self-management), interpersonal skills and attitudes (i.e., social awareness and relationship skills), and making ethical and principled choices in personal and social situations (i.e., responsible decision making) (Mahoney, Weissberg, Greenberg, Dusenbury, Jagers, Niemi, Schlinger, Schlund, Shriver, VanAusdal, & Yoder, 2020).

Current research studies do not demonstrate the extent to which teacher identity development shapes teachers and their practice and can be transferred to social and emotional wellness. Teacher identity development is a complex and individualized process. The purpose of this chapter is to contribute to the body of knowledge identifying how teachers' social and emotional wellness contribute to their professional identity development and the desire to remain in the teaching profession.

Teacher Identity

According to Collaborative for Academic, Social, and Emotional Learning (CASEL), Social and emotional learning is an integral part of education and human development. CASEL states that people acquire and apply knowledge, skills, and attitudes to develop healthy identities. Teacher identity development as a concept in academic literature has grown over the years. During the last two decades, much research has been done on the nature and characteristics (Rodgers & Scott, 2008) as well as the development of teachers' professional identity as the result of the interaction between personal and professional aspects of teaching (Kissling, 2014; Meijer, 2011). Interest has focused on the formation and development of teacher identity. In the Handbook of Research on Teacher Education, Rogers and Scott (2008) summarize identity formation.

Contemporary conceptions of identity share four basic assumptions: (1) that identity is dependent upon and formed within multiple contexts which bring social, cultural, political, and historical forces to bear upon that formation; (2) that identity is formed in relationship with others and involves emotions; (3)

that identity is shifting, unstable, and multiple; and (4) that identity involves the construction and re-construction of meaning through stories over time (p. 733).

Becoming a teacher is a process that results from the interaction between personal beliefs, feelings, and norms. It also includes professional demands from teacher education institutes and schools, including broadly accepted values and standards about teaching (Beijaard, Meijer, & Verloop, 2004). This process may involve periods of exploration, uncertainty, and conflict, eventuating in some incorporation of personal identity with professional identity (Meijer et al., 2011). Teacher identity is likely to undergo considerable development as teachers progress through their careers.

Teachers' life experiences appear to be strongly interwoven with their work as teachers in the classroom. It is one's identity, the perception of oneself as a teacher, and the teacher one wishes to become that guides the behavior and development of teachers (Pinnegar, 2005). It is the personal attributes in becoming a teacher (such as one's own beliefs and previous learning experiences as a student) that seems to stimulate teachers' professional learning and identity development (Darling-Hammond, 2010). SEL helps to advance healthy identity development through authentic learning environments and experiences that feature trusting and collaborative relationships, rigorous and meaningful curriculum and instruction, and ongoing evaluation. (CASEL, 2020).

Learning communities consist of teachers working together and sharing common students, areas of responsibilities, roles, interests, or goals. Learning communities focus on internal and external expertise and resources to strengthen practice and student learning. These opportunities to work with other educators prevent teachers from feeling isolated. When teachers participate in learning communities, they meet, talk, and work with others who see teaching "as a way to live in the world" (Brown & Wynn, 2009; Cochran-Smith, 2004). Teachers who participate in learning communities feel supported and valued.

Teachers generally love their students. They seek professional development to improve their abilities to reach students, and they sacrifice their personal time, and often money, to ensure their students get what they need to succeed in school. Teacher/student relationships are a key component of the teaching profession. Many teachers may become frustrated by aspects of their jobs, but the actual experience and craft of teaching and the relationships with their students are usually the reasons they remain in the profession and continue to provide support to their students (Cochran-Smith, 2004; Freedman & Appleman, 2008).

The quality of leadership can influence teacher wellness and social interactions within a school. In fact, teachers often identify the quality of administrative support as more important to their decision than salaries. Brown and Wynn, (2009), found that improvements in school leadership were strongly related to reductions in teacher turnover. Administration builds positive working relationships and empowers teachers. High levels of administrative support and clearly communicated expectations takes many forms, including providing emotional and instructional support as well as support with instructional resources, teaching materials, and professional learning opportunities (Boyd et al., 2011; Geiger & Pivovarova, 2018; Hughes, 2012; Swars, Meyers, Mays & Lack, 2009). Brown and Wynn (2009) discovered that principals who provided conditions and resources needed to support teachers in their continuous learning, growth, and emotional and professional development were able to reduce teacher isolation, increase teacher responsibility and understanding, and improve teacher satisfaction, morale, and commitment.

Principals can initiate conversations with teachers, observe instruction, provide feedback, monitor progress, and facilitate relationships. Vierstraete's (2005) study suggested fostering of reflective practice within a mentoring relationship that includes the principal, the mentor and the new teacher is important to the ongoing professional learning and social and emotional development of the new teacher within the school community. First year teachers, who were in schools where the socialization by, and interactions with, the principal focused on student learning, teaching practice, and fostering relationships, encountered fewer problems. "Principal support is essential, whether it be in attitude or actions. Lower levels of teacher attrition and migration have consistently been found in schools with more administrative support for teachers" (Brown & Wynn, 2009, p. 58).

Varied theoretical approaches relate to teacher identity; some researchers stress the social and cultural nature of identity, whereas other researchers focus on its broad and narrative nature. Most contemporary approaches, however, agree that identity is constructed in a social context and that rather than being stable and fixed it is shifting and dynamic (Rodgers & Scott, 2008). Teachers who identify with their teaching role are emotionally attached to this role, and it informs their worldview (Holland & Lachicotte, 2007). When one becomes emotionally attached to the teacher role, that role becomes part of who that person is; it becomes an organizing element in teachers' lives (Akkerman & Meijer, 2011). The development of a teacher identity is an ongoing process of interpretation and reinterpretation of who one considers oneself to be and who one would like to become (Beijaard, Meijer & Verloop, 2004).

When defining teacher identity, one could infer that it is the personal and cultural characteristics and experiences of teachers. Teachers are diverse individuals with varied experiences that brought them to teaching. Teachers have their own priority needs, desires, and social and emotional expectations. "Professional identity thus is a set of attributes that are imposed upon the teaching profession either by outsiders or members of the teaching fraternity itself. It provides a shared set of attributes, values and so on so that enable the differentiation of one group from another" (Sachs, 2001. P. 153).

Some research suggests that identity is dependent upon the contexts in which teachers immerse themselves: schools, teacher education programs, study groups, family, religious groups, political parties and so forth (Gee, 2001; Beijaard et al.,2004). Gee also pointed out that relationship is essential to identity primarily because to have an identity one must be recognized as a particular "kind of person" by others. "The 'kind of person' one is recognized as 'being,' at a given time and place, can change from moment to moment in the interaction, can change from context to context, and of course, can be ambiguous or unstable" (p. 99).

Friesen and Besley (2013) examined the development of teacher identity in a cohort of first year student teachers from a developmental and social psychological perspective. Friesen and Besley hypothesized that greater personal identity development would be associated with increased professional teacher identity. The study found that there is potential value of pursuing an understanding of professional teacher identity as a developmental and social psychological process because those who have a well-formed sense of personal identity are more likely to be ready to begin the process of forming a professional identity and have a stronger social and emotional connection.

The findings by Friesen and Besley (2013) may have a positive effect on understanding identity regarding teachers' social and emotional wellness. Friesen and Besley suggest that teachers be encouraged early in their training to explicitly examine their personal beliefs, philosophies, and life-course experiences, and to compare critically and reflectively these to the philosophies and ideologies of their teacher educators, supervisors, and/or mentors. Teachers' professional identities can develop through a productive dialog in contrast to the adoption of rigid and I assumptions which can lead to dissatisfaction in the teaching profession and ultimately a social and/or emotional breakdown.

Freedman and Appleman (2008) followed the development of teacher identities and career choices of a cohort of graduates to identify elements that would help teachers stay in urban schools. The idea was that in developing professional identities in the teacher education program, the teachers would remain in high poverty, low performing urban schools. The findings indicated that the program components influenced the teachers as they developed, refined, and tested their emerging teacher identity. The key component to their identity development was the social aspect of forming a cohort. Freedman and Appleman found that the teachers in the cohort formed professional identities together through support. Additionally, 96 percent of the cohort stayed teaching in high poverty, urban school settings after the first year with 92 percent staying at their same school.

Teacher Experiences

Many aspects of teaching have been researched to understand how teachers develop an understanding of themselves and their social and emotional wellness and how it relates to teacher professional identity development and retention. Positive identity transformation developed through social and emotional wellness could possibly be one of the most important intended learning outcomes for teacher retention and as such needs deliberate and focused attention. A study was conducted with teachers who had longevity in Title 1 schools in a southwestern state school district. Title 1 was first enacted in 1965 as part of the "War on Poverty." Title 1 was part of the Elementary and Secondary Education Act (ESEA) to ensure equal educational opportunities for all students and close the achievement gap between poor and affluent children. All students should have a fair, equal, and significant opportunity to obtain a high-quality education and Title 1 schools try to provide those opportunities. The purpose was to understand the reasons these teachers have remained in the teaching profession, how they understand their professional identity, and if that identity development is significant to their social and emotional well-being.

The study consisted of 5 white female teachers and 2 white male teachers. Teachers ranged in age from 36-56. Six of the teachers graduated from a traditional four-year program and one teacher completed a one-year certificate program. Two teachers teach Kindergarten-2nd grade, four teachers teach 4th-5th grade, and one teacher is a specialist teaching the gifted and talented program (GATE). No teachers of color offered to participate at the time of the study. Teachers told their own unique story and were given pseudonyms for confidentiality and privacy. The teachers are Lisa, Shelby, Melissa, Shannon, Molly, Mark, and Nick. The teachers' longevity in the classroom ranged from six to sixteen years with all teachers working in Title 1 schools. The teachers worked at Title 1 schools either throughout or during most of their careers.

Past research has provided evidence for many factors that influence teacher retention but has not demonstrated the extent to which teacher identity development shapes teachers and their practice and can be transferred to retention. The role of social and emotional wellness of teachers has not been studied as a key component to professional identity development to help influence teacher retention. The development of a teacher's identity is an ongoing process of interpretation and reinterpretation of who one considers oneself to be and who one would like to become (Beijaard, Meijer & Verloop, 2004). Rodgers and Scott (2008) described external and internal aspects of identity formation. They suggested that relationships and contexts are external, and stories and emotions are internal aspects of identity formation. Rodgers and Scott propose that the internal aspects are the "meaning-making" aspects of identity development.

The following stories are from seven teachers who volunteered to participate in a study and meaning was constructed from their stories. The purpose was to understand the reasons these teachers have remained in the teaching profession, how they understand their professional identity, if their social and emotional wellness contributed to their identity, and if that identity development is significant to their retention. Each teacher provided reasons for remaining at their current school and how their identities developed throughout their career. The teachers discussed social and emotional issues that they have experienced throughout their careers.

Lisa

Lisa knew she wanted to become a teacher since high school. She herself had a teacher that inspired her during her junior and senior year of high school. She saw the impact this teacher made on her life as well as her friends and decided that she wanted to do the same thing. However, during college, she became tired of school and decided to enter the military. She was active duty for 5 years and when she returned, she spent a year "becoming a civilian again." Once again, Lisa knew that she wanted to be a teacher and returned to school to finish her degree in Elementary Education.

Upon graduation, Lisa could not find a job in her Midwestern state, so she applied in a southwestern state and was called within four hours by her first principal and hired to teach 3rd grade at a Title 1 school. Lisa left her family to move to the southwest to begin her teaching career. Once school started, Lisa found that her student teaching had not prepared her for the type of environment she was in. Additionally, she was not provided a mentor and felt she had no support. Her teaching team consisted of her, another first-year teacher, and a long-term sub working on her teaching degree. Lisa remembers crying in one another's classrooms because they were new and felt so lost.

I remember calling my parents on my drive home every single day crying, and I'm a tough girl! I don't just break down and cry for no reason, but I was just like, what am I doing here? Did I make the right choice? (Lisa, 2019).

Lisa's father encouraged her to stay and finish out the year. She agreed because she does not see herself as a quitter. She finished her first year of teaching relatively happy. Lisa remained at this Title 1 school for three more years. During the 4th year, however, tension arose between her and the assistant principal. Her principal was having some personal issues, so Lisa was forced to deal with the assistant principal during her workdays. She describes the situation as "hostile" and "crazy." Lisa felt that she was being personally attacked by this assistant principal and it affected her desire to remain teaching at this school, but she did not want to leave the profession. Lisa began looking for another job at another school.

I enjoy teaching, I just didn't enjoy her. I was like, as long as I can get to a different school; nothing can be worse than this school (Lisa, 2019).

Lisa applied at another Title 1 School and was hired to teach 5th grade at School A. There, Lisa says her team is good and one of the other teachers is now her best friend.

I'm good here. I like this place. I'm getting friends, I have people that actually care, my admin seems supportive, and it is just much better (Lisa, 2019).

Shelby

Shelby knew since she was in 2nd grade that she wanted to become a teacher. She always loved kids and knew she would be either a pediatrician or a teacher. Shelby realized that she did not want to give shots or do surgery, so she knew that being a teacher would be the way for her to work with kids. Although she knew since the 2nd grade that teaching was for her, it took her many years to realize her dream. In high school she was good in math and received straight A's in accounting, so she pursued a career in accounting.

While going to school to become an accountant, Shelby met with a career counselor who told her that she should be a teacher and an accountant would be the worst thing for her. She decided to leave school and get a job. She worked for a home builder in accounts payable for fifteen years. Shelby decided to go back to school part time to once again, pursue her teaching degree. While taking classes, she met her husband, got married, and then got pregnant with their daughter. School would once again be placed on hold as she did not want to be away from her daughter. Shelby was laid off from her job and her husband actively supported her returning to school to obtain her teaching degree. He told her she needed to go back to school full time and earn her degree.

Shelby graduated but had trouble getting a job mid-year. She was a substitute teacher at her children's school which she dreamed of working at because she knew so many people and considered the teachers her friends. During the summer, the principal called her a month before school started and asked her if she wanted a job teaching 3rd grade. She graciously accepted. This was the first Title 1 school that she worked at.

Shelby says that her first year was a great year. There were instructional coaches, she had a mentor, and she says her principal was very positive.

Everything was a challenge, but I had a great grade level. I had a mentor who was amazing, and she helped me so much. Everyone says the first year is the hardest, I think the first year was almost easiest because they were so supportive (Shelby, 2019).

Shelby found that teaching was more challenging than college had prepared her for. She dealt with a student with ADHD, she had to find time for testing, student interventions, and many other things that she did not feel ready for. She realized during this first year that there was more to teaching than she originally thought. During the second year at this school, the principal moved, and a new principal was hired. Shelby said the new principal was not supportive at all. She managed to stay for three years but says that each year it was miserable and got worse and worse. By the end of year three, Shelby knew she had to leave.

When she moved to School B, three of her teacher friends moved with her. Once again, she found a supportive principal and she really liked him. She was learning a lot and appreciated the support she was receiving. However, she was not getting along with her grade level chair. She found it hard to communicate with her and the support was not there. Despite liking her administration and her grade level, the grade level chair was making her doubt herself.

I'm like, maybe teaching is not for me. Maybe I should leave because I didn't have the support that I needed in my grade level and I felt like I was not doing a good job, that was when I really started saying maybe I should find something else (Shelby, 2019).

In addition, Shelby was working extremely long hours, nights, and weekends. The time away from her family was taking a toll on her. She was feeling guilty and felt like she was putting other kids in front of her own. She considered moving to a private or charter school. However, the more she thought about it, the more she knew she wanted to stay in a Title 1 school.

I knew I wanted to stay in Title 1 because these kids, they just needed so much and for the most part, they are so sweet and the parents look up to you as a teacher, and that's where I feel most comfortable, in that demographic (Shelby, 2019).

Melissa

Melissa teaches at her "Dream School" and she hopes to continue teaching 2nd grade there. Melissa has taught at three Title 1 schools in her career. As a child, Melissa pretended to teach her stuffed animals and says she wanted to be a teacher as long as she can remember. Becoming a teacher was "something that was always there." Her other career option was becoming a mortician, but there was not a school close by, so she went with her first choice which was teaching.

Melissa sought a degree in child development for three years. She moved and got a job that prevented her from completing her observation hours and other requirements for her teaching degree. At the time money and keeping a roof over her head was her driving force, so she changed her major to Criminal Justice. Melissa was laid off from her job, so she took a couple years to think and "soul search." She decided to go back to teaching.

Melissa pursued her master's degree in Education and was given the opportunity to participate in a cohort program that allowed her to complete her practicums and her student teaching in one year. She was hired at a Title 1 school. She stayed there for two years but felt that there were too many "cliques" at the school. Additionally, the office manager was sharing her personal business and made it an uncomfortable work environment. Melissa found herself at another Title 1 school while pregnant with her daughter. She was in the third year of her probation period and was worried that taking time off would add another year of probation to her, but her principal "was a blessing" during this time and she was not retained on probation. However, when she returned to school, things changed within the school and with the principal.

It was really weird, it was almost like he wasn't running the school, it was whoever his "pets" were at the time, so to speak. We got a couple of student teachers and, I'm sure there's more to it, but just from my personal perspective, when these two people came, it changed everything, and it wasn't for the better (Melissa, 2019).

A year later, the two student teachers were hired, and Melissa says the principal acted like, "they walked on water." They were given student teachers to mentor in their first year of teaching; a job they were not ready for, nor did they do. That year, everything declined. Melissa stayed for two more years, but the situation continued to get worse. During her third year, the principal announced his retirement, so she was going to give it a chance because of new people coming in. However, a new opportunity would present itself to her.

Melissa was hired at another Title 1 school. She taught kindergarten and 1st grade there. Melissa is the first to admit that she is a very private person, so she does not let a lot of people in. She even keeps a little wall up with her students and families because she does not want her heart to get "to involved." She sets boundaries. However, she credits some of her relationships within the school for helping her stay.

Shannon

Shannon has been a teacher for 8 years and has taught 4th and 5th grade, but currently teaches GATE (Gifted and Talented Education). She has taught at two Title 1 schools. Shannon did not know she wanted to be a teacher until she was in college. She was a biology major for three years working towards becoming a veterinarian. One summer, she went to work for a veterinarian, and she disliked it. At that point, she did not know what she was going to do. Her mother encouraged her to take other classes to try and decide what she would like to pursue. She randomly took an education class and loved it.

Shannon was hired at a Title 1 school for her first year of teaching and found herself crying every day. She felt unprepared for the school because it was in a rough area of the city and the kids were very low academically. She did not feel like she was helping them.

I felt like I wasn't good at it and I was just crying all the time. I had a kid that was banging his head into the wall every day. I had another kid who attacked me because I took his butterfly necklace and I had to get him moved out of my room. It was kind of crazy (Shannon, 2019).

The assistant principal took her under his wing so she would go into his office and sit down and cry. She is surprised she made it as a teacher. However, she really loved the kids and the principal helped her a lot, otherwise, she would not have made it in the profession.

The assistant principal was very involved, and he came into Shannon's room to watch her teach. He suggested she work on teaching one subject well each year and then add another subject the following year. She felt this made it more manageable for her to think about it by subject instead of "everything at once." Her second year, she felt more confident by focusing on one subject at a time. She felt better, got more creative, and did things that were fun with the students.

After two years, Shannon changed schools. The supportive principal from her first school was moving and asked her to come with him. Additionally, she moved because she did not have a lot of friends at the school and it was far from her home. She said because all the teachers were traveling to get to the school, they did not try to be friends with one another. Shannon was hired at a school closer to home. It had a younger staff and she made some of her best friends there and they are still her best friends to this day. Having friends made work fun because her and the other teachers could laugh hysterically at everything that the kids did and the "craziness."

Her sixth year of teaching, Shannon had the hardest student of her life and she almost quit that year.

So, I felt like I was, you know, pretty experienced at that point, but I had never had… I'd had lots of behavior problems, but the student was just extreme. He attacked other students all the time. He attacked me all the time. I mean he tried to stab kids with scissors, he tried to stab me with scissors and tacks (Shannon, 2019).

She could not teach because of this student disrupting class with chanting, explosive behaviors, and tearing apart her classroom. Shannon lost confidence because this student's behaviors became worse and she could not manage them. Eventually, she helped him get placed in a self-contained classroom for emotionally disturbed students.

Shannon still had a good relationship with her principal so that helped her. She felt valued because she was given a student teacher. To her, that meant her administration trusted her and it made her feel good about what she was doing and that she was respected as a teacher. Giving her a student teacher made her want to do a good job. Then, something changed. Her and the principal began "butting heads." Shannon does not know why, but he started making her "a little bit miserable." She felt that he was purposefully stacking her classes with difficult students. Other teachers had told her that he did that all the time, but she did not believe them. She had a little argument with him and the next year, she had the worst class. He also moved her down a grade level against her will. Shannon almost quit, but she was very invested in teaching.

Once you get past 10 years, I think it's hard to quit. Before 10 years, I think it would have been much easier for me to quit, but once I'm past 10 years, then it's harder. You're just so invested. That being your career at that point that it's such a change. I don't even know at that point what I would have done (Shannon, 2019).

Shannon has been at this Title 1 school for 8 years. She has gone through three principals, but feels she is important to her new principal. She likes to feel important and this principal relies on her a lot for curriculum and has her help. The principal has Shannon on the leadership team, the RTI team, and she does a lot of "extra stuff" for being a GATE teacher. She appreciates and likes it.

Molly

My mom always tells the story that I had been in preschool for all of 15 seconds and I was like, I'm going to be a teacher when I grow up (Molly, 2019).

When Molly was applying to colleges after high school, elementary education was automatically what she went to. She never wanted to be in a different line of work. It had always been about kids for her. In fact, in high school, she participated in a program that allowed her to teach for a day. She took over a freshman biology course when she was a senior.

Molly taught preschool to pay her way through college. She loved it and loved the kids. She enjoyed what she learned from them. During student teaching, she had no transportation, so she had to take a bus to get to her school which was far away from where she lived. The university did not want her to have a job during student teaching, and she was struggling to pay her rent and buy food. The cohort leader that supervised her asked her if she was sure she really wanted to teach. That was enough to shake her confidence.

Because I was struggling just to get through life, it did show up in my teaching. Looking back on it and I can see it. It showed up in everything I was doing, but instead of saying, "What's going on? What can I do to help?" He just went off on me and I was like, nope, shut down, and walked away (Molly, 2019).

Molly needed one class to graduate, but she walked away and moved back home with her family. She worked at another preschool and remained there for 10 years teaching the toddler program.

Molly felt she was not going anywhere in her career, so she needed a change and moved with her brother to the southwest. She told her boss at the preschool that she was moving. Her boss knew people in the city she was moving to, so she got her an interview. She was hired as a kindergarten aid at a preschool. When she got to the school, the kindergarten teacher had quit and since Molly had enough college credits, the preschool put her in as a long-term substitute teacher. She taught kindergarten for three years as a long-term substitute teacher. After three years, the preschool brought in another teacher to co-teach with her. Molly and the new teacher had very different styles and she felt the preschool was not standing up for her, so Molly transferred to another school within the company.

Molly went back to school while working at the new preschool and they helped pay for her to finish her undergraduate program. She had to retake some courses that did not transfer over, so she was able to work and get financial assistance. As soon as she finished her degree, she was immediately hired. When the first Title 1 school called her, she was not prepared to teach there. It was 99% ELL and she felt that they needed a more experienced teacher who knew what they were doing to help these students. She declined the position. Another school called and the science teacher at that school had been her science professor in college, so she recommended Molly to the assistant principal and she was hired.

During her first couple of years, she explains "I got my feet under me." She had basal readers and a math program, so she did her best to figure everything out that she needed. When the basal readers were no longer meeting the needs of the students, she was part of a group that pushed interactive read aloud stories and other new ideas. She had immediately gone back to school to work on her master's degree upon completing her bachelor's degree. She worked hard to develop a solid program in 5th grade to help her students as well as other 5th graders.

We went through a couple bosses, some up people, some good stuff, some bad stuff, but nothing was overly major. I loved my kids. Everybody knew me. Everything was good until about four years ago. My then boss just started acting really psycho, not just to me, but to a lot of people. I was just done and so it was like, okay, I'm going to transfer (Molly, 2019).

Before Molly left, a new principal came in so she hoped things would improve. However, things only got worse. The new principal watched tv on her phone all day, she would not discipline students, and she "let the mean girls run loose." Her 5th grade team was together for 8 years, but last year, the entire team left. During her 14 years at this school, she says she had 4 different principals and 5 assistant principals.

Mark

Mark did not know he wanted to become a teacher until he was almost finished with college. He was a student athlete and played for his university and was also drafted to a minor league team. During his offseason, he wanted to make some extra money, and someone suggested that he substitute teach. He was a substitute for high school students and enjoyed it. During this time, he never was a substitute teacher in elementary school.

After three years of playing sports, he weighed the decision if he should keep playing or get back into school. He had already attended school for three years, so he considered getting into communications. After some consideration, he decided that he really could not do anything with that degree, so he needed something else.

I had better get into something that'll be solid, recession proof. I knew I could get a job right away. I knew I could get a job right away because they really, at that time, and still do, they needed teachers. So, I was like, that sounds good. I think I can do this (Mark, 2020).

While going to school and substitute teaching, Mark worked in the afterschool program at his current school. He spoke with the principal and asked if he could complete his student teaching there. The principal worked it out and he completed his student teaching in a third-grade classroom. When the school year ended, there were several positions that opened for the following year, so he was hired to teach 5th grade. Mark did not want 5th grade and at first, he declined the offer.

Then I said, what am I doing? I should just be happy that I'm getting hired. He's offering me a job, whatever he wants, I'll do. I called him up and said, okay, I'll do fifth (Mark, 2020).

Mark worried that he would not be able to connect with 5th graders as easily as he did with 3rd graders. He got an extremely rough group with challenging behaviors. Because he was new, he did not really know what he was doing, he just tried to find his way and made it through the year somehow. He received advice from mentor teachers, and they told him to give himself a couple of years before it would really "start to stick." The advice resounded with him. The following year he switched to 4th grade and fell in love on day one.

Mark always had a lot of support at his school because of not only working the afterschool program, but also student teaching there. He knew a lot of teachers right away. Anytime he needed something or was frustrated, he had a lot of people that he could lean on and that would help him out. It was mostly having people tell him everything was going to be okay.

Overall, Mark says he has had a great career. The toughest part of the job for him is the unrealistic expectations put on teachers. The challenges come when people "higher up" place demands about how to teach. If they are not in the classroom, then they do not know what is going on. He feels fortunate to have gotten along with all his administrators and that they have been great. He was with the administrator that hired him for 13 years. When he left, another principal came in for 4 years and they got along well. Now, his principal is the former assistant principal, and they have a nice relationship.

I haven't had that administrator problem where you hear about like butting heads. I've been very fortunate. I know how fortunate I am. I was fortunate to end up here, how it worked out. I've had administrators that I've gotten along with. At the same time though, just because I got along with them, it doesn't mean that I always agreed with them. That's the place I'm at. That's why I think that I love it because I don't let it bother me (Mark, 2020).

Nick

Nick thought about teaching since he was in high school, but he pursued other things first. He was originally in broadcasting. He was not moving up as fast as he had hoped, so he thought about education again. Nick wanted to be a high school teacher. He became a substitute teacher to "try it out." He subbed at elementary schools and decided that elementary was more fun than high school. He went to a university to obtain his teaching certificate. He worked in the classroom during the day and took classes at night for one year. Each course was five to six weeks long.

After Nick received his teaching credentials, he was hired in the city he lived in, but then a new principal came into that school and brought his own teachers. There was no longer a job for Nick. He knew other states were looking for teachers and his wife said she would move if he got a job. One month before school started, he was hired to start teaching 3rd grade at a Title 1 school.

So, I told my wife, I'm going to start in August. We've got to put our house for sale. I moved out by myself until the end of January, without my little kids, without my wife. It was tough. I flew back a lot, but it was hard. They were babies still. They were little and it was hard, but we managed (Nick, 2020).

His first year was challenging. He worked at a school with a lot of transiency. Nick is the first to admit his behavior management was lacking and he felt overwhelmed. He had many students who could not speak English, could not read, and who saw stuff that "little kids shouldn't see." He says it was rough. A new assistant principal was hired, and she was the one to help Nick survive his first year. He also had a lot of teacher support at the school.

By the second year, Nick was the principal's favorite. She gave him a great class his third year. That was his "best class ever." The fourth year, something changed. His principal became mean with everybody and called him a "know it all." He did not understand why she would do this since she would praise him in front of the staff and discuss strategies he was using. She decided to move him to 1st grade without his consent, so he left and went to another Title 1 school.

One thing that Nick really enjoyed at the new school, was that there was a lot of male teachers, so it was easy for him to bond with people. He was able to see men's teaching styles. He saw a woman's style often, but not a man's style. That opened his eyes a little bit because there were so many men teachers at this new school. He made a lot of friends and had support from his administrator and colleagues. The problem Nick had with this school was that it was very far from his home. He wanted to work closer to his house and possibly at his child's school. That finally happened for him.

Nick went to teach 4th grade at a high-performing school. His first two years went well, but then the principal got upset with him and made his last three years there terrible for him. He made a mistake using social media to describe his rough teaching day and the principal was not happy about it. He deleted the post and apologized, but the principal had already changed her opinion about him.

It was never the same. I was always cringing whenever she came in the room because I knew she probably thought I was a low dirt bag. I didn't mean to be. Again, I couldn't convince her that I wasn't making fun of a kid, it was just the situation. I deleted it, I apologized, I didn't spread it around (Nick, 2020).

Nick now teaches at another school and he says it is a blessing. There is not a lot of parental supporters and comradery is missing between the teachers, but he has a new principal and says she is great. He enjoys working with his current grade level. He teaches science and social studies to the 4th graders. He says he has a good group of students. If the principal does not "go crazy on me" he does not plan on leaving.

Social and Emotional Contributors

Each of these teachers shared similar stories; they all struggled during their first couple of years, they all looked for support, and, more importantly, they all remained in the classroom. There are many factors that contribute to teacher identity development, but these stories have shown that there is external as well as internal factors that can influence identity based on social and emotional support. External factors refer to the teachers' social environment, family, friends, co-workers, and school community. Internal factors refer to the teacher's perceptions, attitudes, motivation, feelings, and roles that connect to social and emotional support.

Teachers discussed social and emotional issues that influenced their retention and through those stories, their identities were discovered. Teachers shared stories of the importance of feeling loved and respected by students, parents, colleagues, and administration. A significant reason that teachers remain teaching is due to a supportive administration. The stories about the supportive administration and feeling respected overlapped. The teachers did a lot of self-evaluation and during their toughest times on themselves, they found ways to make connections with students. Even at times when their identity was that of an ineffective teacher, they felt like they were making an impact on the students' lives, so they looked for emotional support and remained teaching. Teachers can be critical about their teaching, but they always remained optimistic. The optimism came from the relationships they had with their students. Self-evaluative and optimism were two different components of their identity and both connected with student relationships. Student relationships are a reason for their strong social and emotional connection to the profession. The teachers are all dedicated to teaching and the students. That part of their identity was evident. Social and emotional support through the relationships with other teachers is a main factor of teacher dedication. The support they receive from other teachers and their friendships play a critical role in their retention.

Two common areas of emotional support that arose in both identity and retention were emotions and perseverance. Each teacher discussed their emotions with regards to their identity and as a reason they remain teaching. Perseverance was a part of who they are and a reason they are still teaching today. All the stories were interwoven with perseverance and emotions and appear to be a part of the teachers' identities. The teachers' stories revealed the social and emotional aspect of teaching and how it is incorporated in teacher's personal identity.

Professional identity has an influence on retention, but retention also has an influence on identity. These factors appear to be dependent on one another. For example, teachers discussed the social and emotional components of being loved and respected as a part of their identity. They also said that supportive administration was a reason for their retention. The teachers felt respected when their administrators complimented them, asked them for help, and gave them more responsibility within the school. This respect became a part of their identity. That identity of being respected contributed to their retention. So, the interactions between these factors contributed to both identity and retention. Feeling socially and emotionally supported and valued became a part of their professional identity.

Self-evaluation was a part of their identity and their connection with students was a reason for their retention. Many of the teachers self-evaluated themselves and many felt they were not "good enough" or "not a good teacher." During this self-evaluation, they were still making connections with students and they realized the positive impact they were having. That would cause their self-evaluation to have some optimistic aspects to it. The connections with students, which is a reason for retention, also helped with their self-evaluations. The self-evaluations caused them to want to be better teachers for students which helped them make student connections. Once again, their identity and reasons for retention supported one another. Teacher optimism was influenced by connections with students. Teachers were optimistic that they could impact student learning, behavior, and help students become better people. The connections they had with students provided them with this optimism and the optimism helped them connect with their students. This social and emotional aspect was not only valuable for the teachers, but for student social and emotional support as well.

CONCLUSION

The teachers' identities included dedication to not only students, but their schools and other teachers. The relationships they built with other teachers contributed to their retention. The teachers discussed, in depth, the relationships and friendships they had with other teachers. Several of them specifically stated that they remained teaching because of the relationships they have with other teachers. Their dedication comes from the support they have from other teachers and these relationships lead to their dedication and retention. The continuous occurrences between dedication and relationships and emotional support with other teachers consistently support one another. For the teachers in this study, professional identity influences retention, but the reasons for retention support professional identity.

Teachers had a unique way of sharing their stories and focused on areas that were significant to them. Despite their individual styles, they majority of their stories had common themes which fit into their cultural scene as Title 1 teachers. The teachers are socially and emotionally content with their school and their careers because of the impact they have on students, their relationships with other teachers and the support they receive. Even though they are happy, there are aspects of teaching at their Title 1 school that does not make them happy. Such as, too much paperwork, excessive testing of students, lack of time, and student behaviors in which discipline is too lenient. However, the teachers can separate the areas of teaching that they do not like or have control over with the social relationships with students and their colleagues.

The professional identity of these teachers is very personal. The strongest components of their identity formation are their emotions, perseverance, and dedication. Each teacher defined professional identity through their stories and personal experiences. While none of them gave a concrete definition about what professional identity means or even what their professional identity is, their stories brought out who they are not only as teachers, but as people through their strong emotions and social connections. Their identity development was of a social and emotional aspect. Teaching is not only a professional career, but a personal one. It is additionally clear that teaching is quite personal when the teachers' main reasons for retention include support, relationships, and their own emotions. Many of these teachers knew they would become teachers at a very young age and others knew it was where they belonged once they were around students. This personal aspect of their identity has impacted their longevity as teachers.

Vygotsky (1978) framed identity as a situational dynamic process of individuals developing conceptions of themselves as rational beings over time. More recent studies defined identity using sociocultural theory as, "a loose cluster of complementary, sometimes competing, contributions from social psychology, social anthropology, sociolinguistics, and philosophy that focus on the self in practice; on the various interdependencies among person, context, history, and others; and on the situated, continuous nature of self-development" (Olsen, 2008, p. 4).

Teachers who identify with their teaching role are emotionally attached to this role, and it informs their worldview (Holland & Lachicotte, 2007). When one becomes emotionally attached to the teacher role, that role becomes part of who that person is; it becomes an organizing element in teachers' lives (Akkerman & Meijer, 2011). The development of a teacher identity is an ongoing process of interpretation and reinterpretation of who one considers oneself to be and who one would like to become (Beijaard, Meijer & Verloop, 2004).

Sociocultural theory was utilized as a lens to view teacher identity. As stated previously, many of the teachers did not have a definite definition of professional identity, but they have many emotions about teaching. Emotions were not only a component of their identity, but of their retention. The social aspect of teaching was significant to constructing, challenging, and modifying the teachers' professional identity. Teaching is incorporated in teachers' personal identity. It is a personal profession. The characteristics of each teacher's personality influences their identity which affects their retention. The personal nature of the profession causes the teacher's professional identity to promote retention and allows reasons for retention to influence their identity.

Teacher turnover impacts student achievement especially for students in Title 1, hard to staff schools. Schools that are unable to maintain highly effective teachers are unable to provide all students with an equitable and quality education. Teacher retention is essential to student success. The personal nature of teaching requires teachers to have strong relationships with colleagues, administrators, and students. Teachers need to feel supported, respected, and valued to develop a strong, positive professional identity as a teacher. Professional identity is important to teacher retention at not only a Title 1 school, but for the teaching profession. Providing social and emotional support for teachers is a critical component of professional identify development and teacher retention.

REFERENCES

Akkerman, S. F., & Meijer, P. C. (2011). A dialogical approach to conceptualizing teacher identity. *Teaching and Teacher Education*, *27*(2), 308–319. doi:10.1016/j.tate.2010.08.013

Beijaard, D., Meijer, P. C., & Verloop, N. (2004). Reconsidering research on teachers' professional identity. *Teaching and Teacher Education*, *20*(2), 107–128. doi:10.1016/j.tate.2003.07.001

Boyd, D., Grossman, P., Ing, M., Lankford, H., Loeb, S., & Wyckoff, J. (2011). The influence of school administrators on teacher retention decisions. *American Educational Research Journal*, *48*(2), 303–333. doi:10.3102/0002831210380788

Brown, K. M., & Wynn, S. R. (2009). Finding, supporting, and keeping: The role of the principal in teacher retention issues. *Leadership and Policy in Schools*, *8*(1), 37–63. doi:10.1080/15700760701817371

Cochran-Smith, M. (2004). Stayers, leavers, lovers, and dreamers: Insights about teacher retention. *Journal of Teacher Education*, *55*(5), 387–392. doi:10.1177/0022487104270188

Darling-Hammond, L. (2010). Teacher education and the American future. *Journal of Teacher Education*, *61*(1-2), 35–47. doi:10.1177/0022487109348024

Freedman, S. W., & Appleman, D. (2008). What else would I be doing?": Teacher identity and teacher retention in urban schools. *Teacher Education Quarterly*, *35*(3), 109–126.

Friesen, M. D., & Besley, S. C. (2013). Teacher identity development in the first year of teacher education: A developmental and social psychological perspective. *Teaching and Teacher Education*, *36*, 23–32. doi:10.1016/j.tate.2013.06.005

Gee, J. P. (2001). Identity as an analytic lens for research in education. In W.G. Secada (Ed.), Review of research in education. Washington, DC: American Educational Research Association

Geiger, T., & Pivovarova, M. (2018). The effects of working conditions on teacher retention. *Teachers and Teaching, 24*(6), 1–22. doi:10.1080/13540602.2018.1457524

Holland, D., & Lachicotte, W. (2007). Vygotsky, Mead, and the new sociocultural studies of identity. *The Cambridge Companion to Vygotsky*, 101-135.

Hughes, G. D. (2012). Teacher retention: Teacher characteristics, school characteristics, organizational characteristics, and teacher efficacy. *The Journal of Educational Research, 105*(4), 245–255. doi:10.1080/00220671.2011.584922

Ingersoll, R. M. (2001). Teacher turnover and teacher shortages: An organizational analysis. *American Educational Research Journal, 38*(3), 499–534. doi:10.3102/00028312038003499

Jackson, I., Paretti, L., Quinn, L., Bickmore, D., & Borek, M. (2019). Retaining Nevada's Teachers: Issues and Solutions. *Policy Issues in Nevada Education, 3*, 1.

Jagers, R. J., Rivas-Drake, D., & Williams, B. (2019). Transformative social and emotional learning (SEL): Toward SEL in service of educational equity and excellence. *Educational Psychologist, 54*(3), 162–184. doi:10.1080/00461520.2019.1623032

Kissling, M. T. (2014). Now and Then, in and out of the Classroom: Teachers Learning to Teach through the Experiences of Their Living Curricula. *Teaching and Teacher Education, 44*, 81–91. doi:10.1016/j.tate.2014.08.003

Mahoney, J. L., Weissberg, R. P., Greenberg, M. T., Dusenbury, L., Jagers, R. J., Niemi, K., Schlinger, M., Schlund, J., Shriver, T. P., VanAusdal, K., & Yoder, N. (2020, October 8). Systemic Social and Emotional Learning: Promoting Educational Success for All Preschool to High School Students. *The American Psychologist*. Advance online publication. doi:10.1037/amp0000701 PMID:33030926

Meijer, P. C. (2011). The role of crisis in the development of student teachers' professional identity. In *Navigating in Educational Contexts* (pp. 41–54). Sense Publishers. doi:10.1007/978-94-6091-522-2_3

Olsen, B. (2008). Introducing teacher identity and this volume. *Teacher Education Quarterly*, 3–6.

Pinnegar, S. (2005). Identity development, moral authority, and the teacher educator. In G. F. Hoban (Ed.), *The missing links in teacher education design* (pp. 259–279). Springer. doi:10.1007/1-4020-3346-X_14

Rodgers, C. R., & Scott, K. H. (2008). *40 The development of the personal self and professional identity in learning to teach*. Academic Press.

Sachs, J. (2001). Teacher professional identity: Competing discourses, competing outcomes. *Journal of Education Policy, 16*(2), 149–161. doi:10.1080/02680930116819

Swars, S. L., Meyers, B., Mays, L. C., & Lack, B. (2009). A two-dimensional model of teacher retention and mobility: Classroom teachers and their university partners take a closer look at a vexing problem. *Journal of Teacher Education, 60*(2), 168–183. doi:10.1177/0022487108329116

Vierstraete, S. (2005). Mentorship: Toward Success in Teacher Induction and Retention. *Catholic Education: A Journal of Inquiry and Practice, 8*(3), 381-392.

Vygotsky, L. S. (1978). Mind in society (M. Cole, V. John-Steiner, S. Scribner, & E. Souberman, Eds.). Academic Press.

KEY TERMS AND DEFINITIONS

Attrition: Attrition occurs when public school teachers (K-12) begin public school teaching in one school year, leave public school teaching during or at the end of that school year, and do not return the following school year.

Hard to Staff Schools: Used to describe an organization that has difficulty finding or keeping employees: Hard-to-staff schools find it difficult to attract and retain qualified teachers.

Identity: Dynamic rather than stable, a constantly evolving phenomenon. It involves both a person and a context: within a context, teachers learn professional characteristics that are adopted by individuals in unique ways.

Identity Development: Identity development is (a) an ongoing process, (b) the relationship between the professional and context, and (c) active agency within a community (Beijaard, Meijer, & Verloop, 2004).

Mentor: A mentor is a tenured teacher who has been partnered with a preservice or novice teacher to help him or her become accustomed to the classroom and the policies of the school where he or she works.

Professional Identity: One's professional self-concept based on attributes, beliefs, values, motives, and experiences.

Teacher: A person who helps students to acquire knowledge, competence or virtue. Those who are employed, as their main role, to teach others in a formal education context, such as at a school.

Teacher Retention: Teacher retention refers to the proportion of teachers in one year who are still teaching in the same school the following year.

Teacher Turnover: The rate at which teachers exit schools is known as teacher turnover. It consists of both teacher migration ("movers," those who transfer or migrate to teaching positions in other schools) and teacher attrition ("leavers," those who leave teaching altogether).

Title 1 School: A school receiving federal funds for Title 1 students. The basic principle of Title 1 is that schools with large concentrations of low-income students will receive supplemental funds to assist in meeting student's educational goals.

Chapter 7
Elevating Social and Emotional Learning Throughout the Day:
Ten Teaching Practices That Promote SEAD in Culturally Responsive Ways

Nick Yoder
National University, USA

Pat Conner
Collaborative for Academic, Social, and Emotional Learning, USA

Tyrone Martinez-Black
CASEL, USA

Richie Ressel
Inspire Teaching and Learning, USA

ABSTRACT

The important role of social and emotional learning (SEL) to promote the holistic development of students, improve academic instruction, and prepare students for the world of work and civic life has been well-established. Although wide consensus has emerged about the importance of SEL, understanding the primary role SEL plays within academic learning and how to more fully embed SEL throughout the school day still appears to be elusive. Compounded by efforts to use SEL as a lever for equity and excellence, educators need practical tools and guidance about approaches that help them attune to the social, emotional, and academic needs of their students. In this chapter, the authors review 10 teaching practices that promote social, emotional, and academic development and ways in which each of these practices can be implemented in classrooms in a culturally responsive way.

DOI: 10.4018/978-1-7998-6728-9.ch007

INTRODUCTION

The important role of social and emotional learning (SEL) to promote holistic development of students, improve academic instruction, and prepare students for the world of work and civic life has been well established (Mahoney, Weissberg, Greenberg et al., 2020). SEL has the potential to promote equity and excellence when SEL is used to intentionally create equitable learning environments, create opportunities for students to understand and nurture their interests and talents, focus on relationships and relationship building, examine root causes of inequities to be able to interrupt those policies and practice, and collaborate with families and community partners to ensure all students receive the education they deserve (Jagers, Rivas-Drake & Borowski, 2018; Schlund, Jagers & Schlinger, 2020).

Although educators agree about the importance of SEL and believe it is a key aspect of their profession, they often feel they do not have the time to promote SEL due to pressures to focus on academic instruction (EdWeek, 2019). Further, the demand from educators about how to implement culturally responsive practices has been on the rise in the past decade, yet the educators need more information about how to implement these practices (Larson, Pas & Bradshaw, 2018). Due to the demand to better understand practices that can leverage SEL in support of equity and excellence, and an additional demand to understand culturally responsive practices, it is important to analyze how educators can implement SEL approaches that honor students' voices, their cultures and families, and breaks down barriers to learning.

Educators can promote student social, emotional, and academic development (SEAD) through three general approaches that typically work best in combination with each other: (a) explicit skill instruction; (b) integration with academic subjects; and (c) general practices that promote a positive learning environment (Dusenbury, Calin, Domitrovich et al., 2015; National Commission on Social, Emotional, and Academic Development [NC-SEAD], 2019). Recent research demonstrates that schools do not typically take this multi-pronged approach, but those that do believe they are more apt to meet their SEL goals (Bryant, Crowley & Davidsen, 2020). Educators need support to promote each of these approaches, in particular how to intentionally promote and develop social and emotional competencies (SECs) (Jones & Bouffard, 2012; Yoder, 2014). To further exacerbate the issues of intentional SEL integration, educators may need support to develop skills for how to embed culturally responsive practices to more fully embolden student development that honors student cultures and lived experiences, particularly for youth who have been most marginalized within the current education system.

To support SEL integration, Yoder (2014) identified 10 teaching practices that promote SEL within classroom instruction. Through a review of literature on SEL evidence-based programs that focus on proactive forms of teaching and learning that promote SEAD, he identified the integrative practices that we will focus on in this chapter. See table 1 for an overview and example of SECs students develop when engaging in these practices.

Table 1. 10 Teaching Practices and Related SECs

Teaching Practice	Definition	Related Example Social and Emotional Competencies
1. Student- centered discipline	Disciplinary strategies that are developmentally appropriate in which the teacher shares power and ownership in how students manage themselves.	*Self-management skills*, such as impulse control and self-discipline.
2. Teacher language	Type of teacher talk focused on encouraging students in ways that are meaningful for the student.	*Self-awareness skills*, such as accurate self-perceptions and self-confidence, and *relationship skills,* such as communication and social engagement.
3. Responsibility and choice	Opportunities for students to make responsible decisions in the classroom that are relevant to students and reflect student interests.	*Responsible decision-making skills,* such as analyzing situations and problem solving.
4. Warmth and support	A classroom environment where all students feel cared for, receive feedback in culturally responsive ways, and develop adult and student relationships.	*Self-awareness skills*, such as enhancing self-efficacy, and *relationship skills*, such as seeking or offering help when needed
5. Cooperative learning	Students work together in diverse groups toward a collective goal in accomplishing an instructional task relevant to the students.	*Relationship skills*, such as collaborative problem solving, and *responsible decision-making skills*, such as evaluating and reflecting.
6. Classroom discussions	Students and teachers have a dialogue about content which honors students' background knowledge and language.	*Social awareness skills*, such as respect for others and acknowledge diverse social norms, and *relationship skills*, such as effective communication and cultural competency.
7. Self-assessment and self-reflection	Opportunities for students to actively think about their own work and the ways in which they engage with their work.	*Self-awareness skills*, such as recognizing virtues and identifying personal assets, and *responsible decision-making skil*ls, such as analyzing situations and examining effects on well-being.
8. Balanced instruction	Teachers implement multiple instructional strategies that are based on student needs, interests, and background so students can maximally learn content.	*Self-management skills*, such as setting personal and collective goals, and planning and organization skills.
9. Academic press and expectations	Educators provide meaningful and challenging work, believe that all students can achieve rigorous work, and support them in doing so.	*Self-awareness skills*, such as linking feeling, values, and thoughts, and *self-management skills*, such as personal and collective agency.
10. Competence building	The teacher helps develop students' social and emotional skills through the typical instructional cycle, such that they explicitly teach, model, and reinforce social and emotional skills in ways that align with student cultures.	Opportunity to develop any SEC.

Although researchers, policymakers and practitioners have examined these 10 teaching practices in their integration of social, emotional, and academic development, the practices have yet to be examined in ways that align with and promote culturally responsive practices. In this chapter, we provide a detailed overview of each of these practices, explore examples of ways in which they work in practice, and identify how educators can use them to more intentionally align with and promote students' cultures. We will also explore ways in which school leaders can intentionally support these practices within schools and classrooms.

ONE APPROACH TO USE SEL AS A LEVER FOR EQUITY AND EXCELLENCE

A deep connection exists between the academic, social, and emotional aspects of learning, yet educators tend to think of each one in isolation rather than how they intersect (NC-SEAD, 2019; Science of Learning and Development [SOLD] Alliance, 2020). Research demonstrates that individuals learn best when they are able to manage their emotions, thoughts, and behaviors (Jones & Khan, 2017). For example, when students feel connected to the content, to their classmates, and to the teacher, they are more likely to engage more deeply with the content, thereby enhancing student learning. These intersections make it important to learn within healthy and secure relationships (Immordino-Yang, Darling-Hammond & Krone, 2018). Learning and development are further influenced by the contexts, environments, and cultures in which one lives, making it incredibly important to have an intra- and inter-personal and cultural assets-based approach to SEL (Jagers et al., 2018).

Given the intersection of social, emotional, and academic development, SEL focuses on creating the conditions necessary to maximize student success in and outside of school. According to the Collaborative for Academic, Social, and Emotional Learning (CASEL), "social and emotional learning involves a coordinated set of evidence-based programs and practices for enhancing social-emotional-cognitive development, positive behavior, and academic performance" (Mahoney et al., 2020). SEL is not just about developing skills, but attuning to the environments in which those skills are developed and applied. Through safe and supportive learning environments, grounded in warm, supportive relationships, students can intentionally learn and have opportunities to apply their SECs, such as critical thinking, problem solving, self-regulation, awareness of others, communication skills, and perspective taking—skills necessary and foundational for learning (Darling-Hammond, Flook, Cook-Harvey et al., 2019).

The SECs most often cited come from CASEL. Educators use the CASEL framework, or competencies identified in SEL curriculum or found in state SEL standards (Dusenbury, Yoder, Dermody et al., 2020), to create a scope and sequence of which SECs to explicitly teach and when. They can also use the framework to determine which competencies to reinforce throughout the day (Berman, Chaffee & Sarmiento, 2018). CASEL views these competencies as student and adult assets that should affirm everyone's identities, values, and cultures (Schlund et al., 2020). The five core competencies and recently developed equity elaborations are found in Table 2 (CASEL, 2020a; Jagers, Rivas-Drake & Williams, 2019). The equity elaborations demonstrate the evolution of CASEL's definition of the competencies and are here incorporated to more explicitly recognize and honor cultural assets and historical inequities. We separated them here to showcase part of that evolution.

Table 2. CASEL Social and Emotional Competencies and Equity Elaborations

Competency	Definition	Equity Elaborations
Self-awareness	The abilities to understand oneself, one's emotions, strengths, and limitations; personal and social identities; as well as having a positive mindset, self-efficacy, and sense of purpose.	Understanding one's biases, the connections between personal and cultural identities and histories, and how thoughts, feelings, and behaviors are connected across contexts.
Self-management	The abilities to manage emotions, thoughts, and behaviors, such as delaying gratification, managing stress, persevering through challenges, and motivating oneself, as well as goal setting (personal and collective) and other organizational skills.	Advocating for self and for collective goals and objectives.
Social awareness	The abilities to take the perspective of and empathize with others, particularly with those from diverse backgrounds, cultures, and contexts. This also includes abilities to understand social and historical norms for behavior in multiple contexts, and abilities to identify supports and help when needed for individual and collective well-being.	Engaging in a critical historical understanding and perspectives of those from the same and different cultures.
Relationship skills	The abilities to establish and maintain healthy relationships including the ability to communicate and listen clearly, demonstrate cooperation and collaboration, resolve conflict constructively, and seek and offer help when needed.	Navigating diverse settings that include varying norms and demands based on culture and context.
Responsible decision-making	The abilities to solve problems and make constructive choices based on personal and social norms across multiple settings, and includes the realistic understanding of consequences for actions on personal, social, and collective well-being.	Making constructive choices about group behavior across interpersonal and institutional settings, and incorporates interpersonal and institutional consideration in making decisions that also focus on the collective well-being.

Educators and adults operating in- and out-of-school time promote SECs through building relationships in safe, supportive environments and engaging students in a rigorous curriculum that is identity-affirming. Educators can engage in critical self-reflection about how they create environments that meet students where they are, honor their cultures, recognize that students develop over time based on their contexts and their relationships, and ensure students make meaning through their unique lived experiences (SOLD Alliance, 2020). In this section, we review why it is important to implement SEL through general teaching practices, provide an overview of culturally responsive practices, and describe the importance of integrating the two approaches.

SEL through General Teaching Practices

As previously noted, educators can take three approaches to promote SEAD in an educational context (in- or out-of-school time): explicit instruction, integration into academic instruction, and practices that promote a safe and supportive learning environment (Dusenbury et al., 2015; NC-SEAD, 2019). Each strategy is important because students need opportunities to explicitly learn about and apply their competencies through embedded instruction in safe learning environments (Berman, et al., 2018; Jones, Brush, Bailey et al., 2017). This chapter primarily focuses on ways to integrate and embed SEL practices within academics and creating a schoolwide culture.

Connecting SEL with instructional strategies is still an emerging area within SEL (Jones & Bouffard, 2012). Even though SEL and academic integration has been an important topic for over a decade, the science has evolved to demonstrate that SEL and academics are not polarized endeavors but rather both are core to learning and development. For example, in their guiding principles to teaching and learning, Darling-Hammond and colleagues (2019) note the importance of SEL integration: students learn best when they make meaning of content that is connected to their prior learning and knowledge; use their competencies to manage their own learning (e.g., awareness of current understanding, collaboration, communication, and help-seeking); and co-construct norms of interactions with their classmates.

As educators use integrated practices, they must use them in a context of warm, caring relationships, in which they develop emotionally and physically safe environments where students feel safe to take risks (Osher, Cantor, Berg et al., 2018). By engaging students in authentic practices, educators create opportunities that promote maximal development. Immordino-Yang and her colleagues (2018) illustrate this point by saying, "[Providing] purposeful learning opportunities for young people—and strategic opportunities for brain development—requires educators to attend to the development of the whole child in context, and to the need for aligned partnerships throughout the community that can support children's and their families' health and well-being." (Immordino-Yang et al., 2018, p. 16).

Culturally Responsive and Adaptive Practices

While learning social and emotional competencies, in and of themselves, is important, potential harm can occur if they are not taught and developed in environments that intentionally address systemic barriers of learning, particularly for students of color and other marginalized students (e.g., LGBTQ, students receiving services, English Language Learners). By creating culturally nurturing environments, educators send the signal to students they are valued, rather than needing to be fixed (Duchesneau, 2020). Further, when educators engage in a culturally responsive lens to SEL, they provide opportunities for students to develop vital skills, such as critical consciousness, that youth will employ as they organize for change (Madden-Dent, 2021).

Culturally responsive practices (similar, yet distinct, concepts include culturally relevant and culturally sustaining) present a commitment to an instructional orientation that aims to hold high expectations for all students, provide culturally affirming materials and strategies, and provide opportunities to deconstruct inequitable social structures. They further promote building an equitable learning environment, routinizing inclusive activities, and emphasizing youth voice and agency (Gay, 2013; Ladson-Billings, 2014; Paris 2012). Educators need to be fully equipped with skills and strategies to adeptly include and value different backgrounds, such as the following:

- Increase cultural representation in curricular programs, problem and story contexts, and expert mentors from around the world, affirming culture as an asset (Paris & Alim, 2014).
- Connect with students as people and activate the value of their backgrounds through their own words and experiences (e.g., through games, cooperation, storytelling, and allowing peers to learn about cultural backgrounds of each other), where teacher acts as facilitator (Hammond, 2015).
- Foster diverse models of knowing and of success (including through affirming feedback and opportunities for revision) that normalize failure as opportunity for growth and align achievement with persistence and effort rather than achievement as an intrinsic part of their identities (Aronson & Inzlicht, 2004).

- Provide opportunities for students to reflect on what is important to them, including their interests and values, and to identify ways in which they have grown and developed (i.e., develop a growth mindset).

Curricula and evidence-based programs and practices that value difference and welcome cultural variation should be more widely adopted as well (Gay, 2013). *Culturally adaptive practices* recognize that evidence-based programs and practices (EBPPs) are typically tested on homogeneously White populations; however, adaptive practices *adapt* EBPPs to demonstrate their utility to other populations by honoring and respecting the cultures of communities where they are implemented. This includes taking into account the relevance of cultural differences, encourages cultural grounding in the creation and testing of the same interventions, and includes members of subculture communities in the evaluation of results (Booth & Lazear, 2015). Culturally adaptive practices ask programs and practices to match content with student language, connect content to student development and educational needs and interests, and apply practices within the lives of learners (e.g., how does your program promote a culturally-rooted agentic identity for young people or how does it support a social awareness conducive to participatory critical analysis of community conditions?) (Castro, Barrera & Holleran Steiker, 2010).

Integrating Two Approaches

To fully support the social, emotional, and academic development of all students, educators can take into account the cultural norms and values of their students, understanding that if the adults do not put in the extra work to understand students, then the burden falls on students, especially students of color (Duchesneau, 2020). As a core component of equity-focused SEL, CASEL notes that districts who are at the forefront of integrating SEL and equity are incorporating multiple strategies to systematically embed equity and culture within instructional practices that promote SECs and through SEL curriculum (Schlund et al., 2020). For example, Teaching Tolerance demonstrates that SEL, academics and anti-bias instruction can be integrated with educator friendly tools (Scharf, 2016). Similarly, Jagers and colleagues present multiple approaches to bring transformative SEL into schools (Jagers et al., 2018; 2019), for example:

- *Cultural integration*, which encourages self-reflection on a person's own life and society, while also bringing in cultural assets, connecting to academics, and allowing others to learn about their own and other cultures.
- *Community-building*, which includes practices where students and adults are able to come together to build positive environments through morning meetings, teacher language, classroom and individual goals, and balanced disciplinary practices.
- *Promotion of racial-ethnic identity*, which provides practices that allow students to explore their racial-ethnic identity (which can be for both White and students of color), and strategies to overcome stereotype threat.
- *Equity integration into academics*, where educators explicitly reference issues of race and equity within academic subjects like social studies and literature arts.
- *Project-based, experiential, and participatory methods*, which provide opportunities for students to engage in inquiry, or projects (such as service learning) that allow students to engage more fully in content and develop social conscientiousness.

The remainder of this chapter provides concrete recommendations on ways in which SEL, culturally responsive practices, and good teaching and learning can be integrated more fully within schools and afterschool programs.

10 TEACHING PRACTICES THAT PROMOTE SEL THROUGH A CULTURALLY RESPONSIVE LENS

The 10 teaching practices provide one approach to more fully embed student and adult SECs within academics and other content areas (Yoder, 2014). As educators review these practices, they probably recognize they use some of these instructional moves already with students. General teaching practices provide opportunities for students to apply and further develop their SECs during academic activities, allow educators to reinforce skills throughout the day, incorporate more rigorous and engaging learning opportunities, and engage students to reflect on and analyze their SECs (Berman et al., 2018; Jones & Bouffard, 2012). The 10 practices align with some common observation rubrics, such as Danielson's and Marzano's (Yoder, 2014), and have been further refined in a series of resources developed by the Tennessee Department of Education[1] in collaboration with the Center on Great Teachers and Leaders and the Appalachian Comprehensive Center (Tennessee Department of Education, n.d.).

The goal of this chapter is to further flush out these 10 teaching practices, with corresponding research and explicit examples, and to intentionally connect them to culturally responsive practices.

Student-Centered Discipline

Overview and Research

Student-centered disciplinary practices are built on the idea that students can regulate their own behavior when adults provide them the necessary tools, resources, and skills (Bear, 2010). These practices are more about how adults help students manage behavior, rather than student behavior itself (Duchesneau, 2020). Discipline, then, should not be about punishment or exclusion, but rather providing students a learning opportunity and facilitating more meaningful relationships (Osher, Bear & Sprague, 2010). When schools use more positive practices to discipline, students are more likely to engage in the classroom, reduce negative behaviors, improve behavior, and do better in class, particularly for students of color who disproportionately receive exclusionary discipline (Osher, Moroney & Wlliamson, 2018).

To promote student-centered discipline, educators can help students develop the skills to manage themselves, provide students opportunities to correct their own behavior, and create consistent and predictable structures. When educators use student-centered discipline, they develop and use SECs such as: become aware of their triggers, identify ways to manage their stressors, and use social skills to ask for help as needed. Further, educators help students to balance managing their emotions with the ability to advocate for themselves and their needs.

Student-centered discipline maintains a balance of power between educators and students, avoiding extrinsic rewards and punishments to maintain control and inviting students to be active participants in the management of the classroom. Five specific strategies educators can use to promote student-centered discipline include the following:

1. *Teach self-control.* Self-control is one's ability to stop automatic responses to social cues. To develop self-control, students can use strategies to stop these automatic responses and control their emotions, cognition, and behavior, for example: noticing when one begins to get upset (Origins Program, 2014; Willingham, 2011), and learning how to channel emotions to advocate for oneself.
2. *Promote self-discipline.* Self-discipline requires students to make decisions about how to behave and take responsibility for those choices. The motivation for their behavior is intrinsic, making it important to have critical conversations about the connections between emotions, thoughts, and behavior (Bear, 2010).
3. *Implement advisory periods or morning meetings.* The goal of advisories and classroom meetings is to create a time and space for students to meet as a group, helping them form a group identity, develop a better connection to school, and solve interpersonal concerns (e.g., through bubble maps, cue cards, and group discussions).
4. *Use restorative practices.* Restorative practices center on the idea that misconduct and negative behaviors should be a learning opportunity. The goal of restorative practices is to repair any tensions or harm that has occurred, taking into account the needs of the victim and the offender (International Institute for Restorative Practices, 2012).
5. *Correct misbehavior through self-discipline.* Adult and student problem solving are important when helping correct misbehavior, as both adults and students share an active role in taking responsibility for the misbehavior and identifying strategies each can take to promote positive behaviors.

Example Approaches to Implement the Practice through a Culturally Responsive Lens

Most exclusionary disciplinary practices, such as suspensions and removal from classrooms, do *not* occur because of violence or serious misconduct. Rather, they occur because of *nonviolent* infractions, including disrespectful behavior, dress code violations, and disruptions to the classroom, which disproportionately influence students of color and students with disabilities (Skiba, Reynolds, Graham, et al., 2006).

Discipline disparities exist, in part, due to implicit biases. Implicit biases are unconscious beliefs individuals may have about others that influence thoughts and behaviors, which can occur even among those that have the best intentions (Staats, 2014). Educators can reduce implicit biases, for example, by becoming aware of those biases. To develop self-awareness, educators may want to record how often they call on students, provide positive praise and feedback, or reprimand—determining if there are patterns of interaction. Similarly, educators can determine if there is a cultural mismatch between student behavior and educator interpretation of that behavior (Safir, 2016).

Teacher Language

Overview and Research

The type of language educators use with students, particularly the feedback they provide about student performance and behavior, has a dramatic effect on students and the ways in which they succeed and behave in classrooms (Mueller & Dweck, 2011; Smith, Brumskill, Johnson et al, 2018). Asking questions and using reinforcing language gives educators an opportunity to discover where students are coming from, connect academics and SEC, and build vocabulary for students to identify and express emotions.

Effective teacher language encourages student effort and work and reinforces positive student behaviors while avoiding language that is humiliating or sarcastic (Denton, 2008).

When effective teacher language is used in the classroom, educators and students create a more supportive environment, built on meaningful relationships. Positive language helps students feel competent, motivates students to improve work habits, and gives students some control and voice in the classroom. Students also develop and apply multiple SECs, including awareness of student strengths and limitations, management of thoughts and behaviors, and making positive choices in class.

There are four types of teacher language that support SEAD, which educators can use in combination with one another. The four types include the following (Denton, 2008):

1. *Use reinforcing language.* Reinforcing language occurs when educators encourage students to continue academic and social behaviors. To motivate students intrinsically, replace praise with language that reinforces student behavior.
2. *Use reminding language.* Reminding language helps students remember for themselves what they are supposed to do and how to behave in a way that will help them achieve their goals. Educators can remind students about next steps or past discussions, for example.
3. *Use redirecting language.* Redirecting language is used when students are too emotional to think reasonably, may harm themselves or others, or may have a difficult time behaving in an expected manner without assistance.
4. *Use reflecting language.* Reflecting language is used to help students think critically about and reflect upon both their social and academic behavior.

Communication is also conveyed through nonverbal behaviors. This can be through the tone of voice or position of arms while talking. Body language helps get the message across and lets students know the tone the educator wants to set.

Example Approaches to Implement the Practice through a Culturally Responsive Lens

The type of language individuals use is directly connected to their culture and identity—language and expressions can vary by culture (Howard, 2019). Educators should thus be aware of cultural patterns within language, including nonverbal behaviors to ensure that clear communication exists between educators, students, and families. Educators' communication patterns signal their beliefs about students, how warm and secure the educator is, and how emotionally and intellectually safe the student can be with the educator. If educators and students do not come from the same culture, it is critical for educators to connect with students and families to better understand their communication patterns so misunderstandings do not arise. Educators can also demonstrate humility in their communications with students, particularly those who are culturally or linguistically different, ensuring that the educator makes the effort to actively listen and understand the students. This affirms the shared responsibility of adults and youth when miscommunications potentially lead to mismatched behaviors.

Responsibility and Choice

Overview and Research

Responsibility and choice occur when educators provide opportunities for students to make their own decisions and take accountability for their interactions (social, emotional, and academic) in the school setting. On the surface, responsibility and choice may appear simple to implement; however, responsibility and choice is more than having a classroom job or having an option or two. Researchers note that the act of choosing, in and of itself, is *not* motivational, but becomes motivational when choices are meaningful, culturally relevant, age-appropriate, and personalized to students' interests and lives (Evans & Boucher, 2015; Katz & Assor, 2007).

Educators should not impose responsibility on students but rather help students realize they have influence on their learning environment, making them feel greater motivation and sense of control (Fishman, 2014). Students develop multiple SECs when engaged in practices such as: managing thoughts and behaviors, strategies to guide learning, setting and monitoring goals, and problem-solving skills (Bierman, Domitrovich, Nix, et al., 2008).

Educators can use the following practices to integrate responsibility and choice in the classroom:

1. *Provide effective choices.* Choices have to be "just right" for students, or they can have negative consequences. Some students can feel overwhelmed if they do not feel like they have a clear understanding of what they are being asked to do. Researchers suggest effective choices include providing processing time, ensuring they are meaningful, and creating relatively similar options (so they are not too different). Choices can be cut across three domains: organizational (e.g., how classrooms operate), procedural (e.g., how learning happens), or cognitive (e.g., content of learning) (Beymer & Thomson, 2015).
2. *Implement self-directed learning.* Educators can take three steps to teach students to become self-directed learners: planning for, monitoring, and evaluating their learning (Ertmer & Newby, 1996).
3. *Create democratic norms.* When developing norms, educators can ensure the norms balance personal and social responsibilities and provide opportunities for group and individual self-reflection (Graham, 2017).
4. *Engage in student-led conferences.* Student-led conferences provide opportunities for students to accept the responsibility for reporting progress on their goals, including their academic, social and personal, and health and physical goals.
5. *Promote service learning and peer tutoring.* Opportunities to give back to their classroom, school, or larger community are great ways educators can provide students responsibility and choice. Educators help students identify goals, create learning experiences, and provide reflection time to process learning.

Example Approaches to Implement the Practice through a Culturally Responsive Lens

Students from all backgrounds and developmental levels can engage in responsibility and choice practices, although the way that they engage in those practices might differ. For example, students who come from cultures that promote independent thinking and interactions are more likely to value making their own choices, whereas students from more communal cultures are more intrinsically motivated when presented with choices that have more value to the group or are decided on with an elder (d'Ailly, 2004).

Helping students identify strategies to become agents of change is critical in developing responsibility and choice. For example, critical engagement activities occur when students take action towards critical issues that are important to them, in addition to promoting equity and justice within their schools and classrooms (Scharf, 2016). Further, students need opportunities to identify topics that are important to them, co-construct solutions, and analyze ways in which they can be agentic within the classroom or school—enhancing student voice.

Warmth and Support

Overview and Research

Warmth and support refer to the academic and social support that students receive from their teacher and their peers. Students who have close, positive, and supportive relationships with their teachers obtain higher levels of achievement compared to students with more conflict in their relationships with their teachers (Rimm-Kaufman & Sandilos, 2018). Educators who use warmth and support strategies create an environment that affords each student the opportunity to demonstrate their value and importance to the classroom community, to develop positive peer and teacher relationships, to promote a sense of comfort and security, and to provide opportunities for students to advocate for themselves.

As students experience a warm and supportive classroom, they develop SECs such as learning to communicate more effectively, providing quality feedback to others, considering the perspectives of others, taking risks and sharing ideas, negotiating the use of resources, and resolving conflicts as they arise. Educators will need to use their own SECs to successfully implement warm and supportive practices.

Many specific practices exist under warmth and support, including the following:

- *Implement relationship-building strategies.* Educators form relationships with students in two capacities: individual with each student and with the whole classroom (Marloes, Hendrickx, Mainhard, et al., 2016). To promote positive relationships, educators can let students know they are aware of their concerns, ask students questions about their lives, help them process misconceptions, provide feedback, and encourage intellectual risk taking (Pianta, Hamre & Mintz, 2012).
- *Engage in peer feedback.* Peer feedback occurs when students provide their peers feedback on a piece of student learning or even the learning process. To promote peer feedback: have clear learning objectives, provide feedback stems, teach students how to receive and provide feedback, and have students reflect on feedback (Sackstein, 2017).
- *Promote conflict resolution.* Educators can teach and reinforce multiple steps in the conflict resolution process, for example, cool off, share perspectives, take responsibility for actions, brainstorm solutions, and enact a solution (Crowe, 2009).
- *Implement advisory periods or morning meetings.* Advisory or morning meetings create a more cohesive classroom community, providing students and educators opportunities to get to know each other better.

Example Approaches to Implement the Practice through a Culturally Responsive Lens

To build warm and supportive classrooms through a culturally responsive lens, educators demonstrate respect for what the students bring to the classrooms from their home, cultures, and peers, resulting in students' perceptions that they are valued and their cultural identities are affirmed. Educators recognize that they set the tone for the classroom, demonstrate humility, and are open to learn about who students are and the assets they bring (Scharf, 2016). They also recognize students from marginalized backgrounds may feel skeptical that school is a safe space for them to share their own realities, whereas they have experienced school not as a place of inclusivity, but rather a place to combat stereotypes (Howard, 2019).

Educators can then create an environment that enables students to feel comfortable sharing their perspectives, backgrounds, and culture, and that they have opportunities to reflect on the multiple "ways of being human" (Howard, 2019). Educators should also be aware that emotional expression and identification of responsible decisions vary by cultural groups. For example, ways in which happiness or anger get expressed can vary by culture. This makes it incredibly important for adults to get to know the communities, families, and students in the schools they serve (Duchesneau, 2020).

Cooperative Learning

Overview and Research

Cooperative learning is more than informally assigning students to a small group and asking them to work together. Cooperative learning requires students to work together, share resources, assume complementary roles, and learn to interact effectively to reach group goals. The educator holds students accountable for both individual and group goals, and provides students an opportunity to reflect on the process (Baloche & Brody, 2017).

When students engage in cooperative learning, student achievement and motivation increases, learning and productivity improves, retention of materials increases, more positive peer relationships develop, and social development improves (Gillies & Boyle, 2010). One reason for the effectiveness of cooperative learning is because it affords student application of SECs, such as collaboration, problem solving when issues arise, managing oneself, negotiating shared resources, and processing multiple perspectives (Knight, 2015).

Effective cooperative learning requires careful planning and group facilitation. To implement cooperative learning effectively, Johnson and Johnson (1999) recommends that educators implement the following core practices:

- *Create positive interdependence.* Educators ask each group member to complete a distinct component of the shared group goal or task.
- *Apply social and emotional competencies.* Educators teach and reinforce a variety of SECs as students work together to set timelines, assume roles and responsibilities, troubleshoot challenges, and complete tasks.
- *Incorporate individual accountability.* Educators hold students responsible for completing their assigned role and for their contributions to the group, helping students understand their contributions have implications for the accomplishment of group goals.

- *Promote one another's success.* Students exhibit a variety of social and emotional competencies, such as active listening, encouraging peers' ideas and work, and being empathetic as they promote and encourage each other.
- *Provide group processing time.* Group processing time is reserved for group debriefing and processing of the experience. The educator provides structures for students to reflect on, clarify, and improve the effectiveness of how the group worked together and the final product.

Example Approaches to Implement the Practice though a Culturally Responsive Lens

Educators have employed cooperative learning with diverse student groups including English language learners, students of all ability levels, students with disabilities, gifted students, and students of different races and ethnicities (Gillies, 2014). Cooperative learning is appropriate for all students and any subject, and when done well, reflects principles of culturally responsive practices. To further promote anti-bias education through cooperative learning, educators need to ensure that multiple perspectives are encouraged, particularly from a diverse cross-section of the student population. Educators encourage diversity as an asset during cooperative groups and assign roles and responsibilities that help break down gender, class, racial, and other stereotypes, encouraging collective ownership (Scharf, 2016).

Classroom Discussions

Overview and Research

Classroom discussions provide students opportunities to communicate their ideas and to learn from their peers and educators. When implementing effective classroom discussions, educators thoughtfully plan them in advance, intentionally and purposefully lead the discussion, implement them with learning in mind, balance the talk between educator and student, and prompt students to engage in more conversations (Center for Instructional Development and Research, 1999). Engagement in classroom discussions can bring students' voices and perspectives to the surface, motivate students, facilitate collaboration and conversation in purposeful ways, promote skills to express and support their viewpoints, help shape the way students see themselves and others in the learning context, and develop a sense of curiosity about the content.

When students engage in content conversations, they not only tap traditional academic skills to interpret, integrate, and synthesize content knowledge, they also develop social and emotional competencies. For example, students become more aware of themselves and others; manage their own behaviors and their interactions with others; use communication skills that they need to be successful in school, work, and life; and develop self-confidence to share their ideas and process misunderstandings.

Example practices that facilitate effective discussions within classrooms of all developmental levels include the following:

- *Questioning.* Questioning is often an area in which learners express reluctance—both to answer questions and to ask questions. Yet, questioning is one of the few ways in which students can pursue their intellectual curiosities, probe for details and elaboration, check for accuracy, and clarify their contributions to discussions. To help students form questions, educators can help them brainstorm questions, improve upon them, prioritize questions, and then think of follow-up questions (Rothstein & Santana, 2011).

- *Perspective taking.* Teaching students how to perspective-take can be challenging, but it is critically important in order to hold effective, respectful discussions. To promote perspective taking, educators and students develop norms that engender openness and free and respectful expression; provide opportunities for posing questions and reflecting on responses; and promote possibilities for amicable disagreement.
- *Accountable talk.* Accountable talk is a mechanism for fostering meaningful classroom discussions and academic discourse that helps students cultivate the habits necessary for perspective taking, specifically to help students determine the degree to which their peers' ideas are similar to or different from their own. To do this, educators provide specific prompts for students to use during a discussion, such as "that is an important point" or "what I hear you saying is…" (Fisher & Frey, 2013).
- *Routines for promoting quality discussions.* Educators can use three instructional routines to promote classroom discussions. These include annotation (marking text prior to discussing), text rendering (discussing ambiguous texts), and Socratic seminars (teacher as facilitator) (Fisher & Frey, 2013).

Example Approaches to Implement the Practice through a Culturally Responsive Lens

Classroom discussions provide ample opportunities for students to discuss their cultures, their own histories, background knowledge, and structural inequities in developmentally appropriate ways. Educators support students to develop an awareness that they are the experts of their own lives, while also acknowledging the importance of understanding the perspectives and lived experiences of others (Scharf, 2016). In effective discussions, students consider their own and others' background experiences and knowledge as they engage with others to solve problems or make sound arguments about content. As educators create this space, students feel comfortable to be able to interpret events based on their previous backgrounds and lived experiences.

Self-Assessment and Self-Reflection

Overview and Research

Self-assessment and self-reflection are two distinct but interrelated practices to help students identify where gaps in knowledge or skills exist and identify strategies to meet desired results. Self-assessment occurs when students evaluate their own work, identifying gaps in performance relative to desired performance. Self-reflection occurs when students reflect on their learning progress, the strategies used to achieve results, and how they can use those strategies to improve work in the future (Costa & Kallick, 2008).

When educators implement strategies that promote self-assessment and self-reflection, they can improve students' motivation to learn, their desire to master academic standards, and their capacity to apply a variety of SECs (McMillan & Hearn, 2008). The SECs that students may develop when engaging in these practices include the identification of what a student does and does not know, self-efficacy, and self-monitoring skills (Costa & Kallick, 2008; McMillan & Hearn, 2008). Through the self-assessment process, educators help students ask themselves three general questions: "Where am I going, where am I now, and where to next?" (Zubrzycki, 2015).

Educators can take five steps to help students engage in a self-assessment and self-reflection, which include the following (Brooke & Andrade, 2013; Costa & Kallick, 2008):

- *Define well-defined performance targets.* The educator—with input from students—develops learning objectives and performance standards. To define SEC learning objectives, educators can use state or district SEL standards or competencies (Dusenbury et al., 2020) or objectives outlined in SEL curriculum. To help define performance, educators can create checklists or rubrics to monitor progress towards outcome.
- *Check progress.* Educators provide students an opportunity to reflect on progress towards performance targets, enabling students to identify their strengths, areas for improvement, and strategies to improve. This could be done through simple cue cards or gestures, as well as more complex tasks such as cover sheets, portfolios, or exit tickets.
- *Revise work.* Students revise their work based on the self-assessment, attempting to close the gap between where they are and where they want to be.
- *Connect current learning to previous learning.* Students reflect on what or how they are currently learning as it relates to previous learning in class. Students may process this connection with their peers through interviews, group processing time, or memos to teachers or their peers.
- *Connect current learning to future learning.* Students identify effective strategies in their current learning experience they would like to use in future learning experiences

Example Approaches to Implement the Practice through a Culturally Responsive Lens

Culturally responsive practices typically use activities that promote student reflection on their own and others' cultures, lives, and society (Aronson & Laughter, 2016; Schlund et al., 2020). Not only can they be used as strategies to critically examine one's role in society and practice how to examine interpersonal and institutional barriers, but self-assessment and self-reflection also help students develop skills they need to critically examine themselves and society. For example, students can self-assess on how they collaborate and how they engage with multiple perspectives, among other critical skills to engage with others who may be different from them. Students also cultivate their identities as students and understand the value of their effort when they are able to objectively reflect on their work and in environments that affirm who they are (Scharf, 2016).

Balanced Instruction

Overview and Research

Balanced instruction supports a thoughtfully designed curriculum that addresses the multidimensional needs and experiences of learners in an enriched environment in a way that ensures a well-rounded education (Diamond, & Hopson, 1999). As defined in this chapter, balanced instruction encourages a deep conceptual understanding of content through a combination of problem-based tasks with explicit instruction needed to accomplish those tasks (Darling-Hammond et al., 2019). When educators create balanced instruction, they create positive emotional support for active participation and risk taking, exploration, inquiry, and choice, and rigorous and differentiated learning opportunities that appropriately challenge students individually and through social interactions.

Students need multiple SECs to engage in multidimensional learning experiences. For example, students manage themselves during direct instruction; develop, monitor, and evaluate their goals during individual and collective action; and ask for help when needed across tasks. Students also need relationship skills as they engage in project-based learning—taking the perspective of their peers to successfully complete the project, and making evidence-based decisions to effectively accomplish inquiry-based tasks.

Although multiple practices exist to engage in balanced instruction, including many of the others discussed in this chapter, three practices that support balanced instruction are the following:

- *Implement direct instruction.* Direct instruction includes teacher-directed interaction guided by clear goals and outcomes; teacher modeling; and explicit instruction. The teacher guides learners to connect new knowledge with prior knowledge (Luke, 2014). Direct instruction is most successful when teachers know when to use it and with whom, typically used in combination with more active forms of instruction.
- *Use project-based learning.* Project-based learning (PBL) calls for learners to explore conditions, circumstances, and possibilities that help students solve questions posed to them (Larmer & Mergendoller, 2010). Typically, PBL includes authentic tasks that tap into student interests.
- *Implement competency-based education.* Competency-based education focuses on mastering specific skills and concepts, calling for more conceptual understanding and active learning. For instance, competencies equate with explicit, measurable, transferable learning objectives that result in the learner's empowerment. Educators use assessment for the learner, both positive and meaningful (Patrick & Sturgis, 2013).

Example Approaches to Implement the Practice through a Culturally Responsive Lens

Because students need multiple opportunities to learn content and develop their competencies, balanced instruction incorporates differentiated instruction, ensuring that educators are using multiple modalities and activities so that all students can be successful (Scharf, 2016). Researchers believe that PBL is an effective way to teach students from a variety of cultural, demographic, and geographic backgrounds a broad array of content, including core content and higher order thinking skills (Schwalm & Tyleck, 2012).

Educators can also purposefully use balanced instruction to help students learn about their own and others' cultures, and examine inequitable systems (Aronson & Laughter, 2016). For example, educators can provide inquiries where students analyze a problem through a multicultural lens. Similarly, students can engage in a project where they examine inequities within their classrooms, school, or broader community. For example, in youth-participatory action research, students engage in real world research projects that have implications within their own lives (Jagers et al., 2019).

Academic Press and Expectations

Overview and Research

Academic press and expectations are two distinct but highly interrelated practices that influence student behavior and outcomes (Gewertz, 2005). Academic press refers to the implementation and encouragement of students to complete meaningful and challenging work. Expectations are educators' beliefs that all students can and will succeed, specific to content, behaviors, and skills (Rubie-Davies, Hattie & Hamilton, 2006). Educator expectations are beliefs that influence both student and teacher behavior (Spiegel, 2012). Expectations influence educator actions, speech, and non-verbal cues, and they also result in student perceptions of those behaviors, making it important for educators to understand how students perceive their experiences in schools.

To successfully hold high expectations, educators ensure that students feel valued and heard (Bondy & Ross, 2008), ensuring that students have the necessary support to meet those expectations (Cannata, Smith & Taylor Haynes, 2017). Given the higher demand of coursework, and increased interaction between students and teachers, students use multiple SECs, such as the abilities to thoughtfully understand their current knowledge related to the coursework, to manage stress that may come from more rigorous work, and to seek help and resources when are needed.

Practices that promote academic press and expectations include the following:

- *Demonstrate positive regard.* Demonstrating positive regard moves educators beyond praising a student for obtaining correct answers, and instead recognizes a more complete picture of the student in their interactions. For example, educators are proactive, rather than reactive, in getting to know students and allowing students to get to know the educator (Jenkins, 2015).
- *Encourage participation.* Educators encourage students to engage in classrooms through multiple mechanisms including letting students know the expectation for participation, knowing which students are more or less comfortable engaging in cooperative tasks, and providing multiple modalities for students to engage with content and with each other (Pianta et al., 2012).
- *Provide support and feedback.* Students feel supported and feel that educators believe in their success when they receive authentic feedback. Educators can affirm students, cite reasons for praise, and follow up on educator comments or questions to students to demonstrate that they believe in their students (Gewertz, 2005).
- *Engage in rigorous curriculum.* Educators need to know students well enough to ensure each student receives the necessary level of rigor, inclusive of their social and emotional development (Gamoran, Porter, Smithson & White, 1997).

Example Approaches to Implement the Practice through a Culturally Responsive Lens

Educator expectations are influenced by multiple factors, including the race, ethnicity, gender, socioeconomic status, behavior, and past performance of their students (Cherng, 2017). Typically, all educators want all of their students to achieve; however, expectations can differ based on unconscious biases. For example, an educator may unconsciously vary in wait time, tone of voice, or type of feedback. Similarly, a delay in response by one student may be perceived as lazy, whereas in another student it is perceived as contemplation.

Low expectations may also be accompanied by microaggressions, which are subtle comments or actions that stereotype a group of students. For example, microaggressions against students of color may be that they are praised for speaking eloquently, unconsciously provided less feedback, or not provided access to advanced coursework (Schlund et al., 2020). To combat these unconscious beliefs, educators can reflect on their actions, and obtain feedback from students about how they are feeling in class. Educators can also learn to adopt conscious beliefs that recognize the giftedness and historical excellence of students of color and train their expectations for abundance rather than deficits (Jackson, 2006; Muhammed, 2018).

Competence Building

Overview and Research

Competence-building instruction, for the purposes of this chapter, is a series of practices that systematically and explicitly develop student social and emotional competencies through the instructional cycle. When implementing competence-building, educators purposefully reinforce SECs through each part of the instructional cycle—either as stand-alone lessons, mini-lessons, or integration with academic content (Yoder, 2014). Further, the educator models and embodies the SECs they reinforce helping students process the SECs the educator uses through self-talk, self-care strategies, and other SECs in their interactions with students, colleagues, and families.

When explicitly teaching and reinforcing student SECs, research demonstrates that educators should be purposeful and systematic in their approach. For example, in their meta-analysis of SEL evidence-based programs, Durlak and colleagues (2011) found that SEL instruction should be sequenced, active, focused, and explicit—or *SAFE*. Although the researchers identified these principles through analyzing SEL programs, educators can apply the same practices with or without programs.

Educators can embed, explicitly teach and reinforce SECs, in the context of safe and supportive learning environments through the following set of practices within the instructional cycle:

- *Establish SEC goals or objectives.* Educators can create a scope and sequence of the SECs they want to teach and reinforce, defining specific SEL goals or objectives. Educators can use state (Dusenbury et al., 2020) or curricular objectives to define the SECs, ensuring that they are developmentally appropriate (Denhem, 2018).
- *Introduce new material.* Similar to academic standards, educators can develop strategies to introduce identified SEC objectives. When introducing new material, educators can explicitly name the competency, help students connect competency with other material, garner background knowledge about the competency, and define relevance of competency to their lives.
- *Provide group and individual practice.* Educators can provide multiple opportunities for students to apply their SECs across settings in schools and afterschool programs. SEL programs use a variety of instructional techniques to develop student SECs, such as discussions, read-alouds, games, role-plays, visuals, embedding into academic instruction, and more (Jones et al., 2017). No matter which strategy an educator chooses, it provides multiple opportunities to develop and apply their skills.

- *Provide a conclusion and reflection.* Feedback—when implemented well—is one of the most important and critical pieces to teaching and learning (Hattie & Clark, 2019). Feedback is an emotional endeavor, requiring educators to understand how students receive and interpret feedback, while also developing the SECs students need to receive and reflect upon that feedback (Varlander, 2008).

Example Approaches to Implement the Practice through a Culturally Responsive Lens

Students develop their social and emotional competencies through a cultural lens. These competencies are developed in the historically grounded systems and structures that oftentimes provided inequitable opportunities and inequitable acknowledgement of the cultural assets of all individuals (Jagers et al., 2018). As educators teach content, including SECs, they reference student cultures and cultural references in how and when skills and content are used (Aronson & Laughter, 2016). The educators also help students understand how they can leverage their competencies to create a more equitable and just society (Schlund et al., 2020). Students learn how and when to advocate for themselves and for others and fight inequitable treatment of others in or out of school. This makes family-school-community connections critically important. These connections also help identify those skills that students use and how they use them in their homes and families and provides multiple opportunities to develop and use those skills.

SUPPORTING TEACHERS TO IMPLEMENT PRACTICES

Although this chapter focused on educator implementation of these practices, all adults—principals, families, community partners—need to partner together to support the social, emotional, and academic development of students (Berman et al., 2018). So, what can other stakeholders do to support educators as they implement these practices? Below we provide some high-leverage practices for other stakeholders:

- *Communicate the importance of SEL.* Leaders and families, in particular, can communicate the importance of SEL as a key component within schools and classrooms. Leaders can come together—with educators, families, community members and students—on ways in which all can agree on the *what* and *how* of SEL within the local community (CASEL, 2020b).
- *Appreciate and support.* Teaching, whether in school or in afterschool programs, is no easy task. Educators, including afterschool staff, need to feel valued and appreciated. By having a community that champions educators, a culture of support in the educational environment is created (Jennings, Minnici & Yoder, 2019).
- *Provide opportunities for educators to reflect on their social and emotional competencies.* Research demonstrates the importance of educators' own social and emotional competencies for student development (Jennings & Greenberg, 2008). Leaders can create safe spaces for educators to reflect on their own SECs, including the language they use with their students, how they interact with different groups of students, the ways in which they model competencies, and how they develop collegial relationships (Berman et al., 2018).
- *Engage in collective planning and learning.* SEL is similar to other content domains: it requires collective planning and learning for effective implementation. Professional learning communities

(PLCs), for example, provide opportunities to cooperatively learn, discuss, and act on their own practices that promote SEAD. At times, collective planning should also include families and community partners (CASEL, 2020b).

- *Promote culturally responsive practices.* Educators should continue to engage in professional development on cultural competencies, alongside their SEL practices. Multiple community organizations can partner with educators to help achieve greater diversity and cultural competency in the classroom (Duchesneau, 2020).
- *Allow for educator autonomy.* Leaders can provide educators opportunities to be responsible for SEL efforts. For example, leaders can encourage educators to adapt lessons to meet the needs of their students, or create an educator leadership team that will guide decisions about SEL integration. Autonomy moves teachers' practices beyond compliance to personal motivation for implementation (Knight, 2019).
- *Provide coaching and support.* Changing educator practices takes time. It is important to understand educator beliefs about their own practice and provide coaching and support to help them identify levers for change. It is important for leaders to match educator needs with appropriate coaching techniques (Yoder & Gurke, 2014).
- *Identify community resources.* It is important that educators have the resources they need to implement SEL and culturally responsive practices. Identify community assets, potential partnerships (e.g., youth-serving organizations, mental health providers), effective strategies, and voices to elevate to ensure the school's SEL efforts are aligned with and grounded in the lived experience of the community (CASEL, 2020b).
- *Partner with families and caregivers.* Equitable learning environments are built on relational trust and mutual respect for funds of knowledge existing in students' cultures and communities. Welcoming parents and families as co-creators of young people's academic, social, and emotional learning leads to improved outcomes (Mapp & Kuttner, 2013). Home visits, for example, can forge meaningful and lasting relationships to support young development and academic achievement (Sheldon & Jung, 2015).
- *Create a culturally diverse workforce.* Projections of shifting racial and ethnic demographics continue to anticipate increasing numbers of students of color in the U.S. public school system, while White teachers are the greatest percentage in the school workforce. There is evidence that race congruity has particular benefits for lower-performing Black and White students (Egalite et al., 2015), making it important for leaders to make active attempts to diversify the workforce. This can occur through actively recruiting educators of color, improving working conditions to retain educators of color, and by prioritizing the recruitment and retention of bilingual educators (Duchesneau, 2020).

Many stakeholders play a valuable role in creating the kind of educational learning environments that support these teaching practices. Interestingly, the practices leaders use to support educators resemble the practices that educators must implement to support their students—reflection, responsibility and choice, warmth and support, and coaching and development. Each of these practices reflect key principles identified in the science of learning and development at any age (Darling-Hammond et al., 2019). When educators receive support from stakeholders at all levels, they are more likely to create environments that develop and emulate social and emotional competencies across the school community.

CONCLUSION

Oftentimes SEL is considered as something separate, added on, or only an intervention for students who adults perceive to have emotional or behavioral concerns. Yet we need to move beyond that (Berman et al., 2018), recognizing that academic learning is social and emotional. Based on the 10 teaching practices and related supports, we know that SEL is more comprehensive than a singular program or a set of practices. Rather SEL is a key component of general pedagogical knowledge that educators need to use in combination with content knowledge. If we are truly to realize the impact that SEL can have as a lever for equity and excellence, SEL needs to be more fully integrated into overall school functioning, including the use of data for continuous improvement, adult SEL, professional learning, and ensuring adults and students have opportunities to use their SECs in and out of school (CASEL, 2020b). We also know that we need to connect to the other environments in which students live, and more authentically bring families into the conversation on SEL and equity. We need to address the histories and cultures of all students, leveraging the power of SEL to promote student and adult development of the beliefs, knowledge, and skills that will facilitate the creation of solutions to some of our most complex problems, while also creating meaningful environments that will help students thrive.

REFERENCES

Aronson, B., & Laughter, J. (2016). The theory and practice of culturally relevant education: A synthesis of research across content areas. *Review of Educational Research*, *86*(1), 163–206. doi:10.3102/0034654315582066

Aronson, J., & Inzlicht, M. (2004). The ups and downs of attributional ambiguity: Stereotype vulnerability and the academic self-knowledge of African American college students. *Psychological Science*, *15*(12), 829–836. doi:10.1111/j.0956-7976.2004.00763.x PMID:15563328

Baloche, L., & Brody, C. M. (2017). Cooperative Learning: Exploring Challenges, Crafting Innovations. *Journal of Education for Teaching*, *43*(3), 274–283. doi:10.1080/02607476.2017.1319513

Bear, G. (2010). *School discipline and self-discipline: A practical guide to promoting prosocial student behavior*. Guilford Press.

Berman, S., Chaffee, S., & Sarmiento, J. (2018). *Supporting students' social, emotional, and academic development: Consensus statements of practice from council of distinguished educators*. Aspen Institute. Retrieved from http://nationathope.org/wp-content/uploads/cde-practice-base_final.pdf

Beymer, P. N., & Thomson, M. M. (2015). The effects of choice in the classroom: Is there too little or too much choice? *Support for Learning*, *30*(2), 105–120. Advance online publication. doi:10.1111/1467-9604.12086

Bierman, K. L., Domitrovich, C. E., Nix, R. L., Gest, S. D., Welsh, J. A., Greenberg, M. T., Blair, C., Nelson, K. E., & Gill, S. (2008). Promoting academic and social-emotional school readiness: The Head Start REDI Program. *Child Development*, *79*(6), 1802–1817. doi:10.1111/j.1467-8624.2008.01227.x PMID:19037951

Bondy, E., & Ross, D. D. (2008). The teacher as warm demander. *Educational Leadership, 66*(1), 54–58. http://www.ascd.org/publications/educational-leadership/sept08/vol66/num01/The-Teacher-as-Warm-Demander.aspx

Booth, C., & Lazear, K. (2015, June). *Cultural adaptation (Resource Brief 1).* CLC Hub Resource Brief 1. Washington, DC: The Cultural & Linguistic Competence Hub of the Technical Assistance Network for Children's Behavioral Health. http://cfs.cbcs.usf.edu/projects-research/_docs/CLC_ResearchBrief1.pdf

Brooke, G., & Andrade, H. (2013). *Student-centered self-assessment.* Jobs for the Future. Retrieved from https://jfforg-prod-prime.s3.amazonaws.com/media/documents/4_SATC_AssessTools_SelfAssessment_042613.pdf

Bryant, G., Crowley, S., & Davidsen, C. (2020). *Finding your place: The current state of K-12 social emotional learning.* Tyton Partners. Retrieved from https://tytonpartners.com/library/k-12-social-emotional-learning/

Cannata, M. A., Smith, T. M., & Taylor Haynes, K. (2017). Integrating academic press and support by increasing student ownership and responsibility. *AERA Open, 3*(3), 1–13. doi:10.1177/2332858417713181

Castro, F. G., Barrera, M. Jr, & Holleran Steiker, L. K. (2010). Issues and challenges in the design of culturally adapted evidence-based interventions. *Annual Review of Clinical Psychology, 6*(1), 213–239. doi:10.1146/annurev-clinpsy-033109-132032 PMID:20192800

Center for Instructional Development and Research. (1999). Teaching through discussion. *Teaching and Learning Bulletin, 2.* Retrieved from: http://www.washington.edu/teaching/files/2012/12/Discussion.pdf

Cherng, H. Y. S. (2017). If they think I can: Teacher bias and youth of color expectations and achievement. *Social Science Research, 66*, 170–186. doi:10.1016/j.ssresearch.2017.04.001 PMID:28705354

Collaborative for Academic, Social, and Emotional Learning. (2020a). *Core SEL competencies.* Chicago, IL: Author. Retrieved from https://casel.org/core-competencies/

Collaborative for Academic, Social, and Emotional Learning. (2020b). *Guide to schoolwide SEL.* Chicago, IL: Author. Retrieved from https://schoolguide.casel.org/focus-area-3/classroom/integration-of-sel-and-instruction/using-interactive-pedagogy/

Costa, A. L., & Kallick, B. (2008). Learning through reflection. In A. L. Costa & B. Kallick (Eds.), *Learning and leading with habits of mind: 16 essential characteristics for success.* ASCD. Retrieved from http://www.ascd.org/publications/books/108008/chapters/Learning-Through-Reflection.aspx

Crowe, C. (2009). *Solving thorny behavior problems. In Coaching Children in Handling Everyday Conflicts.* Responsive Classrooms. Retrieved from https://www.responsiveclassroom.org/coaching-children-in-handling-everyday-conflicts/

d'Ailly, H. (2004). The role of choice in children's learning: A distinctive cultural and gender difference in efficacy, interest, and effort. *Canadian Journal of Behavioural Science, 36*(1), 17–29. doi:10.1037/h0087212

Darling-Hammond, L., Flook, L., Cook-Harvey, C., Barron, B., & Osher, D. (2019). Implications for educational practice of the science of learning and development. *Applied Developmental Science, 24*(2), 97–140. doi:10.1080/10888691.2018.1537791

Denham, S. (2018). *Keeping SEL developmental: The importance of a developmental lens for fostering and assessing SEL competencies.* Establishing Practical Social-Emotional Competence Assessments Work Group. Retrieved from https://casel.org/wp-content/uploads/2020/04/Keeping-SEL-Developmental.pdf

Denton, P. (2008). The power of our words. *Educational Leadership, 66*(1), 28–31. http://www.ascd.org/publications/educational-leadership/sept08/vol66/num01/The-Power-of-Our-Words.aspx

Diamond, M., & Hopson, J. (1999). *Magic trees of the mind: How to nurture your child's intelligence, creativity, and healthy emotions from birth through adolescence.* Plume.

Duchesneau, N. (2020). *Social, emotional, and academic development through an equity lens.* EdTrust.

Durlak, J. A., Weissberg, R. P., Dymnicki, A. B., Taylor, R. D., & Schellinger, K. B. (2011). The impact of enhancing students' social and emotional learning: A meta-analysis of school-based universal interventions. *Child Development, 82*(1), 405–432. doi:10.1111/j.1467-8624.2010.01564.x PMID:21291449

Dusenbury, L., Calin, S., Domitrovich, C., & Weissberg, R. (2015). *What does evidence-based instruction in social and emotional learning actually look like in practice? A brief on findings from CASEL's program reviews.* Collaborative for Academic, Social, and Emotional Learning.

Dusenbury, L., Yoder, N., Dermody, C., & Weissberg, R. (2020). *An examination of frameworks for social and emotional learning (SEL) reflected in state K-12 learning standards.* Collaborative for Academic, Social, and Emotional Learning.

EdWeek. (2019). *Safety and social and emotional learning: Results of a national survey.* Bethesda, MD: Education Week Research Center. Retrieved from https://www.edweek.org/media/safety-and-sel-national-survey-education-week-research-center-2019.pdf

Ertmer, P., & Newby, T. (1996). The expert learner: Strategic, self-regulated, and reflective. *Instructional Science, 24*(1), 1–24. doi:10.1007/BF00156001

Evans, M., & Boucher, A. R. (2015). Optimizing the power of choice: Supporting student autonomy to foster motivation and engagement in learning. *Mind, Brain and Education: the Official Journal of the International Mind, Brain, and Education Society, 9*(2), 87–91. doi:10.1111/mbe.12073

Fisher, D., & Frey, N. (2013). *Engaging the adolescent learner: Fostering classroom discussion about complex ideas and texts.* International Reading Association.

Fishman, E. J. (2014). With great control comes great responsibility: The relationship between perceived academic control, student responsibility, and self-regulation. *The British Journal of Educational Psychology, 84*(4), 685–702. doi:10.1111/bjep.12057 PMID:25251935

Gamoran, A., Porter, A. C., Smithson, J., & White, P. A. (1997). Upgrading high school mathematics instruction: Improving learning opportunities for low-achieving, low-income youth. *Educational Evaluation and Policy Analysis, 19*(4), 325–338. doi:10.3102/01623737019004325

Gay, G. (2013). Teaching to and through cultural diversity. *Curriculum Inquiry, 43*(1), 48–70. doi:10.1111/curi.12002

Gewertz, C. (2005). *Training focuses on teachers' expectations* [Blog post]. Education Week. Retrieved from https://www.edweek.org/ew/articles/2005/04/06/30tesa.h24.html

Gillies, R. M., & Boyle, M. (2010). Teachers' Reflections on Cooperative Learning: Issues of Implementation. *Teaching and Teacher Education, 26*(4), 933–940. doi:10.1016/j.tate.2009.10.034

Graham, E. J. (2017). Authority or democracy? Integrating two perspectives on equitable classroom management in urban schools. *The Urban Review*. Advance online publication. doi:10.100711256-017-0443-8

Hammond, Z. (2014). *Responsive cultural teaching and the brain*. Corwin Press.

Hattie, J., & Clark, S. (2019). *Visible learning: Feedback*. Routledge. doi:10.4324/9780429485480

Howard, D. C. (2019). Social-emotional learning won't happen without a culturally relevant start. *EdWeek: Teacher Blog*. Retrieved from https://blogs.edweek.org/teachers/intersection-culture-and-race-in-education/2019/02/social_emotional_learning_wont_happen_withouth_culturally_relevant_pedagogy.html

Immordino-Yang, M. H., Darling-Hammond, L., & Krone, C. (2018). *The brain basis for integrated social, emotional, and academic development: How emotions and social relationships drive instruction*. Aspen Institute. Retrieved from http://nationathope.org/wp-content/uploads/aspen_research_final_web.pdf

International Institute for Restorative Practices. (2012). *What is restorative practices?* Retrieved from https://www.iirp.edu/what-is-restorative-practices.php

Jackson, Y. (2011). *The pedagogy of confidence: Inspiring high intellectual performance in urban schools*. Teachers College Press.

Jagers, R., Rivas-Drake, D., & Borowski, T. (2018). Equity and social and emotional learning: A cultural analysis. In *Frameworks brief, special issues series*. Collaborative for Academic, Social, and Emotional Learning. Retrieved from https://casel.org/wp-content/uploads/2020/04/equity-and-SEL-.pdf

Jagers, R., Rivas-Drake, D., & Williams, B. (2019). Transformative social and emotional learning (SEL): Toward SEL in service of educational equity and excellence. *Educational Psychologist, 54*(3), 162–184. doi:10.1080/00461520.2019.1623032

Jenkins, R. (2015). The power of positive regard. *The Chronicle of Higher Education*. Retrieved from https://www.chronicle.com/article/The-Power-of-Positive-Regard/232547

Jennings, P. A., & Greenberg, M. T. (2009). The prosocial classroom: Teacher social and emotional competence in relation to student and classroom outcomes. *Review of Educational Research, 79*(1), 491–525. doi:10.3102/0034654308325693

Jennings, T., Minnici, A., & Yoder, N. (2019). Creating the working conditions to enhance teacher social and emotional well-being. In D. Osher, M. J. Mayer, R. Jagers, K. Kendziora, & L. Wood (Eds.), *Keeping Students Safe and Helping Them Thrive: A Collaborative Handbook on School Safety, Mental Health, and Wellness*. Praeger/ABC-CLIO. Retrieved from https://publisher.abc-clio.com/9781440854149/225

Johnson, D. W., & Johnson, R. T. (1999). Making Cooperative Learning Work. *Theory into Practice, 38*(2), 67–73. doi:10.1080/00405849909543834

Jones, S., Brush, K., Bailey, R., Brion-Meisels, G., McIntyre, J., Khan, J., Nelson, B., & Stickle, L. (2017). *Navigating SEL from the inside out: Looking inside and across 25 leading SEL programs, a practical resource for schools and OST providers*. Harvard Graduate School. Retrieved from https://www.wallacefoundation.org/knowledge-center/Documents/Navigating-Social-and-Emotional-Learning-from-the-Inside-Out.pdf

Jones, S., & Khan, J. (2017). *The evidence base for how we learn: Supporting students' social, emotional, and academic development*. Aspen Institute. Retrieved from http://nationathope.org/wp-content/uploads/final_cds-evidence-base.pdf

Jones, S. M., & Bouffard, S. M. (2012). Social and emotional learning in schools: From programs to strategies (Social Policy Report). *Sharing Child and Youth Development Knowledge, 26*(4), 3–22. Retrieved from http://www.ncflb.com/wp-content/uploads/2013/02/Social-and-Emotional-Learning-in-Schools-From-Programs-to-Strategies.pdf

Katz, I., & Assor, A. (2007). When choice motivates and when it does not. *Educational Psychology Review, 19*(4), 429–442. doi:10.100710648-006-9027-y

Knight, J. (2019). Why teacher autonomy is central to coaching success. *Educational Leadership, 77*, 14–20. http://www.ascd.org/publications/educational-leadership/nov19/vol77/num03/Why-Teacher-Autonomy-Is-Central-to-Coaching-Success.aspx

Knight, L. (2015). *Building Social-Emotional Learning Skills Through Cooperative Learning*. ASCD In Service. Retrieved from https://inservice.ascd.org/building-social-emotional-learning-skills-through-cooperative-learning/

Ladson-Billings, G. J. (1994). *The Dreamkeepers*. Jossey-Bass Publishing Co.

Ladson-Billings, G. J. (2014). Culturally Relevant Pedagogy 2.0: A.k.a. the Remix. *Harvard Educational Review, 84*(1), 74–84. doi:10.17763/haer.84.1.p2rj131485484751

Larmer, J., & Mergendoller, J. R. (2010). Seven essentials for project-based learning. *Giving Students Meaningful Work, 68*(1), 34–37.

Larson, K. E., Pas, E. T., Bradshaw, C. P., Rosenberg, M. S., & Day-Vines, N. L. (2018). Examining How Proactive Management and Culturally Responsive Teaching Relate to Student Behavior: Implications for Measurement and Practice. *School Psychology Review, 47*(2), 153–166. doi:10.17105/SPR-2017-0070.V47-2

Luke, A. (2014). *On explicit and direct instruction*. Australian Literacy Educators' Association. ALEA Hot Topics. Retrieved from https://www.alea.edu.au/documents/item/861

Madden-Dent, T. (2021). Advancing equity through culturally responsive social-emotional education: Addressing international student integration. In N. Yoder & A. Skoog-Hoffman (Eds.), Advances in Motivation and Achievement: Vol. 21. *Motivating the SEL Field Forward Through Equity*. Emerald Publishing Limited. doi:10.1108/S0749-7423201719

Mahoney, J. L., Weissberg, R. P., Greenberg, M. T., Dusenbury, L., Jagers, R. J., Niemi, K., Schlinger, M., Schlund, J., Shriver, T. P., VanAusdal, K., & Yoder, N. (2020, October 08). Yoder, N. (2020). Systemic social and emotional learning: Promoting educational success for all preschool to high school students. *The American Psychologist*. Advance online publication. doi:10.1037/amp0000701 PMID:33030926

Mapp, K. L., & Kuttner, P. J. (2013). *Partners in education in a dual capacity-building framework for family–school partnerships*. Southwest Educational Development Laboratory. Retrieved from https://sedl.org/pubs/framework/FE-Cap-Building.pdf

Marloes, M. H. G., Hendrickx, M., Mainhard, T., Boor-Klip, H. J., Cillessen, A. H. M., & Brekelman, M. (2016). Social dynamics in the classroom: Teacher support and conflict and the peer ecology. *Teaching and Teacher Education*, *53*, 30–40. doi:10.1016/j.tate.2015.10.004

McMillan, J. H., & Hearn, J. (2008). Student self-assessment: The key to stronger motivation and higher achievement. *Educational Horizons*, *87*, 40–49. https://files.eric.ed.gov/fulltext/EJ815370.pdf

Mueller, C. M., & Dweck, C. S. (1998). Praise for intelligence can undermine children's motivation and performance. *Journal of Personality and Social Psychology*, *75*(1), 33–52. doi:10.1037/0022-3514.75.1.33 PMID:9686450

National Commission on Social, Emotional, and Academic Development. (2019). *Nation at hope*. Aspen, CO: Aspen Institute. Retrieved from http://nationathope.org/

Osher, D., Bear, G., Sprague, J., & Doyle, W. (2010). How we can improve school discipline. *Educational Researcher*, *39*(1), 48–58. doi:10.3102/0013189X09357618

Osher, D., Cantor, P., Berg, J., Steyer, L., & Rose, T. (2018). Drivers of human development: How relationships and context shape learning and development. *Applied Developmental Science*, *1*. Advance online publication. doi:10.1080/10888691.2017.1398650

Osher, D., Moroney, D., & Williamson, S. (2018). *Creating safe, equitable, engaging schools: A comprehensive, evidence-based approach to supporting students*. Harvard Education Press.

Paris, D. (2012). Culturally sustaining pedagogy: A needed change in stance, terminology, and practice. *Educational Researcher*, *41*(3), 93–97. doi:10.3102/0013189X12441244

Paris, D., & Alim, H. S. (2014). What are we seeking to sustain through culturally sustaining pedagogy? A loving critique forward. *Harvard Educational Review*, *84*(1), 85–137. doi:10.17763/haer.84.1.982l873k2ht16m77

Patrick, S., & Sturgis, C. (2013). *Competency works issue brief: Necessary for success: Building mastery of world-class skills: A state policymakers guide to competency education*. International Association for K–12 Online Education. Retrieved from https://www.competencyworks.org/wp-content/uploads/2013/02/inacol_cw_issuebrief_building_mastery_final.pdf

Pianta, R. C., Hamre, B. K., & Mintz, S. (2012). *Classroom Assessment Scoring System – Secondary Manual*. Teachstone.

Rimm-Kaufman, S., & Sandilos, L. (2018). *Improving Students' Relationships with Teachers to Provide Essential Supports for Learning*. American Psychological Association. https://www.apa.org/education/ce/1360423

Rothstein, D., & Santana, L. (2011). Teaching students to ask their own questions: One small change can yield big results. *Harvard Education Letter*, *27*, 1–6.

Rubie-Davies, C., Hattie, J., & Hamilton, R. (2006). Expecting the best from students: Teacher expectations and academic outcomes. *The British Journal of Educational Psychology*, *76*(3), 429–444. doi:10.1348/000709905X53589 PMID:16953955

Sackstein, S. (2017) Peer feedback in the classroom: Empowering students to be the experts. *ASCD*. Retrieved from http://www.ascd.org/ASCD/pdf/siteASCD/publications/books/PeerFeedbackInTheClassroom_Sackstein.pdf

Safir, S. (2016). 5 keys to challenging implicit bias. *Edutopia*. Retrieved from https://www.edutopia.org/blog/keys-to-challenging-implicit-bias-shane-safir

Scharf, A. (2016). *Critical practices for anti-bias education*. Teaching Tolerance. Retrieved from https://www.tolerance.org/sites/default/files/2017-06/PDA%20Critical%20Practices_0.pdf

Schlund, J., Jagers, R., & Schlinger, M. (2020). *Emerging insights on advancing social and emotional learning (SEL) as a lever for equity and excellence*. CASEL. Retrieved from https://bit.ly/CASELEquityInsights

Schwalm, J., & Tyleck, K. S. (2012). Systemwide implementation of project-based learning: The Philadelphia approach. *Afterschool Matters*, 1–8.

Science of Learning and Development Alliance. (2020). *How the science of learning and development can transform education: Initial findings*. Retrieved from https://5bde8401-9b54-4c2c-8a0c-569fc1789664.filesusr.com/ugd/eb0b6a_24f761d8a4ec4d7db13084eb2290c588.pdf

Sheldon, S. B., & Jung, S. B. (2015). *The family engagement partnership student outcome evaluation*. Johns Hopkins University School of Education, Center on School, Family, and Community Partnerships., https://www.researchgate.net/publication/319226886_The_Family_Engagement_Partnership_Student_Outcome_Evaluation

Skiba, R., Reynolds, C. R., Graham, S., Sheras, P., Conoley, J. C., & Garcia-Vazquez, E. (2006). *Are zero tolerance policies effective in the schools? An evidentiary review and recommendations*. A report by the American Psychological Association Zero Tolerance Task Force. Retrieved from https://www.apa.org/pubs/info/reports/zero-tolerance-report.pdf

Smith, T., Brumskill, R., Johnson, A., & Zimmer, T. (2018). The impact of teacher language on students' mindsets and statistics performance. *Social Psychology of Education*, *21*(4), 775–786. doi:10.100711218-018-9444-z

Spiegel, A. (2012). *Teachers' expectations can influence how students perform*. Retrieved from https://www.npr.org/sections/health-shots/2012/09/18/161159263/teachers-expectations-can-influence-how-students-perform

Staats, C. (2014). *Implicit racial bias and school discipline disparities: Exploring the connection. Kirwan Institute Special Report*. Kirwan Institute. Retrieved from http://kirwaninstitute.osu.edu/implicit-bias-training/resources/ki-ib-argument-piece03.pdf

Tennessee Department of Education. (n.d.). *Social and personal competencies*. Retrieved from https://www.tn.gov/education/health-and-safety/school-climate/social-and-personal-competencies.html

The Origins Program. (2014). *Developmental Designs 1: Resource book*. Author.

Varlander, S. (2008). The role of students' emotions in formal feedback situations. *Journal of Teaching in Higher Education*, *13*(2), 145–156. doi:10.1080/13562510801923195

Willingham, D. (2011). Ask the cognitive scientist: Can teachers increase students' self-control? *American Educator*, *35*(2), 22–27. https://www.aft.org/sites/default/files/periodicals/Willingham_3.pdf

Yoder, N. (2014). *Teaching the whole child: Instructional practices that support social-emotional learning in three teacher evaluation frameworks*. Center on Great Teachers and Leaders. Retrieved from http://www.gtlcenter.org/sites/default/files/TeachingtheWholeChild.pdf

Yoder, N., & Gurke, D. (2017). *Social and emotional learning coaching toolkit: Keeping SEL at the Center*. American Institutes for Research. Retrieved from https://www.air.org/sites/default/files/downloads/report/Social-and-Emotional-Learning-SEL-Coaching-Toolkit-August-2017.pdf

Zubrzycki, J. (2015). *Students 'self-assess' their way to learning*. Retrieved from https://www.edweek.org/ew/articles/2015/11/11/students-self-assess-their-way-to-learning.html

ENDNOTE

1 Two of the authors of the current chapter (Nick Yoder and Pat Conner) were primary authors of the Tennessee Department of Education resources.

Chapter 8
Social Emotional Learning as a Lever for High School Student Mental Health and Academic Success:
A Reflective Analysis

Kimberly Reed
Sierra Nevada University, USA

Tara Madden-Dent
Sierra Nevada University, USA

ABSTRACT

The following case study demonstrates how one high school Social Studies teacher embedded social emotional learning (SEL) into content and classroom management practices for eight years at a large urban school in the American Southwest. The collected data (e.g., teacher reflections, student reflections) provide a variety of viewpoints around how SEL influenced the teacher and student experience. Through collective analysis, this study's qualitative data contributes to new understanding of the importance of social, emotional, and academic development practices in high schools for students and teachers, especially around supporting classroom safety, mental health, and wellness.

INTRODUCTION

There is a crisis in America; a national concern for wellness and safety in schools. Increases in youth gun violence, suicides, substance abuse and over-doses (National Institutes of Health, 2020), increases in violence and crime rates (National Coalition Against Domestic Violence, 2020), and increases in mental health concerns such as depression, apathy, anxiety, fear, feelings of being overwhelmed, and hopelessness (National Alliance on Mental Illness, 2020), demonstrate a hurting populous within struggling

DOI: 10.4018/978-1-7998-6728-9.ch008

educational systems. According to the Anxiety and Depression Association of America (2020), Anxiety disorders affect 25% of children between ages 13 and 18 years and research demonstrates that untreated anxiety disorders contribute to children becoming higher risk to perform poorly in school, miss out on important social experiences, and engage in substance abuse. (Anxiety and Depression Association of America, 2020). Moreover, increasing youth social media addictions and screen-time usage contributes to withdrawn behaviors and feelings of depression (Hurley, 2020; Maker, 2018).

To help address these harmful stressors, schools can provide safe and predictable learning environments with positive, nurturing adult relationships who actively participate in explicit and culturally responsive social-emotional learning activities (EducationLinks, 2018). As demonstrated by more than twenty-five years of research, culturally responsive social-emotional education contributes to safer, healthier, more equitable, and successful educational environments and student outcomes (Cantor et al., 2018; Jones & Kahn, 2017; Kerr, Madden-Dent, & Shalabi, 2020; Madden-Dent, 2021; Osher et al., 2018; Durlak, Weissberg, Dymnicki, Taylor, & Schellinger, 2011; Taylor et al., 2017). Furthermore, SEL education is linked with decreases in unhealthy behaviors, mental health issues, and drop-out rates (Kautz, Heckman, Diris, Bas ter Weel, & Borghans, 2014).

Beyond the student experience, teachers and student support professionals also face high stress levels and adversity (Cipriano & Brackett, 2020). According to the American Federation of Teachers Educator Quality of Work Life Survey (2017), 61% of teachers indicated that their jobs were always or often stressful and 58% of respondents cited poor mental health as a result of that stress. As with the benefits of SEL support for students, studies have found that educators who practice social-emotional and mindfulness interventions experience a reduction in stress, anxiety, emotional exhaustion, improved attention, engagement, emotional regulation, and reduction in burnout (Flook, Goldberg, Pinger, Bonus, & Davidson, 2013; Patti & Tobin, 2003; 2005). Moreover, educators who practice and model regular SEL skills enhance self-efficacy, job satisfaction, and professional identity development (Arroyo, 2021; Elias et al., in press; Jones & Weissbourd, 2013), are less likely to report burnout (Brackett et al., 2010), and have higher levels of relational trust with their peers at work (Bryk & Schneider, 2002; Madden-Dent, Jackson, & Cason, 2021).

SEL and SEAD

This chapter subscribes to the well-established definition of Social and Emotional Learning (SEL) developed by the Collaborative for Academic, Social, and Emotional Learning (CASEL), as being the "process through which all young people and adults acquire and apply the knowledge, skills, and attitudes to develop healthy identities, manage emotions and achieve personal and collective goals, feel and show empathy for others, establish and maintain supportive relationships, and make responsible and caring decisions." (CASEL, 2020). According to the CASEL Five SEL Competencies (CASEL, 2020, p. 2), the skills include:

Self-Awareness: *The abilities to understand one's own emotions, thoughts, and values and how they influence behavior across contexts. This includes capacities to recognize one's strengths and limitations with a well-grounded sense of confidence and purpose.*

Self-Management: *The abilities to manage one's emotions, thoughts, and behaviors effectively in different situations and to achieve goals and aspirations. This includes the capacities to delay gratification, manage stress, and feel motivation & agency to accomplish personal/collective goals.*

Social Awareness: *The abilities to understand the perspectives of and empathize with others, including those from diverse backgrounds, cultures, & contexts. This includes the capacities to feel compassion for others, understand broader historical and social norms for behavior in different settings, and recognize family, school, and community resources and supports.*

Relationship Skills: *The abilities to establish and maintain healthy and supportive relationships and to effectively navigate settings with diverse individuals and groups. This includes the capacities to communicate clearly, listen actively, cooperate, work collaboratively to problem solve and negotiate conflict constructively, navigate settings with differing social and cultural demands and opportunities, provide leadership, and seek or offer help when needed.*

Responsible Decision-Making: *The abilities to make caring and constructive choices about personal behavior and social interactions across diverse situations. This includes the capacities to consider ethical standards and safety concerns, and to evaluate the benefits and consequences of various actions for personal, social, and collective well-being.*

In education, Social, Emotional, and Academic Development (SEAD) practices is the integration of social-emotional learning (SEL) and academics to reinforce equitable and human-centered educational environments (Aspen Institute, 2018). One example of a SEAD practice is a school-community partnership to embed SEL into student and family afterschool programs at local community centers. Another example may include school-family partnerships to provide culturally responsive SEL education at parent and family outreach events. Lastly, school-university partnerships can include SEAD trainings for all new and returning educators and staff members through continuing education programs. SEAD practices woven into the fabric of educational systems can support the modeling and instruction of SEL skills within all subject content areas and within authentic partnerships between the student, school, family/caregivers, and community (Miller, 2020).

In the primary grades, there has traditionally been more SEL curriculum compared to middle and high schools (Grant et al., 2017). By the time students reach high school there is limited explicit SEL included in the curriculum (Gulbrandson, 2019). Often times, high school teachers and students primarily focused on core subjects associated with standardized tests, but due to negative outcomes of 2020 COVID-19 Pandemic (e.g., Mental health issues), there has been greater focus to incorporate SEL at the high school level. This shift was one reason for the following collective analysis of teacher and student reflections on high school SEL. The following section will provide insights into one teacher's SEL experiences and how her students perceived SEL in their school experience.

SOCIAL EMOTIONAL LEARNING REFLECTIONS

The following section examines how SEL had influenced instruction and classroom management for eight years within one teacher's Social Studies class at a large, affluent, urban high school with more than 3,400 students. As part of normal, on-going practice, the teacher collected journal entries of significant professional events which included written reflections. After eight years, the teacher conducted a collective analysis of multiple qualitative data sources (e.g., Teaching materials; Journal notes; Student reflections), to identify in which ways SEL influenced her teaching experience and effectiveness, in addition to student experiences. This section is organized first by the teacher's reflections and is then followed by a section describing students' reflections on their high school perspectives and experiences. A Discussion section is then offered to demonstrate connections between the teacher and student reflections of SEL at the high school level.

Teacher Reflections

The following section is organized to first provide four specific high school class events which either incorporated SEL through SEAD classroom management and instructional practices or were absent of SEL, and some of the resulting outcomes from those relationships. The scenarios demonstrate a relationship between SEAD classroom practices and student experiences, including but not limited to classroom safety and mental health. The following scenarios were consolidated from teacher reflections and journal entries.

Scenario #1: Equitable SEAD Classroom Management Supporting Mental Health

Like many educators who have not completed formal SEL classes at the higher education level (Schonert-Reichl, Kitil, Hanson-Peterson, 2017), this case study's teacher had received no formal training in SEL or SEAD prior to becoming a teacher. Her university did not offer SEL instruction within its teacher training programs or Masters in Education coursework. Learning the SEL competencies was acquired through independent study and on-going professional development. One journal reflection stated,

I really wish I would have had SEL knowledge in middle school, high school, and in higher education. In college, I sought out and practiced self-reflection, goal setting, mindfulness, cultural competence, communication skills, relationship skills, and responsible-decision making skills so I could become a more effective high school teacher.

This teacher's high school was also absent of SEL professional development opportunities although its unique campus culture and climate often indicated need for it. Although the school had strong student achievement scores and marketed itself as a top performing learning institution, school safety and student health indicators were of increasing concern which reflected a different message.

Depression, substance abuse, bullying, racism, anxiety, and tension had increased every year according to student discipline data and climate surveys. These school reports also demonstrated that the majority of its students, who were predominately Caucasian and self-classified as a high socioeconomic status, had access to educational resources and support but struggled with loneliness and isolation. Often times, students expressed being alone at home without supervision and without trusting relationships with parents or caregivers. School teachers and administrators learned that many of the students were addicted to drugs, alcohol, sex, social media, and other unhealthy and illegal behaviors. Heroin and opioid pills were especially common practice among students on campus. Many students struggled with coping strategies to manage their emotions and behaviors which resulted in poor academic performance, poor health, and fatalities (e.g., Drug over-doses; Suicides).

To address these challenges, the Social Studies teacher began intentionally incorporating explicit SEL lessons and activities within class daily practices. First, each class became a "Team" and its members co-created classroom norms and expectations. Team members discussed the importance of having the class be their safe-zone where open, confidential dialog was encouraged within a respectful learning community. Students collectively set team goals and then worked together to accomplish goals for the day, week, and semester. Over the eight years, each team had its own personality and culture; which required a culturally responsive teaching approach every year develop the awareness of the significance and value of students' backgrounds (including historical context), and then intentionally integrate their customs and values into class curriculum and the classroom environment.

With this SEAD approach to creating a human-centered educational experience that supported the whole-child, each student was heard and valued. The Social Studies class created the conditions to cover more than politics, history, and religion, but included sensitive topics such as bullying, anxiety, depression, abuse, violence, divorce, alcoholism, drug use, over-doses, suicides, homelessness, etc. The SEL-grounded classroom was an environment where students felt safe discussing sensitive topics and gained confidence to receive ongoing support from the teacher and school counselors if they wanted. This approach was important because when students were struggling with strong emotions like anxiety or fear, learning stopped for them, and often others around them. This is demonstrated in the following written reflection.

Throughout my first years of teaching, I was continually trying to figure out ways to teach the whole-student. It was pointless trying to teach them to memorize historical facts when they were completely obsessing over a fight they had with their parents, or worried that they were pregnant, or wondering where they were going to get their drugs from that afternoon. I knew that the subject material would not matter unless I put the students first. We started doing a lot of lessons and activities that connected learning objectives with personal life events. Students often would project themselves into historical scenarios and write reflections to assignment prompts that linked feelings and behavior choices. They didn't realize that they were practicing and developing SEL skills.

This is further illustrated in the following journal excerpt of a class event which details how one student's emotions had blocked teaching and learning opportunities while creating an unstable learning climate.

As I learned more about my students, they would present how they learned best and when they were entirely checked-out. One particular Sophomore started attending fifth period angry and emotionally overwhelmed. His behavior repeated for several days and often resulted in yelling and then isolation. The commotion effected his team (classmates), who expressed a wide array of strong feelings (e.g., fear, anxiety, sadness, annoyance), and shared that they were distracted from learning. The student had been getting in trouble for fist fights and other aggressive behavior on campus with students and adults. The student had difficultly trusting teachers to help as he expressed that many of them had only escalated the emotionally-charged situations and/or just sent him to the Dean's Office. Our class took a different approach.

One of the most intensive days, this student arrived in a state of rage, punching desks, and ready to fight. He needed to leave the room, quickly and in a way that kept him and other safe. After notifying the Hall Monitors, I gave him a hall pass to practice self-management and self-awareness skills through a kinesthetic activity. The overwhelmed student asked to run around the school outside which was still on campus property until he felt grounded, calm, and back in control of his faculties. In only five minutes, he returned to class, red-faced, sweaty, catching his breath, but calm, rational, and smiling. He silently sat down, took out his notebook, and joined our class assignment. Soon after, I privately asked him if it helped and how he felt. He shared that he felt better and thanked me for the activity instead of sending him to the Dean's office.

After class, the student and I met. He said that no other teacher had ever helped him in that way before. This running activity became a normal SEL practice for him and other students who needed five minutes to become grounded, centered, and refocused. As the year moved on, this particular student became more confident in managing his emotions and behavior in my class until he no longer had to run and could mindfully recognize his feelings and then quietly self-regulate through breathing and writing activities. After graduation, he returned to school and thanked me again for caring about him and taking the time to support his mental and emotional health during a painful time in his life.

Scenario #2: Outdoor SEAD Practices Supporting Mental Health

Although it was a Social Studies class, SEL classroom management practices contributed to students' social-emotional skills that aided with their abilities to manage emotions and behaviors; a transferrable skill into other academic and professional applications. One example of an effective SEL classroom management practice was revisiting the class team's co-created norms and student behavior expectations which were developed during the first week of every class. These were reviewed to consistently check into how our learning environment was meeting the needs of all students, at the time they needed support, and with the appropriate support and resources.

One discussion centered on how they learned best when learning was supported in safe environments and included physical activities. For example, most students discussed that there were days, especially around testing or holidays, when the majority of the class felt strong emotions and/or experienced heightened excitement, rowdiness or restlessness, and exhaustion. Changing the classroom environment and students' energy levels was one strategy that students wanted to incorporate into their classroom norms. This type of SEL classroom management practice helped increase student engagement and class team relationship building. This is illustrated in the following teacher reflection about studying outdoors and incorporating physical movement into class studies.

Teams often had class outside to do school work in the courtyard or group discussion while walking around the school. School leadership was supportive of this classroom management practice so in seasons of pleasant weather, students would incorporate outdoor learning experiences as much as possible. It was a great way to get oxygen to our brains and bodies while clearing our minds and setting intentions for re-entering the classroom or school setting. Students really enjoyed the outdoor learning activities and practicing SEL skills through group discussions, reflections, and small groupwork. Students had shared that this classroom management practice was especially helpful for them during stressful weeks around final examinations or amidst times of personal or societal trauma (e.g., The Columbine High School Shooting).

Scenario #3: Group Sharing to Support Mental Health

Another classroom activity that contributed to SEL skill development, Team trust, and student health was called, Large Circle; it was a student-favorite every year. Question prompts that aligned with course learning objectives guided student discussions in this activity once a week. Each activity started and ended with consensus for respectful, confidential, and active listening in addition to a reminder of available ongoing support resources for students after the activity (e.g., School counselor; School psychologist; etc.). Students also acknowledged that they could respond to or skip any question that they wanted.

Students prepared for the activity by moving classroom desks and stacking chairs before sitting on the ground in a giant circle. One person would share at a time with their response to the weekly prompt and then ask the Team a follow-up question. In order to share, students needed to be holding the totem figure, while everyone not holding the totem was respectfully quiet. Early in the year, the activity's weekly prompts asked simple questions (e.g., Names; favorite foods; hobbies, etc.) as to familiarize students with the activities process. By the end of the year, students were able to express themselves through more authentic story-telling as trust for each other and confidence in sharing with the Team had increased. This activity was an opportunity for students to explore course lessons, practice SEL skills, and learn from each other about healthy and unhealthy options to manage similar life situations. This human-centered student activity bridged academics with behavior and emotions. Students had shared feeling comforted and supported by their peers after sharing which contributed to the care, empathy, and trust development among Team members.

This Large Circle activity was especially helpful in supporting classroom safety and learning during times of trauma and stress. Throughout the eight years at the urban high school, students had experienced several deaths of their peers from car accidents, suicides, and over-doses. Moreover, students often expressed experiencing increased anxiety, fear, and uncertainty during national tragedies such as school shootings. The following teacher journal entry demonstrates how the Large Circle SEL activity helped support mental health and wellness during the stressful periods at school.

I will always remember when our school initiated a "Hard Lock Down". It occurred during a year that had multiple high-profile mass shootings. Class was interrupted by a school announcement notifying us that the Hard Lock Down initiated and to follow emergency procedures. We locked the classroom door, covered the windows, turned off the lights, and hid under the desks. It was not a drill and although students sat still and quiet, they were expressing fear and concern for their safety.

After fifteen minutes, which felt much longer, the Principal provided an update on the school intercom. There had been a shooting incident next door to our campus and after law enforcement had arrested the shooter and secured our campus, we were released form the Hard Lockdown.

The class sighed but remained quiet. Students began to cry, hug, and expressed their emotional and physical exhaustion. Students texted family and friends to reassure of their safety and then, students asked to debrief the shared experience with a Large Circle activity. We spent the remainder of our class time in the Large Circle activity. Students' shares were authentic and emotional. Some expressed feeling that this campus threat was an increasingly common student experience in our society and felt almost numb to its significance. We listened, shared, and encouraged each other to meet with school support professionals (e.g., School counselor).

Later, students expressed that the activity provided them a safe space to deconstruct the stressful and painful experience because of the relationships and trust that had been built throughout the year. Students felt supported to practice self-care and responsible decision-making for ongoing wellness practices. We continued the SEL activity every week and for students who opted out of meeting with a student support professional, the Large Circle activity provided a structured method to express themselves.

Scenario #4: The Absence of SEAD Practices and its Mental Health Support

This following scenario was an event that occurred towards the beginning of this teacher's career. Feeling motivated, enthusiastic, nervous, and physically and mentally exhausted, the novice teacher recognized the need for her own SEL skills but it was not yet part of her regular routine and classroom management practices. The following reflection provides insight into how instructional and learning experiences can be influenced by the absence of SEL within classroom norms, expectations, and classroom management practices.

Teaching is one of the most mentally and physically demanding and taxing jobs. I remember one specifically stressful events and how it set in motion a new SEL-focused teaching and classroom management mindset for the rest of my career. It was a time when I incorporated traditional, punitive disciplinary practices instead of SEL-based restorative practices. Plus, the lack of my own lack of self-management skills during times of class conflict seemed to escalate students' emotions and contributed to additional disciplinary actions. The following event in still evokes painful feelings and regret.

It was the final quarter of the year and our class had been together for over 100 days of class time. There was one student, Nick (pseudonym), who although had been my greatest challenge, we had a mutual understanding and respect. One day, Nick entered the classroom incredibly agitated with another student. When the opening bell rang and students took their seats, Nick turned around to the other student and started yelling. He was using profanity and demonstrating an increasingly agitated state. Instead of taking him outside and having a respectful conversation with clarifying questions and offering supportive resources (e.g., School counselor services), I engaged him in a pubic confrontation in front of the class. It was not long until we both became increasingly agitated. Nick became so angry that he said, "I'm going to blow up the school." Intensifying this statement was its contextual timing, which occurred soon after a nationally broadcasted large school shooting and a series of other local events of public violence. Class participants felt scared and were unable to focus on their studies.

The school had a zero-tolerance policy for threats of violence and I was obligated to report him. I told him that his statement was unacceptable and if he said it again, I would be forced to send him to the Dean's office. I set Nick up a counterproductive condition for Nick through this public challenge and he accepted it by repeating the threat in a loud voice and made direct eye contact with me. I immediately had the Hall Monitor remove Nick from class and take him to the Dean's office.

Class learning had stopped. Students were experiencing an array of feelings, as was I. Students were silent, still, upset, scared, and confused. After I completed the required disciplinary report, the class debriefed the event to share thoughts and feelings. This was the best part of the event as students expressed their thoughts about how the situation could have been managed differently; to which, I learned through student voice on ways to approach conflict in the future. At the end of the day, I went to discuss the event with Administration and the student. Nick was calm and grounded by this time. He said that his words were an impulsive reaction to an anger-attack and did not want to blow up the school. He shared feeling remorse about the comment but struggled with self-hatred and thoughts of suicide.

With administrative and parental consent, Nick agreed to go with school police to a behavioral health institute for three days to ensure that Nick would receive support and resources to monitor his mental health. The concern was that he would hurt himself. One of the most painful and lasting details of this event was that Nick never returned to school. He transferred to another school and I never saw him again. This story haunts me and I still think about it often. It now serves me as an inspiration to continually seek, acquire, and practice culturally responsive SEL skills and incorporate them within classroom management practices. It also inspired me to collaborate more with student support professionals through a multitiered system of support framework to implement student supports at the time they need it. Nick's story has helped reshape how I approach teaching, building relationships with students and the families, and address conflict.

Classroom conflict and student mental health concerns are part of the educational experience for youth and adults. As an educator, it is my responsibility to address these challenges in healthy and restorative ways by developing my own SEL skills, modeling them to my students, embedding them into instruction and classroom management practices, and collaborating with student support professionals that can reinforce evidence-based SEL strategies in the classroom. The absence of a SEL approach in the preceding classroom event contributed to damaged relationships, unhealthy learning environment, hurtful student outcomes, and high teacher stress.

Student Reflections

The following section provides five student perspectives of their experiences with SEL activities in respective Social Studies classrooms between 2008 – 2016. Pseudonyms are used for students within each written narrative.

Alex (2011)

As I understand it, Social and Emotional Learning is made up of five elements - self-awareness, self-management, social awareness, relationship skills, and responsible decision making. While I can now see how these elements were omnipresent in class, social awareness stands out to me. Being LGBTQ in high school in 2008-2011 was not easy, however, I have incredibly fond memories of my Social Studies classroom being a safe-haven. The teacher promoted open-mindedness and acceptance, which resulted in classes that felt more like an engaged group rather than a sum of random students. We also placed an emphasis on relationship skills, which I personally benefited from as communication and conflict resolution were not stressed in my home. Finally, I'd like to highlight the student-teacher interactions, which I felt were always fostered with patience and understanding. At times I think I received more emotional support than was fair to take from a teacher, but I am beyond grateful to have had her guidance in tough years.

Alex reflects on the overall classroom environment which was supported by SEL lessons and SEAD classroom management practices. One particular activity that Alex referenced was called "Question of the Day" which was designed to support a student-centered environment where open, respectful group discussions helped practice social awareness skills, self-awareness skills, and communication skills. The activity provided reflective writing prompts for students to engage in a self-awareness activity that related to course content or current events. After students completed their written reflection, they had the option to share what they wrote. Those that were not sharing, remained respectfully quiet with the intentional responsibility to practice mindful active listening skills, to stay engaged within that moment without judgement, and consider asking a follow-up clarifying question if the sharing student invited questions (students always had the option to not invite follow-up questions).

In accordance with co-created classroom norms and student-developed Team agreements, students announced that the goal of this activity was not to achieve group consensus on a discussed topic and that disagreement was a natural human experience. The Team sought to recognize differences, practice open-mindedness, and look for how differences could be assets in the classroom, civic life, and workforce settings. Learning from each other, valuing differences, and showing respect was the goal and outcome.

Bailey

One of the biggest keys to life is resiliency and thriving through the adversity life throws at you, especially when you're in school and just beginning to figure out who you are. Having teachers that were able to acknowledge this and teach you how to respond to the curveballs thrown at you made all the difference. Looking back, some of the lessons that stick out the most had less to do with the topic and more to do with discussions and who led the discussions. In one of my favorite Social Studies classes, I vividly remember having a discussion about the upcoming election. Emotions were high, defenses were up, and there were few spaces that we could talk freely without judgment. Instead of shying away from these kinds of tense conversations and taut atmospheres, we learned how to talk through them in class. It didn't matter what political side you were on, who you were rooting for, or even if we agreed with our counterparts at the end. We learned how to find common ground. We each had a chance to say our peace and explain why we felt so strongly about the specific candidate or topic, taught our friends and classmates how they personally affected our lives, and then willingly listened to their point of view. Even if our beliefs didn't falter or stance didn't change, it helped us to listen and managing our emotions with our healthy debate and gain perspective where we probably hadn't looked.

Those lessons bettered us not only as students but teenagers on their way to become young adults. By learning how to open your mind to another's opinion, you allow yourself the chance to learn and to grow which only further helped me get to where I am today. Learning a topic, studying it profusely and incorporating it through team building games that put you on the same team as students you wouldn't normally choose, and having to count on them, changes how you might tackle an obstacle on your own in the future. While it may not be ideal, it's the hand you were dealt and how you respond to it that eventually becomes second nature in adapting and overcoming a sticky situation. Life is hardly ever fair but the faster you accept that and learn when to let your emotions fuel you and when to rein them in, you naturally begin to figure out that no obstacle is too big or too difficult - you just have to find the weak spot and work your way through it.

Bailey referred to an activity designed to build self-awareness, self-management, and social awareness skills through practicing communication and relationship skills. The SEL activity was called, "The Fence". Students picked a topic relevant to the current course content or a related current event (e.g., Presidential Election), and reflected on their values and related experiences which contributed to their opinions about the reflection topic. Students had three days to formulate a written response of "Yes – they were in support or agreement to the topic", "No – they were opposed to or disagreed with the topic", or "On-the-Fence – they were undecided". Each response included their opinion about the topic or current event, why they responded with yes, no, or on-the-fence (including personal experiences and values), and supporting research or artifacts that reinforced their position on the topic.

Students shared their responses one-at-a-time while others practiced mindfulness and active listening skills. In accordance with co-created classroom norms and Team agreements, it was reinforced before each activity that group consensus was not the goal; disagreement was a natural human experience and students were asked to recognize differences, practice open-mindedness, and seek the value in differing perspectives and experiences. Students were able to practice these SEL skills within the activity. Many often shared their appreciation for the rare opportunity to exchange thoughts around sensitive topics in a safe and respectful learning environment where all participants were seen and heard.

Trexton

In my high school class, we focused on goal setting at the beginning of each month. We were taught that having a start date like the beginning of the month or even beginning of the week could help achieve desired and intentional goals easier. I do not remember every goal I set during that time, but the principle of goal setting and especially leveraging the beginning of the month or start of a new week has been something I've used regularly. I often use the strategy of contemplating on the past month and then figuring out what I want to change in the new month just like we practiced as a class. It has helped me to refocus on my course work in my pre-doctoral program as well as get more results in the gym. Learning how to set goals and achieve them has had a major positive impact in all aspects of my life.

This SEL activity was known simply as "Goal Setting" and designed to increase self-awareness, self-management, and responsible decision-making skills while reinforcing student success skills and academic achievement in class. Trexton's narrative reflects the importance of developing the skill to reflect on values, behaviors, and decisions, identify meaningful and intentional goals, and strategically move towards achieving those goals. In the class, students were asked to create personal and academic SMART goals with timeline benchmarks and specific daily action steps. Students reflected on their current habits and if they were aligned with their goals. If they were out of alignment, student would explore strategies to pivot and adjust.

This SEL activity allowed students the flexibility within a safe and trusting learning community to explore what was important for them and to try new approaches for wholistic wellness. Each student had the option of sharing their goals. Students spoke one-at-a-time while other students practiced mindful active listening skills. In accordance with co-created classroom norms and Team agreements, it was emphasized before each Goal Setting activity that group consensus was not the goal; but seeking to learn from one another's experiences, values, and abilities was the goal. Students were asked to practice open-mindedness and consider how differing perspectives contribute to our class, civic life, and the workforce in positive ways. Students were able to practice their SEL skills with this activity and appreciated the safe and respectful learning environment where all participants felt acknowledged and valued.

J.P.

The following former student is now a successful professional in the professional sports industry. His written reflection shares his experience in the high school class how its introduction to SEL activities inspired self-confidence and student leadership. J.P. was a highly engaged high school student who recognized the value of developing SEL skills and wanted to help others build their own. The entire school soon benefitted from J.P.'s leadership when he applied SEL course concepts and activities to a new after-school club founded on building students' SEL skills. Eight years after his high school graduation, J.P. reflects on his experience within the following written narrative.

I remember you as one of the best teachers that I have ever had! The class topic was not my favorite subject but the class structure kept learning real. We accepted everyone for who they were and class allowed me to openly share and attempt to tell (usually bad) jokes. The course structure allowed students to freely express themselves and experience the freedom of being themselves. The after-school SEL club was a next step for practicing relationship building skills. It helped me practiced going outside of my familiar social circle to try and be friends with everyone. I still intentionally practice this.

Kelsie

Curriculum embedded with SEL created opportunities for students to practice self-awareness, self-management, social awareness, relationship skills, and responsible decision-making skills. These skills reinforced class learning objectives and student success. Students were encouraged to learn from each other and develop their respectful communication skills especially in the midst of emotionally-charged and sensitive discussions. The following former student reflected on one of those sensitive group discussion topics (e.g., Child abuse; Neglect) and how the SEL approach shaped her life.

I want to let you know that one of the most memorable activities in your class was reading, "A Child Called It." I now work in child welfare and mental health and that story with our class discussions impact my life every day. I often talk about how my teacher in high school read us this book as part of study activities and how it helped us explore connections between class content and personal values. Thank you for all you did as a teacher!

DISCUSSION

The above section provided written narratives describing how SEL classroom management practices and instruction influenced one teacher's experience and how students were influenced by the SEL activities. The following three themes emerged from the narrative data: 1.) *Safety, Health, & Climate*; 2.)

Self-Management Skills; and 3.) *Professional Development*. The following section describes each theme and connections with literature.

The first theme, *Safety, Health, & Climate*, encompasses the consistent reflection data that discussed how SEL contributed to safer and more respectful human-centered learning environment that recognized individual needs and abilities and supported students' physical and mental health. Multiple data points illuminated this theme as students and the teacher expressed how they felt and what they experienced when a SEL approach was present or absent in class. For example, several reflections mentioned a sense of collective ownership to the Team's co-constructed classroom norms and agreements. Narratives explained how this SEL classroom management practice had helped establish an inclusive safe-zone and supported collective efficacy in upholding the shared norms and agreements. Reflections often described how a SEL lesson or activity had helped students gain confidence in being vulnerable and authentic, to trust their peers, engage in sensitive class discussion topics, and how the act of reflection and sharing allowed for greater development of SEL skills.

According to reflection data, SEL classroom management practices helped shape a learning atmosphere that was welcoming and encouraged a sense of belonging. Moreover, through student and teacher narratives, this theme describes an appreciation for the classroom's inclusive, non-judgmental educational environment which allowed students to study course lessons while developing SEL skills that supported their physical and mental wellness. Moreover, one of the teacher's reflective scenarios demonstrated how the absence of SEAD classroom management practices could contribute towards escalated conflicts and feelings of anxiety, stress, anger, and fear. This theme reinforces current research that demonstrates that students will be better able to retain the information being taught to them when they feel safe and respected in their classroom environment (Committee for Children, 2014), and that social-emotional interventions and practices can contribute towards safer, more respectful learning environments (Cantor et al., 2018; Jones & Kahn, 2017; Madden-Dent, 2021; Osher et al., 2018; Durlak, Weissberg, Dymnicki, Taylor, & Schellinger, 2011; Taylor et al., 2017).

The second theme, *Self-Management Skills*, describes common findings that emerged from the reflective narrative data on how SEL lessons and activities contributed to increased SEL abilities to identify emotions, control impulses, and choose healthy behaviors. The variety of embedded SEAD practices in the Social Studies class were often described to have positively influenced stress levels, mental health, engagement, and responsible life decisions. This theme reinforces current research demonstrating that SEL in education is linked with decreases in unhealthy behaviors, mental health issues, and drop-out rates (Kautz, Heckman, Diris, Bas ter Weel, & Borghans, 2014).

Multiple student reflections indicated how the SEL lessons and activities that they experienced in high school were still positively influencing their lives today. The reflections demonstrated that the gained SEL skills continue to support their current work, personal relationships, and individual pursuits. One example was the SEL Self-Management skill of goal-setting and how it continues to reinforce perseverance especially during trials of adversity. This is consistent with other research findings that SEL interventions contribute to long-term positive impacts on the individual student and community at large (Bailey et al., 2015; Jones, Crowley, & Greenberg, 2017; Osgood et al., 2013; Spoth, Guyll, & Shin, 2009).

The third theme, Professional Development, describes common findings within teacher and student narratives around the need for early and on-going SEL training for educators. Students demonstrated the ability to recognize the teacher's application of SEL skills that contributed to their positive learning experience. The teacher recognized that a deficiency in SEL skills negatively affected her teaching experience while the application of SEL skills both encouraged physical and mental health conditions in addition to instructional effectiveness and satisfaction. This theme is consistent with current research demonstrating that educators who practice mindfulness and SEL interventions experience a reduction in stress, anxiety, emotional exhaustion, improved attention, engagement, emotional regulation, and reduction in burnout (Flook, Goldberg, Pinger, Bonus, & Davidson, 2013; Patti & Tobin, 2003; 2005). Moreover, educators experience enhanced self-efficacy and job satisfaction (Elias et al., in press; Jones & Weissbourd, 2013), are less likely to report burnout (Brackett et al., 2010), and have higher levels of relational trust with their peers at work (Bryk & Schneider, 2002; Madden-Dent, Jackson, & Cason, 2021).

Through the teacher reflections, Professional Development was discussed as a missing piece to her pre-service educator programs of study at the higher educational level in addition to her on-going in-service school-provided training. This theme describes a need for more SEL and SEAD professional development within formal education programs and extended studies of continuous learning. This finding is consistent with current literature that demonstrates an absence of explicit SEL classes within Colleges of Education (Schonert-Reichl, Kitil, Hanson-Peterson, 2017), while the demand for educators to know and apply SEL is increasing across the U.S. (CASEL, 2020).

Based on this chapter's findings, recommendations for practice encourage schools and school districts to consider increasing intentional and explicit culturally responsive social-emotional learning into classroom management practices, schoolwide policies, and professional development options for its teachers and staff. Of note, although stand-alone social-emotional interventions or curriculum packages offered by third-party SEL providers can offer a helpful starting place to introduce SEL within a class unit, school administrators are encouraged to consider embedding SEL within all content areas and campus practices. According to CASEL, SEL implementation is most effective when it is applied schoolwide and engages families and community stakeholders (CASEL, 2020). To truly have an immersive SEL program, the teachers can incorporate CASEL's 5 SEL Competencies into all lessons regardless of subject, classroom management, conflict resolution, parent/teacher activities, and restorative practices.

The three themes from the teacher and student reflections described in this chapter also suggest that institutions of higher education may also consider supporting culturally responsive SEAD education in pre-service programs of study and ongoing faculty development to embed SEL competencies into instruction that prepare aspiring and in-service educators across the industry spectrum. Future research may consider examining larger numbers of teacher and student experiences with SEL in the classroom through a mixed-methods design to collect longitudinal data on the influence of culturally responsive SEL interventions.

CONCLUSION

The issues our students and adults face in today's society will continue to present challenges within educational systems. Mental health, political divisiveness, violence, mass consumerism, sedentary lifestyles, substance abuse, and Social Media addictions continue to negatively impact students and that is why the SEL competencies discussed in this chapter are concepts that educators can develop within their own capacity and to embed within their instructional content and practices. Our world is becoming increasingly more technology driven and isolated. Both youth and adults need to learn how to manage their emotions and behaviors through Social Emotional Learning practices. Once they have a deep understanding of those practices it can then be fully integrated into the classroom. Today's students are our future and they must be taught how to navigate their emotions and remain empathetic through trying times. As educators, it is our duty to see that this happens.

REFERENCES

American Federation of Teachers. (2017). *Teacher Survey*. Retrieved at https://www.aft.org/sites/default/files/2017_eqwl_survey_web.pdf

Anxiety and Depression Association of America. (2020). *Fast fact & statistics*. Retrieved at https://adaa.org/about-adaa/press-room/facts-statistics

Arroyo, M. (2020). *The relationship between teacher identity and teacher retention in Title I schools: A multiple case study*. Dissertation from the University of Nevada, Las Vegas. ProQuest Number: 27999584.

Aspen Institute. (2018). *Pursuing Social and Emotional Development Through a Racial Equity Lens: A Call to Action*. Retrieved at https://www.aspeninstitute.org/publications/pursuing-social-and-emotional-development-through-a-racial-equity-lens-a-call-to-action/

Bailey. (2015). *Persistence and fadeout in the impacts of child and adolescent interventions*. Working paper in the ARC Center of Excellence for Children and Families over the Life Course, University of Queensland, Australia.

Busteed, B. (2019). *Why aren't graduates ready for work? They're the least working generation in U.S. history*. Retrieved at https://www.forbes.com/sites/brandonbusteed/2019/03/29/why-arent-graduates-ready-for-work-theyre-the-least-working-generation-in-us-history/#7cd974ae5e58

Cantor, P., Osher, D., Berg, J., Steyer, L., & Rose, T. (2018). Malleability, plasticity, and individuality: How children learn and develop in context. *Applied Developmental Science*. Advance online publication. doi:10.1080/10888691.2017.1398649

Cipriano, C., & Brackett, M. (2020). *How to support teachers' emotional needs right now. Schools can develop a plan to help teachers who are feeling anxious and overwhelmed*. Retrieved at https://greater-good.berkeley.edu/article/item/how_to_support_teachers_emotional_needs_right_now

Collaborative for Academic, Social, and Emotional Learning (CASEL). (2020). *CASEL's SEL framework: What are the core competence areas and where are they promoted?* Retrieved at https://casel.org/what-is-sel/

Committee for Children Second Step. (2014). *Safe, Supported, and Ready to Learn*. Retrieved at https://www.cfchildren.org/wp-content/uploads/programs/docs/Second-Step_White-Paper_Safe-Supported-Ready-to-Learn_FA18.pdf

Domitrovich, C. E., Syvertsen, A. K., & Calin, S. S. (2017). *Promoting social and emotional learning in the middle and high school years*. Edna Bennett Pierce Prevention Research Center, Pennsylvania State University.

Durlak, J. A., Weissberg, R. P., Dymnicki, A. B., Taylor, R. D., & Schellinger, K. (2011). The impact of enhancing students' social and emotional learning: A meta-analysis of school-based universal interventions. *Child Development*, *82*(1), 405–432. doi:10.1111/j.1467-8624.2010.01564.x PMID:21291449

Educationlinks, U. S. A. I. D. (2018). *Education in crisis and conflict. Social and emotional learning in crisis and conflict settings*. Retrieved at https://www.edu-links.org/learning/social-and-emotional-learning-crisis-and-conflict-settings

Elias, M. J., Leverett, L., Duffell, J., Humphrey, N., Stepney, C. T., & Ferrito, J. J. (in press). Integrating social-emotional learning with related prevention and youth-development approaches. In J. A. Durlak, C. Domitrovich, R. P. Weissberg, & T. P. Gullotta (Eds.), Handbook of social and emotional learning (SEL): Research and practice. Academic Press.

Grant, S., Hamilton, L. S., Wrabel, S. L., Gomez, C. J., Whitaker, A., Leschitz, J. T., Unlu, F., Chavez-Herrerias, E. R., & Baker, G. (2017). *Social and emotional learning interventions under Every Student Succeeds Act: Evidence Review*. Rand Education Commissioned by The Wallace Foundation. Retrieved at www.rand.org/t/RR2133

Gulbrandson, K. (2019). *Committee for children, high schoolers voice the value of social-emotional learning: Middle school SEL matters*. Retrieved at https://www.cfchildren.org/blog/2019/04/high-schoolers-voice-the-value-of-social-emotional-learning-middle-school-sel-matters/

Hurley, K. (2020). *Social media and depression: New research links the problems, especially in teens.* Retrieved at https://www.psycom.net/social-media-depression-teens

Jones, D., Crowley, D. M., & Greenberg, M. T. (2017). *Improving social emotional skills in childhood enhances long-term well-being and economic outcomes*. Edna Bennet Pierce Prevention Research Center, Pennsylvania State University.

Jones, S., & Khan, J. (2017). *The evidence base for how we learn: Supporting students' social, emotional, and academic development*. Aspen Institute. Retrieved at http://nationathope.org/wp-content/uploads/final_cds-evidence-base.pdf

Kautz, Diris, & Borghans. (2014). Fostering and measuring skills: Improving cognitive and non-cognitive skills to promote lifetime success. Paris, France: Organization for Economic Cooperation and Development.

Kerr, D. B., Madden-Dent, T., & Shalabi, N. (2020). Cultural competency interventions: Three case studies with guiding theoretical frameworks. In *Cultural Competencies for Continuous Learning* (2nd ed.). Oxford University Press. Retrieved at https://www.oxfordhandbooks.com/view/10.1093/oxfordhb/9780197506707.001.0001/oxfordhb-9780197506707-e-6?utm_content=148183851&utm_medium=social&utm_source=linkedin&hss_channel=lcp-19900 doi:10.1093/oxfordhb/9780197506707.013.26

Madden-Dent, T. (2021). Advancing equity through culturally responsive social-emotional education: Addressing international student integration. In *Advances in Motivation and Achievement. Motivating the SEL Field Forward Through Equity* (Vol. 21). Emerald Publishing Limited. Retrieved at https://www.emerald.com/insight/publication/issn/0749-7423 doi:10.1108/S0749-7423201719

Madden-Dent, T., Jackson, I., & Cason, J. (2021). Culturally-responsive social emotional academic development. In *Leading Schools with Social Emotional Academic Development (SEAD)*. IGI Global Publication. Retrieved at https://www.igi-global.com/book/leading-schools-social-emotional-academic/256645

Maker, A. (2018). Screen time: The impact on kids and parenting. *Psychology Today*. Retrieved from https://www.psychologytoday.com/us/blog/helping-kids-cope/201808/screen-time-the-impact-kids-and-parenting

Mayo Foundation for Medical Education and Research (MFMER). (2017). *Mayo Clinic*. Retrieved from https://www.mayoclinic.org/diseases-conditions/depression/in-depth/depression-and-exercise/art-20046495

Miller, J. S. (2020). *Confident parents, confident kids: Raising emotional intelligence in ourselves and our kids from toddlers to teenagers*. Fair Winds Press. Retrieved at https://confidentparentsconfidentkids.org/the-book/

National Alliance on Mental Illness (NAMI). (2020). *Mental health by the numbers*. Retrieved at https://nami.org/mhstats

National Center on Safe Supportive Learning Environments. (2020). *Emotional Safety*. American Institutes for Research. Retrieved at https://safesupportivelearning.ed.gov/topic-research/safety/emotional-safety

National Coalition Against Domestic Violence (NCADV). (2020). *Domestic violence statistics*. Retrieved at https://ncadv.org/statistics

National Institutes of Health (NIH). (2020). *National Institute on Drug Abuse*. Retrieved at https://www.drugabuse.gov/drug-topics/opioids/opioid-overdose-crisis

Osgood, D. W., Feinberg, M. E., Gest, S. D., Moody, J., Ragan, D. T., Spoth, R., Greenberg, M., & Redmond, C. (2013). Effects of PROSPER on the influence potential of prosocial versus antisocial youth in adolescent friendship networks. *The Journal of Adolescent Health*, *53*(2), 174–179. doi:10.1016/j.jadohealth.2013.02.013 PMID:23885960

Schonert-Reichi, K. A., Kitil, J., & Hanson-Peterson, J. (2017). To reach the students, teach the teachers: A national scan of teacher preparation and social & emotional learning. Report prepared for the Collaborative for Academic, Social, and Emotional Learning (CASEL). University of British Columbia.

Spoth, R., Guyll, M., & Shin, C. (2009). Universal intervention as a protective shield against exposure to substance use: Long-term outcomes and public health significance. *American Journal of Public Health*, *99*(11), 2026–2033. doi:10.2105/AJPH.2007.133298 PMID:19762678

Taylor, R. D., Oberle, E., Durlak, J. A., & Weissberg, R. P. (2017). Promoting positive youth development through school-based social and emotional learning interventions: A meta-analysis of follow-up effects. *Child Development*, *88*(4), 1156–1171. doi:10.1111/cdev.12864 PMID:28685826

Yoder, N., Dusenbury, L., Martinez-Black, T., & Weissberg, R. P. (2020). *Emerging insights: From insights to action, redefining state efforts to support social and emotional learning*. Collaborative for Academic, Social, and Emotional Learning. Retrieved from www.casel.org

KEY TERMS AND DEFINITIONS

Cultural Responsiveness: Refers to the process of developing awareness of the significance of our students' backgrounds (including historical context), then intentionally integrating their customs and values into our curriculum, instruction, and school environment (Rose, Leverson, & Smith, 2020).

Culture: Sets of socially transmitted ways of thinking, feeling, interacting, and communicating through shared value in traditions and customs distinguishing members of one organization from another (Hofstede, 2001, Kluckhohn, 1951; Lustig & Koester, 2003; Wohl, 2012).

Relationship Skills: The abilities to establish and maintain healthy and supportive relationships and to effectively navigate settings with diverse individuals and groups. This includes the capacities to communicate clearly, listen actively, cooperate, work collaboratively to problem solve and negotiate conflict constructively, navigate settings with differing social and cultural demands and opportunities, provide leadership, and seek or offer help when needed.

Responsible Decision-Making: The abilities to make caring and constructive choices about personal behavior and social interactions across diverse situations. This includes the capacities to consider ethical standards and safety concerns, and to evaluate the benefits and consequences of various actions for personal, social, and collective well-being.

Self-Awareness: The abilities to understand one's own emotions, thoughts, and values and how they influence behavior across contexts. This includes capacities to recognize one's strengths and limitations with a well-grounded sense of confidence and purpose.

Self-Management: The abilities to manage one's emotions, thoughts, and behaviors effectively in different situations and to achieve goals and aspirations. This includes the capacities to delay gratification, manage stress, and feel motivation & agency to accomplish personal/collective goals.

Social Awareness: The abilities to understand the perspectives of and empathize with others, including those from diverse backgrounds, cultures, & contexts. This includes the capacities to feel compassion for others, understand broader historical and social norms for behavior in different settings, and recognize family, school, and community resources and supports.

Social, Emotional, and Academic Development (SEAD): The integration of social-emotional learning (SEL) and academics that reinforces equitable and human-centered educational environments (Aspen Institute, 2019).

Social-Emotional Learning (SEL): A lifelong process through which all people learn and apply culturally responsive, "knowledge, skills, and attitudes to develop healthy identities, manage emotions and achieve personal and collective goals, feel and show empathy for others, establish and maintain supportive relationships, make responsible and caring decisions" (CASEL, 2020).

Chapter 9
Understanding the Why of Behavior Through Regulation

Kristin Martinsen Robison
Independent Researcher, USA

ABSTRACT

This chapter will review the many foundational theories that outline an historical understanding of behavior. Occupational therapy (OT) and psychology have provided a consistent framework for addressing and defining behavior. Behavior communicates self-awareness and self-management which are key competencies upon which social and emotional learning occur. Perception affects the definition and assumption of behavior, and this is affected by knowledge. Various considerations such as sensory processing, executive functioning, nervous system functions, and environmental factors affect the feedback loop that governs a child's ability to regulate. How we assess this process will determine our expectations and responses. When disciplinary programs do not address the whole child, behavior seldom improves. Embracing the big picture of behavior allows it to be viewed through a different lens to establish a supportive relationship with a student and empower them to achieve self-actualization and skills they will use for a lifetime.

INTRODUCTION

Social and emotional development are critical for happiness; they are also the foundation for resilience and cognitive growth. Emotional intelligence is every bit as important as academic intelligence, yet it is easy to overlook the pieces involved in this process. Addressing self-awareness leads to self-management which are two of the CASEL social and emotional learning competencies. To change the aptitude of our students we must begin to see their behavior differently. When a child is seen as a bully, disrespectful, out of control, or lazy, this behavior can define how we see this child, altering our response to them. Understanding and exploring the *why* behind various behaviors can increase the tolerance and acceptance of the *people* behind the behavior.

We have all experienced times when our behavior is hard to manage and we cannot find success anywhere. How we respond to these moments can build resilience, mental strength, and emotional intel-

DOI: 10.4018/978-1-7998-6728-9.ch009

ligence. If expectations or demands are insurmountable, physiological responses take over and we simply survive. The speed of our present-day world, an archaic educational discipline system, and the impact of technology use have all created stress. Constant stress means we must adjust, but not all kids are good at adjusting, so this creates more stress. They cannot grow emotionally or cognitively when they are in a survival state of fight, flight, or freeze. How we address their behavior determines how they feel about themselves and whether they will succeed.

These kids begin to believe they are the problem, that they are a failure, which sets the tone for who they believe themselves to be. This belief tends to spiral downward with self-doubt, more failure, and unhappiness. When schools employ discipline programs that do not address the actual problem and continue to use the same repeated consequences with no effect on behavior, our kids suffer more and learn less. But why? Are the consequences not enough to mold their behavior? When we begin to see that a child would, if they could, suddenly the problem takes on new meaning. Are there things we have missed in this puzzle of behavior and is this why the consequences make no impression on the child?

Educators and parents have an innate desire to help children be happy and embrace learning, yet the knowledge and tools are not always readily available. Our approach to behavior is only as good as the assumption of the problem, and for this we must change our perspective. Many inter-related elements have evolved, founded in solid theory to affect regulation and emotional intelligence. This chapter will first review some of the foundational theories that contribute to the knowledge of understanding behavior. It will then further define the critical elements to changing the way behavior is perceived and thus addressed. Uncovering the meaning behind behavior will support teaching practices that improve self-awareness, strengthen self-management and empower students to be the best they can be.

BACKGROUND: FRAMES OF REFERENCE AND FOUNDATIONAL THEORIES

The Basis for a Behavioral Approach

The Theory of Self-Actualization asserts that individuals are motivated to reach their full potential. Psychologist Abraham Maslow discussed a hierarchy of needs with the basic physiological demands for survival at the bottom that must be satisfied for further growth and self-fulfillment to occur (Fig 1). When basic needs are not met, a child cannot reach a level of active learning or self-actualization. This theory is foundational to everything related to assessing behavior, and critical for regulation. Psychological needs that represent relationships and feeling capable of responding to the demands put upon us, must also be attained. Finally, the top level of self-actualization represents a capacity for learning, adaptability, flexibility and empowerment.

The Pyramid of Learning discussed by Taylor and Trott (1991) and Williams and Shellenberger (1996) focuses on a similar hierarchy in which the foundation of learning is now relevant to the sensory system (Fig 2). Occupational therapy is a field that specializes in regulation and sensory processing. Recognizing this theory's basis, supports its use in addressing behavior necessary for learning to occur. If the sensory system is not working properly, the response will be affected. If a child cannot accurately perceive their body in space, they might crash into their friend because the vestibular and proprioceptive systems are not effectively communicating with the brain. This is behavior we assess. This basic sensory deficit will also affect the next level. Their postural security might be poor, and this child is rolling or slumping into their neighbor when asked to sit on a carpet square. This provides more behavior to assess.

Is this child rowdy, disruptive, acting like a bully? Maybe. But understanding *why* this behavior occurs certainly changes our overall judgement and response to this child. The sensory system correlates with Maslow's basic needs, all of which must remain key considerations when assessing behavior.

Figure 1. Theory of Self-Actualization and the Hierarchy of Needs (Rowley, 1996. Maslow, 1982)

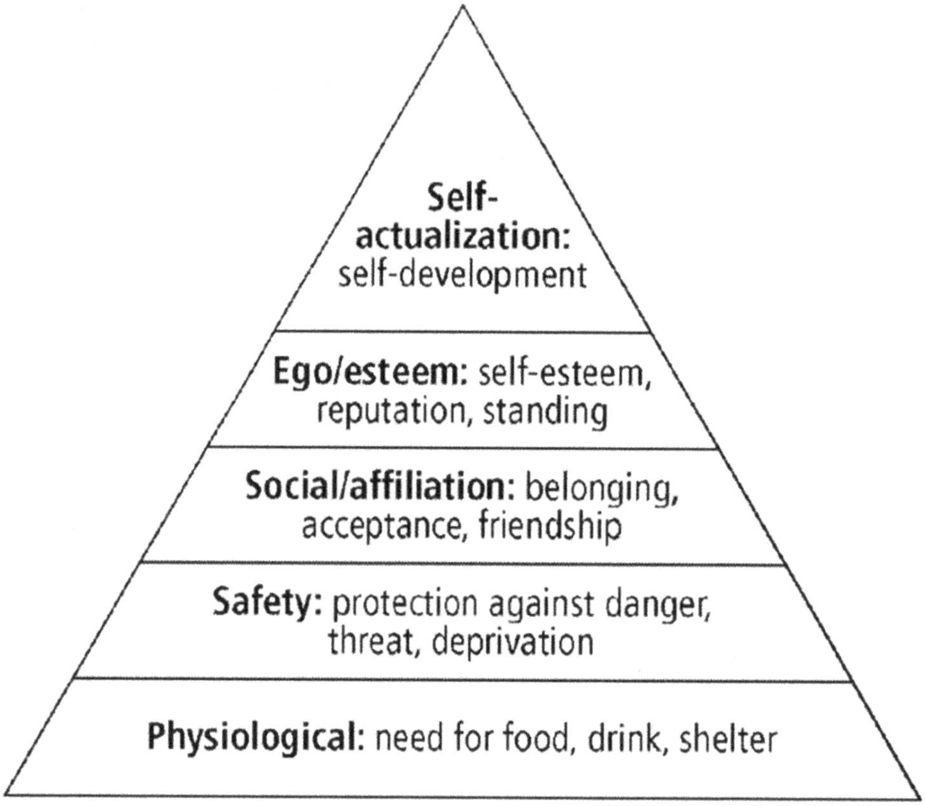

The Spiral of Self-Actualization is a conceptual model of sensory integration. Originally, Jean Ayres (an OT with training in neuroscience and educational psychology) defined sensory integration as a "neurological process that organizes sensation from one's own body and from the environment and makes it possible to use the body effectively within the environment… sensory integration is information processing." (Ayres, 1989). We need to take in, organize and use the sensations from our body and environment to manage behavior. This is also the premise of the Pyramid of Learning. The spiral process of self-actualization looks at the integration of sensory information and depicts a parallel sub-spiral related to volitional factors and motivation. Each time sensory information is taken in, we are made aware of how the body feels, and then we produce a response that affects the environment. This response contributes to motivation and belief in self. This process evolves as adaptive behavior occurs, to reach a point of occupational performance that is functional for the situational and environmental demands.

Figure 2. The Pyramid of Learning (Taylor & Trott, 1991 and Williams & Shellenberger, 1996)

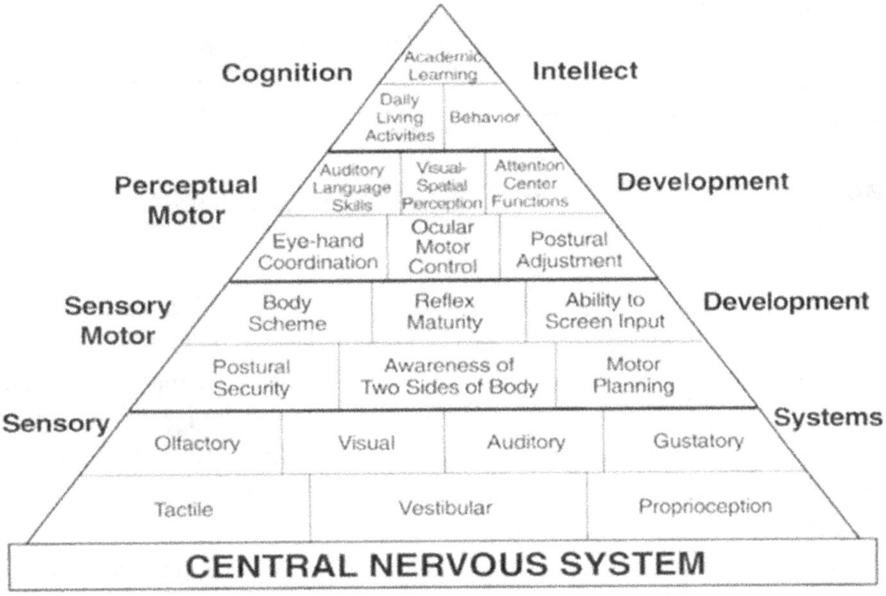

The iterative application of this model is constant. For example, a teacher puts their hand on a child's shoulder. This touch input registers in the nervous system, and the brain responds based on the assessment of this signal. If the child looks up and smiles, this adaptive response may be met with a wink and a smile. This information is remembered in the system and more complex adaptive behavior can occur. This child now feels safe and might trust in this interaction so that growth can occur. If this touch signal was processed differently and the child pulled away, this would likely affect the teacher's response. The impact of this very different social environment shapes this child's sense of safety and in turn their feelings of acceptance. Growth toward occupational performance is affected by the environment and neuronal models impact growth because they represent the system's understanding of how to do what is requested. If this child is affected by sensory issues, sensory motor, or perceptual motor issues (as seen in the Pyramid of Learning), growth will be altered.

The Developmental Frame of Reference emphasizes enabling function through normal stages of development (Creek, 2014). The application of this frame of reference highlights the importance of working through the basic steps before more complex steps can be functionally attempted. If a child is asked to do algebra but they do not yet know addition, the displayed behaviors may be solely because this child is missing a major foundational math skill. Development is dynamic, and everyone develops at their own rate of growth. The developmental rate is dependent on the mastery and integration of previous stages. This is critical when forming expectations because what you see a peer or sibling do might not be developmentally appropriate for this child and will affect behavior. Adjusting expectations related to algebra might now allow this child to find success.

The Cognitive Behavioral frame of reference looks at specific areas critical in assessing and managing behavior (Duncan, 2011). It is necessary to consider how the environment influences behavior, which often alters the physiological response we see. When environmental demands exceed skills, this stress can produce a maladaptive behavioral response. The sensory system also impacts this response because signals in the nervous system affect thoughts and behavior, determining emotions and mood. This cycle creates behavior patterns that can easily become habits and affect feelings of self-belief and self-worth. The five specific areas of life and experience included in this frame of reference are thoughts, behavior, emotions or mood, physiological response, and the environment. All these affect behavioral responses and are similar to the other foundational theories.

The Integration of Knowledge for Perception and how it Alters our Approach to Behavior

Regulation is at the core of social and emotional development because it is the ability to function even when circumstances are not ideal. Adaptive behaviors help us master a challenge and further our learning to reach the next level of development. The hierarchy of stages that must be completed for further growth, and various influences such as the environment and internal factors, are all relevant to regulation. Brain chemistry, previous experiences, knowledge and perspective are all critical things that affect what transpires in our assumption of a situation. If we can begin to see poor behavior as a breakdown in any of these areas, we can determine where things are going wrong and how to address them.

A child's success might depend on our perspective alone. We can change the lens through which we view behavior if we understand the many pieces involved in the very complexity that is human behavior. Different explanations to the behavior we see affect how we engage with a student to teach them how to better understand why they continue to encounter the same barriers. Many of our kids today feel attacked by the people in their world and their own conscience, so they are stuck. Often they do not understand the problem and so they cannot solve it. When we begin to look at regulating behavior by increasing self-awareness of the problem, self-management will occur. Now the child can be mindful of possible problems that have actual solutions.

The following case study is presented for application of the many processes that affect perception. Adults are good at assuming the *why* of behavior, and personal perspectives often lend themselves to conclusions. As you read through the following sections, reflect on your initial assessment of this case. When a student struggles with behavior issues, there is usually more going on than we realize.

Case Study

Josh is a seventh-grade student who is bright but always in detention. He is often late, rarely has class materials, and never turns in homework so he has few passing grades. When the teacher talks, he is doodling, tapping his pencil or engaging with a peer to the point of full class disruption. His parents say he also has trouble at home. He is never ready for school on time and spends the entire night on homework but rarely gets it done. If he gets it done, he forgets to turn it in, or it is discovered under the couch cushions. Often, when he is asked to do something, he does not respond. He has become more defiant in recent months and is now labeled rude, disrespectful and lazy by the adults in his world.

The Integration of Systems in the Quest for Regulation

There are many necessary puzzle pieces we must consider when attempting to understand and affect behavior. It is important to appreciate the role of the nervous system because there are factors here that we cannot change. We can still help a child achieve regulation despite maladaptive functions. The effectiveness of sensory processing to create signals and executive functioning skills will determine if an adaptive response can be achieved (Fig 3). If growth is to continue, there must be some way to monitor the entire process so the system can adjust. Success means finding more of what works and eliminating what does not. The environment, as discussed with most foundational theories, can impact this cycle at any point. It is a huge factor for all people, but children are especially vulnerable. They do not yet have the experience to handle or compensate for an environment that is not conducive to growth and self-actualization.

Regulation is the ability to self-manage which is a key area of competency for social and emotional learning. Regulation means a child can focus even when there are distractions. They can handle plans that change and recover after a disappointment. All of this requires that they monitor what is going on inside to adjust their behavior, thoughts, or feelings. If a child is regulated, they can learn, realize their potential and achieve self-actualization. Regulation can be easier for some than others because of the complexities within the nervous system. These are unique to each individual and affected by the environment, so all previously mentioned theories still apply.

Figure 3. Cycle of regulation with the various factors that affect the feedback loop and behavioral outcome

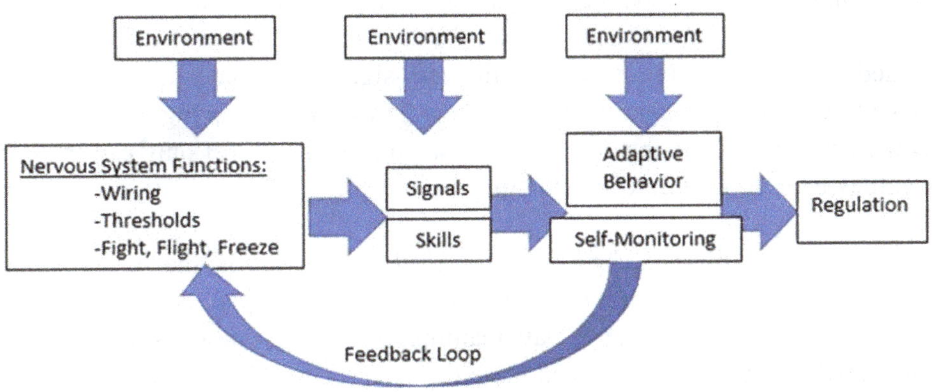

Environment in this discussion refers to anything a child is exposed to such as people, stress, physical objects and sensations. Factors such as time (i.e., the pace of an activity), intensity (i.e., interaction with others) and expectations are also aspects of an environment that will impact this cycle. Our goal is to read behavior, consult with the child, help adjust the environment and assist in finding regulation. There are times we cannot do anything about the environment, or we do not have the necessary skills or tools to affect engagement. Perception and looking through a different lens are now vital. Some kids do not have the skills to adapt successfully and others might go home at night to a place that undermines all we have tried to do. The environmental factor is huge in understanding and guiding the intervention and interaction we have with this child. When a child is merely surviving in an out-of-control environment, a major point of intervention is to provide the opportunity for control, somewhere. Control can affect a seemingly impossible piece of the regulation puzzle.

Self-monitoring is the ability to examine internal signals and communicate these findings to the brain. Even with dysfunction, regulation can occur if this child learns to adapt. When this self-awareness is not intact, it is difficult to adapt. The first step to regulation and self-management is knowing something is off so you can adjust behavior. If you are not aware that your tank is out of gas, you will not know why the car will not start. Self-monitoring helps with regulation because it draws attention to the fact that something is off. Now there is a problem to solve and the *why* of behavior can be assessed.

Adaptive Behavior occurs throughout development and is dependent on exposure to various experiences. When adaptive behavior is positive, this contributes to regulation and creates positive learned skills. Self-monitoring contributes to a feedback loop which communicates what is working and what should happen again (Fig 3). When something does not feel right and a response is negative, we see maladaptive behavior that prevents regulation. Now feedback communicates that this experience should not happen again. If we cannot adapt, we will avoid. We can affect adaptive behavior with a child if they learn to self-monitor, assess the negative feedback and adjust or utilize a strategy. To help a child adapt, we must be mindful of nervous system functions, signals and skills, and self-monitoring for self-management to occur.

Signals and Skills

Sensory Processing creates signals to tell us how our body feels. Basic sensations such as feeling tired or overwhelmed, hunger, thirst, temperature or pain will affect the regulation cycle. These signals allow us to relay what is going on in the outside world (such as the pace of the world). Signals go up to the brain for a skilled response. The brain learns with every signal that comes in, so if the signals are not communicating effectively, kids cannot figure out what they are experiencing. Too many or not enough signals affect the process of planning, starting, and staying focused. Not only can they not figure out what is wrong, they have no idea how to get help.

- If there are too many signals, the brain gets bombarded and overwhelmed and will not respond appropriately. The brain cannot make sense of anything because it tries to weed out which signals to pay attention to and which to ignore. Daydreaming, behavioral outbursts, fear, and anxiety are all related to signals. This child might need more time to process what is said. They may show rigidity and not be able to compromise. A child who cannot manage the many signals coming in can easily over-stimulate and avoid fun things like recess. When things get really bad, a more primitive nervous system function kicks in called fight, flight, or freeze, which completely negates anything that might occur socially or cognitively.
- If there are not enough signals, the brain does not have the information necessary to make an organized response. When the signals do not reach the brain, there may be no response or a very delayed response so this child might need more time to process what you have just said. They may not accurately feel the high-five they gave a friend, so they end up in the principal's office. They might not hear all the instructions, so they cannot do their homework when they get home.

Executive Functioning Skills are necessary for behavioral regulation and responses because they analyze, process, respond and learn from signals. If the signals arrive but the skills are under-developed, we have a problem. Similar to various development hierarchies, if we push too hard before skills are developed, we will see frustration, poor behavior, and more obstacles. Executive skills are developmental and like any other skill can improve with exposure and opportunity. When we allow kids to *do* more, they improve their ability to navigate the demands of childhood which increases proficiency with the complexities of adulthood.

Regulation comes with a balance of signals and skills. Executive functioning and sensory processing are inter-dependent. We need signals and we need skills for regulation. If you want to know the *why* of behavior, you must be aware of both. When signals come in, skills determine the response. No response, or a delayed response can look like intentional behavior, defiance or a lack of motivation. Think about the case study and Josh's behavioral responses. Can you think of another explanation for some of the behaviors he displays based on your knowledge of signals and skills?

Nervous System Functions

Many factors are unique to the individual and related to genetics, environment and exposure. Some will not change without chemical intervention and others can be positively influenced if the child is given the right support. Understanding the complexities of the nervous system, which includes sensory processing and executive functioning, should provide more explanations for behavior. This can be a significant part of the *why*. Understanding why behavior happens will determine where in the cycle the breakdown is occurring. Nervous system functions include individual wiring, nervous system thresholds, and fight, flight, or freeze responses.

Wiring is a nervous system function and what many refer to as personality. It is how someone comes into the world and is the static piece of the puzzle; it does not change with strategies or time. When there are issues, especially related to brain chemistry, pharmaceuticals can alter the function and appearance of behavior, but it will not change who this person is. Since we cannot change the chemical aspect of the brain without medical intervention, it is enough to simply understand the role wiring plays in behavior. If someone is wired busy, they often do better when they can move. If they are asked to sit still and listen, they will likely have trouble regulating focused attention. If someone is wired quiet, they might not like too much going on around them, which will impact behavior. Understanding wiring will influence our expectations for an individual student's behavior. Some people are wired in certain ways that make self-awareness challenging, so they may struggle with "reading the room" or knowing how they feel inside. They may be consistently more volatile or agitated. When we observe behavior knowing how wiring affects it, we gain a new perspective of *why*. This awareness and altered perspective can now help us assist a student in finding success.

Thresholds are nervous system functions that determine if and how we make a response to our world. We need to hit this threshold to engage, attend, and focus, but we also do not want to hit it too often (Dunn, 2007). People are prone to a certain threshold because of their wiring. Still, the behavior we see is a direct result of a person's threshold at that moment, with that activity, and with various strategies in place. Behavioral responses can appear similar but differ in origin; some responses can be due to over-stimulation, others because of under-stimulation. Awareness that the nervous system is not getting what it needs is the critical factor. There are different ways we can find balance with threshold responses.

- Exercise, caffeine, and fidgeting are all strategies that help someone reach a high threshold. People who are wired busy need to move a lot and if they do not get enough input, they might under-respond because there are not enough signals to tell the brain what to do.
- Taking a break, finding some quiet time, or meditation can help someone who has had their lower threshold hit too frequently. People who are wired more sensitive tend to not need as much input and when they get too, they might over-respond because too many signals bombard the system.

Most adults have figured out socially appropriate ways to reach their threshold because they have been exposed to different sensory experiences throughout the years. They also know through self-awareness what helps them regulate and they can usually get, *or avoid*, input without disturbing others. Children lack experience, so they often have not perfected the skill of gracefully reaching their threshold appropriately. Trying to find or manage a threshold need may be the only reason you see the behavior you do. Thresholds are pliable which means they can change depending on input. Is it possible a child is trying to reach their threshold with talking and moving? Maybe their rigidity and poor behavior is because they are simply surviving in this moment of a low threshold. They may not verbalize it, but they cannot do what we ask if they cannot regulate. And to do this, they must satisfy their threshold… we all need to.

Fight, flight, or freeze is our physiological response to stress and another important nervous system function. When our system gets bombarded with too much input, like when signals go astray or we struggle with a low threshold moment, it can quickly put us into fight, flight, or freeze. This is our most primitive system, and we tend to end up here when we experience extreme stress. We do not have to be going through an actual "life or death" experience because our perception of danger can be enough to trigger this response.

The mechanism of fight, flight, or freeze relies on signals, so again we discuss balance. When the amygdala perceives stress, a signal is sent to the prefrontal cortex to determine if this threat is real or not. If it is presumed that this threat is real, a signal goes to the hypothalamus to turn on hormones for a survival response (Fig 5). The hormones released during the fight, flight, or freeze response prepare the body for protection and these physiological changes divert blood to the big muscles for fighting or fleeing.

- Adrenaline increases blood flow to the muscles and causes an increase in breathing.
- Cortisol constricts or narrows arteries which increases blood pressure. It floods the body with glucose which is energy for our big muscles.
- Norepinephrine increases heart rate and blood pressure.

The Prefrontal regions of the brain affect skills or cognitive processes such as attention and working memory. They also contribute to how various signals are interpreted, directly impacting communication that would create a response. There are two significant areas to focus on and while they control many functions, they also impact the signals directly (Fig 4).

- The Dorsal anterior cingulate cortex (dACC) increases the signals from the Amygdala
- The Ventromedial prefrontal cortex decreases the signals

If this threat is perceived as a false alarm, the brain ignores the signal. Through this process, the hippocampus remembers familiar patterns and these can be quickly recalled eliciting the appropriate response. Ignore or react… this is how we survive.

Toxic stress is a response that occurs when a child experiences intense, recurrent, or prolonged adversity without adequate adult support (Franke, 2014). Physical or emotional abuse, chronic neglect, exposure to violence, caregiver mental illness or substance abuse, and extended family hardship affect the brain in ways that can have long-term effects. Research indicates a cumulative effect when high cortisol levels are in the system and this wears down the body. Toxic stress affects the immune system and is linked to increases in inflammation, heart disease, diabetes, depression and brain structure changes (Koch, Klumpers, Zhang, Hashemi, Kaldewaij, van Ast, Smit, Roelofs, 2017).

Figure 4. Illustration: Rosas, 2020. Primary areas of the brain for fight, flight, or freeze

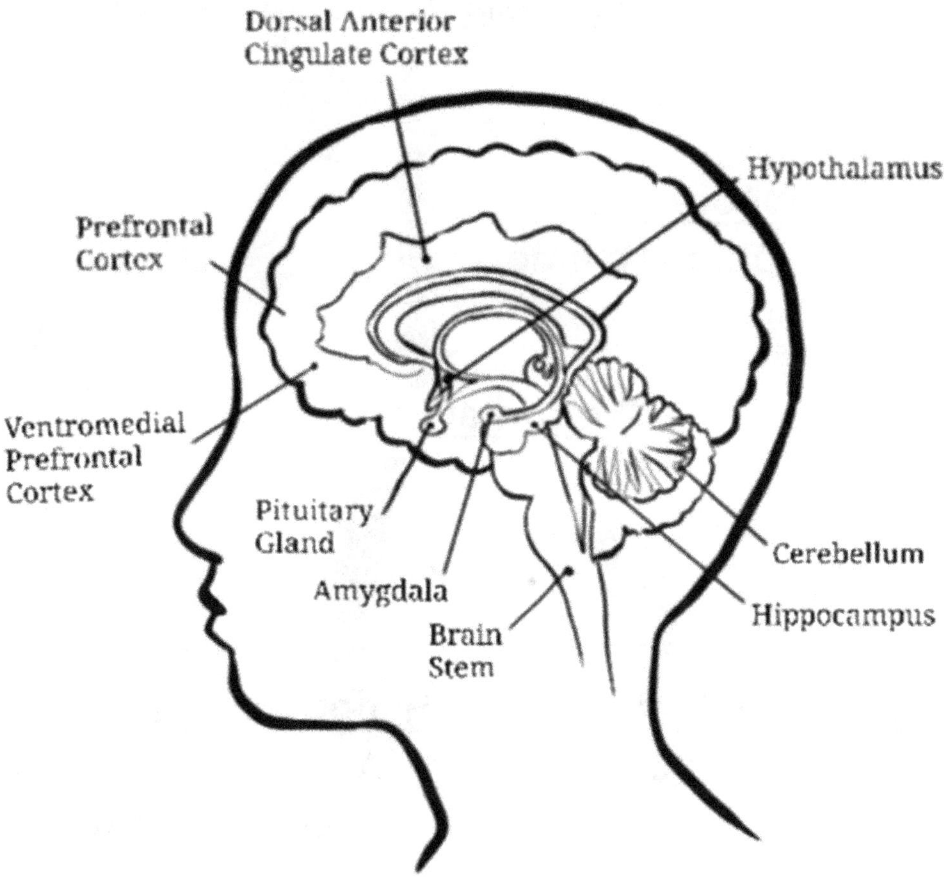

Stress is a nervous system reaction to situations that occur both inside and outside the body. Stress can be helpful, and its response has been hard-wired into our human physiology for survival. For example, imagine you are hiking in the forest and are confronted with a bear. The body's natural fight, flight, or freeze response results in adrenaline and cortisol being pumped into your blood stream to help you fight harder and run faster. The body's stress response is beneficial to help you survive this potentially life-threatening encounter. Cortisol is effective in small doses because it provides glucose and energy to respond. It is also helpful when completing a big project at school, but critical when faced with actual danger. A problem occurs when the bear is always around, as might be perceived by a 5-year-old whose single working mother struggles with substance abuse and poverty. This child experiences stress day after day and this cortisol now begins to break down the body and change the way the brain functions. Children are especially vulnerable to this repeated stress activation because their brains and bodies are still developing. This will affect how a child responds behaviorally.

Figure 5. Fight, Flight, or Freeze

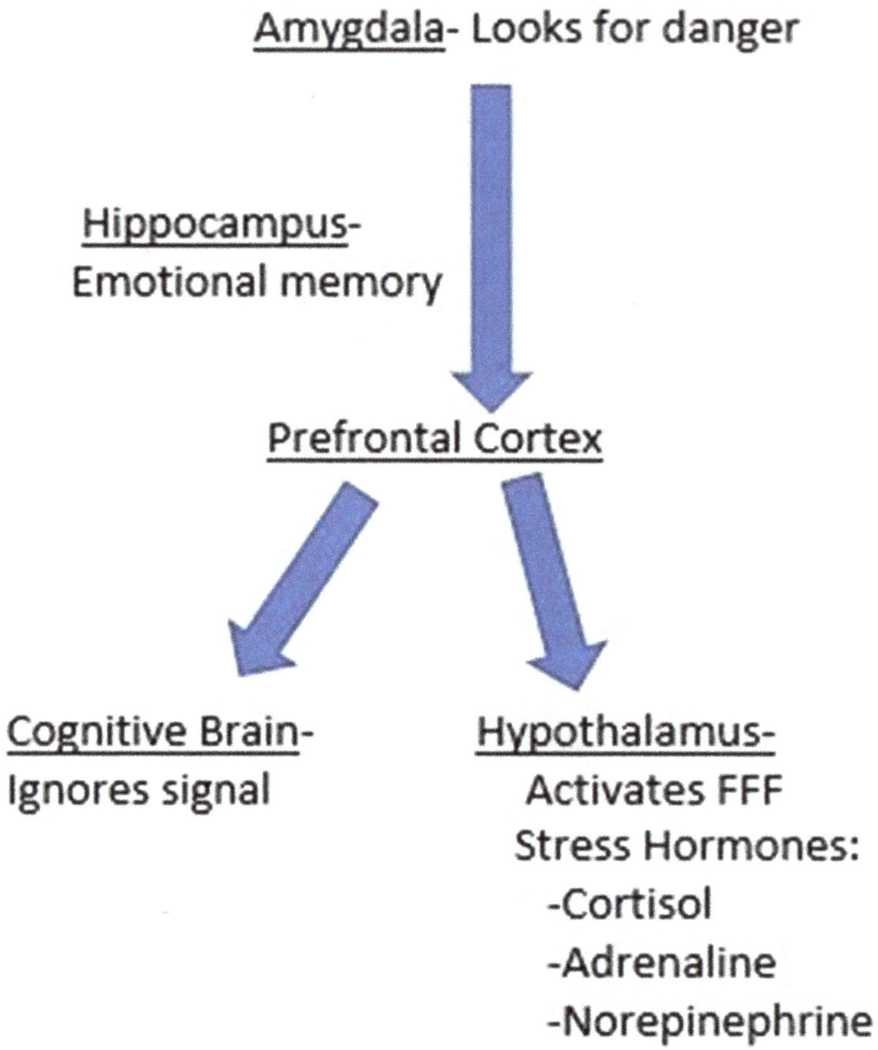

Managing Behavior Through Sensory Processing Signals: Perspective, Expectations and Strategies

CASEL.org defines social and emotional learning as "the process through which all young people and adults acquire and apply the knowledge, skills, and attitudes to develop healthy identities, manage emotions and achieve personal and collective goals, feel and show empathy for others, establish and maintain supportive relationships, and make responsible and caring decisions." For this to happen, the roots of behavior must involve awareness of sensory processing to support the whole child in cultivating a climate that achieves these competencies. When adults are aware of the various puzzle pieces involved in behavior, they can more effectively model the belief that behavior should not define the person. If this can empower a child to act similarly, they may also begin to see their peers and community through a new lens, thus achieving the goals set forth for social and emotional learning competencies.

Changing your Perspective: How brain chemistry, brain types, processing speed and discipline affect behavior

Behavior is often viewed as a way to get or avoid something, which affects our judgment and perspective. A child's tantrum may be to get a toy or avoid something they do not want to do. But behavior also communicates vital information and therefore has significant meaning beyond obvious volitional factors. Maladaptive behavior indicates that there is something in the nervous system preventing success.

Certain brain types, or wiring, create an imbalance in critical parts of the brain. Dr. Thomas Brown, a researcher and creator of The Brown Model of ADD/ADHD, uses the metaphor of an orchestra playing without a conductor to describe what is going on in the brain of someone with ADHD. This brain type will affect how a child responds to various environmental and situational demands. Research indicates that cortical brain development can be developmentally delayed by several years in individuals with attentional deficits (Shaw et al, 2007, 2012). If there are delays in the brain's prefrontal region, specifically the dACC area, we may not get an increase in signals, so the brain will not know to respond. The same is true for the child who has too many signals and depends on the Ventromedial Prefrontal Cortex to decrease the signals. If this area of the brain is developmentally delayed, the signals do not decrease and this child is suddenly over-stimulated, overwhelmed, and in fight, flight, or freeze very quickly. Wiring defines brain type and developmental maturity which completely influences behavior.

Brain chemistry is important in the analysis of behavior and is related to wiring and thresholds. Hormones and neurotransmitters in our body influence threshold levels and these chemicals are all related to wiring. The way a person is wired can be partly explained by the chemicals in the brain. Forgetfulness, disorganization and difficulty with focused attention are some of the trademark symptoms of ADHD. These are affected by the neurotransmitter dopamine. ADHD brains tend to have less dopamine which means memory, mood and motivation will be affected. Individuals with anxiety or depression tend to have less serotonin and GABA which produce a calming effect in the brain and improve mood. The neurotransmitters' levels and the effectiveness of receptors for these chemicals are often related to genetic factors that predispose individuals to certain behaviors or clinical conditions. All of this will impact signals, skills and ultimately, behavior.

Processing speed affects the assumption of behavior because if a child does not respond in the time we expect, we might conclude that they are lazy or not trying hard enough. The reality is that kids who struggle with slower processing speed are anything but lazy; most of the time they are actually trying harder than other kids. If a child could, they would (Greene, 2014). Processing speed can affect verbal, visual and motor responses, and we know that school requires all of these and often all at one time. Visual motor skills are needed to copy notes from the board. Reading aloud requires a visual, motor *and* verbal response. If a child has learning or attentional issues, they may need up to 7-10 seconds to respond, which exacerbates other issues that affect their ability to find success. Processing speed might explain much of the behavior you are seeing.

School discipline programs try to manage behavior using rewards and consequences. If we present a reward, certainly we will see improved focus longer and improved work. If a negative consequence is the result of no work or poor behavior, kids will adapt. Except when they cannot. Repeated consequences such as detention that aim to affect behavior, only work if they *affect* behavior. The frequent fliers in the detention room clearly do not benefit from the consequence and many of these kids have never been able to access rewards. If a child could, they would. This concept is very important to remember. Why are they not finding success? If discipline is attempting to address the motivation and nothing is changing, it is time to look at the child's ability or adjust the expectations. There is no amount of motivation that can come if the signals are not communicating or the skills are not intact. Their behavior communicates that a problem has not been solved so they cannot adjust their behavioral responses.

Acknowledging Expectations

It is hard not to *expect* a certain response and therefore expectations are important to monitor. Behavior communicates what the nervous system can handle. When we see smiles, work completion and engagement we know this child has the self-management for the demands requested. This is a perfect example of the just-right-challenge, a concept created by Jean Ayres. We can remedy maladaptive behavior by making the gap smaller between a situation's demands and the child's skill. This might mean we adjust the expectation or assist more with the skill; the goal is to create an achievable opportunity (Fig 6).

Figure 6. The Just-Right-Challenge

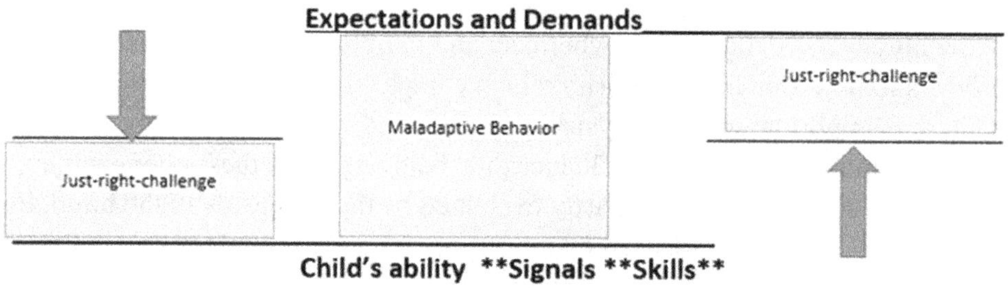

If an expectation or demand is inappropriate for a certain type of wiring or threshold need, this child will never meet it. If a child is wired busy yet you *expect* them to come in and sit for an hour of reading, the response might appear disruptive and certainly not what was requested. The goal of an activity is important to remember too. If the goal is reading, they must be regulated in order to focus and learn. If they need to move or doodle while listening to regulate, this is now a strategy, not maladaptive behavior. Acknowledging how a child is wired and then exploring how this impacts their threshold will allow for more realistic and achievable expectations. It will help define the behavior we see. If this child is learning, but standing in the back or pacing, have they not achieved the goal? Alter the expectation, provide strategies or adjust input based on wiring and thresholds, and we will help a child find regulation.

Strategies for Signal Issues

Internal signals and sensory processing must be considered when trying out strategies for regulation. Where most adults go wrong is with the assumption that they understand the problem based only on their observations. Understanding all the different systems at play that determine behavior is important, but one of the most effective starting points when coming up with the "what now" is found in the child. Watch what they are drawn to and what they avoid. Ask them if they have any ideas. This information will provide insight into how you can address a problem that has prevented a child from self-management.

To increase self-awareness, body scans encourage the child to slow down and focus on each body part, starting at the top of their head. This self-monitoring technique allows them to determine if they are feeling too many signals or nothing at all. It also tells you where they might be feeling these signals. If they feel it in their head, they might be over-stimulated and need less going on around them. If they notice something in their stomach, they might need to think about how they feel emotionally. If they feel nothing at all but they are also not responding appropriately to the cues around them, they can begin to address the idea that they need more input so signals can talk to their brain. All this valuable insight can be obtained through an all-class or individual approach and can be used immediately to create strategies. Kids can also apply this knowledge to better understand the behavior they observe around them which will further enhance their relationships and encourage mindfulness.

Strategies for school must be simple and easy to implement. The following reviews some ideas that will influence how various systems affect a child's ability to regulate.

- When a consequence is needed, try an exercise break instead of recess. Kids still get movement, but free time play is what they have lost.
- Try heavy work such as erasing the board, stacking chairs, carrying lunch bags, or running errands for the teacher. Quiet desk time can be modified by wrapping a TheraBand, or resistive tubing, around the legs of the desk or chair so they can push, pull, or bounce their feet on it as they work.
- Share positive strategies for transition times. Have them put a hand on their belly so they can focus on their breath as they walk; they can count the number of times they breathe from class to class. Now they are calmer, potentially more focused, and able to monitor their breathing.
- Position kids in line for transitions according to their needs. Kids that do not like unexpected touch might do better in the front or back versus the middle of the line where kids could bump them from all sides.
- Provide items or fidgets to carry but ensure all fidget tools or any other things a child might use to improve regulation are used as tools, *not toys.*
- Jobs or tasks can make transitions easier. Have students count how many specific letters they can find on their walk, bring heavy books to music class, or count how many steps it takes to get to the library, etc.
- Discuss and demonstrate that everyone has a bubble of one size or another. This can give a visual for why some kids get agitated or aggressive when people come too close and get in their bubble.
- Headphones or noise-canceling options such as earplugs or hoodie sweatshirts can help distract and block out unexpected noises.
- Seat buddies can help share notes and make focusing easier because they provide a good example and peer motivation.
- Allowing kids to feel out a situation before jumping in can prevent fight, flight, or freeze. We need to pick our battles. Calling on a student to come to the front of the room to do a demonstration in front of everyone might defeat the academic purpose you are trying to achieve.
- Do not demand eye contact or verbal responses.
- Oral anything is good for focus. Gum, water bottle with a straw, and snacks like salty, sweet, or chewy, are ways to improve focused attention.
- Dynamic sitting options can include stomach time with dry erase boards to write on, sitting on a large yoga ball, wobble cushion or chair, or allowing the child to stand in the back of the room or away from distractions.

- Environmental changes can include different lighting, adding music, keeping a corner of the room empty of clutter, or sections with different sitting options.
- Strategies must align with the specific needs of a student and usually these tools are best utilized before or during work.
- If a child must earn the yoga ball by working, they may never meet that demand because they need the movement to regulate and work.
- Help a child replace a behavior that is not working for them with one that would be more appropriate. If they are moving around and distracting others, instead of telling them to sit still, give them a wobble stool or chance to stand. This allows their nervous system to continue getting the input it needs without the behavioral obstacles getting in the way.

Managing Behavior through Executive Functioning Skills: Perspective, Expectations and Strategies

When signals are finally communicating with the brain, the skills are necessary if there is going to be an appropriate response. Executive skills are brain-based behaviors involved in just about everything we do. If the doing (or lack of doing) is the problem, executive functioning needs to be considered. Self-management will be difficult if there are weak skills that prevent a child from successful engagement. What does it look like when dealing with weak executive skills? Planning, reading others' emotions, managing frustration, seeing our involvement in a situation, taking responsibility for our actions, and starting an undesirable task are all brain-based skills. These skills involve numerous parts of the brain, and sometimes these areas develop at different times than they might for a peer or a sibling. Sometimes we will see issues that surprise us.

- A child might be a great reader, but they might not care about school if they have no friends.
- They may have an affinity for math, but if they always forget a pencil, they miss critical instructions and math becomes very hard.
- When a child struggles with the many skills involved with being a successful student, they often have trouble demonstrating their knowledge. If they never hand in homework it is impossible to know if their grade is more a reflection of weak executive skills or poor content knowledge.

The various executive functioning skills that affect behavior can help the adult and the child begin to find a solution that makes life easier. Understanding that there are often many skills impacting ability will also help mold our view of behavior. Activities such as writing, for instance, involve over nine of these skills so it is easy to see how this seemingly simple task can present a complicated obstacle for a student. Executive functioning issues will affect performance which will determine how a child feels about themself and this reflects in their behavior. The following represents the different executive skills and how they impact learning and performance.

Executive Functioning Skills (adapted from Dawson, 2009)

- Response Inhibition: Do they start before instructions are given or act without all the facts? They might interrupt conversations and have trouble with behavior regulation.

- Working Memory: Can they manage facts, details or complete multiple-stepped instructions? If math facts are required to complete math homework, this might be why they cannot start.
- Flexibility: Does the unknown throw them off? Can they shift between activities? Difficulty with flexibility when the schedule or activity changes can result in fight, flight, or freeze.
- Task Initiation: Can they start a task or get back to work after a break? Starting a task that is not preferred (video games are very different than math) can look like they are choosing defiance.
- Emotional Control: Is performance affected by emotions? Can they control behavior or adjust behavior when things are not perfect?
- Sustained Attention: Can they focus on non-preferred activities long enough to complete them? A lack of focus will prevent follow through with tasks like classwork.
- Planning and Prioritization: Can they plan out their day and prioritize accordingly? Do they have the materials they need for class? This can also affect their results on tests because they might not know what to focus on when studying.
- Time Management: Do they procrastinate? Are they late? Can they estimate how long it takes to finish all the important tasks on time?
- Organization: How does their desk or binder look? Disorganized writing, messy work, and very few words on the page are common issues we see when kids struggle.
- Metacognition: Can they evaluate their performance? Do they review work after it is completed? Poor self-monitoring and goal setting prevent accurate evaluation of how they are doing. This affects the ability to learn from experience, so the same mistakes are made over and over.
- Goal-Directed Persistence: Can they follow through on long, non-preferred tasks?
- Stress Tolerance: Do they crumble with pressure? Is change and unpredictability difficult?

Think back to our case study with Josh. Do you think any of the weaknesses mentioned above might be explanations for his behavior?

Expectations

When discussing the gap between ability and demands there is more involved than simply signals because a child's developmental level will always impact ability. Expectations and recognizing the just-right-challenge are as important as ever today as children struggle to find success or manage behavioral responses. Skills mature as the brain develops, which drives expectations; a child's ability to respond is based on their developmental level. We know a toddler cannot manage a multiple-stepped, complicated set of demands, so this is not expected. If the assumption of a child's developmental ability is inaccurate, this will shape the perspective we have for their capabilities. If a child could, they would. The just-right-challenge means a child can find success because the activity is appropriate for the developmental level. When there is an imbalance that prevents regulation, the difference between a child's ability and potential can be huge.

There are times when we feel our expectations are appropriate for a student, but they still fail to reach them. Executive skills develop with time, and as adults and educators, we have an idea of what a child should do at a certain age. When kids begin middle school for instance, expectations include managing multiple teachers, classes and assignments with less support. This expectation is based on child and brain development so we assume it must be appropriate. We have established that certain brain types or wiring create different timelines for development. We might not realize that some kids are not ready for our sixth-grade expectations and this is when the implications of an individualized spatial-temporal window come into play. (Ward and Jacobsen).

For most people, planning occurs in a different space and time than the execution; this is the temporal-spatial window. Spatial refers to the space where we make a plan, and the window is how far away from this space the execution will occur. Temporal refers to the time between when a plan is made and when execution occurs. For instance, when we teach a toddler to put on shoes, we might give simple instructions and demonstrations with their shoe sitting next to them. We plan, demonstrate and execute in the same space and time because developmentally this toddler has a small spatial-temporal window. This is a just-right-challenge because we have acknowledged development, which affects our expectation for this task and this child. If the expectation involved independent execution from instructions given yesterday to this toddler, task completion would look quite different because the spatial-temporal window was not accurately taken into account.

Expectations for an older child would assume more proficient execution, requiring planning in a different space and time because developmentally their spatial-temporal window should be bigger. The expectation for a seventh-grade student might include coming to class on time with the materials they need to work. For this to occur, a plan must be made before class starts if they are going to have proficient execution. This child *should* know what they need from their locker and which class they go to first. There can be more space and time between planning and execution so when they arrive at school, execution is not only possible but also efficient. But if a child's brain has a different developmental timeline, our expectations and assumptions might be off because planning and execution are executive functions. They may not be able to navigate this task successfully because this child's spatial-temporal window is not as we expected so the gap between ability and demand is too large. This awareness can affect your perception of this child's behavior when they continue to show up late to class. It is also a huge factor in the determination of appropriate expectations.

The concept of time is not only something children need to learn, but also something adults need to understand. Processing time will affect behavior and the just-right-challenge if it is not what we expect. Like the spatial-temporal window, an adult's assumption of appropriate processing time will affect the expectations for a child who might not be developmentally prepared for the demands put upon them. Multiple sources indicate that wait time between instruction and a typical child's response is between 3 and 5 seconds (Rowe, 1972; Stahl, 1990). This is an exceptionally long time. Many adults make a request with the expectation of an almost immediate response so seemingly maladaptive behavior might simply be the time this child needs to process what was requested. Children who have issues with signals and skills will need even more time to respond because of the many processes that take time in their nervous system.

Strategies for Specific Skills involving Executive Functioning

Coaching teaches kids how to improve their self-awareness to compensate for lagging executive skills. This collaborative relationship between an adult and child is also crucial to the attainment of social and emotional learning concepts that empower children to contribute to their community and the social climate around them. Realistic goals and expectations are created during coaching sessions *with* the child to address problems the child identifies, not just adult assumptions based on observation. Coaching should consider all the factors from discipline, expectations, processing speed, signals, and skills so a child can better understand their behavioral responses. Once the child sees that their behavior stems from something specific, it is easier to find a solution. There is an accountability piece with coaching because the adult can track the student's goals and help them adjust. This metacognition can be difficult but creates momentum for future endeavors that are challenging. Unmet goals are no longer failures. They are simply part of the learning process for regulation. When goals are met, positive acknowledgement helps with future motivation and a feeling of self-competency.

The concept of time is an important executive skill that can be problematic for kids to master; it also affects most academic tasks. Focused attention can increase, and work is better prioritized when kids know how long something will take. A concept of time will also help prevent procrastination. When kids cannot visualize what time looks like, in essence they are flying blind. Teachers are good at chunking work, but if kids do not see how these chunks fit into their schedule, they may never feel the urgency that initiates a response. Seeing the big picture and planning where these chunks of work fit into this picture can help motivate them. When they see the fun time chunked beside the work time, they might try to push a little harder. Even evaluations require a concept of time because students must gauge their pace and adjust to complete their demonstration of knowledge. Coaching sessions with a child can incorporate all these concepts to increase motivation, work completion, and regulation.

The ability to see into the future and plan is not something that comes naturally, and often it does not develop with time alone. Planning will help improve processing speed, the concept of time, and always results in more effective execution. Sarah Ward and Kristen Jacobsen (Cognitive Connections, EFpractice) provide continuing education to improve executive functioning and support kids when skills are not at the level of situational demands. They teach planning through a process that involves discussing the end of a work cycle first because this is where motivation comes in. Presenting a picture of the completed assignment or the fun activity that a child can do once it is finished can make starting work more manageable. Once the end of a task is discussed, the plan must include how to get ready. When kids do not have the materials to complete their work, it is often because planning did not occur, and now multiple distractions affect successful work completion. When they begin to review the work process and can visualize it, planning gets better. Now what the adult envisions is the same as what the child envisions. The more they plan, the better this skill becomes.

Figure 7. Plan Backward to Move Forward. Adapted from a Concept of Cognitive Connections (Sarah Ward & Kristen Jacobson)

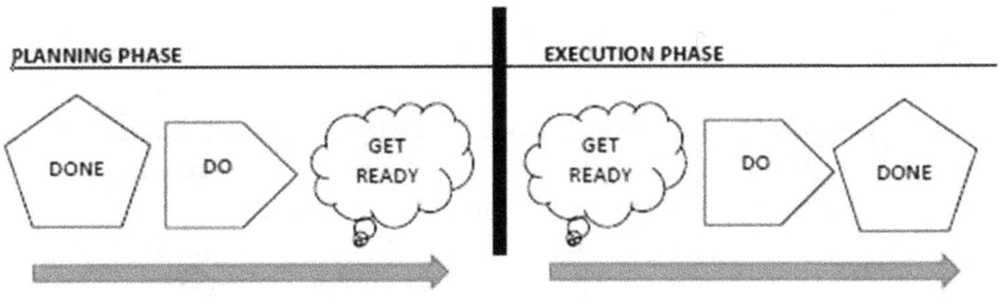

The ability to see into the future and plan is not something that comes naturally, and often it does not develop with time alone. Planning will help improve processing speed, the concept of time and always results in more effective execution. Sarah Ward and Kristen Jacobsen (Cognitive Connections, EFpractice) provide continuing education to improve executive functioning and support kids when their skills are not at the level of situational demands. The end is the first thing to discuss and address because this is where motivation comes in (Fig 7). Presenting a picture of the completed assignment or the fun activity a child can do at the end can make starting work much more manageable. Once the end of a task is discussed, the plan must include how to get ready. When kids do not have the materials to complete their work, it is often because planning did not occur, and now multiple distractions affect successful work completion. When they begin to review the work process and see it in their head, planning gets better. Now what the adult envisions is the same as what the child envisions. The more they plan, the better this skill becomes.

Coaching kids through the various skills and ways to meet school demands is ideal for improving their self-efficacy and capacity for learning. The case study presented in the beginning is a textbook example of a student that would benefit from coaching and the various strategies that improve self-management and regulation. All of this is critical in the attainment of social and emotional learning. The following list of questions address the various pieces in the puzzle of behavior. Understanding the many factors in the cycle of regulation changes how a problem is defined and completely alters the process of finding a solution.

Think back to the case study. Has your appraisal changed or are there explanations for behavior you did not initially consider? When an adult can see behavior in a different way, they can also support children in the awareness of various explanations to their own behavior so they can adjust. When consequences make no impression and obstacles are too much to manage successfully, these questions should be at the forefront of how we begin supporting a child.

- Is Josh getting signals so he can adjust behavior and not always be in trouble?
- Does he have the executive skills to plan through what he needs to respond efficiently, not be late and actively participate in class?
- Is Josh able to respond according to the timeline the adult expects?
- Is the doodling, tapping or peer engagement disrespect or is this his attempt to hit his threshold?
- When he gets home, does he have the notes he needs to do his work? Does he struggle to listen and write at the same time; does this affect the legibility of his notes?
- Does his difficulty with task completion at home also support the idea that he does not have enough signals to make an effective response? If the signals are intact, is it possible he does not have adequate skills for a response?
- Is his workspace at home or at school distracting so he struggles to start, persist and complete work?
- Does he have the skills to complete the work cycle? Maybe he gets the work done but loses the page when he takes a break on the couch. Maybe his binder is so disorganized that he does not put finished work there because he knows he will never find it again.
- Is his defiance and disrespect an indicator of his frustration level? Could his inability to find success prevent him from seeing learning and school as something positive?
- Has he failed too many times to know how to get up on his own?
- Is the list of missing assignments so big that he does not know where to start? Is his behavior an attempt to find control or an indicator that he feels no control over his situation?
- Is detention working? Has his behavior changed because of these consequences? Is his behavior intentional and because he does not care?

CONCLUSION

This chapter began by reviewing original theories that are foundational to understanding behavior and regulation. Research and experience have revealed that there is much to know beyond these original concepts. Sensory processing and executive functioning are part of a regulation cycle that must be considered if an accurate assumption of behavior is possible. Potentially with this new view of the student in mind, a relationship is forged from understanding and knowledge. It starts with the adult taking a different perspective which can change the engagement they have with a child to bolster their emotional literacy. Our children need help understanding that there are circumstances beyond simply the behavior that might come to define them. Social and emotional growth makes life meaningful and is fundamental for developing stress management, self-awareness, a social awareness and ultimately, relationships. When adults can embrace mindful interactions and practice the art of kindness and understanding, our children see this. They feel this. Addressing the whole child is foundational to helping them see that they are not a problem. Finding the balance between the many facets of regulation can empower all of us to see behavior differently to change the world one child at a time.

REFERENCES

Ayres, A. J. (1989). *Sensory Integration and Praxis Tests*. Western Psychological Service.

Ayres, A. J. (2000). *Sensory integration and learning disorders*. Western Physiological Services.

Brown & Kennedy. (n.d.). *The Brown Model of ADD/ADHD: Brown ADHD Clinic: United States*. Brown ADHD Clinic. www.brownadhdclinic.com/the-brown-model-of-add-adhd

Bundy, A. C., Lane, S. J., & Murray, E. A. (2002). *Sensory integration: Theory and practice*. F.A. Davis Company.

Creek, J. (2014). Approaches to practice. In W. Bryant, J. Fieldhouse, & K. Bannigan (Eds.), *Creek's occupational therapy and mental health* (5th ed., pp. 50–69). Churchill Livingstone.

Dawson, P. (2009). *Smart but scattered: The revolutionary "executive skills" approach to helping kids reach their potential*. Academic Press.

Duncan, E. A. S. (2011). The cognitive behavioural frame of reference. In E. A. S. Duncan (Ed.), *Foundations for practice in occupational therapy* (5th ed., pp. 153–164). Churchill Livingstone.

Dunn, W. (2007). Supporting Children to Participate Successfully in Everyday Life by Using Sensory Processing Knowledge. *Infants and Young Children, 20*(2), 84–101. doi:10.1097/01.IYC.0000264477.05076.5d

Franke, H. A. (2014). Toxic Stress: Effects, Prevention and Treatment. *Children (Basel, Switzerland), 1*(3), 390–402. doi:10.3390/children1030390 PMID:27417486

Greene, R. W. (2014). *Lost at school: Why our kids with behavioral challenges are falling through the cracks and how we can help them*. Scribner.

Koch, S., Klumpers, F., Zhang, W., Hashemi, M. M., Kaldewaij, R., van Ast, V. A., Smit, A. S., & Roelofs, K. (2017). The role of automatic defensive responses in the development of posttraumatic stress symptoms in police recruits: Protocol of a prospective study. *European Journal of Psychotraumatology*, *8*(1), 1412226. doi:10.1080/20008198.2017.1412226 PMID:29321826

Maslow, A. H. (1982). *Toward a Psychology of Being (An Insight Book)* (2nd ed.). Van Nostrand Reinhold.

Rowe, M. B. (1972, March 31). *Wait-Time and Rewards as Instructional Variables: Their Influence on Language, Logic, and Fate Control.* Retrieved from https://eric.ed.gov/?id=ED061103

Rowley, J. (1996). Motivation and academic staff in higher education. *Quality Assurance in Education*, *4*(3), 11–16. doi:10.1108/09684889610125814

Shaw, P., Eckstrand, K., Sharp, W., Blumenthal, J., Lerch, J. P., Greenstein, D., Clasen, L., Evans, A., Giedd, J., & Rapoport, J. L. (2007). Attention-deficit/hyperactivity disorder is characterized by a delay in cortical maturation. *Proceedings of the National Academy of Sciences of the United States of America*, *104*(49), 19649–19654. doi:10.1073/pnas.0707741104 PMID:18024590

Shaw, P., Malek, M., Watson, B., Sharp, W., Evans, A., & Greenstein, D. (2012). Development of cortical surface area and gyrification in attention-deficit/hyperactivity disorder. *Biological Psychiatry*, *72*(3), 191–197. doi:10.1016/j.biopsych.2012.01.031 PMID:22418014

Stahl, R. J. (1994, April 30). *Using "Think-time" behaviors to Promote Students' Information Processing, Learning, and On-task Participation: An Instructional Model.* Retrieved from https://www.ericdigests.org/1995-1/think.htm

The Importance of the Pyramid of Learning. (n.d.). Retrieved from https://www.yourkidsot.com/blog/the-importance-of-the-pyramid-of-learning

The Theory of Self-Actualization. (2013, August 13). Retrieved from https://www.psychologytoday.com/us/blog/theory-and-psychopathology/201308/the-theory-self-actualization

Ward, S., & Jacobsen, K. (n.d.). *Cognitive Connections.* www.efpractice.com/

Chapter 10
Nurturing Spiritual Intelligence in the Classroom

V. Vineeth Kumar
https://orcid.org/0000-0002-1841-3407
Manipal University Jaipur, India

Geetika Tankha
Manipal University Jaipur, India

ABSTRACT

Humans have a unique intelligence known as spiritual intelligence that tends to seek meaning and purpose in their lives, ask questions about one's existence, and render resolute conclusions to one's actions. Today, school teachings align with the industry's demands and are nurturing students' cognitive attributes. As the demand for technological innovations increases, the demand for focusing on vocational skill-focused education is also increasing. However, in the era of rapid technological innovations, nurturing the men's psyche behind the technology-driven progress is equally important. The chapter discusses the relevance of spiritual intelligence in schools. Further, the chapter explores spiritual intelligence's relationship with psychological wellbeing, mental health, quality of life (QOL), happiness, and academic performance. The way forward measures to enhance students' spiritual intelligence are also discussed for achieving students' holistic development.

INTRODUCTION

Technological innovations are dynamically altering the way people use to live, travel, and communicate. Every aspect of human life is getting altered because of new technological innovations. Artificial intelligence (AI) development has enabled systems and processes for facilitating day-to-day activities with minimum human interaction. Thus, for some, technological innovations are 'the solution' to most of the human problems. However, how these technological innovations are used has to be ensured. Because at the beginning and end of any technological innovation or change, there will be a human being. The psyche of human beings creating, implementing, and changing these technologies will have a significant

DOI: 10.4018/978-1-7998-6728-9.ch010

impact not only on the system they create but also on the society and the nation. Perhaps education or schooling is the only tool that the communities have to nurture the psyche of young minds driving these technological revolutions of the future.

In primitive times, the primary purpose of education was to teach self-preservation skills and nothing else. However, in modern times education is an essential tool to bring specific desirable changes to the students. In these modern times, the purpose of education is to enable the students to live a purposeful and meaningfully satisfying life with well-developed analytic, emotional, and spiritual qualities. Furthermore, facilitating them in acquiring a perspective in life helps them meet the larger world with higher self-confidence and self-awareness.

Thus, education and educators' roles cannot be taken lightly if we wish to prepare students' current generation for a fulfilling life and make them happy and satisfied both personally and professionally. The fundamental aim of education should be to educate so that the individual is ready to receive and give back to society in a meaningful and constructive way. To fulfill the above aim, the students should have analytical skills (Intelligence Quotient), emotional maturity and balance (Emotional Quotient), and the ability to create inner synergy and develop a socially relevant purpose in life (Spiritual Quotient). Such education has to be multifaceted and includes social, emotional, and academic development (SEAD) practices that equip individuals to meet competition challenges at an intellectual level by achieving grades with the modern syllabi and technology grounded in social-emotional learning (SEL) skills. Next, SEAD education must nurture abilities to withstand the blows of failure and winds of success in a balanced and mature manner. Lastly, the student should move ahead of these individual goals to the stage of self-realization and satisfaction of contributing to the broader community." Social, Emotional, and Academic Development (SEAD) is, in other words, the integration of five SEL skills - Self-awareness; Self-management; Social awareness; Relationship skills; and Responsible decision-making, into the academic system to reinforce more equitable and human-centered educational environments (Aspen Institute, 2019). The implementation of SEAD practices is aimed to increase social-emotional learning (SEL) skills, a lifelong process through which all people learn and apply culturally responsive, "knowledge, skills, and attitudes to develop healthy identities, manage emotions and achieve personal and collective goals, feel and show empathy for others, establish and maintain supportive relationships, and make responsible and caring decisions" (CASEL,2020). By implementing SEAD practices into school processes and policies, its educators, staff, students, parents/families, and community members have the opportunity to practice SEL skills throughout their day consistently.

Thus, education needs to be a mix of both emotional and spiritual intelligence (SI) skills. Both emotional quotient and spiritual quotient can be developed through the SEAD (Social Emotional and Academic Development) based practices. They have similar core competencies like self-awareness, self-management, social awareness, and responsible decision making. Such education will make them a complete person and holistically develop their personality through the social and emotional learning-based curriculum. Individuals nurtured in this way will become competent to think holistically and compassionately. Thus, enabling them to transcend the barriers of individual and small personal goals.

The present education system has evolved and has made the student community capable of achieving intellectual and emotional maturity. However, the ability to see beyond personal growth and development is still to be achieved. There is a need for developing higher intelligence or the ability to see beyond the visible concrete world in the current times. The need of the hour is to have an education based on universalism, compassion, and commitment. Education imbibes in the students the values of being responsible and accountable for their choices and their decisions in life. A high level of intellect without rationally judging can adversely impact the larger community's outcome. It can also be dangerous to society, as the highly intelligent person's selfish and ulterior motives will block him from seeing the horrific consequences of his actions on the community at large. Thus, this ruthless human development devoid of values of compassion, meaningfulness, constructive growth, and transcendence will only lead to humanity's downfall. The integration of SEL-based teaching practices in schools can prove a promising method for effectively teaching these skills early through young adulthood.

It is here that the role of spiritual intelligence (SI), as it is commonly referred to, becomes essential. Danah Zohar (1997) popularized spiritual intelligence as a concept. Zohar (2000) defined spiritual intelligence as a concept with the underlying 12 principles, namely, compassion, humility, holism, self-awareness, a celebration of diversity, positive use of adversity, field independence, ability to reframe, tendency to ask why, sense of vocation, being vision and value-led, and having spontaneity.

Emmons defines spiritual intelligence as:

The adaptive use of spiritual information to facilitate everyday problem solving and goal attainment. [Emmons, 2000]

King defines spiritual intelligence as:

A set of abilities that contribute to the awareness, integration, and adaptive application of the nonmaterial and transcendent aspects of one's existence leads to such outcomes as deep existential reflection, enhancement of meaning, and recognition of a transcendent self, and mastery of spiritual states. [King, 2008]

Kumar and Mehta have defined Spiritual intelligence as:

An individual's capacity to possess a socially relevant purpose in life by understanding 'self' and to have a high degree of conscience, compassion, and commitment to human values. [Kumar and Mehta, 2011a]

Spiritual intelligence is the intelligence, which empowers an individual to discriminate, change the rules, and alter the situations. It gives the ability to transcend beyond individualistic and materialistic goals and redefine personal goals, which helps reach the highest cognitive, emotional, and social development levels. It enables an individual to live an authentic life without any burden of guilt or regret of making wrong choices or decisions. Thus, SI is strongly associated with five core SEC (Social Emotional Competency) clusters defined by CASEL (2020): self-awareness, self-management, social awareness, relationship skills, and responsible decision-making. These components emphasize developing intrapersonal competencies that include self-awareness and self-management and interpersonal competencies that include social awareness and relationship skills.

SPIRITUAL INTELLIGENCE, MENTAL HEALTH, AND QUALITY OF LIFE

Mental health is of utmost importance for any individual to perform efficiently in any sphere of life. Mental health is measured in terms of emotional, social, and behavioral well-being and quality of life (QOL). The students' mental health, both adolescents and adults, is influenced and related to spiritual intelligence. As defined by the proponents of intelligence, spiritual intelligence is beyond solving day-to-day problems or managing our and other's emotions. It is the ability to find meaning in life and purpose in life-related to the broader community. Thus, it can be an important marker for well-being and good quality of life for the individual. The studies have also indicated a positive relationship between the adolescent and young adult students' mental health and well-being.

Singh et al. (2010), in a large-scale study on a sample of 934 Indian school students, aimed to find the predictors of adolescent students' mental health. The role of variables like spiritual intelligence, altruistic behavior, school environment, and academic achievement was examined as predictors of mental health. The study's findings reported that SI, jointly with altruism and school environment (dimensions of rejection and control), contributed as an essential predictor of mental health in adolescent students.

Ebrahimi et al. (2012), in a study on 100 Iranian students, explored the relationship of Spiritual Intelligence, resiliency, and mental health (GHQ). The study results were in line with the earlier studies as SI indicated a significant and negative relationship with all GHQ dimensions, indicating that high SI results in better mental health. The students reported less mental health disorders and psychological morbidity. SI also had a positive and significant relationship with resilience in the students. Besides, a ten percent variance in the resilience of the students was ascribed to spiritual intelligence. It was thus indicating that spiritual intelligence enhances the ability to meet with life stressors and is a critical contributing component in improving students' mental health.

Bolghan-Abadi et al. (2014) attempted to study the relevance of spiritual intelligence in predicting the QOL in a sample of 143 students of Quechan University and reported that spiritual intelligence does play an influential role in predicting the QOL (WHOQOL). Nobari and Shokri (2014) replicated similar findings in another study, and they reported a moderately positive and significant relationship of spiritual intelligence with the students' quality of life. Ansari (2015) examined the association of spiritual intelligence with quality of life in a sample of 358 girl students of Tonekabon Azad University. The study's findings revealed that spiritual intelligence played an important role in predicting the quality of life. Quality of life measures included both mental and physical health, social relations, and the living environment. Spiritual intelligence indicated a strong relation with all the factors of QOL.

More recently, Nemati et al. (2017) explored the relationship of SI with students' mental health at Tehran Shahid Beheshti University of Medical Sciences. The researchers used GHQ as a measure of psychological morbidity and SIRI-24 as a measure of spiritual intelligence. The findings indicated a negative relationship between the two variables, suggesting that spiritual intelligence is a predictor of good mental health. The regression analysis results indicated a forty-three percent variance in mental health attributed to spiritual intelligence. The researchers suggested that enhancing the spiritual intelligence could make the students more capable of meeting the stressors and pressures in life.

Bozorgi and Bozorgi (2017) examined the relationship of spiritual intelligence and mental health with the help of King's (2008) measure of SI and Goldberg's (1972) measure of GHQ-12 in a sample of 300 students of Islamic Azad University, Iran. The study's findings revealed a negative and significant relationship between spiritual intelligence and mental disorders. Furthermore, the regression analysis results indicated that spiritual intelligence accounted for fourteen percent of the students' mental health variance. In another study, Pant and Srivastava (2019) aimed to study the relationship between spiritual intelligence and mental health of Arts and Science students enrolled in the government degree colleges of the holy town of India, Haridwar. The findings indicated a significantly positive association between spiritual intelligence and mental health among both Arts and Science faculties and both genders.

Jain and Meena (2013) have reported a significant positive relationship between Spiritual intelligence and adjustment in a sample of 100 female adolescent students. They reported that spiritual intelligence had a significant and positive relationship with all aspects of adjustment (social, educational, health, and emotional) except home adjustment. Kumar and Mehta (2011a) also reported similar findings with school students.

Brar (2017) has corroborated the findings and reported similar results while examining the relationship between spiritual intelligence and adjustment in young adolescents studying high school. Devi et al. (2017) has corroborated similar findings in a sample of 240 college students pursuing Arts and Science courses in India. Similarly, Nair and Paul (2017) studied the association between spiritual intelligence and social adjustment in school students, and the findings indicated a significantly positive association between the two variables. Eldiasty and Ibrahim (2018) explored the relationship between spiritual intelligence and the adaptation to college life in a sample of 302 students. The findings indicated a positive impact of spiritual intelligence on academic, social, personal, and emotional adaptation and a commitment to achieving students' goals. In a recent study, Giannone and Kaplin (2020) attempted to examine spiritual intelligence's role in mental health (depression, anxiety, and drug addiction). The sample of their study comprised of 353 undergraduate psychology students. Spiritual intelligence did not show any significant relationship with anxiety, depression, or substance use. Some researchers have also explored spiritual intelligence as an intervention tool. Charkhabi et al. (2014) conducted a study to determine the effect of spiritual intelligence training as an intervention technique on high school students' mental health indicators in Iran. Their experimental study's findings indicated that spiritual intelligence training reduced mental health conditions like somatization, depression, anxiety, aggression, phobia, paranoid ideation, and psychosis. Spiritual intelligence training as an intervention technique improved the mental health of the students. These findings are consistent with other researchers (Goodarzi, 2012; Hamid et al., 2013).

SPIRITUAL INTELLIGENCE, WELL-BEING, AND HAPPINESS

Psychological well-being and happiness are significant predictors of a fully functioning individual. In other words, it includes self-belief and satisfaction with oneself, along with the other significant people and social interactions. Sood and associates (2006) studied the relationship of spiritual intelligence with the students' psychological well-being. Their study's findings indicated that spiritual intelligence and psychological well-being have a significant and positive relationship in the student community.

Marzieh et al. (2013) explored spiritual intelligence's relationship with happiness in students pursuing courses like medicine, nursing, and midwifery in Iran's medical university. Their findings indicated a moderately significant relationship of spiritual intelligence with happiness. They concluded that spiritual intelligence enhances the happiness level to some extent in the students. Ansari (2015) studied the relationship between spiritual intelligence and happiness in girl students, further reported similar results. However, in recent times Jasmindebora et al. (2019) conducted a study on 250 nursing students pursuing the nursing course in a nursing college in Andhra Pradesh, India, with the aim was to assess the relationship between spiritual intelligence with psychological well-being. The students ranged in the age group of 17 to 35 years and were administered SIRI-24 (King, 2008) and psychological well-being scale by Carol Ryff. The results of the study indicated a high positive correlation between the two factors. It was thus suggesting that spiritual intelligence enhances the psychological well-being of the students across different age groups. A study by Razia (2019) assessed the relationship between spiritual intelligence and well-being in a sample of 203 B. Ed students of an Indian university corroborated similar findings. The findings suggested that spiritual intelligence had a moderately positive relationship with the students' mental, emotional, and overall well-being. Midi, Cosmas, and Sinik (2019) conducted a study on 250 adolescent school students in a village in Malaysia to investigate the impact of spiritual intelligence and psychological well-being. The findings of the investigation found spiritual intelligence to be a significant predictor of psychological well-being. Spiritual intelligence predicted a twenty-five percent variance of psychological well-being among the students.

Few researchers have also explored the training aspect of spiritual intelligence and used it as an intervention technique to enhance young students' well-being and quality of life. Marashi et al. (2012) also reported that psychological well-being could be enhanced by giving students spiritual intelligence training. In an experimental study, they tested the impact of spiritual intelligence training on the six dimensions of Ryffs psychological well-being. They reported significant differences in all the six dimensions of psychological well-being in the experimental group. Rani et al. (2017) further reinforced the finding that giving spiritual intelligence training enhances students' psychological well-being. The researchers in the study developed a forty days training module on SI for Malaysian university students. Post-training, they experienced better relationships and became more focused and motivated and improved in managing their emotions. The authors recommended that spiritual intelligence enhances students' overall lives, both personally and professionally. It can help them release stress and focus more on their goals.

SPIRITUAL INTELLIGENCE AND ACADEMIC PERFORMANCE

Spiritual intelligence brings purpose and meaningfulness in life, which gives the individual the motivation to be persistent and goal-oriented. Thus, it is expected that a higher level of spiritual intelligence will enhance performance in life's academic sphere. The research also supports the positive impact of spiritual intelligence on the academic performance of the students.

Marzieh et al. (2013) explored spiritual intelligence's relationship with academic achievement in students pursuing courses like medicine, nursing, and midwifery in Iran's medical university. Their findings indicated a low but significant relationship with academic achievement. They concluded that spiritual intelligence and academic performance are associated to some extent in the students. Abadi, Tabbodi, and Rahgozar (2013) investigated the association between spiritual well-being and academic achievement among students of different disciplines like Arts, Humanities Management, Engineering, Sciences, and Architecture. The results indicated a significant positive correlation between Spiritual intelligence and academic achievement only among management, economics, and humanities. More recently, Midi et al. (2019) also investigate the impact of spiritual intelligence on academic performance. The findings of their investigation found spiritual intelligence to be a significant predictor of academic achievement. Spiritual intelligence predicted forty percent of the variance in academic performance of the students. It was thus specifying that spiritual intelligence has a vital role in enhancing adolescent youth's academic performance.

On the other hand, some researchers have reported a weak, non-significant, or inverse relationship of spiritual intelligence with students' academic achievement. Smartt (2014) examined spiritual intelligence's relationship with academic achievement (composite score on the American College Test) while controlling for gender and age in secondary school students. The doctoral study's findings indicated a small and non-significant inverse relationship of spiritual intelligence with the students' academic achievement.

Spiritual intelligence was also not found to be a predictor of academic achievement. Similarly, Aydin (2018) has also reported a weak though a significant relationship between Spiritual intelligence and self-regulation skills and a non-significant relationship with academic achievement.

Similarly, Sharma (2019) also reported a non-significant relationship between spiritual intelligence and academic achievement in a sample of 150 students from Somalia pursuing higher studies at an Indian university. Nurfarojandari and Maftuhah (2019) have also found similar results in a study on a sample of 100 students from South Jakarta, Indonesia. They also reported no significant influence of spiritual intelligence in predicting academic achievement in the students.

Despite the contradictory findings regarding the relationship of spiritual intelligence with academic achievement, recent research by Rayung and Ambotang (2018) attempted to examine the impact of emotional and spiritual intelligence on student outcomes. Their study reported that sixty percent of graduate students' failure in job interviews was due to the low level of emotional intelligence and spiritual intelligence in Malaysian students. Besides, they also reported that the majority of misconduct behaviors in the students were due to a lack of mastery of spiritual and emotional intelligence skills. Thus, they strongly recommended that education policymakers should lay a strong emphasis on developing spiritual and emotional intelligence in the student community.

The literature review's expanse indicates that spiritual intelligence can enhance the quality of life across the dimensions of emotional, social, psychological, and academic well-being. The researchers suggest that any adolescent or young adult's academic phase is caught between fulfilling the self and significant others' expectations. They are under constant pressure to perform well on the academic, social, emotional, and mental levels. In present times when stakes are high to perform well amidst tough competition, there is a need for something more than just cognitive and emotional intelligence, which would differentiate the individual from their cohorts. Thus, there is a scope for exploring developing spiritual intelligence as a useful tool for enhancing students' well-being in the current scenario.

SPIRITUAL INTELLIGENCE, HOLISTIC WELL-BEING, AND PERFORMANCE

Intelligence can determine the level of individual emotional intelligence performance can help them sustain at that level. However, spiritual intelligence is vital to go beyond the barrier of success and failure in life. In current times as pressure to do well and outperform others is expected from a very young age, the individuals with a higher level of intelligence or Spiritual intelligence are better adjusted and adept in facing life pressures and stressors.

A well-performing or high achiever is usually a student who is satisfied and happy with himself/herself. Thus to be satisfied, one needs to have clarity of one's goals in life. Studies have repeatedly stated that spiritual intelligence can see things from a broader perspective and align with the higher purpose of life. Thus an individual with a high level of spiritual intelligence will always be ready to face both success and failures in the right perspective. For instance, the researches mentioned earlier in the chapter indicate that spiritual intelligence has a positive relationship with the psychological well-being of the students across various nations like India (Jasmindebora et al., 2019; Sood & Associates, 2006) Iran (Abadi et al., 2013), Pakistan (Khosravi & Nikmanesh,2014), Malaysia (Midi et al., 2019). Similarly, mental disorders have also indicated a significant and negative relationship with spiritual intelligence (Bozorgi & Bozorgi, 2017; Ebrahimi et al., 2012; Nemati et al., 2017).

The relationship of spiritual intelligence with academic achievement has also been explored (Abadi et al., 2013; Marzieh et al., 2013; Midi et al., 2019) and others a non-significant (Aydin, 2018; Nurfarojandari & Maftuhah, 2019; Sharma, 2019; Smartt, 2014). Furthermore, when used as an intervention technique, spiritual intelligence has enhanced students' well-being and mental health (Charkhabi et al., 2014; Goodarzi, 2012; Hamid et al., 2013). The students who were given training through the modules based on enhancing spiritual intelligence indicated a reduction in mental health conditions like anxiety, depression, and somatization.

The basic concepts or determinants of spiritual intelligence, namely a purpose in life, concern for self, conscience, and compassion to work for others, creates a need to perform in a student (Kumar & Mehta, 2011b). The Bhagwad Gita describes the characteristics of a person who has realized his spiritual self by transcending the mental plane of opposites, such as pleasant and unpleasant. Such a person is said to be beyond the vicissitudes of life, *anasakt* (detached), and established in steady wisdom. Thus, spiritually intelligent students develop detachment towards the fruits of their actions.

However, high spiritual intelligence induces in students the moral courage to stand up for something they believe is wrong and bear its responsibility to accept their actions' inevitability in the common good's interest. Students with spiritual intelligence believe that their purpose or goal will be beneficial for all human beings. So they are even ready to take the overall responsibility of the failure if needed.

Although emotional intelligence makes a person street smart, it does not guarantee that they will always do socially beneficial or relevant things. Spiritual intelligence not only develops a socially relevant purpose or goal in an individual's life but also stirs the conscience in an individual, begetting high moral values and inner strength. Hence, in students, emotional intelligence coupled with spiritual intelligence aids them in dealing with ambivalent situations. Such students can resolve their id-superego complex healthily and can protect their ego against all odds. Resultantly, they never blame others for their wrongdoing and try to find the reason for the actual problem to take a future lesson. As Brown (1996) stated rightly, responsibility, reciprocity, and empathy for others are universally recognized as the moral codes across all the cultures of the world. All religions profess and propagate values like a commitment to self-transcending, respect, and care for other human beings, and looking beyond individualistic thinking. These values have been here for so long that they have become embedded in human society and are now widely recognized as universal qualities. These core qualities are desirous for grooming an individual to an ideal state.

Students with spiritual intelligence can identify their purpose in life. They realize that educational success is of foremost importance in determining their future. Undeterred by youthful life's fantasies and a healthy competitive spirit, they strive hard to succeed in schools. With a strong conscience, the flexibility of thoughts, and compassion towards others, spiritually intelligent students can plan their work, play schedules in a better manner, and remain focused throughout their academic sessions.

Spiritually intelligent students with higher self-awareness can concentrate more readily on the school instructions and use them adequately as desired. However, less spiritually intelligent students lack a purpose in life, which decreases their motivation, and interest in studies resulting in an overall low educational performance. They enjoy their adolescence to the fullest and may waste their entire energy in purposeless ways with a procrastinate attitude. This attitude decreases their ability to adjust to their curriculum, teachers, and schoolmates. Moreover, lack of conscience, flexibility, and compassion also makes the matter worse for them. Thus, it seems SI is very much in sync with the approach of SEL based curriculum. The SEL-based curriculum predicted reduced likelihood to skip classes, drop out, or engage in risky behavior (e.g., sexual, substance-related), and greater resilience to peer pressure (Elias, et al., 1997; Payton, et al. 2000). Thus, spiritually intelligent adolescents will be more goal-directed and academically and socially high performing individuals in their life.

During this period of development, for the first time in their lives, most of the events happen, whether it is the maturational changes, state/ national level exam, career, first mobile, the first vehicle of their own, and their new friends. These multiple role-conflicts acts as significant stressors, and coping with the same becomes a herculean task. Freudian Id asks for immediate pleasure while the super-ego restricts their thoughts and actions as per the social norms. Due to their sound sense of purpose in life, spiritually intelligent students can deal with these conflicts very swiftly while maintaining inner peace and outer equanimity. With a clear vision ahead, they focus on the target, following the society's ethical norms and using their vibrancy to energize their drive towards the goal. In no way do they fall prey to the petty pleasures of day-to-day lives; instead, they find pleasure in serving others, sharing their ideas, and gaining new knowledge to work for society. However, students with low spiritual intelligence lack the attributes to deal with the multiple conflicts of early life. They cannot realize their potential. Further, due to the lack of compassion and flexibility of thoughts in them, they cannot deal effectively with real-life situations. Nurturing SI in schools also help students from weaker and downtrodden sections of society.

Even though the students from downtrodden sections of the society have faced prolonged social deprivation, spiritual intelligence instigates a fire to rise higher in life and show their abilities to the world. To fulfill the same, they work hard on themselves and try to correct their inner weaknesses. In the process, they develop a better conscience, compassion for others, and altruistic nature. Resultantly, they can adequately handle emotional distress and adapt positively to various challenging situations. On the other hand, for students who have not experienced the social apathy as faced by students from weaker sections of society, spiritual intelligence instigates a desire to excel and become successful. Spiritual intelligence cultivates the capability to understand 'self' and a high degree of compassion, conscience, and commitment to human values. Human values are the same across different cultures. These values enable an individual to understand one's own emotions and also others. Thus, enhancing the emotional adjustment of an individual. Thus, spiritual intelligence has a similar effect on emotional adjustment across different groups.

The ability to perceive and understand things from different perspectives and see the relationship between perception, belief, and behavior determines an individual's spiritual intelligence. When individuals can exercise wisdom and compassion in relating to other people, do not discriminate based on gender, creed, age, and ethnicity, and respect all forms of life, they are spiritually and emotionally mature. Thus, the students who develop heightened interpersonal and intrapersonal sensitivity can better adjust to their peers, teachers, family, and community at large.

Developing Spiritual Intelligence: The way Forward

Nurturing students' spiritual intelligence can be achieved by the combined efforts of teachers, parents, counselors, educational policymakers, and associations involved in the students' welfare activities. Currently, the focus is on developing an individual for his/her career advancement. However, a holistic SEAD approach is required in this regard, i.e., education should aim for over-all personality development with due emphasis on SI. The following can be incorporated to develop SI in schools:

- Curriculum Designing: The syllabi must be more insightful, encouraging compassion more than competitiveness, professing wisdom to develop and sustain healthy social groups, which cherishes the aspects of selfless service. The SEL based curriculum can be one of the most important steps in this regard.

- A lesson for Teachers: Teachers should stress the students' scholastic performance and focus on breeding their Spiritual and Emotional Intelligence. The paucity of such attributes has been shown to affect the students' educational achievement directly. The training and refresher courses for teachers should include capsules related to the inculcation of 'spiritual and emotional mannerisms' in themselves and their students. The SEL based teachers training programs can be a facilitative move in this direction.
- Assessment/Evaluation of Students: Assessment should focus on recognizing, encouraging, and rewarding excellence in varied areas among young students. For achieving the objective, there is a need to nurture their ability to relate their learnings to their day-to-day experiences in life and assimilate the knowledge within themselves. More so, they foster their ability to frame questions about the learned content in unique ways and, significantly, enhance their capacity to see unconventionality in their 'lessons' from the right and wrong idea.
- Value-Added Programs: Schools should not become the centers of rote learning, but they should also impart life skills training to students for preparing them for present and future challenges. The whole of education has to be value-oriented rather than impart it as a separate bit of education; Personality development programs imparting training in schools for nurturing conscience, compassion, and commitment to humanity are the need of the hour.
- Psychological well-being of Adolescents: Developing spiritual intelligence will enhance psychological well-being and emotional maturity. This can help reduce the juvenile delinquencies, youth unrest, and, most importantly, the suicidal tendencies that are prominently in vogue.
- Counseling: Counselors and clinicians should always remember the importance of spirituality while conducting and facilitating individual and group counseling. Similarly, personality development programs should also focus on nurturing the spiritual intelligence of students.
- Wake-up call for Child-rearing Institutions: Family/ School should rear the child in a realistic environment rather than a pampered one. A child should be intrinsically motivated to achieve success with his efforts and should be made to learn from his failures. From the beginning, the child must be aware of what is possible and what is not. Unrealistic expectations from parents and school - teachers lead to unusual frustration in children when they face minor failures. In challenging situations, emotionally weak students easily give up, showing maladaptive behaviors and inadequate reactions to the impending frustration. It is high time that the children should be taught to approach and experience the hardships in life rather than avoiding them and taking a safer and unethical way out for their problems.
- Spiritual Workouts: Promote spiritual workout programs like yogic exercises and meditation for students' holistic well-being in schools. This will enable them to cultivate a positive attitude and resilience to deal with stressful situations maturely.
- Role of Other Agents: Education management professionals, consultants, psychologists, and NGO groups are directly involved in efforts to alter society's environment through intervention programs in the education sector. By implementing spiritual intelligence in their programs and projects, they can enhance the participation of students.
- Public Education Programs: Public education programs for holistic well-being and personality development (focused on students' spiritual intelligence) should be encouraged. Strategies to achieve this goal could include advertising campaigns using print and social media. IEC material (e.g.,

short videos, short stories of role models, lectures by appropriate speakers) can be distributed in schools through social media platforms. Further, parents can also be involved in these campaigns. The SEAD based practices can be beneficial for moving beyond the classroom and integrating the beyond classroom experience by involving parents and the community in a manner that promotes holistic development.

FUTURE RESEARCH DIRECTIONS

Although Spiritual Intelligence has emerged as one of the most significant factors associated with mental health, quality of life, and psychological well-being among students, there is a paucity of research studies elaborating on the direct relationship between SI and academic performance. Cognitive factors have majorly been the focus of research when studying academic success. Cognition is a multi-dimensional construct that includes a wide range of mental processes like perception, attention, memory, learning, language, problem-solving, and decision-making. These processes work in different combinations, which allow us to interpret any information in our environment. These cognitive processes cannot be nurtured in isolation. For realizing, the full potential of any overall student, development both inside and outside the classroom is essential. A plethora of research indicates a significant relationship of spiritual intelligence with psychological well-being, adjustment, stress, mental health, and QOL. However, studies exploring the relationship between IQ, spiritual intelligence, and academic performance to SEAD practices can further validate spiritual intelligence's role in the modern education system.

Similarly, cross-cultural studies exploring the role of spiritual intelligence on academic performance should also be conducted. Similarly, longitudinal studies across life span should be initiated to study the implications of nurturing students' nurturing spiritual intelligence. Future research can be directed to exploring the possibilities of developing SQ through the CASEL based programs and then to compare the pre-and post-effect on the enhancement of SQ and academic performance of the adolescent students.

CONCLUSION

Spiritual intelligence enables an individual to realize his potential and use the potential to work in less ordinary ways for the greater common good. Spiritual Intelligence is associated with mental health, psychological well-being, QOL in students. Holistic well-being is a crucial factor for performance in any field. Thus, the holistic development of students should be the aim of any educational system. Nurturing spiritual intelligence ensures that the students become resilient, goal-oriented, compassionate individuals whose purpose in life is in tune with the community and socially relevant goals.

Thus, to nurture spiritual intelligence, efforts need to be made to have classrooms where vitality, excitement, and aliveness are promoted, which stirs the students' minds. The classroom culture should be such that judgments are avoided, and peace, connectivity, and diversity are encouraged. There should be moments of peace and stillness where ideas flow and are not forced. At the same time, a place, which encourages curiosity, mystery, awe, and wonders. It will only then be possible to churn out students who will have spiritual intelligence and technical intelligence to meet life's personal and professional challenges. Spiritual intelligence can be fostered through SEL based teaching practices.

REFERENCES

Abadi, M. M. M., Tabbodi, M., & Rahgozar, H. (2013). The relationship between spiritual well-being and academic achievement. *European Online Journal of Natural and Social Sciences, 2*(3), 3440-3445. https://european-science.com/eojnss/article/view/2233

Ansari, M. (2015). Investigating the relationship between spiritual intelligence and happiness and quality of life for girl students. *International Journal of Humanities and Cultural Studies,* 1678-1685. http://www.ijhcs.com/index.php/ijhcs/article/view/1943

Aspen Institute. (2018). *Pursuing social and emotional development through a racial equity lens: A call to action.* Retrieved from: https://assets.aspeninstitute.org/content/uploads/2018/05/Aspen-Institute_Framing-Doc_Call-to-Action.pdf?_ga=2.44974119.2040306106.1585434015-147 9461922.1582989130

Aydin, D. (2018). Relationship between the spiritual intelligence and self-regulation skills of education faculty students. *Journal of Education and Training Studies*, *6*(12), 227–234. doi:10.11114/jets.v6i12.3481

Bolghan-Abadi, M., Ghofrani, F., & Abde-Khodaei, M. S. (2014). Study of the spiritual intelligence role in predicting university students' quality of life. *Journal of Religion and Health*, *53*(1), 79–85. doi:10.100710943-012-9602-0 PMID:22528289

Bozorgi, M. D., & Bozorgi, Z. D. (2016). The relationship between spiritual intelligence, coping strategies, and mental health among students. *International Journal of Humanities and Cultural Studies,* 636-646. https://www.ijhcs.com/index.php/ijhcs/article/view/962

Brar, S. K. (2017). Study of adjustment among adolescents in relation to spiritual intelligence. *International Journal of Academic Research and Development*, *2*(6), 511–514.

Brown, S. A. (1996). Talent for living success, says Daniel Goleman, requires skill in handling emotions, not just being smart. *People*, *45*(19), 85–86.

Charkhabi, M., Mortazavi, A., Alimohammadi, S., & Hayati, D. (2014). The effect of spiritual intelligence training on the indicators of mental health in Iranian students: An experimental study. *Procedia: Social and Behavioral Sciences*, *159*, 355–358. doi:10.1016/j.sbspro.2014.12.387

Collaborative for Academic, Social, and Emotional Learning (CASEL). (2020). *Resources: SEL background and research.* https://casel.org/resources-learn/

Devi, R. K., Rajesh, N. V., & Devi, M. A. (2017). Study of spiritual intelligence and adjustment among arts and science college students. *Journal of Religion and Health*, *56*(3), 828–838. doi:10.100710943-016-0225-8 PMID:27007602

Ebrahimi, A., Keykhosrovani, M., & Dehghani, M. (2012). Investigation of the relation between resiliency, spiritual intelligence and mental health of a group of undergraduate students. *Life Science Journal*, *9*(1), 67–70.

Eldiasty, A. M. A., & Ibrahim, A. T. H. (2018). The relationship between spiritual intelligence and a student's adaptation to college life: Implications for social work practice. *The Egyptian Journal of Social Work*, *1*(5), 21–46.

Elias, M. J., Zins, J. E., Weissberg, R. P., Frey, K. S., Greenberg, M. T., Haynes, N. M., & … . (1997). *Promoting social and emotional learning: Guidelines for educators*. Association for Supervision and Curriculum Development.

Emmons, R. A. (2000). Is spirituality an intelligence? *The International Journal for the Psychology of Religion*, *11*, 27–34.

Giannone, D. A., & Kaplin, D. (2020). How does spiritual intelligence relate to mental health in a western sample? *Journal of Humanistic Psychology*, *60*(3), 400–417. doi:10.1177/0022167817741041

Goldberg, D. P. (1972). *The detection of psychiatric illness by questionnaire*. Oxford University Press.

Goodarzi, K. (2012). *Interactive effects of spiritual intelligence and life skills education on students' mental health: A case study* [Unpublished doctoral dissertation]. Azad Islamic University Branch Borujerd, Iran.

Hamid, N., Keikhosravani, M., & Babamiri, M. (2013). The relationship between mental health spiritual intelligence with resiliency in student of Kermanshah University of medical sciences. *Jentashapir Journal of Cellular and Molecular Biology, 3*(2), 331-338. https://www.sid.ir/en/journal/ViewPaper.aspx?id=254154

Jain, M., & Meena, S. (2013). A study of relationship of spiritual intelligence and adjustment of adolescents. *Indian Journal of Psychological Science*, *3*(2), 12–16.

Jasmindebora, S., Sudheer, T., Vasantha, M., Bhavani, M., & Rohith, J. (2019). Relationship between spiritual intelligence and psychological well-being. *International Journal of Indian Psychology*, *7*(1), 990–996. doi:10.25215/0701.113

Khosravi, M., & Nikmanesh, Z. (2014). Relationship of spiritual intelligence with resilience and perceived stress. *Iranian Journal of Psychiatry and Behavioral Sciences*, *8*(4), 52–56. PMID:25798174

King, D. B. (2008). *Rethinking claims of spiritual intelligence: A definition, model, & measure* [Unpublished Masters dissertation]. Trent University, Peterborough, ON, Canada.

King, D. B., & DeCicco, T. L. (2009). A viable model and self-report measure of spiritual intelligence. *International Journal of Transpersonal Studies*, *28*(1), 68–85. doi:10.24972/ijts.2009.28.1.68

Kumar, V. V., & Mehta, M. (2011a). Gaining adaptive orientation through spiritual and emotional intelligence. In A. K. Chauhan & S. S. Nathawat (Eds.), *New Facets of Positivism* (pp. 281–301). Macmillan Publishers India.

Kumar, V.V., & Mehta, M. (2011b). *Scale for Spiritual Intelligence* [Electronic Database]. PsycTests. . doi:10.1037/t16725-000

Marashi, S., Naami, A., Beshlideh, K., & Zargar, Y. (2012). The impact of spiritual intelligence training on psychological well- being, existential anxiety, and spiritual quotient among the students of Ahvaz faculty of petroleum. *Journal of Education & Psychology*, *19*(1), 63–80. https://www.sid.ir/en/journal/ViewPaper.aspx?id=307584

Marzieh, R., Hoda, A. T., Saiedeh, H., Esmat, J., Zahra, J., & Ahmad, B. S. (2013). Relationship between spiritual intelligence, happiness and academic achievement in students of QOM University of Medical Sciences. *Indian Journal of Medical Education, 13*(5), 431–440.

Midi, M. M., Cosmas, G., & Sinik, S. (2019). The effects of spiritual intelligence on academic achievement and psychological well-being of youths in Kanibungan village, Pitas. *Southeast Asia Psychology Journal, 9*(3), 1–14.

Nair, K. A., & Paul, G. (2017). A study on spiritual intelligence among higher secondary students in relation to their social adjustment. *Journal of Research in Humanities and Social Science, 5*(3), 38–42.

Nemati, E., Habibi, M., Vargahan, F. A., Mohamadloo, S. S., & Ghanbari, S. (2017). The role of mindfulness and spiritual intelligence in students' mental health. *Journal of Research & Health, 7*(1), 594–602. doi:10.18869/acadpub.jrh.7.1.594

Nobari, L., & Shokri, M. (2014). Evaluating the student's spiritual intelligence and quality of life relationship at Payam-E-Noor University in Kaleibar branch. *Arabian Journal of Business and Management Review, 3*(12), 123–131. doi:10.12816/0016558

Nurfarojandari, A., & Maftuhah, M. (2019, September). *Student academic achievement: The role of emotional and spiritual intelligence* [Paper presentation]. 5th International Conference on Education in Muslim Society, ICEMS 2019, Jakarta, Indonesia. https://eudl.eu/doi/10.4108/eai.30-9-2019.2291124

Pant, N., & Srivastava, S. K. (2019). The impact of spiritual intelligence, gender and educational background on mental health among college students. *Journal of Religion and Health, 58*(1), 87–108. doi:10.100710943-017-0529-3 PMID:29192361

Payton, J. W., Wardlaw, D. M., Graczyk, P. A., Bloodworth, M. R., Tompsett, C. J., & Weissberg, R. P. (2000). Social and emotional learning: A framework for promoting mental health and reducing risk behavior in children and youth. *The Journal of School Health, 70*(5), 179–185. doi:10.1111/j.1746-1561.2000.tb06468.x PMID:10900594

Rani, A. A., Hashim, H., Ali, F., Abidin, I., & Ahmad, A. (2017). *Inculcating spiritual intelligence to enhance students' psychological well-being*. The European Proceedings of Social & Behavioural Sciences. doi:10.15405/epsbs.2017.10.23

Rayung, M. N., & Ambotang, A. S. (2018). The influence of emotional and spiritual intelligence on the high school student outcomes. *Journal of Education & Social Policy, 5*(1), 211-20. http://jespnet.com/journals/Vol_5_No_1_March_2018/23.pdf

Razia, B. (2019). Effect of spiritual intelligence on well-being of prospective teachers. *Research and Reflections on Education, 17*(3), 18-26. http://sxcejournal.com/jul-sep-2019/paper3.pdf

Sa'adati, H., & Lashani, L. (2012). Spiritual intelligence relationship with coping strategies. *Archives of Rehabilitation, 12,* 75-81. http://rehabilitationj.uswr.ac.ir/article-1-1028-en.html

Sharma, S. (2019). Spiritual intelligence in relation to academic achievement among Somalia students. *History Research Journal, 5*(6), 798–800.

Singh, A., Kour, P., & Singh, T. (2010). Spiritual intelligence, altruism, school environment, and academic achievement as predictor of mental health of adolescents. *Journal of Exercise Science and Physiotherapy*, *6*(1), 34–38.

Smartt, M. J. (2014). *The relationship of spiritual intelligence to achievement of secondary students.* Doctoral Dissertations and Projects. 820. https://digitalcommons.liberty.edu/doctoral/820

Sood, S., Bakhshi, A., & Gupta, R. (2012). Relation between personality traits, spiritual intelligence and well-being in university students. *Journal of Education and Practice*, *3*(10), 55–60.

Zohar, D. (1997). *Re-wiring the corporate brain: Using the new science to rethink how we structure and lead organizations*. Berrett-Koehler Publishers.

Zohar, D. (2000). *SQ: Connecting with our spiritual intelligence*. Bloomsbury.

KEY TERMS AND DEFINITIONS

Academic Performance: The student's assessment is based on the scores or grades achieved in the different study courses during the school and college years.

Adaptation: Ability to modify and change oneself to align with the surrounding environment or life demands.

Adjustment: The ability to be flexible and open to adapt or change according to the demands of the environment

Emotional Intelligence: Emotional intelligence is also known as the emotional quotient (EQ). It is the ability to recognize and manage one's own emotions, adapt to the environment, and empathize with others. It consists of five major components: self-awareness, self-regulation, motivation, empathy, social skills.

Happiness: A mental state of positive and pleasant emotions and feelings due to the experience of satisfaction with the prevailing life conditions. It can be both short term and long term.

Mental Health: The emotional, social, and behavioral well-being in an individual's life.

Quality of Life: It is an individual's self-perception about their well-being and satisfaction on a physical, psychological, social, and environmental level in the context of their culture.

Resilience: It is an Individual's ability to cope with adverse events and make a comeback or spring back in life after facing tough times.

Social, Emotional, and Academic Development (SEAD): SEAD is the integration of five social-emotional learning (SEL) skills, namely self-awareness, self-management, social awareness, relationship skills, and responsible decision-making.

Social-Emotional Learning (SEL): SEL is the process through which all young people and adults acquire and apply the knowledge, skills, and attitudes to develop healthy identities, manage emotions and achieve personal and collective goals, feel and show empathy for others, establish and maintain supportive relationships, and make responsible and caring decisions.

Spiritual Intelligence: It is an individual's capacity to possess a socially relevant purpose in life by understanding 'self' and to have a high degree of conscience, compassion, and commitment to human values.

Chapter 11
Social and Emotional Learning (SEL) Assessment in After-School Care:
How Accessible Evaluation Can Lead to Widespread Quality Implementation

Dana Minney
Texas State University, USA & St. Edward's University, USA

ABSTRACT

An abundance of research links children's social-emotional competence with positive school and life outcomes, but many barriers to widespread, high quality social-emotional learning (SEL) exist. Studies also found SEL delivered consistently and in coordination with other programs, both in and out of school, is more effective, but lack of unified standards, a supportive framework, and systematic approach prevent consistency and coordination of delivery. Process monitoring and impact evaluation help overcome barriers and improve implementation. After-school programs provide opportunities for quality SEL delivery and evaluation. This chapter reports results of an evaluation comparing pre- and post-program survey data from elementary school children (n = 98) in an after-school program that has incorporated an SEL curriculum. Results showed significant increases in the SEL competencies of self-management, social awareness, and social skills. The author also explored advantages of providing both SEL instruction and low-cost evaluation in after-school care settings in addition to schools.

INTRODUCTION

The term "emotional intelligence" (EQ) was first widely publicized by Daniel Goleman nearly 25 years ago (Goleman, 1995). Since then, two decades of child development and educational research confirm the value, if not the necessity, of attending to children's emotional and social well-being, and the benefit of doing so on their academic and life outcomes. Children who participate in quality social-emotional

DOI: 10.4018/978-1-7998-6728-9.ch011

learning (SEL) experience reduced likelihood of drug use, aggression, and other high-risk behaviors, as well as improved self-control, emotional regulation, and academic performance (Belfield et al., 2015; Domitrovich et al., 2017; Durlak et al., 2010).

Long-term positive outcomes include higher likelihood of high school graduation, workplace success, and lower rates of incarceration (Domitrovich et al., 2017; Moffitt et al., 2011). Students participating in SEL programs have 76% higher levels of social skills than students who are not in these programs (Bridgeland et al., 2013), and teachers and administrators may even be more likely to stay at a school with evidence-based campus-wide SEL than at one without (Jones & Kahn, 2018).

Not only is the positive impact of school-based SEL on children's academic and life outcomes a near certainty, but exposure to evidence-based SEL during out-of-school time (OST) is also beneficial (Jones et al., 2017). Durlak et al. (2010) established a clear link between social-emotional well-being and academic performance in a meta-analysis. These researchers found children who participated in after-school programs (ASPs) that aimed to promote personal and social skills reported an 11% increase in their school grades. Furthermore, research indicates consistent, coordinated, and evidence-based SEL implementation during OST (i.e., ASPs, parent training or community organizations) supports and reinforces the positive impact of school-based SEL (Durlak, et al., 2010; Jones et al., 2017).

An analysis of ASPs that integrate some kind of SEL content in their program delivery model indicated these may be ideal settings for students to develop their social and emotional skills (Hurd & Deutsch, 2017). One reason is that ASPs have the potential to give continuity and reinforcement to the SEL to which children are exposed during the school day (Durlak, et al., 2010). In addition, ASPs are not subject to the same demands on academic performance as schools, and can usually choose their own curriculum and areas of focus (Hurd & Deutsch, 2017). Instead, curriculum in schools is generally determined by district or state policy.

Unfortunately, widespread implementation of quality SEL is still elusive for schools, districts, and ASPs. A lack of valid, time-effective, and cost-effective formative assessments leads to low quality or non-evidence-based SEL implementation, and a widely used approach in measuring SEL program impact in ASPs currently does not exist (Gullotta, 2015). This chapter describes an organization that offers an ASP (i.e., Extend-A-Care [EAC]) and that designed, implemented, and evaluated its SEL curriculum using pre- and postprogram data. The author proposes that, when appropriate resources are accessible, organizations that provide ASPs have the potential to develop and implement their own SEL curriculum as well as provide their own rudimentary evaluation.

LITERATURE BACKGROUND

Collaborative for Academic, Social, and Emotional Learning (CASEL) is considered as the most prominent and trusted source of information about SEL. Their definition is as follows:

SEL is the process through which all young people and adults acquire and apply the knowledge, skills, and attitudes to develop healthy identities, manage emotions and achieve personal and collective goals, feel and show empathy for others, establish and maintain supportive relationships, and make responsible and caring decisions. (CASEL, 2020, para. 1)

A group of researchers and child advocates (including Daniel Goleman, Roger Weissberg, and Richard Boyatzis) met to discuss children's well-being at the Fetzer Institute in 1994. Their discussion of strategies to enhance students' mental health and academic and healthy social development led them to coin the term "SEL" (Elias et al., 1997). Thus, CASEL was formed.

Simultaneously, interest in emotional intelligence was growing in the field of psychological research, and later spread to the military and organizational psychology. Studies in workplace performance and job success consistently showed a link between the identified EQ constructs and positive career outcomes (Goleman, 2005; Goleman et al., 2002).

Multiple researchers began to develop their own theoretic models (Goleman, 2001). The original conceptualization of EQ consisted of four components, self-management, self-awareness, social awareness, and relationship management (Goleman, 2001). Cherniss et al., (2006) further refined the definition by describing two overarching categories: "Perception of emotions," which encompassed both awareness of one's own emotions and awareness of others' emotions, and "management of emotion," which encompassed management of one's own emotions and management of others' emotions. Further research including validity testing revealed the importance of these competencies in life satisfaction, success, and leadership effectiveness. It was also found that EQ represented a skillset distinct from personality traits or cognitive ability (Brackett & Mayer, 2003; Cherniss et al., 2006).

Interest in SEL continued on multiple fronts, and applying the research to students in schools became a priority. The US Department of Health and Human Services (2001) published a report on children's well-being which described emerging trends in society that seemed to put children's emotional well-being at increasingly higher risk. Researchers agreed, saying schools faced unprecedented challenges to educate an increasingly multicultural and multilingual student body and to address the widening social and economic gaps of students' families (Elias et al., 1997; Weissberg et al., 2003). Other research was published citing the danger of easier access to media that encouraged health-damaging behavior to children's social, emotional, and moral development. A study reported 30% of 14- to 17-year-olds engaged in behaviors that negatively impacted their potential for life success (Dryfoos, 1997). Furthermore, Greenberg et al. (2003) noted approximately 20% of young people experienced mental health problems during the course of a year; yet, 75% to 80% of them did not receive appropriate interventions.

While schools faced increasingly high expectations by parents, community members, and the state as to how to successfully address these serious challenges, pressure mounted to improve students' academic performance. However, some claimed using only academic measures to gauge success was too limiting (Shriver & Buffett, 2015), and pushed for policies and practices supporting evidence-based and coordinated youth development programming. Some schools began delivering programs on topics such as drug prevention, violence prevention, sex education, promoting healthy behavior, character education, service learning, and civic education. Durlak and Wells (1997) found children who participated in emotion education and interpersonal problem-solving training experienced mean effect sizes ranging from .24 to .93. Similarly, Catalano et al. (2002) found that "promotion and prevention programs that address positive youth development (PYD) constructs are definitely making a difference in well-evaluated studies" (p. 62).

Social-Emotional Learning in After-School Programs

ASPs first came into existence to provide a safe place for children to be supervised in between the hours of 3:00 p.m. and 6:00 p.m., while parents or caregivers worked. Later, these settings began to be seen as a place for social enrichment and skill-building (Gullotta, 2015). Researchers in child development coined the term PYD, which then began to inform some ASPs such as Big Brothers/Big Sisters and the Promoting Alternative Thinking Strategies (PATHS) Project (Laughlin, 2013). Programs began to offer a range of skill-building content, from social to technical, art or athletic skills. More recently, research indicated ASPs may be able to offer SEL curricula while bypassing some of the barriers that traditional schools face (Hurd & Deutsch, 2017).

For example, schools are more likely to be bound by academic expectations from the district, which leads to school resources and trainings funneled toward improving academic results, rather than SEL (Elias et al., 2015). Organizations that offer ASPs, on the other hand, are usually able to determine their own areas of focus, and are not bound by district policies. In addition, while their employees are not teachers, they may have more opportunities to connect and form relationships with the children they serve. This can benefit the child's social development, since SEL is said to occur within the context of a warm relationship between the child and an older and more skilled person, based on microinteractions throughout the day (Weissberg et al., 2015). With a less regimented schedule than a teacher would have in a typical school day, an ASP provider could more easily form a relaxed and friendly connection with a child (Hurd & Deutsch, 2017).

ASPs can also complement and reinforce SEL instruction that is provided in traditional school settings. In fact, research suggested school curriculum should be integrated with ASPs as much as possible for SEL to work to its maximum potential (Greenberg et al., 2003). In schools, a campus-wide adoption of SEL works best (Durlak et al., 2015; Elias et al., 2006). Likewise, in ASPs, facility-wide adoption of SEL and commitment to training all staff in their social-emotional development are necessary for SEL to be most effective (Elias et al., 2006).

Despite the benefits of SEL in ASPs, there are challenges to high-quality delivery, just as there are challenges with school-based SEL (Gullotta, 2015). Catalano et al. (2002) analyzed 161 PYD programs, concluded that only 25 were effective, and acknowledged the need for standards for SEL assessment measures. SEL curricula specifically designed for use in ASPs are not widely available, and are difficult to design (the incredible years program is an exception) (Webster-Stratton & Herman, 2010). School-based SEL curricula are not transferable to ASPs (where multiple grades are often combined) because school-based lessons are usually age- or grade-specific (Belfield et al., 2015; Gullota, 2015).

Evaluation and assessment tools for SEL in ASPs are even more scarce. Those tools that do currently exist are usually designed with school-based programs in mind. These assessments are not conducive to after-school care settings. One reason assessment is more difficult in ASPs is children do not attend ASPs as regularly as they attend school, which leads to incomplete results. Additionally, assessments are often grade-specific (i.e., only for kindergarten students, as in Deveraux Early Childhood Asssessment) and not generalizable to multiple age groups (Denham, 2015). Further, ASP employees are not trained in giving assessments as most teachers are. Lastly, many ASPs are nonprofits that do not have funds to purchase assessment tools, which can range from $198 to $342 and up, nor are they able to provide the necessary training to administer the assessments (Denham, 2015; Hurd & Deutsch, 2017). Nevertheless, in order to offer high-quality SEL in an ASP, finding or creating adequate assessment and evaluation tools is essential. Leaders at EAC, the ASP the author describes in this chapter, worked to overcome the above-mentioned challenges.

HOW EVALUATION ENSURES HIGH-QUALITY IMPLEMENTATION

Both educators and the scientific community concur that effective SEL requires fostering social and emotional competencies through explicit, consistent, and sequenced instruction (Catalano et al., 2002). They concur that programming should include school-wide or facility-wide policies and practices fostering collaboration, problem-solving, and warm communication among staff members and administrators. Further, researchers affirm that planned, ongoing, systematic, and structured manuals and curricula should be used to support consistency and coordinated SEL delivery (Greenberg et al., 2003).

Although guidelines such as these indicate how to create the ideal environment and how to most effectively deliver SEL, school districts and childcare settings across the US still lack high-quality and consistent SEL implementation. High-quality and evidence-based delivery in an SEL-friendly environment (both in and out of school settings) requires program evaluation to play a role. Evaluation and continuous progress monitoring can increase the likelihood SEL delivery will comply with SAFE (i.e., sequenced, active, focused, and explicit) standards (Durlak et al., 2010, 2011), inform policy-makers to set guidelines and designate funding, and provide evidence to create a supportive ecological framework. Evaluation data, both formative (i.e., progress monitoring for student learning and implementation) and summative (i.e., assessment of learning), can inform the creation of standards, provide tools to reinforce these standards, and therefore lead to the creation of structures for system-wide implementation.

Programs which are plagued by poor implementation (i.e., uncoordinated, unsubstantiated by validity or reliability assessment or lack of attention to fidelity and consistency) are unlikely to show positive effects (Greenberg et al., 2003), but, unfortunately, are very common. Hallfors and Godette (2002) reported the results from a study with 81 school district curriculum coordinators across the US. Their findings indicated that 59% of these coordinators had selected a research-based curriculum for implementation, but only 19% of the coordinators reported their schools were implementing these programs with fidelity. Part of the problem was that parents and community members demonstrated having widely varied understanding, awareness, and acceptance of research-based SEL (Hamilton et al., 2019a). Other research confirms principals and teachers agree on the importance of SEL assessment, but, unfortunately, the majority of them do not know how to do it. In fact, only 37% of principals are aware of methods to assess SEL, even though 90% of them believe in the importance of assessing SEL (DePaoli et al., 2017).

In order to address inconsistent implementation, McGown (2015) and Weissberg et al. (2015) advocated for developing valid and easy-to-use assessment tools that can be used in the regular school context and can be competently, quickly, and efficiently administered and interpreted. Dusenbury et al. (2015) reported there continues to be a need for well-developed assessment tools that align with SEL standards, and cited several resources for these types of tools. Denham (2015) described several of the most reliable SEL assessment tools. Unfortunately, most, if not all, cost money, take at least 10 minutes per child (some as much as 25 minutes), and may involve purchase of technology or software. Schools often do not have the budget for evaluation when first initiating a program, and none of these would be feasible.

Greenberg et al. (2003) concluded SEL programs that were not coordinated, monitored, evaluated, and improved over time were unlikely to be sustainable or to impact student behavior. However, consistent SEL delivery can occur in coordination with other programs (including academic and out-of-school activities). Standardized measures and evaluation are needed to assess youth development constructs and ensure program integrity (Hallfors & Godette, 2002).

Evaluation Starts with Standards

Business managers are told to "inspect what you expect" to underscore the importance of measurement in attaining high standards in their procedures. Program evaluation is the educational equivalent, and is an appropriate way to measure SEL impact and implementation. Research indicates low-quality SEL implementation is fairly common (Durlak & DuPre, 2008) and leads to poor or ambiguous outcomes. Indicators of low-quality implementation may include inconsistency of dosage, nonadherence in delivery, multiple competing or noncoordinated programs cooccurring, lack of evidence-based materials and lessons, and low-quality or no teacher training. Instead, programs that are implemented well have nearly three times the likelihood to show positive impact, and programs that are evaluated are more likely to be implemented well (Durlak & DuPre, 2008).

Standards and subsequent measurement and reinforcement of these standards allow evidence-based quality programs to progress and expand. Denham (2015) noted assessment is an indispensable part of strategic program planning and expansion that include clear goals and benchmarks (standards), evidence-based curricula, and progress monitoring. In order to fulfill this recommendation, schools and districts must develop or obtain standards (i.e., what students should know and be able to do at each school level), specific criteria, and tools for SEL measurement (Dusenbury et al., 2015).

Illinois was the first state to adopt comprehensive SEL standards for all grade levels. The *Illinois Goals and Standards* provide very specific performance descriptors for different development levels. For example, Goal 1 is to "develop self-management and self-awareness skills" and the performance indicator is "identify and manage one's own emotions and behavior" (Dusenbury et al., 2015). Experts recommend standards serve as a blueprint for curriculum design, evaluation, and high-quality professional development (Dusenbury et al., 2015).

Not only does evaluation support high-quality SEL implementation by helping to establish and maintain unified standards, but evaluation is valuable for replication, adaptation, and diffusion of SEL innovation. The goal of widespread and evidence-based SEL requires reaching as many students as possible with evidence-based and well-implemented curriculum. High-quality and high-fidelity (i.e., extent to which the innovation corresponds to the originally intended program) implementation is only sustainable, and possibly only exists, when programs are evaluated (Durlak & DuPre, 2008).

Only after standards are set and multiple types of SEL assessments (e.g., implementation and impact) are accessible, is widespread adoption of high-quality SEL possible. Adoption depends on exposure to information. Conversely, disseminating information about successful programs leads to adoption by increasing numbers of sites. According to Rogers (2002), the adoption of a school-based innovation takes place over time and is marked by five distinct stages: Dissemination, adoption, implementation, evaluation, and sustainability. If any of the five stages of the process are not carried out effectively, low-quality programs may be adopted and will not be sustainable. The cycle from diffusion to adoption, and eventually sustainability, can most efficiently be ushered along with data from assessments ensuring efficiency and success at each stage.

A System-Wide Framework of Support

A systemic approach to implementation and coherent school-wide improvements is consistent with the federal government's comprehensive school reform (CSR). The CSR recognizes school ecology and climate should be a central focus of intervention, and program success is enhanced by combining emphases on changing not just children's behaviors, but also teacher and family behavior and home and school relationships. This systemic or widespread adoption of high-quality SEL delivery depends on extensive diffusion and subsequent adoption of a message to prioritize high-quality SEL implementation and evaluation (Mahoney et al., 2018).

Students adopt the desired attitudes and behaviors at a higher rate when classroom SEL instruction is combined with environmental support and reinforcement from peers, family, school staff, and community members, both in school and OST (Greenberg et al., 2003). Researchers Mart et al. (2015) called for a system-based focus, and an overall coordinated strategy to effectively integrate multiple programs. Therefore, an ecological perspective is useful to enlist support from political, social, institutional, economic, community, and family structures (Mahoney et al., 2018). Obstacles such as lack of resources, lack of infrastructure, and lack of teacher training (Schonert-Reichl et al., 2017) can be overcome. Indeed, funding can become available, communities can provide collaboration, administrators can give their support, and policy-makers can integrate evidence-based SEL standards into legislation. Achieving widespread and consistent implementation of beneficial programming calls for educational policies that require accountability at both a state and federal level (Catalano et al., 2002).

State Support

Evaluation can provide evidence which enhances adoption, adaptation, and replication of SEL delivery (Mahoney et al., 2018). For example, cost-benefit analysis of SEL has shown time and money invested in improving SEL programs are well-spent (Belfield et al., 2015; Durlak et al., 2011). Results of such an evaluation can be presented to funders for increases or continuation of SEL program funding, as well as provide guidance on where future messaging needs to be targeted.

Stronger federal support–for example, adopting the SEL standards Illinois has set for K-12 students–would be an important step toward widespread high-quality SEL implementation (Bridgeland et al., 2013; Weissberg et al., 2015). At a state level, Texas created the *Common Core State Standards*, which include standards for skills in the interpersonal and intrapersonal domains, and which other states are adopting (Dusenbury et al., 2015). These domains are linked to the SEL competency clusters of social awareness, self-awareness, and social skills (Brown & Kappes, 2012), although they do not map onto the five SEL competencies as identified by CASEL.

Setting state or federal standards for high-quality implementation and teacher training can enable schools to receive the necessary resources–funding, quality materials, and technology–for student social-and-emotional enrichment, rather than just academic support. Evaluation, whether it is ongoing or annual, can inform administrators, stakeholders, and policy-makers as to how closely the SEL is adhering to the vision that researchers set out. This can provide the evidence administrators, policy-makers, teachers, and parents need in order to know why and how they should support the SEL measures being implemented.

A Culture of Adoption

The necessary cultural shift can occur to widespread adoption and prioritizing of SEL, but only with proof of positive impact. Evidence illustrating how social-and-emotional well-being supports campus goals like improved academic performance and enhanced student engagement. Further, according to some research, even increases in quality teacher retention (Jones & Kahn, 2018) can begin to sway public opinion. Evaluation data can be submitted when putting together school budgets, applying for center grants or state monies, and asking the community for more support through partnerships and collaboration.

With school and community leaders championing SEL campus-wide, district-wide, and even community-wide coordinated effort, they can uphold a vision of school change. Funding for explicit training for teachers and childcare workers on how to provide an SEL-friendly classroom (i.e., one that is well managed, feeds warm relationships with students, and supports teachers modelling SEL behavior) (Williford & Wolcott, 2015) can be provided with a learning model. The following section illustrates a case study of an after-school care center that created its own curriculum and evaluation at no cost.

SOCIAL-EMOTIONAL LEARNING EVALUATION IN AFTER-SCHOOL CARE: A WORKING MODEL

Although SEL is not found in ASPs as often as in schools, a meta-analysis has evidenced that children in ASPs promoting personal and social skills reported an 11% increase in their academic achievement (Durlak et al., 2010). Research also shows that, when SEL lessons learned during OST are consistent with lessons learned in school, the child benefits from this added reinforcement and continuity (Hurd & Deutsch, 2017; Jones et al., 2017). Therefore, continuing to improve SEL delivery in ASPs by evaluating the impact of SEL curriculum is crucial for children's development and for ASP design.

The organization highlighted in this chapter is a working model of how to implement quality SEL in an after-school care setting, as well as how to conduct a time- and cost-effective, and age-appropriate SEL assessment. This working model consists of a detailed examination of how the operations director modified school-based SEL curriculum to accommodate an after-school environment, as well as a description of the methods and results of the accompanying program evaluation. Through a collaboration with graduate students from a neighboring university, program evaluation interns were able to design survey questions, research age-appropriate measures, and conduct an impact evaluation of the SEL pilot.

Background of the After-School Care Center Extend-A-Care

EAC provides after-school care in pop-up sites at elementary schools located throughout Central Texas. The organization serves over 3,500 children aged 4-12 during the school year and nearly 800 during the summer programs. Their mission is to provide an environment for PYD by enhancing cognitive, social, and physical development of children, and assisting working families and communities by providing enriching, affordable, and licensed childcare. As part of this commitment to children's enrichment, EAC began offering a SEL curriculum delivered by group leaders approximately once per week in 2015-2016 and EAC's staff, numbering 380 people, were trained to lead these lessons.

Social-Emotional Learning Curriculum

Although organizations such as Second Step, Promoting Alternative Thinking Strategies, and Responsive Classroom provide evidence-based SEL materials and curriculum to schools (Rimm-Kaufman & Hulleman, 2015), ASPs often do not have the funding to obtain it. This was the case for EAC, a nonprofit. Therefore, EAC's Operations Director and Curriculum Director decided to take matters into their own hands and create a hybrid SEL curriculum. Their initial goal was to help children learn and understand how to regulate their emotions, have more self-control, and deal with challenging situations (i.e., bullying and conflict).

An analysis of evidence-based SEL programming in ASPs found the offerings to be scant (Gullotta, 2015). However, three programs were identified that could be incorporated into ASPs with minor modifications: All Stars Prevention Curriculum (for middle school aged children), Promoting Alternative Thinking Strategies (PATHS), and Life Skills Training (promoting self-management and social skills). Programs such as Life Skills Training require funds and training. Materials typically consist of a manual, PDFs, CDs or online instruction (Gullotta, 2015). Training may be in-person or online, and can range from $250 to over $1000 for two days of instruction. EAC, being a nonprofit, did not have funds for external training nor for materials. They found another solution.

By first reaching out to local school district officials, they were able to form a partnership that gave them access to resources for content they normally would not have been able to access. Partnering with the school district also gave EAC access to district-wide teacher training materials including Peace Path (Abadesco & Savage, 2015) and the Mindfulness Revolution training (Boyce, 2011), as well as Second Step curriculum (i.e., classroom-based social skills curriculum with specific lessons for each grade) (Jennings & Frank, 2015) and the Anti-Defamation League's No Place for Hate. These materials had to be modified for use in an after-school care setting, but the theoretical basis and impact evaluation evidence were solid (Rimm-Kaufman & Hulleman, 2015).

EAC ensured high-quality materials by creating lessons from content that was previously tested for validity and effectiveness and then vetted by the SEL department of a school district. They also adhered as closely as possible to implementation procedures by following best practices. While not all ASPs are in the proximity of a school district with a well-developed SEL department and evaluation department, some materials are available for free online from nonprofit organizations, such as Panorama and CASEL, which contributes to the knowledge-base, curriculum creation, and publishing of research on the topic. An additional benefit of partnering with the local school district was that training and curriculum resources provided consistent language children could understand and could reinforce what they learned in school.

The hybridized lessons created by the Operations Director and SEL Director at EAC were then put into a weekly activity guide and distributed to all group leaders at all sites at the beginning of each week, along with a packet of any needed materials corresponding with the lessons. SEL lessons occurred Monday through Friday for 10 to15 minutes and were conducted by group leaders in segments called "group meetings." At EAC, children are divided by age into groups of 12 to 17 children. Each group has a group leader, who is responsible for the activities of their group every day, and a site supervisor, who oversees all groups and group leaders at each location. Group meetings occurred in one group of children at a time, with children being invited to sit in a circle or around a "Feelings Rug" to learn how to routinely calm themselves down when upset, to empathize with others, and to talk about their own emotions. For example, children viewed pictures of faces displaying various emotions and identified the face representing their current feelings. After identifying how they felt, they were invited to share with the group their reason for feeling that way.

The activities which were outlined in the manuals group leaders received for SEL sessions were created with a clear set of goals. Jones et al. (2018) suggested articulating a series of outcomes that are reasonable goals or expectations for the effort is a best practice for effective programs. Jones et al. (2017) further suggested that the program aligned with the ASP mission and pedagogy and with the needs of the students. All activities should fit within an appropriate timeframe and should be congruent with children's developmental stage. Jones et al. (2017) advocated for adapting existing in-school lessons as

EAC did, since SEL programs specific to ASPs are rare. In addition, ASP directors can use worksheets provided by Jones et al. (2017) to help prioritize the needs of their student population, determine how much time should be allotted to the sessions, and evaluate which programs already in existence may be a good fit. For example, a program with songs or stories may work well for younger children or students with attention control difficulties.

All EAC staff attended SEL instruction training in how to lead these activities and implement SEL best practices, and subsequently participated in review sessions periodically. As of this writing, Second Step was researching and developing a curriculum for ASPs and included some implementation data provided by EAC in their research. The SEL curriculum created by EAC aimed to improve children and adolescents' understanding of emotions and create and maintain positive relationships

In the interest of gaining both formative and summative feedback about the implementation and impact of this SEL curriculum, impact evaluations were conducted at three randomly selected sites during the 2017-2018 school year, and again in the 2018-2019 school year. Results from 2017-2018 were published in a previous report (Minney et al., 2019) and showed statistically significant increases in children's levels on two SEL constructs (i.e., self-management and social awareness) from the pretest to the posttest. Most importantly, the impact evaluation was time- and cost-effective, and was conducted with very little disruption to class activities.

Evaluation Question

The purpose of this evaluation was to determine if there were changes in SEL, as measured by self-management, self-awareness, and social awareness, in children who participated in EAC's SEL curriculum. Impact was measured by comparing children's pretest scores at the beginning of the school year and posttest scores at the end of the school year to determine if there were significant differences.

A secondary goal was to increase the validity of the instrument by collecting data from a second reporter. In this case, the second reporter was the group leader who filled out a questionnaire assessing similar constructs for each child at the same time the pretests and posttests were given to the children.

Additionally, a factor analysis with SPSS was planned to find whether or not correlations for question clusters existed. This type of analysis would reveal if responses to questions related to the same construct clustered together (Bhattacherjee, 2012). Lastly, this evaluation serves as an example of a nonprofit using resourcefulness to create an instrument and conduct a low-cost and efficient SEL evaluation.

METHOD

Participants

The evaluator randomly chose three EAC sites (out of 80) for the curriculum evaluation by numbering each site and using a random number generator software (i.e., SPSS). Collectively, 120 children participated in the study, but only children who completed both pretest and posttest (N = 98) were included in the analyses. The children ranged in age from 4 to 11 years old (M = 7.28). A slightly higher percentage of participants were males (53.3%). Figure 1 illustrates children's ages.

Figure 1. The children ranged in age from 4 to 11 years old

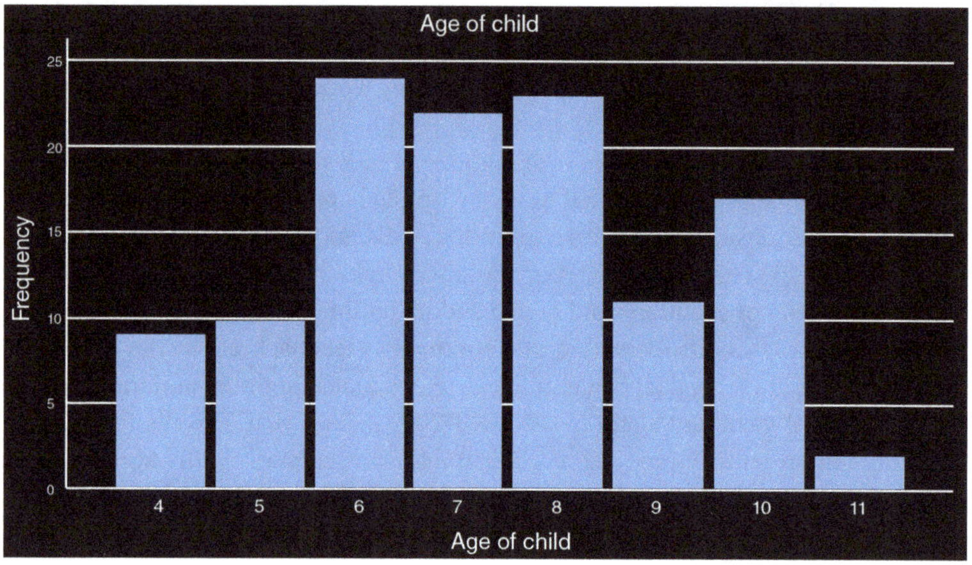

The study was approved by the Texas State University's Institutional Review Board. Informed consent was obtained from most of the parents, and the children without parental consent were omitted from the final analysis and report. No information on ethnicity of the children was obtained, in compliance with procedures approved by the Institutional Review Board's waiver.

Procedures

Evaluation pretests were administered a few weeks after beginning the school year. Children gave assent prior to data collection. Parents gave consent with the understanding that aggregate data gathered through these evaluation activities may be published. EAC directors and the evaluator developed a modified version of an SEL self-report survey which was originally based on the CASEL-5 Model (CASEL, 2012), with an emphasis on self-awareness, self-management, social skills, and social awareness. However, after a literature review of SEL evaluation in adolescents (Borgers et al., 2003; Crowe et al., 2011; Doll & Elliott, 1994; McKown, 2015), several questions were modified. Researchers report children identify more with vignette-style questions on self-report surveys because they are more likely to think in concrete than conceptual terms.

At each site, the evaluator handed out the pretest surveys to the children of 8 years and older. They were instructed to fill them out on their own after a short explanation about confidentiality and explaining that the questions are "about your thoughts and feelings, so every answer you give is the right answer." Due to younger children's less-developed literacy skills (Borgers et al., 2003), the evaluator interviewed children between the ages of 4 and 7 years old individually. The posttest surveys were administered in April, a few weeks prior to the end of school in the same manner.

Evaluation and Data Collection

Measure

The CASEL 5 Model (2012) served as the source for EAC directors when they designed their original SEL evaluation tool. The evaluator modified the questions and the procedures conducting the evaluation (Minney et al., 2019) in the first year of evaluation (school year 2017-2018). Table 1 displays the original survey.

Table 1. Evaluation questions and response choices, school year 2017-2018

Evaluation Questions and Response Choices: School year 2017-2018.

Competency	Question	Response Option
Self-management	1. It is (blank) to calm myself down when I'm feeling upset.	1 = Very Hard to 4 = Very Easy
	2. Can you think of three ways to calm yourself down when you are upset?	Open-ended question
Social awareness	1. It is (blank) for me to know what people might be feeling by the look on their face.	1 = Very Hard to 4 = Very Easy
	2. If I accidentally hurt my friend's feelings, it is (blank) to figure out what to do to make them feel better.	1 = Very Hard to 4 = Very Easy
Self-awareness	1. It is (blank) for me to think about what might happen before I decide what to do.	1 = Very Hard to 4 = Very Easy

The next year (school year 2018-2019), the evaluation instrument was further modified. Evaluators considered the five SEL competencies identified by CASEL (2003): Self-awareness (ability to assess personal feelings accurately), self-management (ability to handle one's emotions and behavior productively, self-soothe), social awareness (ability to take others' perspectives, empathy), relationship and social skills (promote positive and effective exchanges with others), and responsible decision-making (analyzing social situations and problems, and setting prosocial goals). In an effort to simplify the evaluation process and keep the instrument short, two measures were used to assess social skills and social awareness in combination, and one measure each was used for self-management and for self-awareness. Since the definitions of the competencies are broad and may overlap, researchers have recommended choosing a narrower scope when first introducing SEL curriculum and subsequent evaluation (Hamilton & Schwartz, 2019). Additionally, research has shown "responsible decision-making" is not an appropriate standard for younger children (Dusenbury et al., 2015).

All the questions in the 2018-2019 version of the survey, except one, were made to be vignette style with four-point Likert scale response sets. Therefore, a high score indicated higher levels of the construct.

Questions were designed to assess the constructs of self-management (three items), social skills and social awareness (four items), and self-awareness (one item) (Table 2).

Table 2. Evaluation questions and response choices, school year 2018-2019

Evaluation Questions and Response Choices: School year 2018-2019.

Competency	Question	Response Option
Self-management	Q3. If you get mad at another child on the playground, you will probably find a way to stay calm.	1 = Not true to 4 = Really true
	Q8. Can you think of three ways to calm yourself down when you are upset?	Open-ended question
	Q4. If you are doing a puzzle that's so hard you feel like quitting, how hard or easy is it to keep trying at it?	1 = Very Hard to 4 = Very Easy
Social awareness/ Social skills	Q1. If you see one of your friends walking with their head down and a frown on their face, you most likely would try to talk to them about feeling sad.	1 = Not true to 4 = Really true
	Q5. If I accidentally hurt my friend's feelings, I can probably figure out what to do to make them feel better.	1 = Very Hard to 4 = Very Easy
	Q2. When you are at Extend-A-Care and you need help, how hard or easy is it to talk to a grownup?	1 = Very Hard to 4 = Very Easy
	Q7. When someone is mean to you, how hard or easy is it to tell them they hurt your feelings?	1 = Very Hard to 4 = Very Easy
Self-awareness	Q6. If someone makes you angry while you are playing-like taking away a toy-you can usually notice when the feelings first start.	1 = Not true to 4 = Really true

The last question (Q8) was open-ended and asked the child to list three self-soothing methods ("Can you name three ways to calm yourself down when you're upset?"). For this question, a score of 3.0 meant the child could name at least three methods of self-soothing.

A second measure was administered to the group leaders of the children in the evaluation. They were asked questions related to a particular child and his/her conduct based on their observations of the child (Table 3) in the areas of self-management (SM; two items), social awareness/social skills (SASS; two items), and self-awareness (SA; one item). This survey was given to the group leaders at the same time as the pretest and posttests were given to students. Adding a second reporter is a commonly used method to test reliability of a measurement instrument (Bhattacherjee, 2012).

Table 3. Group leader evaluation questions and response choices

Group Leader Evaluation Questions and Response Choices

Competency	Question	Response Option
Self-management	Q2. When encountering an obstacle or a new activity, (child name) expresses confidence and self-assurance (e.g. "I can do it", or "I'd like to try it").	1 = Almost never (0-1) to 4 = Almost always (>4)
	Q5. (Child name) uses observable strategies to calm him/herself down if upset (e.g. goes to the peace corner, talks about it, or takes deep breaths).	1 = Almost never (0-1) to 4 = Almost always (>4)
Social awareness/ Social skills	Q3. (Child name) shows helpfulness and/or cooperation toward grownups and other children (e.g. puts things away when asked, assists another child in distress).	1 = Almost never (0-1) to 4 = Almost always (>4)
	Q4. (Child name) can easily ask for help from/express needs to EAC staff (e.g. verbalizes need to be listened to, need for snack/supplies/toy, need for comfort, etc.)	1 = Almost never (0-1) to 4 = Almost always (>4)
Self-awareness	Q1. (Child name) expresses his/her personal feelings to me, to another child or to another grownup (e.g. says things like "I miss my mom", or "I am mad").	1 = Almost never (0-1) to 4 = Almost always (>4)

RESULTS

Pretest and Posttest Differences

Pretest and posttest scores were compared using paired samples t-tests in SPSS to assess changes in SM, SASS, and SA. Effect sizes of the results were found by dividing the mean difference by the standard deviation (Cohen, 1988). It is recommended that effect sizes be viewed in the context of other research (Durlak et al., 2010); in a meta-analysis of 75 SEL programs in the US, the average effect size for change in prosocial behavior was .29.

Table 4 displays the results including effect size, pre- and posttest means, and statistical significance. The average scores reflect only the responses of the 98 children who had both pre- and posttest data. The number of paired responses is listed next to each question because the number of respondents varied depending on whether or not a question was skipped.

Table 4. Pretest and posttest outcomes of SEL curriculum evaluation

	Q3	98	2.57	2.96	0.39	0.28	0.007
	Q4	98	2.74	2.83	0.08		0.537
	Q2	98	2.85	3.17	0.33	0.24	0.018
	Q7	98	2.5	2.69	0.19		0.13

Average scores increased on all of the questions, with 5 out of 8 questions showing statistically significant improvement [p<.05] based on the children's self-reports. On two of the three questions relating to the construct self-management (Q3 and Q8), mean scores increased by .39 and 1.08, with an effect size of .28 and .90, respectively. The third question relating to self-management (Q4) showed a mean increase of .08, but was not found to be statistically significant.

On the first question (Q1) measuring SASS, the average score increased by .45, with an effect size of .35. The number of students who responded "True" or "Extremely true" increased from 63% to 88% (Figure 2).

*Figure 2. Children who answered "True" or "Really true" to the question "If I saw a friend walking with his/her head down and a frown, I would try to understand why they feel sad" (Q1) increased from 63% to 88%***
***p<.01*

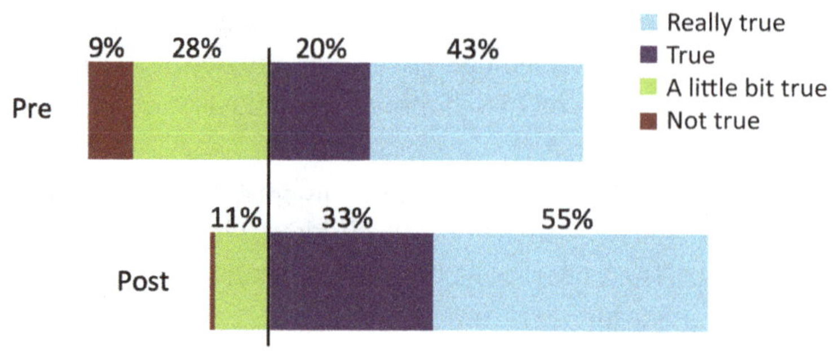

On another question (Q2) addressing SASS, the average score increased by .33, with an effect size of .24. Further, the number of children who responded “Often” or “Almost always” increased from 65% to 81% (Figure 3).

*Figure 3. Children who answered “Often” or “Almost always” to the question “How often do you feel you can talk to a grownup at Extend-A-Care when you need help?” (Q2) increased from 65% to 81%**
**p<.05*

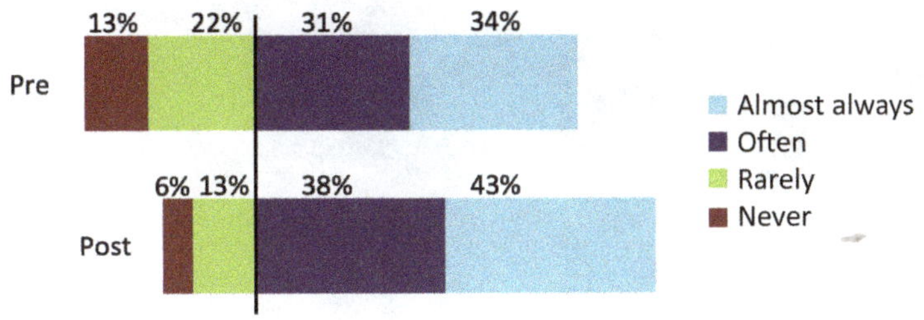

The other two questions pertaining to SASS (Q5 and Q7) increased by .16 and .19, respectively, which were not found to be statistically significant differences. Lastly, the question relating to self-awareness (Q6) increased by .51, with an effect size of .36, and the number of students who responded “Often” or “Almost always” increased from 47% to 70% (Figure 4).

*Figure 4. In the measure of self-awareness (Q6), children answering “True” or “Really true” to the question “If someone makes you angry when you are playing, you notice when the angry feelings first start” increased from 47% to 70%***
***p<.01*

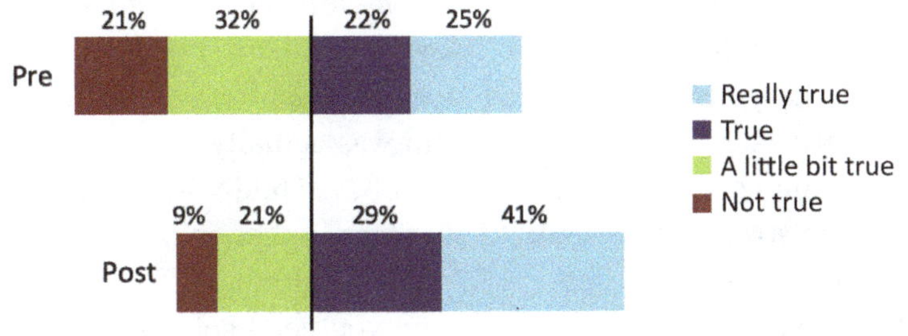

It is worth noting that the mean scores on Q8 (i.e., the open-ended question addressing self-management) increased from 1.87 to 2.95 (Table 5). In the pretest, many children (15%) were unable to name a single self-soothing strategy, while only 1% could not name one at posttest. At the pretest, only 42.5% of the children could name three, while, at the posttest, 97% could. Answers ranged from “hug someone” to “take belly breaths” (Figure 5).

*Figure 5. Lastly, in a self-management measure (Q8), when children were asked to name three methods they use to calm themselves down when they are upset, the number who could think of three methods for coping increased from 42% to 97%. The number who could think of no methods for coping decreased from 17% to 1%.****
****p<.001*

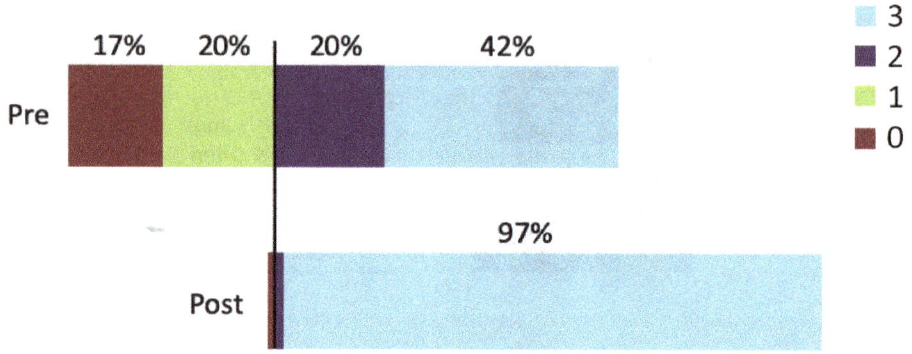

Exploratory Factor Analysis

An exploratory factor analysis was run in SPSS using a principal axis factor analysis to look for relationships between responses to questions related to the same presumed construct (Table 5). In the pretest data, the Kaiser-Meyer-Olkin measure of sampling adequacy had a value of .64, and two factors were identified which explained 30% of the variance. The first factor explained 21% and the second explained 9%. The following questions loaded together on factor one: Q1, Q3, Q5, and Q7. All of these, except for Q3, were created to measure SASS. The item Q3 was created to measure SM. However, the wording of the item described a scenario involving an interaction with another child ("If you get mad at another child on the playground, you will probably find a way to stay calm") with responses ranging from "Not true" to "Really true." The response set was on a four-point Likert scale, therefore a high score indicated higher levels of the constructs. It is possible this item was actually a better indicator for SASS than it was for SM, thereby explaining why it loaded onto SASS. A child who recognized that staying calm in the interaction makes good social sense would likely score higher on SASS.

Also surprising was that Q2 loaded high on factor two, although it was created as an indicator for SASS. The item "When you are at Extend-A-Care and you need help, how hard or easy is it to talk to a grownup?" was created to measure how well a child could navigate a social interaction where he/she needed to ask for help. However, it could also measure a child's SA (factor two) in recognizing that he/she needs help.

Additionally, Q4 was deleted after the extraction process because it did not demonstrate discriminant validity (its values were similar on both factor one and two). Also, the results of the difference between pre- and posttest mean scores on this question were not significant, and therefore the question may not be a good measure or it may measure two constructs that strongly overlap.

Table 5. Reproduced correlations

	Q1-SASS	Q2-SASS	Q3-SM	Q4-SM	Q5-SASS	Q6-SA	Q7-SASS
Q1-SASS	.154a	0.118	0.23	0.092	0.244	0.14	0.147
Q3-SM	0.23	0.115	.351a	0.12	0.393	0.201	0.219
Q5-SASS	0.244	-0.057	0.393	0.078	.502a	0.188	0.231
Q7-SASS	0.147	0.115	0.219	0.089	0.231	0.134	.141a
Q2-SASS	-0.015		0.013	0.007	-0.006	0.019	-0.014
Q4-SM	0.066	0.007	-0.027		0.009	-0.041	-0.007
Q6-SA	-0.001	0.019	-0.046	-0.041	0.028		0.035

Reliability Analysis

In an effort to analyze construct validity (i.e., the degree to which an instrument measures what it is supposed to measure) and reliability (i.e., an instrument that generates similar results at different points in time and with different raters), a reliability analysis was conducted (Bhattacherjee, 2012). First, the analysis was run with Q1, Q3, Q5, and Q7; the factors that loaded together in the factor analysis and the reliability statistic were .56. A second analysis was run on Q2 and Q6, which resulted in a reliability statistic of .33. Both these values are lower than what is generally considered acceptable (Netemeyer et al., 2003). Further analysis and pilot testing of additional questions are recommended with larger sample sizes. The results of this analysis serve as a baseline for EAC as they continue to refine their instrument.

Second Reporter Correlations

Overall, the scores given by the children to themselves correlated higher with the scores given to them by the teachers on the same constructs in the pretests than the correlations between these two sets of scores at the posttest (Table 6). For example, on a measure of SM, children's self-reports and group leader pretest reports were similar (2.54 compared to 2.58), with a correlation of .19. However, at the posttest, the differences were greater (2.90 compared to 2.52), with a correlation of .05 (.14 points lower than at the pretest).

A similar pattern continued for other constructs. For questions on the pretest assessing SASS, teacher report scores were similar to child self-report scores (2.77 compared to 2.78), with a correlation of .18. At the posttest, however, scores differed greatly (3.17 compared to 2.69, respectively), with no correlation. Furthermore, on a different measure of SASS the pretest scores of the children's self-reports and teacher reports were exactly the same (2.96), but posttest scores varied greatly between children's self-reports (3.41) and teacher reports (2.78).

Table 6. Correlations between child self-report and teacher report

Construct	child pre	teacher pre	correlation	p-test	child post	teacher post	correlation	p-test
	2.54	2.58	0.19	0.040*	2.9	2.2	0.05	0.654
	2.96	2.96	0.21	0.024*	3.41	2.78	0.09	0.357

High correlations between teacher report and child self-report, at least on the pretest, could indicate reliability. However, the discrepancy between the children's self-reports and teacher reports at the posttest indicates otherwise. It could indicate the children perceived more improvement in themselves than their teachers recognized. There could have been other possible explanations why children rated themselves higher in their SEL skills at the end of the year than what the teachers perceived.

For one, students were sometimes shuffled between groups throughout the school year, due to a group leader being transferred or quitting or children dropping out of after-school care and the remaining children being combined with a different group. A different group leader may have had different perceptions of the children than the one from the beginning of the year (at the pretest) or they may have only spent a short time with the child and not had the advantage of observing them over time. Group leaders could also benefit from training on how to observe and impartially rate children's behavior pertaining to SEL skills. Nevertheless, the strong correlations at the pretest are promising and invite further inquiry.

Exploratory Correlation Analysis

As the author stated in the introduction, the instruments (i.e., teacher report survey and child self-report survey) used in this evaluation were created by EAC and the evaluator. The child survey was modified after the first year's evaluation. Correlation measures between teacher reports and children's self-reports as well as factor analysis were used, in order to begin to establish validity and reliability.

Additionally, in an exploratory correlation analysis, several of the questions within the same construct had high correlations with each other (Table 7). For example, a correlation of .58 was found between two items measuring SM ("When encountering an obstacle or a new activity, *child name* expresses confidence and self-assurance" and "*Child name* uses observable strategies to calm him/herself down if upset"). A strong correlation (.49) was found between two questions measuring SASS ("*Child name* shows helpfulness and/or cooperation toward grownups and other children" and "*Child name* can easily ask for help from or express personal needs to EAC staff members"). In a third example, two items measuring SM ("When encountering an obstacle or a new activity, *child name* expresses confidence and self-assurance" and "*Child name* uses observable strategies to calm him/herself down if upset") were highly correlated (.59), indicating strong construct validity.

On the other hand, an unexpected outcome was the high correlation (.62) between one item measuring SM ("*Child name* uses observable strategies to calm him/herself down if upset") and another measuring SASS ("*Child name* shows helpfulness and/or cooperation toward grownups and other children"). Similarly, a correlation of .39 was found between two child report measures, one for SM ("If you get mad at another child on the playground, you will probably find a way to stay calm") and one for SASS ("If I accidentally hurt my friend's feelings, I can probably figure out what to do to make them feel better").

Table 7. Unexpected findings from exploratory correlation analysis matrix including child report and teacher report

		Child report								Teacher report				
		Q1-SASS	Q2-SASS	Q3-SM	Q4-SM	Q5-SASS	Q6-SA	Q7-SASS	Q8-SM	Q1-SA	Q2-SM	Q3-SASS	Q4-SASS	Q5-SM
Child report	Q1-SASS	1	0.09	0.22	0.16	0.25	0.13	0.11	0.06	0.07	0.13	0.21	0.13	0.12
	Q2-SASS		1.00	0.11	0.21	-0.07	0.20	0.12	0.15	0.18	0.01	0.00	0.05	-0.02
	Q3-SM			1.00	0.08	0.39	0.15	0.28	0.00	0.15	0.18	0.25	0.20	0.19
	Q4-SM				1.00	0.08	0.06	0.06	0.04	0.09	0.10	0.13	0.11	0.13
	Q5-SASS					1.00	0.21	0.18	0.02	-0.01	0.08	0.21	-0.06	0.09
	Q6-SA						1.00	0.15	0.08	0.02	0.20	0.02	-0.08	-0.01
	Q7-SASS							1.00	-0.04	-0.05	0.12	0.13	0.03	0.05
	Q8-SM								1.00	0.05	0.14	0.14	-0.03	0.15
Teacher report	Q1-SA									1.00	0.28	0.17	0.33	0.27
	Q2-SM										1.00	0.48	0.34	0.58
	Q3-SASS											1.00	0.49	0.62
	Q4-SASS												1.00	0.39
	Q5-SM													1

Three possible reasons may explain why some of the results indicate correlations between items meant to measure different constructs. For one, it may have been due to the possibility the items assess a child's overall SEL competence, which is a composite of skill clusters anyway, rather than specific aspects of SEL. Alternatively, it could be that the items tap into ability level of both SM and SASS in the child. Lastly, there could be another quality, or latent variable, not identified by the named constructs.

As a whole, these results demonstrate moderate validity of the instrument, but more research needs to be done to improve the questions' likelihood of targeting very specific abilities in children.

DISCUSSION

For the second year in a row, this evaluation of EAC's innovative SEL delivery showed children can receive quality SEL curriculum in an after-school care setting. The importance of including SEL in OST is evidenced by the link previous research highlighted between increased SM and improved academic performance, as well as increased prosocial behavior (i.e., reduced aggression, bullying, and delinquency) (Durlak et al., 2010; Zins et al., 2007). The statistically significant increase in scores of the children on all three of the constructs of the evaluation (SM, SASS, and SA) suggests the students at EAC benefitted from the SEL curriculum between the pretest and the posttest.

Key findings in this study were that students' scores increased on all assessment questions, and 5 out of 8 of the results were statistically significant. On Q1, which measured SASS, the number of students who responded "True" or "Extremely true" increased by .25 percentage points. On Q2, which also addressed SASS, the number of children who responded "Often" or "Almost always" increased by .16 percentage points. On Q6, which addressed SA, the number of students who responded "Often" or "Almost always" increased by .23 percentage points. Most notably, on Q8 (the open-ended question addressing self-management), only 42.5% of children could name three methods of self-soothing, while, at the posttest, 97% could.

EAC overcame the many challenges that most organizations that offer ASPs face with high-quality SEL implementation. One of these challenges was lack of SEL content for ASPs, and another one was inability to use data to guide decision-making about implementation and improvement of the strategies they used.

A third challenge common in organizations that offer ASPs was the high turnover rate of ASP workers (Hurd and Deutsch, 2017). These positions are usually part-time and therefore do not attract trained professionals. EAC was innovative in overcoming this challenge in that ongoing professional development was a requirement for staff and new hires. Also, all staff received training in SEL.

The implications of this study are that EAC can be viewed as a working model for overcoming challenges in delivering effective SEL in ASPs. While their strategies may not work for all ASPs, their example can provide a new perspective on how a grassroots effort, creativity, and resourcefulness can bring about results. These strategies can also be adapted to suit various populations and delivery models. In EAC's case, a partnership with a school district and access to high-quality SEL content from Second Step enabled them to reach their goals.

This evaluation serves as evidence and encouragement to childcare centers that, through resourcefulness and smart partnerships, time- and cost-effective evaluation, and data-driven program improvement is attainable.

Limitations

One limitation of this evaluation is the inability to imply causality due to the absence of a control group. All children at EAC were exposed to SEL curriculum as a necessary part of the program, so a control group made up of children not exposed to SEL was not possible. A future impact evaluation could be conducted with a quasi-control group or a group of randomly selected children who do not attend EAC's ASP, either because they attend another program that does not offer SEL or because they go home after school.

Additionally, the number of subjects generally recommended for factor analysis is 200, with a minimum of seven variables for each factor. This study had 98 subjects and three factors, which does not meet the minimum recommended criteria. However, if more items were developed to meet the criteria, the survey would be much longer, thus defeating the purpose of a simple and time-efficient SEL measure. A future evaluation with a greater number of participants should be considered. Further, since this was only the second year the curriculum was evaluated, only an exploratory factor analysis was run. A confirmatory factor analysis would provide more information on the reliability of the items in the survey instrument (Bhattacherjee, 2012). Lastly, further research into how to assess student's SM and SASS independent from each other could be pursued. Future iterations of the instrument should replace items Q4 and Q2.

CONCLUSION

Current threats to success and effectiveness of SEL are inconsistency, competing or noncoordinated programming, and low-quality and nonevaluated programs. Similarly, in ASPs, successful and effective SEL delivery is threatened by lack of affordable and accessible content materials, and lack of affordable and accessible evaluation. Although much work has been done in developing assessments, program evaluation, and cost benefit analyses of SEL in school settings, there is more work to be done. In order to achieve widespread and high-quality implementation and evaluation for both school and out-of-school settings, more efforts are necessary from the education, research, and administration fields. It requires professional development that prepares and supports educators to implement programs effectively, it requires a collective awareness at all levels–social, political, family, and community–and, it requires standardized measures to assess youth development constructs.

In many ways, current achievements have surpassed the original vision of SEL researchers. Over 500 SEL programs have been evaluated and all 50 states in the US have some social and emotional standards for preschoolers (a few states even have standards all the way through high school), providing guidance and emphasizing the importance for schools to provide SEL curriculum. Foster et al. (2005) found that 59% of US schools reported having directed resources toward implementing curriculum-based programs to enhance the social and emotional functioning of their students. Some states passed legislation requiring school districts to incorporate social and emotional development into their educational programs and to ensure that all students meet social and emotional learning standards as part of their state learning requirements.

However, barriers to high-quality and widespread SEL implementation still exist. State educational policies must require accountability in order to achieve widespread and consistent implementation. Districts, cities, and states need to hold higher standards. Supporting this goal necessitates dissemination of time- and cost-effective methods of evaluation. Each administrator, teacher preparation professor or after-school care director needs to begin to form research questions: Is our SEL curriculum working? Is more training needed? What resources or materials can we use? What outcomes can be measured? Are we consistent? What is our long-term plan?

By asking the above questions, organizations that offer ASPs may start to access the resources that are already within reach. A state university or community college psychology department may be willing to collaborate by providing service learning students or free materials. An organization that provides school-based SEL may be available for partnership by contributing its own curriculum as a pilot project for an ASP. Interns or apprentices from local elementary schools may want to provide evaluation under the guidance of a mentor at no cost. In addition, organizations such as CASEL, Panorama, and Second Step provide resources and content for free on their Web site (although their main products and services are fee-based).

SEL program evaluation may seem daunting to school administrators and after-school care center directors. However, through creativity and resourcefulness, a nonprofit offering an ASP was able to effectively design and administer an impact evaluation of an SEL curriculum. The activities at this center of first modifying the SEL curriculum to that which would be fitting in an out-of-school environment and further conducting an impact evaluation can be replicated.

A study in 2014 found that nearly 1 in 4 families in the United States had a child enrolled in an after-school program (Afterschool Alliance, 2014). This number has risen by almost 4 million since 2004 (from 6.5 to 10.4 million children). Improving and standardizing schools' and ASPs' ability to effectively care for and foster children's SEL has the potential to change the trajectory of millions of lives. Improving emotional, social, and mental health and academic outcomes can give students tools to live an active, engaged, and productive life, and enable them to reach their full potential.

Systematic monitoring and evaluation must be accessible to guide school and youth development program improvement. Until SEL implementation and impact assessment are more accessible and widespread, high-quality SEL will not be a reality for students. Denham (2015) stated:

Much work needs to be done—from the very acknowledgment of the importance of SEL to the creation of standards and better assessment tools to the connections with assessment an instruction, and professional development for teachers in both SEL instruction and assessment. (p.298)

Children learn and develop as whole human beings; high-quality SEL delivery honors the way children learn and develop by addressing the whole child. Now, policy-makers, district leaders, and ASP directors need to answer the call for appropriate and accessible measurement tools for SEL implementation, wide-scale dissemination, and continual monitoring (Mahoney et al., 2018).

ACKNOWLEDGMENT

A hearty thank you goes out to Dr. Norma Perez-Brena, Program Evaluation professor at Texas State University and my Service Learning Project Supervisor, and Dr. Elizabeth Blunk, my Practicum Advisor. Additionally; I owe a debt of gratitude to Dr. Joan Altobelli and COO Jaime Garcia at Extend-A-Care/YMCA. You all were my A-Team! Without you, none of this work would have been possible, and it certainly would not have been so much fun!

REFERENCES

Abadesco, V., & Savage, J. (2015). *Soul shoppe peace path guidebook*. http://www.onthepeacepath.com/wp-content/uploads/2018/07/peace-path-guide_final.pdf

Afterschool Alliance. (2014). *America after 3 pm: Afterschool programs in demand*. Retrieved on April 12, 2018 from: http://www.afterschoolalliance.org/documents/AA3PM-2014/AA3PM_National_Report.pdf

Belfield, C., Bowden, A., Klapp, A., Levin, H., Shand, R., & Zander, S. (2015). The economic value of social and emotional learning. *Journal of Benefit-Cost Analysis*, *6*(3), 508–544. doi:10.1017/bca.2015.55

Bhattacherjee, A. (2012). *Social science research: Principles, methods, and practices*. Textbooks Collection. 3. https://scholarcommons.usf.edu/oa_textbooks/3

Borgers, N., Hox, J., & Sikkel, D. (2003). Response quality in survey research with children and adolescents: The effect of labeled response options and vague quantifiers. *International Journal of Public Opinion Research*, *15*(1), 83–94. doi:10.1093/ijpor/15.1.83

Boyce, B. E. (2011). *The mindfulness revolution: Leading psychologists, scientists, artists, and meditation teachers on the power of mindfulness in daily life*. Shambhala Publications.

Brackett, M. A., & Mayer, J. D. (2003). Convergent, discriminant, and incremental validity of competing measures of emotional intelligence. *Personality and Social Psychology Bulletin*, *29*(9), 1147–1158. doi:10.1177/0146167203254596 PMID:15189610

Bridgeland, J., Bruce, M., & Hariharan, A. (2013). *The missing piece: A national teacher survey on how social and emotional learning can empower children and transform schools. A report for CASEL*. Civic Enterprises.

Brown, S., & Kappes, L. (2012). *Implementing the Common Core State Standards: A primer on*. Aspen Institute.

Catalano, R. F., Berglund, M. L., Ryan, J. A. M., Lonczak, H. S., & Hawkins, J. D. (2002). Positive youth development in the United States: Research findings on evaluations of positive youth development programs. *Prevention & Treatment*, *5*, 15. http://journals.apa.org/prevention/volume5/pre0050015a.html

Cherniss, C., Extein, M., Goleman, D., & Weissberg, R. P. (2006). Emotional intelligence: What does the research really indicate? *Educational Psychologist*, *41*(4), 239–245. doi:10.120715326985ep4104_4

Cohen, J. (1988). *Statistical power analysis for the behavioral sciences* (2nd ed.). Erlbaum.

Collaborative for Academic, Social, and Emotional Learning. (2005). *Safe and sound: An educational leader's guide to evidence-based social and emotional learning programs. Illinois edition.* Author.

Collaborative for Academic, Social, and Emotional Learning. (2020, December 21). *SEL is...* https://casel.org/what-is-sel/

Consortium on the School-based Promotion of Social Competence. (1994). The school-based promotion of social competence: Theory, research, practice, and policy. In R. J. Haggerty, N. Garmezy, M. Rutter, & L. R. Sherrod (Eds.), *Stress, risk, and resilience in children and adolescents: Processes, mechanisms, and interventions* (pp. 268–316). Cambridge University Press.

Crowe, L., Beauchamp, M., Catroppa, C., & Anderson, V. (2011). Social function assessment tools for children and adolescents: A systematic review from 1988 to 2010. *Clinical Psychology Review, 31*(5), 767–785. doi:10.1016/j.cpr.2011.03.008 PMID:21513693

Denham, S. A. (2015). Assessment of SEL in educational contexts. In J. A. Durlak, C. E. Domitrovich, R. P. Weissberg, & T. P. Gullotta (Eds.), *Handbook of social and emotional learning: Research and practice* (pp. 285–300). The Guilford Press.

DePaoli, J. L., Atwell, M. N., & Bridgeland, J. (2017). *Ready to lead: A national principal survey on how social and emotional learning can prepare children and transform schools. A report for CASEL.* Civic Enterprises.

Doll, B., & Elliott, S. N. (1994). Representativeness of observed preschool social behaviors: How many data are enough? *Journal of Early Intervention, 18*(2), 227–238. doi:10.1177/105381519401800209

Domitrovich, C. E., Durlak, J. A., Staley, K. C., & Weissberg, R. P. (2017). Social-emotional competence: An essential factor for promoting positive adjustment and reducing risk in school children. *Child Development, 88*(2), 408–416. doi:10.1111/cdev.12739 PMID:28213889

Dryfoos, J. G. (1997). The prevalence of problem behaviors: Implications for programs. In R. P. Weissberg, T. P. Gullotta, R. L. Hampton, B. A. Ryan, & G. R. Adams (Eds.), *Healthy children 2010: Enhancing children's wellness* (pp. 17–46). Sage.

Durlak, J. A., Domitrovich, C. E., Weissberg, R. P., & Gullotta, T. P. (2015). *Handbook of social and emotional learning: Research and practice.* Guilford Press.

Durlak, J. A., & DuPre, E. P. (2008). Implementation matters: A review of research on the influence of implementation on program outcomes and the factors affecting implementation. *American Journal of Community Psychology, 41*(3-4), 327–350. doi:10.100710464-008-9165-0 PMID:18322790

Durlak, J. A., Weissberg, R. P., Dymnicki, A. B., Taylor, R. D., & Schellinger, K. B. (2011). The impact of enhancing students' social and emotional learning: A meta-analysis of school-based universal interventions. *Child Development, 82*(1), 405–432. doi:10.1111/j.1467-8624.2010.01564.x PMID:21291449

Durlak, J. A., Weissberg, R. P., & Pachan, M. (2010). A meta-analysis of after-school programs that seek to promote personal and social skills in children and adolescents. *American Journal of Community Psychology, 45*(3/4), 294–309. doi:10.100710464-010-9300-6 PMID:20300825

Durlak, J. A., & Wells, A. M. (1997). Primary prevention mental health programs for children and adolescents: A meta-analytic review. *American Journal of Community Psychology, 25*(2), 115–152. doi:10.1023/A:1024654026646 PMID:9226860

Dusenbury, L. A., Newman, J. Z., Weissberg, R. P., Goren, P., Domitrovich, C. E., & Mart, A. K. (2015). The case for preschool through high school state learning standards for SEL. In J. A. Durlak, C. E. Domitrovich, R. P. Weissberg, & T. P. Gullotta (Eds.), *Handbook of social and emotional learning: Research and practice* (pp. 532–548). The Guilford Press.

Elias, M. J., Leverett, L., Duffell, J. C., Humphrey, N., Stepney, C., & Ferrito, J. (2015). Integrating SEL with related prevention and youth development approaches. In J. A. Durlak, C. E. Domitrovich, R. P. Weissberg, & T. P. Gullotta (Eds.), *Handbook of social and emotional learning: Research and practice* (pp. 33–49). Guilford Press.

Elias, M. J., O'Brien, M. U., & Weissberg, R. P. (2006). Transformative Leadership for Social-Emotional Learning. *Principal Leadership: High School Edition, 7*(4), 10–13. Retrieved from http://libproxy.txstate.edu/login?url=http://search.ebscohost.com.libproxy.txstate.edu/login.aspx?direct=true&db=eue&AN=507936535&site=eds-live&scope=site

Elias, M. J., Zins, J. E., Weissberg, R. P., Frey, K. S., Greenberg, M. T., Haynes, N. M., & … . (1997). *Promoting social and emotional learning: Guidelines for educators.* Association for Supervision and Curriculum Development.

Foster, S., Rollefson, M., Doksum, T., Noonan, D., Robinson, G., & Teich, J. (2005). School mental health services in the United States 2002–2003 (DHHS Pub. No. (SMA) 05–4068). Center for Mental Health Services, Substance Abuse and Mental Health Services Administration.

Goleman, D. (1995). *Emotional intelligence. Why it can matter more than IQ.* Bantam Books.

Goleman, D. (2001). Emotional intelligence: Issues in paradigm building. In C. Cherniss & D. Goleman (Eds.), *The emotionally intelligent workplace* (pp. 13–26). Jossey-Bass.

Goleman, D. (2005). *Emotional intelligence.* Bantam Books.

Goleman, D., Boyatzis, R., & McKee, A. (2002). *Primal leadership: Realizing the power of emotional intelligence.* Harvard Business School Press.

Greenberg, M. T., Weissberg, R. P., O'Brien, M. U., Zins, J. E., Fredericks, L., Resnik, H., & Elias, M. J. (2003). Enhancing school-based prevention and youth development through coordinated social, emotional, and academic learning. *The American Psychologist, 58*(6-7), 466–474. doi:10.1037/0003-066X.58.6-7.466 PMID:12971193

Gullotta, T. P. (2015). After-school programming and SEL. In J. A. Durlak, C. E. Domitrovich, R. P. Weissberg, & T. P. Gullotta (Eds.), *Handbook of social and emotional learning: Research and practice* (pp. 260–266). Guilford Press.

Hallfors, D., & Godette, D. (2002). Will the "Principles of Effectiveness" improve prevention practice? Early findings from a diffusion study. *Health Education Review, 17*(4), 461–470. doi:10.1093/her/17.4.461 PMID:12197591

Hamilton, L. S., Doss, C. J., & Steiner, E. D. (2019a). *Support for social and emotional learning is widespread: Principals and teachers give insight into how they value, address, and measure it, and which supports they need.* Rand Corporation. https://www.rand.org/pubs/research_briefs/RB10064

Hamilton, L. S., Doss, C. J., & Steiner, E. D. (2019b). *Teacher and principal perspectives on social and emotional learning in America's schools: Findings from the American Educator Panels*. Rand Corporation. https://www.rand.org/pubs/research_reports/RR2991.html

Hamilton, L. S., & Schwartz, H. L. (2019). *Get smart about social and emotional learning measurement*. American Enterprise Institute. https://www.aei.org/research-products/report/get-smart-about-social-and-emotional-learning-measurement/

Hurd, N., & Deutsch, N. (2017). SEL-focused after-school programs. *The Future of Children*, *27*(1), 95–115. doi:10.1353/foc.2017.0005

Jennings, P. A., & Frank, J. L. (2015). Inservice preparation for educators. In J. A. Durlak, C. E. Domitrovich, R. P. Weissberg, & T. P. Gullotta (Eds.), *Handbook of social and emotional learning: Research and practice* (pp. 422–437). The Guilford Press.

Jones, S., Bailey, R., Brush, K., & Kahn, J. (2018). *Preparing for effective SEL implementation*. Harvard Graduate School of Education Easel Lab. https://www. wallacefoundation.org/knowledgecenter/Documents/Preparing-for-Effective-SEL-Implementation.pdf

Jones, S., Brush, K., Bailey, R., Brion-Meisels, G., McIntyre, J., Kahn, J., Nelson, B., & Stickle, L. (2017). *Navigating SEL from the inside out. Looking inside and across 25 leading SEL programs: A practical resource for schools and OST providers*. Harvard Graduate School of Education.

Jones, S. M., & Kahn, J. (2018). The evidence base for how learning happens: A consensus on social, emotional, and academic development. *American Educator*, *41*(4), 16.

Laughlin, L. (2013). Who's minding the kids? Child care arrangements: Spring 2011. Current Population Reports. U.S. Census Bureau.

Lopes, P. N., Grewal, D., Kadis, J., Gall, M., & Salovey, P. (2006). Evidence that emotional intelligence is related to job performance and affect and attitudes at work. *Psicothema*, *18*(Suppl.), 132–138. PMID:17295970

Mahoney, J. L., Durlak, J. A., & Weissberg, R. P. (2018). An update on social and emotional learning outcome research. *Phi Delta Kappan*, *100*(4), 18–23. doi:10.1177/0031721718815668

Mart, A. K., Weissberg, R. P., & Kendziora, K. (2015). Systemic support for SEL in school districts. Handbook of social and emotional learning: Research and practice, 482-499.

McKown, C. (2015). Challenges and opportunities in the direct assessment of children's social and emotional comprehension. In J. A. Durlak, C. E. Domitrovich, R. P. Weissberg, & T. P. Gullotta (Eds.), *Handbook of social and emotional learning: Research and practice* (pp. 320–335). The Guilford Press.

Minney, D., Garcia, J., Altobelli, J., Perez-Brena, N., & Blunk, E. (2019). Social-emotional learning and evaluation in after-school care: A working model. *Journal of Youth Development*, *14*(3), 130–145. doi:10.5195/jyd.2019.660

Moffitt, T. E., Arseneault, L., Belsky, D., Dickson, N., Hancox, R. J., Harrington, H., Houts, R., Poulton, R., Roberts, B. W., Ross, S., Sears, M. R., Thomson, W. M., & Caspi, A. (2011). A gradient of childhood self-control predicts health, wealth, and public safety. *Proceedings of the National Academy of Sciences of the United States of America, 108*(7), 2693–2698. doi:10.1073/pnas.1010076108 PMID:21262822

Netemeyer, R. G., Bearden, W. O., & Sharma, S. (2003). *Scaling procedures: Issues and applications.* Sage Publications. doi:10.4135/9781412985772

Rimm-Kaufman, S. E., & Hulleman, C. S. (2015). Social and emotional learning in elementary school settings: Identifying mechanisms that matter. In J. A. Durlak, C. E. Domitrovich, R. P. Weissberg, & T. P. Gullotta (Eds.), *Handbook of social and emotional learning: Research and practice* (pp. 151–166). The Guilford Press.

Rogers, E. M. (2002). Diffusion of preventive innovations. *Addictive Behaviors, 27*(6), 989–993. doi:10.1016/S0306-4603(02)00300-3 PMID:12369480

Schonert-Reichl, K. A., Kitil, M. J., & Hanson-Peterson, J. (2017). *To reach the students, teach the teachers: A national scan of teacher preparation and social and emotional learning*. University of British Columbia.

Shriver, T., & Buffett, J. (2015). The uncommon core. In J. A. Durlak, C. E. Domitrovich, R. P. Weissberg, & T. P. Gullotta (Eds.), *Handbook of social and emotional learning: Research and practice* (pp. xv–xvi). The Guilford Press.

Sigmar, L. S., Hynes, G. E., & Hill, K. L. (2012). Strategies for teaching social and emotional intelligence in business communication. *Business Communication Quarterly, 75*(3), 301–317. doi:10.1177/1080569912450312

US Department of Health and Human Services. (2001). *Trends in the well-being of America's children and youth, 2001*. US Government Printing Office.

Webster-Stratton, C., & Herman, K. C. (2010). Disseminating Incredible Years Series early-intervention programs: integrating and sustaining services between school and home. *Psychology in the Schools, 47*(1), 36-54. doi:20450 doi:10 1002/pits

Weissberg, R. P., Durlak, J. A., Domitrovich, C. E., & Gullotta, T. P. (Eds.). (2015). Social and emotional learning: Past, present, and future. In J. A. Durlak, C. E. Domitrovich, R. P. Weissberg, & T. P. Gullotta (Eds.), Handbook of social and emotional learning: Research and practice (pp. 3-19). The Guilford Press.

Weissberg, R. P., Walberg, H. J., O'Brien, M. U., & Kuster, C. B. (Eds.). (2003). *Long-term trends in the well-being of children and youth*. Child Welfare League of America Press.

Williford, A. P., & Wolcott, C. S. (2015). SEL and student-teacher relationships. In J. A. Durlak, C. E. Domitrovich, R. P. Weissberg, & T. P. Gullotta (Eds.), *Handbook of social and emotional learning: Research and practice, 634*. The Guilford Press.

ADDITIONAL READING

Siegel, D. J. (2014). *Brainstorm: The power and purpose of the teenage brain*. Tarcher Perigree Publisher.

The National US Department of Education. (2013). *The evaluation of enhanced academic instruction in after-school programs: Findings after the first year of implementation*. Institute of Education Sciences.

KEY TERMS AND DEFINITIONS

After-School Programs (Sometimes Called OST or Out-of-School Time Programs): Serve children and youth of all ages, and encompass a broad range of focus areas including academic support, mentoring, positive youth development, arts, sports and recreation. They can be offered on a campus, after the school day ends, or off-campus, hosted by a for-profit or non-profit organization.

Ecological Framework: A framework or model originally defined by Bronfenbrenner (1990) as 5 levels of influence, or layers in a person's environment. In the model, reciprocal relationships exist within and between these layers and each layer influences the individual in different ways. This framework of influence can also be used in analyzing organizations and communities and in policy practice.

Emotional Intelligence: Emotional intelligence (otherwise known as emotional quotient or EQ) is the ability to understand, use, and manage your own emotions in positive ways to relieve stress, communicate effectively, empathize with others, overcome challenges and defuse conflict.

Program Evaluation: A systematic method for collecting, analyzing, and using information to answer questions about projects, policies, and programs, particularly about their effectiveness and efficiency.

SEL Curriculum: Any content, exercises or learning material that includes a wide variety of ideas and skills related to self-awareness, self-management, social awareness, relationship skills, and responsible decision making.

Self-Management: The ability to regulate one's emotions, thoughts, and behaviors effectively in different situations.

Self-Soothing: Any behavior an individual uses to regulate their emotional state by themselves. These behaviors are often developed in the early years of life, are repetitive or habitual in nature, and are often viewed by a child or adolescent as calming or comforting.

Social-Emotional Learning: The process through which children and adults acquire and effectively apply the knowledge, attitudes, and skills necessary to understand and manage emotions, set and achieve positive goals, feel and show empathy for others, establish and maintain positive relationships, and make responsible decisions.

Chapter 12
A More Mindful Approach to College and Career Counseling

Alexandra Ellison
Davidson Academy of Nevada, USA

ABSTRACT

While social and emotional learning practices are now more common in American classrooms, counselors often have limited time and resources to devote to college counseling at all, let alone a type of counseling grounded in social and emotional awareness. The American School Counselor Association recommends a student-to-counselor ratio of 250 to 1, but the current ratio is 430 to 1. Few high school counselors have the rare luxury of only needing to focus on college and career readiness. They are up against pressures from parents, and sometimes administrators, who want to see more AP courses, higher GPAs, higher ACT and SAT scores, and more elite college acceptances. These pressures can blur a counselor's view of what is actually suitable for each individual student; this means the counselor needs to understand financial fit, social and emotional fit, and academic match for each college-bound student. This kind of holistic understanding of a student is the only way to restore a focus on student wellbeing to the college and career planning process.

INTRODUCTION

Each year, March is the long-awaited month when teenagers around the world begin receiving acceptances or rejections from U.S. colleges. Students usually plan college visits in the first 2 weeks of April for "admitted student weekends" at the schools that have made them offers of admission. Parents, students, and counselors meet in the days leading up to May 1st, the traditional commitment date, to discern the best match, fit, and price that students have before them. But in the spring of 2020, less than a month after the COVID-19 pandemic brought the United States to a halt, Art & Science Group published a poll that would be one of the most alarming, and one of the most talked about, findings for higher education. The student poll surveyed 487 graduating seniors (86% from public schools), with 64% identifying as female and 74% identifying as caucasian; the respondents reported an average annual household income of $88,000 (Art & Science Group, 2020). The report had some startling numbers:

DOI: 10.4018/978-1-7998-6728-9.ch012

52% of students reported that a parent or guardian had lost their job or had been furloughed as a result of the pandemic; 40% of students were uncertain they could attend their first-choice school now; and perhaps most shattering, 12% of students who had *already deposited* at their top-choice institution had changed their plans and could no longer enroll full-time at a 4-year college or university. Like the 2020 pandemic, the American higher education system knows no borders; it touches the lives of students studying abroad at their international campuses, and at their home campuses, where some 1 million students study each year (Educationdata, 2020).

This forced pause ushered in a new conversation about what college, and education at large, would look like in the future. But the pause also brought to mind questions around the burdens teens carry as they navigate college admission; it called into question the heavy performance culture and a kind of "cult" around college prestige that permeate college preparations. Bribes, scandals, and celebrity plea deals have become bi-products of an admission process that is not equitable, transparent, or mindful.

The Collaborative for Academic, Social, and Emotional Learning (CASEL) has a social and emotional learning (SEL) framework that addresses how to instill young people with the agency, confidence, and self-awareness to make responsible decisions for themselves and the societies in which they are active players (CASEL, 2020a). While these social and emotional competencies are integral to a successful and holistic academic experience, they are equally important to the increasingly complex college counseling process. With so many choices, a great deal of money on the line, there is a desperate need for a counseling curriculum infused with SEL competencies, namely, self awareness and responsible decision making.

STRESS AND ANXIETY IN COLLEGE AND CAREER PLANNING: HOW DID WE GET HERE AND IS THERE A BETTER WAY?

History marks World War II and the resulting GI Bill as the transitional point from elite, exclusive higher education to open, mass education. The GI Bill made funds available to veterans returning home, forced to reimagine their professional lives as civilians, to help pay for post-secondary education. While elite and exclusive universities certainly still exist today, the end of WWII was the beginning of a new way of thinking about higher education in America: Everyone had the *opportunity* to gain entry to this exclusive club, but not every would have equal access to it. The narrative began to shift in this country from "My socioeconomic position in life is fixed, and higher education is not within my grasp," to "My socioeconomic position is fluid; I can control the outcome." Simultaneously liberating and burdensome, this new way of thinking seems to be uniquely American, and it is essential to start from this point in order to understand how the American approach to college and career planning became what it is today.

As society began to view one's position as fluid and higher education as the entry point to a higher social standing, the flood gates opened, but not the gates at every university. As of 2017, there were roughly 2,800 4-year, Title IV, post-secondary institutions in the United States (U.S. Department of Education, 2019). While it would seem that increased options allows for greater access for more students, the reality looks different. If not equipped or properly counseled to filter through the options, students can feel overwhelmed by this tyranny of choices. As a result, many students limit their options by focusing on the schools they have heard of, the schools represented in popular culture, or those that are the most selective (assuming these must be the "best"). Just 19 of the thousands of options students have in the United States alone admit less than 10% of the students who apply, and these tend to be the schools talked about most. The schools that receive the greatest share of applications, four of which are University of

California institutions, are simply becoming more selective because the number of seats available is not increasing with the number of new applicants each year. To hedge their bets, more students are applying to more colleges. In 1990, just 9% of rising college freshmen applied to seven or more schools; in 2016, this number had increased to 35%. According to 2018 admission data, the University of California at Los Angeles received more than 102,000 applications for roughly 6,000 freshmen openings (Hess, 2019). These applicants represent some of the highest achieving students around the world, so narrowing the pool is no easy task; in 2018, the majority of applicants had GPAs above 3.45. The admittance rate was just 14% that year.

While the majority of colleges admit the majority of students who apply, students and parents fixate on the most selective colleges and universities because they are most often mentioned in the public arena. The *U.S. News and World Report* rankings of colleges has aided in creating a hierarchy of schools, which in turn, has students ranking themselves against their peers based on admission to elite colleges. The result can be overwhelming fatigue, angst, and depression, which can last throughout high school and continue even after they have gained admission to a college or university. The pecking order that students may find themselves in does not disappear once they are admitted; once this hierarchical mindset is adopted, it can be difficult to shed. Once students buy into the performance culture they see all around them, it is difficult not to see life as a series of costs and benefits, risks and rewards -- a very binary view of the world. Students often begin to think that the elite college acceptance is proportional to the amount of work put in throughout high school. Therefore, the thinking goes: *If I cannot get into a highly selective college, my hard work will have been for nothing.* It is dangerous to believe that hard work always leads to rewards; as soon as the rewards do not arrive or they are not what was expected, the work appears to be futile. Students who see admission to an elite college as the ultimate reward for their work output in high school, may eventually become college students who see getting the most prestigious internship as the reward for their work output in college, and will eventually become adults who see the highest paying job as the only acceptable reward for their collective work output in their young lives.

The observant reader will see another glaring flaw in this mentality: Not only are rewards not always given for hard work, but often, rewards are given for very little work. Herein lies the red herring in the modern mass education system. While the move toward more open, "mass" education should have opened more doors to more students, in fact it merely succeeded in making more students aware of more opportunities to which they did not have equal access. While the universities of the 17th and 18th centuries were exclusive and admittedly so, the universities of the 19th and 20th centuries multiplied in number, creating more open spots for more college-bound students, but the most selective universities held onto their traditional positions as elite universities, designed to educate elite families. The median family income of a student from Harvard is $168,800, and 67% come from the top twenty percent. What about the argument that schools like Harvard can catapult students to a higher income bracket? Only about 1.8% of students at Harvard who came from poor families became rich adults. The overall mobility index (a measure of the likelihood that a student has to move up two or more income quintiles) at Harvard is around 11% (The Upshot, 2017). If social mobility and elite college attendance are not as clearly connected as some would believe, the modern-day college and career counselor might wonder why low-income and high-income families alike place such an extraordinary burden on their children when it comes to elite university admission. To be fair, the burden is not only coming from families, but from the colleges themselves too, causing students and their parents to take drastic measures to better their chances in the selective enrollment process. In reaction to a sliding decline in acceptance rates at the most well-known colleges and universities, families act out of stress and fear, sometimes taking drastic measures. In perhaps the most extreme case of corruption in college admission, a case known as "Operation Varsity Blues," thirty-three parents of college applicants, including celebrities Lori Loughlin and Felicity Huffman, were accused of paying more than $25 Million to ring leader, Rick Singer, who used part of these payments to inflate test scores and bribe university coaches in order to enhance the students' chances of admission. While one would assume the pressure is greatest among students from low-income families who may see higher education attainment as an entry ticket to a higher socioeconomic status, some reports suggest the most social and emotional impacts of all this mounting pressure are hitting more affluent kids.

In 2018, Suniya Luthar, a professor emerita at Columbia University's Teachers College told NPR, "What we've found is that kids in high-achieving, relatively affluent communities are reporting higher levels of substance abuse than inner-city kids and levels of anxiety and depressive symptoms are also commensurate — if not greater." In her research, she found rates of substance abuse remain high among upper-middle-class kids, as they enter early adulthood. The alcohol or drugs are a form of self-medication (Aubrey & Greenhalgh, 2018). Since 2007, there has been a steady increase in mental health services utilization by U.S. college students. Both treatment and lifetime diagnoses of college students saw an increase, perhaps due in part to an overall decline in stigma around mental health (Lipson, Lattie, & Eisenberg, 2018). Research shows that an integrated SEL curriculum can help to reduce anxiety as well as substance abuse (CASEL, 2020b). This happens, in part, because students learn how to become more aware of their emotions and reactions to stressful situations, and in turn, they gain greater clarity to make responsible decisions in their lives .

Recognizing the tainted ethics and self-absorbed objectives that arise from high-pressure college planning, Harvard's Graduate School of Education spearheaded the Making Caring Common Project with several other university leaders (Allman & et al., 2016). The project resulted in a comprehensive report with recommendations to improve the admission process in three main areas:

1. promoting more meaningful contributions to others, community service and engagement with the public good;
2. assessing students' ethical engagement and contributions to others in ways that reflect varying types of family and community contributions across race, culture and class;
3. redefining achievement in ways that both level the playing field for economically diverse students and reduce excessive achievement pressure (Allman & et al., page 2).

The report's recommendations are meant not only for the counselors who are seeking to guide students in a more holistic and mindful way, but also for the colleges who have the power to evaluate students differently in the admissions process, giving students "points" for things like meaningful community engagement and family contributions. Colleges can pose essay prompts on college applications that ask students about a time they have contributed to their community without any formal recognition, or about times they had to miss out on a fun opportunity with friends in order to support their families. While some might point to the well-known act of "padding a resume" as a negative, padding a resume with meaningful experiences, responsibilities, and commitments, even if initially done to impress colleges, will ultimately be enriching for the student. In August of 2019, the Making Caring Common project shared an article and companion quiz titled: "For Families: Red Flags for Parents—Are You Putting Too Much Pressure on Your Child During the College Admission Process?" The quiz includes questions like, "During dinner conversations, do you talk often about your child's grades and college applications, often forgetting to ask your child what he or she finds interesting and fun about school?" and "Do you sometimes allow your child to exaggerate or lie about the extent of his or her community service because it will help him or her get into a selective college?" While the content is directed at families, school counselors would likely find tremendous benefit using such queries in sessions with college-bound students and their parents. The quiz concludes with recommendations to change course during the college admissions process, and encourages parents to engage in healthier parenting practices with their teens.

Much of the stress and fear around college admissions, on the part of students and parents, arises out of a perception of lack; there are only so few spots available, so few options, and so few dollars. Starting from a place of lack can lead to the anxiety-inducing sensation that the walls are closing in. Counselors and educators are well-positioned to create a more mindful culture around college and career readiness, starting with a more expansive presentation of the wide array of options available to students. Without overwhelming students with too many choices, counselors can curate lesser-known pathways to college and career opportunities that give students permission to explore less-traveled, and less competitive, routes that suit their needs. Counselors are also educated and trained to recognize emotional responses from their students, including those brought on by college application. Kaitlin Levesque, a school counselor at Middletown High School in Connecticut, wrote in 2018: "A senior came into my office hysterical over a denial from an Ivy League college, reiterating how every decision she made in high school was in preparation for an acceptance letter. Although I explained how competitive such schools are and congratulated her on many other accomplishments, the student's devastation could have been lessened through a comprehensive social-emotional curriculum" (Levesque, 2018). It's true that a social-emotional curriculum is well-suited for the high school counseling office, as the counselor is typically well-acquainted with the importance of emotional well-being to a student's academic success.

PRESENTING THE OPTIONS: DIVERSE PATHS FOR DIVERSE STUDENTS

"What SAT score do I need to get into college?"

"How many service hours do colleges want to see on an application?"

"What is the minimum GPA that colleges will accept?

These oversimplified questions commonly come from students who see college admissions as a linear, defined, one-right-way process. It is natural to want to simplify a complex process; it would be so much easier if college admissions in the United States was based merely on a single test (some countries do operate college admissions this way). However, in the United States, standardized test scores (such as those from the SAT or ACT), grades, level of high school rigor, community engagement, leadership experience, and research are all parts that make up the whole of an institution's evaluation process; and each institution evaluates its applicants differently, placing different point values on different factors. It is arguably an overly complex system, and one that is impossible to see fully and transparently. However, the variety of institutions to choose from, all of which place different weight on different student characteristics and achievements, allows students to seek out the best-fit institutions given their accomplishments, learning needs, and future goals. What a disservice to students to hand them a set of boxes to check off in high school in order to be competitive at only one type of institution.

What's the answer to these questions posed above? It is impossible to answer them without first asking, "What kind of post-secondary experience do you want?" As part of CASEL's SEL framework, *responsible decision making* is the pillar most exercised in mindful college counseling (CASEL, 2020a). Students who may have never been given the agency to make their own decisions, suddenly find themselves tasked with making a major one: where to go and what to pursue after high school graduation.

When considering all of the types of colleges and universities in this country alone, it is helpful to divide them into groups or "buckets" and present these buckets to students when they are first beginning to consider their higher-education options. It is not helpful to begin a counseling session with a student by simply asking what they are looking for; in all likelihood, they lack the exposure and full understanding of what their options are to be able to answer that question honestly. There is no one right way to group colleges, and each counselor may develop different groupings that resonate with their student population, but the chart below offers suggested buckets with a few examples in each category as a reference:

Table 1. Chart showing sample of college "buckets" or categories

Research Universities House multiple colleges with specific areas of study, research and publishing are regarded highly, typically larger in size, and offer graduate degrees	**Polytechnic and Technical Institutions** Tend to offer degrees centered around science, technology, engineering, and math, academic focus is more career-oriented, specialized, and technical	**Liberal Arts Colleges** Offer a traditionally broad, interdisciplinary course of study without separate colleges for specific areas of study	**Community Colleges and Technical Colleges** Offer a-la-carte courses open to all members of a community, often offer special programs tied to a top industry or company in the community they serve	**Performing and Visual Arts Institutions** Specialize in arts disciplines, often requiring students to complete a foundational program of study in multiple art domains	**Service Academies** Offer a broad range of majors, but all students have an interest in and are willing to commit to service in one of five branches of military service
-University of Illinois at Urbana-Champaign -University of North Carolina at Chapel Hill -University of California, Los Angeles	**-Massachusetts Institute of Technology -Rochester Institute of Technology -California Polytechnic State University**	**-Swarthmore College -Pitzer College -St. Olaf College**	**-Santa Barbara City College -Lake Area Technical College -Fox Valley Technical College**	**-Rhode Island School of Design -California College of the Arts -Oberlin Conservatory of Music**	**-United States Air Force Academy -United States Merchant Marine Academy -United States Military Academy -United States Naval Academy -United States Coast Guard Academy**

Keeping a database of past students who attend a range of colleges around the country, and the world, will enrich a counseling office by creating student networking opportunities. When future students hear from current students about the social and academic experience on campus, the school becomes more familiar than it ever would from the pages of a book or a website. When prospective students talk to future students, they also begin to see themselves on campus, giving them something more tangible to grasp and considero. Furthermore, counselors can invite past students to campus to talk about their current college experience, or host a virtual college panel with students. It's impossible for a counselor to visit every college and university in the United States, so by inviting current students (especially those who attended the same high school) back for a college talk, prospective students can begin to see themselves on a campus they may never have considered, let alone visited in person.

When hosting college nights or inviting college representatives to the high school, counselors can be mindful of the above buckets, and do their best to provide representation across these (and other) institutional categories. In doing so, a counselor can offer diverse learners the chance to see themselves as "college material" rather than saving that designation for AP and honor students alone. The term "college material" ought not to take on one, singular definition on a high school campus; rather, it has the opportunity to mean something slightly different for every student.

It is important to recognize that the work of presenting diverse options requires innovative and progressive thinking and an ability to consider options that do not presently exist. Mindful counseling today means preparing students for unpredictable and shifting situations. Jobs like drone operator, app developer, driverless car engineer, and big data analyst came on the scene within these teens' lifetimes, and it is likely that new job descriptions and entire industries will emerge before they are in their 30s. Young workers change jobs every couple of years nowadays, often for better work and higher pay. Today, almost half of working millennials (those born between roughly 1980 and 1994, depending on the source), are freelancing, and this unique workforce grew 3x faster than the overall U.S. workforce since 2014 (Pofeldt, 2017).

All of this shifting is due in part to skepticism around what jobs will actually exist in 10-20 years. Compared to the days of choosing one industry, one company, and one occupation for 30 years and retiring with a gold watch, young workers today see agility as the safer bet; they feel more in control when they can decide when and where to pivot as the economy shifts. By introducing students to entrepreneurs, solopreneurs, and innovators, counselors can do more to present variety in post-secondary options. These presentations can also capture the attention of students who struggle to see themselves in any one occupation, and so remove themselves from career and college counseling activities altogether.

The modern, mindful counselor is also likely to be working with more students who have more angst about college, career, and adulthood in general. It's not uncommon for this new wave of teens to forgo traditional markers of the entry into adulthood. Jean Twenge, PhD, a researcher and professor, has done tremendous research on generational differences. In her book, *iGen: Why Today's Super Connected Kids are Growing Up Less Rebellious, More Tolerant, Less Happy—and Completely Unprepared for Adulthood—and What that Means for the Rest of Us*, she presents the newest research on this new generation, born between 1995 and 2012. One of her findings is that teens today are much more practical, sensible, risk-averse and realistic. They tend to be less interested in going out, which means they are drinking less, having sex later and learning to drive later, compared to previous generations. They seem to be doing less of everything outside of the home and more inside by themselves. More risk averse than the Millennials before them, this generation appears to be okay with lengthening adolescence, putting off traditional coming-of-age markers like drinking at a party or getting a driver's license (see Ellison, 2019). With a desire to prolong adolescence, it begs the question, are parents and counselors putting undue pressure on teens by promoting a direct entry into college immediately after high school graduation? Many students might see the linear and prescribed path of college following high school with any break as the safest and surest, but they may simultaneously feel overwhelmed by this, what they see as their only option. Both parents and students may feel a sense of relief when a counselor presents a less-conventional option, such as a year break between high school and college. Some students would benefit greatly from a year out of formal schooling to engage in informal learning through travel, community college classes, internships, volunteerism, and quiet introspection. A counselor could help a student map out a self-designed "gap" year, or consult websites such as www.gapyearassociation.org to review accredited gap-year programs, which offer structured and facilitated programs for young people. While some students are eager to get to college and continue their education, others find the pressure to decide where to go and what to study too crippling a task at 17 or 18 years old. An offer of a gap year may just be the hall pass that a student was waiting for.

When framed as the decision of a lifetime, choosing a college and a major can feel like simultaneously choosing an occupation and setting a life course. It's unreasonable and unrealistic to ask any adolescent to do such a thing, but intentionally or unintentionally, this is the message coming from counselors, educators, peers, and parents. As a result, students are experiencing anxiety and are unnecessarily overwhelmed. The counselor can work to dispel myths and fears around the linear connection between major and career or university acceptance and future income potential. It can serve as an illuminating example to host a parent night to address college admissions and ask the parent audience how many had a college major that directly related to their current occupation. It's not uncommon for a few hands to fly up with confidence, while the rest of the audience smiles as they realize just how non-linear their own paths have been. Students will be shocked to hear that they have the freedom to choose almost any major and still have doors open to almost any career. There are few career fields (engineering comes to mind) that favor those who began relevant study from day one of their undergraduate career. However, the major the student chooses only matters if the content interests them. In other words, students who choose majors that don't interest them, assuming these will lead directly to lucrative careers, will suffer throughout their undergraduate years, studying something that bores them to tears. However, when a student chooses a major that is engaging with a majority of classes that the student genuinely enjoys, the level of engagement will be high, as well as grades, and letters of recommendation will be glowing; all of this will serve to impress a future employer more than the name of the major.

Giving a student permission to study what they want to study, regardless of its practicality, can relieve a student from unnecessary stress and premature career commitments. Students can relax knowing that the most common path to a fulfilling career involves organic introductions, curiosity, trial and error, and insightful conversations with industry leaders.

Presenting a wider range of options is no easy task for a counselor, especially if given a huge case load and only limited time with each student. To simply put more brochures in the counseling office and more posters on the wall is to merely contribute to the *tyranny of choice* and ensuing angst. Rather, the mindful counselor helps a student to filter through the noise by helping them really understand who they are and what they value, and then presenting options that fit the student *before* the student starts changing who they are to fit a college.

TOOLS AND METHODS FOR SELF-AWARENESS AND ASSESSMENT

Research-based assessments can provide an objective conversation starter for the counselor and the student. For counselors with a large caseload, assessments can be taken by the student in advance of a meeting and discussed in a one-on-one session. The counselor will get to know the student better, enabling them to make more accurate recommendations, and the student will gain more clarity around their most natural aptitudes and interests. An assessment that culminates in a list of career recommendations can also be illuminating, and provide the student with a starting point to begin their exploration. However, it's important for the counselor to walk the student through the results, making sure they understand how to identify common features among all of the recommendations so as to prevent the student from getting too stuck on limiting career titles. For example, a student might get the following career recommendations after an assessment: logistician, crime scene investigator, fraud examiner, and auditor. Perhaps the student is not immediately interested in any of these specific occupations, but more important is to look for common threads: investigation, attention to detail, convention and structure, analytical thinking, etc. With an analysis of the tasks, features, and educational requirements of a handful of careers, the student and counselor can have a more meaningful conversation about other possible occupations and college majors, and more importantly, about activities that the student may enjoy right now, while still in high school. Perhaps this student would enjoy taking a forensic science class, or maybe there is an opportunity to take a more specialized course at a local college to better understand these fields.

The most accurate, and most helpful, assessments test both *aptitudes* and *interests*. To only analyze one or the other is to neglect half of the factors necessary in guiding a student. Only look at interests and no regard for ability is taken into account; only look at aptitudes and passion and enjoyment are overlooked. The problem of too many competing aptitudes can also arise; such can be the case for students whose aptitudes are evenly distributed, making it difficult to choose activities, programs or study, or careers if not for the interest assessment that accompanies the aptitude analysis. Some students will look with skepticism at such assessments, refusing to be put into a box, but it's helpful to look at assessments as starting points and introductions to an array of possibilities. Without such a tool, the choices a student is aware of either seem overwhelming or underwhelming; they have either seen or heard of too many options and lack the self-awareness to filter, or they have had too little exposure to feel confident about choosing from such a small selection.

While formal, research-based assessments are perhaps the most accurate when it comes to understanding a student's current and future knacks and preferences, high school counselors can create their own questionnaires and surveys to assess their students in myriad ways. Such surveys can also be sent to parents and guardians as a way to compare and contrast the wishes and goals of parents with those students. Counselors can even follow the style of popular personality quizzes that teens are more familiar with in order to gauge college interest, readiness, and learning styles. These types of informal assessments can serve the purpose of starting a conversation, but should never be used in isolation as a counseling tool or as a prescriptive device in college and career planning. While paper and online tools can be easy and inexpensive to buy or create, it's often the case that self-awareness and confidence in goal setting come from exposure to new people and opportunities. Exposure provides context, and context provides clarity when it comes to a student's self-awareness and future plans.

Job shadowing and early exposure to industry are essential parts of schooling and future planning in Switzerland. The *Schnupperlehre* or trial apprenticeship is like a sneak peak week for students, and it provides a glimpse into a given industry before students begin to narrow their educational and career-training trajectories. Students can participate in multiple Schnupperlehre, along with career counseling, to thoughtfully plan for their futures. While there are material differences in college and vocational pathways in Switzerland and the United States, namely, 70% of Swiss students opt for a vocational education pathway over traditional university, U.S. schools and districts could benefit from adopting the Schnupperlehre concept, if nothing else (see Ellison, 2019). Students in high school today rarely get as much as a career fair before they graduate high school. While not pressuring students to choose too early, vocational exposure can serve to alleviate anxieties that come about due to a lack of exposure and context. A student who engages in job shadowing and professional mentoring may benefit from increased self-awareness by *imagining* themselves in different occupations, settings, and lifestyles. Seeing a day-in-the-life of different adults entertains the imagination and allows students to begin to see different versions of their future selves. While initially time-consuming to develop, professional job shadowing and mentoring networks can include leadership and support from across campus and the community. Organizing a board of community and school leaders will ensure buy-in and long-term sustainability. Industry professionals have an interest in these kinds of programs beyond pure altruism because employers want to fill the school-to-work pipeline with educated, engaged, and enthusiastic young people. School districts may quickly learn they too benefit from such programs because unengaged students without post-secondary plans may be better equipped to articulate their plans after high school graduation once they have a chance to learn more about their real-world options beyond the walls of their high school. With counselor-facilitated reflection and discussion to complement the experience, job shadowing and mentorship opportunities can ease some angst around choosing the best path after high school graduation and aid a student's lifelong journey of self discovery.

A Team Effort: Creating Coaches out of Parents, Teachers, Administrators, and Mentors

While social and emotional learning practices are now more common in American classrooms, counselors often have limited time and resources to devote to college counseling at all, let alone a type of counseling grounded in social and emotional awareness. The American School Counselor Association recommends a student-to-counselor ratio of 250 to 1, but the current ratio is 430 to 1. Surprisingly, this is the lowest it's been in 30 years. A 2018-2019 report noted that in reaction to school shootings, mental health challenges, and bullying, the number of school counselors has actually been increasing (Barshay, 2020). While some might have liked to see this be a proactive rather than a reactive move on the part of districts, the increase in new hires is an improvement. Still, even if more high school counselors have the rare luxury of only needing to focus on college and career readiness (one big hat to wear), they are up against pressures from parents, and sometimes administrators, who want to see more AP courses, higher GPAs, higher ACT and SAT scores, and more elite college acceptances. If students only have an opportunity to meet with their counselor once each month (or less), the counselor's efforts to decrease anxieties, reveal diverse options, and provide the student with tools for self-awareness and discovery will likely be short-lived and drowned out amid the noise coming from a rumor mill run by fellow students and well-intentioned adults.

A *coaching students to college and careers* training, webinar, or manual is something that a counselor can design once, update annually, and distribute or offer at the beginning of each school year. Counselors can identify those teachers and administrators on staff who show a natural interest in and passion for guiding students along the college and career readiness journey. There are those teachers in every high school who informally mentor and guide countless students. The counselor's job is to harness that natural inclination and, without presenting a load of new responsibilities, provide updates regarding college admission trends, changing requirements, new and exciting opportunities, and financial aid resources. By providing updated information and resources, the teacher mentors have facts and data to accompany their natural love for shepherding students through college admission. Community mentors (perhaps those same mentors who are willing to host job shadows) can also be guided through an easy and approachable training and provided with an updated manual to serve as a reference. The school counselor may find that by providing a timely and easy-to-follow resource guide, more volunteers may come forward to fill the role of college and career coach.

Beyond college and career guidance, mentorships for adolescents provide numerous benefits. According to YouthMentor.org, some of the benefits that arise out of caring mentorship connections include:

- Students who meet regularly with their mentors are 52% less likely than their peers to skip a day of school and 37% less likely to skip a class.
- Youth who meet regularly with their mentors are 46% less likely than their peers to start using illegal drugs and 27% less likely to start drinking.
- Seventy-six percent of at-risk young adults who had a mentor aspire to enroll in and graduate from college versus half of at-risk young adults who had no mentor. They are also more likely to be enrolled in college.
- Mentoring reduces "depression symptoms" and increases "social acceptance, academic attitudes and grades."

Counselors can look to successful community-based mentoring programs near their schools for partnership opportunities or to refer at-risk, high-need students. Programs such as Questbridge, Chicago Scholars, POSSE, AVID, The Boys and Girls Club, College Bound, College Possible, Genesys Works, and many more provide college guidance, mentorship, and scholarships to eligible students.

While parent over involvement has already been addressed, this should not be misinterpreted to mean that parents play no role in college and career coaching at all. According to a 2017 Gallup report, students get most of their information about prospective majors from their *informal social network,* a network that includes family, friends, and community leaders (Gallup & Strada Education Network, 2017). While counselors provide key guidance tips, students are making decisions based on more informal conversations with people they trust. Parents have been known to nudge students in one direction or another on long car rides or around the dinner table, so it's beneficial if they are knowledgeable about college and career options and provide relevant information as their students navigate college admission. Counselors can host parent information nights, one-on-one family meetings, and send out news trends and updates in weekly or monthly newsletters. Establishing a position as a reliable source of information will make the counselor's job easier as well; when parents act on and share misinformation about college admissions, the counselor may have to remedy the situation and provide triage for a misguided student. By providing an annually-revised *coaching guide* and list of tasks and need-to-know dates, parents will feel knowledgeable, in control, and useful. By engaging parents, counselors can also have more success keeping students on track with tasks related to graduation requirements and college deadlines. For communication and broadcasts, it is useful to maintain a parent and student combined list, a student-only list by grade level, and a parent-only list. While it's important that students feel a sense of agency over their college and career planning process, there are situations that call for including parents in communications, especially if a student has proven to be non-responsive to outreach. It should go without saying that parents must be involved in the financial planning process for college; while students may not rely on them as much as other sources for information about college, no one will be happy if a student is admitted to top-choice colleges none of which are affordable to the family. Determining financial fit requires parent involvement, just as determining social and academic fit require full participation from the student.

Committed, integrated, and holistic guidance counseling will rely on a team of reliable and supportive adults in a student's life, but passionate mentorship alone won't be enough in a rapidly evolving college and career landscape. The high school counselor can act as a sort of impresario, bringing together important players around a common cause, and providing the tools, methods, and resources to empower mentors to be both knowledgeable and committed.

Culture Change: Adjusting the Mood and Language Around College and Career Planning

High school class rank used to be an important metric that was reported on the high school transcript and in college applications. Now, more than half of all US high schools have done away with class rank (College Board, 2020). The rationale behind this seemingly bold move on the part of high schools appears to be in the best interest of students. It would appear that removing class rank would improve the overall culture, especially at competitive high schools, thwarting students' inclination to compare and compete with each other. But according to a recently-revised report by the National Association of of Secondary School Principals, many of the schools that led the charge to do away with school rankings were private and selective high schools that saw removing the class rank metric as a strategic move to get more of their students into more selective colleges (National Association of Secondary School Principals, 2020). This example illustrates the necessity of deep-rooted, student-centric, SEAD principles in schools that have wide buy in and acceptance from students, teachers, and administrators. Even more recent conversations about changing grading policies to be more holistic or competency-based will not improve the social-emotional wellbeing of students if their wellbeing is not central to the decision.

In the spring of 2020, many high schools around the country moved to a pass/fail grading system, given the dramatic shift in instruction delivery due to the COVID-19 pandemic. Suddenly, teachers had to become online instructors, using new technologies. Students, regardless of their style, had no choice but to learn at home from a packet or a computer. Many students found themselves without internet, without the free lunches, and without quiet workspaces. Some students couldn't attend even online classes, asked instead to look after younger siblings who now had no childcare. Despite this sudden onset of new challenges for large swaths of students, it didn't take long for more income-secure students to use the pass/fail option to their advantage. Some students who had a choice between letter grades and pass/fail, chose letter grades, knowing this last quarter of the school year would be less demanding given all the fluctuations in instruction. Before long, students began to use their "choice" to stand out in the college admissions process, believing that opting for letter grades during a pandemic proved their grit and perseverance.

This same phenomenon could be seen in the arena of standardized testing (Fair Test, 2020). The pandemic put into motion a quick domino effect of modified testing requirements in admissions offices across the country. Several hundred colleges and universities in the US had adopted a test-optional policy pre pandemic, but they were largely less-selective institutions. By September of 2020, roughly ⅗ of 4-year colleges and universities had gone test-optional, bringing the total number of institutions that no longer required the ACT or SAT to 1570 in that month, including institutions that had long remained loyal to standardized tests, such as the University of California and members of the Ivy League. It didn't take long for educators and students alike to realize that high-scoring test takers could impress the test-optional schools to which they were planning to apply by submitting their stand-out scores in a sea of applicants with no scores. Questions bubbled up around how scores that were submitted would be weighed and if test-optional *really* meant optional. Here again, students with the advantage of test-prep or early testing opportunities could use their "edge" even during a pandemic.

The class rank, pass/fail, and standardized test examples illustrate how policy changes that would appear to give students more options and less angst can actually backfire, creating even more hierarchy among students. Rather than give students the option between letter grades and pass/fail, complete adoption of pass/fail for all students could work to create a more cooperative and less competitive culture on high school campuses, just as adoption of a pure "test-blind" policy, one that ignores test scores altogether, could work to balance the pecking order that students naturally create when some have the stand-out scores and others don't.

It would be overly simple to imply that removing competition improves campus culture in high school. Healthy competition is welcome at any school committed to SEAD programs and methods, but without a social-emotional framework that places student wellbeing at the center (not college acceptances), competition around rank, GPA, and test scores is likely to become the focus. Putting student-wellbeing at the center of all decisions should not be conflated with putting student *achievement* at the center. Rather, a mindful counseling approach emphasizes the importance of shared success, and offers new definitions of success and achievement.

While changing vocabulary might seem like a superficial adjustment, it is a starting point. Of course, it is a meaningless effort if not adopted widely on campus. Just as SEAD cannot exist in a single silo on campus, mindfulness around college admission cannot merely be seen or heard in the counseling office. Below is a sample list of words and phrases that are tossed around frequently in college and career planning conversations. Simply paying more attention to how this language affects the way students think about their own abilities and goals could act to nudge the entire school community toward a healthier and more mindful culture.

We are applying to____ college/university

I got my student into ____ college/university

Our students get into these colleges/universities

Good/bad schools or Good/bad students

Back up colleges/universities

The best schools or The best students

Apply just to see if you get in!

Additionally, even when used humorously, language about "stressful admission seasons" or "senior year college stress" can only heighten the angst that many students are already experiencing and introduce angst to those who weren't feeling any such emotions. Students and parents will often adopt the mentality of the counselor, so rather than assuming stress, fear, and anxiety around college admission, the mindful counselor responds according to what the student expresses.

Furthermore, while it can be helpful for families to see where other students from the same high school have gone to college, such "college acceptance" lists should be used as tools to connect prospective students with current students, as mentioned earlier when talking about exposing students to more options. Unfortunately, these lists are too often used as marketing tools, opening up the door for toxic comparisons and oversimplified evaluations of high schools and their counselors. It's a narrow assessment to be impressed by a college acceptance list with "Harvard," "Stanford," and "MIT" and to be concerned about a list without these names. If such lists are to be posted at all in the halls or on the school website, they can be framed with the phrase, "You have peers from this high school at these colleges and universities!" And then provide opportunities for students to connect with these college students, after receiving permission.

The *Making Caring Common Project* provides these additional recommendations for what secondary school teachers, counselors, and administrators ought to focus on in order to improve culture, alleviate stress and anxiety, and emphasize collaboration in secondary schools:

- meaningful, sustained community service
- collective action that takes on community challenges
- authentic, meaningful experiences with diversity
- service that develops gratitude and a sense of responsibility for the future
- contributions to one's family
- assessing students' daily awareness of and contributions to others
- prioritizing quality—not quantity—of activities
- awareness of overloading on AP/IB courses
- discouraging "overcoaching"
- options for reducing test pressure
- expanding students' thinking about "good" colleges

CONCLUSION

Secondary school guidance counselors are not responsible for preventing the seemingly rampant stress culture that is permeating so many campuses around the country, nor should they bear the burden of changing strong-held ideologies around college and career planning. However, counselors are in a unique position as liaisons between colleges, community members, teachers, and administrators and the students they serve. Often the only point of contact for students wanting to learn about life beyond high school, counselors have a profound opportunity to introduce diverse college and career opportunities to students in an optimistic and enthusiastic manner, affecting the way students see themselves and their role in society.

School counselors can also serve as filters; they can control the valve between the noise, the misinformation, and rumors and their students. Surely, counselors cannot keep students in a bubble, but as a trusted source of information on campus, they can position themselves as the grounded, mindful, and knowledgeable first point of contact for students and families to turn to before they turn to untrustworthy or outdated sources. By sharing their approach and perspective with administrators, teachers, and parents, counselors can build a team of *coaches* who can provide trusted and reliable support that is both customizable to the students they mentor as well as consistent and up-to-date.

A socially- and emotionally-aware approach to college and career planning will infuse a counseling office with greater calm and mindfulness that will permeate the school and the families it serves. While college admission is fraught with challenges and toxicity, it is also an arena that is perhaps the most thirsty for a better way, a more mindful way, and a way that puts student wellbeing at the forefront.

REFERENCES

Allman, M. B., Anci, D., Babington, C., Ballinger, P., Beseda, M., Bland, T., Bock, J., Browning, J., Chan, F. Z., Chermonte, D. J., Cohen, J., Cohen, K. C., Dileno, S., Evans, Z., & Farmer, S. M. (2020). *Impact of the COVID-19 pandemic on college-going high school seniors*. Retrieved from: https://www.artsci.com/studentpoll-covid19

Aubrey, A., & Greenhalgh, J. (2018, June 11). The perils of pushing kids too hard and how parents can learn to back off. *National Public Radio*. https://www.npr.org/sections/health-shots/2018/06/11/616900580/back-off-how-to-get-out-of-the-high-pressure-parenting-trap

Barshay, J. (2020, April 27). *Lowest student-to-school-counselor ratio since 1986*. Retrieved from: https://hechingerreport.org/lowest-student-to-school-counselor-ratio-since-1986/

CASEL. (2020a). *Casel's SEL framework: What are the core competence areas and where are they promoted?* Retrieved from: https://casel.org/wp-content/uploads/2020/12/CASEL-SEL-Framework-11.2020.pdf

CASEL. (2020b). *SEL is…* Retrieved from: https://casel.org/wp-content/uploads/2020/12/CASEL-SEL-Framework-11.2020.pdf

College Board. (2020, September 10). *Class rank & college admission: To rank or not to rank*. https://professionals.collegeboard.org/guidance/applications/rank#:~:text=Class%20rank%20was%20once%20a,no%20longer%20report%20student%20rankings

Educationdata. (2020). *International student enrollment statistics*. Retrieved from: https://educationdata.org/international-student-enrollment-statistics

Ellison, A. (2019). *Go your own way: 7 student-centered paths to the best college experience*. Dunce, LLC.

Fissinger, M. X., Fitzsimmons, W. R., Flagel, A., Fretwell, K., & Zakrzewski, V. (2016, January 20). *Turning the tide: Inspiring concern for others and the common good through college admissions*. Making Caring Common Project. Retrieved from: https:///Downloads/20160120_mcc_ttt_report_interactive.pdf

Gallup and Strada Education Network. (2017). *On second thought: U.S. adults reflect on their education decisions*. Retrieved from: http://stradaeducation.gallup.com/reports/208535/gallup-strada-education-ecp-inaugural-report-2017.aspx

Hess, A. (2019, September 28). *Make it: The 10 US universities that receive the most applications*. Retrieved from: https://www.cnbc.com/2019/09/28/the-10-universities-that-receive-the-most-applications.html

Levesque, K. (2018, October 4). A school counselor puts social-emotional learning first. *Social-Emotional Learning in Action, 14*(4). Retrieved from: http://www.ascd.org/ascd-express/vol14/num04/A-School-Counselor-Puts-Social-Emotional-Learning-First.aspx

Lipson, S. K., Lattie, E. G., & Eisenberg, D. (2018). Increased rates of mental health service utilization by U.S. college students: 10-year population-level trends (2007-2017). *Psychiatric Services, 70*, 60-63. doi:10.1176/appi.ps.201800332

Mentor, Y. (2020, September 14). *The stats*. https://www.youthmentor.org/thestats

National Association of Secondary School Principals. (2020, March 11). *Class rank, GPA, and grading*. Retrieved from: https://www.nassp.org/policy-advocacy-center/nassp-position-statements/class-rank-gpa-and-grading/#:~:text=As%20schools%20and%20districts%20moved,the%20basis%20of%20class%20rank

Pofeldt, E. (2017, October 17). Are we ready for a workforce that is 50% freelance? *Forbes*. Retrieved from: https://www.forbes.com/sites/elainepofeldt/2017/10/17/are-we-ready-for-a-workforce-that-is-50-freelance/#e3713a3f82b2

Test, F. (2020). *The national center for fair & open testing*. https://www.fairtest.org/

The Upshot Harvard University. (2017). *The New York Times*. Retrieved from: https://www.nytimes.com/interactive/projects/college-mobility/harvard-university

Twenge, J. (2018). *iGen: Why today's super-connected kids are growing up less rebellious, more tolerant, less happy—and completely unprepared for adulthood—and what that means for the rest of us*. Atria Books. Retrieved from: https://www.cnbc.com/2019/09/28/the-10-universities-that-receive-the-most-applications.html

U.S. Department of Education, National Center for Education Statistics. (2019). *Digest of Education Statistics*. Retrieved from: https://nces.ed.gov/fastfacts/display.asp?id=84

Chapter 13
Strengthening College and Career Readiness With Social and Emotional Learning:
Integrating Explicit SEL in CTE

Kara Sidorowicz
IMAGO, USA

Anthony Yang
IMAGO, USA

ABSTRACT

Social-emotional skills are essential for navigating the rapidly evolving world, especially for students who will become the makers and doers of tomorrow. The literature suggests that a technology-driven shift in needs is fueling a skills gap within a workforce needing social-emotional competencies. These shifts have grown the need for students to develop their social-emotional skills for professional and personal success. Experts suggest infusing social and emotional learning (SEL) in career and technical education (CTE) to address this. This study documents and explores a strategy for explicit SEL in CTE at Clark County School District in Nevada, USA during the 2019-2020 school year. Usage and student answers suggest promising value of SEL in CTE for student learning, but a need to better support teacher adoption. Findings from this study contribute preliminary guidance on program development and implementation upon which future educators and researchers can build.

INTRODUCTION

Preparing high-school students for college & career is important for both their own success, and the collective success of communities and businesses they will engage in. This depends on an education strategy that can effectively equip students with the skills needed today, and to adapt in the future. Experts are calling for prioritization of social-emotional skills to address the skills gap (Casner-Lotto &

DOI: 10.4018/978-1-7998-6728-9.ch013

Barrington, 2006; Committee for Children, 2016; Deming, 2017; Johnson & Wiener, 2017; Lippman et al., 2015; Rainie & Anderson, 2017; Yoder et al., 2020). Curricula and instruction must adapt to innovation and changes in work and societal norms to effectively prepare students for success in their present and future realities.

Researchers suggest integrating social and emotional learning (SEL) into career and technical education (CTE) to address this (Committee for Children, 2016; Yoder et al., 2020). Due to the nascent space of formalizing the teaching of *social-emotional skills* for college and career readiness (CCR), there exist many challenges that hamper the seamless implementation of SEL frameworks and programs in school districts. The present study explored the implementation and value of an approach to explicit SEL in the Clark County School District's CTE program during the 2019–2020 school year. Program design, implementation, and study insights for future practice and research of SEL and CCR are discussed throughout this chapter.

LITERATURE REVIEW

SEL is the development and practice of cognitive, emotional, and social competencies that promote productive mindsets and habits for setting and navigating goals, building and managing relationships, regulating behavior, and interpreting experiences (Harvard Graduate School of Education, n.d.). SEL has many documented benefits such as improved academic performance and well-being (Durlak et al., 2011; Taylor et al., 2017), and the initiative to infuse SEL in education has gained momentum as 50 states adopted SEL standards from 2015 to 2019 (Dusenbury et al., 2018). In today's fast-paced, high-tech society, these skills are increasingly valued by employers and becoming more important to learn for professional success and personal well-being, warranting the need to comprehensively integrate them in education (Committee for Children, 2016; Deming, 2017; Lippman et al., 2015; Yoder et al., 2020).

Skills for the 21st Century

Technological innovations have automated more rudimentary tasks, consequently, increasing demand for non-technical skills in project and people management (World Economic Forum, 2020). Ultimately, the current workforce needs a combination of both technical and social-emotional skills (Autor et al., 2003; Casner-Lotto & Barrington, 2006; Deming, 2017; Johnson & Wiener, 2017; Pew Research Center, 2016; Yoder et al., 2020). This trend will continue in the future, with social-emotional competencies becoming increasingly important in the workforce (Deming, 2017; Manyika et al., 2017; Rainie & Anderson, 2017). The World Economic Forum (2020) found that 13 out of the top 15 skills projected for the year 2025 were part of a broader social and emotional competency (see Table 1).

Table 1. Top 15 Skills for 2025 and Related Social and Emotional Competencies

#	Skill	Social-Emotional Competency
1	Analytical thinking and innovation	Global Awareness
2	Active learning and learning strategies	Self-Management
3	Complex problem-solving	Ethical Decision Making
4	Critical thinking and analysis	Global Awareness
5	Creativity, originality, and initiative	Self-Management
6	Leadership and social influence	Relationship Skills
7	Technology use, monitoring and control	N/A
8	Technology design and programming	N/A
9	Resilience, stress tolerance, and flexibility	Self-Management
10	Reasoning, problem-solving, and ideation	Ethical Decision Making
11	Emotional intelligence	All Sections
12	Troubleshooting and user experience	Relationship Skills
13	Service orientation	Relationship Skills
14	Systems analysis and evaluation	Global Awareness
15	Persuasion and negotiation	Relationship Skills

Note. *Social-emotional competencies are based on IMAGO's framework for social and emotional intelligence.*

The Skills Gap

Despite the value and demand for social-emotional skills, there is a gap & diminished confidence in the education system's ability to address it. Employers consistently struggle to find individuals with needed skills, such as complex problem-solving, teamwork, and communication (Casner-Lotto & Barrington, 2006; Committee for Children, 2016; Yoder et al., 2020). Pew Research Center (2016) found that 60% of over 5,000 respondents believed that public education was responsible for this preparation; however, only 16% felt that a four-year degree effectively prepares people for today's jobs, and 72% believed that much of the preparation ultimately falls on the individual. These results suggest that, while people see the important role that education plays, schools do not effectively teach to meet labor demands.

As society and the workforce change with the pace of technology, the education system will need to recalibrate itself to prepare individuals for 21st-century demands. We are still teaching students how to think, behave, and interact with each other primarily in mechanistic and linear ways, when conversely, the real world is non-mechanistic, is non-linear, and requires people to adapt according to any situation socially and emotionally—and then apply their technical knowledge. Providing a 19th- or 20th-century education in an evolving 21st-century environment will leave individuals unprepared.

Connecting CTE and Social-Emotional Skills

To address the need to better prepare students for the workforce, many school districts have established CTE programs involving multiyear sequences of courses that integrate technical occupational and leadership curricula with core academic subjects. In a CTE program, students select an industry-aligned pathway consisting of a pathway-specific course of study in order to gain technical knowledge and skills to prepare for postsecondary pursuit of a career in that pathway. Many CTE programs also emphasize teaching leadership and employability skills to equip students with tools for successfully pursuing a career after high school. The language and framework for these skills vary (i.e., leadership skills, employability skills, soft skills, 21st-century skills), but are all essentially SEL (Committee for Children, 2016; Johnson & Wiener, 2017; Jones et al., 2016; Yoder et al., 2020).

CTE programs often formally refer to these types of learning objectives as Employability Skills. The U.S. Department of Education's Office of Career, Technical, and Adult Education (2012) developed the Employability Skills Framework (see Table 2) as part of an initiative to guide instruction and assessment of the skills. CTE programming must address locally relevant employability skills to receive federal Perkins funding, and multiple states have developed their own employability standards modeled after this framework.

Table 2. Employability Skills Framework

Domain	Skill	Indicator
Applied Knowledge	Applied Academic Skills	Reading writing, math, and science skills
	Critical Thinking Skills	Thinks creatively and critically Makes sound decisions Solves problems Reasons Plans/organizes
Effective Relationships	Interpersonal Skills	Understands teamwork and works with others Responds to customer needs Exercises leadership Negotiates to resolve conflict Respects individual differences
	Personal Qualities	Demonstrates responsibility, self-discipline, willingness to learn, integrity, and professionalism Adapts and shows flexibility Works independently Takes initiative Displays a positive attitude and sense of self-worth Takes responsibility for professional growth
Workplace Skills	Resource Management	Manages time, money, resources, and personnel
	Information Use	Locates, organizes, uses, and communicates information
	Communication Skills	Communicates verbally Listens actively Comprehends written material Conveys information in writing Observes carefully
	Systems Thinking	Understands, uses, monitors, and improves systems
	Technology Use	Understands and uses technology

Note. *Adapted from U.S. Department of Education (2012).*

The most widely recognized SEL framework, The CASEL 5 (Collaborative for Academic, Social, and Emotional Learning [CASEL], 2020) defines SEL as a set of five interrelated competencies (see Table 3). The competency descriptions reveal the overlap of employability skills with SEL.

Table 3. The CASEL 5 Framework

Competency	Description
Self-Awareness	Abilities to understand one's own emotions, thoughts, and values and how they influence behavior across contexts.
	Capacities to recognize one's strengths and limitations with a well-grounded sense of confidence and purpose.
Self-Management	Abilities to manage one's emotions, thoughts, and behaviors effectively in different situations and to achieve goals and aspirations.
	Capacities to delay gratification, manage stress, and feel motivation and agency to accomplish personal/collective goals.
Social Awareness	Abilities to understand the perspectives of and empathize with others, including those from diverse backgrounds, cultures, & contexts.
	Capacities to feel compassion for others, understand broader historical and social norms for behavior in different settings, and recognize family, school, and community resources and supports.
Relationship Skills	Abilities to establish and maintain healthy and supportive relationships and to effectively navigate settings with diverse individuals and groups.
	Capacities to communicate clearly, listen actively, cooperate, work collaboratively to problem solve and negotiate conflict constructively, navigate settings with differing social and cultural demands and opportunities, provide leadership, and seek or offer help when needed.
Responsible Decision Making	Abilities to make caring and constructive choices about personal behavior and social interactions across diverse situations.
	Capacities to consider ethical standards and safety concerns, and to evaluate the benefits and consequences of various actions for personal, social, and collective well-being.

Teachers are often expected to provide opportunities for students to acquire and develop these skills within their CTE courses, but often lack the knowledge and tools to do so as a consequence of inconsistent language and structure across these frameworks (Jones et al., 2016; Yoder et al., 2020). Considering this, along with the overlap of CTE program objectives with SEL, experts suggest integrating SEL into CTE (Committee for Children, 2016; Yoder et al., 2020). Explicit SEL could help CTE programs more feasibly and successfully teach to address all their objectives, subsequently developing stronger students equipped with the skills to succeed in the near and far future as paralleling research supports (Kerr et al., 2020).

Because much is unknown about incorporating SEL in CCR programming, researchers have expressed a need to design and investigate approaches to teach social-emotional skills in youth and young adults in technical education (Lippman et al., 2015). In this study, the researchers detail and explore the development of a solution for explicitly embedding SEL in CTE and initial findings surrounding the successes and challenges of implementation at a large school district in the southwestern United States. Study findings will contribute to the SEL and CCR literature and provide direction in adopting explicit SEL instruction in CCR programs.

METHODS

The Career and Technical Education (CTE) Department in Clark County School District (CCSD), Nevada, partnered with IMAGO to implement a comprehensive program to develop students' CCR through the lens of SEL (i.e., emotional intelligence). CCSD is one of the nation's five largest school districts, with over 300,000 students in 360 schools. CCSD's student population is over 46% Hispanic/Latino, 24% Caucasian, and 14% Black/African American. During the 2018–2019 school year, CTE enrollment exceeded 67,000 students (CCSD, 2020).

The CTE department's philosophy is to "ensure that all students have access to quality programs that lead to marketable skills for the 21st century" (CCSD, n.d.-b, para. 1), with a vision that focuses on quality in education so all students will be equipped with "the knowledge, skills, attitudes, and values necessary to achieve academically, prosper economically, and contribute in a global society" (CCSD, n.d.-a, para. 2).

IMAGO is an educational technology company whose mission is to help students develop the skills, knowledge, and mindsets to successfully navigate and find fulfillment in their personal and professional lives. They provide over 200 digital lessons covering SEL and career-related topics, and deliver SEL-focused professional development and training. IMAGO takes a student-centered approach, which focuses first on self-exploration, and then on understanding and engaging with the world through a problem-solving lens.

The sample in this study includes CTE teachers and students with access to IMAGO during the 2019–2020 school year. This included 282 teachers from 20 high schools who logged in to the IMAGO platform from their own accounts at least once during the school year, and 3,726 students who were digitally assigned IMAGO lessons.

Materials

The IMAGO lessons were provided on a digital learning platform accessible via web browsers. Teachers and students logged-in to the platform to access SEL lessons. Lessons consist of five to eight short videos (1–3 minutes per video). Each lesson includes study guide questions after each video. Study guide questions are intended to help check and extend student understanding of lesson concepts. Study guide questions vary from recall to concept application and extended thinking to address the different depth-of-knowledge (DOK) levels. Responses to study guide questions provide insight into student perspectives and current skills, as well as the impacts of lessons on the students. This report includes several findings from analyzing these responses.

Facilitator guides accompany each lesson and can be accessed by teachers on the platform. The guides are documents that include an outline of lesson objectives, think-ahead questions, discussion questions, activities, and additional resources to help teachers explain the lesson topics. Teachers were strongly encouraged, but not required, to incorporate extension activities and conversations from facilitator guides with assigned lessons.

The *Mindsets* lessons were CCSD's primary focus. Each of the 42 Mindsets lessons provided an introduction to skills underlying one of the six key components of IMAGO's model of emotional intelligence (i.e., social-emotional competencies; see Figure 1). This model was created based on the epistemological question: Before a person does anything, what can (or should) a person understand first? This is reflected in the essence of emotional intelligence—described by Peter Salovey and John Mayer as the ability to understand oneself and others in order to think, behave, and navigate one's surroundings in contextually appropriate ways.

Figure 1. IMAGO's emotional intelligence framework

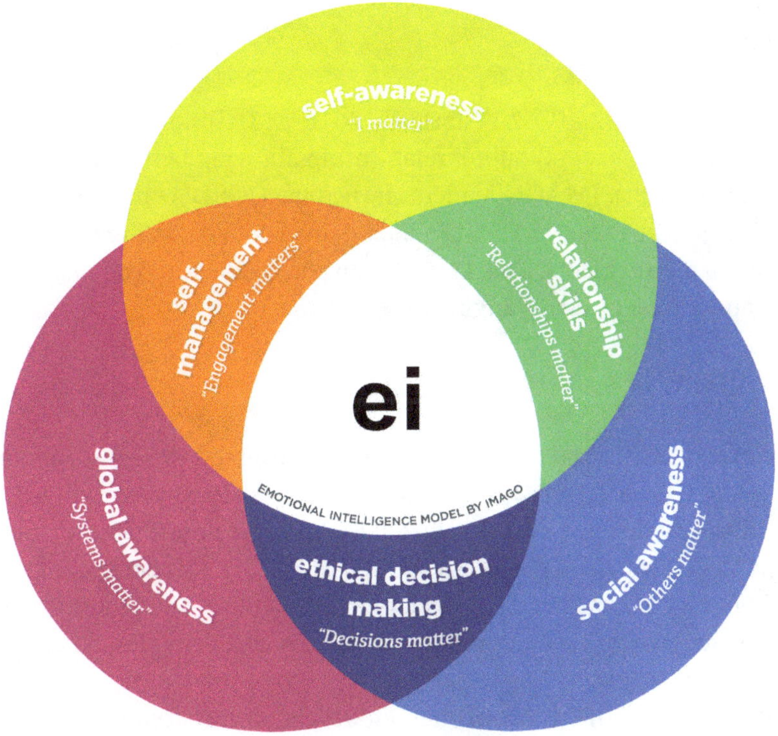

Other IMAGO lessons framed through the lens of SEL were also available to CCSD teachers (see Table 4). The curricula address three primary focuses: career preparation (e.g., designing resumes and interview preparation), career exploration (e.g., industry exploration), and SEL (e.g., self-awareness and management, social awareness).

Table 4. All Types of IMAGO Lessons Available to CCSD

Lesson Category	Description of Lessons
Mindsets	Foundational knowledge of social-emotional skills
Industries	Broad descriptions of different professional industry sectors and global problems they address
Life Skills	Guides for developing and successfully exercising the skills and behaviors introduced in the Mindsets lessons
Career Pathways	Guides that walk students through exploring all available careers in each industry, identifying those they are most interested in pursuing, and developing action plans to prepare for their chosen careers
Work Skills	Guides on interviewing, jobs search, and maintaining professionalism in work settings
Career Dives	In-depth descriptions of the duties, experiences, requirements, and education path for various careers provided by local professionals working in each career
Life After High School (LAHS)	Guides teaching high school students how to set goals, and develop and execute plans that will help them successfully transition into independent lifestyles after graduating

Note. *Career Dives currently only cover careers in the medical field.*

Procedure

Program Fit-Verification

The partnership between IMAGO and CCSD started in 2016, and will continue into 2021. First, the CCSD and IMAGO project directors (leaders) built a relationship allowing both parties to gauge feasibility of the partnership. During this time, IMAGO leaders learned the CCSD's objectives and desired benefit of using IMAGO, and teacher capacity; the CCSD leader gained understanding of IMAGO's content offerings and implementation requirements. This helped both parties identify and discuss potential obstacles of implementation and ultimately verify alignment.

Planning and Program Design

After deciding to partner, CCSD and IMAGO leaders co-designed program rollout and implementation to fit CCSD's goals and needs. First, the leaders operationalized program goals and expectations in a meeting with IMAGO's director of research. CCSD's leader described the outcomes they hope to achieve with IMAGO. In defining what success looks like, CCSD's leader specified how they envision its measurement. From this information, the leaders planned for IMAGO to evaluate perceived value and benefit of IMAGO to students' social-emotional skills by analyzing lesson usage and student study guide responses.

Next, the CCSD's leader identified school sites and teachers who would be the most willing and best positioned to pilot IMAGO and incorporate SEL content by considering various teacher characteristics. IMAGO recommended identifying a leader at each site who demonstrates passion for supporting student success and would recognize the beneficial possibilities of SEL for both students and their own workload, and selecting teachers who:

- are comfortable with technology and incorporating it in their teaching practices;
- would be willing to facilitate lessons with the intention of discussing potentially unfamiliar topics in an unstructured, exploratory manner;
- would be willing to share their own stories while leaving room to actively listen to student experiences and perspectives to encourage lively discussion;
- would be willing to attend IMAGO's training to learn implementation strategies to support a good user experience and a smooth rollout.

Teacher Training

The CCSD's leader invited the identified teachers to a 7-hour IMAGO training at the end of August. The training occurred during a school day and the CCSD leader's department hired substitutes for all teachers who attended. Training covered CCSD's objectives and expectations for teachers, SEL through IMAGO's lens, and IMAGO's platform functionality and lesson content. IMAGO provided an interactive demonstration of lesson facilitation, including activities from facilitator guides, for three Mindsets lessons: *Systems Thinking*, *Values and Attitudes* and *Organization*. Teachers had time to explore IMAGO's platform and ask questions at the end of the training.

Implementation and Follow-Up

Teachers started using lessons at their leisure following the training. Even if teachers did not attend training, they were still provided access to IMAGO's platform. To digitally use lessons, teachers had to first create a digital class within the platform and select the lessons they wanted to assign to the class. Then, teachers instructed students to create accounts on IMAGO and join the digital class. Teachers had the flexibility of implementing lessons using any combination of the following approaches: facilitating in class, assigning as homework, assigning as individual in-class work, guiding in-class conversations on lesson topics, and incorporating facilitator-guide activities. Teachers who wanted to use a more traditional instructional approach could present lessons from their own IMAGO account to their class and print hard copies of study guides for students to complete.

Throughout the school year, IMAGO followed-up with teachers to ensure they were comfortable and using the content properly. Follow-up involved on-site visits with participating teachers to attend meetings, share best-practices, and co-facilitate lessons for further personalized training when requested. IMAGO coordinated these visits roughly a month following training, and upon request throughout the school year. The program was piloted in Spring, 2018 and in the 2018–2019 school year, and fully implemented with CCSD CTE in the 2019–2020 school year.

RESULTS

Data Collection and Analysis Procedures

The researchers obtained usage and study guide data from the IMAGO learning platform. Datasets included both qualitative and quantitative data, used in tandem to clean, code, and conduct analyses in RStudio and Microsoft Excel. Prior to analysis, datasets were cleaned by removing duplicate cases.

Usage Analysis Procedure

To understand the extent of teacher and student engagement with IMAGO, the present study analyzed teacher-login and lesson-usage data. Teacher-login data was used to gauge teacher engagement by analyzing the total number of logins and time spent on the IMAGO platform. Lesson-usage data was used to gauge student engagement by analyzing the number of lessons according to completion status: *not started (assigned)* included lessons that were assigned and never accessed, *incomplete* included lessons that were started but not completed during the school year, *complete* included lessons with a completion date during the school year, and *accessed* included incomplete and complete lessons.

Study Guide Analysis Procedure

The researchers targeted and analyzed questions to which responses can provide insight to student comprehension and value of the lessons. Seven open-ended questions asking students to apply and synthesize lesson concepts from five lessons were analyzed to explore student comprehension and application of Mindsets lessons (see Table 5). Qualitative data analysis was conducted on each question separately to extract question-specific themes. The initial phase of analysis involved the identification of problematic responses. Because these were open-ended questions and students were required to answer all questions in a study guide before completing each lesson, this study guide data contained some irrelevant (i.e., readable but did not address any part of the question) or unclear (i.e., gibberish, blank spaces, or grammatically illegible) responses. In consideration of this, the researchers determined such responses to be indicative of either disengagement or error. Therefore, these responses were excluded from further analyses on a question-by-question basis.

Table 5. Seven Open-Ended Study Guide Questions Analyzed for Comprehension and Application

Lesson		Question
Accountability	1	Where could you start applying these [accountability] steps to hold yourself or others accountable?
Adaptability	2	Why is it important to know that people aren't born good or bad, but instead that people can change as they develop over time?
Empathy	3	Where would you like to be shown more empathy?
	4	How does recognizing how others are feeling help you interact with them at home, school, or work? How does this help with conflict resolution and/or solving problems?
Resilience	5	When you fail or do not accomplish something, how does it make you feel? How can you learn from this failure and turn this experience around to make you a better person?
Self-Control	6	We all have things we can work on and develop to become better. In terms of self-control, what is something you would like to begin working on and be better at?
	7	What has this lesson taught you about self-control that you didn't know before?

The specific approach used to code the open-ended responses varied by question, depending on the question context and time considerations that emerged with the progression of analysis. The researchers initially employed a conventional thematic content analysis on questions in which it made sense to extract specific themes surrounding the topical nature of the responses (e.g., "Where could you start applying these [accountability] steps to hold yourself or others accountable?"); however, in consideration of time and minimal comparative value-add of this approach, the researchers employed a more basic content analysis technique to analyze the remaining questions. This involved coding and quantifying responses to the five remaining questions according to whether or not they addressed the objective of the question in a meaningful way.

To explore the relevance of Mindsets lessons to students, the researchers aggregated and analyzed all 20 Mindsets study guide questions that asked students to rate how helpful the lesson was. These questions were embedded in the final study guide of 20 different Mindsets lessons. Questions varied slightly in their wording and scale anchors—using lesson-specific verbiage, and either a 3- or 5-point rating scale. Both variations of rating scales were structured similarly: options below the midpoint corresponded to *not helpful* or *minimally helpful*, the midpoint corresponded to *not sure* or *neutral*, and options above the midpoint corresponded to *helpful* or *extremely helpful*. To combine and compare these questions, the researchers recoded responses such that all responses below the midpoint were coded as *not helpful*, all midpoint responses were coded as *not sure*, and all responses above the midpoint were coded as *helpful*.

Usage Findings

Of the teachers provided access to IMAGO, 130 teachers (46.10%) from 15 sites created classes and digitally assigned lessons to students. Collectively, teachers digitally assigned 21,374 lessons to their 3,726 students on the platform ($M = 5.74$, $SD = 6.67$). Of these students, 2,756 (74%) accessed (i.e., at least started) 9,541 lessons ($M = 2.56$, $SD = 3.64$). Teachers assigned 173 (70.90%) of the 244 unique lessons available to CCSD during the 2019–2020 school year. In addition to the primary focus, which was Mindsets (i.e., 42 SEL lessons), teachers found value in and utilized (i.e., assigned) 122 other lessons from different categories (see Table 6).

Table 6. Lesson Usage Across all Assigned Lesson Categories

Lesson Type	Complete	Started (Incomplete)	Accessed
Mindsets	4,904	745	5,649
Life Skills	2,236	330	2,566
Life After HS	561	101	662
Career Dives	390	21	411
Career Pathways	87	41	128
Work Skills	103	10	113
Industries	11	1	12
Core Skills	0	0	0

Mindsets Only

Of the facilitators who digitally assigned lessons, 89 (68.46%) assigned all 42 Mindsets lessons. Collectively, facilitators assigned 11,682 Mindsets lessons to 2,330 learners ($M = 5.01$, $SD = 5.00$)—62.50% of all CCSD learners on platform. From this, 1,670 learners (71.67%) accessed a total of nearly 6,000 Mindsets lessons ($M = 2.42$, $SD = 3.71$). Usage across each subcategory of Mindsets lessons is displayed in Table 7.

Table 7. Mindsets Usage by Subcategory

Category	Complete	Started (Incomplete)	Assigned (Not Started)	Total
Self-Awareness	2,129	113	864	3,106
Relationship Skills	1,576	103	2,010	3,689
Social Awareness	537	168	506	1,211
Ethical Decision Maker	341	182	966	1,489
Self-Management	279	166	1,507	1,952
Global Awareness	42	13	180	235

STUDY GUIDE FINDINGS

Student Comprehension and Application

Accountability

Accountability involves taking responsibility for your own actions. The Accountability lesson explains what accountability is and why it is important, and provides students with steps for being and holding others accountable. One of the questions from this lesson asked students how they could personally apply the accountability steps to hold themselves or other people accountable. Analysis of these responses can provide insight into both learning and the applicability of lesson concepts.

Responses to this question were thematically coded. The first phase of coding revealed 22 students who provided unclear or irrelevant answers, and these students were excluded from remaining analysis of this question. The remaining responses ($N = 255$) underwent two additional coding phases to identify and collapse related themes into broader concepts. The final phase of thematic coding revealed seven final themes (see Table 8). Most students said they could use the accountability steps to better engage and succeed in school, followed by applying accountability steps to better navigate and accomplish goals.

Excluding students who provided *not sure* responses, 246 students (96.47%) indicated that they see value in using accountability steps in their own lives. Students who said they could use the accountability steps everywhere may have seen value in using the steps, but their responses did not include sufficient detail to suggest more meaningful learning. Excluding the theme *everywhere*, 226 (88.63%) students were able to apply what they learned in a personally meaningful way by identifying specific aspects of their own lives where they can start using accountability steps.

Adaptability

Adaptability involves altering your thoughts and behaviors. It is important to understand that you are capable of changing the way you think and behave, both long-term and situationally. This mindset underlies one's own adaptability and belief in the ability of other people to change in a positive direction. In the final study guide in the Adaptability lesson, students were asked, "Why is it important to know that people aren't born good or bad, but instead, that people can change as they develop over time?"

Responses to this question were coded according to whether the student provided an explanation of the significance. There were 25 students who answered this question, and 19 (76.00%) of them were able to articulate the importance of this knowledge. The remaining 6 students did not believe that people were capable of changing or were uncertain. The following are some of the explanations that students provided:

- It means they aren't doomed to be what they are. By being able to change, it means the person can decide what they want to be.
- It is important because it tells you yourself you were not born good or bad but teachable.
- To realize that no one is going to be perfect or ideal from the jump, everything takes time.
- It is important to know that people aren't born good or bad because it shows that over time, they are capable of changing for the better or for the worst thus, showing that people can change as they develop over time and start to experience life lessons or life experience.

Table 8. Summary of Themes from the Question, "Where could you start applying these steps to hold yourself or others accountable?"

Theme	n	%	Sample Responses
In School	110	43.14	I could start by getting good grades and get no tardies/ absences.
			I could start applying these steps in school for projects and other things like that. It would help me know that I can do whatever I put my mind to and it would motivate me.
			I could start applying these steps on the next long homework/ project (assignment) I have to do. Then it would make it easier . . . because I have everything I need to do laid out.
			Capstone project. Make it easier
Improve Goal Planning and Attainment	66	25.88	Start setting reminders each day to make you complete your goal. Yes i do feel like this would help me remember but my goal
			Start applying the 3 steps for my own personal goals. It could impact them by actually being completed
			You can start by putting on a calendar your goals and what you want to accomplish by that day
			I could apply these steps to my life by practicing using them . . . to reach my personal goals. This will allow me to reach my goals more efficiently and effectively.
Improve Personal Habits and Behaviors	28	10.98	Start focusing on more focus on being paicet [*sic*] and keeping my self positive
			Don't procrassonate [*sic*] anymore
			I could start by holding myself accountable and doing my work and doing my stuff and learning to be own my own
Everywhere (Nonspecific)	20	7.84	I could apply this to anything in my life and it will help me.
			In my everyday life. this would improve my life substantially.
			Anywhere and everywhere
At Home	11	4.31	At home. I would be less distracted by external factors, and focused on my main goal.
			If I start becoming more accountable for my actions at home then I will have a better relationship with my parents
			I can start applying these steps in my household so my youngins can grow up accountable and responsible. It would make accomplishing goal much easier.
Collaborating with Others	11	4.31	During group projects; This would allow the work to be distributed more evenly and allow it to be managible [*sic*] for each person
			I could start applying these steps on my soccer team. Everyone is accountable to control their part of the field in order to be the most successful.
			I could apply these steps to group projects and it would impact my goal by giving me a plan.
Not Sure	9	3.53	I don't know where to these steps can help day to day life.
			I dont get this

Empathy

Empathy affects both our intra- and interpersonal interactions. This lesson covers the different types of empathy, their value, and how to become more empathetic. One of the study guide questions from this lesson asked students where they personally would like to be shown more empathy by other people. Results from this question can reveal both student understanding and interpersonal needs.

Responses to this question were thematically coded. The first phase of coding revealed 32 students who provided unclear or irrelevant answers, and these students were excluded from remaining analysis of this question. Some of the remaining 511 students provided multiple answers to this question, bringing the total number of responses to 543. Two additional coding phases were conducted to identify and collapse related themes. From the final coding phase of the qualitative analysis, nine response themes emerged (see Table 9). Excluding 2 themes—*Don't need it* and *Not Sure*—465 students (91.00%) applied what they learned by describing one or more aspects of their own life where they would like more empathy. Students most commonly reported desire for more empathy at school, followed by more understanding of their personal situations and compassion during hardships.

Another study guide question in the Empathy lesson asked, "How does recognizing how others are feeling help you interact with them at home, school, or work? How does this help with conflict resolution and/or solving problems?" Unclear and irrelevant responses ($n = 17$) were identified and excluded from analysis. Responses to this question were coded according to whether or not the student explained the value of empathy in interpersonal interactions. Of the 587 remaining students, 541 (92.16%) were able to identify a benefit. There were 41 students (6.98%) who either said that this does not help (e.g., "It doesn't") or provided responses that were too vague and failed to address the question (e.g., "By there [*sic*] physical appearance like crying"; "It makes it easier"). The remaining five students (0.85%) said they did not know how to answer the question. Responses from students who were able to answer this question included the following:

- Knowing how someone is feeling helps you interact with them because it helps you know what things to say and what things to avoid in a conversation. This helps with solving problems because seeing how someone feels might help you understand the problem better and in a different perspective.
- Empathy allows us to interact well with people in different environments. When resolving conflicts, it allows us to understand why someone is disagreeing with you or opposing your perspective and improvise or negotiate with them.
- When you take an interest in what others think, feel and experience, you'll develop a reputation for being caring, trustworthy and approachable. It helps to build trust and strengthen relationships.
- Recognizing how others feel help you know how you should approach someone. This will help you know what to say/do to help someone feel better and calm down.
- It helps me know when it is the right time to talk to them about myself or about them and what they are feeling. . . .This help [*sic*] with conflict resolution and/or solving problems because you would know if someone in the relationship is feeling a type of way about the other and it helps solve problems by knowing what they are going thought [*sic*].
- It helps you . . . because you can feel more comfortable talking about emotions with others. It can help you relate and/or prepare for conflicts. This helps because people has experiences that they can deal with, and/or can give us advice on ways to deal with it.

- Recognizing how other are feeling helps interact with them because it helps to understand the type of person that they are and how they handle certain things. This helps with conflict resolution and solving problems because you can take the time to see their point of view and understand why they feel that way to fix it.

Table 9. Summary of Themes from the Question, "Where would you like to be shown more empathy?"

Theme	n	%	Sample Responses
At School	169	31.12	I would like to be shown more empathy at school. People don't know what others do through on a daily basis, so I think that everyone could be shown more empathy at school.
			At school, sometimes teachers get mad about lack of participation, but a lot of times there is a reason behind the student not wanting to do their work.
			I would like to be shown more empathy at school because at school, I feel like I'm not cared for and that some people don't like me.
			Absolutely in school. Children especially think that it's alright to joke around too much and be jerks to one another they create this toxic atmosphere where no one really cares about each other only about physical things or how funny someone is.
Toward Personal Needs, Troubles, and Values	87	21.55	I'd like to [be] shown empathy when it comes to family issues, I don't tell anyone about stuff like that because the last time they did they didn't take it seriously.
			I would like to be shown more empathy in my faults and mistakes. I haven't necessarily experienced the worse of things, but it's nice to know that people are there to support you.
			When people dont understand that i have stricted parents and i cant go everywhere & people being annoyed when i cancel places over school.
			Being stressed about school; going through a rough time with my life; past experiences with relationships.
At Home	81	16.02	At home because my parents think I do nothing all day when i'm actually doing my homework.
			I would like to be shown more empathy when I get in trouble because of my little sister.
			I would like to be shown more empathy at home because i feel like parents dont understand how stress we can actually get. They call it "baby stress"
In Interpersonal Relationships and Interactions	57	10.5	I would like to be treated fairly and listened to.
			I would like to be shown more empathy from my friends because I often feel that they don't understand how I feel because I don't directly state how I feel.
			I would like to be shown more empathy when it comes to cognitive empathy. Some people I have conflicts with tend to be closed minded and never really see my point of view.
Everywhere	44	8.1	Throughout my life
			EVERYWHERE
			In everything I am sensitive
Don't Need It	36	5.34	I don't need empathy
			I think I get enough empathy from everyone in my life.
			I wouldn't, I don't need their pity.
Not Sure	29	3.13	Not sure
			idk
At Work or During Extracurricular Activities	19	2.4	I would like to be shown more empathy at my place of work. Some customers act like they've never had a bad day in their life and can't understand that I'm trying my best. In society overall, people need to be more empathetic in public.
			I would like to be shown more empathy during fast-paced games because if you mess up once your team dislikes you.
Prefer to Show to Others	17	1.84	I don't need anymore [*sic*] empathy, but a lot of others do, and I'd like to see those struggling to live receive much more empathy.
			I would like to show more empathy when someone is angry

Self-Control

Self-control requires thinking about the consequences of your actions before choosing to act and learning to monitor and self-regulate any emotional influence. This lesson covers the relationship between actions and consequences. One of the questions from the end of the lesson was, "We all have things we can work on and develop to become better. In terms of self-control, what is something you would like to begin working on and be better at?" Responses to this question can provide insight into student understanding and ability to apply what they learned by identifying where they can personally start practicing self-control.

Responses to this question were coded according to whether or not the student identified some aspect of themselves that they would like to work to improve. The first phase of coding revealed 53 students who provided unclear or irrelevant answers, and these students were excluded from remaining analysis of this question. Of the 272 remaining students, 241 (89.64%) described how they could start practicing self-control for self-improvement. Twelve students (4.41%) said they did not need to improve anything, two students (0.74%) said they were incapable of improving, and 17 students (6.25%) were uncertain. Responses from students who were able to identify a personal application of self-control included the following:

- I would like to begin working on doing stuff on time and not waiting until the last minute to do it.
- I think that I should work on thinking before I say things because you never know how it can affect someone.
- In terms of self-control, I would like to be able to express my feelings in a calm manner instead of keeping them in because I don't want to risk hurting others. I could instead let out my feelings in a way in which nobody ends up hurt.
- I need to work on my attitude, and I need to have more so control of my anger. I would like to work on this because I know I'm not the easiest person to deal with and to talk with but I really want to try to become better.
- I would like to work on my tone, attitude and word choice because when I get mad I go UP and I can get disrespectful at times
- Something I would want to get better at in terms of self-control is controlling my cravings. This is hard for me, especially since I like to give in to what I want in terms of snacks.
- I would like to work on not being so stuck to my phone all the time because it is constantly glued to me and I sometimes need a break from it and I know that but I don't stop.

Another question in the final study guide of the Self-Control lesson explicitly asked, "What has this lesson taught you about self-control that you didn't know before?" Responses to this question were coded according to whether or not the student described something new they learned. Unclear and irrelevant responses (n = 63) were identified and excluded from analysis. Of the 257 remaining students, 208 (80.93%) reported learning something new about self-control. The remaining students did not learn anything new (4.67%) or were uncertain (6.61%). The following are some examples of what students said they learned:

- You can show that you're feeling a certain way without being violent of [*sic*] letting your emotions get the best of you.

- It taught me that not having self-control in situations can lead to bad consequences.
- It taught me that you have to think before you act.
- This has taught me that you have to practice self-control to be good at it, and that everyone struggles with it.
- When im really mad i dont think about the consequences, i have too start doing that [*sic*].
- That self control isn't impossible, it just takes effort.
- Ways to cope with the frustration you are dealing with to control yourself.
- That when you have self control it reflects upon others to have self control.

Resilience

Resilience is about hard work and is a factor that influences success. This lesson highlights how resilient people have a growth mindset and view failures as valuable learning opportunities. One of the questions from the end of the lesson asked, "When you fail or do not accomplish something, how does it make you feel? How can you learn from this failure and turn this experience around to make you a better person?"

Responses to this question were coded according to whether the student described how to approach failure and mistakes in a manner conducive to learning and growth. The first phase of coding revealed 82 students who provided unclear or irrelevant answers, and these students were excluded from remaining analysis of this question. Of the 141 remaining students, 129 (91.49%) described a proactive approach to overcoming failure; 2 students (1.42%) said it was not possible or important to learn from failure or mistakes. The remaining 10 students (7.10%) were uncertain. Responses from students who explained how to approach and learn from mistakes included the following:

- You can learn from it by seeing what you did wrong and building on that. It is important to learn from them so you won't make the same mistake again.
- Think a failure is not a dead end, it is just an obstacle in the road and it is your decision to get past it or not.
- Take it as a learning experience, but it might make me feel disappointed and embarrassed depending on the circumstance, but I'll work on that as I reflect. . . . I will create solutions for the next time, keep myself positive & motivated, and make sure that I know my mistake to [avoid] doing it again, and possibly try to prevent other upcoming mishaps. Doing that will definitely make me understand what it is to be a leader, which also makes me a better person to myself and others.
- To learn from it, I can keep experimenting and find something that works and use that failure as a way for me to learn. Why? Because nobody is perfect. There WILL be bumps in every road you choose, but you have to know how to deal with them. In other words, learn to use failure as a motivation.
- Look to find out why I failed and how I could improve. You could learn from failure by working more on what you struggle with. Never give up because you'll never succeed if you stop trying. It's important to learn from mistakes so you can better yourself and succeed.

Perceived Helpfulness

Across all 20 of these lessons, 1,408 learners collectively accessed and provided helpfulness ratings for 4,064 lessons. Excluding one lesson (i.e., Tenacity), the majority of students who accessed each lesson rated the lesson as helpful. Altogether, 1,208 students (85.80%) rated at least one of the Mindsets lesson they accessed as helpful. Considering the number of accessed lessons, 3,257 (80.14%) were rated as helpful by the students who accessed them. A breakdown of helpfulness ratings and access totals for each lesson is provided in Table 10.

Table 10. Distribution of Students Across Perceived Helpfulness of Each Lesson

Lesson	Helpful		Not Helpful		Not Sure		Total
	n	%	n	%	n	%	n
Accountability	395	88.76	22	4.94	28	6.29	445
Adaptability	16	64.00	3	12.00	6	24.00	25
Building Relationships	165	79.71	42	20.29	0	0.00	207
Choose Your Path	36	70.59	15	29.41	0	0.00	51
Civic Engagement	10	83.33	1	8.33	1	8.33	12
Conflict Resolution	415	89.63	48	10.37	0	0.00	463
Digital Ethics	55	56.12	8	8.16	35	35.71	98
Digital Safety	10	55.56	4	22.22	4	22.22	18
Effective Listening	411	84.39	76	15.61	0	0.00	487
Empathy	285	58.16	61	12.45	144	29.39	490
Ethics	17	94.44	1	5.56	0	0.00	18
Heuristics	186	74.40	21	8.40	43	17.20	250
Introspection	197	81.74	44	18.26	0	0.00	241
Organization	249	82.45	34	11.26	19	6.29	302
Personal Development	206	87.29	30	12.71	0	0.00	236
Perspective	17	56.67	13	43.33	0	0.00	30
Purpose	203	87.50	29	12.50	0	0.00	232
Resilience	375	84.84	67	15.16	0	0.00	442
Systems Thinking	6	85.71	1	14.29	0	0.00	7
Tenacity	3	30.00	1	10.00	6	60.00	10

Note. This includes only the 20 Mindsets lessons that contained a helpfulness-rating study guide question (N = 1,408). Many of these students accessed and rated multiple lessons, totaling 4,064 accessed lessons and corresponding ratings.

DISCUSSION

This study's goals were to document a strategy for incorporating explicit SEL instruction in CTE at CCSD, Nevada and explore the subsequent adoption and value during the 2019–2020 school year. To explore the extent and value of adoption by CTE teachers and students, the present study analyzed usage data from both facilitators and students, and study-guide response data from students. The findings are discussed throughout this section.

Program Implementation and Usage

In the process of collaboratively designing and piloting an implementation strategy, CCSD CTE and IMAGO discovered:

- Adoption is stronger if aligned with state and district mandates. Although teachers have the best intentions and see the value, the age-old saying, "If it's not measured, it's not taught," stands true. IMAGO and CCSD CTE had success cross-walking specific lessons with Nevada standards for employability skills.
- Educators generally believed that SEL was valuable, but they often had difficulty embedding the content into more traditional subjects like math and science. A district-assigned specialist helped remove those barriers and boosted teacher usage.
- SEL requires thoughtful and intentional professional development. The more a teacher is trained, the higher their confidence to deliver content to students will be. Districts should plan for extended teacher professional development for SEL.
- Repeating and revamping the training to not only cover the content but also how to connect and implement the content in their class was key to success for teachers and IMAGO.
- Asking for feedback throughout the process was key to learning and improving the experience for both parties.

Usage data included 3,726 students who were digitally assigned IMAGO lessons by 130 teachers. Altogether, 282 teachers accessed the IMAGO platform during the 2019–2020 school year, and 2,756 students digitally accessed (i.e., at least started) 9,541 lessons. It is important to note, however, that 53.90% ($n = 152$) of these teachers never created any digital classes. Teachers had the flexibility of implementing lessons with students outside the platform by presenting the lessons from their own facilitator account. Unless facilitators who used this approach also digitally assigned lessons to those students and asked them to complete the accompanying study guide from their own account in the IMAGO platform, usage was not tracked for these students. Currently, the only way to track IMAGO lesson usage is to digitally assign lessons to students and ask them to access the lesson and its study guide from their own account. Given this, data may be missing from students who participated in lessons outside of the platform, and therefore the results provided in this report may not accurately reflect the usage and experiences of all CCSD users who engaged with IMAGO lessons.

Teacher login data can help shed some light on a more accurate summary of lesson usage but still does not paint an entirely clear picture. Of the 152 teachers who never created any digital classes in which they digitally assigned lessons to students, 130 (83.53%) logged in multiple times. Sixteen (10.53%) of these teachers with multiple logins each spent an average of between 30 minutes and an hour on the platform each time they logged in. It takes roughly an hour to facilitate a full lesson, including extension activities and conversations, but they can be partially facilitated in as little as 30 minutes if activities and conversations are assigned as preliminary or follow-up homework. Considering this, it is possible that 16 teachers used lessons with students outside of the platform. Although any teachers who implemented in

Table 11. Percentage of Students who Successfully Answered each Open-Ended Question [a]

Lesson	Question[b]	n	%
Accountability	Q1	255	88.63
Adaptability	Q2	25	76.00
Empathy	Q3	511	91.00
	Q4	587	92.16
Resilience	Q5	141	91.49
Self-Control	Q6	272	89.64
	Q7	257	80.93

Note. Sample sizes represent the total number of students who answered each question, excluding students who provided unclear or irrelevant responses. Total N = 1,033.

[a]Successful answers include students who either were able to apply lesson concepts to their own lives or provided meaningful answers to non-application questions. Questions are the seven open-ended study guide questions analyzed in the study.

[b]See Table 5 for questions.

this manner likely created a more engaging and meaningful experience for their students, it is impossible to truly discern this from the available data.

Looking specifically at the adoption of Mindsets lessons, just over 68% of teachers who digitally assigned lessons assigned Mindsets lessons. Similarly, almost 63% of students on the IMAGO platform were assigned Mindsets lessons. Almost 72% of these students accessed Mindsets lessons, but this equates to under 45% of all students on the platform. Because students must be assigned lessons in order to access them, this means that roughly 37% of students on the IMAGO platform did not have access to Mindsets, and this is consequently reflected in the relatively low access rate for these lessons. Considering that Mindsets lessons were the driving force behind CCSD's decision to utilize IMAGO, this is undesirable.

Comprehension and Value

The present study analyzed student responses to seven open-ended study guide questions spanning five different Mindsets lessons to explore student learning and ability to apply SEL concepts covered in the Mindsets lessons. Results from thematic content analyses revealed that, for each of the seven questions, most students who provided legible answers were able to interpret and apply lesson concepts to address the question in contextually appropriate and meaningful ways (see Table 11). Most of these questions were embedded in study guides at the end of lessons. Findings from these questions demonstrate that most CCSD students could analyze and apply SEL concepts covered in Mindsets lessons by the end of those lessons. Considered in conjunction with the details of the direct responses students provided, these findings provide evidence that students at least understand and reflecting on the social-emotional skills addressed in the Mindsets lessons they access by reviewing and reflecting on these concepts using metacognitive processes.

Looking specifically at results for the first Empathy question, over 90% of students identified where they would like to be shown more empathy. Combined with findings from IMAGO's preliminary exploration of the Effective Listening and Empathy lessons during the pilot years, these findings suggest that these students, in general, may not feel like they are being heard by others. When employed strategically, addressing student responses to study guide questions similar to this Empathy question can help give students more voice and feel like they are better heard. Such questions are embedded across all Mindsets lessons. Looking at results for the Accountability question, almost 89% of students identified where they could use what they learned to better hold themselves or others accountable, and most of them described a need to be better accountable at school. Teachers could use information from this and similar questions in other Mindsets lessons to identify needed skills they can help students improve.

To explore whether the concepts covered by Mindsets lessons were valuable to CCSD CTE students, the present study analyzed 20 questions from 20 different Mindsets lessons asking students to rate how helpful the lesson was. The rationale behind deducing value and relevance from helpfulness ratings was that, if an individual considers something to be useful, then it must be relevant to that person in a practical way, and things that are practical and relevant are valuable additions to one's arsenal of knowledge or other resources. Altogether, most students felt the lessons were useful, suggesting that these lesson concepts are in fact relevant and valuable to CCSD CTE students, and therefore, worthwhile to incorporate in their education. This finding coincides with literature identifying a growing need for strong social-emotional skills in the workforce (Autor et al., 2003; Casner-Lotto & Barrington, 2006; Committee for Children, 2016; Deming, 2017; Pew Research Center, 2016; Yoder et al., 2020).

Looking at individual lessons, all except one were considered useful by most of the students. Tenacity was considered *not useful* more often than *useful*. It is possible that the small sample of students who answered this question ($n = 10$) introduced bias from some shared experience that confounded results for this lesson; however, it could also be due to some shortcoming in the lesson content. Without further researching this lesson, it is not possible to conclude definitively. Several other lessons that were rated predominately as useful also included data for very few students, and many of these included helpfulness ratings from fewer than 20 students (i.e., Civic Engagement, Digital Safety, Ethics, Systems Thinking, and Tenacity). Ratings from these lessons with relatively small samples of students are more prone to bias and may not be truly representative of all students.

Aggregated results here should be considered with caution, due to variations in question content and only partial representation of all Mindsets lessons. The structure and verbiage of questions and rating scales varied across these lessons. Although they were recoded, the variations may have added nuanced meaning to seemingly similar scale anchors when isolated from other rating questions. Additionally, fewer than half of the Mindsets lessons included study guide questions asking for helpfulness ratings. Although this analysis included a considerable number of lessons spread across all SEL areas, it is possible that these lessons share some quality unique from the rest of the Mindsets lessons and may not provide an accurate representation of the value of all SEL concepts to students. For these reasons, continued use of Mindsets lessons by CCSD CTE warrants continued monitoring of the degree to which students feel they are useful.

Findings from student responses to study guide questions are promising, but it is important to note that many rely on self-report of understanding and behaviors, and the validity of using self-rating and multiple-choice assessment to gauge their development of social-emotional skills is controversial. Such approaches are subject to social-desirability bias, inaccuracy due to poor self-awareness, and primed responses when assessed quiz-style.

SOLUTIONS AND RECOMMENDATIONS FOR PRACTICE

When designing and coordinating explicit SEL instruction in a school or district, administrators and coordinators should consider the following:

- Prior to selecting an SEL solution, verify curricula content-alignment with program goals and recognized standards.
- Employ a district-assigned specialist to help with curriculum mapping, instructional coaching, and integration.
- Invest in extended training. A good rule of thumb is a 1:3 ratio of content delivery to discussion and group work during training. Iterate training as needed, and repeat the process each school year with both former and new IMAGO teachers.
- Encourage and support a blended-teaching approach.
- Clearly communicate organizational goals and expectations, providing detailed instructions explaining which lessons to use and how to use them. This can be addressed during training and should be repeated throughout the school year.
- Develop a strategy for evaluating and providing feedback on student performance that is appropriate for organizational needs and teacher capacity.
- Ask for user feedback to learn how teachers used the lessons and integrated assessment/feedback to identify opportunities to improve experiences.

Teachers should facilitate SEL lessons in a blended-teaching style—incorporating conversations about lessons and activities from facilitator guides, and asking students to digitally complete associated study guides in the platform either during or after facilitation. This ensures student-usage tracking, and has been found to support the best retention of explicit SEL (IMAGO, 2017).

Educators should evaluate and provide timely feedback on student SEL with respect to the specific topics to which they have been exposed. This can be accomplished systematically by grading study guide responses or, more effectively, by facilitating and engaging in class-wide student conversations on study guide questions from each lesson. The latter approach can provide teachers a sense of student understanding, growth, and needs, and build a path to a more harmonious and productive class culture—potentially making their jobs easier in the end. For example, many questions in the Mindsets lessons, such as those discussed from *Empathy* and *Accountability*, can serve as an opportunity to increase student voice to help students feel heard and understood, and can also help teachers identify and strategically target the skills students need to improve.

There is a promise of impact, but this will depend on the approach each teacher takes to implement. To ensure all students have equal opportunity to receive the maximum benefit from these lessons, aim to ensure their experiences are similar. Remind teachers that Mindsets lessons are only a starting point in developing students' social-emotional skills and should be accompanied by ongoing opportunities for students to practice and receive feedback.

FUTURE RESEARCH DIRECTIONS

There is a need to identify ways to integrate SEL in technical education for youth and young adults (Lippman et al., 2015), and dearth of research on the impacts of high school programming intended to develop both technical and social-emotional skills that incorporates explicit SEL (American Institutes for Research, 2015; Rosen et al., 2018). Therefore findings from this study contribute program-design guidance and initial evidence supporting explicit SEL in CTE programming to research in the fields of SEL and CCR. Because much is still unknown about best practices and the impact of explicit SEL as part of a CCR strategy, directions for future research primarily entail more rigorous investigation of the strategies and outcomes of such programming. Future studies should aim to ensure implementation approaches are either experimentally controlled or documented to help reduce the number of potentially confounding extraneous variables and allow for appropriate controls and comparisons when analyzing data. Additionally, this study lacked sufficient experimental controls to generalize findings to other students outside of this study. Future studies should try replicating this study using appropriate methodology to accommodate generalizability of findings, and compare them with those presented in this chapter.

Future research should also aim to study long-term outcomes of SEL in CTE. CTE research has neglected to investigate long-term student outcomes of CTE programs (Jacob, 2017). Furthermore, gaps in the extant literature reveal value in studying long-term influence of SEL on adult career outcomes (Deming, 2017). Comparing long-term student outcomes across CTE programs that do and do not include SEL programming would be highly valuable to the field. An additional direction for future research is to identify and design CTE-aligned SEL assessment tools and strategies that are valid and feasible for CTE teachers to use (Committee for Children, 2016; Lippman et al., 2015). These tools should accommodate rapid summarization of student skills related to the SEL lessons they completed and provide timely feedback to students connecting these skills to their CTE goals. Tools should also provide teachers with a quick way to identify common underlying needs and interests addressed within student responses. Future research should then use these tools to more robustly measure and statistically evaluate program impact.

CONCLUSION

This study sought to describe the development and incorporation of explicit SEL in CTE at CCSD, and to explore the subsequent adoption and value during the 2019–2020 school year. Usage findings reveal promising adoption by teachers and students, but also expose Mindsets usage patterns that were incongruent with CCSD's implementation objectives. Most of the findings on student comprehension and relevance of lessons emerged from study guide questions placed at the end of Mindsets lessons that ask students to demonstrate or report their understanding of the lesson topics. Findings from these questions provide evidence that most CCSD students could analyze and apply SEL concepts covered in Mindsets lessons in meaningful ways, and most students felt there was value in these lessons.

CTE educators should aim to incorporate explicit SEL instruction to better equip students for success in a manner conducive to consistent implementation of blended learning for all students. Additionally, CTE educators should design and implement a feasible approach to observe and provide timely feedback on student performance. Future research should seek to evaluate both short- and long-term outcomes of SEL in CTE. Additionally, research should identify and design realistic SEL assessment tools to enable

CTE teachers to gauge student learning and any potential needs easily and quickly. Considered as a whole, findings from the present study provide preliminary evidence that there exists realistic opportunity to improve student social-emotional skills through explicit SEL instruction in a CTE program, and there is value in student use of the IMAGO Mindsets lessons as the initial step of a strategically designed SEL and career exploration strategy to support students' college and career readiness. CTE educators should use the methods and suggestions in this chapter as guidance for incorporating SEL in a manner adapted to fit their specific program needs. Program leaders should evaluate the success of their design and iterate to address any challenges. Being in uncharted territory with many unknowns, it is important that program leaders disseminate their experiences in order to support future research and practice that will further enhance our understanding and ability to lead students toward a path to success.

ACKNOWLEDGMENT

We want to extend gratitude to Snehal Bhakta and from CCSD and his educators using IMAGO, our friends and colleagues from IMAGO, our supportive friends and family, and those who contributed to this chapter: Dalia Haitayan, Melissa Murphy, Edgar Blunt, and Simran Nagra. This research received no specific grant from any funding agency in the public, commercial, or not-for-profit sectors.

REFERENCES

American Institutes for Research. (2015). *Ready for work? How afterschool programs can support employability through social and emotional learning*. https://www.air.org/sites/default/files/downloads/report/Afterschool-Programs-Support-Employability-Brief-Dec-2015.pdf

Autor, D. H., Levy, F., & Murnane, R. J. (2003). The skill content of recent technological change: An empirical exploration. *The Quarterly Journal of Economics*, *118*(4), 1279–1333. doi:10.1162/003355303322552801

Casner-Lotto, J., & Barrington, L. (2006). *Are they really ready to work? Employers' perspectives on the basic knowledge and applied skills of new entrants to the 21st century US workforce*. Partnership for 21st Century Skills. https://files.eric.ed.gov/fulltext/ED519465.pdf

Clark County School District. (2020). *Pocket guide: A little book about all of the big things happening in the Clark County School District—2019–2020*. https://newsroom.ccsd.net/wp-content/uploads/CCSD-Pocket-Guide-January-2020.pdf

Clark County School District. (n.d.a). *About Clark County School District*. https://teachvegas.ccsd.net/our-district/about-clark-county-school-district/

Clark County School District. (n.d.b). *Career and technical education*. https://www.ccsd.net/departments/career-technical-education/

Collaborative for Academic, Social, and Emotional Learning. (2020). *CASEL'S SEL framework*. https://casel.org/wp-content/uploads/2020/12/CASEL-SEL-Framework-11.2020.pdf

Committee for Children. (2016). *Why social and emotional learning and employability skills should be prioritized in education.* https://www.cfchildren.org/wp-content/uploads/policy-advocacy/sel-employability-brief.pdf

Deming, D. J. (2017). The growing importance of social skills in the labor market. *The Quarterly Journal of Economics, 132*(4), 1593–1640. doi:10.1093/qje/qjx022

Durlak, J. A., Weissberg, R. P., Dymnicki, A. B., Taylor, R. D., & Schellinger, K. B. (2011). The impact of enhancing students' social and emotional learning: A meta-analysis of school-based universal interventions. *Child Development, 82*(1), 405–432. doi:10.1111/j.1467-8624.2010.01564.x PMID:21291449

Dusenbury, L., Dermody, C., & Weissberg, R. P. (2018). *State scorecard scan.* CASEL. https://casel.org/wp-content/uploads/2018/09/csi-scorecard-sept2018.pdf

Harvard Graduate School of Education. (n.d.). *About SEL.* Explore SEL. http://exploresel.gse.harvard.edu/about/

IMAGO. (2017). *Duncan mindsets pilot.* IMAGO.

Jacob, B. A. (2017). *What we know about career and technical education in high school.* https://www.brookings.edu/research/what-we-know-about-career-and-technical-education-in-high-school/

Johnson, H., & Wiener, R. (2017). *This time, with feeling: Integrating social and emotional development and college- and career-readiness standards.* Aspen Institute. https://eric.ed.gov/?id=ED577037

Jones, S., Bailey, R., Brush, K., Nelson, B., & Barnes, S. (2016). *What is the same and what is different? Making sense of the "non-cognitive" domain.* Harvard Graduate School of Education, EASEL Lab. https://easel.gse.harvard.edu/files/gse-easel-lab/files/words_matter_paper.pdf

Kerr, D. B., Madden-Dent, T., & Shalabi, N. (2020). Cultural competency interventions. In The Oxford Handbook of Lifelong Learning. Academic Press.

Lippman, L., Ryberg, R., Carney, R., & Moore, K. (2015). *Key "soft skills" that foster youth workforce success: Toward a consensus across fields.* Child Trends. https://www.childtrends.org/publications/key-soft-skills-that-foster-youth-workforce-success-toward-a-consensus-across-fields

Manyika, J., Lund, S., Chui, M., Bughin, J., Woetzel, J., Batra, P., Ko, R., & Sanghvi, S. (2017). *Jobs lost, jobs gained: Workforce transitions in a time of automation.* McKinsey Global Institute. https://www.mckinsey.com/~/media/McKinsey/Industries/Public%20and%20Social%20Sector/Our%20Insights/What%20the%20future%20of%20work%20will%20mean%20for%20jobs%20skills%20and%20wages/MGI-Jobs-Lost-Jobs-Gained-Executive-summary-December-6-2017.pdf

Pew Research Center. (2016). *The state of American jobs.* https://www.pewsocialtrends.org/2016/10/06/the-state-of-american-jobs/

Rainie, L., & Anderson, J. (2017). *The future of jobs and jobs training.* https://www.pewresearch.org/internet/wp-content/uploads/sites/9/2017/05/PI_2017.05.03_Future-of-Job-Skills_FINAL.pdf

Rosen, R., Visher, M., & Beal, K. (2018). *Career and technical education: Current policy, prominent programs, and evidence.* MDRC. https://eric.ed.gov/?id=ED590008

Taylor, R. D., Oberle, E., Durlak, J. A., & Weissberg, R. P. (2017). Promoting positive youth development through school-based social and emotional learning interventions: A meta-analysis of follow-up effects. *Child Development*, *88*(4), 1156–1171. doi:10.1111/cdev.12864 PMID:28685826

U.S. Department of Education, Office of Career, Technical, and Adult Education. (2012). *Employability skills framework*. https://s3.amazonaws.com/PCRN/docs/Employability_Skills_Framework_OnePager_20180212.pdf

World Economic Forum. (2020). *The future of jobs report*. http://www3.weforum.org/docs/WEF_Future_of_Jobs_2020.pdf

Yoder, N., Atwell, M. N., Godek, D., Dusenbury, L., Bridgeland, J. M., & Weissberg, R. (2020). *Preparing youth for the workforce of tomorrow: Cultivating the social and emotional skills employers demand*. Collaborative for Academic, Social, and Emotional Learning. https://casel.org/wp-content/uploads/2020/06/Preparing-Youth-for-the-Workforce-of-Tomorrow-Final.pdf

KEY TERMS AND DEFINITIONS

Accountability: The fact or condition of being accountable; responsibility.

Adaptability: The quality of being able to adjust to new conditions.

Career Technical Education (CTE): Programs involve a multiyear sequence of courses that integrate core academic subjects with career-specific technical and occupational knowledge.

College and Career Readiness (CCR): Ensures students graduate from high school prepared to enter and succeed in postsecondary opportunities—whether college or career—without need for remediation. To be college and career ready, students must graduate with the knowledge, skills, and dispositions necessary to succeed.

Emotional Intelligence (EI): As defined by Peter Salovey, John Mayer, and others, one's ability to understand oneself and others in order to think, behave, and navigate one's surroundings in ways that are contextually appropriate.

Empathy: The ability to understand and share the feelings of another.

Facilitator Guides: Documents accompanying each Mindsets lesson that identify the lesson objectives, and include think-ahead questions, discussion questions, activities, and additional resources to help teachers explain the topics.

Resilience: The capacity to recover quickly from difficulties; toughness.

Self-Control: The ability to control oneself, in particular, one's emotions, desires, or behaviors resulting from them, especially in difficult situations.

Social and Emotional Learning (SEL): The process of acquiring knowledge and developing self-awareness, social awareness, global awareness, self-management, relationship skills, and ethical decision-making.

Chapter 14
Developing Social Emotional Learning Competencies Through Virtual Internships

Daniel Basil Kerr
St. Joseph's College, USA

Tom Gore
Kaya Responsible Travel, UK

ABSTRACT

This chapter explores the experiences of four virtual interns working with organizations tackling social issues in Ecuador, Morocco, South Africa, and Vietnam. These internships provided a unique opportunity to develop and apply the social, emotional, and academic development (SEAD) competencies of self-awareness, self-management, social awareness, relationship skills, and responsible decision-making. Schlossberg's transition theory provides a framework for transitioning to another culture and cultural mapping is used as a tool to identify, plan, and mitigate differences in cultural orientations between interns and colleagues in their host countries. The chapter draws upon student narratives and reflections, and supervisor feedback to capture what they learned and the challenges they faced as they completed their virtual internships. The results contribute to the literature related to the development of SEAD competencies through virtual internships for high school and college students.

MITIGATING AN UNANTICIPATED CHANGE IN PLANS

A young female university student from Michigan was signed up for a medical internship in Morocco. She was to be based in the maternity ward of a hospital in the city of Rabat, beginning in May 2020. All of the arrangements were confirmed in February. Once the Covid-19 pandemic was declared by the WHO in March, her school banned all international travel for students and Morocco closed its borders to all international visitors shortly thereafter.

DOI: 10.4018/978-1-7998-6728-9.ch014

She first contacted a European-based internship company in early 2019 and began planning her internship in September. The cancellation of her internship was a tremendous disappointment as she was "looking forward to it immensely." Once this disappointment set in, she asked the company she was working with if there were any virtual alternatives available. When she found out the company had recently begun offering virtual internships, and explored the alternatives available, she chose not to join a virtual placement in Morocco but selected one in Vietnam instead. She told the company she "had every intention to still physically complete her internship in Morocco in the future once this is possible, and wanted to experience a different culture as part of her virtual internship experience."

While this young woman would have ideally liked to travel abroad for her internship placement, she had been thinking through alternative options for her internship experience. The virtual internship still allowed her to join a placement related to her studies, and through a variety of experiences planned for her by the company, she would the learn about the culture of Vietnam virtually. Later in this chapter we will illustrate her virtual internship experience.

THE IMPACT OF THE COVID-19 PANDEMIC ON THE INTERNATIONAL INTERNSHIP MARKET

The COVID-19 pandemic has affected many industries worldwide, with nearly every organization seeing the pandemic's impact on their business operations in one way or another. Many businesses experienced adverse effects from the pandemic due to disrupted business operations, demand for products, and supply chains worldwide. Many businesses have experience reduced demand for their services, lowering revenues, net incomes, and the businesses' overall financial condition (Elleby et al., 2020). The pandemic has disrupted lives, businesses, economic health and pushed the healthcare system to its limits. "The economic crisis is unprecedented in its scale: the pandemic has created a demand shock, a supply shock, and a financial shock all at once" (Bauer, 2020).

Prior to the Covid-19 pandemic, the International Internship market had been a growing field over the past few years. Especially in the US, over the past few years an increasing number of students have been looking to join international internships in a variety of different fields to gain practical experience. More and more colleges in the US have also been encouraging and/or requiring students to join international internship placements, so that they can gain practical experience to complement their studies also grow through working in a new cultural setting.

Students from some colleges in the US are also able to gain academic credit for doing an internship abroad, so this is another factor for increased interest in this area. That, coupled with increasing host communities requesting interns with experience in a specific area, has resulted in more companies moving into the International Internship market.

With travel coming to a standstill in March 2020 because of the Covid-19 pandemic, the proceeding months have seen many international internship organizations trying to move their programs online. Some organizations have not been able to adapt to this sudden change, and 2020 has seen some of them go out of business as a result. Perhaps the biggest example of was this was STA Travel, as an organization that offered various types of travel experiences, including both international internship and volunteer programs to customers, and the ability to book flights through them. Because of their dependence on in-person travel and offering flights in particular, the business went into insolvency in August 2020, only a few months after the pandemic began.

As of December 2020, the number of travel organizations that have moved most of their programs online, temporarily at least, is evident when looking for online internship opportunities online. The travel directory website GoOverseas.com, for example, lists 75 different program options for virtual internships. While another travel directory website, GoAbroad.com, lists 258 different virtual programs. This shows how many different travel organizations have had to adapt by diversifying and moving their programs online and keep supporting local communities in alternative ways. Travel organizations now offering virtual internships for the first time including organisations such as CIS Abroad, BSAE (Barcelona Study Abroad), GVI (Global Vision International) and Intern Abroad HQ.

Companies are offering a variety of virtual internship experiences. For example, while some virtual internships focus mostly or only on the placement itself, other virtual programs offer more cultural components that complement that placement and encourage further learning alongside their internship to make the most out of their experience. Usually, an in-person intern would research the culture and history of the country they were travelling to and then be immersed in that culture by being in the country during their internship in ways such as, for example, staying with a host family, working with locals during their placement, as well as interacting with locals during their free time.

It is harder to develop SEAD competencies virtually because virtual interns are often working from home and do not have the environment and culture of their virtual internship country physically around them day-to-day. This is why implementing cultural components into the virtual experience such as the GlobeSmart training, cultural workshop and buddy chat reflections are even more important to make sure that virtual interns are engaged, are learning about the culture and their placement in an international context, and are developing their cross cultural skills.

SEAD competencies are especially important in a virtual realm given some of the challenges that come about on a virtual program that would not be as much of an issue during a traditional in-country internship (e.g., time zone difference, not meeting people in-person, technical difficulties).

VIRTUAL INTERNSHIPS

In "normal times," internships in other countries provide high school and college students during their "gap year" (i.e., a year between high school and college or after graduating from college) or during summer breaks and/or between semesters, an opportunity to develop and apply the Social, and Emotional Learning (SEL) competencies of self-awareness; self-management; social awareness; relationship skills; and responsible decision-making. This chapter illustrates the experiences of four virtual interns at one of the leading firms in the International Internship market.

Since 2008, Kaya Responsible Travel has arranged sustainable volunteering projects and internships in 27 countries across Africa, Asia-Pacific, and Latin America. Kaya's mission is to promote sustainable social, environmental and economic development, empower communities and cultivate educated, compassionate global citizens through responsible travel.

The mission of Kaya Responsible Travel is deeply rooted in the experience of their founder. During a gap year trip to Thailand in 2004, she was fortunate enough to make a last-minute change to her itinerary which resulted in her not being on the beaches of Thailand, as planned, for the Christmas holidays. She arrived just two days after the world's deadliest tsunami killed 230,000 people and worked for four months as a volunteer with a Thai NGO in the town of Khao Lak, one of Thailand's worst hit regions. These were the most emotional, memorable, impactful and immersive travel experiences of her life. From her experience, she wanted others to have the chance to do the same and Kaya Responsible Travel was born. Kaya is a word that has many meanings in number of countries where they arrange their unique types of internships. In the Waray language of the Philippines it means "I can do it!" In the Zulu language of South Africa, it means "my spiritual home." The Trikaya symbol Kaya uses as its logo is a Buddhist symbol that means "the enlightened body" (Kaya Responsible Travel, 2020).

Kaya has been a finalist for "Best Volunteering Organisation" at the British Youth Travel every year since 2012, and has won the gold award on two occasions. They have also been listed for International Business of the Year at the E3 Business Awards, which celebrates diversity of business across the Northwest of England, Green Match's 2017 Sustainable Voluntourism Award, which promotes the top 'Eco-Traveling Enthusiasts', and in 2020 they were listed for GoAbroad's Innovative New Program (Volunteer) award, for their Enchanted Forest Art Therapy Volunteering Program in Belize.

In response to the recent Covid-19 travel restrictions, Kaya joined with its community partners in Ecuador, Morocco, South Africa and Vietnam to offer virtual internships that support capacity-building projects for organizations tackling social or environmental issues in their local communities. These internships are all community-driven, and they are eager to engage with students remotely so that they continue to progress the great work they have been doing.

These interns join interactive weekly cultural workshops led by Kaya's In-Country Directors and are also paired with a "local buddy" eager to share their culture and learn about the culture of the virtual interns. The cultural workshops provide instant connections to local people who invited them behind closed doors and into the day-to-day lives of the local people. They learn about the cuisine, music, and cultural traditions, and also get to know the culture on a deeper level, understanding both personal and professional relationships in the context of their host country (Kaya Responsible Travel, 2020).

These virtual internships are aligned with Kaya's mission to promote sustainable social, environmental, and economic development and provided the students with relevant cross-cultural work experience that would improve their future job prospects and also make a long-lasting impact in a community in their host country.

With the world going virtual in the wake of Covid-19, many schools and businesses are bringing work and learning online. To keep up with these changes, it is especially important for students to learn effective virtual work methods. These virtual internships provide a valuable experience of virtual work in their field of interest in which expectations were set and guidance provided by remote supervisors and mentors. Each intern had the opportunity to work on a special project from start to finish and to enhance their teamwork, organization, and time management skills.

Working virtually with colleagues in another country provides even more opportunities for employable skills. The experiences of working with a variety of cultures, work styles, and languages differentiates a resume. For example, a "Marketing Internship with Ecuadorian Company" sounds more impressive than a "Marketing Internship;" it tells a future employer that a job candidate has the ability to adjust, adapt and collaborate.

SCHLOSSBERG'S TRANSITION THEORY

Nancy Schlossberg described Transition Theory as any event or non-event that results in changed relationships, routines, assumptions, and roles. The theory identifies three types: anticipated, unanticipated, and nonevents. Anticipated transitions are predictable and would include, graduating from high school or embarking on a virtual internship like the four students in this chapter. Unanticipated transitions are unpredictable changes, such as death of a family member, or a friend, or the restrictions put in place to control the coronavirus. Under this theory, nonevents occur when something we expected, does not occur, like going abroad for an internship during a gap year. (Goodman, Schlossberg, & Anderson, 2006).

Transition theory provides a framework for how individuals go through transition. This is referred to as "taking stock" as individuals evaluate their situation, their support, themselves, and their strategies (Chickering & Schlossberg, 1995). p. 49). As the virtual interns in this chapter experienced, transition does not depend on any one of these factors, and they will make the transition to working with another culture with both resources and deficits which can change over time. Taking stock includes the "4Ss" of Situation, Self, Support and Strategies (Evans, Forney, & Guido-DiBrito, 1998).

Situation refers to how an individual assesses the transition in terms of its impact, timing, type, and onset. Self refers to the strengths and weaknesses individuals have as they begin their transition, reflective of their previous experience, their feeling of empowerment, the control they can expect of their situation, and their level of optimism. Support describes the help and guidance that is available to them from work colleagues, family members, organizations, etc., during the transition. Strategies relate to the ability to develop coping strategies, change their way of looking sat a situation, managing stress and emotions during transition, and remaining flexible through transition (Chickering & Schlossberg, 1995; Schlossberg, 1990).

Transition Theory also describes three stages of transition: "moving in," the point when individuals are faced with a transition or change; "moving through," the period in which individuals cope with the transition, and "moving out," the end of the transition cycle (Chickering & Schlossberg, 1995; Evans et al., 1998; Goodman et al., 2006).

Guided by Transition Theory (Evans et al., 1998), a recent Oxford University Press case study illustrated how engaging Asian university students in volunteer work with community service not-for-profit organizations were an effective strategy to facilitate their transition into Canadian culture. Although the case was before Covid-19 pandemic, the authors suggested additional research be done to identify the attributes of effective service-learning programs for international students as well as explore other strategies for enabling them to attain learning experiences to help them successfully navigate the cultural challenges of work and study in other countries (Kerr, Madden-Dent & Shalabi, 2020).

This chapter explores whether virtual internships with organizations tackling social issues in Ecuador, Morocco, South Africa, and Vietnam can have a similar impact on interns working remotely with colleagues in these countries.

SOCIAL, EMOTIONAL, AND ACADEMIC DEVELOPMENT

The Aspen Institute (2019) described Social, Emotional, and Academic Development (SEAD) as the integration of social-emotional learning (SEL) and academics that reinforces equitable and human-centered educational environments. SEAD has been linked with cultural competencies, linguistic skills, and academic success (Madden-Dent, 2014).

To be successful, students working on internships abroad, whether traditional or virtual, need to develop and apply the five competencies identified by the Collaborative for Academic, Social, and Emotional Learning (CASEL, 2017): Self-Awareness; Self-Management; Social Awareness; Relationship Skills; Responsible Decision-Making. The chart below school provides a summary and description of these competencies.

Figure 1.

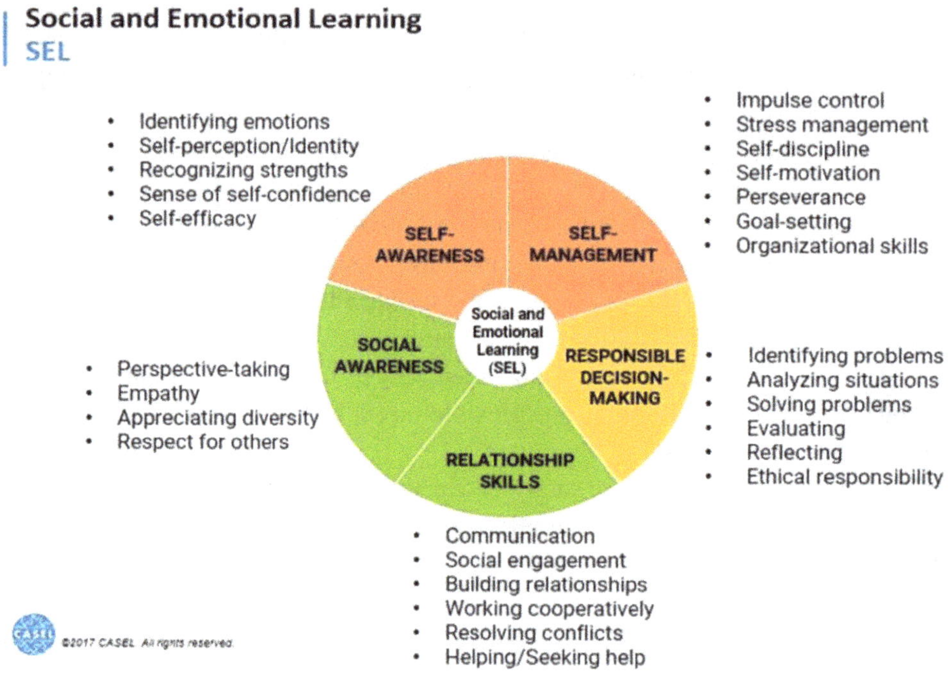

Throughout their virtual internships, each of the four students examined their own cultural orientations (Self-Awareness) before comparing/contrasting those to the norms of their host country (Social-Awareness), developed strategies to bridge cultural and language differences with their foreign work colleagues (Relationship Skills), managed stressful workplace situations (Self-Management Skills), and set and attempted to achieve specific goals during their eight-week virtual internships (Responsible Decision-Making).

CULTURAL MAPPING

Both theorists (Hofstede, 1980; Kluckhohn and Strodtbeck, 1961 Trompenaars & Hampden-Turner, 1998) and practitioners (Hall, 1960; Marquart & Engel, 1993) have described culture as having many layers, much like an onion. It is what is at the center of the "onion," that which we cannot see when encountering people from another culture, that has the biggest impact on behavior. The outer layers of culture include symbols (e.g., words, gestures, pictures), heroes (persons, real or imagined that serve as role models), and rituals (e.g., ways of greeting, social and religious ceremonies). The inner layer is formed of values and underlying assumptions that are not easily understood by others from a dissimilar culture and are most resistant to change. They are taught to the young and most children have their basic value system established at a young age as reflected by Hofstede (2001, p. 36) who stated, "Thence my assumption that by age ten, maximally twelve, a young person's mental programs, especially his or her values, are firmly in place and unlikely to change even if that person migrates to another culture later."

Due to this ingrained value system, miscommunication and conflict can easily occur when first encountering people from different cultures. These differences introduce several incompatible practices related to academics, communication and interaction styles, health, safety, legal practices, and workplace behaviors. Students and employees of all ages are likely to encounter values very different than their own when they work or study in a culture different than the one they grew up in.

When traveling to another city or country, it is often useful to have a map to help you find your way. In the arena of culture, several cultural maps have emerged. In "The Silent Language of Overseas Business" (Hall, 1960) identified the cultural dimensions of Time, Space, Things, Friendships, and Agreements that guide cultural differences. Kluckhohn and Strodtbeck (1961) developed the Cultural Orientations Framework after analyzing ethnographic descriptions of many countries and identified challenges faced by all cultures: Relation to the Environment, Relationships Among People, Mode of Normal Activity, Orientation to time, Belief About Human Nature, and Use of Space.

Hofstede founded and managed the Personnel Research Department of IBM Europe in the 1960s. During this period, he had access to IBM's employee survey which surveyed equivalent, stratified samples of workers in many countries. The IBM survey included 32 items that Hofstede described as work-related values. He analyzed the results of each nation-sample. Through correlation and factor analysis, he identified four dimensions which he used to map the values of nations (Hofstede, 1980): Individualism, Power Distance, Uncertainty Avoidance, and Masculinity. Years later, he added a fifth value: Confucian Dynamism (Hofstede, 1997). This empirical mapping of major nations of the world galvanized social scientists and made Hofstede one of the most often cited social scientists of all time. As Bond (2002, p. 73) observed, "Hofstede had mapped the values of nations much as former Dutch explorers had mapped the geography of terra incognita." Several other researchers built upon Hofstede's work. For example, the GLOBE project (Global Leadership and Organizational Behavior Effectiveness) extended Hofstede's work across other organizations and countries (Javidan et.al., 2004) and identified nine cultural dimensions. Schwartz developed another map that focused on the individual's interaction with society (Sagiv and Schwartz, 2000). Kerr and Madden-Dent (2019) demonstrated the successful application of cultural mapping in pre-departure training for East Asian undergraduate students preparing for study in the United States.

Lane and Maznevski (2019) recently reviewed and summarized several of the more well-known cultural maps currently in use, and stated (p. 62) "When we map cultures for mindful international management, we find the GlobeSmart tool provides the best combination of validity and practical application. The Cronbach's Alpha reliability scores of all five of the GlobeSmart dimensions exceed 0.70 (Doherty, 2016). The GlobeSmart Profile (GSP) is summarized below and integrated into two of the case studies in this chapter.

Research by The Georgetown Consortium Project (Vande Berg, Connor-Linton, & Paige, 2009) shows that it is not the amount of knowledge one has about cultures, the time spent engaging with people in country, or even learning a new language that increase a person's cultural competence. It is the intentional, persistent and focused attention of a person's self-reflection on their learning over time, that leads to greater understanding and competence.

The GSP provides a valuable point of self-reflection for learning to interact with different cultures. In addition to the GSP, the GlobeSmart platform includes just-in-time cultural briefings on 97 countries and several self-directed learning programs focused on cultural competence. It is a cultural intelligence tool that helps individuals understand their own preferences and tendencies for interacting with others, and allows for comparisons with other individuals, groups they may belong to, as well as with other countries. The GSP also provides specific recommendations to users on ways to enhance their effectiveness interaction with others that have different cultural orientations.

The GSP is intended to stimulate discussions about the impact of culture on our preferred style of engaging with others. It is comprised of five dimensions that compare the following phenomena that are found in all cultures. Based on a brief survey, participants receive a personalized report that shows where they fall on each of the dimensions summarized below (Doherty, 2016).

Table 1. GlobeSmart Cultural Dimensions

The individualism/collectivism dimension focuses on how do we derive our identity?	
Independent	**Interdependent**
Place great importance on individual identity Derive identity from personal choices and achievements Prefer taking action on their own	Place great importance on group harmony and cooperation Derive identity from group affiliation Feel a sense of duty, obligation to ascribed groups
The egalitarianism/status dimension compares what are our preferences for how our groups should be structured and power should be distributed?	
Egalitarianism	Status
Comfortable challenging the views of superiors Flexible about roles Treat everyone the same Assume power and authority should be shared broadly among a group	Prefer not to challenge those above Deferential to superiors Adapt behavior depending on relative status Assume power and authority should be reserved for a few members of a group
The risk/certainty dimensions examine how do we make decisions in uncertain or ambiguous situations?	
Risk	Certainty
Prefer rapid decision-making and quick results Place great importance on flexibility and initiative Value speed over thoroughness	Spend significant time on background research Establish proper procedures before starting a project Value thoroughness over speed
The direct or indirect dimension compares how do I communicate requests, tasks, and feedback?	
Direct	Indirect
Come to the point quickly Forthright in asking questions in most settings Comfortable making requests, giving direction, or disagreeing with others Give negative feedback directly	Spend time explaining the context before coming to the point Avoid asking questions in public settings Express disagreement in subtle ways Give negative feedback indirectly
The task/relationship dimension compares when working on new projects, do I prefer to address tasks first, or relationships first?	
Task	Relationship
Place high values on reaching goals and objectives on schedule Prioritize accomplishing tasks over maintaining relationships Focus on what people achieve more than who they know	View time building relationships as key to achieving good results Prioritize maintaining relationships over accomplishing tasks on time Focus on who people know as much as what they themselves can achieve

Although the interns in this chapter worked in their own homes, and were physically surrounded by a familiar environment, they were all worked with a very different culture; and to be effective they needed to develop the skills to help bridge these differences. This chapter describes the experiences of four virtual interns. They all worked remotely for eight weeks and were expected to work between 15 and 30 hours per week.

Kaya was aware of how GlobeSmart had been used for in-person internships and found it useful in setting expectations and reducing culture shock. When Kaya shifted to a virtual space, the company concluded the need for cultural understanding and the ability to style switch (i.e., suppress your own cultural preference and demonstrate the preference of your host culture) was even more important as there would be less opportunity to "naturally soak up the local culture." It positioned GlobeSmart as a just-in-time resource for interns as they encountered challenges working virtually; the company sought to empower interns to start a respectful discussion around the differences in cultures.

Kaya used GlobeSmart to teach the virtual interns about their own working style (SEL Skill: Self-Awareness). By completing the survey and seeing their Profile, virtual interns learn more about their working style and can compare that with the country profile of their remote internship (SEL Skill: Social Awareness). They saw their colleagues' potential work styles and how to navigate those differences should they arise (SEL Skill: Relationship Skill).

Additionally, Kaya shared the student's Profiles with the interns' local organizations so that they, too, could learn about the student's work style. Virtual interns research their internship destination through the Culture Guides on GlobeSmart, particularly the "Core Knowledge," "Communication," "Relationship Building," "Local Business Environment," and "Protocol" sections.

Students found it helpful to compare GlobeSmart cultural profiles. They saw where the most significant differences would likely be and could keep them in mind as they went through their internship. For example, students who knew they are very task-oriented and rigid in their schedules needed to adjust to work cultures that were more organic and relaxed. Knowing this ahead of time and helped set expectations and helped mitigate negativity or workplace frustration. For example, recent feedback from three virtual interns - two in South Africa, and one in Morocco is illustrative of insights provided through GlobeSmart.

"I found it very interesting to compare my profile to South Africa's work culture. I also liked reading the cultural guide - these elements really helped me to prepare for my internship."

"The comparison between the work styles of South Africa and my own was actually super helpful, especially after I have gradually been able to observe them at play within my own internship."

"I loved the rating scale (directness vs. indirectness, etc.) and found this component to be the most useful working with Moroccan colleagues!"

Kaya recommended interns use the GlobeSmart comparison tool and looking through the country profiles. The company believes it is essential to get a well-rounded view of the country and culture, including history, climate, social norms, and traditions, etc.

Additionally, Kaya recommended that students explore GlobeSmart before they start their internships to help them get over their nerves, and instead, get excited about working in a different culture.

FOUR CASE STUDIES

The experiences of the four virtual internships are more fully described in the sections that follow. The researchers prepared dossiers for each of the four virtual interns. They reviewed the interns' reflective journals, feedback received from the organizations the students were placed with, as well as the feedback the students themselves submitted to Kaya during and after their placement. They extracted unedited quotes from each of the four interns relevant to the SEAD competencies and Schlosberg's Transition theory. After reviewing the dossiers, the researchers searched for examples of how each of the four interns demonstrated growth in each of the five SEAD competency areas and any linkages between the challenges they faced and the comparison of their GlobeSmart profile to that of their host country.

Virtual Intern #1

Virtual Intern #1 was a female university student from Indiana. She was placed with an organization that has several health centers in Quito, Ecuador and some rural communities; they take health services to their territories, training them on sexual education and reproductive health, family planning, female empowerment, responsible paternity, and more.

This is an institution with a long history of providing comprehensive services in sexual and reproductive health, training and research, with a rights-based approach, applying quality standards, to meet the needs of the population and contribute to the country's development. The Foundation has 23 multi-service centers located in urban, marginal urban and rural areas in 10 provinces of Ecuador and a central government office. The medical centers include medical care with multiple services, such as gynecology, prenatal care, pediatrics, family planning, and other specialties; there are also complementary services, clinical laboratory, ultrasound, colonoscopy, dentistry, first aid kits and comprehensive community development programs, aimed especially at priority groups such as adolescents, mothers, children and families in the middle and poor sectors.

Interns at this organization work do related to Family planning, Early Detection of Cervical and Breast Cancer at impoverished rural communities, HIV, Domestic Violence, Infant Mortality, Maternal Mortality, Morning-after Emergency Contraceptive Pill for proper use, and Post - Abortion care.

When the Virtual Intern #1 compared her GlobeSmart profile to the norms for Ecuador, she discovered both similarities and differences in cultural orientations.

Table 2. **GlobeSmart Dimension**

Intern #1	Ecuador
Interdependent	Interdependent
Egalitarianism	Status
Certainty	Certainty
Direct	Indirect
Task	Relationship

Intern #1's preference for Egalitarianism over Status would likely raise some challenges for her working virtually with colleagues from Ecuador. While she would be comfortable challenging the views of superiors and would be flexible about roles, her work colleagues would likely be deferential to superiors and adapt their behavior depending on relative status of who they were interacting with.

Her preference for Direct over Indirect would likely raise some challenges for her working virtually with colleagues from Ecuador. While she would naturally be comfortable getting to the point quickly, making requests, giving direction, disagreeing with others, and giving negative feedback directly, her hosts would be more concerned with context, avoid asking questions in group settings, express disagreement in subtle ways, and prefer to give negative feedback indirectly.

Intern #1's preference for Task over Relationship would likely raise some challenges for her working virtually with colleagues from Ecuador. While she places high values on reaching goals, staying on schedule, and completing tasks; her Ecuadorian colleagues view time building relationships as key to achieving good results and prioritize maintaining relationships over accomplishing tasks on time.

Virtual Intern #1 developed educational and communication materials (brochures, videos), supplementary proposals on sexual and reproductive health, and a flow chart for better care in case of sexual violation.

The following unedited quotes were extracted from her reflective journal.

"I loved the not-for-profit I worked with. This organization focuses on sexual and reproductive health education, which fit perfectly for me because I am very interested in public health."

"I liked the cultural workshops! While it was nothing like what it would be like if we had been able to travel in-country, it was a great substitute!"

"It was difficult to talk to my buddy because she often did not respond."

"My favorite element of the remote internship experience were my bi-weekly meetings with my project supervisors."

"My greatest achievement was completing two funding proposals, while also designing a campaign to help reduce the levels of teen pregnancy in Ecuador."

"The main challenges I encountered during this internship were with technical difficulties and communication issues, but they were often easily fixed."

"Looking back, I do feel like I accomplished these goals. While working remotely is never ideal, and I would have preferred to be physically in Ecuador, I made many great connections with the other workers and also learned a lot to help advance my professional goals this summer."

"The advice I would give to someone who has the same nerves about a language barrier and doubts their language skills is to just go for it. Everyone is super understanding about the fact that learning a second language is very difficult and are very helpful with translations, so do not let your nerves hold you back!"

"I think my greatest strength during this internship was my willingness to be uncomfortable and try new things. I was very out of my comfort zone learning about some of these topics all while speaking in a non-native language, but I faced the challenge head on and had a great time doing it."

"A difficult challenge I faced during this internship was with a lack of clarity of instructions on assignments. The instructions I was given for assignments were fairly vague every week, and combining that with the instructions all being in a non-native language made it difficult at first for me to know exactly what my supervisors expected me to accomplish. I overcame this barrier, however, simply by asking for information. Sending explicit emails to my supervisors allowed them to realize where they were being unclear, as well as allowed me to gain a greater understanding of the type of deliverables they were expecting."

"A unique thing that I learned while working in a cross-cultural setting was that there are different taboos in Ecuador than there are in the United States when dealing with sexual and reproductive health. I learned that talking with your parents about your sexual and reproductive health is seen as a very awkward thing and would not be discussed without judgement, which is something I have never experienced here in the United States."

"While working in a remote setting I learned how to deal with unforeseen complications, such as Wi-Fi trouble and difficulty connecting to Zoom meetings. I also learned what type of work environment and schedule work best for me, as I am most productive in the morning and tend to procrastinate more if I save my work for later in the day."

"All of my meetings during this internship were conducted in Spanish, and thus I boosted my Spanish proficiency immensely throughout the internship. The fact that my meetings were all in a different language also allowed me to improve my active listening skills, as if I spaced out and did not pay attention I would miss out on information."

"I have always been eager to learn more about other cultures and experience different ways of life, but I think this internship greatly boosted, not my willingness to do this, but my understanding of different work styles and cultural life. This internship gave me great insight into what a typical work day/ schedule look like in Ecuador vs. in the United States, and this will prove extremely helpful in my pursuit of international work for the future."

"One of the best things I gained from this internship was being able to be comfortable in asking and receiving help from others. At the beginning of my work, I was extremely wary of asking for clarification on instructions or help in any way, as I perceived that to be a sign of weakness or ignorance. As the internship progressed, however, I began to realize that asking questions to others is a part of working with a team, and became much more comfortable in approaching my supervisors for the help I needed to ensure that I was turning in the best deliverables I could."

"This Covid-19 pandemic and the subsequent internship I procured during it allowed me to develop a great sense of humor during stressful and unexpected situations. There are very few things in life we can control, and one of those things is our attitude in the way we approach things. While it is unfortunate when plans get cancelled and things change unexpectedly, there is no point in being angry over things we cannot control. We simply must put a smile on our face and focus on what we can control to succeed."

After interviewing Intern #1 and reviewing her reflective journals, the Kaya Responsible Travel placement manager observed linkages between the challenges the intern faced resulting from their cultural profile and the hosts country.

Intern #1's preference for direct over indirect is demonstrated in how she encountered some challenges with vague directions and unclear translations from Spanish to English during her virtual internship, "but nothing that couldn't be fixed upon further questioning." Intern #1 also mentioned when she was unclear with instructions or any assignments, "she would send explicit emails to her supervisors allowing them to where they were being unclear" confirming she was direct in her communication style and less concerned with status and challenging her supervisors if there was a lack of direction when she was given a task.

While much of Intern #1's feedback was focused on the work and tasks she did as part of her internship placement, which suggests her preference for task over relationship, interestingly she mentioned that her favorite element of the remote internship was her bi-weekly meetings with her project supervisors, suggesting she was able to develop her relationship skills and really valued her relationship with her placement supervisors.

After interviewing Intern #1 and reviewing her reflective journals, the Kaya Responsible Travel placement manager made the following assessment of her SEAD competencies.

- Self-awareness: She was aware of the fact that her Spanish was rusty and out of practice, especially the speaking part, and she felt worried about it, but then she realized that her Spanish speaker colleagues and contacts were there to help and were trying to make things easier for her as much as possible. She didn't have the tendency to ask for better instructions or to repeat the tasks given as she saw this as a weakness, but then she realized that if she wanted to succeed in her goals, she needed this push to ask.

- Self-management: She knew she was going to be out of her comfort zone and occasionally she would feel uncomfortable, but she embraced it as part of the experience and faced the challenges head on.
- Responsible decision-making: She recognized that the instructions given by her supervisor were vague and she didn't understand them, so she decided to communicate her concerns and ask for better instructions for next times.
- Relationship skills: She had a lot of conversations in Spanish with her colleagues and was able to strengthen her connections with the staff at her placement as a result. She also talked to her local buddy every day, even though they both had challenges finding times to meet, showing she kept in touch to maintain that relationship despite their busy schedules. She also met her in-country directors and project supervisors twice a week, maintaining communication with them throughout her internship.
- Social-awareness: She recognized that in Ecuador talking about sexuality and reproductive health is still a taboo even within someone's family. This is so different than in the States, but she enjoyed working on campaigns to raise awareness on these topics.

Virtual Intern #2

Virtual Intern #2 was a female University student from Michigan and was placed with a foundation in Morocco, a transit country for Sub-Saharan African and Middle East and North Africa (MENA) region migrants travelling across the Strait of Gibraltar to Europe. Many people are attempting to escape political unrest, civil wars and economic turndowns trying to get to European's most popular cities. However, many end up staying in Morocco as they fear getting caught and be deported back in their home countries.

The foundation was conceived as a bridge between the two shores of the Mediterranean, the mission of the foundation its mission is to address the difficulties of migrants, refugees and the disadvantaged youth, and to promote employability by setting up socio-educational and professional training centers. The foundation also works for the support of diversity, and for the appreciation and respect of all cultures. It organizes events to promote cultural diversity. It supports migrants and refugees by providing them with education, professional training, social assistance and workshops and classes to help them assimilate.

Interns at the foundation provided online lessons to teach the migrants, prepared a test online to gauge the level of the participants, created workshops and ideas to work on during the online teaching sessions, wrote reports on key statistics, and worked on the design of the foundation's website.

When Virtual Intern #2 compared her GlobeSmart profile to the norms for Morocco, she discovered both similarities and differences in cultural orientations.

Table 3. GlobeSmart Dimension

Intern #2	Morocco
Independent	Interdependent
Egalitarianism	Status
Certainty	Certainty
Direct	Indirect
Relationship	Relationship

Intern #2's preference for Independent over Interdependence would likely raise some challenges for her working virtually with colleagues from Morocco. While she places great importance on her individual identity, derives identity from personal choices and achievements, and prefers taking action on her own, her hosts likely give more importance to group harmony and cooperation and derive their identity from group affiliation.

Her preference for Egalitarianism over Status would likely raise some challenges for her working virtually with colleagues from Ecuador. While she would be comfortable challenging the views of superiors and would be flexible about roles, her work colleagues would likely be deferential to superiors and adapt their behavior depending on relative status of who they were interacting with

Intern #2's preference for Direct over Indirect would likely raise some challenges for her working virtually with colleagues from Morocco. While she would naturally be comfortable getting to the point quickly, making requests, giving direction, disagreeing with others, and giving negative feedback directly, her hosts would be more concerned with context, avoid asking questions in group settings, express disagreement in subtle ways, and prefer to give negative feedback indirectly.

Virtual Intern #2 taught English to local migrants, refugees and disadvantaged youth students via Zoom.

The following unedited quotes were extracted from her reflective journals.

"Though the cultural workshops have been led very well by Ali and I am enjoying the content, it hasn't been at a great time for me, so I've had to miss some of them."

"My buddy chats were great, but a little hard to coordinate schedules."

"Though I appreciated getting to know the organizer for us interns on the ground in Morocco, I didn't find the cultural workshops that effective for getting to know the culture. Perhaps having guests come in for the cultural workshops to share certain aspects of the culture from different perspectives?"

"Using Zoom was a challenge when many students didn't have access to good internet or a way to access Zoom. Organizing the students when many of them couldn't attend was difficult."

"I wished I could have organized the students better over Zoom and also learning more about Zoom and its functionality before-hand, but it was very challenging given the fact many students didn't have a reliable connection or couldn't access Zoom."

"My favorite elements of my remote internship experience have been getting to teach English classes on Zoom and getting to know my students and the culture of Morocco a little bit at the same time!"

"My greatest achievement was learning how to effectively teach and finding activities that are helpful and enjoyable at the same time - small victories, but still feel like big achievements. Getting to know and teach the group of migrants/native Moroccans!"

"To observe and hear feedback that the students improved in their English and enjoyed the classes."

"My advice to future virtual interns is to make sure you actually want to get to know your country's culture and the people you are working with! If you come into it only looking for work experience and forget that it takes engaging with people, it would be really hard to get anything out of it. Wanting to get to know Morocco and the organization I am with has made this a super enjoyable experience so far!"

'I really enjoyed my placement! There were some things I wished could have been better, like navigating using Zoom and organizing the students, but overall, it was great, especially under abnormal circumstances."

After interviewing Intern #2 and reviewing her reflective journals, the Kaya Responsible Travel placement manager searched for linkages between the challenges the intern faced resulting from their cultural profile and the hosts country. The placement manager struggled to find direct linkages but noted some of the recurring challenges the intern faced.

Coordinating schedules seemed difficult, especially the timing of the cultural workshops which she struggled to work into her schedule. The placement manager speculated might have been related to the fact she did not find the cultural workshops that effective for getting to know the culture, and suggested that having some different guests come in to share certain aspects of the culture from different perspectives might improve these.

She also had some difficulties working virtually, such as using Zoom and organizing the students in an online setting, as well as learning how to teach effectively and find activities for the students that were helpful and enjoyable at the same time.

After interviewing Intern #2 and reviewing her reflective journals, the Kaya Responsible Travel placement manager made the following assessment of her SEAD competencies.

- Self-awareness: Her assumption that "everybody has internet access" proved to be false and she underestimated the learning curve in teaching on the Zoom platform. She needed to work through the frustrations she felt and regain her confidence.
- Self-management: She managed to make improvement in providing effective teaching with fun and helpful activities despite the tech challenges. Also, she gradually got better at using Zoom and make the best of the circumstances in Covid-19 stricken times.
- Social-awareness: She clearly understands that it is vital for a successful placement to wanting to learn more about the culture and the company.
- Relationship skills: She had a great time chatting with her buddy in Morocco, despite it being difficult to arrange meet-up times. Also, she spent time to getting to know the organization she worked with and the people so this has made her experience more enjoyable.
- Responsible decision-making: She realized that sometimes cultural workshops and buddy chats did not make her fully understand the Moroccan culture. She suggested that it would be useful sometimes to have a guest to these events so that people can get different perspectives on the culture and habits of the country.

Virtual Intern #3

Virtual Intern #3 was a female high school student from Canada and was placed with a a not-for-profit football academy in Cape Town, South Africa. The academy provides community interventions aimed at empowering and improving the lives of girls in high-risk areas through football. They create alternative life paths for girls and women in high-risk communities. The academy provides safe spaces where girls develop football skills, build strong relationships, and tap into mentorship and guidance from a representative leadership and peer group. They have a formal partnership with a low-income high school, where they manage the football coaching for their girls. They also run activations with schools in various low- to no-income areas, holding football tournaments for their girls and fundraising for sporting equipment for schools who would not ordinarily be able to afford it.

They hold a long-term lease on a sports grounds in the center of Cape Town, with Table Mountain as its backdrop. They have an amazing opportunity to create a vibrant sports club for the surrounding community, while still ensuring that school girls from high risk areas receive excellent football and mental coaching. They requested "creative and hard-working individuals" to help them in the strategizing, planning, costing and rollout of current and new programs.

When Virtual Intern #3 compared her GlobeSmart profile to the norms for South Africa, she discovered she had different orientations on each of the five dimensions.

Table 4. GlobeSmart Dimension

Intern #3	South Africa
Interdependent	Independent
Status	Egalitarianism
Certainty	Risk
Indirect	Direct
Relationship	Task

Intern #3's preference for Interdependence or Independent would likely raise some challenges for her working virtually with colleagues from South Africa. While she places great importance on group harmony and cooperation, her hosts place great importance on individual identity and derive identity from personal choices and achievements, and prefer taking action on their own.

Her preference for Status over Egalitarianism over would likely raise some challenges for her working virtually with colleagues from South Africa. While she would be likely be deferential to superiors and adapt her behavior depending on relative status of who she was interacting with, her hosts would be more comfortable challenging the views of superiors, treat everyone the same, assume power and authority should be shared broadly among a group, and would be flexible about roles.

Intern #3's preference for Certainty over Risk would likely raise some challenges for her working virtually with colleagues from South Africa. While she would likely spend significant time on background research, establish proper procedures before starting a project, and value thoroughness over speed, her hosts would likely prefer rapid decision-making and quick results, place great importance on flexibility and initiative, and value speed over thoroughness.

Her preference for Indirect over Direct would likely raise some challenges for her working virtually with colleagues from South Africa. While she would naturally be concerned with context, avoid asking questions in group settings, express disagreement in subtle ways, and prefer to give negative feedback indirectly, her hosts would likely be comfortable getting to the point quickly, making requests, giving direction, disagreeing with others, and giving negative feedback directly

Intern #3's preference for Relationship over Task would likely raise some challenges for her working virtually with colleagues from South Africa. While she views time building relationships as key to achieving good results and prioritizes maintaining relationships over accomplishing tasks on time, her hosts likely place high values on reaching goals, staying on schedule, and completing tasks.

Virtual Intern #3 worked closely with another intern at the Not-for-Profit Football Academy on how to incorporate social-emotional and soft skill aspects into each training sessions. They delivered tangible outputs that the Academy is now using with their Head Coach to plan the return of school sport after the Covid-19 regulations ease in South Africa. She was able to develop her knowledge around social emotional learning and how these aspects can be incorporated into sports training.

The following unedited quotes were extracted from her reflective journals.

"My placement was a perfect fit for my interests and am so happy to be able to help Academy."

"The cultural workshops were amazing. I love learning about South Africa in a way that is both informative and interactive."

"I loved my buddy! We have had some amazing conversations and she has been able to answer all my questions about the amazing country of South Africa!"

"My favorite element is definitely buddy chats! I love talking to my new friend."

"My check-ins with my in-country director and project supervisor been regular and very helpful!"

"The only challenge I came across is learn to step outside of my comfort zone and be able to communicate effectively virtually."

"Although I would have liked to visit Cape Town in person, I have still been able to meet some incredible people and truly experience the South African culture within the comfort of my own home. I feel I am making a difference in these girls lives While they are changing mine. I have been participating in fun cultural workshops and weekly buddy chats with my new friend in South Africa."

"This experience has helped me gain perspective, think creatively, and explore my interests. I have had a great experience with Kaya Volunteer from the very beginning on my program and I would definitely recommend this internship!"

"I have just finished my remote internship where I was working on putting together a sports program design for a group of underprivileged girls based in South Africa. Although I would have liked to visit Cape Town in person, I have still been able to meet some incredible people and truly experience the South African culture within the comfort of my own home. I feel I have made a difference in these girls lives While they have changed mine. While participating in fun cultural workshops and weekly buddy chats with my new friend in South Africa, I was able to learn and experience as much of South Africa as possible remotely."

"The buddy chats were always the highlight of my week and are something I will truly miss. This experience has helped me gain perspective, think creatively, and explore my interests."

"Some goals I had before starting this internship were to meet new people, complete my soccer program in its entirety and help these girls. I feel I have reached all of my goals and am not left with and regrets or unfinished business!"

After interviewing Intern #3 and reviewing her reflective journals, the Kaya Responsible Travel placement manager observed linkages between the challenges the intern faced resulting from their cultural profile and the host country.

Ironically, despite having different orientations on each of the five dimensions, Intern #3 was the intern that had the least challenges during her virtual internship. The only challenge Intern #3 raised was having to learn to step out of her comfort zone and trying to communicate effectively in a virtual setting.

Other than that, both Intern #3's feedback and that of her workplace and buddy suggest there were very few challenges that arose during her placement, despite the difference in GlobeSmart profiles, and the feedback given from both sides suggest the placement was a great success for everyone involved. The placement manager speculated that this intern was especially adept and "style switching" (i.e., suspending her preference and adopting the preferences of her hists).

After interviewing Intern #3 and reviewing her reflective journals, the Kaya Responsible Travel placement manager made the following assessment of her SEAD competencies.

- Self-awareness: She never did something like this so she was aware she was going to have to step out of her comfort zone. She grew a lot during the internship and especially she gained new perspectives on things, she started to think more creatively and explored more of her interest. She realized she had the potential to change the girls' lives working on the sport project and she thinks she did in to a certain extent.
- Self-management: She had set goals before starting the placement and she feels like she managed to achieve them all through communication and hard work. Also, her supervisor confirmed that she met each deadline in a timely manner and her work was always well done.
- Social awareness: She was from the beginning very interested in South African culture and the differences between that and Canada. She also took time to observe and listen to the people she was working with and learn from them.
- Relationship skills: In the buddy chats she had a sense if the buddy needed to step out and talk about something else, as some topics could be upsetting, therefore she'd interrupt the chat and talk about something different, like life in general, and other things to ease the vibe. This is something her buddy noticed and appreciated greatly. She was also prepared to really listen and focus on the people talking around her to learn from them, instead of always talking herself. She was also assigned to work with another intern, and despite the physical distance, they were able to work very well together.
- Responsible decision making: She took ownership of some projects and delivered them timely, such as the design of football trainings.

Virtual Intern #4

Intern #4 was a female university student from Michigan has been placed with a small local NGO in Vietnam that conducts research, provides clinical help and works to improve the well-being of children with developmental issues in Vietnam. They operate three interventions operating together in Hanoi, Vietnam.

Interns perform a variety of tasks including preparing documents in English for international school students with special needs; preparing lesson plans for training for staff and parents on sanitation issues, eating problems, and physical activity/therapy for children with developmental disorders. Interns also observe (via Skype/Zoom) intervention activities and the social skills class, teaching English to the staff, designing and participating in intervention activities, and participating and assisting in the research of the center. Interns put together training plans on neurodevelopmental disorders and English lessons for beginners.

When Virtual Intern #4 compared her GlobeSmart profile to the norms for Vietnam, she discovered both similarities and differences in cultural orientations.

Table 5. GlobeSmart Dimension

Intern #4	Vietnam
Interdependent	Interdependent
Egalitarianism	Status
Certainty	Certainty
Direct	Indirect
Relationship	Relationship

Intern #4's preference for Egalitarianism over Status would likely raise some challenges for her working virtually with colleagues from Vietnam. While she would be comfortable challenging the views of superiors and would be flexible about roles, her work colleagues would likely be deferential to superiors and adapt their behavior depending on relative status of who they were interacting with.

Her preference for Direct over Indirect would likely raise some challenges for her working virtually with colleagues from Vietnam. While she would naturally be comfortable getting to the point quickly, making requests, giving direction, disagreeing with others, and giving negative feedback directly, her hosts would be more concerned with context, avoid asking questions in group settings, express disagreement in subtle ways, and prefer to give negative feedback indirectly.

Virtual Intern #4 worked with an intervention center working with children with developmental delays. She was proactive on asking for more tasks. By the end of her internship she was in charge of the center's social media and also teaching English for their staff. With local buddies and our cultural sessions, she was also actively contributing to the sessions. Though she did not have a lot of prior interactions with Vietnamese culture, she was described by her supervisor as one of the most friendly and active students in the cultural exchanges.

The following unedited quotes were extracted from her reflective journals.

"I would suggest allowing us to sometimes have our cameras turned off for video chats considering it's usually late here in the US and I prefer my privacy sometimes! This can be challenging when we are asked to have our cameras on. Otherwise, everything has been great."

"My check-ins with my in-country director and project supervisor have been going well; but sometimes there is a lack of direction when I'm given a task, but I appreciate that they trust me to figure things out on my own as well. Otherwise, I've really loved working with my project supervisor."

"Time difference is a large challenge. I find myself almost falling asleep sometimes when our meetings go past 11 pm. Definitely something I have been trying to adapt to."

"I would tell someone who was looking into doing a virtual internship it's very challenging and you will sometimes have several tasks assigned at once. Additionally, time differences may be a component as well."

"It's important to reach out if you need help with something, especially if you're struggling with your technology or service. It is ok to not understand something and for things to be rocky in the beginning, but forming relationships makes the experience much more enjoyable. Participate as much as you can!"

"I loved my placement, as I got to contribute to the work being done at the Hung Dong center. I got to observe so many wonderful children and staff members working together, and I loved watching their development over time."

"I loved learning in all the cultural workshops. They were all so different and interesting and allowed us all to have fun and connect virtually."

"Buddy chats were awesome and definitely the heart of this program. It was such an amazing way to connect with the host organization and other students from around the world. I valued our time together every week."

"There was a slight lack of understanding between the company I was working for and myself- I think some more clarified guidelines and expectations should be set before the intern starts! For example: I would be assigned to do things last minute, and sometimes very late at night due to the time difference. Additionally, the time difference was challenging to navigating and sometimes confusing when assigning dates to things. "

"My favorite part was meeting people from Vietnam. They are now great friends that I plan to meet someday in person. The buddy chats really help develop those relationships, so I would say that the relationships I was able to form was the highlight of this experience."

"The Vietnamese team and local buddies are phenomenal and I hope I can meet them in person someday. They've already taught me so much about Vietnamese culture and have really made it a point to get to know me. We speak every day and they always show so much love and support."

"My greatest achievement was I was able to translate the Hung Dong center Facebook page entirely to English to help expand their organization globally and the training I formatted on Neurodevelopmental disorders and an English lesson for beginners."

"The check-ins with my in-country director and project supervisor were always joyous! Typically, not very organized, but I always enjoyed connecting with my supervisor and discussing upcoming tasks."

"The time difference and communication were my two biggest challenges."

After interviewing Intern #4 and reviewing her reflective journals, the Kaya Responsible Travel placement manager observed linkages between the challenges the intern faced resulting from their cultural profile and the hosts country.

Intern #4's preference for direct over indirect is demonstrated in how she struggled with communication at times during her virtual internship, and mentioned her advice to any future interns is that '

"it's important to reach out if you need help with something, especially if you're struggling with your technology or service. It is ok to not understand something and for things to be rocky in the beginning, but forming relationships makes the experience much more enjoyable." This also suggests that Intern #4 would be less concerned with status and is comfortable challenging, or at least questioning, her supervisor or other superiors if there was a lack of direction when she was given a task.

After interviewing Intern #4 and reviewing her reflective journals, the Kaya Responsible Travel placement manager made the following assessment of her SEAD competencies.

- Self-awareness: She realized that for some late meetings she was sleepy as they were at 11pm US time, but she really wanted to attend and pushed through. Time difference was definitely a factor to take into account.
- Self-management: She was sometimes given vague instructions or the tasks given were last minute, but she appreciated the fact that they trusted her with figuring out things for herself. Although when she was stuck and couldn't complete the tasks, she'd ask for help and support. Also, she was managing her time very well and occasionally she'd ask for more tasks. Lastly, she was successful at running her own projects like the translation of the social media page and teaching English to the organization staff.

- Social awareness: She was very friendly and active in contributing to the cultural workshops and chats with the buddy. She was always trying to learn more about the Vietnamese culture by asking questions. She says that those weekly and bi-weekly check-ins really were the highlight of her experience. Despite the lack of organization and structures of the calls, she appreciated them.
- Relationship skills: She wanted from the first moment to form relationships with the organization and everyone involved in the work to make her experience more enjoyable.
- Responsible decision-making: She'd recognize the lack of instructions and would ask for help when she needed it, but as said above, she also first tried to manage the tasks on her own to see if she could do them. She was also confident and had the management skills to take up more tasks if needed. Lastly, she decided to participate in some meetings even though at late hours in the US because she wanted to be present and do her best.

DISCUSSION AND CONCLUSION

The four virtual internships described in this chapter provided examples on an initiated event under Schlossberg's Transition Theory and a Covid-19 world where the opportunity for students to do an internship abroad are currently severely restricted.

Although their interactions with their foreign colleagues were virtual, they nevertheless went through the "taking stock" or "4Ss" described in the theory. Each intern assessed their situation; considered their strengths and weaknesses, sought out support from colleagues at both their volunteer organizations and Kaya Responsible Travel, and developed strategies to manage stress and emotions and remain flexible throughout their virtue virtual internships.

Furthermore, the description of the virtual internship design and the students' reflections illustrate the three stages of transition included in Transition Theory: "moving in," the point when individuals are faced with a transition or change; "moving through," the period in which individuals cope with the transition, and "moving out," the end of the transition cycle.

It is clear from the students' reflections that they deepened their knowledge of the cultures of Ecuador, Morocco, South Africa, and Vietnam through their virtual volunteer work at organizations tackling social issues in these countries.

The five competencies identified by the Collaborative for Academic, Social, and Emotional Learning (CASEL, 2017) provided a useful lens to evaluate each of the four students experiences regarding social and emotional learning. Throughout their virtual internships, each of the four students examined their own cultural orientations (Self-Awareness) before comparing/contrasting those to the norms of their host country (Social-Awareness), developed strategies to bridge cultural and language differences with their foreign work colleagues (Relationship Skills), managed stressful workplace situations (Self-Management Skills), and set and attempted to achieve specific goals during their eight-week virtual internships (Responsible Decision-Making).

Although there is ample opportunity to make the SEAD competencies more integral to the virtual internship experience, the Kaya Responsible Travel placement managers review of the reflective journals and discussions with in-country teams provided evidence of growth in each of the competency areas.

The GlobeSmart profiles provided a useful lens to identify, explore, and mitigate cultural differences. Having a cultural map provided both the interns and their foreign colleagues a shared frame of reference for exploration of ways to trust, teamwork, communications and team performance. The structured dialogue around the GlobeSmart cultural dimensions and how to work across the differences and resolve disputes and misunderstandings.

Virtual interns enhanced their knowledge of their host countries through the Culture Guides on GlobeSmart, particularly the "Core Knowledge," "Communication," "Relationship Building," "Local Business Environment," and "Protocol" sections.

The experiences of four virtual interns working with organizations tackling social issues in Ecuador, Morocco, South Africa and Vietnam demonstrated these types of experiences provide a unique opportunity to develop and apply the Social, and Emotional Learning (SEL) competencies of self-awareness; self-management; social awareness; relationship skills; and responsible decision-making. Schlossberg's Transition Theory provided a framework for the virtual interns transitioning to another culture. Cultural Mapping proved to be a useful tool to identify, plan, and mitigate differences in cultural orientations between interns and colleagues in their host countries. The results contribute to the literature related to the development of SEAD competencies through virtual internships for high school and college students.

The feedback of the virtual interns also included recommendations for improving future virtual internships:

- Virtual interns described their frustration with the availability of the internet to people they were working with. As more and more internships become virtual, internet availability might be designed into the role that virtual internships are assigned.
- Zoom features prominently in these virtual internships. Perhaps future interns should complete Zoom training as a pre-requisite to beginning their internships.
- The quality of the Cultural Workshops seems to have varied. It might be helpful for Kaya Responsible Travel to assess the qualities of those that went well and describe best practice for future Cultural Workshops.
- The quality of the interaction with country buddies varied; there were issues related to their availability. Perhaps the criteria for buddy selection can be tightened in this regard.

SUGGESTIONS FOR FUTURE RESEARCH

This chapter was perhaps the first to explore they experiences of gap year virtual interns through the lenses of Schlossberg's Transition Theory, Collaborative for Academic, Social, and Emotional Learning (SEAD) competencies, and cultural mapping. It is the hope and expectation of the co-authors that this chapter will stimulate additional research in this area.

The four virtual internships in this study were all female; three were from the United States and one from Canada. It would be informative to explore the experiences of males and also the experiences of European and Asian interns to see if they differ.

The placement managers made an assessment of evidence of development of the SEAD competencies after the internships were complete. A future study might include a pre and post evaluation of the SEAD competencies by the virtual intern and development a post internship assessment by their in-country supervisor as well.

It might be helpful to integrate the SEAD competencies into the reflective journals of the virtual interns, encouraging them to capture their experiences in the context of SEAD companies.

Another alternative for the SEAD competencies Assessment would be for participants to complete the Intercultural Effectiveness Scale (IES) at the beginning and at the end of the program. This assessment measures competencies essential for effective interaction with people from different cultures including Continuous Learning, Interpersonal Engagement, Hardiness and Overall Cultural Effectiveness. The pre-Virtual internship and post-virtual internship scores would provide an objective measure of the extent the virtual internship experience enhanced cultural competency (Kerr and Madden-Dent, 2019).

Future researchers also might want to compare and contrast the results from virtual internships and traditional internships once the Covid-19 restrictions on travel are lifted.

REFERENCES

Aspen Institute. (2019). *What is Social, Emotional, and Academic Development?* Retrieved at https://www.aspeninstitute.org/publications/pursuing-social-and-emotional-development-through-a-racial-equity-lens-a-call-to-action/

Bauer, B. K. L. E. (2020, September 18). *Ten Facts about COVID-19 and the U.S. Economy.* Brookings.Edu. https://www.brookings.edu/research/ten-facts-about-COVID-19-and-the-u-s-economy/#:%7E:text=The%20decline%20in%20business%20revenue,seen%20in%20an%20entire%20 year

Bond, M. H. (2002). Reclaiming the individual from Hofstede's ecological analysis – A 20-year odyssey: Comment on Oyserman et al. (2002). *Psychological Bulletin, 128*(1), 73–77. doi:10.1037/0033-2909.128.1.73 PMID:11843548

Chickering, A. W., & Schlossberg, N. K. (1995). *Getting the most out of college.* Allyn and Bacon.

Collaborative for Academic, Social, and Emotional Learning (CASEL). (2017). *Making the Case for SEL* (PowerPoint). Retrieved at https://docs.google.com/presentation/d/1Tb9WundNcsURexo2RTvVGVIVlzD_q9i6Vv4jcNtqZjI/edit#slide=id.p4

Doherty, W. J. (2016). *Psychometric Properties of the GlobeSmart Profile.* Aperian Global.

Dorfman, P., Javidan, M., Hanges, P., Dastmalchian, A., & House, R. (2012). GLOBE: A Twenty-Year Journey into the Intriguing World of Culture and Leadership. *Journal of World Business, 47*(4), 504–518. doi:10.1016/j.jwb.2012.01.004

Elleby, C., Domínguez, I. P., Adenauer, M., & Genovese, G. (2020). Impacts of the Covid-19 pandemic on the global agricultural markets. *Environmental and Resource Economics, 76*(4), 1067–1079. doi:10.100710640-020-00473-6 PMID:32836856

Evans, N. J., Forney, D. S., & Guido-DiBrito, F. (1998). *Student development in college theory, research, and practice.* Jossey-Bass.

Goodman, J., Schlossberg, N. K., & Anderson, M. L. (2006). Counseling adults in transition: Linking practice with theory (3rd ed.). New York: Springer.

Hall, E. T. (1960). The Silent Language in Overseas Business. *Harvard Business Review, 38*, 87–96.

Hofstede, G. (1980). *Culture's Consequences: International Differences in Work Related Values*. Sage Publications.

Hofstede, G. (1997). *Cultures and Organizations: Software of the Mind*. McGraw-Hill.

Javidan, M., Gupta, V., House, R. J., Hanges, P. J., & Dorfman, P. W. (2004). *Culture, Leadership, and Organizations: The GLOBE Study of 62 Societies*. Sage Publications.

Kaya Responsible Travel. (2020). *About Kaya – How It All Began*. Retrieved at https://www.kayavolunteer.com/responsible-travel

Kaya Responsible Travel. (2020). *What is a Remote Internship?* Retrieved at https://www.kayavolunteer.com/what-is-a-remote-internship

Kerr, D. B., & Madden-Dent, T. (2019). Cultural Transition and Adjustment of International East Asian Undergraduate Students. In S. E. Brock & P. J. McAliney (Eds.), *Discourses on Business Education at the College Level: On the Boundaries of Content and Praxis*. Touro University Press Books.

Kerr, D. B., Madden-Dent, T., & Shalabi, N. M. (in press). Cultural Competency Interventions: Three Case Studies with Guiding Theoretical Frameworks. In M. London (Ed.), *Oxford Handbook of Lifelong Learning* (2nd ed.). Oxford Press.

Kluckhohn, R., & Strodtbeck, F. (1961). *Variations in Value Orientations*. Row, Peterson.

Lane, H. W., & Maznevski, M. L. (2019). *International Management Behavior: Global and Sustainable Leadership*. Cambridge University Press. doi:10.1017/9781108637152

Madden-Dent, T. (2014). *A phenomenological study of cultural transition and adjustment of Asian undergraduate international students using different cross-cultural treatments*. Retrieved from http://hdl.handle.net/11714/2895

Marquardt, M. J., & Engel, D. W. (1993). *Global human resource development*. Prentice Hall.

Sagiv, L., & Schwartz, S. H. (2000). A New Look at National Culture: Illustrative Applications to Role Stress and Managerial Behavior. In The Handbook of Organizational Culture and Climate. Sage Publications.

Schlossberg, N. K. (1981). A model for analyzing human adaptation to transition. *The Counseling Psychologist*, *9*(2), 2–18. doi:10.1177/001100008100900202

Schlossberg, N. K. (1990). Training counselors to work with adults. *Generations (San Francisco, Calif.)*, *90*(14), 7.

Trompenenaars, F., & Hampden-Turner, C. (1998). *Riding the waves of culture: understanding cultural diversity in global business* (2nd ed.). McGraw Hill.

Vande Berg, M., Connor-Linton, J., & Paige, M. R. (2009). The Georgetown Consortium Project: Interventions for Student Learning Abroad. *Frontiers: The Interdisciplinary Journal of Study Abroad*, *18*(1), 1–75. doi:10.36366/frontiers.v18i1.251

Compilation of References

Abadesco, V., & Savage, J. (2015). *Soul shoppe peace path guidebook.* http://www.onthepeacepath.com/wp-content/uploads/2018/07/peace-path-guide_final.pdf

Abadi, M. M. M., Tabbodi, M., & Rahgozar, H. (2013). The relationship between spiritual well-being and academic achievement. *European Online Journal of Natural and Social Sciences, 2*(3), 3440-3445. https://european-science.com/eojnss/article/view/2233

Academy of Achievement. (1961). *Find my role model.* https://achievement.org/find-my-role-model/

Afterschool Alliance. (2014). *America after 3 pm: Afterschool programs in demand.* Retrieved on April 12, 2018 from: http://www.afterschoolalliance.org/documents/AA3PM-2014/AA3PM_National_Report.pdf

Akkerman, S. F., & Meijer, P. C. (2011). A dialogical approach to conceptualizing teacher identity. *Teaching and Teacher Education, 27*(2), 308–319. doi:10.1016/j.tate.2010.08.013

Allensworth, E. M., Farrington, C. A., Gordon, M. F., Johnson, D. W., Klein, K., McDaniel, B., & Nagaoka, J. (2018). *Supporting social, emotional, & academic development: Research implications for educators.* University of Chicago Consortium on School Research.

Allensworth, E. M., & Hart, H. (2018). *How do principals influence student achievement?* University of Chicago Consortium on School Research.

Allman, M. B., Anci, D., Babington, C., Ballinger, P., Beseda, M., Bland, T., Bock, J., Browning, J., Chan, F. Z., Chermonte, D. J., Cohen, J., Cohen, K. C., Dileno, S., Evans, Z., & Farmer, S. M. (2020). *Impact of the COVID-19 pandemic on college-going high school seniors.* Retrieved from: https://www.artsci.com/studentpoll-covid19

Almlund, M., Duckworth, A. L., Heckman, J. J., & Kautz, T. (2011). Personality psychology and economics. In E. A. Hanushek, S. Machin, & L. Wößmann (Eds.), *Handbook of the economics of education.* Elsevier. doi:10.1016/B978-0-444-53444-6.00001-8

Almlund, M., Duckworth, A. L., Heckman, J. J., & Kautz, T. (2011). Personality psychology and economics. In E. A. Hanushek, S. Machin, & L. Wößmann (Eds.), *Handbook of the economics of SEADation.* Elsevier. doi:10.3386/w16822

Altay, I. F. (2005). Developing cultural awareness. *Journal of Language and Linguistic Studies, 1*(2), 171–182.

American Federation of Teachers. (2017). *Teacher Survey.* Retrieved at https://www.aft.org/sites/default/files/2017_eqwl_survey_web.pdf

American Institutes for Research. (2015). *Ready for work? How afterschool programs can support employability through social and emotional learning.* https://www.air.org/sites/default/files/downloads/report/Afterschool-Programs-Support-Employability-Brief-Dec-2015.pdf

Ansari, M. (2015). Investigating the relationship between spiritual intelligence and happiness and quality of life for girl students. *International Journal of Humanities and Cultural Studies,* 1678-1685. http://www.ijhcs.com/index.php/ijhcs/article/view/1943

Anti-Defamation League. (n.d.). *What do safe, respectful and inclusive virtual classrooms look like?* https://www.adl.org/education/resources/tools-and-strategies/what-do-safe-respectful-and-inclusive-virtual-classrooms

Anxiety and Depression Association of America. (2020). *Fast fact & statistics.* Retrieved at https://adaa.org/about-adaa/press-room/facts-statistics

Aronson, B., & Laughter, J. (2016). The theory and practice of culturally relevant education: A synthesis of research across content areas. *Review of Educational Research, 86*(1), 163–206. doi:10.3102/0034654315582066

Aronson, J., & Inzlicht, M. (2004). The ups and downs of attributional ambiguity: Stereotype vulnerability and the academic self-knowledge of African American college students. *Psychological Science, 15*(12), 829–836. doi:10.1111/j.0956-7976.2004.00763.x PMID:15563328

Arroyo, M. (2020). *The relationship between teacher identity and teacher retention in Title I schools: A multiple case study.* Dissertation from the University of Nevada, Las Vegas. ProQuest Number: 27999584.

Aspen Institute. (2017). *Leading for equity: Opportunities for state education chiefs.* https://www.aspeninstitute.org/publications/leading-equity-opportunities-state-education-chiefs/

Aspen Institute. (2018). *Equity statement.* https://assets.aspeninstitute.org/content/uploads/2018/06/Aspen-Education-equity-statement_6.27.2018_Final.pdf

Aspen Institute. (2018). *Pursuing Social and Emotional Development Through a Racial Equity Lens: A Call to Action.* Retrieved at https://www.aspeninstitute.org/publications/pursuing-social-and-emotional-development-through-a-racial-equity-lens-a-call-to-action/

Aspen Institute. (2018). *Pursuing social and emotional development through a racial equity lens: A call to action.* Retrieved from: https://assets.aspeninstitute.org/content/uploads/2018/05/Aspen-Institute_Fra ming-Doc_Call-to-Action.pdf?_ga=2.44974119.2040306106.1585434015-147 9461922.1582989130

Aspen Institute. (2019). *Integrating social, emotional and academic development: An action guide for school leadership teams.* Education and Society Program. https://www.aspeninstitute.org/publications/integrating-social-emotional-and-academic-development-sead-an-action-guide-for-school-leadership-teams/

Aspen Institute. (2019). *What is Social, Emotional, and Academic Development?* Retrieved at https://www.aspeninstitute.org/publications/pursuing-social-and-emotional-development-through-a-racial-equity-lens-a-call-to-action/

Aubrey, A., & Greenhalgh, J. (2018, June 11). The perils of pushing kids too hard and how parents can learn to back off. *National Public Radio.* https://www.npr.org/sections/health-shots/2018/06/11/616900580/back-off-how-to-get-out-of-the-high-pressure-parenting-trap

Autor, D. H., Levy, F., & Murnane, R. J. (2003). The skill content of recent technological change: An empirical exploration. *The Quarterly Journal of Economics, 118*(4), 1279–1333. doi:10.1162/003355303322552801

Aydin, D. (2018). Relationship between the spiritual intelligence and self-regulation skills of education faculty students. *Journal of Education and Training Studies, 6*(12), 227–234. doi:10.11114/jets.v6i12.3481

Ayres, A. J. (1989). *Sensory Integration and Praxis Tests.* Western Psychological Service.

Ayres, A. J. (2000). *Sensory integration and learning disorders.* Western Physiological Services.

Bailey. (2015). *Persistence and fadeout in the impacts of child and adolescent interventions.* Working paper in the ARC Center of Excellence for Children and Families over the Life Course, University of Queensland, Australia.

Balcazar, F. E., Suarez-Balcazar, Y., & Taylor-Ritzler, T. (2009). Cultural competence: Development of a conceptual framework. *Disability and Rehabilitation, 31*(14), 1153–1160. doi:10.1080/09638280902773752 PMID:19802931

Baloche, L., & Brody, C. M. (2017). Cooperative Learning: Exploring Challenges, Crafting Innovations. *Journal of Education for Teaching, 43*(3), 274–283. doi:10.1080/02607476.2017.1319513

Banks, J. A. (1991). A curriculum for empowerment, action, and change. In C. E. Sleeter (Ed.), *Empowerment through multicultural education* (pp. 76–88). Southern Illinois University Press.

Barshay, J. (2020, April 27). *Lowest student-to-school-counselor ratio since 1986.* Retrieved from: https://hechinger-report.org/lowest-student-to-school-counselor-ratio-since-1986/

Bauer, B. K. L. E. (2020, September 18). *Ten Facts about COVID-19 and the U.S. Economy.* Brookings.Edu. https://www.brookings.edu/research/ten-facts-about-COVID-19-and-the-u-s-economy/#:%7E:text=The%20decline%20in%20business%20revenue,seen%20in%20an%20entire%20year

Bear, G. (2010). *School discipline and self-discipline: A practical guide to promoting prosocial student behavior.* Guilford Press.

Beijaard, D., Meijer, P. C., & Verloop, N. (2004). Reconsidering research on teachers' professional identity. *Teaching and Teacher Education, 20*(2), 107–128. doi:10.1016/j.tate.2003.07.001

Belfield, B., & Klapp, L. (2015). The economic value of social and emotional learning. New York, NY: Center for Benefit-Cost Studies in Education: Teachers College, Columbia University.

Belfield, B., & Klapp, L. (2015). The economic value of social and emotional learning. New York, NY: Center for Benefit-Cost Studies in SEADation: Teachers College, Columbia University.

Belfield, C., Bowden, A., Klapp, A., Levin, H., Shand, R., & Zander, S. (2015). The economic value of social and emotional learning. *Journal of Benefit-Cost Analysis, 6*(3), 508–544. doi:10.1017/bca.2015.55

Bem, D. J. (1972). Self-Perception Theory. In L. Berkowitz (Ed.), (pp. 1–63). Advances in Experimental Social Psychology. Academic Press.

Berman, S., Chaffee, S., & Sarmiento, J. (2018). *The Practice Base for How we Lear: Supporting Students' Social, Emotional, and Academic Development.* https://www.aspeninstitute.org/wp-content/uploads/2018/03/CDE-Practice-Base_FINAL.pdf

Berman, S., Chaffee, S., & Sarmiento, J. (2018). *Supporting students' social, emotional, and academic development: Consensus statements of practice from council of distinguished educators.* Aspen Institute. Retrieved from http://nationathope.org/wp-content/uploads/cde-practice-base_final.pdf

Beymer, P. N., & Thomson, M. M. (2015). The effects of choice in the classroom: Is there too little or too much choice? *Support for Learning, 30*(2), 105–120. Advance online publication. doi:10.1111/1467-9604.12086

Bhattacherjee, A. (2012). *Social science research: Principles, methods, and practices.* Textbooks Collection. 3. https://scholarcommons.usf.edu/oa_textbooks/3

Bierman, K. L., Domitrovich, C. E., Nix, R. L., Gest, S. D., Welsh, J. A., Greenberg, M. T., Blair, C., Nelson, K. E., & Gill, S. (2008). Promoting academic and social-emotional school readiness: The Head Start REDI Program. *Child Development, 79*(6), 1802–1817. doi:10.1111/j.1467-8624.2008.01227.x PMID:19037951

Bolghan-Abadi, M., Ghofrani, F., & Abde-Khodaei, M. S. (2014). Study of the spiritual intelligence role in predicting university students' quality of life. *Journal of Religion and Health*, *53*(1), 79–85. doi:10.100710943-012-9602-0 PMID:22528289

Bond, M. H. (2002). Reclaiming the individual from Hofstede's ecological analysis – A 20-year odyssey: Comment on Oyserman et al. (2002). *Psychological Bulletin*, *128*(1), 73–77. doi:10.1037/0033-2909.128.1.73 PMID:11843548

Bondy, E., & Ross, D. D. (2008). The teacher as warm demander. *Educational Leadership*, *66*(1), 54–58. http://www.ascd.org/publications/educational-leadership/sept08/vol66/num01/The-Teacher-as-Warm-Demander.aspx

Booth, C., & Lazear, K. (2015, June). *Cultural adaptation (Resource Brief 1)*. CLC Hub Resource Brief 1. Washington, DC: The Cultural & Linguistic Competence Hub of the Technical Assistance Network for Children's Behavioral Health. http://cfs.cbcs.usf.edu/projects-research/_docs/CLC_ResearchBrief1.pdf

Borgers, N., Hox, J., & Sikkel, D. (2003). Response quality in survey research with children and adolescents: The effect of labeled response options and vague quantifiers. *International Journal of Public Opinion Research*, *15*(1), 83–94. doi:10.1093/ijpor/15.1.83

Boyce, B. E. (2011). *The mindfulness revolution: Leading psychologists, scientists, artists, and meditation teachers on the power of mindfulness in daily life*. Shambhala Publications.

Boyd, D., Grossman, P., Ing, M., Lankford, H., Loeb, S., & Wyckoff, J. (2011). The influence of school administrators on teacher retention decisions. *American Educational Research Journal*, *48*(2), 303–333. doi:10.3102/0002831210380788

Bozorgi, M. D., & Bozorgi, Z. D. (2016). The relationship between spiritual intelligence, coping strategies, and mental health among students. *International Journal of Humanities and Cultural Studies,* 636-646. https://www.ijhcs.com/index.php/ijhcs/article/view/962

Brackett, M. A., & Mayer, J. D. (2003). Convergent, discriminant, and incremental validity of competing measures of emotional intelligence. *Personality and Social Psychology Bulletin*, *29*(9), 1147–1158. doi:10.1177/0146167203254596 PMID:15189610

Brar, S. K. (2017). Study of adjustment among adolescents in relation to spiritual intelligence. *International Journal of Academic Research and Development*, *2*(6), 511–514.

Bridgeland, J., Bruce, M., & Hariharan, A. (2013). *The missing piece: A national teacher survey on how social and emotional learning can empower children and transform schools*. Collaborative for Academic, Social, and Emotional Learning. https://www.casel.org/wp-content/uploads/2016/01/the-missing-piece.pdf

Bridgeland, J., Bruce, M., & Hariharan, A. (2013). *The missing piece: A national teacher survey on how social and emotional learning can empower children and transform schools. A report for CASEL*. Civic Enterprises.

Brooke, G., & Andrade, H. (2013). *Student-centered self-assessment*. Jobs for the Future. Retrieved from https://jfforg-prod-prime.s3.amazonaws.com/media/documents/4_SATC_AssessTools_SelfAssessment_042613.pdf

Brown & Kennedy. (n.d.). *The Brown Model of ADD/ADHD: Brown ADHD Clinic: United States*. Brown ADHD Clinic. www.brownadhdclinic.com/the-brown-model-of-add-adhd

Brown, K. M., & Wynn, S. R. (2009). Finding, supporting, and keeping: The role of the principal in teacher retention issues. *Leadership and Policy in Schools*, *8*(1), 37–63. doi:10.1080/15700760701817371

Brown, S. A. (1996). Talent for living success, says Daniel Goleman, requires skill in handling emotions, not just being smart. *People*, *45*(19), 85–86.

Brown, S., & Kappes, L. (2012). *Implementing the Common Core State Standards: A primer on*. Aspen Institute.

Bryant, G., Crowley, S., & Davidsen, C. (2020). *Finding your place: The current state of K-12 social emotional learning*. Tyton Partners. Retrieved from https://tytonpartners.com/library/k-12-social-emotional-learning/

Bundy, A. C., Lane, S. J., & Murray, E. A. (2002). *Sensory integration: Theory and practice*. F.A. Davis Company.

Busteed, B. (2019). *Why aren't graduates ready for work? They're the least working generation in U.S. history*. Retrieved at https://www.forbes.com/sites/brandonbusteed/2019/03/29/why-arent-graduates-ready-for-work-theyre-the-least-working-generation-in-us-history/#7cd974ae5e58

Cannata, M. A., Smith, T. M., & Taylor Haynes, K. (2017). Integrating academic press and support by increasing student ownership and responsibility. *AERA Open*, *3*(3), 1–13. doi:10.1177/2332858417713181

Cantor, P., Osher, D., Berg, J., Steyer, L., & Rose, T. (2018). Malleability, plasticity, and individuality: How children learn and develop in context. *Applied Developmental Science*. Advance online publication. doi:10.1080/10888691.2017.1398649

Carver-Thomas, D., & Darling-Hammond, L. (2017). *Teacher turnover: Why it matters and what we can do about it*. Learning Policy Institute. https://learningpolicyinstitute.org/sites/default/files/product-files/Teacher_Turnover_REPORT.pdf

CASEL. (2020, March). *The CASEL Guide to Schoolwide SEL Essentials*. Retrieved January 8, 2021, from https://schoolguide.casel.org/uploads/sites/2/2019/09/School-Guide-Essentials-5.2020.pdf

CASEL. (2020a). *Casel's SEL framework: What are the core competence areas and where are they promoted?* Retrieved from: https://casel.org/wp-content/uploads/2020/12/CASEL-SEL-Framework-11.2020.pdf

CASEL. (2020b). *SEL is …* Retrieved from: https://casel.org/wp-content/uploads/2020/12/CASEL-SEL-Framework-11.2020.pdf

CASEL. (2021). *Adult SEL Self-Assessment*. Retrieved January 8, 2021, from https://schoolguide.casel.org/resource/adult-sel-self-assessment/

Casner-Lotto, J., & Barrington, L. (2006). *Are they really ready to work? Employers' perspectives on the basic knowledge and applied skills of new entrants to the 21st century US workforce*. Partnership for 21st Century Skills. https://files.eric.ed.gov/fulltext/ED519465.pdf

Castro, F. G., Barrera, M. Jr, & Holleran Steiker, L. K. (2010). Issues and challenges in the design of culturally adapted evidence-based interventions. *Annual Review of Clinical Psychology*, *6*(1), 213–239. doi:10.1146/annurev-clinpsy-033109-132032 PMID:20192800

Catalano, R. F., Berglund, M. L., Ryan, J. A. M., Lonczak, H. S., & Hawkins, J. D. (2002). Positive youth development in the United States: Research findings on evaluations of positive youth development programs. *Prevention & Treatment*, *5*, 15. http://journals.apa.org/prevention/volume5/pre0050015a.html

Center for Instructional Development and Research. (1999). Teaching through discussion. *Teaching and Learning Bulletin, 2*. Retrieved from: http://www.washington.edu/teaching/files/2012/12/Discussion.pdf

Center on Great Teachers & Leaders. (2020, April). *Educator Resilience and Trauma-Informed Self-Care Self-Assessment and Planning Tool*. Retrieved from https://gtlcenter.org/sites/default/files/Educator-Resilience-Trauma-Informed-Self-Care-Self-Assessment.pdf

Center on Positive Behavioral Interventions and Supports. (2019). *Tier 3*. https://www.pbis.org/pbis/tier-3

Charkhabi, M., Mortazavi, A., Alimohammadi, S., & Hayati, D. (2014). The effect of spiritual intelligence training on the indicators of mental health in Iranian students: An experimental study. *Procedia: Social and Behavioral Sciences*, *159*, 355–358. doi:10.1016/j.sbspro.2014.12.387

Cherng, H. Y. S. (2017). If they think I can: Teacher bias and youth of color expectations and achievement. *Social Science Research*, *66*, 170–186. doi:10.1016/j.ssresearch.2017.04.001 PMID:28705354

Cherniss, C., Extein, M., Goleman, D., & Weissberg, R. P. (2006). Emotional intelligence: What does the research really indicate? *Educational Psychologist*, *41*(4), 239–245. doi:10.120715326985ep4104_4

Chickering, A. W., & Schlossberg, N. K. (1995). *Getting the most out of college*. Allyn and Bacon.

Cipriano, C., & Brackett, M. (2020). *How to support teachers' emotional needs right now. Schools can develop a plan to help teachers who are feeling anxious and overwhelmed*. Retrieved at https://greatergood.berkeley.edu/article/item/how_to_support_teachers_emotional_needs_right_now

Clark County School District. (2020). *Pocket guide: A little book about all of the big things happening in the Clark County School District—2019–2020*. https://newsroom.ccsd.net/wp-content/uploads/CCSD-Pocket-Guide-January-2020.pdf

Clark County School District. (n.d.a). *About Clark County School District*. https://teachvegas.ccsd.net/our-district/about-clark-county-school-district/

Clark County School District. (n.d.b). *Career and technical education*. https://www.ccsd.net/departments/career-technical-education/

Cochran-Smith, M. (2004). Stayers, leavers, lovers, and dreamers: Insights about teacher retention. *Journal of Teacher Education*, *55*(5), 387–392. doi:10.1177/0022487104270188

Cohen, J. (1988). *Statistical power analysis for the behavioral sciences* (2nd ed.). Erlbaum.

Collaborative for Academic, Social, and Emotional Learning (CASEL). (2017). *Making the Case for SEL* (PowerPoint). Retrieved at https://docs.google.com/presentation/d/1Tb9WundNcsURexo2RTvVGVIVlzD_q9i6Vv4jcNtqZjI/edit#slide=id.p4

Collaborative for Academic, Social, and Emotional Learning (CASEL). (2017). *Making the case for SEL* [PowerPoint slides]. CASEL. https://docs.google.com/presentation/d/1Tb9WundNcsURexo2RTvVGVIVlzD_q9i6Vv4jcNtqZjI/edit#slide=id.p4

Collaborative for Academic, Social, and Emotional Learning (CASEL). (2020). *CASEL's SEL framework: What are the core competence areas and where are they promoted?* Retrieved at https://casel.org/what-is-sel/

Collaborative for Academic, Social, and Emotional Learning (CASEL). (2020). *Resources: SEL background and research*. https://casel.org/resources-learn/

Collaborative for Academic, Social, and Emotional Learning (CASEL). (2020). *What is SEL?* Retrieved at https://casel.org/what-is-sel/

Collaborative for Academic, Social, and Emotional Learning. (2005). *Safe and sound: An educational leader's guide to evidence-based social and emotional learning (SEL) programs*. https://casel.org/wp-content/uploads/2016/06/safe-and-sound.pdf

Collaborative for Academic, Social, and Emotional Learning. (2005). *Safe and sound: An educational leader's guide to evidence-based social and emotional learning programs. Illinois edition*. Author.

Collaborative for Academic, Social, and Emotional Learning. (2019). *SEL 3 signature practices playbook: A tool that supports systemic SEL.* https://schoolguide.casel.org/resource/three-signature-sel-practices-for-adult-learning/

Collaborative for Academic, Social, and Emotional Learning. (2020). *CASEL'S SEL framework.* https://casel.org/wp-content/uploads/2020/12/CASEL-SEL-Framework-11.2020.pdf

Collaborative for Academic, Social, and Emotional Learning. (2020, December 21). *SEL is...* https://casel.org/what-is-sel/

Collaborative for Academic, Social, and Emotional Learning. (2020a). *Core SEL competencies.* Chicago, IL: Author. Retrieved from https://casel.org/core-competencies/

Collaborative for Academic, Social, and Emotional Learning. (2020b). *Guide to schoolwide SEL.* Chicago, IL: Author. Retrieved from https://schoolguide.casel.org/focus-area-3/classroom/integration-of-sel-and-instruction/using-interactive-pedagogy/

Collaborative for Academic, Social, and Emotional Learning. (n.d.a). *Examining biases for cultural competence.* https://schoolguide.casel.org/focus-area-2/learn/examining-biases-for-cultural-competence/

Collaborative for Academic, Social, and Emotional Learning. (n.d.b). *Focus area 4 – practice data for continuous improvement.* https://drc.casel.org/practice-continuous-improvement/share-with-stakeholders-and-take-action/

College Board. (2020, September 10). *Class rank & college admission: To rank or not to rank.* https://professionals.collegeboard.org/guidance/applications/rank#:~:text=Class%20rank%20was%20once%20a,no%20longer%20report%20student%20rankings

Committee for Children Second Step. (2014). *Safe, Supported, and Ready to Learn.* Retrieved at https://www.cfchildren.org/wp-content/uploads/programs/docs/Second-Step_White-Paper_Safe-Supported-Ready-to-Learn_FA18.pdf

Committee for Children. (2016). *Why social and emotional learning and employability skills should be prioritized in education.* https://www.cfchildren.org/wp-content/uploads/policy-advocacy/sel-employability-brief.pdf

Consortium on the School-based Promotion of Social Competence. (1994). The school-based promotion of social competence: Theory, research, practice, and policy. In R. J. Haggerty, N. Garmezy, M. Rutter, & L. R. Sherrod (Eds.), *Stress, risk, and resilience in children and adolescents: Processes, mechanisms, and interventions* (pp. 268–316). Cambridge University Press.

Costa, A. L., & Kallick, B. (2008). Learning through reflection. In A. L. Costa & B. Kallick (Eds.), *Learning and leading with habits of mind: 16 essential characteristics for success.* ASCD. Retrieved from http://www.ascd.org/publications/books/108008/chapters/Learning-Through-Reflection.aspx

Creek, J. (2014). Approaches to practice. In W. Bryant, J. Fieldhouse, & K. Bannigan (Eds.), *Creek's occupational therapy and mental health* (5th ed., pp. 50–69). Churchill Livingstone.

Crowe, C. (2009). *Solving thorny behavior problems. In Coaching Children in Handling Everyday Conflicts.* Responsive Classrooms. Retrieved from https://www.responsiveclassroom.org/coaching-children-in-handling-everyday-conflicts/

Crowe, L., Beauchamp, M., Catroppa, C., & Anderson, V. (2011). Social function assessment tools for children and adolescents: A systematic review from 1988 to 2010. *Clinical Psychology Review, 31*(5), 767–785. doi:10.1016/j.cpr.2011.03.008 PMID:21513693

Cunningham, W. V., & Villasenor, P. (2016). Employer voices, employer demands, and implications for public skills development policy connecting the labor and education sectors. *The World Bank Research Observer, 31*(1), 102–134. doi:10.1093/wbro/lkv019 d'Ailly, H. (2004). The role of choice in children's learning: A distinctive cultural and gender difference in efficacy, interest, and effort. *Canadian Journal of Behavioural Science, 36*(1), 17–29. doi:10.1037/h0087212

Dahl, M. (2019). *InSPIRE check-in*. Mindful SEAD. https://www.mindfulsead.org/uploads/1/7/1/7/17176054/inspire_check-in_for_srs_copy.pdf

Dahl, M. (2018). *YOUTH positive middle school workbook*. YOUTH Positive Publishing.

Dahl, M. (2019). *YOUTH positive teacher's guide: A deep dive into mindfulness, positive education, and SEL*. YOUTH Positive Publishing.

Darling-Hammond, L. (2010). Teacher education and the American future. *Journal of Teacher Education, 61*(1-2), 35–47. doi:10.1177/0022487109348024

Darling-Hammond, L., Flook, L., Cook-Harvey, C., Barron, B., & Osher, D. (2019). Implications for educational practice of the science of learning and development. *Applied Developmental Science, 24*(2), 97–140. doi:10.1080/10888691.2018.1537791

Dawson, P. (2009). *Smart but scattered: The revolutionary "executive skills" approach to helping kids reach their potential*. Academic Press.

Deming, D. J. (2015). *The growing importance of social skills in the labor market* (NBER Working Paper No. 21473). Cambridge, MA: National Bureau of Economic Research.

Deming, D. J. (2017). The growing importance of social skills in the labor market. *The Quarterly Journal of Economics, 132*(4), 1593–1640. doi:10.1093/qje/qjx022

Denham, S. (2018). *Keeping SEL developmental: The importance of a developmental lens for fostering and assessing SEL competencies*. Establishing Practical Social-Emotional Competence Assessments Work Group. Retrieved from https://casel.org/wp-content/uploads/2020/04/Keeping-SEL-Developmental.pdf

Denham, S. A. (2015). Assessment of SEL in educational contexts. In J. A. Durlak, C. E. Domitrovich, R. P. Weissberg, & T. P. Gullotta (Eds.), *Handbook of social and emotional learning: Research and practice* (pp. 285–300). The Guilford Press.

Denton, P. (2008). The power of our words. *Educational Leadership, 66*(1), 28–31. http://www.ascd.org/publications/educational-leadership/sept08/vol66/num01/The-Power-of-Our-Words.aspx

DePaoli, J. L., Atwell, M. N., & Bridgeland, J. (2017). *Ready to lead: A national principal survey on how social and emotional learning can prepare children and transform schools. A report for CASEL*. Civic Enterprises.

Devi, R. K., Rajesh, N. V., & Devi, M. A. (2017). Study of spiritual intelligence and adjustment among arts and science college students. *Journal of Religion and Health, 56*(3), 828–838. doi:10.100710943-016-0225-8 PMID:27007602

Diamond, M., & Hopson, J. (1999). *Magic trees of the mind: How to nurture your child's intelligence, creativity, and healthy emotions from birth through adolescence*. Plume.

Doherty, W. J. (2016). *Psychometric Properties of the GlobeSmart Profile*. Aperian Global.

Doll, B., & Elliott, S. N. (1994). Representativeness of observed preschool social behaviors: How many data are enough? *Journal of Early Intervention, 18*(2), 227–238. doi:10.1177/105381519401800209

Domitrovich, C. E., Durlak, J. A., Staley, K. C., & Weissberg, R. P. (2017). Social-emotional competence: An essential factor for promoting positive adjustment and reducing risk in school children. *Child Development, 88*(2), 408–416. doi:10.1111/cdev.12739 PMID:28213889

Domitrovich, C. E., Syvertsen, A. K., & Calin, S. S. (2017). *Promoting social and emotional learning in the middle and high school years*. Edna Bennett Pierce Prevention Research Center, Pennsylvania State University.

Domitrovich, C., Bradshaw, C., Poduska, J., Hoagwood, K., Buckley, J., Olin, S., Romanelli, L. H., Leaf, P. J., Greenberg, M. T., & Ialongo, N. (2008). Maximizing the Implementation Quality of Evidence-Based Preventive Interventions in Schools: A Conceptual Framework. *Advances in School Mental Health Promotion*, *1*(3), 6–28. doi:10.1080/1754730X.2008.9715730 PMID:27182282

Donahue, C. (2020). *Advice: Building positive relationships with fellow educators*. Retrieved at www.nea.org

Dorfman, P., Javidan, M., Hanges, P., Dastmalchian, A., & House, R. (2012). GLOBE: A Twenty-Year Journey into the Intriguing World of Culture and Leadership. *Journal of World Business*, *47*(4), 504–518. doi:10.1016/j.jwb.2012.01.004

Draeger, C. (2017). Developing professional relationships that work. *Education Week*. Retrieved at https://www.edweek.org/education/opinion-developing-professional-relationships-that-work/2017/09

Dryfoos, J. G. (1997). The prevalence of problem behaviors: Implications for programs. In R. P. Weissberg, T. P. Gullotta, R. L. Hampton, B. A. Ryan, & G. R. Adams (Eds.), *Healthy children 2010: Enhancing children's wellness* (pp. 17–46). Sage.

Duchesneau, N. (2020). *Social, emotional, and academic development through an equity lens*. EdTrust.

Duckworth, A. L., & Seligman, M. E. P. (2005). Self-discipline outdoes IQ in predicting academic performance of adolescents. *Psychological Science*, *16*(12), 939–944. doi:10.1111/j.1467-9280.2005.01641.x PMID:16313657

Duncan, E. A. S. (2011). The cognitive behavioural frame of reference. In E. A. S. Duncan (Ed.), *Foundations for practice in occupational therapy* (5th ed., pp. 153–164). Churchill Livingstone.

Dunning, D. L., Griffiths, K., Kuyken, W., Crane, C., Foulkes, L., Parker, J., & Dalgleish, T. (2019). Research Review: The effects of mindfulness-based interventions on cognition and mental health in children and adolescents - a meta-analysis of randomized controlled trials. *Journal of Child Psychology and Psychiatry, and Allied Disciplines*, *60*(3), 244–258. doi:10.1111/jcpp.12980 PMID:30345511

Dunn, W. (2007). Supporting Children to Participate Successfully in Everyday Life by Using Sensory Processing Knowledge. *Infants and Young Children*, *20*(2), 84–101. doi:10.1097/01.IYC.0000264477.05076.5d

Durlak, J. A., Domitrovich, C. E., Weissberg, R. P., & Gullotta, T. P. (2015). *Handbook of social and emotional learning: Research and practice*. Guilford Press.

Durlak, J. A., & DuPre, E. P. (2008). Implementation matters: A review of research on the influence of implementation on program outcomes and the factors affecting implementation. *American Journal of Community Psychology*, *41*(3-4), 327–350. doi:10.100710464-008-9165-0 PMID:18322790

Durlak, J. A., Weissberg, R. P., Dymnicki, A. B., Taylor, R. D., & Schellinger, K. (2011). The impact of enhancing students' social and emotional learning: A meta-analysis of school-based universal interventions. *Child Development*, *82*(1), 405–432. doi:10.1111/j.1467-8624.2010.01564.x PMID:21291449

Durlak, J. A., Weissberg, R. P., & Pachan, M. (2010). A meta-analysis of after-school programs that seek to promote personal and social skills in children and adolescents. *American Journal of Community Psychology*, *45*(3/4), 294–309. doi:10.100710464-010-9300-6 PMID:20300825

Durlak, J. A., & Wells, A. M. (1997). Primary prevention mental health programs for children and adolescents: A meta-analytic review. *American Journal of Community Psychology*, *25*(2), 115–152. doi:10.1023/A:1024654026646 PMID:9226860

Dusenbury, L., Dermody, C., & Weissberg, R. P. (2018). *State scorecard scan.* CASEL. https://casel.org/wp-content/uploads/2018/09/csi-scorecard-sept2018.pdf

Dusenbury, L. A., Newman, J. Z., Weissberg, R. P., Goren, P., Domitrovich, C. E., & Mart, A. K. (2015). The case for preschool through high school state learning standards for SEL. In J. A. Durlak, C. E. Domitrovich, R. P. Weissberg, & T. P. Gullotta (Eds.), *Handbook of social and emotional learning: Research and practice* (pp. 532–548). The Guilford Press.

Dusenbury, L., Calin, S., Domitrovich, C., & Weissberg, R. (2015). *What does evidence-based instruction in social and emotional learning actually look like in practice? A brief on findings from CASEL's program reviews.* Collaborative for Academic, Social, and Emotional Learning.

Dusenbury, L., Yoder, N., Dermody, C., & Weissberg, R. (2020). *An examination of frameworks for social and emotional learning (SEL) reflected in state K-12 learning standards.* Collaborative for Academic, Social, and Emotional Learning.

Ebrahimi, A., Keykhosrovani, M., & Dehghani, M. (2012). Investigation of the relation between resiliency, spiritual intelligence and mental health of a group of undergraduate students. *Life Science Journal, 9*(1), 67–70.

Educationdata. (2020). *International student enrollment statistics.* Retrieved from: https://educationdata.org/international-student-enrollment-statistics

Educationlinks, U. S. A. I. D. (2018). *Education in crisis and conflict. Social and emotional learning in crisis and conflict settings.* Retrieved at https://www.edu-links.org/learning/social-and-emotional-learning-crisis-and-conflict-settings

Edutopia. (2010). *Social emotional learning.* https://www.edutopia.org/social-emotional-learning

EdWeek. (2019). *Safety and social and emotional learning: Results of a national survey.* Bethesda, MD: Education Week Research Center. Retrieved from https://www.edweek.org/media/safety-and-sel-national-survey-education-week-research-center-2019.pdf

Eldiasty, A. M. A., & Ibrahim, A. T. H. (2018). The relationship between spiritual intelligence and a student's adaptation to college life: Implications for social work practice. *The Egyptian Journal of Social Work, 1*(5), 21–46.

Elias, M. J., Leverett, L., Duffell, J., Humphrey, N., Stepney, C. T., & Ferrito, J. J. (in press). Integrating social-emotional learning with related prevention and youth-development approaches. In J. A. Durlak, C. Domitrovich, R. P. Weissberg, & T. P. Gullotta (Eds.), Handbook of social and emotional learning (SEL): Research and practice. Academic Press.

Elias, M. J., O'Brien, M. U., & Weissberg, R. P. (2006). Transformative Leadership for Social-Emotional Learning. *Principal Leadership: High School Edition, 7*(4), 10–13. Retrieved from http://libproxy.txstate.edu/login?url=http://search.ebscohost.com.libproxy.txstate.edu/login.aspx?direct=true&db=eue&AN=507936535&site=eds-live&scope=site

Elias, M. J., Leverett, L., Duffell, J. C., Humphrey, N., Stepney, C., & Ferrito, J. (2015). Integrating SEL with related prevention and youth development approaches. In J. A. Durlak, C. E. Domitrovich, R. P. Weissberg, & T. P. Gullotta (Eds.), *Handbook of social and emotional learning: Research and practice* (pp. 33–49). Guilford Press.

Elias, M. J., Zins, J. E., Weissberg, R. P., Frey, K. S., Greenberg, M. T., Haynes, N. M., & … . (1997). *Promoting social and emotional learning: Guidelines for educators.* Association for Supervision and Curriculum Development.

Elleby, C., Domínguez, I. P., Adenauer, M., & Genovese, G. (2020). Impacts of the Covid-19 pandemic on the global agricultural markets. *Environmental and Resource Economics, 76*(4), 1067–1079. doi:10.100710640-020-00473-6 PMID:32836856

Ellison, A. (2019). *Go your own way: 7 student-centered paths to the best college experience.* Dunce, LLC.

Emmons, R. A. (2000). Is spirituality an intelligence? *The International Journal for the Psychology of Religion, 11*, 27–34.

Ertmer, P., & Newby, T. (1996). The expert learner: Strategic, self-regulated, and reflective. *Instructional Science*, *24*(1), 1–24. doi:10.1007/BF00156001

Evans, M., & Boucher, A. R. (2015). Optimizing the power of choice: Supporting student autonomy to foster motivation and engagement in learning. *Mind, Brain and Education: the Official Journal of the International Mind, Brain, and Education Society*, *9*(2), 87–91. doi:10.1111/mbe.12073

Evans, N. J., Forney, D. S., & Guido-DiBrito, F. (1998). *Student development in college theory, research, and practice.* Jossey-Bass.

Every Student Succeeds Act of 2015, 20 U.S.C. § 8101(42). https://www2.ed.gov/policy/elsec/leg/essa/legislation/title-ii.pdf

Every Student Succeeds Act of 2015, 20 U.S.C. § 8101(44). https://www2.ed.gov/policy/elsec/leg/essa/legislation/title-ii.pdf

Every Student Succeeds Act of 2015, Title II Part A, 20 U.S.C. §6601 *et seq.* https://www2.ed.gov/policy/elsec/leg/essa/legislation/title-ii.pdf

Ferguson, R. (2012). Let's find a way to learn about our rights: Communities of practice as "spaces" for women and girls to learn about their human rights. In C. R. Roux (Ed.), *Safe spaces: Human rights education in diverse contexts* (pp. 131–150). Sense. doi:10.1007/978-94-6091-936-7_9

Fisher, D., & Frey, N. (2013). *Engaging the adolescent learner: Fostering classroom discussion about complex ideas and texts.* International Reading Association.

Fishman, E. J. (2014). With great control comes great responsibility: The relationship between perceived academic control, student responsibility, and self-regulation. *The British Journal of Educational Psychology*, *84*(4), 685–702. doi:10.1111/bjep.12057 PMID:25251935

Fissinger, M. X., Fitzsimmons, W. R., Flagel, A., Fretwell, K., & Zakrzewski, V. (2016, January 20).*Turning the tide: Inspiring concern for others and the common good through college admissions.* Making Caring Common Project. Retrieved from: https:///Downloads/20160120_mcc_ttt_report_interactive.pdf

Fitzgerald, B. K., & Sigelman, M. (2018). *The new foundational skills of the digital economy: Developing the professionals of the future.* Burning Glass Technologies. Retrieved from www.burning-glass.com

Forman, S. G., Olin, S. S., Hoagwood, K. E., Crowe, M., & Saka, N. (2008). Evidence-Based Interventions in Schools: Developers' Views of Implementation Barriers and Facilitators. *School Mental Health*, *1*(1), 26–36. doi:10.100712310-008-9002-5

Foster, S., Rollefson, M., Doksum, T., Noonan, D., Robinson, G., & Teich, J. (2005). School mental health services in the United States 2002–2003 (DHHS Pub. No. (SMA) 05–4068). Center for Mental Health Services, Substance Abuse and Mental Health Services Administration.

Franke, H. A. (2014). Toxic Stress: Effects, Prevention and Treatment. *Children (Basel, Switzerland)*, *1*(3), 390–402. doi:10.3390/children1030390 PMID:27417486

Freedman, S. W., & Appleman, D. (2008). What else would I be doing?": Teacher identity and teacher retention in urban schools. *Teacher Education Quarterly*, *35*(3), 109–126.

Freeman, J., Sugai, G., Simonsen, B., & Everett, S. (2017). MTSS coaching: Bridging knowing to doing. *Theory into Practice*, *56*(1), 29–37. doi:10.1080/00405841.2016.1241946

Frey, N., Fisher, D., & Smith, D. (2019). *All learning is social and emotional: Helping students develop essential skills for the classroom and beyond.* ASCD.

Friesen, M. D., & Besley, S. C. (2013). Teacher identity development in the first year of teacher education: A developmental and social psychological perspective. *Teaching and Teacher Education*, *36*, 23–32. doi:10.1016/j.tate.2013.06.005

Fullam, J. P. (2017). From seeing to believing: Using instructional video to develop culturally responsive teaching. *Journal for Multicultural Education*, *11*(2), 131–148. doi:10.1108/JME-09-2016-0053

Gallup and Strada Education Network. (2017). *On second thought: U.S. adults reflect on their education decisions*. Retrieved from: http://stradaeducation.gallup.com/reports/208535/gallup-strada-education-ecp-inaugural-report-2017.aspx

Gallup. (2014). *State of American Schools*. Retrieved from https://www.gallup.com/education/269648/state-america-schools-report.aspx

Gamoran, A., Porter, A. C., Smithson, J., & White, P. A. (1997). Upgrading high school mathematics instruction: Improving learning opportunities for low-achieving, low-income youth. *Educational Evaluation and Policy Analysis*, *19*(4), 325–338. doi:10.3102/01623737019004325

Gay, G. (2013). Teaching to and through cultural diversity. *Curriculum Inquiry*, *43*(1), 48–70. doi:10.1111/curi.12002

Gay, G. (2018). *Culturally responsive teaching: Theory, research, and practice* (3rd ed.). Teachers College Press.

Gee, J. P. (2001). Identity as an analytic lens for research in education. In W.G. Secada (Ed.), Review of research in education. Washington, DC: American Educational Research Association

Geiger, T., & Pivovarova, M. (2018). The effects of working conditions on teacher retention. *Teachers and Teaching*, *24*(6), 1–22. doi:10.1080/13540602.2018.1457524

Gewertz, C. (2005). *Training focuses on teachers' expectations* [Blog post]. Education Week. Retrieved from https://www.edweek.org/ew/articles/2005/04/06/30tesa.h24.html

Giannone, D. A., & Kaplin, D. (2020). How does spiritual intelligence relate to mental health in a western sample? *Journal of Humanistic Psychology*, *60*(3), 400–417. doi:10.1177/0022167817741041

Gillies, R. M., & Boyle, M. (2010). Teachers' Reflections on Cooperative Learning: Issues of Implementation. *Teaching and Teacher Education*, *26*(4), 933–940. doi:10.1016/j.tate.2009.10.034

Goldberg, D. P. (1972). *The detection of psychiatric illness by questionnaire*. Oxford University Press.

Goleman, D. (1995). *Emotional intelligence. Why it can matter more than IQ*. Bantam Books.

Goleman, D. (2001). Emotional intelligence: Issues in paradigm building. In C. Cherniss & D. Goleman (Eds.), *The emotionally intelligent workplace* (pp. 13–26). Jossey-Bass.

Goleman, D. (2003). *Destructive emotions: A scientific dialogue with the Dalai Lama*. Bantam Dell.

Goleman, D. (2005). *Emotional intelligence*. Bantam Books.

Goleman, D., Boyatzis, R., & McKee, A. (2002). *Primal leadership: Realizing the power of emotional intelligence*. Harvard Business School Press.

Goleman, D., & Davidson, R. J. (2017). *Altered traits, Science reveals how meditation changes your mind, brain, and body*. Avery.

Goleman, D., & Senge, P. (2014). *The triple focus; A new approach to education*. More Than Sound.

Goodarzi, K. (2012). *Interactive effects of spiritual intelligence and life skills education on students' mental health: A case study* [Unpublished doctoral dissertation]. Azad Islamic University Branch Borujerd, Iran.

Goodman, J., Schlossberg, N. K., & Anderson, M. L. (2006). Counseling adults in transition: Linking practice with theory (3rd ed.). New York: Springer.

Gorton, S. D., & DuFresne, M. (2021). Implementing SEAD statewide: A three-year case study of SEAD support for educators. In *Leading Schools with Social Emotional Academic Development (SEAD).* IGI Global Publication. Retrieved at https://www.igi-global.com/book/leading-schools-social-emotional-academic/256645

Graham, E. J. (2017). Authority or democracy? Integrating two perspectives on equitable classroom management in urban schools. *The Urban Review*. Advance online publication. doi:10.100711256-017-0443-8

Grant, S., Hamilton, L. S., Wrabel, S. L., Gomez, C. J., Whitaker, A., Leschitz, J. T., Unlu, F., Chavez-Herrerias, E. R., & Baker, G. (2017). *Social and emotional learning interventions under Every Student Succeeds Act: Evidence Review.* Rand Education Commissioned by The Wallace Foundation. Retrieved at www.rand.org/t/RR2133

Greenberg, M. T., Weissberg, R. P., O'Brien, M. U., Zins, J. E., Fredericks, L., Resnik, H., & Elias, M. J. (2003). Enhancing school-based prevention and youth development through coordinated social, emotional, and academic learning. *The American Psychologist*, *58*(6-7), 466–474. doi:10.1037/0003-066X.58.6-7.466 PMID:12971193

Greene, R. W. (2014). *Lost at school: Why our kids with behavioral challenges are falling through the cracks and how we can help them.* Scribner.

Griggs, C., & Strauss, T. (2018). *iConscious*. https://drcarolegriggs.com/about-iconscious

Gulbrandson, K. (2019). *Committee for children, high schoolers voice the value of social-emotional learning: Middle school SEL matters.* Retrieved at https://www.cfchildren.org/blog/2019/04/high-schoolers-voice-the-value-of-social-emotional-learning-middle-school-sel-matters/

Gullotta, T. P. (2015). After-school programming and SEL. In J. A. Durlak, C. E. Domitrovich, R. P. Weissberg, & T. P. Gullotta (Eds.), *Handbook of social and emotional learning: Research and practice* (pp. 260–266). Guilford Press.

Hall, E. T. (1960). The Silent Language in Overseas Business. *Harvard Business Review*, *38*, 87–96.

Hall, E. T. (1976). *Beyond culture*. Doubleday.

Hallfors, D., & Godette, D. (2002). Will the "Principles of Effectiveness" improve prevention practice? Early findings from a diffusion study. *Health Education Review*, *17*(4), 461–470. doi:10.1093/her/17.4.461 PMID:12197591

Hamid, N., Keikhosravani, M., & Babamiri, M. (2013). The relationship between mental health spiritual intelligence with resiliency in student of Kermanshah University of medical sciences. *Jentashapir Journal of Cellular and Molecular Biology, 3*(2), 331-338. https://www.sid.ir/en/journal/ViewPaper.aspx?id=254154

Hamilton, L. S., & Doss, C. J. (2020). *Supports for social and emotional learning in American schools and classrooms: Findings from the American teacher panel.* RAND Corporation. https://www.rand.org/pubs/research_reports/RRA397-1.html

Hamilton, L. S., & Schwartz, H. L. (2019). *Get smart about social and emotional learning measurement*. American Enterprise Institute. https://www.aei.org/research-products/report/get-smart-about-social-and-emotional-learning-measurement/

Hamilton, L. S., Doss, C. J., & Steiner, E. D. (2019a). *Support for social and emotional learning is widespread: Principals and teachers give insight into how they value, address, and measure it, and which supports they need.* Rand Corporation. https://www.rand.org/pubs/research_briefs/RB10064

Hamilton, L. S., Doss, C. J., & Steiner, E. D. (2019b). *Teacher and principal perspectives on social and emotional learning in America's schools: Findings from the American Educator Panels*. Rand Corporation. https://www.rand.org/pubs/research_reports/RR2991.html

Hammond, Z. (2014). *Responsive cultural teaching and the brain*. Corwin Press.

Hammond, Z. (2015). *Culturally responsive teaching and the brain: Promoting authentic engagement and rigor among culturally and linguistically diverse students*. Corwin Press.

Harvard Graduate School of Education. (n.d.). *About SEL*. Explore SEL. http://exploresel.gse.harvard.edu/about/

Hattie, J., & Clark, S. (2019). *Visible learning: Feedback*. Routledge. doi:10.4324/9780429485480

Hess, A. (2019, September 28). *Make it: The 10 US universities that receive the most applications*. Retrieved from: https://www.cnbc.com/2019/09/28/the-10-universities-that-receive-the-most-applications.html

Hofstede, G. (1980). *Culture's Consequences: International Differences in Work Related Values*. Sage Publications.

Hofstede, G. (1997). *Cultures and Organizations: Software of the Mind*. McGraw-Hill.

Hofstede, G. (2001). *Cultural consequences. Comparing values, behaviors, institutions, and organizations across nations* (2nd ed.). Sage.

Holland, D., & Lachicotte, W. (2007). Vygotsky, Mead, and the new sociocultural studies of identity. *The Cambridge Companion to Vygotsky*, 101-135.

Holt-Lunstad, J. (2020). *The double pandemic of social isolation and COVID: Cross-sector policy must address both*. Health Affairs Blog., doi:10.1377//hblog2020609.53823

Howard, D. C. (2019). Social-emotional learning won't happen without a culturally relevant start. *Education Week*. Retrieved from https://blogs.edweek.org/teachers/intersection-culture-and-race-ineducation/2019/02/social_emotional_learning_wont_happen_without_culturally_relevant_pedagogy.html

Howard, D. C. (2019). Social-emotional learning won't happen without a culturally relevant start. *EdWeek: Teacher Blog*. Retrieved from https://blogs.edweek.org/teachers/intersection-culture-and-race-in-education/2019/02/social_emotional_learning_wont_happen_withouth_culturally_relevant_pedagogy.html

Hughes, G. D. (2012). Teacher retention: Teacher characteristics, school characteristics, organizational characteristics, and teacher efficacy. *The Journal of Educational Research*, *105*(4), 245–255. doi:10.1080/00220671.2011.584922

Hurd, N., & Deutsch, N. (2017). SEL-focused after-school programs. *The Future of Children*, *27*(1), 95–115. doi:10.1353/foc.2017.0005

Hurley, K. (2020). *Social media and depression: New research links the problems, especially in teens*. Retrieved at https://www.psycom.net/social-media-depression-teens

IMAGO. (2017). *Duncan mindsets pilot*. IMAGO.

Immordino-Yang, M. H., Darling-Hammond, L., & Krone, C. (2018). *The brain basis for integrated social, emotional, and academic development: How emotions and social relationships drive learning*. The Aspen Institute National Commission on Social, Emotional, and Academic Development. https://www.aspeninstitute.org/publications/the-brain-basis-for-integrated-social-emotional-and-academic-development/

Immordino-Yang, M. H. (2016). *Emotions, learning, and the brain: exploring the educational implications of affective neuroscience*. W. W. Norton & Company, Inc.

Immordino-Yang, M. H., & Damasio, A. (2007). We feel, therefore we learn: The relevance of affective and social neuroscience to education. *Mind, Brain and Education: the Official Journal of the International Mind, Brain, and Education Society*, *1*(1), 3–10. doi:10.1111/j.1751-228X.2007.00004.x

Immordino-Yang, M. H., Darling-Hammond, L., & Krone, C. (2018). *The brain basis for integrated social, emotional, and academic development: How emotions and social relationships drive instruction.* Aspen Institute. Retrieved from http://nationathope.org/wp-content/uploads/aspen_research_final_web.pdf

Ingersoll, R. M. (2001). Teacher turnover and teacher shortages: An organizational analysis. *American Educational Research Journal*, *38*(3), 499–534. doi:10.3102/00028312038003499

International Institute for Restorative Practices. (2012). *What is restorative practices?* Retrieved from https://www.iirp.edu/what-is-restorative-practices.php

Jackson, I., Paretti, L., Quinn, L., Bickmore, D., & Borek, M. (2019). Retaining Nevada's Teachers: Issues and Solutions. *Policy Issues in Nevada Education*, *3*, 1.

Jackson, I., Sealey-Ruiz, Y., & Watson, W. (2014). Reciprocal love: Mentoring Black and Latino males through an ethos of care. *Urban Education*, *49*(4), 394–417. doi:10.1177/0042085913519336

Jackson, Y. (2011). *The pedagogy of confidence: Inspiring high intellectual performance in urban schools.* Teachers College Press.

Jacob, B. A. (2017). *What we know about career and technical education in high school.* https://www.brookings.edu/research/what-we-know-about-career-and-technical-education-in-high-school/

Jagers, J. J., Rivas-Drake, D., & Borowski, T. (2018). *Equity & social and emotional learning: A cultural analysis.* Collaborative for Academic, Social, and Emotional Learning (CASEL) Frameworks Briefs. https://measuringsel.casel.org/wp-content/uploads/2018/11/Frameworks-Equity.pdf

Jagers, R., Rivas-Drake, D., & Borowski, T. (2018). Equity and social and emotional learning: A cultural analysis. In *Frameworks brief, special issues series.* Collaborative for Academic, Social, and Emotional Learning. Retrieved from https://casel.org/wp-content/uploads/2020/04/equity-and-SEL-.pdf

Jagers, R.-D., Rivas-Drake, D., & Williams, B. (2019). Transformative Social and Emotional Learning (SEL): Toward SEL in Service of Educational Equity and Excellence. *Educational Psychologist*, *54*(3), 162–184. doi:10.1080/00461520.2019.1623032

Jain, M., & Meena, S. (2013). A study of relationship of spiritual intelligence and adjustment of adolescents. *Indian Journal of Psychological Science*, *3*(2), 12–16.

Jasmindebora, S., Sudheer, T., Vasantha, M., Bhavani, M., & Rohith, J. (2019). Relationship between spiritual intelligence and psychological well-being. *International Journal of Indian Psychology*, *7*(1), 990–996. doi:10.25215/0701.113

Javidan, M., Gupta, V., House, R. J., Hanges, P. J., & Dorfman, P. W. (2004). *Culture, Leadership, and Organizations: The GLOBE Study of 62 Societies*. Sage Publications.

Jenkins, R. (2015). The power of positive regard. *The Chronicle of Higher Education.* Retrieved from https://www.chronicle.com/article/The-Power-of-Positive-Regard/232547

Jennings, P. A., & Frank, J. L. (2015). Inservice preparation for educators. In J. A. Durlak, C. E. Domitrovich, R. P. Weissberg, & T. P. Gullotta (Eds.), *Handbook of social and emotional learning: Research and practice* (pp. 422–437). The Guilford Press.

Jennings, P. A., & Greenberg, M. T. (2009). The prosocial classroom: Teacher social and emotional competence in relation to student and classroom outcomes. *Review of Educational Research, 79*(1), 491–525. doi:10.3102/0034654308325693

Jennings, T., Minnici, A., & Yoder, N. (2019). Creating the working conditions to enhance teacher social and emotional well-being. In D. Osher, M. J. Mayer, R. Jagers, K. Kendziora, & L. Wood (Eds.), *Keeping Students Safe and Helping Them Thrive: A Collaborative Handbook on School Safety, Mental Health, and Wellness*. Praeger/ABC-CLIO. Retrieved from https://publisher.abc-clio.com/9781440854149/225

Jkorderm, C. (2017). *Social contract: Capturing kids hearts*. Casey Jkorderm. Retrieved at https://rumblepups.wordpress.com/

Johnson, H., & Wiener, R. (2017). *This time, with feeling: Integrating social and emotional development and college- and career-readiness standards*. Aspen Institute. https://eric.ed.gov/?id=ED577037

Johnson, D. W., & Johnson, R. T. (1999). Making Cooperative Learning Work. *Theory into Practice, 38*(2), 67–73. doi:10.1080/00405849909543834

Jones, S. M. & Kahn, J. (2017, September 13.) *The evidence base for how we learn: Supporting students' social, emotional, and academic development*. Academic Press.

Jones, S. M., & Bouffard, S. M. (2012). Social and emotional learning in schools: From programs to strategies (Social Policy Report). *Sharing Child and Youth Development Knowledge, 26*(4), 3–22. Retrieved from http://www.ncflb.com/wp-content/uploads/2013/02/Social-and-Emotional-Learning-in-Schools-From-Programs-to-Strategies.pdf

Jones, S., Bailey, R., Brush, K., & Kahn, J. (2017). Kernels of practice for SEL: Low-cost, low-burden strategies. EASEL Lab, Harvard Graduate School of Education.

Jones, S., Bailey, R., Brush, K., & Kahn, J. (2018). *Preparing for effective SEL implementation*. Harvard Graduate School of Education Easel Lab. https://www. wallacefoundation.org/knowledgecenter/Documents/Preparing-for-Effective-SEL-Implementation.pdf

Jones, S., Bailey, R., Brush, K., Nelson, B., & Barnes, S. (2016). *What is the same and what is different? Making sense of the "non-cognitive" domain*. Harvard Graduate School of Education, EASEL Lab. https://easel.gse.harvard.edu/files/gse-easel-lab/files/words_matter_paper.pdf

Jones, D., Crowley, D. M., & Greenberg, M. T. (2017). *Improving social emotional skills in childhood enhances long-term well-being and economic outcomes*. Edna Bennet Pierce Prevention Research Center, Pennsylvania State University.

Jones, S. M., & Kahn, J. (2018). The evidence base for how learning happens: A consensus on social, emotional, and academic development. *American Educator, 41*(4), 16.

Jones, S., Brush, K., Bailey, R., Brion-Meisels, G., McIntyre, J., Kahn, J., Nelson, B., & Stickle, L. (2017). *Navigating SEL from the inside out. Looking inside and across 25 leading SEL programs: A practical resource for schools and OST providers*. Harvard Graduate School of Education.

Jones, S., Brush, K., Bailey, R., Brion-Meisels, G., McIntyre, J., Khan, J., Nelson, B., & Stickle, L. (2017). *Navigating SEL from the inside out: Looking inside and across 25 leading SEL programs, a practical resource for schools and OST providers*. Harvard Graduate School. Retrieved from https://www.wallacefoundation.org/knowledge-center/Documents/Navigating-Social-and-Emotional-Learning-from-the-Inside-Out.pdf

Jones, S., & Khan, J. (2017). *The evidence base for how we learn: Supporting students' social, emotional, and academic development*. Aspen Institute. Retrieved from http://nationathope.org/wp-content/uploads/final_cds-evidence-base.pdf

Kabat-Zinn, J. (2013). *Full catastrophe living: Using the wisdom of your body and mind to face stress, pain, and illness.* Bantam Dell.

Katz, I., & Assor, A. (2007). When choice motivates and when it does not. *Educational Psychology Review, 19*(4), 429–442. doi:10.100710648-006-9027-y

Kautz, Diris, & Borghans. (2014). Fostering and measuring skills: Improving cognitive and non-cognitive skills to promote lifetime success. Paris, France: Organization for Economic Cooperation and Development.

Kaya Responsible Travel. (2020). *About Kaya – How It All Began.* Retrieved at https://www.kayavolunteer.com/responsible-travel

Kaya Responsible Travel. (2020). *What is a Remote Internship?* Retrieved at https://www.kayavolunteer.com/what-is-a-remote-internship

Kerr, D. B., & Gore, T. (2021). Developing Social Emotional Learning Competencies Through Virtual Internships. In *Leading Schools with Social, Emotional, and Academic Development (SEAD).* IGI Global Publication. Retrieved at https://www.igi-global.com/book/leading-schools-social-emotional-academic/256645

Kerr, D. B., Madden-Dent, T., & Shalabi, N. (2020). Cultural competency interventions. In The Oxford Handbook of Lifelong Learning. Academic Press.

Kerr, D. B., Madden-Dent, T., & Shalabi, N. (2020). Cultural Competency Interventions: Three Case Studies with Guiding Theoretical Frameworks. In *Cultural intelligence and social-emotional competencies across the lifespan: Cultural Competencies for Continuous Learning* (2nd ed.). Oxford University Press. Retrieved at https://www.oxfordhandbooks.com/view/10.1093/oxfordhb/9780197506707.001.0001/oxfordhb-9780197506707-e-6?utm_content=148183851&utm_medium=social&utm_source=linkedin&hss_channel=lcp-19900 doi:10.1093/oxfordhb/9780197506707.013.26

Kerr, D. B., & Madden-Dent, T. (2019). Cultural Transition and Adjustment of International East Asian Undergraduate Students. In S. E. Brock & P. J. McAliney (Eds.), *Discourses on Business Education at the College Level: On the Boundaries of Content and Praxis.* Touro University Press Books.

Kerr, D. B., Madden-Dent, T., & Shalabi, N. M. (in press). Cultural Competency Interventions: Three Case Studies with Guiding Theoretical Frameworks. In M. London (Ed.), *Oxford Handbook of Lifelong Learning* (2nd ed.). Oxford Press.

Khosravi, M., & Nikmanesh, Z. (2014). Relationship of spiritual intelligence with resilience and perceived stress. *Iranian Journal of Psychiatry and Behavioral Sciences, 8*(4), 52–56. PMID:25798174

Kim, Y. Y. (2001). Becoming intercultural: An integrative theory of communication and cross-cultural adaptation. *Sage (Atlanta, Ga.).*

King, D. B. (2008). *Rethinking claims of spiritual intelligence: A definition, model, & measure* [Unpublished Masters dissertation]. Trent University, Peterborough, ON, Canada.

King, D. B., & DeCicco, T. L. (2009). A viable model and self-report measure of spiritual intelligence. *International Journal of Transpersonal Studies, 28*(1), 68–85. doi:10.24972/ijts.2009.28.1.68

Kissling, M. T. (2014). Now and Then, in and out of the Classroom: Teachers Learning to Teach through the Experiences of Their Living Curricula. *Teaching and Teacher Education, 44*, 81–91. doi:10.1016/j.tate.2014.08.003

Kluckhohn, C. (1951). *The study of culture: The policy sciences.* Stanford University Press.

Kluckhohn, R., & Strodtbeck, F. (1961). *Variations in Value Orientations.* Row, Peterson.

Knight, L. (2015). *Building Social-Emotional Learning Skills Through Cooperative Learning.* ASCD In Service. Retrieved from https://inservice.ascd.org/building-social-emotional-learning-skills-through-cooperative-learning/

Knight, J. (2019). Why teacher autonomy is central to coaching success. *Educational Leadership*, *77*, 14–20. http://www.ascd.org/publications/educational-leadership/nov19/vol77/num03/Why-Teacher-Autonomy-Is-Central-to-Coaching-Success.aspx

Koch, S., Klumpers, F., Zhang, W., Hashemi, M. M., Kaldewaij, R., van Ast, V. A., Smit, A. S., & Roelofs, K. (2017). The role of automatic defensive responses in the development of posttraumatic stress symptoms in police recruits: Protocol of a prospective study. *European Journal of Psychotraumatology*, *8*(1), 1412226. doi:10.1080/20008198.2017.1412226 PMID:29321826

Korbey, H. (2017). *The power of being seen: How well do you know your students?* Edutopia. https://www.edutopia.org/article/power-being-seen

Kumar, V.V., & Mehta, M. (2011b). *Scale for Spiritual Intelligence* [Electronic Database]. PsycTests. . doi:10.1037/t16725-000

Kumar, V. V., & Mehta, M. (2011a). Gaining adaptive orientation through spiritual and emotional intelligence. In A. K. Chauhan & S. S. Nathawat (Eds.), *New Facets of Positivism* (pp. 281–301). Macmillan Publishers India.

Ladson-Billings, G. J. (1994). *The Dreamkeepers*. Jossey-Bass Publishing Co.

Ladson-Billings, G. J. (2014). Culturally Relevant Pedagogy 2.0: A.k.a. the Remix. *Harvard Educational Review*, *84*(1), 74–84. doi:10.17763/haer.84.1.p2rj131485484751

Lane, H. W., & Maznevski, M. L. (2019). *International Management Behavior: Global and Sustainable Leadership.* Cambridge University Press. doi:10.1017/9781108637152

Larmer, J., & Mergendoller, J. R. (2010). Seven essentials for project-based learning. *Giving Students Meaningful Work, 68*(1), 34–37.

Larson, K. E., Pas, E. T., Bradshaw, C. P., Rosenberg, M. S., & Day-Vines, N. L. (2018). Examining How Proactive Management and Culturally Responsive Teaching Relate to Student Behavior: Implications for Measurement and Practice. *School Psychology Review*, *47*(2), 153–166. doi:10.17105/SPR-2017-0070.V47-2

Laughlin, L. (2013). Who's minding the kids? Child care arrangements: Spring 2011. Current Population Reports. U.S. Census Bureau.

Leverson, M., Smith, K., McIntosh, K., Rose, J., & Pinkelman, S. (2019). *PBIS cultural responsiveness field guide: Resources for trainers and coaches.* OSEP Technical Assistance Center. https://www.pbis.org/school/equity-pbis

Leverson, M., Smith, K., McIntosh, K., Rose, J., & Pinkelman, S. (2019). *PBIS Cultural Responsiveness Field Guide: Resources for Trainers and Coaches.* OSEP Technical Assistance Center. Retrieved at: https://www.pbis.org/school/equity-pbis

Levesque, K. (2018, October 4). A school counselor puts social-emotional learning first. *Social-Emotional Learning in Action, 14*(4). Retrieved from: http://www.ascd.org/ascd-express/vol14/num04/A-School-Counselor-Puts-Social-Emotional-Learning-First.aspx

Li, C., & Xu, J. (2019). Trait emotional intelligence and classroom emotions: A positive psychology investigation and intervention among Chinese EFL learners. *Frontiers in Psychology*, *10*, 1–17. doi:10.3389/fpsyg.2019.02453 PMID:31736840

Li, L., Gow, A. D. I., & Zhou, J. (2020). The role of positive emotions in education: A neuroscience perspective. *Mind, Brain and Education: the Official Journal of the International Mind, Brain, and Education Society, 14*(3), 220–234. doi:10.1111/mbe.12244

Lippman, L., Ryberg, R., Carney, R., & Moore, K. (2015). *Key "soft skills" that foster youth workforce success: Toward a consensus across fields.* Child Trends. https://www.childtrends.org/publications/key-soft-skills-that-foster-youth-workforce-success-toward-a-consensus-across-fields

Lipson, S. K., Lattie, E. G., & Eisenberg, D. (2018). Increased rates of mental health service utilization by U.S. college students: 10-year population-level trends (2007-2017). *Psychiatric Services, 70*, 60-63. doi:10.1176/appi.ps.201800332

Lopes, P. N., Grewal, D., Kadis, J., Gall, M., & Salovey, P. (2006). Evidence that emotional intelligence is related to job performance and affect and attitudes at work. *Psicothema, 18*(Suppl.), 132–138. PMID:17295970

Lucas Education Research. (2017). *Home page.* https://www.lucasedresearch.org/

Luke, A. (2014). *On explicit and direct instruction.* Australian Literacy Educators' Association. ALEA Hot Topics. Retrieved from https://www.alea.edu.au/documents/item/861

Lustig, M. W., & Koester, J. (2003). *Intercultural competence: Interpersonal communication across cultures* (4th ed.). Pearson Education, Inc.

Madden-Dent, T. (2014). *A phenomenological study of cultural transition and adjustment of Asian undergraduate international students using different cross-cultural treatments.* Retrieved from http://hdl.handle.net/11714/2895

Madden-Dent, T. (2021a). Advancing equity through culturally responsive social-emotional education: Addressing international student integration. In Advances in Motivation and Achievement. Motivating the SEL Field Forward Through Equity (Vol. 21). Emerald Publishing Limited. doi:10.1108/S0749-7423201719

Madden-Dent, T. (2021b). Bridging academic and industry skills gap via digital collaboration: Preparing scholars for international assignment. In *University-Industry Collaboration Strategies in the Digital Era.* Retrieved at https://www.igi-global.com/book/university-industry-collaboration-strategies-digital/244278 doi:10.4018/978-1-7998-3901-9

Madden-Dent, T., & Donaburska, P. (2019). *Beyond Orientation: International Student Integration.* NAFSA: Association of International Educators National Conference.

Madden-Dent, T., Jackson, I., & Cason, J. (2021). Culturally-responsive social emotional academic development. In *Leading Schools with Social Emotional Academic Development (SEAD).* IGI Global Publication. Retrieved at https://www.igi-global.com/book/leading-schools-social-emotional-academic/256645

Madden-Dent, T. (2014). *A phenomenological study of cultural transition and adjustment of Asian undergraduate international students using different cross-cultural treatments. ProQuest.* UMI Dissertations Publishing.

Madden-Dent, T., Wood, D., & Roskina, K. (2019). A survey of international student services at 200 U.S. universities and colleges. *Journal of International Students, 9*(4), 346–362. doi:10.32674/jis.v9i4.346

Mahoney, J. L., Durlak, J. A., & Weissberg, R. P. (2018). An update on social and emotional learning outcome research. *Phi Delta Kappan, 100*(4), 18–23. doi:10.1177/0031721718815668

Mahoney, J. L., Weissberg, R. P., Greenberg, M. T., Dusenbury, L., Jagers, R. J., Niemi, K., Schlinger, M., Schlund, J., Shriver, T. P., VanAusdal, K., & Yoder, N. (2020, October 8). Systemic Social and Emotional Learning: Promoting Educational Success for All Preschool to High School Students. *The American Psychologist.* Advance online publication. doi:10.1037/amp0000701 PMID:33030926

Maker, A. (2018). Screen time: The impact on kids and parenting. *Psychology Today*. Retrieved from https://www.psychologytoday.com/us/blog/helping-kids-cope/201808/screen-time-the-impact-kids-and-parenting

Maldonado, C. (2019). *Integrating workforce development practices in higher education*. Workforce Development Center, University of Nevada.

Manyika, J., Lund, S., Chui, M., Bughin, J., Woetzel, J., Batra, P., Ko, R., & Sanghvi, S. (2017). *Jobs lost, jobs gained: Workforce transitions in a time of automation*. McKinsey Global Institute. https://www.mckinsey.com/~/media/McKinsey/Industries/Public%20and%20Social%20Sector/Our%20Insights/What%20the%20future%20of%20work%20will%20mean%20for%20jobs%20skills%20and%20wages/MGI-Jobs-Lost-Jobs-Gained-Executive-summary-December-6-2017.pdf

Mapp, K. L., & Kuttner, P. J. (2013). *Partners in education in a dual capacity-building framework for family–school partnerships*. Southwest Educational Development Laboratory. Retrieved from https://sedl.org/pubs/framework/FE-Cap-Building.pdf

Marashi, S., Naami, A., Beshlideh, K., & Zargar, Y. (2012). The impact of spiritual intelligence training on psychological well- being, existential anxiety, and spiritual quotient among the students of Ahvaz faculty of petroleum. *Journal of Education & Psychology*, *19*(1), 63–80. https://www.sid.ir/en/journal/ViewPaper.aspx?id=307584

Marloes, M. H. G., Hendrickx, M., Mainhard, T., Boor-Klip, H. J., Cillessen, A. H. M., & Brekelman, M. (2016). Social dynamics in the classroom: Teacher support and conflict and the peer ecology. *Teaching and Teacher Education*, *53*, 30–40. doi:10.1016/j.tate.2015.10.004

Marquardt, M. J., & Engel, D. W. (1993). *Global human resource development*. Prentice Hall.

Mart, A. K., Weissberg, R. P., & Kendziora, K. (2015). Systemic support for SEL in school districts. Handbook of social and emotional learning: Research and practice, 482-499.

Marzieh, R., Hoda, A. T., Saiedeh, H., Esmat, J., Zahra, J., & Ahmad, B. S. (2013). Relationship between spiritual intelligence, happiness and academic achievement in students of QOM University of Medical Sciences. *Indian Journal of Medical Education*, *13*(5), 431–440.

Maslow, A. H. (1982). *Toward a Psychology of Being (An Insight Book)* (2nd ed.). Van Nostrand Reinhold.

Mayo Foundation for Medical Education and Research (MFMER). (2017). *Mayo Clinic*. Retrieved from https://www.mayoclinic.org/diseases-conditions/depression/in-depth/depression-and-exercise/art-20046495

McIntosh, K., & Goodman, S. (2016). *Integrated multi-tiered systems of supports: Blending RTI and PBIS*. Guilford Press. https://www.guilford.com/books/Integrated-Multi-Tiered-Systems-of-Support/McIntosh-Goodman/9781462524747/reviews

McKown, C. (2015). Challenges and opportunities in the direct assessment of children's social and emotional comprehension. In J. A. Durlak, C. E. Domitrovich, R. P. Weissberg, & T. P. Gullotta (Eds.), *Handbook of social and emotional learning: Research and practice* (pp. 320–335). The Guilford Press.

McMillan, J. H., & Hearn, J. (2008). Student self-assessment: The key to stronger motivation and higher achievement. *Educational Horizons*, *87*, 40–49. https://files.eric.ed.gov/fulltext/EJ815370.pdf

Medina-López-Portillo, A. (2004). Intercultural learning assessment: The link between program duration and the development of intercultural sensitivity. *Frontiers: The Interdisciplinary Journal of Study Abroad*, *10*(1), 179–200. doi:10.36366/frontiers.v10i1.141

Meijer, P. C. (2011). The role of crisis in the development of student teachers' professional identity. In *Navigating in Educational Contexts* (pp. 41–54). Sense Publishers. doi:10.1007/978-94-6091-522-2_3

Mentor, Y. (2020, September 14). *The stats*. https://www.youthmentor.org/thestats

Meyers, D. C., Domitrovich, C. E., Dissi, R., Trejo, J., & Greenberg, M. T. (2019). Supporting systemic social and emotional learning with a schoolwide implementation model. *Evaluation and Program Planning, 73*, 53–61. doi:10.1016/j.evalprogplan.2018.11.005 PMID:30513463

Midi, M. M., Cosmas, G., & Sinik, S. (2019). The effects of spiritual intelligence on academic achievement and psychological well-being of youths in Kanibungan village, Pitas. *Southeast Asia Psychology Journal, 9*(3), 1–14.

Miller, J. S. (2020). *Confident parents, confident kids: Raising emotional intelligence in ourselves and our kids from toddlers to teenagers*. Fair Winds Press. Retrieved at https://confidentparentsconfidentkids.org/the-book/

Mindful SEAD. (2020a). *Comprehensive report: Ongoing SEAD professional development*. Author.

Mindful SEAD. (2020b). *Journal and reference tool: Ongoing SEAD professional development*. Author.

Mindful SEAD. (2021). *Comprehensive report: The Nevada Department of Education SEAD Center*. Manuscript in preparation.

Minney, D., Garcia, J., Altobelli, J., Perez-Brena, N., & Blunk, E. (2019). Social-emotional learning and evaluation in after-school care: A working model. *Journal of Youth Development, 14*(3), 130–145. doi:10.5195/jyd.2019.660

Mizell, H. (2010). *Why professional development matters*. Learning Forward. https://learningforward.org/wp-content/uploads/2017/08/professional-development-matters.pdf

Moffitt, T. E., Arseneault, L., Belsky, D., Dickson, N., Hancox, R. J., Harrington, H., Houts, R., Poulton, R., Roberts, B. W., Ross, S., Sears, M. R., Thomson, W. M., & Caspi, A. (2011). A gradient of childhood self-control predicts health, wealth, and public safety. *Proceedings of the National Academy of Sciences of the United States of America, 108*(7), 2693–2698. doi:10.1073/pnas.1010076108 PMID:21262822

Mueller, C. M., & Dweck, C. S. (1998). Praise for intelligence can undermine children's motivation and performance. *Journal of Personality and Social Psychology, 75*(1), 33–52. doi:10.1037/0022-3514.75.1.33 PMID:9686450

Nair, K. A., & Paul, G. (2017). A study on spiritual intelligence among higher secondary students in relation to their social adjustment. *Journal of Research in Humanities and Social Science, 5*(3), 38–42.

National Alliance on Mental Illness (NAMI). (2020). *Mental health by the numbers*. Retrieved at https://nami.org/mhstats

National Association of Colleges and Employers. (2019). *Career readiness for the new college graduate: A definition of competencies (revised)*. Retrieved from https://www.naceweb.org/career-readiness/competencies/career-readiness-defined/

National Association of Secondary School Principals. (2020, March 11). *Class rank, GPA, and grading*. Retrieved from: https://www.nassp.org/policy-advocacy-center/nassp-position-statements/class-rank-gpa-and-grading/#:~:text=As%20schools%20and%20districts%20moved,the%20basis%20of%20class%20rank

National Center on Safe Supportive Learning Environments. (2020). *Emotional Safety*. American Institutes for Research. Retrieved at https://safesupportivelearning.ed.gov/topic-research/safety/emotional-safety

National Coalition Against Domestic Violence (NCADV). (2020). *Domestic violence statistics*. Retrieved at https://ncadv.org/statistics

National Commission on Social, Emotional, and Academic Development (NC-SEAD). (2019). *Nation at hope*. Aspen, CO: Aspen Institute. Retrieved from http://nationathope.org/

National Commission on Social, Emotional, and Academic Development. (2019). *Nation at hope*. Aspen, CO: Aspen Institute. Retrieved from http://nationathope.org/

National Institutes of Health (NIH). (2020). *National Institute on Drug Abuse*. Retrieved at https://www.drugabuse.gov/drug-topics/opioids/opioid-overdose-crisis

National School Reform Faculty. (2020). *Critical friend*. https://nsrfharmony.org/faq-items/critical-friend/

Neill, J. (2008). *The expatriate venture: What role does cross-cultural training play and what theories guide research in the field?* Schmidt Labor Research Center Seminar Research Series. University of Rhode Island.

Nemati, E., Habibi, M., Vargahan, F. A., Mohamadloo, S. S., & Ghanbari, S. (2017). The role of mindfulness and spiritual intelligence in students' mental health. *Journal of Research & Health*, *7*(1), 594–602. doi:10.18869/acadpub.jrh.7.1.594

Netemeyer, R. G., Bearden, W. O., & Sharma, S. (2003). *Scaling procedures: Issues and applications*. Sage Publications. doi:10.4135/9781412985772

Nevada Association of School Administrators. (2020). *Home page*. https://nvadministrator.org/

Nevada Department of Education. (2018). *Nevada's framework for equitable integrated system of student supports*. http://www.doe.nv.gov/uploadedFiles/ndedoenvgov/content/SafeRespectfulLearning/MTSSGuidanceDoc508.pdf

Nevada Department of Education. (2019a). *SEAD 101 SEAD center* [MOOC]. Pepper PD. https://www.pepperpd.com/courses/NDE/SEAD101/SU2020/cabout

Nevada Department of Education. (2019b, June 26). *Social Emotional, and Academic Development (SEAD)*. http://www.doe.nv.gov/Educator_Licensure/Special_Licenses-Endorsements-Various_Grade_Levels/

Nevada Digital Learning. (2020). *Home page*. https://nvdigitallearning.org/

New Leaders. (2017). *Prioritizing leadership: Opportunities in ESSA for chief state school officers*. https://newleaders.org/wp-content/uploads/2016/10/PrioritizingLeadership_OpportunitiesESSAChiefStateSchoolOfficers.pdf

Nobari, L., & Shokri, M. (2014). Evaluating the student's spiritual intelligence and quality of life relationship at Payam-E-Noor University in Kaleibar branch. *Arabian Journal of Business and Management Review*, *3*(12), 123–131. doi:10.12816/0016558

Nurfarojandari, A., & Maftuhah, M. (2019, September). *Student academic achievement: The role of emotional and spiritual intelligence* [Paper presentation]. 5th International Conference on Education in Muslim Society, ICEMS 2019, Jakarta, Indonesia. https://eudl.eu/doi/10.4108/eai.30-9-2019.2291124

Olsen, B. (2008). Introducing teacher identity and this volume. *Teacher Education Quarterly*, 3–6.

Osgood, D. W., Feinberg, M. E., Gest, S. D., Moody, J., Ragan, D. T., Spoth, R., Greenberg, M., & Redmond, C. (2013). Effects of PROSPER on the influence potential of prosocial versus antisocial youth in adolescent friendship networks. *The Journal of Adolescent Health*, *53*(2), 174–179. doi:10.1016/j.jadohealth.2013.02.013 PMID:23885960

Osher, D., Bear, G., Sprague, J., & Doyle, W. (2010). How we can improve school discipline. *Educational Researcher*, *39*(1), 48–58. doi:10.3102/0013189X09357618

Osher, D., Cantor, P., Berg, J., Steyer, L., & Rose, T. (2018). Drivers of human development: How relationships and context shape learning and development. *Applied Developmental Science*, *1*. Advance online publication. doi:10.1080/10888691.2017.1398650

Osher, D., Moroney, D., & Williamson, S. (2018). *Creating safe, equitable, engaging schools: A comprehensive, evidence-based approach to supporting students*. Harvard Education Press.

Pant, N., & Srivastava, S. K. (2019). The impact of spiritual intelligence, gender and educational background on mental health among college students. *Journal of Religion and Health*, *58*(1), 87–108. doi:10.100710943-017-0529-3 PMID:29192361

Paris, D. (2012). Culturally sustaining pedagogy: A needed change in stance, terminology, and practice. *Educational Researcher*, *41*(3), 93–97. doi:10.3102/0013189X12441244

Paris, D., & Alim, H. S. (2014). What are we seeking to sustain through culturally sustaining pedagogy? A loving critique forward. *Harvard Educational Review*, *84*(1), 85–137. doi:10.17763/haer.84.1.9821873k2ht16m77

Patrick, S., & Sturgis, C. (2013). *Competency works issue brief: Necessary for success: Building mastery of world-class skills: A state policymakers guide to competency education.* International Association for K–12 Online Education. Retrieved from https://www.competencyworks.org/wp-content/uploads/2013/02/inacol_cw_issuebrief_building_mastery_final.pdf

Payton, J. W., Wardlaw, D. M., Graczyk, P. A., Bloodworth, M. R., Tompsett, C. J., & Weissberg, R. P. (2000). Social and emotional learning: A framework for promoting mental health and reducing risk behavior in children and youth. *The Journal of School Health*, *70*(5), 179–185. doi:10.1111/j.1746-1561.2000.tb06468.x PMID:10900594

Pew Research Center. (2016). *The state of American jobs.* https://www.pewsocialtrends.org/2016/10/06/the-state-of-american-jobs/

Pianta, R. C., Hamre, B. K., & Mintz, S. (2012). *Classroom Assessment Scoring System – Secondary Manual*. Teachstone.

Pieter Van Oudenhoven, J., & Van der Zee, K. I. (2002). Predicting multicultural effectiveness of international students: The Multicultural Personality Questionnaire. *International Journal of Intercultural Relations*, *26*(6), 679–694. doi:10.1016/S0147-1767(02)00041-X

Pilhofer, K. (2010). *Cultural knowledge: An ethical deconstruction of the concept as a foundation for respect for cultural differences from a post-colonial and Levinasian perspective*. Copenhagen Business School. Retrieved at http://studenttheses.cbs.dk/bitstream/handle/10417/1677/katharina_pilhofer.pdf?sequence=1

Pinnegar, S. (2005). Identity development, moral authority, and the teacher educator. In G. F. Hoban (Ed.), *The missing links in teacher education design* (pp. 259–279). Springer. doi:10.1007/1-4020-3346-X_14

Pitts, M. J. (2009). Identity and the role of expectations, stress, and talk in short-term student sojourner adjustment: An application of the integrative theory of communication and cross-cultural adaptation. *International Journal of Intercultural Relations*, *33*(6), 450–462. doi:10.1016/j.ijintrel.2009.07.002

Podolsky, A., Kini, T., Bishop, J., & Darling-Hammond, L. (2016). *Solving the teacher shortage: How to attract and retain excellent educators*. Learning Policy Institute. https://learningpolicyinstitute.org/sites/default/files/product-files/Solving_Teacher_Shortage_Attract_Retain_Educators_REPORT.pdf

Pofeldt, E. (2017, October 17). Are we ready for a workforce that is 50% freelance? *Forbes*. Retrieved from: https://www.forbes.com/sites/elainepofeldt/2017/10/17/are-we-ready-for-a-workforce-that-is-50-freelance/#e3713a3f82b2

Pollard, B. A. (2020). What Sparks Critical Learning?: Exploring the Dialogical Teaching Context Facilitated in the LEAD Course. In G. Salinitri (Ed.), *Handbook of Research on Leadership Experience for Academic Direction (LEAD) Programs for Student Success* (pp. 297–322). IGI Global. doi:10.4018/978-1-7998-2430-5.ch016

Rainie, L., & Anderson, J. (2017). *The future of jobs and jobs training*. https://www.pewresearch.org/internet/wp-content/uploads/sites/9/2017/05/PI_2017.05.03_Future-of-Job-Skills_FINAL.pdf

Rani, A. A., Hashim, H., Ali, F., Abidin, I., & Ahmad, A. (2017). *Inculcating spiritual intelligence to enhance students' psychological well-being*. The European Proceedings of Social & Behavioural Sciences. doi:10.15405/epsbs.2017.10.23

Rayung, M. N., & Ambotang, A. S. (2018). The influence of emotional and spiritual intelligence on the high school student outcomes. *Journal of Education & Social Policy, 5*(1), 211-20. http://jespnet.com/journals/Vol_5_No_1_March_2018/23.pdf

Razia, B. (2019). Effect of spiritual intelligence on well-being of prospective teachers. *Research and Reflections on Education, 17*(3), 18-26. http://sxcejournal.com/jul-sep-2019/paper3.pdf

Reed, K., & Madden-Dent, T. (2021). Social emotional learning as a lever for high school student mental health and academic success: A reflective analysis. In *Leading Schools with Social Emotional Academic Development (SEAD)*. IGI Global Publication. Retrieved at https://www.igi-global.com/book/leading-schools-social-emotional-academic/256645

Regional Educational Laboratory (REL) Midwest. (2018). *Integrating a focus on equity into social and emotional learning*. https://ies.ed.gov/ncee/edlabs/infographics/pdf/REL_MW_Integrating_a_Focus_on_Equity_into_Social_and_Emotional_Learning.pdf

Rew, L., Becker, H., Cookston, J., Khosropour, S., & Martinez, S. (2003). Measuring cultural awareness in nursing students. *The Journal of Nursing Education, 42*(6), 249–257. doi:10.3928/0148-4834-20030601-07 PMID:12814215

Rimm-Kaufman, S., & Sandilos, L. (2018). *Improving Students' Relationships with Teachers to Provide Essential Supports for Learning.* American Psychological Association. https://www.apa.org/education/ce/1360423

Rimm-Kaufman, S. E., & Hulleman, C. S. (2015). Social and emotional learning in elementary school settings: Identifying mechanisms that matter. In J. A. Durlak, C. E. Domitrovich, R. P. Weissberg, & T. P. Gullotta (Eds.), *Handbook of social and emotional learning: Research and practice* (pp. 151–166). The Guilford Press.

Rodgers, C. R., & Scott, K. H. (2008). *40 The development of the personal self and professional identity in learning to teach*. Academic Press.

Rogers, E. M. (2002). Diffusion of preventive innovations. *Addictive Behaviors, 27*(6), 989–993. doi:10.1016/S0306-4603(02)00300-3 PMID:12369480

Rose, J., Leverson, M., & Smith, K. (2020). *Embedding culturally responsive practices in Tier I.* Center on Positive Behavioral Interventions & Supports. Retrieved at www.pbis.org

Rosen, R., Visher, M., & Beal, K. (2018). *Career and technical education: Current policy, prominent programs, and evidence*. MDRC. https://eric.ed.gov/?id=ED590008

Rossatto, C. A. (2020). Challenging fear and hate: Caring and compassion as essential components of a critical pedagogy school curriculum. In J. Keengwe (Ed.), *Handbook of Research on Diversity and Social Justice in Higher Education* (pp. 149–159). IGI Global. doi:10.4018/978-1-7998-5268-1.ch009

Rothstein, D., & Santana, L. (2011). Teaching students to ask their own questions: One small change can yield big results. *Harvard Education Letter, 27*, 1–6.

Rowe, M. B. (1972, March 31). *Wait-Time and Rewards as Instructional Variables: Their Influence on Language, Logic, and Fate Control.* Retrieved from https://eric.ed.gov/?id=ED061103

Rowley, J. (1996). Motivation and academic staff in higher education. *Quality Assurance in Education*, *4*(3), 11–16. doi:10.1108/09684889610125814

Rubie-Davies, C., Hattie, J., & Hamilton, R. (2006). Expecting the best from students: Teacher expectations and academic outcomes. *The British Journal of Educational Psychology*, *76*(3), 429–444. doi:10.1348/000709905X53589 PMID:16953955

RULER. (n.d.). Retrieved January 4, 2021, from https://www.rulerapproach.org/about/what-is-ruler/

Sa'adati, H., & Lashani, L. (2012). Spiritual intelligence relationship with coping strategies. *Archives of Rehabilitation, 12,* 75-81. http://rehabilitationj.uswr.ac.ir/article-1-1028-en.html

Sachs, J. (2001). Teacher professional identity: Competing discourses, competing outcomes. *Journal of Education Policy*, *16*(2), 149–161. doi:10.1080/02680930116819

Sackstein, S. (2017) Peer feedback in the classroom: Empowering students to be the experts. *ASCD.* Retrieved from http://www.ascd.org/ASCD/pdf/siteASCD/publications/books/PeerFeedbackInTheClassroom_Sackstein.pdf

Safir, S. (2016). 5 keys to challenging implicit bias. *Edutopia.* Retrieved from https://www.edutopia.org/blog/keys-to-challenging-implicit-bias-shane-safir

Sagiv, L., & Schwartz, S. H. (2000). A New Look at National Culture: Illustrative Applications to Role Stress and Managerial Behavior. In The Handbook of Organizational Culture and Climate. Sage Publications.

Scharf, A. (2016). *Critical practices for anti-bias education.* Teaching Tolerance. Retrieved from https://www.tolerance.org/sites/default/files/2017-06/PDA%20Critical%20Practices_0.pdf

Schlossberg, N. K. (1981). A model for analyzing human adaptation to transition. *The Counseling Psychologist*, *9*(2), 2–18. doi:10.1177/001100008100900202

Schlossberg, N. K. (1990). Training counselors to work with adults. *Generations (San Francisco, Calif.)*, *90*(14), 7.

Schlund, J., & Weissberg, R. P. (2020). *Leveraging social and emotional learning to support students and families in the time of COVID-19.* Learning Policy Institute. https://learningpolicyinstitute.org/blog/leveraging-social-emotional-learning-support-students-families-covid-19

Schlund, J., Jagers, R., & Schlinger, M. (2020). *Emerging insights on advancing social and emotional learning (SEL) as a lever for equity and excellence.* CASEL. Retrieved from https://bit.ly/CASELEquityInsights

Schonert-Reichi, K. A., Kitil, J., & Hanson-Peterson, J. (2017). To reach the students, teach the teachers: A national scan of teacher preparation and social & emotional learning. Report prepared for the Collaborative for Academic, Social, and Emotional Learning (CASEL). University of British Columbia.

Schonert-Reichl, K., Kitil, M. J., & Hanson-Peterson, J. (2017). To reach the students, teach the teachers: A national scan of teacher preparation and social and emotional learning. A report prepared for the Collaborative for Academic, Social, and Emotional Learning (CASEL). University of British Columbia.

Schonert-Reichl, K. A., Kitil, M. J., & Hanson-Peterson, J. (2017). *To reach the students, teach the teachers: A national scan of teacher preparation and social and emotional learning.* University of British Columbia.

Schwalm, J., & Tyleck, K. S. (2012). Systemwide implementation of project-based learning: The Philadelphia approach. *Afterschool Matters*, 1–8.

Science of Learning and Development Alliance. (2020). *How the science of learning and development can transform education: Initial findings*. Retrieved from https://5bde8401-9b54-4c2c-8a0c-569fc1789664.filesusr.com/ugd/eb0b6a_24f761d8a4ec4d7db13084eb2290c588.pdf

SEL. What Are the Core Competence Areas and Where are they Promoted? (n.d.). Retrieved January 11, 2021, from https://casel.org/sel-framework/

Seligman, M. E. P. (2011). *Flourish, A visionary new understanding of happiness and well-being*. Atria Paperback.

Sharma, S. (2019). Spiritual intelligence in relation to academic achievement among Somalia students. *History Research Journal*, *5*(6), 798–800.

Shaw, P., Eckstrand, K., Sharp, W., Blumenthal, J., Lerch, J. P., Greenstein, D., Clasen, L., Evans, A., Giedd, J., & Rapoport, J. L. (2007). Attention-deficit/hyperactivity disorder is characterized by a delay in cortical maturation. *Proceedings of the National Academy of Sciences of the United States of America*, *104*(49), 19649–19654. doi:10.1073/pnas.0707741104 PMID:18024590

Shaw, P., Malek, M., Watson, B., Sharp, W., Evans, A., & Greenstein, D. (2012). Development of cortical surface area and gyrification in attention-deficit/hyperactivity disorder. *Biological Psychiatry*, *72*(3), 191–197. doi:10.1016/j.biopsych.2012.01.031 PMID:22418014

Sheldon, S. B., & Jung, S. B. (2015). *The family engagement partnership student outcome evaluation*. Johns Hopkins University School of Education, Center on School, Family, and Community Partnerships., https://www.researchgate.net/publication/319226886_The_Family_Engagement_Partnership_Student_Outcome_Evaluation

Shriver, T. P., & Weissberg, R. P. (2020). A response to constructive criticism of social and emotional learning. *Phi Delta Kappan*, *101*(7), 52–57. doi:10.1177/0031721720917543

Shriver, T., & Buffett, J. (2015). The uncommon core. In J. A. Durlak, C. E. Domitrovich, R. P. Weissberg, & T. P. Gullotta (Eds.), *Handbook of social and emotional learning: Research and practice* (pp. xv–xvi). The Guilford Press.

Sierra Nevada University. (2019a). *Comprehensive report: Sierra Nevada College pilot 2019 SEAD leadership summit*. Author.

Sierra Nevada University. (2019b). *SEAD educational leadership summit program and journal*. Author.

Sigmar, L. S., Hynes, G. E., & Hill, K. L. (2012). Strategies for teaching social and emotional intelligence in business communication. *Business Communication Quarterly*, *75*(3), 301–317. doi:10.1177/1080569912450312

Singh, A., Kour, P., & Singh, T. (2010). Spiritual intelligence, altruism, school environment, and academic achievement as predictor of mental health of adolescents. *Journal of Exercise Science and Physiotherapy*, *6*(1), 34–38.

Skiba, R., Reynolds, C. R., Graham, S., Sheras, P., Conoley, J. C., & Garcia-Vazquez, E. (2006). *Are zero tolerance policies effective in the schools? An evidentiary review and recommendations.* A report by the American Psychological Association Zero Tolerance Task Force. Retrieved from https://www.apa.org/pubs/info/reports/zero-tolerance-report.pdf

Smartt, M. J. (2014). *The relationship of spiritual intelligence to achievement of secondary students.* Doctoral Dissertations and Projects. 820. https://digitalcommons.liberty.edu/doctoral/820

Smith, M. K. (2020, January 24). *Aristotle and education*. Retrieved from https://infed.org/mobi/aristotle-and-education/

Smith, T., Brumskill, R., Johnson, A., & Zimmer, T. (2018). The impact of teacher language on students' mindsets and statistics performance. *Social Psychology of Education*, *21*(4), 775–786. doi:10.100711218-018-9444-z

Social, Emotional and Academic Development Endorsements. (2019). *NRS 391.019*. https://www.leg.state.nv.us/Register/2018Register/R154-18AP.pdf

Sood, S., Bakhshi, A., & Gupta, R. (2012). Relation between personality traits, spiritual intelligence and well-being in university students. *Journal of Education and Practice*, *3*(10), 55–60.

Spiegel, A. (2012). *Teachers' expectations can influence how students perform.* Retrieved from https://www.npr.org/sections/health-shots/2012/09/18/161159263/teachers-expectations-can-influence-how-students-perform

Spoth, R., Guyll, M., & Shin, C. (2009). Universal intervention as a protective shield against exposure to substance use: Long-term outcomes and public health significance. *American Journal of Public Health*, *99*(11), 2026–2033. doi:10.2105/AJPH.2007.133298 PMID:19762678

Spradley, J. P. (1980). *Participant observation.* Harcourt Brace Jovanovich College Publishers.

Staats, C. (2014). *Implicit racial bias and school discipline disparities: Exploring the connection. Kirwan Institute Special Report*. Kirwan Institute. Retrieved from http://kirwaninstitute.osu.edu/implicit-bias-training/resources/ki-ib-argument-piece03.pdf

Stahl, R. J. (1994, April 30). *Using "Think-time" behaviors to Promote Students' Information Processing, Learning, and On-task Participation: An Instructional Model.* Retrieved from https://www.ericdigests.org/1995-1/think.htm

Swain-Bradway, J., Lindstrom Johnson, S., Bradshaw, C., & McIntosh, K. (2017). *What are the economic costs of implementing SWPBIS in comparison to the benefits from reducing suspensions?* Technical Brief from Center for Positive Behavioral Interventions and Supports. https://assets-global.website-files.com/5d3725188825e071f1670246/5d76c00cb9339d5f3f267ee7_economiccostsswpbis.pdf

Swars, S. L., Meyers, B., Mays, L. C., & Lack, B. (2009). A two-dimensional model of teacher retention and mobility: Classroom teachers and their university partners take a closer look at a vexing problem. *Journal of Teacher Education*, *60*(2), 168–183. doi:10.1177/0022487108329116

Taters, G. (2019). *Making time for mindfulness.* Harvard Graduate School of Education. Retrieved at https://www.gse.harvard.edu/news/uk/19/01/making-time-mindfulness

Taylor, R. D., Oberle, E., Durlak, J. A., & Weissberg, R. P. (2017). Promoting positive youth development through school-based social and emotional learning interventions: A meta-analysis of follow-up effects. *Child Development*, *88*(4), 1156–1171. doi:10.1111/cdev.12864 PMID:28685826

Tennessee Department of Education. (n.d.). *Social and personal competencies.* Retrieved from https://www.tn.gov/education/health-and-safety/school-climate/social-and-personal-competencies.html

Terzi, S., & Celik, A. (2005). Teacher-student interactions in distance learning. *The Turkish Online Journal of Educational Technology*, *4*(1), 54–56.

Test, F. (2020). *The national center for fair & open testing.* https://www.fairtest.org/

The Glossary of Education Reform. (2016, February 18). Retrieved from https://www.edglossary.org/student-engagement/

The Importance of the Pyramid of Learning. (n.d.). Retrieved from https://www.yourkidsot.com/blog/the-importance-of-the-pyramid-of-learning

The Origins Program. (2014). *Developmental Designs 1: Resource book.* Author.

The Theory of Self-Actualization. (2013, August 13). Retrieved from https://www.psychologytoday.com/us/blog/theory-and-psychopathology/201308/the-theory-self-actualization

The Upshot Harvard University. (2017). *The New York Times*. Retrieved from: https://www.nytimes.com/interactive/projects/college-mobility/harvard-university

Thessin, R. A., & Louis, K. S. (2020, April). The principal's role has changed: Is professional learning keeping up? *The Learning Professional, 41*(2). https://learningforward.org/journal/beyond-the-basics/the-principals-role-has-changed/

Training Management Corporation©. (2013). *Cultural Orientations Indicator® technical manual summary*. Retrieved by request from http://www.tmcorp.com/

Training Management Corporation©. (2020). *Cultural Orientations Indicator®*. Retrieved from http://www.tmcorp.com/Online-Learning/Assessments/Cultural-Orientations-Indicator-COI/76/

Trompenaars, F. (1993). Riding the waves of culture: Understanding cultural diversity in business. *Economica Books.*

Trompenenaars, F., & Hampden-Turner, C. (1998). *Riding the waves of culture: understanding cultural diversity in global business* (2nd ed.). McGraw Hill.

Twenge, J. (2018). *iGen: Why today's super-connected kids are growing up less rebellious, more tolerant, less happy—and completely unprepared for adulthood—and what that means for the rest of us*. Atria Books. Retrieved from: https://www.cnbc.com/2019/09/28/the-10-universities-that-receive-the-most-applications.html

U.S. Department of Education, National Center for Education Statistics. (2019). *Digest of Education Statistics*. Retrieved from: https://nces.ed.gov/fastfacts/display.asp?id=84

U.S. Department of Education, Office of Career, Technical, and Adult Education. (2012). *Employability skills framework*. https://s3.amazonaws.com/PCRN/docs/Employability_Skills_Framework_OnePager_20180212.pdf

US Department of Health and Human Services. (2001). *Trends in the well-being of America's children and youth, 2001*. US Government Printing Office.

Vande Berg, M., Connor-Linton, J., & Paige, M. R. (2009). The Georgetown Consortium Project: Interventions for Student Learning Abroad. *Frontiers: The Interdisciplinary Journal of Study Abroad, 18*(1), 1–75. doi:10.36366/frontiers.v18i1.251

Varlander, S. (2008). The role of students' emotions in formal feedback situations. *Journal of Teaching in Higher Education, 13*(2), 145–156. doi:10.1080/13562510801923195

Vierstraete, S. (2005). Mentorship: Toward Success in Teacher Induction and Retention. *Catholic Education: A Journal of Inquiry and Practice, 8*(3), 381-392.

Vygotsky, L. S. (1978). Mind in society (M. Cole, V. John-Steiner, S. Scribner, & E. Souberman, Eds.). Academic Press.

Ward, S., & Jacobsen, K. (n.d.). *Cognitive Connections*. www.efpractice.com/

Webster-Stratton, C., & Herman, K. C. (2010). Disseminating Incredible Years Series early-intervention programs: integrating and sustaining services between school and home. *Psychology in the Schools, 47*(1), 36-54. doi:20450 doi:10 1002/pits

Wehling, S. (2008). Cross-cultural competency through service-learning. *Journal of Community Practice, 16*(3), 293–315. doi:10.1080/10705420802255080

Weissberg, R. P., Durlak, J. A., Domitrovich, C. E., & Gullotta, T. P. (Eds.). (2015). Social and emotional learning: Past, present, and future. In J. A. Durlak, C. E. Domitrovich, R. P. Weissberg, & T. P. Gullotta (Eds.), Handbook of social and emotional learning: Research and practice (pp. 3-19). The Guilford Press.

Weissberg, R. P., Shriver, T. P., Sharmistha, B., & DeFalco, K. (1997). Creating a districtwide social development project. *Educational Leadership*, *54*, 37–39.

Weissberg, R. P., Walberg, H. J., O'Brien, M. U., & Kuster, C. B. (Eds.). (2003). *Long-term trends in the well-being of children and youth*. Child Welfare League of America Press.

Williford, A. P., & Wolcott, C. S. (2015). SEL and student-teacher relationships. In J. A. Durlak, C. E. Domitrovich, R. P. Weissberg, & T. P. Gullotta (Eds.), *Handbook of social and emotional learning: Research and practice, 634*. The Guilford Press.

Willingham, D. (2011). Ask the cognitive scientist: Can teachers increase students' self-control? *American Educator*, *35*(2), 22–27. https://www.aft.org/sites/default/files/periodicals/Willingham_3.pdf

Wohl, A. F. (2012). *Citizenship and social activism: A mixed method case study to understand cultural competence in students of a service-learning based course* (Thesis). North Dakota State University.

Woolf, N. (2020). *A Comprehensive Guide to Adult SEL*. Panorama Education. Retrieved from https://www.panoramaed.com/blog/comprehensive-guide-adult-sel

World Café Community Foundation. (2015). *Café to go! A quick reference guide for hosting world café*. http://www.theworldcafe.com/wp-content/uploads/2015/07/Cafe-To-Go-Revised.pdf

World Economic Forum. (2020). *The future of jobs report*. http://www3.weforum.org/docs/WEF_Future_of_Jobs_2020.pdf

Yang, X., Ge, C., Hu, B., Chi, T., & Wang, L. (2009). Relationship between quality of life and occupational stress among teachers. *Public Health*, *123*(11), 750–755. doi:10.1016/j.puhe.2009.09.018 PMID:19883926

Yoder, N., Atwell, M. N., Godek, D., Dusenbury, L., Bridgeland, J. M., & Weissberg, R. (2020). *Preparing youth for the workforce of tomorrow: Cultivating the social and emotional skills employers demand*. Collaborative for Academic, Social, and Emotional Learning. https://casel.org/wp-content/uploads/2020/06/Preparing-Youth-for-the-Workforce-of-Tomorrow-Final.pdf

Yoder, N., Atwell, M. N., Godek, D., Dusenbury, L., Bridgeland, J. M., & Weissberg, R. (2020). *Preparing youth for the workforce of tomorrow: Culturivating the social and emotional skills employers demand*. CASEL publication. Retrieved at https://casel.org/collaborative-state-initiative/

Yoder, N., Dusenbury, L., Martinez-Black, T., & Weissberg, R. P. (2020). *Emerging insights: From insights to action, redefining state efforts to support social and emotional learning*. Collaborative for Academic, Social, and Emotional Learning. Retrieved from www.casel.org

Yoder, N., Martinez-Black, T., Dusenbury, L., & Weissberg, R. P. (2020). *Systemic social and emotional learning for states: CASEL state theory of action*. Collaborative for Academic, Social, and Emotional Learning. https://casel.org/wp-content/uploads/2020/03/State-Theory-of-Action-Mar.pdf

Yoder, N., Posamentier, J., Godek, D., Seibel, K., & Dusenbury, L. (2020). *From response to reopening: State efforts to elevate social and emotional learning during the pandemic*. CASEL Committee for Children. https://www.cfchildren.org/wp-content/uploads/policy-advocacy/casel-cfc-covid19-response-plan-brief.pdf

Yoder, N. (2014). *Teaching the whole child: Instructional practices that support social-emotional learning in three teacher evaluation frameworks*. Center on Great Teachers and Leaders. Retrieved from http://www.gtlcenter.org/sites/default/files/TeachingtheWholeChild.pdf

Yoder, N., & Gurke, D. (2017). *Social and emotional learning coaching toolkit: Keeping SEL at the Center*. American Institutes for Research. Retrieved from https://www.air.org/sites/default/files/downloads/report/Social-and-Emotional-Learning-SEL-Coaching-Toolkit-August-2017.pdf

Zhu, Y. (2008). From cultural adaptation to cross-cultural discursive competence. *Discourse & Communication*, *2*(2), 185–204. doi:10.1177/1750481307088483

Zianian, T., Sawyer, J., Evans, N., & Gillham, D. (2015, November 25). The Impact of mindfulness meditation on academic well-being and affective teaching practice. *Creative Education*, *6*(20), 2174–2185. doi:10.4236/ce.2015.620222

Zohar, D. (1997). *Re-wiring the corporate brain: Using the new science to rethink how we structure and lead organizations*. Berrett-Koehler Publishers.

Zohar, D. (2000). *SQ: Connecting with our spiritual intelligence*. Bloomsbury.

Zubrzycki, J. (2015). *Students 'self-assess' their way to learning*. Retrieved from https://www.edweek.org/ew/articles/2015/11/11/students-self-assess-their-way-to-learning.html

About the Contributors

Tara Madden-Dent, PhD, is currently serving as the Director of Global Programs at Sierra Nevada University and a Social Emotional Academic Development Specialist for the Nevada Department of Education. She previously taught at the University of Nevada, Reno while finishing her Ph.D. in Educational Leadership. Since then, Dr. Madden-Dent has traveled the world further studying, researching, teaching, and publishing on social emotional learning and cultural intelligence for academic and workforce development.

Deborah Oliver, Ed.D., is a Learning Scientist, with research interests in SEAD, competency based learning and personalized learning. She is an adjunct professor at National University Sanford School of Education where she teaches graduate level courses. She received her Ed.D. in Educational Leadership from Idaho State University. She Co-founded Mindful SEAD, a non-profit organization that inspires innovative teaching and learning through mindful practices by fostering community, personalized learning, developing leadership and embracing each individual's unique genius. She is an accomplished senior executive, entrepreneur, public speaker and learning specialist with more than 30 years of success in K-12 and higher education, international education affairs and non-profits.

* * *

Michelle Arroyo, PhD., is a Visiting Assistant Professor in Teaching & Learning at the University of Nevada, Las Vegas. She teaches both face-to-face and online undergraduate and graduate courses focused on helping teacher candidates learn methods and theories about becoming elementary teachers. Her research interests include teacher retention, teacher mentoring and coaching, and teacher identity development. Dr. Arroyo has numerous years of teaching experience in elementary grades at Clark County School District (CCSD) and Academia Charter Schools in Las Vegas and Henderson, NV. She earned her Ph.D. in Teacher Education from the University of Nevada Las Vegas and taught as a graduate assistant while pursuing her degree. Awards: Dr. Arroyo was selected as the Graduate Teacher of the year in 2019 by the College of Education.

Jo Ann L. Cason, Ed.D., received her doctorate in Urban Leadership from Morgan State University, in Baltimore,MD, M.S. in Education from Towson State University, Towson, MD, and B.S. in Education from Coppin State University, Baltimore, MD. She is a retired administrator with the Clark County School District in Las Vegas, Nevada. She has also served the district as an elementary and middle school math teacher and a dean of students. Before serving in Clark County, Dr. Cason served as an assistant principal, principal, and central office administrator for Baltimore City Public School System and Perry Street Preparatory Charter School in Washington, D.C. She offers training and classes on social emotional learning, self care love, and cultural competency for schools and organizations.

Pat Conner is a Senior Policy and Practice Consultant for CASEL (Collaborative for Academic, Social, and Emotional Learning). As a consultant with CASEL, she provides technical assistance and support to states involved in the Collaborative States Initiative (CSI). An educator for over 34 years, Pat retired from the TN Department of Education as the Executive Director for the Office of Student Support. In that role, she provided oversight to 146 school districts on SEL, school climate, mental health, trauma-informed schools, and extended learning. Her belief is that all children deserve to feel safe, emotionally and physically, at school and that families and the community play an important role in making schools safe places to learn and grow.

Molly Dahl received her M.Ed. from Shenandoah University in 2006. She received her Certificate of Positive Psychology from the Wholebeing Institute with Dr. Tal Ben-Shahar in 2015 and a Teacher Certificate, Cultivating Emotional Balance from the Santa Barbara Institute in 2017. She is the co-founder of Mindful SEAD a non-profit organization focusing on educator professional development and the Author of The Art of Emotional Resilience and YOUTH Positive a High School Curriculum for Mindful SEL. She presents nationally and internationally on mindful practice and building resiliency. She began her career as a high school teacher and coach.

Marie DuFresne received her M.Ed. in Educational Counseling from the University of Phoenix in 2003. In 2004, she was hired as a professional school counselor for the Lyon County School District where she served for sixteen years. In 2013, she was awarded Nevada School Counselor of the Year and was a semifinalist for the American School Counselor of the Year. She is currently the Social Emotional Academic Development Education Programs Professional for the Office for a Safe and Respectful Learning Environment at the Nevada Department of Education. She presents widely on issues concerning social emotional learning.

Alexandra Ellison is an education consultant and college counselor, working with high school students to find great-fit options after high school, and to secure the scholarships necessary to continue their education. She earned her BA in German Business from Northwestern University, her Masters in Public Policy and Administration from the University of Nevada, and her certificate in college counseling from UCLA. Ellison has spoken about education, training, entrepreneurship education, and preparing for the future of work at TEDx University of Nevada, SXSWedu and the Kuala Lumpur International Youth Discourse in Malaysia. She is the author of "Go Your Own Way: 7 Student-Centered Paths to the Best College Experience." Ellison currently works with profoundly gifted students at Davidson Academy of Nevada, as well as counsels students in the Chicago Scholars Launch program.

Tom Gore is Senior Placement Manager at Kaya Responsible Travel, where he helps place students on volunteering and internships in various countries in Latin America, Asia and Africa. He studied at Manchester Metropolitan University, where he graduated with an Undergraduate degree in History. Tom has travelled to over thirty countries across six continents, and has been advising volunteers and interns for more than six years. Tom is currently based in Manchester, UK.

Silvana (Diaz) Gorton is the Title II, Part A, Director-Education Programs Professional for the Office of Educator Development, Licensure, and Family Engagement at the Nevada Department of Education. A Colorado native, she received her Ph.D. in Educational Leadership and Innovation from the University of Colorado in 2008. She has more than 25 years of experience working in education and is currently focused on developing professional learning opportunities that join social emotional learning, multiculturalism and multilingualism, and special education interventions with equitable multi-tiered instructional practices. Her current work encompasses 13 years in the role of bilingual school psychologist. She also has 14 years of experience in professional roles in higher education to increase retention and graduation rates of underrepresented undergraduate students, and to increase educator capacity through bilingual education professional development projects and as adjunct faculty.

Iesha Jackson, Ed.D., is an Assistant Professor of Teacher Education at the University of Nevada, Las Vegas. Her research calls attention to the need for equity-based reforms in education practices and policies across the secondary through post-secondary spectrum. In order to address this, her research is situated in three main areas: student voice, culturally relevant and sustaining pedagogies, and equity-based, macro-level education policies. Dr. Jackson's recent publications shed light on the experiences of pre- and in-service educators of color as they develop skills to more effectively teach marginalized student populations.

Daniel Basil Kerr is an intercultural solutions consultant and partners with organizations and universities to develop cultural competence and inclusive work and study environments. He previously served as Director of Development at Deloitte where he was responsible for their Global New Partner Seminar and other global partner development programs. He currently serves as an adjunct faculty member at Suffolk County Community College, St. Joseph's College, and the College of Business at Stony Brook University. Dan is a CPA (New York) and holds a Master's Degree in Accounting from the CW Post School of Accountancy, as well as a PhD in Business Education/Cultural Studies from New York University.

V. Vineeth Kumar, Ph.D., is an Associate Professor at the Department of Psychology, Manipal University Jaipur, India. He has more than 15 years of experience in teaching, training, and research. His pursuits have been in the arena of positive psychology-based interventions for nurturing holistic well-being in youth. His interest area includes psychometric testing and assessment, educational psychology, positive psychology, and military psychology. He has published several research papers in peer-reviewed national and international journals.

Tyrone Martinez-Black is a former teacher of middle school math and science, an instructional coach for those subjects, and an assistant director of mathematics curriculum. In addition, he has designed and delivered professional learning in the Chicago metropolitan area and across the nation. Especially applicable to his work at CASEL, Tyrone has been a member of projects addressing youth development, design thinking within schools, and integrating SEL competencies with the Common Core Standards for Mathematical Practice. His primary responsibilities include developing and fostering connections between and among district and state teams and with external partners to better understand strategies for leveraging SEL to advance educational equity. Tyrone devotes special attention to integrating SEL across academic content areas and to improving the engagement of families in SEL initiatives and participatory evaluation.

Dana Minney works as a program evaluation analyst for a school district in Central Texas, and applies skills from her experience as an independent consultant and training facilitator. Additionally, she draws from her M.S. in Human Development and Family Studies with an emphasis in Program Evaluation. Dana enjoys using and sharing tools to clarify measurable (and helpful) goals for people, organizations, or families. Her mission is to make learning and development accessible for all people. She continues to pursue her own personal best as demonstrated by her participation in a Doctorate program at St. Edward's University in Leadership in Education with an emphasis on Organizational Change. She also enjoys reading and writing and spending time with her partner and teenage twins in her free time.

Kimberly Reed is an educator and coach with nearly twenty years of experience teaching at the secondary, undergraduate and graduate levels in Nevada. Her teaching and coaching credentials and experience include social studies at the high school level, student teaching field supervisor, graduate level SEAD and Family Involvement and Parental Engagement courses for teachers, Capstone Project Director for graduate students at Sierra Nevada University, a Teacher Coach for University of Nevada, Las Vegas and personal development and running coach at www.coachkimreed.com. She is also an avid trail runner and adventurer with her two children and husband. Her life's passion is to improve people's lives through education, wellness, nutrition and outdoor fun.

Richie Ressel has a background in K-12 education as a classroom teacher, language development specialist, and central office administrator for the Glendale School District in Arizona. Richie also co-founded the nonprofit HEROES For Students, which provided guest speakers to students both for the in-school and out-of-school settings. The program focused on workforce development skills including leadership, innovation, perseverance, and teamwork. After working with Harmony and Inspire in Arizona both as a client and later as a trainer, Richie joined the Harmony and Inspire leadership team at National University System where he now serves as the Director of Teaching and Learning.

Kristin Robison is an author and lecturer who has practiced occupational therapy in clinical and school settings for over twenty years. She has a Master's degree in Occupational Therapy from Midwestern University and a Bachelor's degree in Psychology from the University of Washington. Her unique approach was developed and refined through clinical expertise and real-world experiences to address the social and emotional needs of our youth and to help adults see behavior in a different way so their responses will be more effective. Her current book, "The Secret to Happy," helps families uncover the meaning behind behavior and provides practical strategies to help children navigate the many challenges of their school, home and social worlds. Her clinical practice addresses nervous system concepts, including sensory processing and executive functioning, to help manage the behavioral hurdles that make life challenging for many kids today. She currently practices and resides in Carson City, Nevada with her husband and two children.

Kara Sidorowicz is the Director of Research at IMAGO, where she works to support the development, alignment, and integration of content to promote social and emotional learning for life and career readiness. Her research interests include research methods, teaching methods, and emotional intelligence. Kara earned her MA in experimental psychology from California State University, Fresno, and holds a BS in psychology from Western Michigan University. She lives and works by the doctrine that if knowledge isn't shared, it's wasted.

Eleanor Strand moved to the Lake Tahoe, Nevada region in 2016 after receiving her Bachelors of Arts in Humanity and Nature Studies from Northland College in Ashland, Wisconsin. Eleanor Strand has been working in the classroom at mostly Title 1 schools. She continuously noticed how important relationship building and mindfulness were in the classroom which led her towards getting a Masters in the Arts of Teaching where she began researching connections between teacher Social Emotional Competence and student success. Eleanor considers teaching and learning to be a continuous feedback loop and is constantly trying to improve upon her instructional strategies, content relevancy, and build connections with her students. While in the classroom, Eleanor has found success in tying the elements of Social Emotional Competence and SEAD to a critical literary lens. Throughout her journey of teaching SEAD to adults, Eleanor has noticed her own Social Emotional Competency flourishing. She considers SEAD to be a fundamental part of both herself as well as her classroom.

Brooke Stratton has been teaching Masters of SEADation courses at Sierra Nevada College for 10 years. Teaching and mentoring teachers is her passion and she values her teacher mentor role as a privilege to contribute an improved education for all students. Her academic background includes an undergraduate degree in sociology from Southern Methodist University and master's degrees in special education and educational administration from UNLV. While working in public school as a teacher, mentor, and administrator for 20 years, she recognized that developing empathetic relationships is a primary determiner of student and teacher success. Focused on improving inclusive practices, she has trained and coached teachers in the best practices for educating students with disabilities and second language learners. Additional areas of emphasis include trauma-informed care, culturally responsive teaching, and implementing social-emotional learning (SEL) standards. The opportunity to teach SEL courses at the university level has provided an exciting new avenue to improve education for all students. She believes that as teachers develop their social-emotional awareness, their empathetic student relationships will improve to allow a high level of student learning.

Geetika Tankha, Ph.D., is Professor and Head of the Department of Psychology at Manipal University Jaipur, India. She has more than 20 years of teaching and research experience in the field of Psychology. Her major areas of research interest include clinical psychology, environmental psychology, and applied positive psychology. She has published research papers in several prominent journals, including European Psychologist, Journal of Cross-cultural Psychology, Journal of Health Management, and Indian Journal of Clinical Psychology.

Ashley Wolfe Reilly is a Licensed Clinical Social Worker with her Pupil Personnel Services Credential in School Social Work. She lives in beautiful Northern California, where she works with adolescents as a Mental Health Therapist on a school campus. In the process of doing this work, she developed a passion for social emotional learning and a fascination with strategies for implementing it effectively. In her free time, she pursues additional training and education and spends as much time as possible outdoors and near water. She also loves practicing the various social emotional learning skills with her children and celebrates moments where they use the tools to express themselves.

Anthony Yang, an instructional designer and researcher, has been assessing and evaluating the impact of non-governmental programs since 2010 while he was finishing his MA program in General-Experimental Psychology. Afterwards, he spent several years consulting doctoral level students around research methods and statistical analyses before joining IMAGO in 2015. At IMAGO, Anthony led the corporate shift from focusing on career preparedness for students to developing their social and emotional competencies. In this reorientation, he co-led the content development team in the research, writing, and production of over 40 social and emotional learning lessons that are used today by nearly 90% of IMAGO school districts and Native American partners across the United States.

Nick Yoder, PhD, is the Director of Strategic Initiatives for Harmony SEL and Inspire Teaching & Learning at National University. Harmony SEL, an evidence-based social and emotional learning program (SEL). He oversees the development of a system of support for effective SEL implementation in schools and afterschool programs. Dr. Yoder leads the research agenda at Harmony, collaborating with districts, schools, and other research organizations to identify the effectiveness of the program and ways in which data can be used for continuous improvement. He also partners with other leading SEL organizations focused on promoting a federal, state, and district SEL policy agenda. Prior to Harmony, Dr. Yoder was the Director of Policy and Practice at the Collaborative for Academic, Social, and Emotional Learning (CASEL), a senior technical assistant consultant at the American Institutes for Research, a pre-service instructor and field coach at the University of Michigan while he was receiving his PhD in Education and Psychology, and first grade teacher in Chicago Public Schools.

Index

A

academic performance 75, 122, 152, 187, 192, 197, 201, 203-204, 208, 222, 248
accountability 7, 129, 131, 183, 208, 223, 247, 256, 258, 267-268, 272
Adaptability 167, 247, 258, 272
adaptation 38-39, 41, 141, 191, 198, 201, 207-208, 296
adjustment 38-39, 76, 187, 191, 195, 197-201, 226, 243, 296
adolescents 18, 75, 187, 189, 191, 195-196, 198-199, 201, 211-212, 225-226, 241, 282
adult social emotional learning 42-43, 78
after-school programs 202-204, 226, 228, 230
After-School Programs (Sometimes Called OST or Out-of-School Time Programs) 230
Aspen Institute 1, 3-5, 21, 36, 38-39, 41-42, 57, 75, 78-79, 83, 96-97, 140, 143-145, 150, 162-163, 165, 188, 198, 225, 271, 277, 295
attentional awareness 5-7
attrition 104, 118

B

behavior 8-11, 15-16, 18, 23, 67, 82, 90, 102-103, 109, 113-114, 122, 126-128, 136, 140-141, 144, 149-150, 152-154, 165-174, 176-182, 184-185, 190, 194-195, 200, 204, 206-209, 213, 215, 220, 222, 230, 248, 278-279, 282, 286, 288, 291, 296

C

Campus Climate 62, 148
Career Technical Education (CTE) 272
CASEL 1, 3-6, 10, 15-16, 21, 30, 37, 41-43, 48-54, 57-58, 69, 71, 75, 77-78, 81-82, 85-86, 89, 91, 95-97, 99-100, 102-103, 119, 122-123, 125, 138-143, 146, 149, 161-162, 164-166, 176, 188-189, 197-198, 203-204, 208, 210, 212-213, 224-226, 232, 234, 236, 245, 250-251, 270-272, 277, 293, 295
classroom management 9, 143, 148, 150-151, 153, 155-157, 159-161
College and Career Readiness (CCR) 248, 272
Community of Practice 80, 83, 99
competencies 4-6, 10, 15-17, 20-22, 24, 29-33, 35-36, 38, 41-43, 48-49, 54, 57-58, 60-63, 65-66, 68-69, 71-72, 76-77, 80-83, 85-87, 89-91, 93, 100, 120, 122-124, 131-132, 134-135, 137-139, 141-142, 147, 149, 151, 161, 163, 166, 176, 188-189, 202, 204, 206, 208, 213, 232, 247-250, 252, 273, 275, 277-278, 282, 284, 287, 290, 292-295
COVID-19 pandemic 34, 63, 74-75, 80, 89, 93, 99, 150, 231, 242, 245, 273-274, 277, 284, 295
critical consciousness 20, 23-26, 28-29, 35, 41, 68, 124
Critical Friend 90, 98-99
cultural awareness 23-24, 35-36, 40-41
cultural competence 21, 35-36, 41, 57, 96, 151, 279-280
cultural intelligence 20, 23, 25-26, 28-29, 38, 76, 89, 280
Cultural Knowledge 35, 39, 41
Cultural Responsiveness 21-22, 38, 41, 76, 89, 165
Cultural Sensitivity 41
Culturally adaptive 119, 125
culturally responsive 20-26, 28-37, 39-41, 51, 56-57, 68, 71, 75-77, 89, 95, 119-121, 123-124, 126-129, 131-136, 138-139, 144, 149-150, 152, 156, 161, 163, 165, 188
culturally responsiveness 20, 68
culture 5, 20, 22-29, 31-32, 37-38, 40-43, 50-51, 53, 57, 85, 88-91, 100, 102, 123-125, 128, 131, 138, 151-152, 165, 197, 201, 208, 232-235, 242-244, 268, 273-281, 286-287, 289-296

D

Daniel Siegel 1, 3
distance learning 20, 32, 34-35, 40, 64, 83
Dr. Jean Twenge 231

E

Ecological Framework 202, 206, 230
Ecuador 273, 276-277, 282-286, 293-294
education 1-8, 17-19, 21, 23-29, 32, 35-40, 42-44, 50, 54, 56-60, 62, 69, 74-79, 81, 83, 85, 89-90, 92-98, 102-106, 108-110, 112, 116-118, 120, 126, 132, 134-135, 140, 142-151, 160-161, 163-164, 183-184, 186-188, 193, 195-201, 204, 223, 227-228, 230-234, 238-239, 241, 245-252, 267, 269-272, 282-283, 285, 296
educator 1, 20, 23, 31, 36, 44-45, 49, 53-54, 56, 63, 65-66, 68, 75, 78-83, 85, 90-91, 94-95, 98, 117, 125, 127-128, 131-132, 134, 136-139, 147, 149, 156, 161, 228
Elementary Education 101, 106, 110
Emotional Intelligence (EI) 272
emotions 3, 6-11, 14, 18-19, 21, 30, 38, 41, 49, 57, 62, 76, 82, 92, 97, 102, 105, 114-116, 122, 126-127, 142-143, 147, 149-150, 152-155, 157-158, 160-162, 165, 170, 176, 180-181, 188, 190, 192, 195, 198, 201, 203-204, 207, 210-211, 213, 230, 234, 243, 260, 262, 272, 277, 293
empathy 2-3, 21, 41, 49, 52, 57, 87, 93, 102, 149, 154, 165, 176, 188, 194, 201, 203, 213, 230, 247, 260-261, 266, 268, 272
employability skills 247, 250, 265, 271-272
engagement 2, 5, 22, 29-31, 34, 37, 43-45, 47, 55, 57, 61, 63, 66, 68, 79, 82-83, 88-90, 130, 132, 142, 146, 149, 153, 160-161, 171, 178, 180, 184-185, 208, 234-235, 238, 255, 267, 295
environment 2, 7, 9, 11, 15, 21, 23, 27, 29-31, 35, 41, 49-50, 60-61, 69-70, 79-80, 87, 91, 106, 108, 114, 120, 123-124, 128-131, 134, 138, 152-153, 156-160, 165, 168-171, 173, 190, 196-197, 201, 206, 209, 224, 230, 249, 275, 279-281, 284, 294
equity 20, 27, 36, 38-39, 56, 59, 62-63, 75-76, 80, 83, 89, 95-100, 117, 119-120, 122-123, 125, 130, 140, 142-144, 146, 162-163, 198
executive functioning 6, 9, 166, 170, 172-173, 180, 182-185
expectations 21, 23, 26-28, 33, 39, 46, 58, 67, 70, 74, 87, 103-104, 112, 124, 136-137, 141, 143, 146, 152-153, 155, 166-167, 169, 171, 173, 176-178, 180-182, 193, 196, 204-205, 210, 254, 268, 276, 281, 292

F

facilitator guides 252, 254, 268, 272
fidelity 42-43, 46, 51, 53, 55, 83, 89-90, 206

G

GlobeSmart 275, 279-282, 285-286, 288, 290-291, 293-295

H

happiness 5, 19, 33, 79, 86, 131, 166, 187, 191, 198, 200-201
Hard to Staff Schools 116, 118
Harvard 39-40, 97, 144-146, 227-228, 231, 233-234, 244, 246, 248, 271, 295
high school 4, 20, 22-24, 26-27, 29, 36, 40, 45, 106-107, 110-112, 117, 142, 145, 148, 150-151, 154, 156, 158-160, 162, 191, 200, 203, 223, 227, 231, 233, 235-237, 239-245, 250, 269, 271-273, 275-276, 287-288, 294
higher education 29, 35, 39-40, 56, 58, 74, 77, 85, 90, 95, 143, 147, 151, 161, 186, 231-232, 234

I

identity 23-24, 39, 63, 66, 68, 75, 101-105, 113-118, 125, 127-128, 149, 162, 286, 288
identity development 101-105, 113, 115-118, 149
iGen 237, 246
implementation 1-2, 20-21, 30-35, 42-43, 45-51, 53-55, 57, 61, 79-81, 83, 86, 89, 91, 94, 98, 136, 138-139, 143, 146, 161, 188, 202-203, 206-208, 210-211, 222-224, 226, 228, 230, 247-248, 251, 254-255, 265, 269
implementation strategies 254
inSPIRE Check-in 12-14, 19, 91-92, 97
integration 21, 25, 27-28, 39, 41, 43, 51-52, 55, 57, 76, 83, 86-87, 91, 120-121, 123-125, 137, 139, 144, 150, 163, 165, 168-170, 185, 188-189, 201, 268, 277
international student 27-28, 39, 76, 144, 163, 245
internships 38, 237, 273-278, 281, 293-295

J

job shadowing 239-240

K

Kaya Responsible Travel 273, 275-276, 284, 287, 289-290, 292-294, 296

M

Making Caring Common Project 231, 234, 244-245
mapping 268, 273, 278-279, 294
Martin Seligman 2, 4
Mary Helen Immordino-Yang 1-3
mental health 18, 22, 40, 47, 53-54, 57, 93, 139, 143, 148-151, 153-156, 159-161, 164, 185, 187, 189-191, 194, 197-201, 204, 224, 226-227, 234, 240, 245
mentor 103, 106-108, 112, 118, 224, 240-241, 244-245
Mindfulness-Based SEAD 2, 19
Mindfulness-Based Stress Reduction (MBSR) 1, 19
Morocco 273-274, 276-277, 281, 285-287, 293-294
M-SEL 2, 15-16, 19
M-SEL COMPETENCY BENCHMARKS 16
Multi-Tiered System of Supports 22, 57, 78-79, 99
Multi-Tiered System of Supports (MTSS) 79, 99

O

Occupational therapy (OT) 166
Operation Varsity Blues 231, 234
orientations 23-25, 40-41, 273, 278-280, 282, 285, 288-290, 293-294, 296

P

professional development 23, 35-36, 43-45, 48-49, 51-52, 56, 66, 74, 78, 80-83, 90, 92-93, 98, 103, 139, 151, 160-161, 207, 222-224, 252, 265
professional identity 101-105, 114-118, 149
professional learning 34, 71, 74, 78-81, 85, 88-94, 99, 103-104, 138, 140
program evaluation 202, 206-207, 209, 223-224, 230
psychological wellbeing 187

Q

quality of life 36, 55, 64, 70, 187, 189-190, 192-193, 197-198, 200-201

R

regulation 1, 6-7, 14, 55, 70, 149, 161, 166-167, 170-173, 178-181, 183-185, 203
relationship skills 4, 21, 25, 29, 33, 35-36, 42, 44, 46, 48, 57, 60-62, 65, 67, 82, 102, 135, 150-151, 156, 158-159, 165, 188-189, 201, 230, 272-273, 275, 277-278, 284-285, 287, 290, 293-294
resilience 1-2, 7-10, 14, 17-18, 49, 54, 92-93, 166, 190, 194, 196, 199, 201, 226, 263, 272
responsible decision-making 4, 21, 24-25, 29, 33, 36, 42, 57, 60, 62, 67, 82, 150, 155, 158-159, 165, 188-189, 201, 213, 273, 275, 278, 285, 287, 293-294
Richard Davidson 1, 3, 6

S

Schlossberg 273, 276-277, 293-296
school leader 43, 48, 50, 81
school safety 62, 88, 143, 148, 151
SEAD 1-5, 7-8, 14, 18-24, 29-32, 35-36, 38, 40-44, 47, 50-52, 54-71, 74-83, 85-95, 97-99, 119-120, 123, 128, 139, 149-153, 155, 157, 160-161, 164-165, 188, 195, 197, 201, 231, 242-243, 273, 275, 277, 282, 284, 287, 290, 292-295
Secondary Education 94, 105, 148
SEL 1-7, 14-18, 20-26, 28-39, 41-54, 56-58, 60-62, 64-69, 71-72, 74-76, 78-83, 85-91, 93, 95-97, 99-100, 102-103, 117, 119-120, 122-126, 134, 137-144, 146-163, 165, 188, 194, 196-198, 201-213, 215-216, 220-230, 232, 234, 236, 245, 247-248, 250-254, 257, 264-272, 275, 277, 281, 294-295
SEL curriculum 45, 65, 122, 125, 134, 150, 202-203, 209, 211, 213, 216, 222-224, 230, 234
self-awareness 4, 6-7, 9-10, 12, 14, 16, 21, 24-25, 29, 31, 33-36, 42, 46, 48, 57, 60-62, 67, 82, 85, 91, 102, 127, 149, 153, 156-159, 165-167, 170-171, 173-174, 179, 182, 185, 188-189, 194, 201, 204, 207-208, 211-214, 217, 230, 232, 238-240, 253, 267, 272-273, 275, 277-278, 281, 284, 287, 290, 292-294
self-control 127, 147, 203, 210, 229, 262-263, 272
self-management 4, 7-10, 21, 24-25, 29, 33, 36, 42, 57, 60-62, 65, 67, 82, 102, 150, 153, 155-156, 158-160, 165-167, 170-172, 178, 180, 184, 188-189, 201-202, 204, 207, 210-214, 216-218, 222, 230, 272-273, 275, 277-278, 285, 287, 290, 292-294
self-soothing 214, 217, 222, 230
sensory processing 166-167, 170, 172-173, 176, 178, 185
SI 187-190, 192, 194-195, 197
social and emotional learning 3-4, 29-30, 32, 36-38, 40, 54, 58, 61, 69, 75-76, 86, 96-100, 102, 117, 119-120, 122, 142-147, 149, 156, 162-164, 166, 171, 176, 182, 184, 199-200, 202, 223, 225-229, 231-232, 240, 247-248, 270-272, 293
social and emotional support 101, 114-116
social awareness 3-4, 6, 21, 25, 29, 31, 33, 35-36, 42, 46, 57, 60, 62, 65, 67, 82, 102, 125, 150, 156-159, 165, 185, 188-189, 201-202, 204, 208, 211-214,

230, 253, 272-273, 275, 277, 281, 290, 293-294
Social Emotional Academic Development (SEAD) 40, 54, 76-77, 99, 164
Social Emotional and Academic Development 42, 188
social emotional learning 2, 15, 38, 40, 42-48, 50-53, 55-56, 60, 63, 65, 78, 97, 99-100, 141, 148, 150, 161, 273, 289
Social Emotional Learning Implementation 42
Social, Emotional, and Academic Development (SEAD) 1, 20-21, 38, 41-42, 56-57, 60, 78, 120, 150, 165, 188, 201, 273, 277
South Africa 273, 276-277, 281, 287-289, 293-294
spiritual intelligence 187-201
student success 40, 62, 67, 74, 88, 116, 122, 148, 158-159, 254
students 2-21, 23-32, 35-46, 48-52, 54, 57-58, 60-72, 74, 76-83, 85, 87-89, 91-95, 97-99, 103, 105, 109-111, 113-140, 142-161, 163-167, 179, 183, 186-201, 203-205, 207-211, 215-217, 220, 222-224, 226, 229, 231-245, 247-252, 254-258, 260, 262-279, 281, 286-287, 290-294, 296
systemic 24, 28, 35, 57, 68, 78-80, 86, 93, 95-96, 98-100, 117, 124, 145, 207-208, 228

T

teacher 7, 9, 11, 13, 18, 23, 28-29, 43, 45-47, 51-52, 54, 56, 58, 60, 63-66, 68, 70, 75, 77, 79-80, 82, 85, 88-90, 92, 96-98, 101-119, 122, 124-125, 127-128, 130, 133, 135-136, 141, 143-148, 150-157, 159-162, 164, 169-170, 179, 205, 207-208, 210, 220-221, 223, 225, 228-229, 240, 247, 254-255, 265, 268
teacher identity 75, 101-105, 113, 115-117, 162
teacher retention 75, 82, 101, 105, 116-118, 162, 208
Teacher turnover 96, 103, 116-118
teaching practices 91, 119-121, 123, 126, 139-140, 167, 189, 197, 254
Title 1 101, 105-111, 113, 115-116, 118
Title 1 school 106-111, 113, 115-116, 118
transformative SEL 95, 100, 125
transition 38-39, 76, 87, 92, 94, 179, 273, 276-277, 282, 293-296

U

University 1, 3, 19-20, 24-26, 29, 36, 38-39, 41, 54, 56, 58-59, 62-63, 75-77, 81, 85-88, 96, 99, 101, 110-112, 117, 119, 146, 148, 151, 162-164, 187, 190-193, 198-202, 209, 212, 224, 226, 229, 231-234, 236, 238-239, 242-243, 246, 273, 277, 282, 285, 290, 296
University of California 231-233, 242

V

Vietnam 24, 27, 273-274, 276-277, 290-294
virtual 30, 32-35, 38, 63-64, 67, 74-75, 78, 83, 92, 94, 96, 236, 273-278, 281-295

W

wellness 27, 34, 43-44, 52-53, 61, 64, 70, 79-80, 83, 87, 94-95, 101-105, 143, 148, 154-155, 158, 160, 226

CPSIA information can be obtained
at www.ICGtesting.com
Printed in the USA
BVHW010221160722
642304BV00007B/116

9 781799 867296